THE GERMAN EPISCOPACY AND
THE IMPLEMENTATION OF THE DECREES
OF THE FOURTH LATERAN COUNCIL
1216-1245

STUDIES IN THE HISTORY
OF
CHRISTIAN THOUGHT

EDITED BY

HEIKO A. OBERMAN, Tucson, Arizona

IN COOPERATION WITH

HENRY CHADWICK, Cambridge
JAROSLAV PELIKAN, New Haven, Connecticut
BRIAN TIERNEY, Ithaka, New York
ARJO VANDERJAGT, Groningen

VOLUME LXIV

PAUL B. PIXTON

THE GERMAN EPISCOPACY AND
THE IMPLEMENTATION OF THE DECREES
OF THE FOURTH LATERAN COUNCIL
1216-1245

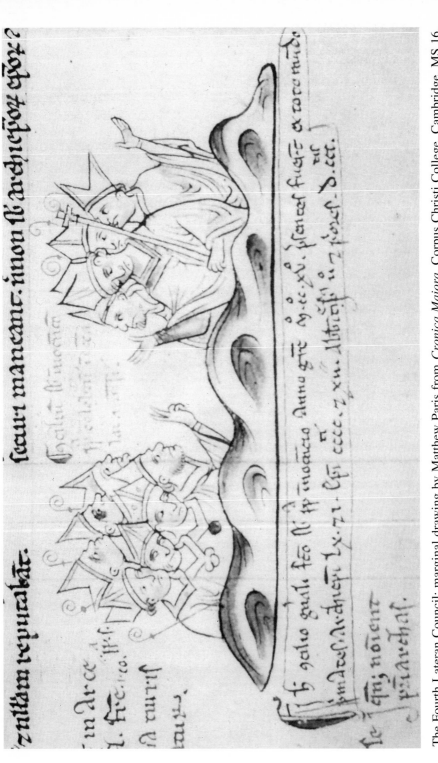

The Fourth Lateran Council: marginal drawing by Matthew Paris from *Cronica Maiora*, Corpus Christi College, Cambridge, MS 16, f.43v (used by permission of the Master and Fellows of Corpus Christi College, Cambridge).

THE GERMAN EPISCOPACY AND
THE IMPLEMENTATION OF THE DECREES
OF THE FOURTH LATERAN COUNCIL
1216-1245

WATCHMEN ON THE TOWER

BY

PAUL B. PIXTON

E.J. BRILL
LEIDEN · NEW YORK · KÖLN
1995

The paper in this book meets the guidelines for permanence and durability of the Committee on Production Guidelines for Book Longevity of the Council on Library Resources.

Library of Congress Cataloging-in-Publication Data

Pixton, Paul B.
   The German episcopacy and the implementation of the decrees of the fourth Lateran Council, 1216-1245 : watchmen on the tower / by Paul B. Pixton.
      p.   cm. — (Studies in the history of Christian thought, ISSN 0081-8607 ; v. 64)
   Includes bibliographical references and index.
   ISBN 9004102620 (alk. paper)
   1. Lateran Council (4th : 1215)   2. Germany—Church history—843-1517.   I. Title.   II. Series.
   BX830 1215.P58   1995
   282'.43'09022—dc20   94-44944
                                                                          CIP

Die Deutsche Bibliothek - CIP-Einheitsaufnahme

Pixton, Paul B.:
The German episcopacy and the implementation of the decrees of the Fourth Lateran Council : 1216 - 1245 : watchmen on the tower / by Paul B. Pixton. – Leiden ; New York ; Köln : Brill, 1995
   (Studies in the history of Christian thought ; Vol. 64)
   ISBN 90-04-10262-0
NE: Concilium Lateranense <4, 1216 - 1245 >; GT

ISSN   0081-8607
ISBN   90 04 10262 0

To Mary Elizabeth Curtis Pixton

TABLE OF CONTENTS

ACKNOWLEDGEMENTS

This book owes its inception to the teaching of Profs. Emil Lucki, Harold Bauman, John Bell Henneman and Donald Wayne Sutherland who fostered my interest in and enthusiasm for the medieval world. An early research proposal was given endorsement by Profs. Robert L. Benson and Christopher R. Cheney, enabling me to spend a year at the Monumenta Germaniae Historica in Munich. Among the many pleasant associates of that institution, especial thanks are due to the former president, Dr. Horst Fuhrmann, and to Drs. Hans Martin Schaller and Alexander Patschovsky for their interest and encouragement. The librarians at the Monumenta, Dr. Hilda Lietzmann, Dr. Norbert Martin and Frau Christa Becker, have made their expertise available to me in countless ways.

No one can conduct research which depends so heavily upon the source collections produced in the previous century without developing a deep appreciation for those early generations of scholars at the Monumenta and elsewhere in Germany whose enthusiasm for discovering and preserving the muniments of the medieval world has made modern scholarship possible. To those who developed the canons of research and who founded journals, published sources and provided the great wealth of secondary literature I express my deepest gratitude.

Librarians at the universities of Iowa, Wisconsin, Minnesota, Bonn, Cologne, and Brigham Young University, as well as those at the Bavarian State Library in Munich, the Landeshauptarchiv in Coblenz, the Bistumsarchiv in Trier, the Bistumsarchiv in Bamberg, and the Center for Canon Law Studies at Berkeley, have provided assistance during the lengthy course of my research.

Portions of the book have been read in one form or another by Prof. Egon Boshof and Dr. Franz-Josef Heyen whose comments have been most appreciated. Prof. Peter Johanek allowed me to read his unpublished Habilitationsschrift; my debt to that work is duly noted in the text.

Financial support for research has been given over many years by the College of Family, Home and Social Sciences at Brigham Young University; two grants from the Deutscher Akademischer Austauschdienst (DAAD) also are appreciated.

I am greatly indebted as well to Prof. Heiko Oberman for his willingness to include this volume in the series *Studies in the History of Christian Thought*.

Above all, I express my deep appreciation to my wife Mary and our four children whose lives have been controlled in many ways by the demands of research for this book. Their willingness to be uprooted periodically and to accept a nomadic lifestyle has allowed me to make use of research opportunities in the United States and in Germany, without which this undertaking would have been impossible.

While recognizing my great debt to others, I nonetheless accept the book's shortcomings to be my own.

LIST OF TABLES

PREFACE

In the year 1215 Pope Innocent III presided over an assembly of some 400 bishops and over 800 abbots and other prelates of the Latin Church in what is generally acknowledged as the greatest ecumenical council of the medieval period. The agenda was twofold: reform of the Church and further promotion of what we now call the Fifth Crusade. In anticipation of the reform measures, the pontiff had solicited memoranda from the provincial and diocesan leaders which helped identify those areas requiring conciliar attention. Out of this process emerged an extensive set of constitutions aimed at every level of Church governance, and touching upon clergy and laity alike.

The impact of this legislation (and that of other councils as well) has been the object of scholarly investigation since at least the eighteenth century when the great collections of conciliar and synodal statutes were published. Beginning in the nineteenth century interpretive studies have also been written, attempting to relate the statutes of a given council or synod to the historical context. Evidence of continued interest in synodal and conciliar activity in the twentieth century can be seen in the increased study of medieval canon law, the establishment of the Institute for Medieval Canon Law by Dr. Stephan Kuttner, the recent agenda of the Monumenta Germaniae Historica under President Horst Fuhrmann, and the publication of journals such as *Traditio* and *Annuarium Historiae Conciliorum*.

This present study began as an inquiry into the ecclesiastical activities of a German archbishop whose pontificate ran from 1212 until 1242, and who was personally present in Rome in 1215. His own enthusiasm for and response to the reforms proposed by Innocent III at the Fourth Lateran Council prompted a more extensive investigation into how the German episcopacy as a whole reacted to the papal charges that they take aggressive action in correcting the abuses of their respective clergy through the use of provincial and diocesan synods, episcopal visitations, triennial general chapters of the monastic orders, and other means. The original intention was to extend the study for some fifty years—until the Second Council of Lyons in 1274. It soon became evident, however, that there was simply too much material for a single volume of that scope: the solution was to pull back to the First Council of Lyons in 1245. What the study thus loses in the longer perspective, it attempts to compensate for in the detail of its examination.

The primary tools of implementing the reform decrees of the general council were the provincial and the diocesan synod, both of which had an extensive history in Germany prior to 1215. From the evidence which we have been able to assemble in this volume for the first time to this degree of comprehensiveness, there emerges a picture of great diversity and great disparity: some German dioceses are well documented, others hardly at all, in the half-century which preceded the council. Part of this may be the result of the fact that we are still learning how to recognize synods—not all recorded synodal acts bear the actual word *synodus* in the text. Scholars in this century have developed the methodology for identifying other gatherings of clerics as synods: if they did the work of synods, if they were comprised of those whose presence would otherwise be hard to explain, they must have been synods. Thus, while the diocesan synod may have been a seldom affair in some areas of Germany before 1215, it was by no means a moribund institution.

To decree a measure is one thing; to see to it that the measure is in fact carried out is altogether different. Crucial to the implementation of Innocent III's reform program was an episcopacy which could be inspired, cajoled or threatened into fulfilling their roles as "watchmen on the tower," recognizing the spiritual enemies of their respective churches and taking the necessary steps in the eradication of such problems. It has thus been necessary to treat at some length the German bishops (both collectively and as individuals), thereby gaining a better appreciation for the varying degrees of support which they gave to the papal precepts.

What emerges in the following study is a mixed image, one which shows great effort on the part of some prelates, and indifference or inability on the part of others. This disparity of commitment and talent was obviously well understood in the Roman curia, so much so that almost at once papal legates went forth to provide more determined direction in the reform efforts. While the best of these legates may have accomplished much of a positive nature, others succeeded only in alienating themselves (and perhaps by extension their papal masters) from the German clergy.

Even those archbishops (or bishops) with the greatest resolve found it impossible to effect the changes which the papacy had demanded: contributing to this failure were the ever-changing political conditions in Germany, the refusal of both secular and regular clergy to abide by the decrees of their ordinaries, the seemingly insatiable appetite of the upper clergy for prebends and benefices, papal practices of granting German ecclesiastical offices to members of the Roman curia or as rewards for services rendered to some member of the curia, and the institution of appeal measures which often removed the decision of local matters to Rome and thereby weakened the effective authority of prelates.

Despite its long-term failure to effect a regeneration of the medieval Church, the Fourth Lateran Council remains as the greatest testimony of Pope Innocent III's vision and authority: its constitutions became an integral part of the Church's law, and its various other acts show a Latin Christendom united under the presidency of the bishop of Rome. The specific instance of medieval Germany demonstrates, however, that despite such claims of papal *plenitudo potestatis*, deep-seated changes in the thought and actions of the clergy had to be more than mere "legislated morality." Without an inner commitment to the principles articulated at the Fourth Lateranum, the German church of 1245 was not fundamentally different from that of 1200 or even 1500.

CHAPTER ONE

PROLEGOMENON

. . . Filii matris meae pugnaverunt contra me, posuerunt me custodem in vineis:
vineam meam non custodivi.
(Canticum Canticorum 1,5)

Vineam domini Sabaoth multiformes moliuntur bestiae demoliri, quarum incursus
adeo invaluit contra ipsam, ut ex parte non modica pro vitibus spinae
succreverint, et, quod gementes referimus, ipsae jam vites proferant
pro uva labruscam, infectae multipliciter et curruptae.
(Pope Innocent III, a. 1213)

On 19 April 1213 Pope Innocent III issued the bull *Vineam domini Sabaoth* summoning ecclesiastical leaders of Christendom to an ecumenical council to be held in the basilica of St. John Lateran at Rome commencing 1 November 1215. The agenda for the council was a lengthy one, expressed in some detail in the encyclical itself:

> Two things lie particularly near my heart: the regaining of the Holy Land and the reform of the whole church. Attention to both can hardly be delayed any longer without grave danger. After praying to God for enlightenment in this matter, and also after frequent consultation with the cardinals and other learned men, I have decided after the manner of the ancient fathers to convoke a general council, by means of which evils may be uprooted, virtues implanted, mistakes corrected, morals reformed, heresies extirpated, the faith strengthened, disputes adjusted, peace established, liberty protected, Christian princes and people induced to aid the Holy Land and salutary decrees enacted for the higher and lower clergy.[1]

Such a council had been projected for many years by this pontiff, but had been delayed by the numerous vexatious problems with which he had been confronted.

While a council would clearly serve to further papal efforts at union with the Greek church, it also provided an opportunity for publicizing and organizing under papal direction a new expedition for recovery of the Holy Land. Over and above this, however, Innocent planned the council as a

---

[1] Migne, *PL* CCXVII, col. 674; Mansi, *Collectio* XXII, cols. 960-961; Potthast, *Regesta* I, Nrs. 4707-4708. The translation used is that of Schroeder, *Disciplinary Decrees* 236-237. Cf. also Foreville, *Lateran I-IV* 278-294; Jedin, *Handbook of Church History* IV 167.

culminating celebration of his previous reform activity. Both the experiences of his own administrative, legislative and disciplinary action over the years, and those of the bishops and prelates invited were to contribute to establishing a model of renewal which would be obligatory for the universal Church. The end result, so believed the pontiff, would be a Christendom less torn by doctrinal dissention, more committed to order and discipline, and regenerated from within.

The following study seeks to assess the impact of this papal program of reform upon the churches within the six German ecclesiastical provinces of Bremen, Cologne, Magdeburg, Mainz, Salzburg and Trier during the three decades between the conclusion of the Fourth Lateranum and the First Council of Lyons (1245). Given the large number of issues raised in 1215 regarding the administration and oversight of the Church, the scope will of necessity have to restrict itself to some of the more easily identifiable aspects of reform. In order that our understanding of such consequences be as complete as possible, however, we must also consider the state of the German church on the eve of Innocent III's great council, and the nature of the German episcopacy at this critical moment in ecclesiastical history.

The papal bull indicated that capable men were being sent to direct the crusade effort. According to a contemporary, Prior Reiner of St. Jacob's at Liège, the papal representative given responsibility for Germany was *magister* Alatrino, papal subdeacon and *capellanus*. Reiner's mention of Alatrino suggests that the latter perhaps engaged in activities in the towns and cities of Brabant, while a second reference to him in a continuation of the *Gesta Treverorum* may indicate that the papal nuncio also sojourned in Lorraine. Johann Friedrich Böhmer's register for legates contains no indications of Alatrino's activities whatever, but Eduard Winkelmann has suggested that he represented the pope as Frederick II issued the Golden Bull at Eger in Thuringia on 12 July 1213.[2] If this conclusion be indeed correct, we may assume that Alatrino promoted the business of the crusade in regions east of the Rhine as well.

Men more familiar with the local situation had already been appointed as crusade preachers as well. For the province of Mainz these included Abbot Eberhard of Salem (Salmansweiler in the diocese of Constanz), Peter, the erstwhile abbot of Neubourg (ca. eighteen miles north of Basel), *magister* Conrad, cathedral dean at Speyer, and provost Sifrid of Augsburg. For the provinces of Bremen and Magdeburg there appear Conrad of

---

[2] Cf. *Reineri Ann.* 667; *Gesta Trev.* 391; also Winkelmann, *Phil. von Schw.* II 342. On the long career of service to three popes by Master Alatrino, see Kenneth Pennington, *Pope and Bishops: The Papal Monarchy in the Twelfth and Thirteenth Centuries* (Philadelphia, 1984) 150-152.

Krosigk, erstwhile bishop of Halberstadt, and Frederick, former abbot of Sichem (Sittichenbach, near Eisleben in Thuringia. For the province of Cologne, *magister* Oliver of Paderborn, cathedral scholastic at Cologne, and *magister* Hermann, dean at St. Cassius in Bonn were named. For Salzburg, Bishop Conrad of Regensburg, and the cathedral provost of Salzburg, Otto, received the appointment. The province of Trier was to be recruited by the Premonstratensian Abbot Rainer of Rommersdorf on the middle Rhine, and the Cistercian Abbot Conrad of Villers in Brabant.[3]

With the exception of recruiting activities by such individuals, details of preparations for the Council at the diocesan level are poorly documented and little known. The primary responsibility for preparing the clergy rested with archbishops, bishops and monastic leaders. One reason why invitations went out so early was to allow time not only for zealous promoting of the crusade, but also for amassing all the *gravamina* or lists of complaints regarding the state of the church, for the settling of which the Council was summoned. Because no reform program could hope for success without broad support from all the clergy, Lateran IV took an important new step in its demand that "cathedral and collegiate chapters also shall send representatives, for with them the Council must also occupy itself."

Personal invitations were also sent to the abbots and to the general chapters of Cîteaux and Prémontré, and to the grand masters of the Templars and the Hospitallers. From the testimony of the pope himself, it appears that complaints about the conduct of the Cistercians had reached the Curia from various corners of Christendom: letters dated 20 June 1213 to the Cistercians of the diocese of Pécs (Fünfkirchen) in Hungary, and 19 July 1214 (possibly to the abbot of Cîteaux and all the abbots of the Order assembled in the general chapter) warn them that if they do not correct certain specific abuses at once, he would do so at the general council.[4] We do not know to what extent the monasteries of White Monks in Germany were guilty of these abuses, but they must have been an integral part of the problems described by the pope.

---

[3] Cf. Paul B. Pixton, "Die Anwerbung des Heeres Christi: Prediger des fünften Kreuzzuges in Deutschland," *DA* 34/1 (1978) 166-191, and drawing on him, James M. Powell, *Anatomy of a Crusade, 1213-1221* (Philadelphia, 1986) 23-24.

[4] The papal chastisements are in Migne, *PL* CCXVI 886-887; Cambridge University Library MS. Ff.4.1 fol. 130va. The Cambridge MS was first published in Christopher R. Cheney, "A Letter of Pope Innocent III and the Lateran Decree on Cistercian Tithe-Paying," *Cîteaux: Commentarii Cistercienses* (1962) fasc. 2, 146-151; reprinted in *Medieval Texts and Studies* 278-284. A French translation from this text is given by Foreville, *Latran I-IV* (1965) 332-333 (German translation, Idem., *Latran I-IV* (1970) 390; cf. discussion of general context, 293-294). The Cistercian abbots actually dealt with these issues at the 1215 General Chapter, the confirmation of which is *c.* 55 of the Lateran IV constitutions; cf. Canivez, *Statuta ord. Cist.* I, Nr. 65.

The Sessions of the Fourth Lateran Council

The great effort which went into preparations for the Council was not lost on the 404 bishops and more than 800 abbots, priors and other ecclesiastical dignitaries who gathered at Rome on 1 November 1215. Delays prevented the start of the first session until the 11th, however, when the pope celebrated Mass at dawn in the presence of the higher prelates alone. With the bishops and abbots formally seated, the basilica was then opened to the throng of lesser clergy and laymen. Innocent III next intoned the hymn *Veni creator spiritus*, which was taken up by all, followed by the collect. An eyewitness to these events claimed that the noise level was so high in the basilica that he could not hear the pope's sermon[5] which was based on the words which Jesus spoke to his twelve disciples on the eve of his arrest and trial: *"Desiderio desideravi hoc Pascha manducare vobiscum, antequam patiar."*[6] Seeing in the restoration of the Temple at Jerusalem under King Josiah a parable for his own day, he expressed his desire that

> . . . in this the eighteenth year of our pontificate, the Temple of the Lord, which is the Church, might be restored and that this passover or *pasha*—to wit, this solemn council, might be celebrated, by means of which a change from vices to virtues might be effected among the Christian people such as indeed has not been made in Israel since the days of the judges and kings—that is, since the days of the holy Fathers and the Catholic princes.[7]

Immediately after the pope had spoken, the patriarch of Jerusalem delivered an impassioned address on the misfortunes of the Holy Land; thereafter the bishop of Agde spoke on the problems of the Albigenses in Languedoc. The choice of these two speakers suggested the major problems with which the Council was concerned.

---

[5] Stephan Kuttner and Antonio Garcia y Garcia, "A New Eyewitness Account of the Fourth Lateran Council," *Traditio* 20 (1964) 115-178, espec. 129-130. The following discussion of the course of the Council relies heavily on Kuttner/Garcia y Garcia's commentary.

[6] Lk 22:15.

[7] For Innocent III's sermon, cf. Mansi, *Collectio* XXII cols. 968-979; Migne, *PL* CCXVII cols. 673-680. The sermon is noted by various contemporary chroniclers, e.g., the Sicilian notary Richard of San Germano; cf. *Ryccardi Chronica* 337: *"Dictus papa Rome apud Lateranum in ecclesia Salvatoris que Constantiniana dicitur sanctam synodum celebravit, in qua cum fuerint patres circiter quadringenti, de reformatione ecclesie in suo sermone preposuit, et libertatione potissimum terre sancte; . . . et sancta synodus 70 capitula promulgavit: dampnavit librum Ioachim Florensis abbatis, quem contra magistrum Petrum Lombardum ediderat de unitate vel essentia Trinitatis."* A longer version of Richard's chronicle containing the entire sermon is in C.A. Garufi, ed., *Ryccardi de Sancto Germano Chronica*, in Muratori, *Rerum Italiacarum Scriptores*, editio nuova, 7.ii (1936-1938) 62-70.

Between the first and second formal sessions, the Curia attended to disputes over bishoprics and other important juridical matters, and presided over solemn celebrations.   E.g., on 12 November discussions regarding the vacant see of Constantinople began; on 13 November the primatial claims of Toledo were addressed; and on Sunday, 15 November, the church of S. Maria in Trastevere was consecrated.   The consecration, which was apparently one of the great public events of the Council, lasted almost all day and the procession returned in the evening to the city with the Roman nobility preceding the clergy and people.   Three days later the feast of the Dedication of Sts. Peter and Paul was celebrated.   According to eyewitnesses, the crowds were so large that the pope could scarcely make his way to the basilica.

Session two commenced on 20 November, at which time the Council fathers considered the question of the Empire.   Our eyewitness again noted that the pope ascended his throne, silence was ordered, and· trumpets sounded; Innocent III then delivered a short allocution, followed by Archbishop Berard of Palermo who read a letter from Frederick II which petitioned the pope in council for approbation of Frederick's imperial election by the German princes 5 December 1212 at Frankfurt and his coronation 25 July 1215 at Aachen.   Milanese ambassadors were then admitted who pleaded for the absolution of the erstwhile emperor, Otto IV, from his several years' old excommunication.   After a storm of protest by Frederick's supporters which required the pope to restore order, the Milanese read Otto IV's letter.   Acrimony followed at once, as the Marquis of Montferat and the Milanese ambassadors hurled insults at one another. The session ended without reaching a final decision.

The third session convened on 30 November, commencing with a high mass and the seating of the pope.   Two dogmatic decrees were read aloud, the first, *Firmiter credimus*, being a solemn profession of faith which touched on the orthodox teachings of the Trinity, the Incarnation, baptism, penance, and matrimony, and which gave canonical sanction to the term *transsubstantiatio* in the doctrine of the Eucharist; it was essentially a condemnation of the teachings of the Cathari and, to a lesser extent, the Waldenses.   The companion decree (*c*. 2) was a rejection of other heresies, most notably those of the Calabrian monk Joachim of Fiore on the Trinity, and the pantheistic views of Amalric of Bène.   Thereupon, the formal question was put to the assembly: "*Creditis hec per omnia?*"   These were adopted by acclamation.

The solemn conciliar excommunication of the English barons who had revolted against King John then was pronounced.   During the discussion of England's relationship to the papacy, the archbishop of Mainz as archchancellor of the Empire rose three times to assert imperial claims over England, and three times was silenced by the pope.   Having defended his action regarding England, Innocent at length returned to the matter of the Empire, ratifying what the German princes had done concerning Frederick II, while ignoring altogether Otto IV's plea for absolution.

Then followed the formal reading and adoption of sixty-eight disciplinary decrees which had been prepared in advance in the papal chancery and were not debated in the Council itself.[8] "Innocent regarded these decrees as universal laws and as a summary of the jurisprudence of his pontificate. Few links with earlier councils survive, those with the third Lateran council being the only relevant ones of which we know."[9] The Council closed with the exposition and adoration of the True Cross which had just recently been brought from Constantinople, the singing of the *Te Deum* and the collect, and the papal benediction.

The seventy decrees issued by the Council give clear expression to the concerns of the Church at the beginning of the thirteenth century.[10] Their importance to the further development of medieval canon law can be seen in the fact that many of them were included in the *Liber sextus* of Pope Innocent IV, in the commentaries of the canonists such as the *Compilatio quarta* of Johannes Teutonicus (1216) and in the *Decretalia* of Gregory IX.[11] To what extent they may also have had an impact upon the various churches of medieval Christendom needs extensive further investigation, however.[12]

---

[8] Thus assumes Binterim, *Concilien* IV 269; confirmed by Kuttner/Garcia y Garcia, "A New Eyewitness Account" 164. See also Cheney, "A Letter of Pope Innocent III and the Lateran Decree on Cistercian Tithe-Paying" in *Medieval Texts and Studies* 278.

[9] Tanner, *Decrees* 228.

[10] The English translation of the decrees in Tanner, *Decrees* 230-271, based on the text established by *Conciliorum Oecumenicorum Decreta*, ed. G. Alberigo, J.A. Dossetti, P.-P. Joannou, C. Leonardi, and P. Prodi, in consultation with H. Jedin (Freiburg-Rome-Vienna, 1962) 203-247, is now used in preference to Schroeder, *Disciplinary Decrees*. The definitive edition of the Council's constitutions is now *Constitutiones Concilii quarti Lateranensis una cum Commentariis glossatum*, ed. Antonio Garcia y Garcia, Monumenta Iuris Canonici, ser. A, vol. 2 (Città del Vaticano, 1981). It provides a full critical apparatus, together with the commentaries of five glossators.

[11] The *Compilatio IV* took in all of the constitutions but 42 and [71—the crusade decree, *Ad liberandum*]; the *Decretalia* omitted 42, 49 and [71]. Cf. Stephan Kuttner, "Johannes Teutonicus, das vierte Laterankonzil und die Compilatio quarta," *Miscellanea Giovanni Mercati*, Studi e Testi 125 (Città del Vaticano, 1946) 608-634; on the relationship of the *Compilatio quarta* to other collections of canon law, cf. Kenneth Pennington, "The Making of a Decretal Collection: The Genesis of Compilatio Tertia," *Proceedings of the Fifth International Congress of Medieval Canon Law* (Salamanca, 21-25 September 1976), ed. Stephan Kuttner and Kenneth Pennington, Monumenta Iuris Canonici Series C: Subsidia, Vol. 6 (Città del Vaticano, 1980) 75-77.

[12] Cf. Gibbs/Lang, *Bishops and Reform*, for the only extended treatment of this question to date. Of a more specialized nature is Phyllis B. Roberts, "The Pope and the Preachers. Perceptions of the Religious Role of the Papacy in the Tradition of the Thirteenth-Century

Synods in Germany Prior to 1215

A major instrument of reform as envisioned by Innocent III was re-affirmed in *c.* 6 of the constitutions which ordained that metropolitans hold annual provincial synods with their suffragans, at which canonical rules were to be enacted and the decrees of general councils—particularly the most recent—were to be reviewed, for the purpose of effecting needed changes among clergy and laymen alike. Bishops were to proclaim the provincial decrees in turn at yearly diocesan synods, and to enforce observance through the imposition of due punishment for transgressors. The episcopal role was further strengthened by *c.* 7 which stipulated that "no custom or appeal can impede the execution of their decisions . . . [to correct] their subjects' offenses, especially of clerics, and [to reform] morals." Cathedral chapters were thus put on notice that if they failed to take the necessary reform measures themselves, the responsibility for such would devolve upon their superiors. *C.* 15 stipulated that clerics who, after being warned, did not abstain from drunkenness, were to be suspended from their offices and benefices. *C.* 16 commanded clerics not to engage in secular pursuits, attend unbecoming exhibitions, visit taverns, or play games of chance; their clothing must also be in keeping with their dignity. *C.* 29 ordained that anyone having a benefice with the *cura animarum* attached was to lose the first if he accepted another, and if he resisted this action, he would lose the second one as well; it furthermore prohibited the possession of several dignities in the same church by a single individual. *C.* 12 commanded conventuals in those orders not accustomed to celebrating such to institute general chapters of abbots and priors, to be held in each ecclesiastical province under the presidency of two neighboring Cistercian abbots and two others chosen from those in attendance. Bishops were further instructed to institute a system of regular visitations for the purpose of effecting reforms among all houses of monks, nuns, and canons-regular (*c. 33*).

The ultimate success or failure of these measures in Germany was heavily contingent upon the willingness and ability of the prelates of that realm to implement them. Would they accept Innocent III's vision of their own pastoral role by revitalizing existing provincial and diocesan synodal practices, or by re-establishing such institutions as had fallen into desuetude, and imparting to them this function of perfecting the Church? How committed were they to improving the discipline and order among the children of their own churches? An investigation of synodal activity in

English Church," *The Religious Roles of the Papacy: Ideals and Realities 1150-1300*, ed. Christopher Ryan, Medieval Studies 8 (Toronto, 1988) 277-297, who examines the impact of Innocent III's call for renewed effort in preaching at the Fourth Lateranum.

Germany in the three decades after 1215, together with an analysis of visitations of religious houses and the holding of triennial general chapters by all monastic orders in response to the measures of Lateran IV, is thus basic to an assessment of the impact of Innocent III's legislation.

The traditions for holding provincial and diocesan synods, upon which *c*. 6 of the Fourth Lateran decrees built, were already quite ancient for the six provinces of Germany by 1215, but the surviving record shows only sporadic holding of such assemblies, especially in the four decades which immediately preceded Innocent III's great Council. Interest in these synods dates back at least to the great collections of Johann Friedrich Schannat, *Concilia Germaniae* (1759-1763), Joseph Hartzheim (who continued the work of Schannat to 1790), and Joannes Dominicus Mansi, *Sacrorum Conciliorum nova et amplissima Collectio* (1759-1789), who reprinted most texts from just one fortuitously-known manuscript which had often been copied in a careless fashion. Critical editions of most German synods included in these works are still lacking.[13]

Anton Joseph Binterim, whose *Pragmatische Geschichte der deutschen National-, Provincial-, und vorzüglichsten Diöcesanconcilien* was published 1835-1848, also planned to issue a supplement to Schannat's *Concilia* which would contain numerous references to as yet unknown manuscripts, but unfortunately this was never carried out.[14] Binterim's work did, however, serve as the basis of Karl Joseph Hefele's *Conciliengeschichte* which was published in 1879 and has undergone several revisions.[15] The brief outline of German synodal activity to about 1215 found in volume III of Paul Hinschius' *System des Katholischen Kirchenrechts* (1883) depends almost entirely on the collections of Hartzheim and Mansi.[16] Even Pietro Palazzini's *Dizionario dei Concili* (1963) depends for Germany at least entirely on older research and offers little new.[17] The only comprehensive presentation of German synodal history of the later Middle Ages which meets modern critical standards is the outline given by Albert Hauck in *Kirchengeschichte Deutschlands*, volumes IV and V; this, however, remains incomplete and no longer represents the current state of research.[18]

---

[13] Johanek, "Synodalia" I 4-5; of a like view is Jedin, *Handbook* III/2 206, who cautions that those found in Mansi, *Collectio* XXII, must also be checked for accuracy.

[14] Cf. Franz Gescher, "Hartzheims Concilia Germaniae und ihre Ergänzung durch Binterim und Floss," *ANrh* 118 (1931) 154-157; Johanek, "Synodalia" I 6.

[15] E.g., 2nd edition, revised and augmented by Alois Knöpfler (Freiburg, 1886); French transl. with corrections by H. Leclercq (Paris, 1913).

[16] III (Berlin, 1883) 473-501, 586-596.

[17] (Rome, 1963); cf. critique thereof in Johanek, "Synodalia" I 7.

[18] (8th unaltered ed.; Berlin, 1954).

The works of Binterim and Hefele sought to provide the historical context within which the statutes noted in the great collections could be viewed, but they offered little more than a brief summary of the decrees without a critical investigation of them. Heinrich Finke recognized this in 1891, as did subsequent regional studies such as those of Karl Hübner for Salzburg, Passau, and Brixen, of Nikolaus Hilling for the Westphalian bishoprics, and of Johannes Maring for Hildesheim.[19] Isolated and generally uncritical texts, based on a single manuscript, have also been published, but no attempt has been made to update the collections for individual bishoprics, let alone all of Germany.[20] There is furthermore no exhaustive catalogue of extant manuscripts for German synods comparable to that compiled by Odette Pontal for France.[21]

Heinz Wolter has recently observed that a very distorted picture of German synods emerges when one restricts the investigation just to the legislative evidence. For the period 916 to 1215 only twenty-eight complete sets of statutes issued at provincial, legatine or supra-provincial synods held in imperial Italy and Germany are known to exist, yet the currently accepted number of synods documented from a variety of sources exceeds two hundred and fifty.[22] The state of preliminary studies has heretofore prevented our having definitive figures for either the regularity or distribu-

---

[19] Cf. *Konzilienst.*; further, Karl Hübner, "Provinzialsynoden im Erzbistum Salzburg bis zum Ende des 15. Jahrhunderts," *DGbll* 10 (1909) 187-236; 14 (1913) 243-248; Idem, "Die Passauer Diözesansynoden, *Jahresbericht des Niederösterreich Landes-Real-und Obergymnasiums in Sankt Pölten* (1911) 3-23; Idem, "Die Brixner Diözesansynoden bis zur Reformation," *Dgbll* 15 (1914) 85-103. Heavily dependent upon Hübner for the period of our interest is Johannes Baur, "Brixner Synoden von ihren Anfängen bis zur Gegenwart," *Der Schlern. Zeitschrift für Heimat- und Volkskunde seit 1920* 24 (Innsbruck, 1950) 305-314; Hilling, *Diözesansynoden*; Idem, "Gegenwart und Einfluss der Geistlichen und Laien auf den Diözesansynoden vornehmlich in nordwestdeutschland," *AKKR* 79 (1899) 203-232; and Maring, *Diözesansynoden*.

[20] Cf. Heinrich August Erhard, "Constitutionen einer Mainzer Synode aus der Zeit des Erzbischofs Wernher von Eppenstein," *ZGAW* 10 (1847), 284-299; Joseph Lipf, *Oberhirtliche Verordnungen und allgemaine Erlasse für das Bisthum Regensburg vom Jahre 1250-1852* (Regensburg, 1853); Franz Joseph Moné, "Kirchenverordnungen der Bistümer Mainz und Strassburg," *ZGO* 3 (1852) 129-150; Idem, "Kirchenverordnungen der Bistümer Mainz und Konstanz aus dem 13. und 16. Jahrhundert," *ZGO* 4 (1853) 257-274; Himmelstein, *Synodicon Herb.*

[21] *Liste des MSS* 79-107. For the period before the mid-eleventh century see Martin Boye, "Quellenkatalog der Synoden Deutschlands und Reichsitaliens von 922-1059," *NA* 48 (1930) 45-96. More recently the task for Germany was begun by Johanek who eventually limited his study to Salzburg and Mainz; cf. "Synodalia" I 12-13.

[22] Cf. "Erfahrungen und Probleme bei der Erforschung und Darstellung der Partikularsynoden Deutschlands und Italiens zwischen 916 und 1215," *AHC* 11 (1979) 38-54. This figure, which Wolter maintains is still too low, nevertheless is far greater than that found in Hefele for the same period. Moreover, many of Hefele's "synods" were some other sort of assembly.

tion of diocesan synods.   This present investigation proposes to bring together the scattered results of numerous local and regional investigations, to provide a more extensive search through printed document collections, and to offer a correction to the prevailing view that on the eve of the Fourth Lateran Council both types of synods were essentially moribund in the German church.

By far the greatest number of synods held between 900 and 1215, and 1216-1245, are known to us from brief references in documents or narrative sources.[23] At times the identification of the type of synod rests solely on an analysis of the witness lists which reveal the names of those present at some synodal act: the evidence of comprovincial bishops allows categorizing a particular assembly as a provincial synod; their absence generally means that it was diocesan. Often, however, the word *synodus* is not used in the document at all, being replaced by other terms which had a synonymous meaning: e.g., a document of 1136 contains the rubric: "*actum Colonie in ecclesia beati Petri . . . in presentia et generali conventu tam episcoporum quam abbatum et multarum venerabilium personarum.*"[24] The realization that such phrases were often interchangeable has resulted in the identification of numerous provincial and diocesan synods of which the great collections had no notion whatsoever. A further indicator that certain assemblies were in fact synods is the date of documents which tell of business transacted there.[25] Taken collectively, these approaches to the synodal activities of medieval Germany produce a very different sort of picture than that found in the great collections.

The Province of Cologne

Cologne provides an excellent case in point. *Colonia Agrippina* was at once the largest city in medieval Germany, the seat of the second most important bishopric, and the center of a far-reaching province which extended across Brabant, the Netherlands, the Lower Rhineland, Westphalia, and Lower Saxony. According to the older view, only three provincial synods were held under the presidency of the archbishop during the period 916 to 1215:

---

[23] Indispensable for synods in all German provinces of the pre-Gregorian period are Martin Boye, "Die Synoden Deutschlands und Reichsitaliens von 992-1069," *ZSRG* KanAbt 18 (1929) 131-284, and Idem., "Quellenkatalog." Definitive for the tenth century is now Ernst-Dieter Hehl, unter Mitarbeitung von Horst Fuhrmann, *Die Konzilien Deutschlands und Reichsitalien 916-1001*, Teil I: 916-960, MGH Concilia VI (Hannover, 1987).

[24] Erhard, *Regg. hist. Westf.* II, Nr. 1570; Günther, *CdRhM* I 221; Knipping, *REK* II, Nr. 320; cf. also discussion in Wolter, "Erfahrungen und Probleme" 40.

[25] See Hilling, *Diözesansynoden* 19ff., for the earliest attempts to use these more critical methods in determining the existence of diocesan synods; more recently they have been used by Claude, *Erzbistum Magdeburg* I 223-230, and by Wolter, "Erfahrungen und Probleme" 38-54.

those of 1023, 1067 and 1104.[26] Equally conservative is the outline of the
Cologne provincial synods in Hauck, which lists five provincial synods for
the eleventh and twelfth centuries (1023, 1138, 1152, 1186 and 1187.[27]
Wolter has expanded this list considerably:[28] 920,[29] end of July 1023,[30]
1067,[31] 20 April 1081/1085,[32] 23 September 1110,[33] 23 March (Palm
Sunday) 1119,[34] 1132,[35] early 1136,[36] 3/17 April 1138,[37] 28 August
1140? under Archbishop Arnold I,[38] 29 June (the Feast of Sts. Peter and

---

[26] Hartzheim, *Concilia* III 757; Phillips, *Diözesansynode* 9. Oediger, *Bistum Köln* 170 note
18, citing Knipping, *REK* I, Nrs. 704 (with incorrect date of 1025), 970; II, Nr. 30, argues
that in the twelfth century imperial and legatine synods replaced the earlier provincial synods.
He further contends that because many cathedral canons also held prebends in other foundations
of the province, there was a communication network which made synods less necessary.

[27] *KGD* IV 20 note 1; Idem. V 133, omits that of 1186.

[28] See Heinz Wolter, "Die Kölner Provinzialsynoden bis zum vierten Laterankonzil im
Jahre 1215," *AHC* 21 (1989) 62-102.

[29] Knipping, *REK* I, Nr. 307; Wolter, "Erfahrungen und Probleme" 41; Idem, "Kölner
Provinzialsynoden" 68; and most recently, Hehl, *Konzilien 916-1001* I 41ff.

[30] Knipping, *REK* I, Nr. 704. Boye, "Synoden Deutschlands" 178 and 235, includes this
"*synodus provincialis*" on his expanded list, as does Wolter, "Erfahrungen und Probleme" 42.
Idem, "Kölner Provinzialsynoden" 71 and 97, alters this position, however, seeing it as having
more the character of a *Reichssynode*.

[31] Knipping, *REK* I, Nr. 970. Once again Wolter, "Erfahrungen und Probleme" 42,
includes this on his list of provincial synods, while Idem, "Kölner Provinzialsynoden" 97, has
omitted it.

[32] Erhard, *Regg. hist. Westf.* I, Nr. 1211 (with date 1083); Knipping, *REK* I, Nr. 1166.

[33] Hartzheim, *Concilia* III 256; Knipping, *REK* II 12, Nr. 73; Wolter, "Kölner Provinzialsynoden" 80.

[34] Hartzheim, *Concilia* III 291, 771; Mansi, *Collectio* XXI, col. 175; Knipping, *REK* II,
Nrs. 153-155; Wolter, "Erfahrungen und Probleme" 42; Idem, "Kölner Provinzialsynoden"
80-81; Oediger, *Bistum Köln* I 170; Palazzini, *Dizionario* II 306 (with incorrect date of 19
March). At this synod, the excommunication of Bishop Alexander of Liège and the election
of his successor were the major issues; deliberations ended in the election of Bishop Frederick.

[35] Knipping, *REK* II 45, Nr. 292 ("*Actum publice in eccl. b. Petri . . . omnibus fere
ecclesie nostre prioribus praesentibus: Alexander Leodiensis episc., Arnoldus prep. de domo
s. Petri, . . .*" Thereupon follow the names of seven provosts of the major collegiate churches,
five abbots, seven deans of collegiate churches, a choirbishop, a subdean and a *magister
scholarum*. The lay witnesses include the most prominent dukes, counts, *nobiles* and
ministeriales of the province. See also Idem, II 46, Nr. 294; Wolter, "Kölner Provinzialsynoden" 84.

[36] Erhard, *Regg. hist. Westf.* II, Nr. 1570; Knipping, *REK* II 50-51, Nrs. 318, 319 ("*Actum
Colonie in eccl. b. Petri . . . in presentia et generali conventu tam abbatum quam prepositorum*"), 320 ("*Actum Colonie in eccl. b. Petri . . . in presentia et generali conventu tam
episcoporum quam abbatum et multarum venerabilium personarum: Andreas Traiectensis,
Wernerus Monasteriensis episc. etc.*"), 322. According to Wolter, "Kölner Provinzialsynoden"
85, the date of the synod fell during the first half of the year.

[37] Hartzheim, *Concilia* III 338; Mansi, *Collectio* XXI 519; Knipping, *REK* II 57, Nr. 357;
Hinschius, *KR* III 486 note 5 and 489 note 1; Hauck, *KGD* IV 20 and V 133; Palazzini,
Dizionario II 306.

[38] Witnessing the public announcement made by the Archbishop of Cologne that out of
consideration for the peace and quiet desired by the monks at Klosterrath, the abbot had

Paul) 1152 at Cologne under Arnold II,[39] 2 August (the Monday after St. Peter *in vincula*) 1166 at Cologne,[40] 1186 at Cologne,[41] and 22 March (Palm Sunday) 1187 at Cologne under Philip, in the presence of a papal legate.[42] A complaint lodged against the Curia 1106/1109 sees the provincial synod as a well-established organ of church government. If this letter is not merely a "canonical reminiscence" on earlier times, it suggests that there were others between 1081/1085 and 1110, the record of which has been lost.[43] There is, however, not the slightest indication that they occurred with the regularity required by the canonical decrees. The huge gap which occurs 920-1081 (if we remove the synods of 1023 and 1067) is not found to this same degree in either Mainz or Trier; Wolter attributes it to the close ties which existed during this period between the archbishopric of Cologne and the imperial court, resulting in the fact that the prelates left the business of provincial synods to the royal court or imperial synods. By contrast, no pontificate of any length in the twelfth century lacked at least one provincial synod (a characteristic also observable in other provinces). This in turn has been linked to the new self-awareness of the archbishops

---

recommended the transfer of the nuns cloistered at that same location to Marienthal (*"in vallem, que prius Hubach, nunc s. Mariae dicitur"*) were a very mixed group of clerics from the province, including the following: Bishop Adalbero of Liège, the cathedral provost of Cologne, the provost of St. Severin at Cologne, two archdeacons from Liège, the provost of St. John and Holy Cross in Liège, the provost of St. Dionysius in Liège, and the provost of St. Mary's in Utrecht; a significant number of the leading nobles from the archdiocese of Cologne; and various archiepiscopal *ministeriales*. See Knipping, *REK* II 64, Nr. 387.

[39] *Wibaldi ep.* Nr. 379; *Chron. reg. Colon.* 90; Hartzheim, *Concilia* III 370; Mansi, *Collectio* XXI 763; Knipping, *REK* II, Nrs. 535, 539, 540; Philippi, *UB Osnabrück* I, Nr. 288; Hauck, *KGD* IV 20 and V 133 note 4; Palazzini, *Dizionario* II 306; Wolter, "Kölner Provinzialsynoden" 89.

[40] Knipping, *REK* II 144-145, Nrs. 840 (*"Acta . . . in prima sinodo presente Alexandro Leodicensi [sic] episcopo, Godefrido Traiectensi ep., Friderico Monasteriensi ep., Philippo Osenbrugensi ep., Wernero Mindensi ep."*) 845, 846 (*"Data Colonie in synodo IIII non. augusti . . . nostri pontificatus primo"*); Lacomblet, *NRUB* IV 780, Nr. 630; Philippi, *Osnabrück UB* I, Nr. 319; cf. Wolter, "Kölner Provinzialsynoden" 91.

[41] According to Aegidius Müller, *Anno II. der Heilige. Erzbischof von Köln und dreimaliger Reichsverweser von Deutschland, 1056-1075: Sein Leben, sein Wirken und seine Zeit* (Leipzig, 1858) 160, the formal canonization of the former archbishop, Anno II, was proclaimed at a synod held in 1186. Wolter, "Erfahrungen und Probleme" 42, includes it on his list, as does Hauck, *KGD* IV 20; Idem V 133, omits it.

[42] Hartzheim, *Concilia* III 438; Mansi, *Collectio* XXII 536; Knipping, *REK* II 253-254, Nrs. 1281, 1282, 1264. The chronicler Henricus de Herfordia recorded that: *"Philippus in festo palmarum sollempnem curiam Colonie tenuit. Cui Phylippus comes Flandrie, Lodwicus lantgravius Thuringie, episcopi Monasteriensis et Eystensis [Traiectensis?] et omnes nobiles terre ac circiter 4000 militum itererant;"* cf. *Liber de rebus memorabilioribus*, ed. August Potthast (Göttingen, 1859) 169. See further Goerz, *MRR* II, Nr. 580; Hinschius, *KR* III 487 note 5; Hauck, *KGD* IV 20 and V 133 note 4; Palazzini, *Dizionario* II 306; Wolter, "Kölner Provinzialsynoden" 93.

[43] Cf. Knipping, *REK* II 9-10, Nrs. 62-63; Oediger, *Bistum Köln* I 133, 170 note 18.

in the aftermath of the Investiture Controversy and to a predisposition to increase their metropolitan power. Tied to this effort was the policy of convening synods in the city of Cologne itself, generally during Lent or on some date near the feast days of Cologne's patron, St. Peter.[44]

On 20 August 1083 Archbishop Siegewin of Cologne convened a diocesan synod at which was proclaimed the "Peace of God."[45] This synod marks the beginning of a more normal routine for the archdiocese, and a return to conducting its internal affairs within the confines of its own ecclesiastical structures. Under Archbishop Frederick I (1100-1131) whose pontificate marked a period of greater importance for provincial synods, at least seven diocesan synods also took place: 1103,[46] 13 April (the Wednesday of Holy Week) 1104,[47] mid-October 1109,[48] 23 September 1110,[49] 1121,[50] 1127,[51] and 1130.[52] Others are known for 1136,[53] 1138,[54]

[44] Ennen, *Quellen* I, Nr. 214 (*"In solempnitate s. Petri, quum synodus episcopalis celebratur"*); Hauck, *KGD* IV 8; Wolter, "Kölner Provinzialsynoden" 98-101.

[45] Philippi, *UB Osnabrück* I, Nr. 199; W. Altmann & E. Bernheim, *Ausgewälte Urkunden zur Erläuterung der Verfassungsgeschichte Deutschlands im Mittelalter* (5th ed.; Berlin, 1920) 226. The most complete study of diocesan synods is that of Franz Gescher, "Geschichte und Recht der kölnischen Diözesansynoden" (Dissertation Köln, 1923) 11ff., the conclusions of which are supported by E. Wisplinghoff, "Friedrich I. Erzbischof von Köln (1100-1131)" (Dissertation Bonn, 1951) 70ff.

[46] Hartzheim, *Concilia* III 775; Lacomblet, *NRUB* I 169, Nr. 262 (". . . *in s. synodo Colon.*"); Knipping, *REK* II 4-5, Nr. 27; Hauck, *KGD* IV 7; Gescher, "Geschichte und Recht" 11.

[47] Hartzheim, *Concilia* III 756; Lacomblet, *NRUB* I 170, Nr. 263; Binterin, *Concilien* IV 215, 756; Phillips, *Diöcesansynode* 50; Knipping, *REK* II 6, Nr. 31; Hauck, *KGD* IV 7; Gescher, "Geschichte und Recht" 11.

[48] Hartzheim, *Concilia* III 255-256; Sloet, *Oorkondenboek* 217, Nr. 219; Lacomblet, *NRUB* I 176, Nr. 272 (*"Acta sunt hec a nobis et banno confirmata in generali synodo nostra . . ."*); Binterim, *Concilien* IV 219; Phillips, *Diöcesansynode* 50; Hinschius, *KR* III 586 note 7, 587 note 1; Hauck, *KGD* IV 7; Gescher, "Geschichte und Recht" 13.

[49] Hartzheim, *Concilia* III 256; Lacomblet, *NRUB* I, Nr. 311; Knipping, *REK* II 12, Nr. 73. The primary event was the elevation of the relics of Wibert of Gembloux. Cf. also Gescher, "Geschichte and Recht" 13-16, who argues that the synod took place during the early part of the year, several months prior to the actual elevation of the bones.

[50] Hartzheim, *Concilia* III 773; Lacomblet, *NRUB* I 191, Nr. 292 (*"Actum Coloniae in celebri conventu cleri et populi"*); Binterim, *Concilien* IV 215; Knipping, *REK* II 29, Nr. 191; Wolter, "Kölner Provinzialsynoden" 76, citing Gescher, "Geschichte und Recht" 16.

[51] Ennen, *Quellen* I 502, Nr. 40; Knipping, *REK* II 36, Nr. 236; Gescher, "Geschichte und Recht" 16-17.

[52] Knipping, *REK* II 39-40, Nr. 253 (*"Actum Colonie in celebri conventu cleri et populi"*); Wolter, "Kölner Provinzialsynoden" 76; Gescher, "Geschichte und Recht" 17; Wisplinghoff, "EB Friedrich I." 70ff.

[53] Goerz, *MRR* I 515, Nr. 1889 (*"Colonie in eccl. b. Petri in generali conventu"*); Günther, *CdRM* I 220, 222; Hauck, *KGD* IV 7; Gescher, "Geschichte und Recht" 17-19.

[54] This diocesan synod which began about 3 April, developed into the provincial assembly which convened before 17 April; cf. Wolter, "Kölner Provinzialsynoden" 87.

1139,[55] 1140,[56] 13 June 1142,[57] 1143,[58] 1146,[59] 1147,[60]
1138/1148,[61] 1153,[62] 1163,[63] 1171,[64] 1173,[65] 1174,[66] 1182,[67]

[55] Goerz, *MRR* I 534, Nr. 1955; Lacomblet, *NRUB* I 222-224, Nr. 334 (*"Actum Colonie in celebri conventu cleri et populi"*); Knipping, *REK* II 60-61, Nr. 374; Binterim, *Concilien* IV 216; Gescher, "Geschichte und Recht" 19.

[56] Ennen, *Quellen* I 510, Nr. 48; Binterim, *Concilien* IV 217 (*"Actum Colonie publice in maiori ecclesia"*); Knipping,*REK* II 65, Nr. 390; Hauck, *KGD* IV 7; Gescher, "Geschichte und Recht" 19-20.

[57] Lacomblet, *NRUB* I 234, Nrs. 346, 347; Knipping, *REK* II 68, Nrs. 404, 405 (*"Actum Colonie in publico conventu"*); Hauck, *KGD* IV 7; Gescher, "Geschichte und Recht" 20; Wolter, "Erfahrungen und Probleme" 40.

[58] Knipping, *REK* II, Nr. 412; Binterim, *Concilien* IV 217 (*"Huius rei testes sunt: Arnoldus maioris ecclesiae praepositus et aulae regiae cancellarius, et eiusdem ecclesiae totum capitulum"*); Hauck, *KGD* IV 7; Gescher, "Geschichte und Recht" 20-25. Hartzheim, *Concilia* III 766, and Ennen, *Quellen* I 498, incorrectly place the synod in the year 1113.

[59] Hartzheim, *Concilia* III 353; Hinschius, *KR* III 587 note 2. The synod dealt with an investigation of accused heretics. The item is missing in Knipping, *REK* II, however.

[60] Lacomblet, *NRUB* I 248, Nr. 361; Knipping, *REK* II 77, Nr. 455 (*"Acta Colonie in publico conventu"*); Gescher, "Geschichte und Recht" 25-27.

[61] Gescher, "Geschichte und Recht" 27-28.

[62] Knipping, *REK* II 94, Nr. 564 (*"Acta sunt hec in facie totius ecclesie . . ."*). Witnessing the confirmation of the order of precedence for archdeacons of the Cologne church were all the major provosts of the diocese and at least six abbots. See also Binterim, *Concilien* V 218. Gescher, "Geschichte und Recht" 43-44, admits the possibility that this was a synod, due to the large number of witnesses to the existing document; the lack of lay witnesses leaves him unconvinced, however.

[63] According to Binterim, *Concilien* IV 218, Eckbert of Schönau exposed the errors of various heretical teachers *"in conspectu totius cleri et multorum de populo civitatis"* at Cologne in 1163; these were then condemned at a synod held shortly thereafter and burned. The relevant source references are in Knipping, *REK* II 124-125, Nrs. 760-761. Since the archbishop was in Italy at the time, serving the emperor as chancellor, any diocesan synod would have been under the direction of the cathedral provost and dean of Cologne, Hermann of Hengebach and Philip of Heinsberg. Gescher, "Geschichte und Recht" 43-45, rejects any attempts to place a diocesan synod in the period 1161-1164, failing to recognize that other diocesan officials could function *in loco episcopi*.

[64] Beyer, *MRUB* II 46, Nr. 9; Goerz, *Regg. zu MRUB* II 726, Nr. 725; Hauck, *KGD* IV 7: "*Ex multitudine synodalis conventus quorundum nomina prelatorum et nobilium in testimonium subscribi iussimus. . . . in generali synodo nostra secundum consuetudinem et iusticiam in ecclesia b. Petri sollemniter et legitime celebrata, acta sunt hec et confirmata.*" See also Binterim, *Concilien* IV 218; Gescher, "Geschichte und Recht" 28.

[65] Two separate issues were dealt with: the first, a compromise between the prior of Cappenberg and the abbess of Neuss; cf. Hartzheim, *Concilia* III 404-405; Erhard, *CdWestf* II 121 Nr. 363 (*"nobis Colonie generaliem sinodum celebrantibus"*); Goerz, *MRR* II 95, Nr. 332; Knipping, *REK* II 182, Nr. 983; Hinschius, *KR* III 587 note 1; Phillips, *Diöcesansynode* 50. The second was the announcement by Archbishop Arnold II (of Wied) that he had established a monastery on family patrimony at Schwarzrheindorf and that he turned this new foundation over to his sister, Abbess Hedwig of Essen, for further development; another of his sisters had been appointed as abbess of the new Benedictine convent; see Lacomblet, *NRUB* I 311, Nr. 445 (*"in generali nostra synodo"*); Goerz, *MRR* II 95, Nr. 331; Knipping, *REK* II 182, Nr. 984; Binterim, *Concilien* IV 219. See also Hauck, *KGD* IV 7; Gescher, "Geschichte und Recht" 28-30.

1183,[68] 1185?,[69] 1188?,[70] 1197,[71] and 1198.[72] Uncertainty exists whether the synod held 4 January 1201 at Herringen near Hamm in Westphalia was diocesan or provincial.[73] At some unspecified time between 1200 and

[66] Binterim, *Concilien* IV 219, lists among the diocesan synods an assembly at Cologne in 1174 at which Archbishop Philip reclaimed for his church advocacy over the town of Rhens on the Rhine which had suffered under the heavy hand of its lay advocate, Count Henry of Saffenberg. Witnessing this rather simple act were the provosts, deans, and *magistri scholarum* of the cathedral and major collegiate church of the archdiocese, as well as the counts of Saffenberg, Hochstaden, and Berg, the count of the city of Cologne, and various *ministeriales*. This impressive gathering had significance far beyond the recorded act: the specific mention of the heads of the five secular schools of the city suggests that the synod addressed matters of particular interest or concern to them. The document is printed in Beyer, *MRUB* II 729, Nr. 740; register in Knipping, *REK* II 189, Nr. 1015. Gescher, "Geschichte und Recht" 43, expresses serious reservations about classifying this as a synod: despite the witness list, he finds little else to support such a contention.

[67] Hartzheim, *Concilia* III 426-427 ("*synodus nostra*"); Lacomblet, *NRUB* I 342, Nr. 484; Phillips, *Diöcesansynode* 62; Knipping, *REK* II 229, Nr. 1194; Hinschius, *KR* III 487 note 5, 586 note 11, 587 note 1. Cf. Hauck, *KGD* IV 7, and Idem, V 133 note 2, who argues that this synod, classified as provincial by Hinschius, was probably only diocesan since no bishops but Philip were present. Gescher, "Geschichte und Recht" 30-31, includes it on his diocesan list.

[68] Gescher, "Geschichte und Recht" 30-31.

[69] Binterim, *Concilien* IV 219, includes the assembly at which Archbishop Philip withdrew the right of advocacy over Lechenich from lay hands following the death of Dietrich of Hengebach, owing to the latter's repressive treatment of the inhabitants of the town. Witnessing this event were once again a large number of prominent ecclesiastical and lay personalities whose presence suggests that there was more to the gathering than what has survived in this document; cf. Knipping, *REK* II 241, Nr. 1237. Gescher, "Geschichte und Recht" 43-45, regards the witness list insufficient evidence to agree with Binterim that this was a diocesan synod.

[70] Lacomblet, *NRUB* I 359, Nr. 511; Knipping, *REK* II, Nr. 1323. The act attested by the document is the grant of an island in the Rhine river between Rees and Wissel to the Cistercian monastery at Camp. The key phrase here is "*Nos quidem in ipsa ecclesia Campensi per codicem sanctorum evangeliorum super altare in conspectu plurimorum circumastantium tam synodalium quam laicarum personarum Christo et b. eius genitrici manu propria obtolimus.*" Hilling, "Geistlichen und Laien" 224f., uses this as proof for his argument that both laymen and clergy attended synods in the twelfth century; Gescher, "Synodales" 362-363, on the contrary maintains that in this instance the term *personae synodales* is used as a synonym for *personae ecclesiastici* and that this event was not a synod at all.

[71] Hartzheim, *Concilia* III 465-467 ("*synodus nostra*"); Knipping, *REK* II 310, Nr. 1527; Hinschius, *KR* III 586 note 11, 587 note 1; Hauck, *KGD* IV 7; Gescher, "Geschichte und Recht" 21-22.

[72] Hartzheim, *Concilia* III 466 ("*generalis synodus*"); Knipping, *REK* II 318, Nr. 1557; Hinschius, *KR* III 586 note 7, 587 note 2; Hauck, *KGD* IV 7; Gescher, "Geschichte und Recht" 32-32; further, Wolter, "Kölner Provinzialsynoden" 95. This synod demonstrates that at times the coercive powers of the church were used: "*C. de Schleyde, qui in partem desisae haereditatis ipsam decimam acceperat, de sentencia priorum et assensu nobilium vivorum excommunicavimus.*"

[73] Knipping, *REK* II 322, Nr. 1572; cf. Wolter, "Kölner Provinzialsynoden" 95. Franz Gescher, "Die kölnischen Diözesansynoden am Vorabend der Reformation (1490-1515),"

1203 a joint diocesan synod involving clergy from the dioceses of Cologne and Liège also was held.[74] Despite the political problems which beset the church of Cologne during the first two decades of the thirteenth century, and which came to a head in 1211/1212, there is also record of a diocesan synod at Cologne in 1211.[75]

Since the days of St. Boniface the week days before Maundy Thursday had been the traditional time for holding diocesan synods in Cologne and many other German dioceses.[76] Between 1142 and 1148 the assemblies met on 29 June (the feast of Saints Peter and Paul), leading some of the older legal-historical literature to conclude that this was the customary day of the year. This was an eccentric practice, however, and until about 1280 Maundy Thursday was the recognized feast day around which diocesan synods were scheduled.[77] The great frequency of diocesan synods led to efforts in 1193 by the Cistercian monastery of Petersberg to seek papal exemption from attendance.[78] That such a privilege was necessary despite the general exemption granted in 1186 to the entire Cistercian Order suggests a refusal by the archbishops to concede the abolition of a long-standing custom within their church, by which the abbots of Cistercian houses had been obligated to attend gatherings of their diocesan clergy. A

ZSRG KanAbt 21 (1932) 225, argues that until the mid-thirteenth century Cologne is the only place mentioned as the venue for diocesan synods (18 times); not until the fourteenth century did they begin to rotate Cologne with their other "archiepiscopal city," Bonn. Should Gescher be correct on this issue, the synod in question would have to be included in the provincial category. Cf. further, Bruno Dauch, "Die Bischofsstadt als Residenz des geistlichen Fürsten," *HSt* 109 (1913) 154ff.

[74] Knipping, *REK* II 338, Nr. 1644; cf. Wolter, "Kölner Provinzialsynoden" 96. The confirmation of this document by the papal-legate Guido of Praeneste was made at some unspecified time after 1204.

[75] Knipping, *REK* III, Nr. 115.

[76] Gescher, "Diözesansynoden am Vorabend der Reformation" 234; for the general practice, cf. H. Barion, *Das fränkisch-deutsche Synodalrecht des Frühmittelalters*, Kanonische-Studien und Texte, ed. A.M. Koeniger, 5/6 (Bonn & Köln, 1931) 47f.

[77] Cf. Franz Gescher, "Der kölner Dom des Mittelalters als Pfarr- und Sendkirche des hohen Adels," in *Der Dom zu Köln*, Veröffentlichungen des kölner Geschichtsvereins 5 (Köln, 1930) 226ff.; further, Idem, "Geschichte und Recht" 72ff. A document dated 13 May 1219 contains the rubric *"In solemnitate s. Petri, quum synodus episcopalis celebratur"*; cf. Ennen, *Quellen* I 214, and Lacomblet, *NRUB* II Nr. 80. Ca. 1280 the archbishop issued a statute declaring that henceforth the synods would convene on the Monday after *Invocavit*, the first Sunday of Lent. This maintained the relationship to the provincial synod stipulated by the Fourth Lateranum, namely that the diocesan synod should follow on the heels of the provincial; cf. Phillips, *Diözesansynode* 63f.; Hinschius, *KR* III 591. In the early fourteenth century, Cologne adopted the practice of holding two synods per year, adding one for the first work day after the feast of St. Remigius (1 October); cf. Gescher, "Diözesansynoden am Vorabend der Reformation" 192 note 5, 234.

[78] Lacomblet, *NRUB* I, Nr. 538; cited in Hilling, "Geistlichen und Laien" 223.

further indication of late-twelfth century synodal practices in the archdiocese of Cologne comes from a document of 1219 in which the obligations of the *ministeriales* of the Cologne church were defined: at the same time as the archbishop convened his synod for the clergy, the members of this class of unfree knights was expected to attend a special synod (*Sendgericht*) conducted by the archiepiscopal *capellanus*.[79]

Osnabrück, one of the oldest suffragan churches in the province of Cologne, records a diocesan synod as early as 835.[80] More recently synods had been held 27 May 1153,[81] 1160,[82] 1163,[83] and 1170.[84] This latter assembly is significant inasmuch as it was personally attended by the Abbess Luidgard of Herford. That the synodal tradition flourished between 835 and 1153, and continued after 1170, is suggested from the obligation placed by Bishop Benno II ca. 1082/4 on the first abbot of the newly-established monastery at Iburg, ". . . *ut, dum episcopus synodalia negotia exercuerit, idem abbas eandem synodum more religiosorum observet,*"[85] and from an 1184 charter which attests that Bishop Arnold had made a grant of the tithe at Wildeshausen to the convent of that same location, the purpose of which was to pay the travel and board expenses of the two chapter representatives who were sent to diocesan synods and other assemblies.[86] Since Wildeshausen was not far from Osnabrück, the expenses will not have been great, yet apparently the monastery had complained about such costs to its corporate resources and had perhaps also sought exemption from regular attendance.

---

[79] See Hilling, "Geistlichen und Laien" 222; cf. also [ ] Frensdorff, *Das Recht der Dienstmännern des Erzbischofs von Köln*, Sonderabdruck aus den *Mitteilungen des Stadtarchivs von Köln* (Köln, 1883) 1ff. More recently, Franz Gescher has discussed the obligations of laymen to attend ecclesiastical courts in "Synodales. Studien zur kirchlichen Gerichtsverfassung und zum deutschen Ständewesen des Mittelalters," *ZSRG* KanAbt 29 (1940) 358-446.

[80] Philippi, *UB Osnabrück* I, Nr. 18; Hauck, *KGD* IV 8.

[81] Philippi, *UB Osnabrück* I, Nr. 288 ("*actum in communi synodo in Osnaburg*"); the heading incorrectly refers to this as the decision of a provincial synod. Neither the printing in Möser, *Sämmtliche Werke* VIII 316, nor Erhard, *Regg. hist. Westf.* II 32, Nr. 1796 (UB Nr. 288) repeats that error. See also Hilling, *Diözesansynoden* 6; Hauck, *KGD* IV 8.

[82] Philippi, *UB Osnabrück* I, Nr. 309 (". . . *in synodum nostram*"); Hilling, *Diözesansynoden* 6; Hauck, *KGD* IV 8.

[83] Philippi, *UB Osnabrück* I, Nr. 314; cf. Hilling, *Diözesansynoden* 19, who includes this assembly on his list of those which have the characteristics of a synod, without the name. The witness list is his chief indicator.

[84] Philippi, *UB Osnabrück* I, Nr. 325 (". . . *in generali synodo*"); Hilling, *Diözesansynoden* 6; Idem, "Geistlichen und Laien" 225; Hauck, *KGD* IV 8.

[85] Philippi, *UB Osnabrück* I, Nr. 196.

[86] Philippi, *UB Osnabrück* I, Nr. 377.

The endowment by the bishop reveals the determination with which he sought to enforce synodal attendance, indicating also that matters pertaining to the cure of souls were included on the agenda. Such efforts to enable representatives from economically distressed houses to attend would not have been necessary had the primary function of the synods been merely juridical or administrative. Whether Hilling's contention is valid as well, that the grant made possible a visit twice yearly and that it can therefore be used as evidence for arguing semi-annual synods at Osnabrück, as at Münster, Halberstadt and Hildesheim, requires further substantiation.[87] It likewise cannot be asserted on the basis of this one example that all monasteries sent two proctors.

The diocesan assembly of 1184[88] and a similar one in 1186,[89] designated as *capitula* by Bishop Arnold, may also have been synods inasmuch as the term was commonly used synonymously throughout northern Germany at this time. The practice ceases at Osnabrück by ca. 1203, however, presumably because the growing power of the cathedral chapter made the appropriation of the term *capitulum* by other ecclesiastical bodies impossible.[90]

Like Osnabrück, the earliest recorded synod at Münster dates from the late ninth century—7 October 889.[91] Thereafter, the record is sporadic, but it nonetheless points to an acknowledged tradition: 1022/1032,[92] 1125,[93] 1179,[94] 1185,[95] and 1193—the last three all during the episcopacy of Hermann II of Katzenellenbogen.[96] That synods were regularly sum-

---

[87] Hilling, *Diözesansynoden* 16.

[88] Philippi, *UB Osnabrück* I, Nr. 377.

[89] Philippi, *UB Osnabrück* I, Nr. 385; Hilling, *Diözesansynoden* 6, 10.

[90] Cf. Hilling, *Diözesansynoden* 6 and 22 note 1; Maring, *Diözesansynoden* 12-13; Hinschius, *KR* III 586 note 11. In Hildesheim the term was modified to signify a synod: "*capitulum generale,*" or "*capitulum plenum.*"

[91] Erhard, *Regg. hist. Westf.* I, Nr. 479 (= *UB* Nr. 40). Börsting, *Bistum Münster* 29, gives date of 18 October 889 without reference to sources; he likewise maintains that in later times synods were held every year in the spring and fall.

[92] Erhard, *Regg. hist. Westf.* I 166, Nr. 917 (= *UB* Nr. 103); Börsting, *Bistum Münster* 34-35, places it in 1022.

[93] Hartzheim, *Concilia* III 776-777; Erhard, *Regg. hist. Westf.* I 233, Nr. 1489 (= *UB* Nr. 190); Phillips, *Diöcesansynode* 52, 175. The synod confirmed the establishment of the Premonstratensian monastery at Kappenberg; cf. Börsting, *Bistum Münster* 45.

[94] Erhard, *Regg. hist. Westf.* I, Nr. 2072 (= *UB* Nr. 401).

[95] Erhard, *Regg. hist. Westf.* I, Nr. 451; cf. Hilling, *Diözesansynoden* 19, who includes this assembly on his "probable" list as well.

[96] Erhard, *Regg. hist. Westf.* I, Nr. 2306 (= *UB* Nr. 529); Hilling, *Diözesansynoden* 5. The synod dealt with the establishment of new regulations for church governance, made necessary by the recent creation of several large archdeaconries; see Börsting, *Bistum Münster* 58.

moned and attendance consistently demanded by the bishops of Münster is revealed by a papal charter of 1198 which attests the exemption from synodal attendance granted that year to the Cistercian monastery of Marienfeld.[97]   An even more positive proof comes from an index of privileges claimed by the Premonstratensian convent Kappenberg, including: "*Item in synodis duabus sedebunt praepositus Capenbergensis et Varlarensis iuxta dominum episcopum et decanum et si quid acquisierit decanus, divider cum illis duobus.*"[98]   From this it is also evident that the semi-annual synod was common practice at Münster.   In the thirteenth century, attendance of abbesses at Münster synods was not mandatory, but was allowed, and according to a charter drafted in 1238, laymen were obligated to attend these assemblies as well as the clergy, a custom which was clearly not an innovation but had existed at earlier times as well.[99]

Some modern scholars have assumed that before the thirteenth century synods were only held in the diocese of Utrecht for specific purposes, rather than as part of a long-standing episcopal practice.[100]   There are, however, a number of recorded assemblies which look very much like synods because of the witnesses present for a specific act, or the wording of the document in which the act itself has been preserved.   On 18 November 1006, e.g., Bishop Ansfrid established a Benedictine cloister dedicated to Sts. Mary and Martin at Hoogehorst near Amersfort, granting it various properties as its initial endowment.   All this was "*Actum . . . publice coram idoneis testibus in basilica S. Marie sanctique Martini in Hohorst, ipso die dedicationis eius . . .*"[101]   This is the first recorded assembly within the diocese of Utrecht since Bishop Ansfrid's return from the great synod held at Dortmund the previous year;[102] it may thus have served as a diocesan synod in addition to its stated purpose, since the clergy who were gathered at Hoogehorst would have been able to receive direct word of matters discussed at Dortmund.

---

[97] Erhard, *Regg. hist. Westf.* II, Nr. 2404 (= *UB* II Nr. 569); cf. further, Hilling, "Geistlichen und Laien" 223.

[98] Dated by Hilling, *Diözesansynoden* 16 and 43, at ca. 1209; cf. also *Westf. UB* III, Nr. 51 note.

[99] Hilling, "Geistlichen und Laien" 225, citing Finke, "Die angebliche Fälschung" 162 note 1; cf. also Hilling, *Diözesansynoden* 43; *Westf. UB* III, Nr. 346.

[100] *Vorreformatorische Kirchengeschichte der Niederlande nach Willem Moll Deutsch bearbeitet nebst 1. einer Polemik gegen die im 1. Bande der Janssen'schen Geschichte des deutschen Volkes erhaltenen Kirchengeschichte Irrtümer und 2. eine Abhandlung über die Bedeutung Kirchengeschichtlicher Bildung für das geistliche Amt* (Leipzig, 1895) 145, with which Hauck, *KGD* IV 8 note 3, disagrees.

[101] Muller, *Oorkondenboek* I 153-154, Nr. 162.

[102] Muller, *Oorkondenboek* I 151, Nr. 159.

In 1027 the vassals of Bishop Adelbold assembled in the general synod,[103] a synod of 25 June 1058 served to publish a recent accord between the bishops of Utrecht and Liège,[104] and on 28 December 1063 the members of the synod witnessed an agreement reached between the bishop and a diocesan abbot.[105] For the next four decades, however, the record is silent.[106] Not until the early twelfth century do we find traces which suggest that diocesan synods were still a regular occurrence. In 1108 Bishop Burchard VIII granted the church at Limmen to St. Mary's church in Aachen: the transfer took place with the assistance of the count of Holland and the advocate, in the presence of numerous dignitaries from the diocese; the charter issued contains the rubric "*Acta est publice hec traditio . . . ,*" allowing the inference (as was also the case in Cologne) that this was a diocesan synod.[107]

A document dated 13 August 1108 contains a similar phrase and may be yet another record of business transacted at this same synod.[108] At some time before 24 September 1116 an agreement was reached between the churches of Utrecht and Tournai whereby the collegiate chapter of St. Mary at Bruges was released from subordination to the chapter of St. Martin at Utrecht. The charter issued in this connection refers to the "*Tornacensi sinodo pristino*"; perhaps a similar synod at Utrecht was the forum at which

---

[103] Hartzheim, *Concilia* III 18: "*praenominati omnes feudales ecclesiae in generali synodo episcopi Traiectensis tenentur et debent personaliter interesse, qui fuedum suum a me receperunt;*" Hinschius, *KR* III 588 note 9, 589 note 3.

[104] Bormans, *Cartulaire* I 33, Nr. 23; Muller, *Oorkondenboek* I 200, Nr. 220: "*Placuit autem successoribus illorum venerabili quidem episcopo Leodicensi Dietwino item Traiectensi pontifici domno Wilhelmo, pie fraternitatis gratia in unum coadunatis, conditionem illam renovare et in synodo Leodicensi in auribus cleri et populi publice recitare, . . .*"

[105] Hartzheim, *Concilia* III 148; Muller, *Oorkondenboek* I 203, Nr. 225 ("*In nomine sancte et individue Trinitatis hec carta consignata et in sinodo confirmata, banno episcopali corroborata*"); Hinschius, *KR* III 587 note 1; Palazzini, *Dizionario* VI 8.

[106] While the possibility exists that Bishop Conrad held a diocesan synod with his clergy on 29 October 1088, at which time he confirmed the privileges of the cathedral chapter and issued regulations for its members, the fact that "*Acta sunt hec in capitulo Maioris ecclesie, presentibus . . .*" in the presence of the Emperor Henry IV, the archbishops of Cologne and Trier, and the bishops of Halberstadt and Münster, reveals this to have been far more than just a local assembly; cf. Muller, *Oorkondenboek* I 226, Nr. 253.

[107] Sloet, *Oorkondenboek* 215, Nr. 216; Muller, *Oorkondenboek* I 255, Nr. 277. See also Muller, *op.cit.* Nr. 278 (1108 "*Actum publice*"). On 9 August 1108 Bishop Burchard resolved a dispute over property lying between Lek and Linge in the presence the cathedral provost and three collegiate provosts, seven other canons from the cathedral and St. Boniface, and numerous *laici liberi*; the size and type of witnessing body suggests that they had been present at a diocesan synod (see Muller, *op.cit.* I 257, Nr. 280).

[108] Sloet, *Oorkondenboek* 216, Nr. 218: "*Acta est publice . . .*"

this accord was publicly announced.[109]   In 1121, at sometime before 13
April, Bishop Godebold transferred the church at Warnsveld to the Utrecht
cathedral chapter, which again *"Actum est publice in Traiecto . . ."*[110]
Another document bears just the year 1129 and records the confirmation of
the founding of the cloister Mariënweerd by a noblewoman named
Alveradis.   It contains the more common *"Actum Traiecta in generali
synodo . . . ,"*[111] but the type of business of which it bears record was
much the same as that mentioned in the other three documents, strengthening   our   conjecture   that   all   four   assemblies   were   essentially   the
same—diocesan synods. A further support for our argument is the fact that
not all episcopal documents contain the *"Acta est publice"* rubric; it was
thus not just some notarial flourish but had a technical meaning.

On 29 May 1132 Bishop Andreas of Utrecht declared before a large
assembly of cathedral and collegiate clergy, abbots, nobles and *ministeriales*
that the burghers of Staveren had freed the church of St. Odulf from all lay
control; at the same time he confirmed the establishment of a monastic
community in the church, for which he established regulations and specified
privileges.[112]   Once again, the event has the character of a diocesan
synod, providing the bishop with the opportunity of restating his episcopal
prerogatives over against religious foundations.

After 1132 there is a hiatus in the evidence for almost three decades. At
some time between 1157/1164 Bishop Godefrid presided over a diocesan
synod at which the complaints of the abbey of Lorsch regarding the
dilapidated condition of the church at Angeren were handled.   The
parishioners were ordered to replace the roof over the sanctuary and on
other buildings and to maintain a perpetual flame in the church.[113]
Godefrid was also present at the provincial synod held at Cologne in early
August 1166,[114] and in 1173 we find record of a diocesan synod at which

---

[109] Muller, *Oorkondenboek* I 264, Nr. 286.

[110] Sloet, *Oorkondenboek* 231, Nr. 236; Muller, *Oorkondenboek* I 274, Nr. 298. Among
te privileges granted to the church was: *"Fecimus etiam ipsam ecclesiam liberam a circatu
episcopi, ab oblatis, ab omni episcopali debito, nisi si episcopus ibi presens synodum habeat
et duas marcas pro servitio accipiat."*

[111] Sloet, *Oorkondenboek* 243-244, Nr. 249: Muller, *Oorkondenboek* I 300, Nr. 327.

[112] Muller, *Oorkondenboek* I 311, Nr. 340 (*"Data autem Traiecti in die sancto
Pentecostes, . . . presentibus testibus idoneis clericis, liberis, ministeralibus."*

[113] Muller, *Oorkondenboek* I 379, Nr. 422 (*"quod legatus abbatis de Lorsa, cum
pulsaretur coram nobis pro aedificiis in Angerem restaurandis, hoc tamen iudicio totius synodi
generalis obtinuit, quod parrochiani in Angerem ecclesiam preter sanctuarium in tecto et in
caeteris aedificiis restaurare . . ."*)

[114] Muller, *Oorkondenboek* I 407, Nr. 454.

a new church service was introduced.[115]   At an assembly held in 1176, the
prelate declared that because of the large numbers of people who previously
had attended the archidiaconal synod (*Send*) at Epe, it had become necessary
to divide them and release the inhabitants of certain locations from prior
obligations.[116]   The decision impacted the lives of parishioners, yet the
decision itself was probably declared in a diocesan synod in the presence of
the archdeacons and other prominent clergy of the Utrecht church.

The tradition of diocesan synods is then interrupted until 1205 when, to
the question of whether it was necessary to have the approval of the patron
in order to erect a new church, a diocesan synod returned an affirmative
answer.[117]   The final reference before 1215 is particularly significant for
the history of German synods because the 1209 assembly is known to us
through a set of statutes which were published.   These decrees stipulated
that three times yearly a *commune capitulum* was to take place—on the
Wednesday after Low Sunday (*Quasimodogeniti*), the Wednesday after
St. Remigius, and on the feast day of St. Blaise.[118]   Like the term "*Actum
est publice*" which appears to have been the standard rubric used to
designate actions taken at a diocesan synod in the early twelfth century, the
phrase "*commune capitulum*" was apparently interchangeable with
"*synodus*" in the late twelfth and early thirteen century.   Although there is
sufficient evidence to conclude that a tradition of regularly-held diocesan
synods existed during the first half of the twelfth century, it is too
fragmentary to allow the assumption that this same frequency persisted up
to the time of the Council of 1215.[119]

---

[115] Hartzheim, *Concilia* III 404 ("*generalis synodus*"); Hinschius, *KR* III 586 note 7;
Hauck, *KGD* IV 9; Palazzini, *Dizionario* VI 8.

[116] Muller, *Oorkondenboek* I 434, Nr. 487: ". . . *exemplo praedecessorum meorum edocti
et ab auctoritate nobis concessa freti, consilio ecclesiae nostrae, propter numerositatem et
multitudinem populi, convenientis ad synodum in ecclesia Eep, illos de Herghe et illos de
Gaedsbergh et illos de Vorichten ab ea divisimus, ita ut prima die synodi quam devote et
religiose in ecclesia de Herghe et in Gaedsberh custodiant et observant, et a sepeliendo
cimiterii, ab aedificatione ecclesiae in Ep, et ab omni iure synodali, quo ipsis de Epe fuerint,
absolvimus et liberor fecimus.   Omnibus autem, qui ad capellam de Fassen et ad capellam de
Unen assignati sunt, firmiter praecipimus, ut illis duobus diebus ad synodum in ecclesia de
Eepe, tanquam in matrici ecclesie, in omni synodali subjecti sint iure, ibique sepes civiterii et
aedificationes ecclesiae procurent.*"

[117] Hartzheim, *Concilia* III 490-491; Hauck, *KGD* IV 17-18.

[118] Hartzheim, *Concilia* III 488-490; Phillips, *Diöcesansynode* 10; Hinschius, *KR* III 487
notes 1 and 4; Palazzini, *Dizionario* VI 8.   Cf. Hauck, *KGD* IV 8-9, who argues that these
statutes are technically *not* a decree of the synod, having been only discussed and accepted by
the organizers.

[119] On the relationship of diocesan synods and the development of the exclusive right of
episcopal election for the cathedral chapter at Utrecht, see Requerus Richardus Post,

Minden's recorded synodal tradition commences just before the beginning of the thirteenth century—in 1197, when an assembly was convened on 4 April, the Friday after Easter.[120]   Another was summoned between 1209 and 1214, the record of which reveals only that the privileges of the monastery at Nenndorf had been investigated.[121]   Judging from the antiquity of synodal practices in neighboring bishoprics, however, we may assume the existence of other, unrecorded synods in the twelfth, and perhaps also the eleventh, century.

The evidence for synods in Liège is likewise scant.   That the tradition was ancient may be inferred from the existence of a *Sermo synodalis* which is attributed to Bishop Ratherius (953-956).[122]   Two assemblies from the tenth century are referred to as "*synodalis conventus*", the first in 968 and the other in 980.[123]   Since the accord reached between Bishops Dietwin of Liège and William of Utrecht at the latter's city on 25 June 1058 (and presumably as part of a diocesan synod) regarding churches at Odilienberg, Linne, and Leenkerken, stipulated that this same agreement be made known to the clergy and people of Liège in a public synod, we can only surmise that such was carried out shortly thereafter.[124]   The *Chronicon sancti Huberti Andagimensis* contains the brief note for the year 1075: "*Hiis actis circa Leodiensem sinodum quae agitur in festo apostolorum Simonis et Iudae [2 July], . . . ,*" informing us as to when synods normally met for the diocese of Liège,[125] but this was no fast rule.   The business for which the document dated 14 June 1096 was fashioned ("*Actum . . . publice Leodii*"),[126] was probably transacted at a diocesan synod.

At a synod held in 1104 at Liège, Bishop Otbert confirmed the return of property to the monastery at Stablo.[127]   On 23 December 1107 at Liège, Henry, king of the Romans, confirmed the ancient privileges of the mother

---

Geschiednis der Utrechtsche Bisschopsverkiezingen tot 1535, Bijdragen van het Instituut voor Middeleeuwsche Geschiedenis der Reijks-Universiteit te Utrecht, ed. O. Oppermann, 19 (Utrecht, 1933) 28-68.

[120] Cf. Hilling, *Diözesansynoden* 8, citing B.C. von Spilcker, "Geschichte der Grafen von Everstein und ihrer Beneficien," *Beiträge zu älterer deutscher Geschichte* (1833), *UB* 25, Nr. 22.

[121] *Westf. UB* VI, Nr. 39; Hilling, *Diözesansynoden* 8.

[122] Phillips, *Diöcesansynode* 57.

[123] Hartzheim, *Concilia* III 647, 662; Hinschius, *KR* III 586 note 11.

[124] Bormans, *Cartulaire* I, Nr. 23.

[125] *MGH SS* VIII 588; Hauck, *KGD* IV 8.

[126] Bormans, *Cartulaire* I 46, Nr. 29.

[127] Binterim, *Concilien* IV 215 ("*Hanc cartam in synodo mea, ut debui, confirmavi.*" See also Phillips, *Diöcesansynode* 138.

church, including its synodal rights,[128] and the following year Bishop Otbert confirmed in his synod a statute of the cathedral chapter regarding deceased canons.[129] Hartzheim also records a synod for 1124.[130] The next recorded synod at Liège went far beyond a mere diocesan assembly, however. On 21 March 1131 Pope Innocent II and King Lothar met there in what was described as a dazzling affair: in addition to the pope and thirteen cardinals, the archbishop of Rheims and other French prelates were present; some counted more than thirty bishops and over fifty abbots participating.[131] The diocesan synod held 1136 must therefore have seemed a minor affair, by contrast, as Stephan, provost of the cathedral church, granted the tithe from property at Marché to his servitor John.[132] In 1139 Bishop Albero transferred ownership of property at *Turnines* to the monastery at Stablo in his synod.[133] The confirmation of a grant to St. Bernard of Clairvaux for the purpose of establishing a Cistercian daughter-house in the bishopric of Liège, probably took place at a diocesan synod held in 1158 as well.[134] In 1196 Abbot Gerard of Prüm was a witness at the *synodus generalis* held at Liège in the church of St. Peter to a charter issued by Bishop Albert in favor of the monastery *Bonae spei*.[135]

From the beginning of the thirteenth century the evidence is more plentiful. Prior Reiner made an entry into his annals for the year 1202, that "*Episcopus ordines sollempnes in pentechoste fecit, et synodum cellebravit.*"[136] On 22 June 1203 Bishop Hugh (of Pierrepont) and the cathedral chapter publicly announced that the count of Loos had surrendered several properties to the bishopric of Liège and had received them back as fiefs. This was a public event, "*Actum est hoc publice et sollemniter in presentia nostra Leodii . . .*"[137] Later that same year the decrees for the church at Liège formulated by Cardinal-legate Guy presumably were read at another

---

[128] Bormans, *Cartulaire* I 50, Nr. 30.

[129] Binterim, *Concilien* IV 215 ("*Confirmatum in capitulo S. Lamberti etc.*")

[130] *Concilia* III 775; Phillips, *Diöcesansynode* 52.

[131] Erhard, *Regg. hist. Westf.* II, Nr. 1531; Hauck, *KGD* IV 147.

[132] Bormans, *Cartulaire* I 63, Nr. 38 ("*Actum est hoc in publico conventu nostro . . .*")

[133] Binterim, *Concilien* IV 216 ("*Huic rei interfuerunt praelati et canonici maioris ecclesiae Fridericus praepositus et archidiaconus etc. . . . Actum est hoc publice Leodii in capitolio s. Mariae sanctique Lamberti.*"

[134] Bormans, *Cartulaire* I 81, Nr. 48; the bishop stated that he took the action "*consilio et consensu tocius Leodiensis ecclesie . . .*"

[135] Goerz, *MRR* II, Nr. 767 ("*Leodii in eccl. b. Petri in nostra synodo generali*"). Albert of Kuyck was elected 11 November 1194, but received consecration as bishop 7 January 1196 at Cologne. This was presumably his initial diocesan synod. See also Hartzheim, *Concilia* X 719; Phillips, *Diöcesansynode* 138.

[136] *Reineri Ann. (a. 1202)* 656.

[137] Bormans, *Cartulaire* I 130, Nr. 83.

diocesan assembly.[138] In 1204 Bishop Hugh made known the decision of his synod regarding the conflict between the abbey of Alne and Hugh of Florennes.[139] These, and the further synods held after 24 May 1209[140] and in 1212,[141] together with the synod summoned shortly after Lateran IV (in 1217) suggest the existence of a long-standing synodal tradition for the diocese of Liège.

The Province of Salzburg

Synodal practices for the province of Salzburg went back to the erection of the metropolitanate in 798, comprising the bishoprics of Brixen, Freising, Regensburg, Passau, and Neuburg-on-the-Danube. The latter church was soon combined with Augsburg and made part of the province of Mainz.[142] Archbishop Arno, elected on 20 April 798, held a series of synods in order to introduce Frankish ecclesiastical practices into his province. The first recorded assembly was on 20 August 798 at Reisbach-on-the-Vils in Bavaria.[143] Five months later, on 20 January 799, he convened another synod at Reisbach, with continuations later that year at Freising and Salzburg.[144] Subsequent synods are noted for 16 June 804,[145] May 805,[146]

[138] Bormans, *Cartulaire* I 132, Nr. 84 (dated after October 1203?); cf. Ch. Two below.

[139] Bormans, *Cartulaire* I 145, Nr. 91 (". . . *quod in generali synodo Leodii nobis presidentibus . . . Quam sententiam nos utpote iustam approbantes, eam nostra et tocius synodi auctoritate confirmavimus, . . .*").

[140] *Reineri Ann.* 661; further, pp. 157-158, below.

[141] *Reineri Ann. (a. 1212)* 664: "*Sinodus Hoii celebratur, tota Leodiensis ecclesia lamentatur, organa deponit et silet. Inter episcopum et ducem treugae dantur usque as octavos sancti Johannis baptiste.*" See further discussion, pp. 173-174, below.

[142] For the history of Salzburg provincial synods, see Hübner, "Provinzialsynoden" 187-236, with corrections by Dopsch, *Geschichte Salzburgs* I 328.

[143] Hübner, "Nachträgliches über die Salzburger Provinzialsynoden" *Dgbll* 14 (1913) 243-244, emending his earlier statement in "Provinzialsynoden" 189 which combined the assemblies of 798 and 799. Cf. also, Albert Werminghoff, "Zu den bayerischen Synoden am Ausgang des VIII. Jahrhunderts," *Festschrift für Heinrich Brunner* (Weimar, 1910) 458-464; more recently the early synodal activity at Salzburg has been treated by Hageneder, *Geistliche Gerichtsbarkeit* 1ff.

[144] Hübner, "Provinzialsynoden" 189-190, places the synod in the year 800; Idem, "Nachträgliches" 244-245, using Hauck's arguments, *KGD* II (3rd/4th ed; Weimar, 1912) 464, revises this to 799. See also, Heidingsfelder, *Regg. Eichst.* I 19, Nr. 38. Hageneder, *Geistliche Gerichtsbarkeit* 1, notes that among the items considered at these synods was the decree of the archbishop that all clerics avoid lay tribunals and seek resolution of their disputes with the counsel of the bishop; cf. *MGH Concilia* II/1 207 (lines 32-36).

[145] Hübner, "Provinzialsynoden" 189.

[146] Hübner, "Provinzialsynoden" 189.

and 16 January 807;[147] Archbishop Arno held two assemblies for his provincial clergy in 810, at Regensburg and at Freising.[148] Others occurred in the winter of 870;[149] July 900 at Reisbach,[150] early 916,[151] 7 October 916 at Regensburg,[152] 14 January 932 at Regensburg,[153] and 16 July 932 at Dingolfing.[154] At a diocesan synod held 1 August 976 at Regensburg, Archbishop Friedrich of Salzburg exchanged properties with one of his *ministeriales;*[155] on 2 August 1023 at Regensburg Archbishop Hartwig exchanged property with two lay nobles of his diocese.[156]

The church reforms of the twelfth century had the greatest impact in Germany within the province and archdiocese of Salzburg. Included in these was an active synodal program. On 31 July 1129 Conrad I convened an assembly at Lauffen,[157] in 1137 at Friesach,[158] 10 October 1139 at

[147] *MGH Concilia* II/1 234, Nr. 32; Hübner, "Provinzialsynoden" 189; Idem, "Nachträgliches." 245; Hauck, *KGD* II 464 (3rd/4th ed., Leipzig, 1912); Hageneder, *Geistliche Gerichtsbarkeit* 2. Heidingsfelder, *Regg. Eichst.* I 20, Nr. 39, gives a provincial synod at Regensburg (806?) at which were present Archbishop Arno, Atto of Freising, Adalwin of Regensburg, Hato of Passau, Einrich of Seben (Säben).

[148] Hübner, "Nachträgliches" 245 note 1, citing Hauck, *KGD* (1912) II 464ff., note 6.

[149] Hübner, "Provinzialsynoden" 189; Idem, "Nachträgliches" 245; Alfons Huber, *Geschichte Österreichs* I (Gotha, 1885) 106ff.; Max Vancsa, *Geschichte Nieder- und Oberösterreichs* I (Gotha, 1905) 176ff.; Hauck, *KGD* (1912) II 723ff.

[150] Presumably the one listed by Hübner, "Provinzialsynoden" 189, for 899; cf. Heidingsfelder, *Regg. Eichst.* I 36, Nr. 86. Present were the archbishop and the bishops of Freising, Eichstätt, Säben (Brixen), Regensburg and Passau; Ried, *CdRatisb.* I 78, Nr. 78.

[151] Cf. Heidingsfelder, *Regg. Eichst.* I 42, Nr. 112 (6 July 916 at Neuburg): the bishop of Eichstätt was present with the archbishops of Mainz and Salzburg, and the bishops of Regensburg, Freising and Verden, at an assembly with King Conrad. The Eichstätt prelate thus probably attended the synod held on the border of his bishopric at Hohenaltheim im Ries.

[152] Heidingsfelder, *Regg. Eichst.* I 42, Nr. 112.

[153] Hartzheim, *Concilia* III 57; Boye, "Quellenkatalog" 49; Heidingsfelder, *Regg. Eichst.* I 43, Nr. 114; Boye, "Synoden Deutschlands" 276; Phillips, *Diöcesansynode* 9; Hehl, *Konzilien 916-1001* I 93ff.

[154] Boye, "Quellenkatalog" 50; Heidingsfelder, *Regg. Eichst.* I 43, Nr. 115. The decrees are published in *Quellen und Erörterungen zur bayrischen und deutschen Gesch.* I 411; most recently in Hehl, *Konzilien 916-1001* I 115ff. This was another Bavarian synod at which representatives of Eichstätt were present, along with the archbishop and the bishops of Regensburg, Passau, Freising and Säben.

[155] Hautaler, *SUB* I 183, Nr. 19 (". . . *coram primatibus synodum Radaspone colentibus in die, quando vincula sancti Petri celebramus, fecit*"); Boye, "Quellenkatalog" 61.

[156] Boye, "Quellenkatalog" 77 ("*Actum . . . in concilio publico*").

[157] *Vita Chuonradi c.* 22, *MGH SS* XI 76f.; Hartzheim, *Concilia* III 308; Hübner, "Provinzialsynoden" 179; Hauck, *KGD* IV 20 note 1, and V 134; Palazzini, *Dizionario* II 233-234; Dopsch, *Geschichte Salzburgs* I 1268 note 260.

[158] *UBLOE* II 178, Nr. 120. Archbishop Conrad granted to the monastery at Reichersberg the salt-basin at Bad Reichenhall, together with other properties. Witnessing this act Bishop Romanus of Gurk and Pabo, the cathedral provost at Gurk; the cathedral provost and a canon

Friesach,[159] and in October 1143 at Reichenhall in Tyrol. This latter synod is now known to us through a fragment of the statutes which were promulgated there.[160] They show clearly that pastoral reform was a major issue, stipulating that every church should have its own priest, and if there were too many chapels within a single parish for one priest to properly serve, then rather than appointing vicars (the word used is *mercenarii*), new parish priests were to be instituted; canons regular who cared for a parish church were also to have full responsibility for all chapels within the parish; and only those who actually possessed parish churches were to be ordained as priests.

On 23 October 1144 Archbishop Conrad granted the tithe at Püten and Bramberg to the monastery at Reichersberg.[161] Two years later he held three provincial synods, the first at Reichenhall on 9 October,[162] the second on 11 November at Passau,[163] and the third on 20 December at Friesach.[164] That he was intent on introducing reform into all royal monasteries within his province can be seen from one of the synodal decrees: monastic reform was seen as the complement to clerical reform

---

at Salzburg, the prior of Klosterneuburg, two abbots, other clerics and several laymen. The event bears all the characteristics of a synod.

[159] *UBLOE* II 183, Nr. 123. Archbishop Conrad restored to the monastery at Admont the tithe at Lungau which had been renounced by a third party; witnessing this event were the bishop of Gurk, the cathedral provosts of Gurk and Salzburg, two abbots and numerous nobles and *ministeriales*.

[160] Weinfurter, *Bistumsreform* 176 note 330, 177 note 331, 186-190; cf. also Czumpelik, *Gurk* 230ff. The decrees are found in clm 12 612, fol. 117^r-117^v (*Ex consilio Hallensi*) from Ranshofen, to which Peter Johanek, "Ein Mandat Papst Hadrians IV. für die Mönche von Seeon und die Ordensreform in der Kirchenprovinz Salzburg," *StMOSB* 83 (1972) 166 note 24, made first reference. See also Dopsch, *Geschichte Salzburgs* I 1268 note 261a.

[161] *UBLOE* II 215, Nr. 146. Witnessing this were the bishop of Gurk, the abbots of Salzburg and Admont, the provosts of Salzburg, Chiemsee and Berchtesgaden, four other priors and numerous clerics and laymen. The witnesses suggest that a provincial synod had been held

[162] Hübner, "Provinzialsynoden" 189, 196-197; Dalham, *Concil. Salisb.* 69 (with date 1145); Meiller, *RAS* 41f., Nr. 224; Idem. 54f., Nrs. 281-285; Hauthaler, *SUB* II Nrs. 246f.; Palazzini, *Dizionario* II 159. Hauck, *KGD* IV 20 note 1, assumes separate synods at [Reichen]-Hall in 1145 and 1146. See also Weinfurter, *Bistumsreform* 161 note 259, and 177; Cornelius Will, *Konrad von Wittelsbach, Cardinal, Erzbischof von Mainz und von Salzburg, deutscher Reichskanzler* (Regensburg, 1880) 76, 203; Dopsch, *Geschichte Salzburgs* I 1268 Note 261.

[163] Dalham, *Concil. Salisb.* 70 (1145); Hauck, *KGD* IV 20 note 1 (who assumes separate synods at Passau in 1145 and 1146); Meiller, *RAS* 54, Nrs. 281 (1146), 284 (1146).

[164] *UBLOE* II 221, Nr. 151. These assemblies appear to have been continuations of the first synod at which the issue of the tithe at Neukirchen was treated. The account of the final session refers to the previous synod at Passau, suggesting that this too should be regarded as part of the synodal record for 1146. Present were Bishops Otto of Freising and Romanus of Gurk, the abbots of Admont and St. Victoria, the provost at Seckau, various archdeacons and priests.

by this prelate. The contemporary *Vita Gebehardi et successorum eius* records that, with the exception of Frauenchiemsee and Göss, there were no houses of regular or secular clergy which were not the object of his reforming efforts.[165] This synod also confirmed the establishment and transfer of the canons-regular foundation Feistritz-Seckau.

Archbishop Eberhard I issued a charter declaring the exchange of property between the monastery of St. Peter and the Salzburg cathedral chapter "*in die autem ordinationis nostrae*," to which Bishops Otto of Freising, Hartmann of Brixen and Romanus of Gurk bore record.[166] Such a solemn occasion may also have been the opportune moment for the new metropolitan to meet with his comprovincial clergy in a synod. More certain is the notice given in the *Annales s. Rudberti* for 18 October 1150: while this entry is far too terse to provide information regarding the synod's agenda, Hübner suggests that it undoubtedly published the statutes from the general Church council held in 1148 at Rheims.[167] Perhaps another assembly was held between 1149 and 1151 as well.[168] While the presence of the bishop of Gurk at an assembly held 20 December 1153 at Leibnitz may not suffice to consider this as a provincial synod,[169] a gathering of many of the most prominent clergy of the province at Salzburg on 8 June 1160 seems without question to have been just that.[170] The fruits of the

---

[165] *MGH SS* XI 44: "*Exceptis enim duobus monasteriis sanctimonialium Chyemsse et Gosse, quae illum audire noluerunt et ipse obedire contempserunt, nulla ecclesia vel monachorum vel clericorum aut sanctimonialium in toto eius episcipo fuit, quae non aut sub ipso constructa aut per eum in rebus interioribus ex exterioribus meliorata et augmentata fuerit.*"

[166] *UBLOE* II 242, Nr. 162, dated 1147.

[167] *Ann. Salisb.* (a. 1150) 775: "*Sinodus quinque episcoporum sub Eberhardo episcopo Salzburg habetur*"; Hübner, "Provinzialsynoden" 189, 198-199; Meiller, *RAS* 63, Nr. 40; Hauck, *KGD* IV 20 note 1, and V 134.

[168] Hansiz, *Germaniae sacrae* II 252, lists another provincial synod for the year 1150 at Regensburg: "*Beatus Eberhardus, sanctae Salzburgensis Ecclesiae Archiepiscopus, in Synodo quam Ratisbonae Suffraganeis suis assistentibus habuit, Octaves Matris Mariae Beatae instituit.*" Following Hansiz are Dalham, *Concil. Salisb.* 73; Hefele, *Conziliengeschichte* V 528; Thaddäus Zauner, *Chronik von Salzburg* I (Salzburg, 1796) 156; Mansi, *Collectio* XXI 749, and Hinschius, *KR* III 486 note 5. Hübner, *op.cit.* 198-199, notes that there is no record of the archbishop at Regensburg in 1150; he was there in 1149 with the suffragans of Regensburg and Gurk, however, and again in 1151 with Regensburg and Freising; perhaps the (1150) synod was in one of these years.

[169] *UBLOE* II 265, Nr. 177. Archbishop Eberhard I declared a concord between the monastery at Stuben and Engelschalk of Leibnitz; witnessing the event were the bishop of Gurk, the cathedral provost of Gurk, the abbot of Salzburg, Prior Gerhoh of Reichersberg, and numerous other clergy.

[170] *UBLOE* II 302, Nr. 204. Archbishop Eberhard granted permission to allow the parish

reform activities of Conrad and Eberhard were at best short-lived, however, being destroyed by the papal schism which pitted one party against the other throughout the Latin church.

Only after the restoration of ecclesiastical order could Archbishop Conrad III (1177-1183) resume regular church activities. Indicative of this return to normalcy was the provincial synod held 1 February 1178 at Hohenau, in which all suffragans participated. There is no record of decrees issued at this assembly, though a letter written by the dean at Tegernsee to his Abbot Rupert makes mention thereof.[171] Hübner also identifies an assembly held 2 February 1180 at Salzburg as a provincial synod, called to deal with problems which arose during the unrest of the recent papal schism, and with claims by the cathedral chapter and *ministeriales* at Gurk to the right of election of their own bishop.[172] Hauck, on the other hand, rejects this, pointing out that Bishop Albert of Freising and Abbot Henry of Heiligenkreuz sat as *delegati iudices a domino papa*.[173] Eberhard I also held two diocesan synods for Salzburg for which we have documentation: in November 1159 at Reichenhall, and during the autumn of 1161 at Friesach.[174] From the pontificate of Adalbert III (1183-1200), there are also four known diocesan synods, 15 December 1187 at Leibnitz, which dealt with an exchange of churches and the termination of a legal process, from which one of the parties withdrew,[175] 31 August 1188 at

church at Bramberg to be cared for by a priest from the monastery at Reichersberg. Witnessing this were the bishops of Brixen and Gurk, the provosts of Chiemsee, Berchtesgaden and the Salzburg cathedral chapter, the abbot of St. Peter's in Salzburg, and the prior of Reichenhall.

[171] *Ann. Salisb.* 506; Hübner, "Provinzialsynoden" 189, 199-200; Hinschius, *KR* III 487 note 1; Hauck, *KGD* IV 20 note 1, and V 134 note 1; Meiller, *RAS* 131, Nrs. 13, 14, 15; Palazzini, *Dizionario* II 159. Pope Celestine III speaks of this synod as the first one held by Archbishop Conrad. The letter is placed by Mansi, *Collectio* XXII 121 in the year 1171, for which he posits a provincial synod as well; Hübner rejects this and argues for 1178 as the date for both the letter and the therein-mentioned synod. See also Dopsch, *Geschichte Salzburgs* I 1279 Note 485.

[172] *Chron. Gurcense, MGH SS* XXIII 10; Jaksch, *MC* I, Nr. 312; Hartzheim, *Concilia* III 424; Hauthaler, *SUB* II, Nr. 424a; Hübner, "Provinzialsynoden" 189, 200; Dopsch, *Geschichte Salzburgs* I 1280 Note 501.

[173] *KGD* IV 20 note 1.

[174] Hübner, "Provinzialsynoden" 199.

[175] Hartzheim, *Concilia* III 441 ("*capitulum universale*"); Dalham, *Concil. Salisb.* 87; Jaksch, *MC* III 505, Nr. 1346; Hauthaler, *SUB* II, Nrs. 447 ("*in capitulo nostra Libniz . . .*"), 456; Meiller, *RAS* 148, Nr. 33; Phillips, *Diözesansynode* 8 note 26, 50; Hinschius, *KR* III 586 note 11, 587 note 1; Hübner, "Provinzialsynoden" 201 note 2.

Lauffen,[176] 1192 at Salzburg,[177] and in mid-November 1195 at Lauf-fen.[178]

The hiatus between 1161 and 1178 for both provincial and diocesan assemblies can in part be attributed to the papal schism; only after the restoration of ecclesiastical order could synodal practices be resumed. The reform-minded Abbot Gerhoh of Reichersberg, and Archbishops Conrad I and Eberhard I during the mid-twelfth century, had utilized provincial and diocesan synods to help accomplish their tasks.[179]   Since their day, however, there had been a marked decline, and Archbishop Eberhard II at the beginning of the thirteenth century had a constant struggle to reverse that condition.   Shortly after his accession, Eberhard secured a bull from Pope Innocent III (dated January 1201), according to which all comprovincial bishops of Salzburg were obligated to attend any and all yearly provincial synods which might be convened.[180]   Despite this, however, in the following fifteen years there were no true synods for the entire province of Salzburg.   The assembly held at Gutaring in Carinthia in late 1201 was attended only by Eberhard's uncle Walther, the new bishop of Gurk, by Meinhalm, the archdeacon of Friesach, Prior Henry of Mariasaal, and various other lesser clergy.[181]   Another synod for the provincial regions of Carinthia and Styria was held at Friesach in 1202, dealing among other things with issues involving the monastery at Admont; present were Bishop Walter of Gurk and numerous nobles.[182]   That same year the archbishop

---

[176] Hauthaler, *SUB* II, Nr. 460 (*"Acta sunt hec . . . in capitulo nostra celebri Loufen . . ."*).

[177] *UBLOE* II 442, Nr. 301.   Archbishop Adalbert confirmed to the monastery at Reichersberg privileges and liberties granted by his predecessors; witnessing this event were various members of the Salzburg cathedral chapter and the prior of Boumburg, leaving somewhat uncertain the nature of the assembly.

[178] Hartzheim, *Concilia* III 459-462 (*"in solemni capitulo"*); Hauthaler, *SUB* II, Nr. 498 (*"Acta sunt hec . . . in sollempni capitulo apud Loufen habito . . . presentibus et assentibus prepositis et abbatibus supra in inscriptionibus suis annotatis et laicis quam plurimis"*); Meiller, *RAS* 160, Nrs. 99, 100; Hinschius, *KR* III 586 notes 10 and 11, 587 note 1; Palazzini, *Dizionario* 233-234. Cf. further the discussion in Hübner, "Provinzialsynoden" 189, 199-201; Phillips, *Diöcesansynode* 8 note 26, 50.

[179] Johanek, *Synodalia* I 87-89.

[180] Potthast, *Regesta* I, Nr. 1251; Meiller, *RAS* Nr. 8; Dopsch, *Geschichte Salzburgs* I 328.

[181] Muchar, *Steiermark* V 34; Hansiz, *Germaniae sacrae* II 315.

[182] Muchar, *Steiermark* V 35; Dopsch, *Geschichte Salzburgs* I 328, denies this "*capitulum*" the status of a provincial synod, or even of a diocesan synod, since it had at best a regional character. That the term "*capitulum*" was synonymous "*synodus*" elsewhere in Germany in the late twelfth/early thirteenth century is clear from our survey of the individual dioceses and provinces, however.

also convened a provincial assembly at his fortress Leibnitz,[183] details of which are very sparse.

In 1203 a synod was convened once more at Friesach. Attended by Bishop Walter of Gurk, Abbot Rudiger of Admont, the abbot of Viktring, Provost Gerald of Seckau, Henry, the dean of Gurk, Henry, the archdeacon of Lavant, and other members of the clergy and laity, it dealt with (among other things) complaints from the cloister at Göss against a self-proclaimed advocate.[184] It was this same community of nuns which had resisted the reforming efforts of the Salzburg prelates half a century earlier; where once they rejected the decisions of the archiepiscopal synod, now they sought its intervention in their behalf. Presumably the assembly which met 8 February 1203 at Lauffen was a diocesan synod, called to deal among other things with the renewal of an indulgence granted to the monastery at Reichersberg in 1192.[185]

The authority of the synod over-against the archbishop was manifested on 10 November 1205 at Leibnitz when the claims by the abbey of St. Lamprecht to appoint the priest at Biber were conceded by Eberhard II in the presence of Abbot Ulrich of St. Paul's, Prior Gerold of Seckau, the archdeacons Meinhard and Henry, and other lesser clergy.[186] Less is known of a synod held 1204/1207 at Lauffen.[187] At the provincial synod convened on 1 May 1209 at Friesach to deal with a dispute over the church at Schönberg in Styria, the bishop of Gurk was once again the only suffragan bishop present, though many lesser clerics also attended.[188] Six weeks later the archbishop presided over a diocesan synod held 14 June 1209 at Werfen, which confirmed the possessions of the monastery at Admont.[189] The bishop of Gurk was once again the only diocesan who attended the yearly provincial synod held 1 May 1210,[190] and though numerous abbots, priors and clerics attended the synod held in 1211 at

---

[183] Dopsch, *Geschichte Salzburgs* I 328, maintains that this assembly of the clergy and people had only a regional character and was thus not even a diocesan synod.

[184] Muchar, *Steiermark* V 42; Froelich, *Dipl. Styriae* I, Nrs. 24-26; Obersteiner, *Gurk* 71.

[185] *UBLOE* II 489, Nr. 339. Witnessing this act were the cathedral provost and dean at Salzburg, the provost at Chiemsee who was also a Salzburg canon, fourteen other cathedral canons, the abbot of St. Victor, the priors at Reichenhall and Garze, and several other clerics.

[186] Muchar, *Steiermark* V 45.

[187] Hauthaler, *SUB* III, Nr. 755. Dopsch, *Geschichte Salzburgs* I 328, argues that this assembly had regional character only, thus failing to qualify as a diocesan synod.

[188] Muchar, *Steiermark* V 56-57; Obersteiner, *Gurk* 73; Froelich, *Dipl. Styriae* I 190-191.

[189] Muchar, *Steiermark* V 58. Present were Provost Albrecht of the Salzburg cathedral, Engelmar the *custos*, Rudiger the head of the infirmary, Henry the *cammerarius*, eleven capitular priests, two capitular deacons, and other clerics.

[190] Obersteiner, *Gurk* 73; Jaksch, *MC* I 427.

Friesach, witnessing the resolution of a conflict between the archbishop and the duke of Austria, there were no other bishops present, suggesting that it was diocesan rather than provincial.[191]

The very mixed nature of synods held during the first fifteen years of Archbishop Eberhard II's pontificate reveal two rather important aspects: the first relates to the prelate's determination to employ this organ of ecclesiastical administration in his efforts to strengthen his position vis-a-vis his diocesan clergy on the one hand, and his suffragan bishops on the other; the second is the equally emphatic refusal by these two groups to surrender their accustomed independence. We shall yet see the degree to which either side in this power struggle succeeded in gaining the upper hand in the decades which followed the Fourth Lateran Council.

Those same suffragan bishoprics had limited synodal traditions of their own, judging from the evidence which has survived. Established in 1072, Gurk exhibits a flurry of synodal activity in the mid-twelfth century which perhaps corresponds to the reform efforts of the archbishops of Salzburg. Assemblies in 1146 and 1150 may have considered the reform decrees issued at Reichenhall in 1143 and 1146;[192] at that held at Gurk in 1178 we may presume the statutes published that same year at the 1178 Salzburg provincial synod were read, in addition to the conduct of business of a more local nature.[193] Surprising is the fact that as often as the Bishop Walter of Gurk was present at Salzburg synods in the early thirteenth century, there is no record of his having presided over a similar gathering of his own clergy.

Documented as early as 572/577 as a suffragan of the province of Aquileia, the see of Säben was transferred into the newly established province of Salzburg in 798, and was obligated to attend synods convened by that metropolitan. In the second half of the ninth century, the episcopal seat was transferred to Brixen in South Tyrol. Its strategic location on the road through the Brenner Pass gave it an importance far beyond its size. On 25 June 1080, e.g., the Emperor Henry IV called a council at Brixen for the purpose of dealing with Pope Gregory VII. Attended by some twenty-one Italian and nine German bishops, this synod (clearly not diocesan!) declared the pontiff deposed.[194] Not until 1186 does the record show

---

[191] Muchar, *Steiermark* V 62, is uncertain about the venue—Friesach, Salzburg, or Leibnitz? Present were numerous abbots, priors and clerics, but no other bishops, suggesting that it was diocesan. Dopsch, *Geschichte Salzburgs* I 328, on the other hand, rejects this *generalsynode* as either a provincial or a diocesan assembly because it had a regional character only.

[192] Jaksch, *MC* I, Nrs. 145, 172.

[193] Cf. Jaksch, *MC* I, Nr. 202.

[194] Philippi, *UB Osnabrück* I Nr. 191; Baur, "Brixner Synoden" 305.

evidence of a diocesan synod for Brixen, which dealt mainly with administrative and legal matters—e.g., tithes from various properties belonging to
the mother church were granted to the foundation (*Stift*) Polling in Upper
Bavaria.[195] If the synod also dealt with pastoral matters, we may assume
that it built on the foundation of the Salzburg provincial synods of 1178 and
1180.[196]

Freising presents an erratic pattern, with tenth century synods recorded
for the years 908,[197] at which a dispute between the bishop and a choir-
bishop was resolved, and 3 April 956,[198] at which various parcels of
church property were exchanged. Thereafter, the record is silent until 1140
when Bishop Otto I met with his clergy "*in universali capitulo*" at
Freising.[199] In the year 1170 a "*plena synodus*" confirmed the grant of
a tithe.[200]

Laymen clearly participated in Passau synods from the Frankish period
as evidenced by a charter issued in 903.[201] About the year 985 synods for
the diocese of Passau held at Lorch and Mautern dealt with various tithe
rights of that bishopric between the river Enns and the Vienna Woods.[202]
Another synod from approximately this same time held at Mistelbach
established the tithe boundaries for five baptismal churches in Upper
Austria.[203] At a synod convened in 1074 at Passau, Bishop Altmann
decreed that the papal bulls then issuing forth from Rome be read, explained
and followed. Particular attention was given to the observance of celibacy.

---

[195] Baur, "Brixner Synoden" 305; Hübner, "Brixner Diözesansynoden" 86; Sparber,
"Brixner Bischöfe" 24-26; G. Tinkhauser, "Studien und Skizzen zur Geschichte der Kirche von
Säben und Brixen," *Katholische Blätter aus Tirol* Jg. 11 (1853) 597-598, prints the text of a
copy no longer extant in the consistorial archive at Brixen. See also, Sinnacher, *Säben und
Brixen* III 618.

[196] The oldest set of synodal statutes for Brixen dates from 1511; cf. Ludwig Rapp, "Die
Statuten der ältesten bekannten Synode von Brixen im Jahre 1511," *Zeitschrift des Ferdinand-
eums für Tirol und Vorarlberg* 22 (Innsbruck, 1878) 1-45.

[197] Hartzheim, *Concilia* II 585-586 ("*publica synodus*"); Hinschius, *KR* III 586 note 8, 587
note 1.

[198] See Boye, "Quellenkatalog" 54; Hinschius, *KR* III 587 note 1.

[199] Hartzheim, *Concilia* III 781-782; Phillips, *Diöcesansynode* 8 note 26; Hinschius, *KR*
III 586 note 11.

[200] Hartzheim, *Concilia* III 365; Hinschius, *KR* III 586 note 11, 587 note 1.

[201] *UBLOE* II 49, Nr. 36 ("*Pataviensis ecclesie presul et . . . choriepiscopus eiusdam sedis
. . . consedentes publicamque synodum tenentes multisque laycis multisque tam comitibus quam
ceteris nobilibus viris presentibus . . .*"); see also Hageneder, *Geistliche Gerichtsbarkeit* 4 note
25.

[202] See Boye, "Quellenkatalog" 62-63.

[203] Boye, "Quellenkatalog" 63.

Apparently the clergy were unreceptive to this directive, however, for the record states that they sought the bishop's life.[204]

Hageneder has identified a significant number of eleventh- and twelfth-century synods, the purpose of which appears to have been for effecting decisions or compromises between ecclesiastical parties, or between a monastery or foundation and some lay antagonist: 1081/1091,[205] 1093,[206] ca. 1155,[207] 1158,[208] 1159,[209] 1162,[210] 1163/1165,[211] 1169-1173,[212] ca. 1180,[213] 1180,[214] ca. 1188,[215] 1188,[216]

---

[204] *Vita Altmanni episc. Pataviensis (cap. 11)* 232: "*Altmannus collecto undique fratrum concilio, in ipso Pataviensis ecclesiae gremio epistolas ab apostolico missas coram omnibus recitari praecepit, canonica iura proposuit, consecratos viros ab uxoribus abstinere censuit.*" See also, Hansiz, *Germaniae sacrae* I 262-263; Hartzheim, *Concilia* III 173-176; Hinschius, *KR* III 587 note 1; Schrödl, *Bistum Passau* 119-125; Palazzini, *Dizionario* III 355. Further discussion in Phillips, *Diöcesansynode* 50; Kerschbaumer, *Sankt Pölten* I 173; G. Allmang, "Altmann (Saint) evèque de Passau," *DHGE* II cols. 826-827.

[205] *Fontes rer. Austr.* II 69 406, Nr. 265; Hageneder, *Geistliche Gerichtsbarkeit* 195.

[206] *UBLOE* II 720, Nr. 10; Hageneder, *Geistliche Gerichtsbarkeit* 6, 195. The recorded issue was a disputed tithe involving the monastery at Kremsmünster and the parish priest Eberhard.

[207] *Mon. Boica* V 323, Nr.38; Hageneder, *Geistliche Gerichtsbarkeit* 194.

[208] *Fontes rer. Austr.* II 31 104f., Nr. 106; Idem. 33 8f., Nr. 6; Hageneder, *Geistliche Gerichtsbarkeit* 6, 195. The issues were disputed tithes between Bishop Otto of Freising and the monastery at Seitenstetten. See also *UBLOE* II 291, Nr. 196, dated 1158 at Mautern, in which Bishop Conrad of Passau grants to the canons-regular at Waldhausen a tithe and the parish rights at Beinwald: "*Acta autem sunt haec a nobis in celebri conventu fratrum nostrorum Mutaren assistentibus venerabilibus fratribus nostris archipresbyteris . . . et abbate Cothwicense, prep. Neuenburg., prep. S. Nicholai, prep. Methnensi etc.*"

[209] Hauthaler, *SUB* II 469ff., Nr. 337; Hageneder, *Geistliche Gerichtsbarkeit* 6, 195. This synod seemed preoccupied with complaints by the monastery of St. Peter of Salzburg against Gumpold of Pollheim who had retracted a grant made by his father to the cloister, and against Adalbert of Perg who claimed a vineyard and a tithe.

[210] *UBLOE* II 317f., Nr. 216; Hageneder, *Geistliche Gerichtsbarkeit* 195.

[211] *UBLOE* II 326f., Nr. 223; Hageneder, *Geistliche Gerichtsbarkeit* 195.

[212] *UBLOE* I 85, Nr. 146; Hageneder, *Geistliche Gerichtsbarkeit* 195.

[213] *UBLOE* I 594f., Nr. 243; Hageneder, *Geistliche Gerichtsbarkeit* 195.

[214] *Mon. Boica* V 312, Nr. 23; Hageneder, *Geistliche Gerichtsbarkeit* 195. See also the document dated 1180 at Passau, attesting the exchange made with the monastery at Arbenburg under Abbot Gebhard involving a tithe: ". . . *quod venerabilis abbas . . vir in sancta professione spectabilis atque fervidus cum suis fratribus nostrisque non paucis fidelibus aput Anesum in nostro sollemni capitulo nos adiit . . . Peracta sunt hec Patavie in celebri capitulo nostro choro presente et universo fidelium nostrorum collegio . . .*" Witnessing this were members of the cathedral chapter and numerous laymen.

[215] *UBLOE* I 587f., Nr. 224; Hageneder, *Geistliche Gerichtsbarkeit* 195.

[216] *UBLOE* II 407f., Nr. 277; *Fontes rer. Austr.* II 33 25, Nr. 16; Hageneder, *Geistliche Gerichtsbarkeit* 6, 194. The synod rejected a claim to property by Bishop Otto of Bamberg against the monastery at Seitenstetten.

1196,[217] ca. 1200,[218] 1200-1204,[219] and ca. 1203.[220]   Other assemblies dated 23 August 1111,[221] 1125,[222] 7 March 1189 at Efferding,[223] and July 1189 at Krems[224] have the characteristics of diocesan synods, though they may have been chapters of the Augustinian canons in the diocese.

The record of the synod held in July 1188/1190 is of particular interest because it notes the fact that representatives of the cathedral chapter, four abbots, eight provosts or deans from foundation churches, and eighteen parish priests witnessed the confirmation of the sale of possessions by the Augustinian chapter at Waldhausen to the cathedral chapter at Salzburg.[225]

---

[217] Hauthaler, *SUB* I 881, Nr. 17 (". . . *celebravit sollempnem synodum in Patavia, ubi diffinitum fuit de eleccione Maticensis.*") See also Hübner, "Passauer Diözesansynoden" 5, citing Erben, *Mattsee* 69, Nr. 17; Idem, 104, Nr. 7; Hageneder, *Geistliche Gerichtsbarkeit* 5, 194. The synod dealt with the composition of a dispute between Bishop Wolfger and the foundation at Mattsee over the right of electing the provost. The cloister complained that the previous three bishops had severely compromised its right to elect its own provost by appointing one of their cathedral canons to the office. Acting as a judicial body, the members of the synod decided in favor of Mattsee. In the end, however, the cloister invoked the bishop's grace (". . . *ut eis in sua iustitia derogari non deberet, nostram misericordiam suppliciter imploraverunt.*")

[218] *UBLOE* I 598, Nr. 254; Idem II 473, Nr. 326; Hageneder, *Geistliche Gerichtsbarkeit* 195. See also *UBLOE* II 470, Nr. 324, dated ca. 1200, which records the resolution of a conflict between the monastery of St. Nicholas and the brothers at Tegernbach regarding the tithe at Tegernbach; witnessing this were a large number of clerics and laymen, including the abbot of Altha, the priors of Reichersberg and Osterhoven, and several cathedral canons.

[219] *UBLOE* II 470, Nr. 324; Hageneder, *Geistliche Gerichtsbarkeit* 18, 194.

[220] Hartzheim, *Concilia* III 482; *UBLOE* II 470f., Nr. 324; Hinschius, *KR* III 586 note 11, 587 note 2; Palazzini, *Dizionario* III 355; Hageneder, *Geistliche Gerichtsbarkeit* 195. At this "*capitulum publicum*" a dispute over a tithe was resolved. See also Othmar Hageneder, "Die bischöflich- passauische Synode des 12. und 13. Jahrhunderts als Gerichtsforum. Bericht über den 7. österreichischen Historikertag in Eisenstadt . . . 1962," *Veröffentlichungen des Verbandes Österreichischer Geschichtsvereine* 15 (Wien, 1963) 156-159.

[221] *UBLOE* II 142, Nr. 98. Bishop Ulrich confirms the liberties of the monastery St. Florian and the possession of two parish churches: "*Acta sunt hec consilio et consensu tam cathedralium quam ministerialium nostrorum, quorum nomina . . .*"

[222] *UBLOE* II 163, Nr. 110. Bishop Reginmar confirms to St. Florian grants made by two laymen: "*Acta sunt hec anno ab incarnatione domini mcxxv . . . per venerabilem pataviensis ecclesie episcopum . . . publice in capitulo suo Patavie banno et presenti sigilato privilegio, ut inconfulsum permaneat, confirmante.*"

[223] *UBLOE* II 415, Nr. 284. Bishop Diepold confirms the request from Abbot Hiltger of Wilhering regarding an exchange of property: "*Acta sunt hec . . . ad capitulum Everdingen.*"

[224] *UBLOE* II 418, Nr. 286. Bishop Diepold confirms anew with the episcopal advocate the sale of property by the monastery at Velburg to the Salzburg cathedral chapter. Witnessing this act were a large number of clerics including the abbot of Kremsmünster.

[225] Hauthaler, *SUB* II, Nr. 457, gives the date as July 1188; *UBLOE* II 420, Nr. 287, ca. 1190. The latter recension of the document notes that Bishops Otto of Bamberg and Otto of Freising were present as witnesses, as was the provost of the Bamberg cathedral chapter; this suggests a direct relationship between this synod and that notes for 1188 (above, Note 214).

Such an impressive showing by the diocesan *plebani*, while assumed elsewhere, is seldom documented.

Sometime between 942 and 966 Bishop Starchand of Eichstätt entered into a prayer-union with the Regensburg church, according to which every priest in the Regensburg diocese was obligated to recite three masses between one synod and the next for the bishops of the Salzburg province and for the neighboring bishops of Salzburg and Eichstätt. Our knowledge thereof comes from a decree from a Regensburg diocesan synod of the tenth or eleventh century preserved in Vienna.[226] Whether annual synods continued unrecorded on a regular basis thereafter until the early thirteenth century we cannot say. On 17 September 1194 Bishop Conrad granted the church and location of Weihmerting to the cloister at Mondsee, an act done *"ex sententia chori nostri et ministerialium ecclesiae nostrae."*[227] Witnessing this were a large number of clerics and laymen, suggesting that this was a diocesan synod. Certainly the practice of holding such assemblies survived into the thirteenth century: in 1209 it was brought to the attention of the bishop at his synod with the leading clergy of the diocese that when the rural priests and deans gathered for their annual assemblies (the archidiaconal *Send*), they hid the fact that they were living openly with concubines, an act which a papal letter of 18 April 1209 charged brought injury to their souls and aroused anger among the people.[228]

The Province of Trier

Re-established as a metropolitanate in about 811-813, Trier included in its ecclesiastical union the Lotharingian bishoprics of Toul, Metz and Verdun. Under Archbishop Hetti (816-847) the comprovincial bishops petitioned for a concerted effort to hold yearly synods as was prescribed in the ancient canons. The direct result of that request is uncertain, but a well-established synodal tradition clearly existed by the end of the century. Beginning with that of 893,[229] provincial assemblies are recorded for 927 at Trier,[230]

---

[226] Heidingsfelder, *Regg. Eichst.* I 47, Nr. 127 (*"Hanc igitur orationis adunationem quandocumque nostri adventaverunt synodi cause parrochiani, de una synodo usque ad aliam sine aliqua minoratione cum subscriptione fieri decrevimus . . ."*); Hefele-Knöpfler, *Conziliengeschichte* IV (2nd ed.) 603f.

[227] *UBLOE* II 447, Nr. 305.

[228] Ried, *CdRatisb.* I 297, Nr. 314 (". . . *cum ad generalem synodum singulis annis accedunt"*); Potthast, *Regesta* I, Nr. 3706; Hauck, *KGD* IV 9; and Janner, *Regensburg* II 55. The decrees of this synod are discussed in the context of Ch. Two, below.

[229] In general, cf. Boye, "Synoden Deutschlands" 151, 233; Heydenreich, *Metropolitangewalt* 80-112; Goerz, *RET* 44.

[230] Boye, "Quellenkatalog" 48; Idem, "Synoden Deutschlands" 140 and 233; Michael Blasen, "Die Canonessammlung des Erzbischofs Ruotger von Trier vom Jahre 927," *Pastor Bonus* 52 (Trier, 1941) 61-72; Idem, "Erzbischof Ruotger von Trier (915-930) und seine Bedeutung für die kirchliche Reichsgeschichte mit einem Auszug seines Capitulare,"

929,[231] 17 November 947 at Verdun,[232] 13 January 948 at Mouzon,[233] 8 September 948 at Trier,[234] 995 at Mouzon,[235] 1030 and 1037 under Archbishop Poppo.[236]

During the Gregorian era synods unique to the archdiocese or province of Trier gave way to the larger imperial or papal synods. As late as 13 March 1127 the papal legate Peter presided over a synod at Toul.[237] As in other metropolitanates, the second quarter of the twelfth century was marked by the vigorous pontificate of a reform-minded archbishop. Following what appears to have been a long hiatus, during which the internal affairs of the ecclesiastical province of Trier were subordinated to the demands of the papal-imperial conflict, Archbishop Albero summoned a provincial synod in 1132 at Diedenhofen,[238] followed in 1135 by one at Metz[239] and another at Rettel.[240] The assembly held 20 January 1136

(Unpublished Dissertation Bonn, 1944); Idem, "Die Bussbücher und die Reformsbestrebungen des Erzbischofs Ruotger von Trier (915-930) auf dem Gebiete der Bussdisziplin. Ein Beitrag zur Rechtsgeschichte des Bistums Trier," *AmKG* 3 (1951); and Peter Brommer, "Die Kanonessammlung Ruotgers von Trier. Quellenuntersuchung und Analyse der Arbeitsweise," 27 *AmKG* (1975) 35-48. See also the critical edition in Hehl, *Konzilien 916-1001* I 75ff.

[231] Heydenreich, *Metropolitangewalt* 111; Goerz, *RET* 47.

[232] Boye, "Quellenkatalog" 51; Idem, "Synoden Deutschlands" 151; Hehl, *Konzilien 916-1001* I 128ff. This synod cut across the ecclesiastical provinces of Trier and Rheims, and was thus not technically a German provincial synod.

[233] Boye, "Quellenkatalog" 51; Idem, "Synoden Deutschlands" 151; Hehl, *Konzilien 916-1001* I 132ff. Once again this was a supra-provincial assembly involving clergy from both Trier and Rheims provinces.

[234] Boye, "Quellenkatalog" 52; Idem, "Synoden Deutschlands" 151; Palazzini, *Dizionario* V 408-410; Hehl, *Konzilien 916-1001* I 164ff. This was a joint synod for the provinces of Trier and Rheims.

[235] Boye, "Synoden Deutschlands" 151. In addition to the clergy from the provinces of Trier and Rheims, representatives of the dioceses of Liège and Münster were also present.

[236] Johannes Jacobi, "Erzbischof Poppo von Trier (1016-1047). Ein Beitrag zur geistlichen und politischen Situation der Reform," *AmKG* 13 (1961) 21; Goerz *RET* 8; Brower/Masen, *Antiq.* 518a. These synods were used to carry out a precise division of property between the bishopric and the cathedral chapter.

[237] *Gesta Godefridi archiep. Trev. (cap. 8)* 203: ". . . *cum episcopis . . . et abbatibus quam pluribus et optimatibus regionis , . . .*"; Hauck, *KGD* IV 170 note 8.

[238] Calmet, *Hist. eccles.* I (2nd ed.) 298; Goerz, *MRR* I 504, Nrs. 1852, 1853 ("*In celebri conventu apud Theodonis Villam coram domino Alberone archiepiscopo rev. Trevirensi, praesentibus quoque tribus episcopis Stephano Metensi, Henrico Tullensi, Alberone Virdunensi*"); Hontheim, *Hist. Trev. dipl.* I 519-520, Nr. 345f.; Martène, *Thesaur.* IV 135-137; Binterim, *Concilien* IV 216; Palazzini, *Dizionario* V 408-410. According to these, restitution was made by Duke Simon of Lorraine before the body of the synod. Hauck, *KDG* V 133, argues, however, that this assembly was not a synod, but a *Fürstentag* (diet of princes). The language of the document is consistent with that used for other provincial synods, however; it thus seems that Hauck is in error.

[239] Calmet, *Hist. eccles.* I (2nd. ed.) 305; Hontheim, *Hist. Trev. dipl.* I 529; Goerz, *MRR* I, Nr. 1875; Idem, *RET* 17; Binterim, *Concilien* IV 216; Hauck, *KGD* IV 20 and V 133.

[240] Mansi, *Collectio* XXI 419; Hartzheim, *Concilia* III 332; Goerz, *MRR* I 510, Nr. 1876; Palazzini, *Dizionario* V 408-410. Hauck, *KGD* V 133, argues that this "*conventus*" cannot be

at Trier, during which Archbishop Albero confirmed the reformation of the monastery of St. Paul at Verdun according to the Premonstratensian model was clearly a provincial synod as well: witnessing this act were the bishops of Metz, Toul and Verdun, together with representatives of the cathedral chapter, the collegiate churches of St. Paulin and St. Simeon, and six abbots.[241]

Archbishop Hillin, clearly one of the most dominant German metropolitans of his generation and one of the more effective occupants of the chair at Trier during the entire twelfth century, exhibited a strong determination to control his province, convening two synods in the year 1152, the first on 18/29 January at Metz,[242] and a second on 16 August in his metropolitan city.[243]   Others are recorded for 1157 at Trier,[244] 9-11 March 1159 at Trier,[245] 1161 at Trier,[246] 1162 at Toul,[247] and 1163 at Trier.[248]

considered a synod. Our survey of German synodalia reveals that this term was commonly used as a synonym for *"synodus,"* allowing us to retain the 1135 assembly on our list.

[241] Goerz, *MRR* I 513-514, Nr. 1891; Hontheim, *Hist. dipl.* I 531; Binterim, *Concilien* IV 216; Rodgero Prümers, *Albero von Montreuil, Erzbischof von Trier 1132-1152* (Göttingen, 1874) 85.

[242] Cf. *Gesta Alberonis Trev. (cap. 28)* 258-259; Brower/Masen, *Antiq.* II 54; Kyriander, *Annales Trev.* 124; Goerz, *MRR* I, Nr. 2124; Palazzini, *Dizionario* III 102.

[243] Hartzheim, *Concilia* IV 571; Mansi, *Collectio* XXI 761; Hontheim, *Hist. Trev. dipl.* I 567, 569; Martène, *Collectio* VII 71; *Gallia Christ.* XIII 507; Goerz, *MRR* II, Nrs. 19, 20; Beyer, *MRUB* I, Nr. 629; Hinschius, *KR* III 486-487 note 5. Hauck, *KGD* IV 20 and V 133, notes that since this assembly does not refer to itself as a synod, he is hesitant to include it unequivocally on his list of twelfth-century synods. Both documents under consideration were witnessed by all three suffragans, four abbots, the major dignitaries of the cathedral chapter at Trier, numerous clerics from the suffragan bishoprics, Duke Matthew of Lorraine, the counts of Namur, Arlon and Ahr, the Wildgraf, several other members of the high nobility, and various *ministeriales*. The synod served as the tribunal where a dispute between the duke of Lorraine and the nuns' cloister Remiremont was decided in accordance with a papal directive; it also witnessed the surrender of the fortress Sayn by the resident counts who then received it back in fee from the archbishop.

[244] *Gallia Christ.* XIII 511; Calmet, *Hist. eccles.* (2nd ed.) I 351; Hontheim, *Hist. Trev. dipl.* I 583; Tabouillot, *Histoire de Metz* III 120; Goerz, *RET* 21; Idem, *MRR* II, Nr. 124 (cf. also Nrs. 116, 117, 125, 126, 127). Binterim, *Concilien* IV 218; Phillips, *Diöcesansynode* 50 note 28. The confirmation of the establishment of the monastery Belchamp took place *"in synodo autumnali."* Of the suffragans, only Bishop Albert of Verdun was present.

[245] Goerz, *MRR* II, Nrs. 151-156; Beyer, *MRUB* I, Nrs. 668, 669, 670, 671. The conjecture that this was a provincial synod is based on the fact that the documents were witnessed by Bishop Albert of Verdun and several abbots of the province.

[246] Goerz, *MRR* II, Nr. 184: Archbishop Hillin of Trier confirmed to the abbey Etival a privilege granted it by Bishop Henry of Toul with the consent of Archdeacon Peter of Toul regarding the cure of souls in the Etival valley. Witnessing this act were Bishop Stephan of Metz, Abbot Siger of St. Maximin in Trier, the cathedral dean of Trier, the Trier archdeacon Rudolf of Wied, and others. The presence of the bishop of Metz allows the assumption that the bishop of Toul was also present and that this was the occasion of a provincial synod. It is also plausible that the undated charter which Goerz places *circa* 1160, containing the confirmation for the abbey of Gorze of a grant made by Bishop Stephan of Metz belongs to this provincial synod as well; cf. *MRR* II, Nr. 182. The synod convened at Trier in the fall of 1162

Diocesan synods also occur quite frequently in the eleventh and twelfth centuries, showing many of the same cluster-characteristics as their provincial counterparts. E.g., the assembly of 1030,[249] was succeeded by those held 12 June 1037 at Trier,[250] 2 September 1038,[251] 23 October 1065 at Trier under Archbishop Eberhard,[252] 1084/1101 under Archbishop Egilbert,[253] 1107 at Trier,[254] 1110 at Trier,[255] 2 May 1129,[256] 1135 at Trier,[257] and 21 June 1139 at Trier.[258] As was true with provincial synods, these diocesan assemblies show the imprint of individual archbishops, most recently Albero.

Such efforts to reassert his metropolitan authority met some opposition, however. On 15 April 1139 the pope granted to the monastery at Springiersbach exemption from attending diocesan synods at Trier, so that we may presume that this privilege was claimed two months later when Archbishop Albero summoned his clergy to his cathedral church.[259] We

was under the direction of Pope Victor and should not be regarded as having the same purpose as episcopal assemblies; cf. Hauck, *KGD* IV 263.

[247] Goerz, *MRR* II 59, Nr. 207: Archbishop Hillin confirmed at Toul grants made to the cloister Epinal by Bishops Stephan of Metz and Henry of Toul; again, the simultaneous appearance of these three prelates suggests a provincial synod.

[248] Hartzheim, *Concilia* III 393-394 ("*in plena synodo*"); Goerz, *RET* 22; Idem, *MRR* II 61-62, Nrs. 215-216; Palazzini, *Dizionario* V 408-410. Hinschius, *KR* III 586 note 9, and 587 note 2, and Phillips, *Diöcesansynode* 62, treat this as a diocesan synod. The presence of Bishop-elect Richard of Verdun as a witness argues in favor of a provincial synod, despite the fact that the recorded business was the resolution of a tithe dispute. Hauck, *KGD* IV 20 and V 133, includes it on his list of provincial assemblies.

[249] Goerz, *RET* 8; Günther, *CdRhM* I, Nr. 111 ("*in generali sinodo*").

[250] Goerz, *RET* 8; Hontheim, *Hist. Trev. dipl.* I 370 ("*in synodo sancta*").

[251] Goerz, *RET* 8 ("*in generali placito*").

[252] Goerz, *MRR* I, Nr. 1402; Beyer, *MRUB* I, Nr. 414; Hontheim, *Hist. Trev. dipl.* I 408. The synod announced the restoration of several churches to the abbey of Prüm.

[253] Goerz, *MRR* I, Nr. 1557; Calmet, *Hist. eccles.* (1st ed.) I 514. The synod confirmed the transfer of income from the church at Mont St. Martin to the abbey of St. Vanne near Verdun.

[254] Hartzheim, *Concilia* III 760-761; Hontheim, *Hist. Trev. dipl.* I 483; Brower, *Metrop.* I 300; Goerz, *RET* 14; Idem, *MRR* I, Nr. 1601; Beyer, *MRUB* I, Nr. 475; Phillips, *Diöcesansynode* 138; Palazzini, *Dizionario* V 408-410. At this "*generalis synodus*" the establishment of the Augustinian canon foundation at Springiersbach was confirmed.

[255] Goerz, *MRR* I, Nr. 1635; Beyer, *MRUB* I, Nr. 478. Binterim, *Concilien* IV 147-148, notes that about the year 1122, at the time of Archbishop Bruno of Trier, heretics appeared at Ivois or Carignan (Ipsch on the river Chier) in the diocese of Metz who denied transubstantiation; two priests and two laymen were brought before the archbishop for judgment (cf. *Gesta Trev.* 193-194). Perhaps a diocesan synod and/or a later provincial synod also dealt with this matter.

[256] Goerz, *RET* 16 ("*in capitulo*").

[257] Hartzheim, *Concilia* III 327-328 ("*in generali synodo*"); Goerz, *MRR* I, Nr. 1882; Idem, *RET* 17; Hinschius, *KR* III 586 note 7; Palazzini, *Dizionario* V 408-410.

[258] Goerz, *MRR* I, Nr. 1948; Idem, *RET* 18; Beyer, *MRUB* I, Nr. 568; Idem, II 692, Nr. 563: the establishment of the monastery at Schiffenburg was confirmed "*in publica synodo.*"

[259] Beyer, *MRUB* I, Nr. 507; cf. also, Hilling, "Geistlichen und Laien" 223.

have noted above that the establishment of this same foundation was confirmed in a synod held in 1107, leading us to conclude that representatives of the house were in attendance at that time. Moreover, the abbots or their proctors had presumably been summoned to all subsequent synods, from which they eventually sought relief. Behind the papal exemption of 1139 there would thus seem to be a certain period of friction between the archbishops and this monastic community, the details of which are lost to us.

At the general synod held after 13 March 1140, grants made over an extended period of time to the monastery of Ravengiersburg on the Hunsrück were confirmed,[260] while the assembly on 22 October 1142 at Trier dealt with the establishment of the nuns-cloister at Lunnech.[261] The matter of Lunnech did not end there, however, for at the diocesan synod which met 24 October 1143 at Trier the decision was made to transfer the nuns from Lunnech to Schönstätt near Valendren.[262] Further synods are recorded for 1145,[263] after 13 May 1147 by directive of the pope,[264] 1152 at Trier,[265] 1154 at Trier,[266] 1161 at Trier,[267] 1162 at Trier,[268] 1167 at Coblenz?,[269] and 1169.[270]

---

[260] Goerz, *MRR* I 535, Nrs. 1958, 1959; Beyer, *MRUB* I 569, Nr. 513 (*"in generali synodo"*); Palazzini, *Dizionario* V 408-410..

[261] Beyer, *MRUB* I, 582-583, Nr. 526; Günther, *CdRhM* I 264; Goerz, *MRR* I, Nrs. 1995, 1996; Idem, *RET* 19 (*"Treveri in generali synodo"*); Binterim, *Concilien* IV 217; Phillips, *Diöcesansynoden* 50; Palazzini, *Dizionario* V 408-410.

[262] Brower/Masen, *Antiq.* II 44; Hartzheim, *Concilia* III 344-345 (*"in generali synodo"*); Goerz, *MRR* I, Nr. 2003; Idem, *RET* 19; Beyer, *MRUB* I, Nr. 585; Günther, *CdRhM* I 284; Idem, III 3; Binterim, *Concilien* IV 217; Phillips, *Diöcesansynode* 50.

[263] Goerz, *MRR* I, Nrs. 2016, 2022; Beyer, *MRUB* II, Nrs. 590, 594; Günther, *CdRhM* I 301; Hontheim, *Hist. Trev. dipl.* I 552 (*"in generali synodo"*). Cf. further, Julius Wegeler, *Das Kloster Laach* (Bonn, 1854) I 167; Idem, II 7.

[264] Goerz, *MRR* I, Nr. 2053; Beyer, *MRUB* I 607, Nr. 548, and II 700, Nr. 599. Archbishop Albero was directed by Pope Eugenius III to take action with his clergy; cf. Prümers, *Albero von Montreuil* 76.

[265] Beyer, *MRUB* I, Nrs. 579 (*"Hanc igitur traditionem et donationem ex consilio reliquiorum archidiaconorum abbatum et reliquarum personarum nostrarum in generali synodo nostra promulgatam"*), 580 (". . . *ex consilio personarum nostrarum et totius capituli nostri in generali synodo promulgatam"*); Hilling, "Geistlichen und Laien" 216.

[266] Goerz, *MRR* II 16, Nrs. 49-51; Beyer, *MRUB* II, Nrs. 634, 635 (the third document listed in Goerz is not printed).

[267] Goerz, *RET* 22; Tabouillot, *Hist. de Metz* IV 125 (*"in synodo generali"*).

[268] Goerz, *MRR* II 58, Nr. 204 (*"in generali synodo"*); Tabouillot, *Hist. de Metz* III 125.

[269] In 1167 an assembly (*"in publico doctorum conventu"*) at Coblenz witnessed Eckbert of Schönau dispute with an heretical teacher from the region of the Mosel; the man recognized his error and converted back to the Catholic faith; cf. Binterim, *Concilien* IV 218. Goerz, *MRR* II 75, Nr. 262, prints the summary of an unpublished charter dated August 1167 at Coblenz which declares that Archbishop Hillin of Trier had made a grant of property to the prior and nuns at Valendra. Witnessing this act were the following:

Rudolf, cathedral provost and archdeacon;

Bruno, archdeacon and provost of St. Florin in Coblenz;

The papal-imperial struggle during the second half of the century may in part account for the virtual disappearance of provincial synods at Trier after 1163. The assembly in 1179 which adjudicated a tithe dispute between the monastery Himmerode and the pastor at Altrea was presumably a diocesan synod.[271] However, the assembly in 1179 at which Archbishop Arnold confirmed the renunciation of claims by several nobles to possessions claimed by the abbey at Orval appears to have been a provincial synod: witnessing the act was Bishop Arnold of Verdun.[272]

Thereafter, however, a schismatic election which occurred in 1183 reflected the partisan nature of German ecclesiastical life during the reign of the Emperor Frederick I and undoubtedly had an impact upon synodal activity for several years. The papal candidate, Folmar of Bliescastel, was consecrated at Verona 1 June 1186 by Pope Clement III, at which time he may also have received the pallium of his archiepiscopal office. Only then could he hold a provincial synod, the first evidence of which is 15 February (Sunday *Invocavit*) 1187 at Mouzon, south of Metz.[273] Two years later

magister Gerard, provost at Pfalzel;

Rudolf, the scholastic at St. Paulin in Trier;

Dietrich, archiepiscopal *capellanus* and a cathedral canon at Trier;

Alard, archiepiscopal *capellanus* and canon at St. Paulin;

Count Eberhard of Sayn;

Reinbold and Gerlach of Isenburg;

9 *ministeriales* of the Trier church.

This very unusual assemblage of clerics seems clearly to be connected with the confrontation which Eckbert of Schönau had with the heretical teacher: as many as four of them were specialists in doctrinal matters, being either in charge of a foundation school, or serving as one of the archbishop's inner circle of priests and advisors. This seems to correspond well with Eckbert's *conventus doctorum*.

[270] Goerz, *RET* 23 ("*in generali synodo*").

[271] Hartzheim, *Concilia* III 421, Hinschius, *KR* III 587 note 1, and Palazzini, *Dizionario* V 408-410, include it among their provincial councils; the entire matter seems to have played itself out over several diocesan synods, however; cf. Goerz, *MRR* II, Nr. 430. Further actions related to this synod appear to be recorded in *MRR* II, Nrs. 431, 432.

[272] Goerz, *MRR* II, Nr. 435.

[273] *Gesta Trev., cont. III (a. 1187)* 387: "*Accepta igitur suae voluntatis plenitudine, statim Treverensibus et suffraganeis aecclesiis concilium indixit apud Mosomum, castrum archiepiscopi Remensis, qui eum eo tempore manutenebat et solatium ei per se et suos in multis exibebat. Universi itaque tam clerici quam prelati suffraganearum aecclesiarum et plurimu pastores aecclesiarum de archidiaconatu, quod inter Treverim et Yvodium castrum constitutum est, timentes ordini suo, ad concilium istud, antecedente eos Metense episcopo, dominica qua cantatur Invocavit convenerunt. Petrus vero Tullensis et Heinricus Virdunensis episcopi, appellatione interposita, non venerunt. Venerunt autem et multi tam magistri quam clerici de Frantia, inter quos etiam quidam episcopi, animantes eum, ut auctoritatis sibi concesssae potestate uteretur et subditos suos a subiectione resilientes censura aecclesiastica cohercert. Horum ergo suffragiis animatus, prelatorum quosdam et clericorum Treverensium excommunicavit, . . .*"; *Chron. reg. Colon.* 135: "*Predictus Volmarus in regno regis Franciae se continens, apud Remis suffraganeis episcopis seu prioribus Trevirensis ecclesiae synodum indicit. Imperator, hoc audito, ne irent, interdicit. Episcopus Mettensis Bertrammus, quia*

Archbishop Folmar presided over a second provincial assembly which convened at Trier.[274]

Elected in 1189, Archbishop John I of Trier sent Abbot Hermann of Himmerode to Rome following his election for the purpose of receiving the pallium. In order to raise the necessary money for this delegation, the prelate mortgaged three manors to the cathedral chapter of Trier, purchasing therewith golden art pieces and jewels which would serve as "gifts" to the Curia.[275] Presumably this symbol of office was obtained shortly after 4 June 1190.[276] Whether he immediately sought to convene provincial synods is problematic, however. On 18 October 1194 Bishop Eudes of Toul declared that Archbishop John had sat in judgment "*in sua synodo generali*" regarding the attack by Duke Simon of Lorraine against the monastery at Remiremont. To the bishop was given the charge to proclaim the judgment publicly.[277] Our survey of references to synods in this and other bishoprics leads to the conclusion that the term "*synodus generalis*" had specific reference to diocesan synods, not provincial assemblies.[278] It would thus seem that Archbishop John had written Bishop Eudes of Toul regarding the decision of his own diocesan synod which had concluded prior to 18 Oc-

---

eundem Volmarum hospicio suscepit, vel quia synodum eius dictus est adisse, per Wernerum de Bolant, nuncium imperatoris, de episcopatu eicitur, bona eius confiscantur, ipse Coloniae apud Sanctum Gereonem, ubi etiam canonicus ante fuit, privatus vixit. Episcopus Virdunensis ob eandem werram episcopatum sponte resignavit. Episcopus Tullensis et priores Trevirenses eadem occasione per Volmarum excommunicantur; quam excommunicationem papa confirmat." The synod is noted in Mansi, *Collectio* XXI 509-510; Brower/Masen, *Antiq.* II 84; Goerz, *MRR* II, Nrs. 555, 570; Paul Scheffer-Boichorst, *Kaiser Friedrichs I. letzter Streit mit der Kurie* (Berlin, 1866) 130; Hefele, *Conciliengeschichte* V 647; Heydenreich, *Metropolitangewalt* 27; Hinschius, *KR* III 487 note 5 and 489 note 1; Hauck, *KGD* IV 20 and 309 note 4, and V 133 note 3; Palazzini, *Dizionario* V 408-410. Presumably it was during or immediately after this synod that the archbishop suspended the abbot of St. Vannes at Verdun; cf. *Ann. S. Vitoni Verdun.* 527; Goerz, *MRR* II 161, Nr. 571.

[274] The evidence of the synod is the charter which published the sale of land to the monastery of St. Matthias near Trier by St. Vitus in Verdun, an act which presumably was done in the synod itself. The document would have been issued afterwards, witnessed by the prior, provost and convent members from St. Vitus, the abbot and several monks from St. Paul's in Verdun, and the abbot and monks from St. Agericus; see Beyer, *MRUB* II 133, Nr. 97; Goerz, *MRR* II, Nr. 617.

[275] Cf. Beyer, *MRUB* II 140, Nr. 103; Heydenreich, *Metropolitangewalt* 27; Hauck, *KGD* V 591 note 7.

[276] Cf. Beyer, *MRUB* II 143, Nr. 105, in which the pope refers to John as "*electus.*" John himself has employed the "*electus*" rubric before this time (cf. *MRUB* II 140), but abandoned it for "*archiepiscopus*" once the pallium was in his possession (cf. *loc. cit.* II 151).

[277] Heydenreich, *Metropolitangewalt* 104 note 160, and Reg. 169; Margret Loenartz Corsten, "Erzbischof Johann I. von Trier (1189-1212)," *Zeitschrift für die Geschichte der Saargegend* 13 (Saarbrücken, 1963) 127-200, especially 140-141, where it is regarded as a provincial synod.

[278] For the technical aspects of various phrases, see Boye, "Provinzialsynoden" 179.

tober 1194, with the expectation that now Eudes would publish that same report within the boundaries of his bishopric.

An undated diocesan synod (1190/1212) gave its consent as the prelate removed the nuns-cloister Horreum/St. Irmenen at Trier from under the protection and supervision of Abbot Richard of Springiersbach and assumed those prerogatives for himself and his successors. At the same time he granted to this religious house the parish church of St. Pauli and established certain regulations.[279] Such a synod in the year 1190 or shortly before may also have been the cause for the Cistercian monastery at Himmerode to seek an exemption from the pope.[280]

The care of monks travelling to synods was dealt with in a document which Archbishop John I issued in 1196. In the process of resolving a conflict between the prior and the collegiate chapter of Münstermaifeld, he declared that: *"Curiam de rore . . . preposito liberam adiudicavimus excepto quod si fratres monasterii ad ordines vel synodum seu pro negotiis ecclesie Treverum adierunt in villa de rore prepositus in eius necessariis providebit."*[281] Presumably those resources would be drawn on regularly. John's assertion of synodal rights is further indicated from a 1208 document in which he declared that the vicar of the church at Ehrang was obligated to attend synods.[282] In a document dated 1210, the prelate proclaimed that in accordance with the decision of his synod held at Trier, the foundation at Carden was to enjoy the same wood and other privileges as the parish of Treis.[283]

Binterim's assertion that John could hardly have summoned either provincial or diocesan synods after 1198 due to the troubled times occasioned by the throne controversy, and that he therefore resorted to a quasi-standing synod—a *curia archiepiscopalis*—made up of the provosts and archdeacons of his diocese, is refuted at least by the above-noted diocesan assemblies. It remains correct however with respect to synods at the provincial level.[284] Although John's successor, Dietrich II of Wied, was

---

[279] Goerz, *RET* 30; Idem, *MRR* II, Nr. 875; Beyer, *MRUB* II 326, Nr. 292: *"Hanc igitur traditionem et donationem consilio et auxilio archidiaconorum, abbatum et reliquarum personarum nostrarum in generali sinodo nostra promulgatum . . . confirmavimus."*

[280] Beyer, *MRUB* II, Nr. 105, dated 1190; cf. also Hilling, "Geistlichen und Laien" 223.

[281] Beyer, *MRUB* II, Nr. 152; further, Hilling, "Geistlichen und Laien" 222.

[282] Beyer, *MRUB* II, Nr. 240; Hilling, "Geistlichen und Laien" 217.

[283] Beyer, *MRUB* II, Nrs. 303, 304; Goerz, *MRR* II, Nrs. 1107, 1109; Idem, *RET* 29: ". . . *constituimus Treveri in synodo generali observandum"*; *"Communicato itaque consilio cum prelatis qui nobis assidebant in audientia totius synodi judictum est . . ."*; *"Acta sunt autem hec in facie generalis synodi . . . coram his testibus . . ."*

[284] Binterim, *Concilien* IV 397. Hilling, "Geistlichen und Laien" 216, incorrectly cites

elected near the end of 1212 and received the pallium between 13 March and 19 April 1213,[285] the earliest apparent opportunity for a provincial synod does not appear until the end of 1214.

In late December 1214 Frederick of Staufen, king of the Romans, held court at Metz, attended by numerous princes of the realm, both temporal and spiritual. Among these were Archbishop Dietrich of Trier and Bishop Conrad of Metz, his suffragan. On 20 December Dietrich was a co-signatory to a covenant made between the bishop of Metz and Duke Theobald of Lorraine.[286] At an unspecified time he was a witness to a charter which Frederick II directed on the king of Denmark,[287] on 29 December he rendered a judgment along with Duke Theobald in a suit brought by certain merchants of Huy against the bishop and townsmen of Metz,[288] and on 8 January 1215 he witnessed the investiture of William of Baux with the kingdom of Arles by Frederick II.[289]

We do not know whether Bishop Rainald of Toul was present during this time. It is consistent with other similar assemblies, however, that the archbishop of Trier would have taken advantage of being present with at least one of his suffragans and presumably clergy from the four bishoprics in his ecclesiastical province to convene a synod for the discussion of matters of common interest and importance. Such a provincial synod would have provided Dietrich II of Trier with the opportunity to discuss the implications of the papal invitation to the Council slated for late 1215, including the pope's invitation for input from the prelates of the Church regarding problems requiring correction. It may also be significant that immediately after the archbishop's return to his metropolitan city from Metz he commenced an ambitious program of reform within his own church. Some hint of this must have been given as he met with his suffragans during December and early January.

Given the numerous Trier synods, it is both noteworthy and disappointing that the record for the suffragan bishoprics is so sparse. The 1135

Beyer, *MRUB* II, Nr. 203, as evidence of a provincial synod for Trier; it was in fact a diocesan synod for the bishopric of Speyer.

[285] Heydenreich, *Metropolitangewalt* 28; Beyer, *MRUB* III 8, 17; Potthast, *Regesta* I, Nr. 4706; Pixton, "Dietrich von Wied" (1974) 73; Löhnert, *Amtsdaten Trier* 37 note 1.

[286] Goerz, *RET* 337; Idem, *MRR* II 338, Nr. 1231; Calmet, *Hist. eccles.* II 424; H-Bréholles, *Hist. dipl.* I 346.

[287] Goerz, *RET* 32; Idem, *MRR* II 339, Nr. 1231; H-Bréholles, *Hist. dipl.* I 348.

[288] H-Bréholles, *Hist. dipl.* I 348-350; that same day the king, the *scabini* of Metz and Bishop Conrad of Metz all confirmed the judgment.

[289] Ficker, *Regg. Imp.* V 195, Nr. 776; Goerz, *MRR* III, Nachtrag II, Nr. 2275; Idem, *MRR* IV, Nachtrag II, Nr. 2323; Böhmer, *Acta imperii inedita* I 105-106, Nr. 125;

provincial synod was held at Metz, as was that convened on 18 January 1152, but there is no evidence that diocesan synods were held there at all during the twelfth century.[290] That synods were not totally unknown at Metz is revealed by a dispute between the monastery of Hastière-on-the-Meuse and the abbey of Waulsort: although originally established as an independent nuns' cloister in the tenth century, Hastière soon became dependent on Waulsort, a relationship which became especially strained in the second half of the twelfth century; in its efforts to re-assert its autonomy, Hastière produced a number of forged documents which were investigated at a diocesan synod held in November 1202 at Metz; the synod rejected the claims, and Hastière remained thereafter a priory subordinate to Waulsort.[291]

Sources are equally sparse for diocesan synods at Verdun prior to 1215. Hartzheim preserves the notice of a *"generalis synodus"* held in 967 which dealt with a dispute over a church,[292] and another for 1197.[293] Though one might assume that the concerns for the general peace and the combatting of heresy which prompted Bishop Eudes de Vaudemont to convene a synod in 1192 produced similar reactions elsewhere in Lorraine, we simply do not know.

Even the diocese for which we possess considerable evidence exhibits a very sporadic pattern of synods. According to Jacques Choux, *«Pour le diocèse de Toul, l'existence des synodes est bien attestée dès l'époque carolingienne; elle semble avoir été régulière pendant tout le Moyen Age et au delà, encore que plus on avance dans le temps, plus le cérémonial ait été négligé.»*[294] In 916 a *"plena synodus"* at Toul dealt with a tithe dispute.[295] Others recorded in the tenth century are 9 October 971,[296] 15

---

[290] According to Hauck, *KGD* IV 8, citing Hartzheim, *Concilia* III 367, synods at Metz were convened after All Saints Day.

[291] Ulrich Nonn, "Die gefälschte Urkunde des Grafen Widerich für das Kloster Hastière und die Vorfahren der Grafen von Luxemburg," *Rheinische Vierteljahrsblätter* 42 (1978) 53.

[292] Hartzheim, *Concilia* II 631; Hinschius, *KR* III 586 note 7, 587 note 2, 588 note 7, and 589 note 4

[293] Hartzheim, *Concilia* III 795 (*"1197 fer. 5. ante Pascha"*); cited by Phillips, *Diöcesansynode* 51.

[294] "Le Synode Diocésain de Toul a la Fin du Moyen Age," *Revue d'Histoire de l'Eglise de France* 45 (Paris, 1959) 63. See also Christian Pfister, "L'évêque Frothaire de Toul," *Annales de l'Est* (Nancy, 1890) 276.

[295] Hartzheim, *Concilia* II 587; Hinschius, *KR* III 586 note 9, 587 note 2.

[296] Boye, "Quellenkatalog" 59-60 (*"Actum Tulli in plenaria synodo"*); Hinschius, *KR* III 586 note 10, 587 note 1.

October 982,[297] and 7 June 988, all under Bishop Gerhard.[298] Only five synods are documented for the eleventh century, and they all seem to fall within the pontificate of Bishop Pibo (1069-1107): 1072,[299] 1074,[300] 1091,[301] 1098,[302] and at an unspecified time.[303] Whereas seven are known from the first half of the twelfth century—1105,[304] 1111,[305] 1116,[306] 1119,[307] 1122,[308] 1123,[309] and 1136,[310] only two are mentioned in the second half: 1190,[311] and on 8 May 1192 when Bishop Eudes convened a synod of his diocesan clergy at Toul where he published ten articles for combatting heresy.[312]

---

[297] Boye, "Quellenkatalog" 62; Hinschius, *KR* III 586 note 10, 587 note 1. From this synod, two pieces of business are known: 1) the confirmation of property belonging to the monastery of St. Mansuetus by Bishop Gerhard (*"Actum Tulli publice in plenaria synodo"*, and 2) the confirmation of a church belonging to the same abbey (*"Actum Tulli publice . . . in plenaria synodo"*).

[298] Boye, "Quellenkatalog" 63; Hinschius, *KR* III 587 note 1.

[299] Hartzheim, *Concilia* III 162; Phillips, *Diöcesansynode* 50. See also Jacques Choux, *Recherches sur le diocèse de Toul au temps de la Réforme grégorienne: L'épiscopat de Pibon* (1069-1107) (Nancy, 1952) 47-50.

[300] Hartzheim, *Concilia* III 174 (*"plenaria synodus"*); Phillips, *Diöcesansynode* 50; Hinschius, *KR* III 586 note 10, 587 note 3.

[301] Hartzheim, *Concilia* III 217 (*"plena synodus"*); Phillips, *Diöcesansynode* 9, 50; Hinschius, *KR* III 386 note 9.

[302] Hartzheim, *Concilia* III 213 (*"synodus nostra"*); Hinschius, *KR* III 586 note 11.

[303] Hartzheim, *Concilia* III 182 (*"plena synodus"*); Hinschius, *KR* III 586 note 9. Choux, "Synode Diocésain" 65, notes that at the end of the eleventh century appears to have been the Wednesday after Trinity and the Wednesday after St. Luke. If one considers the list of attested assemblies, however, one sees that for the ninth through the twelfth centuries the date varied frequently.

[304] Hartzheim, *Concilia* III 249-251 (*"in evidentia generalis synodi"*); Phillips, *Diöcesansynode* 50; Hinschius, *KR* III 586 note 7, 587 note 1.

[305] Hartzheim, *Concilia* III 267-268 (*"synodalis conventus"*); Phillips, *Diöcesansynode* 10; Hinschius, *KR* III 586 note 11, 587 note 2.

[306] Hartzheim, *Concilia* III 270 (*"plena synodus"*); Hinschius, *KR* III 586 note 9.

[307] Hartzheim, *Concilia* III 269; Hinschius, *KR* III 587 note 1.

[308] Hartzheim, *Concilia* III 282-283 (*"generalis synodus"*); Phillips, *Diöcesansynode* 50; Hinschius, *KR* III 586 note 7, 587 note 1.

[309] Hartzheim, *Concilia* III 293-294 (*"plenaria synodus"*); Phillips, *Diöcesansynode* 9; Hinschius, *KR* III 586 note 10, 587 note 1.

[310] Hartzheim, *Concilia* III 333; Hinschius, *KR* III 587 note 1.

[311] Hartzheim, *Concilia* III 213; Phillips, *Diöcesansynode* 175.

[312] MS. Nancy, Arch. dép. H 335 (autographum Belliprati); Hartzheim, *Concilia* III 455-456; Mansi, *Collectio* XXII col. 647-650; Martène, *Thesaur.* IV col. 1177-1180; Migne, *PL* CCV col. 914-918; Hinschius, *KR* III 587 note 4; Binterim, *Concilien* IV 456; Phillips, *Diöcesansynode* 50. Hauck, *KGD* IV 9, sees in the decrees of Radulf of Liège (Hartzheim, *Concilia* III 422) the model for those at Toul in 1192. See further, Pontal, *Liste des MSS* 431-

The Province of Mainz

The metropolitan authority of the church of Mainz owed much to the dominating personality of Boniface who sat there in the second half of the eighth century. During Carolingian times one annual (spring?) provincial synod appeared sufficient, for which there is evidence for the years 829 at Mainz,[313] early October 847 at Mainz,[314] early October 848,[315] October 857,[316] Fall 867 at Mainz,[317] May 890 at Forchheim,[318] and 1 June 932 at Erfurt.[319] It is not known whether a synod called for 4 March 877/878 actually convened.[320]

Under Archbishop Frederick I (937-954), however, an additional autumn synod was added,[321] though the only known synod associated with him was held ca. 951 at Mainz.[322] Thereafter until the early twelfth century there are just a handful which have been recorded: 28 April 976 at

---

2; Idem, *Statuts synodaux du XIIIᵉ s.* I lxxiii note 3.

[313] Heidingsfelder, *Regg. Eichst.* I 17, Nr. 27. For Mainz provincial synods in general, cf. Wenner, *Rechtsbeziehungen* 123-187; for Carolingian synods, see Wilfried Hartmann, ed., *Die Konzilien der karolingischen Teilreiche 843-859*, MGH Concilia III (Hannover, 1984).

[314] Hartzheim, *Concilia* II 151; Mansi, *Collectio* XIV 899ff.; Heidingsfelder, *Regg. Eichst.* I, Nr. 52; Hauck, *KGD* (1912) II 643f. The synod, called by Louis the German, was presided over by Archbishop Hraban; all suffragan bishops were present except Strasbourg. Wenner, *Rechtsbeziehungen* 127-129, regards this as the first true provincial synod, relegating that of 829 to the "mixed" or "national" category.

[315] Heidingsfelder, *Regg. Eichst.* I 24, Nr. 52; Böhmer-Mühlbacher, *Regg. Imp.* I, Nr. 1488cc.

[316] Wenner, *Rechtsbeziehungen* 130.

[317] Wenner, *Rechtsbeziehungen* 130.

[318] Heideingsfelder, *Regg. Eichst.* I, Nr. 53.

[319] Hauck, *KGD* IV 84-85; Hehl, *Konzilien 916-1001* I 97ff. The ordering of the celebration of the apostolic feastdays was among the items of business dealt with.

[320] Wenner, *Rechtsbeziehungen* 132-134.

[321] Hauck, *KGD* IV 6; Idem, II, 243, 735; *Epistolae Moguntinae* Nr. 16, in *Monumenta Moguntina*, vol. 3 of Jaffé, *Bibliotheca*, 344 (". . . *omni anno a synodo ante pascha habita usque eam quae post festivitatem s. Remigii [1 October] colenda esse dinoscitur"*). For the 1225 provincial synod at Mainz, cf. Hartzheim, *Concilia* III 523, Cap. 14: ". . . *ut archiepiscopi, episcopi, etc. in suo singuli concilio annis singulis celebrando eas publicari faciant."* Boye, "Synoden Deutschlands" 140, argues that in the period 922-1059 references to provincial synods at Mainz always imply that they were semi-annual affairs; cf. letters of Aribo of Mainz to Bishop Meginhard of Würzburg and to Bishop Godehard of Hildesheim, *Epist. Mogunt.* 359, Nr. 23, and 365, Nr. 26).

[322] Boye, "Quellenkatalog" 53; Hauck, *KGD* IV 20, citing *Epist. Mogunt.* 344, Nr. 16; Boye, "Synoden Deutschlands" 140 and 196; Wenner, *Rechtsbeziehungen* 144; Hehl, *Konzilien 916-1001* I 173ff. Only the bishops of Worms and Strasbourg were present.

Mainz,[323] 26-28 November 1000 at Gandersheim,[324] 25 May (Pentecost) 1007 at Mainz,[325] 6 October 1019 at Mainz,[326] 2 June 1023 at Mainz,[327] 12 August 1023 at Seligenstadt,[328] 13 May 1024 at Höchst,[329] 17 October

[323] Boye, "Quellenkatalog" 61; Idem, "Synoden Deutschlands" 196 and 234; *Mainzer UB* I 134, Nr. 219; Falck, *Mainz im Mittelalter* 100. A *Schulordnung*—school regulations—for Aschaffenburg issued at this synod by Archbishop Willigis apparently served other schools throughout the province, including the cathedral school at Mainz, as witnessed by the fact that it was copied into the oldest *Copialbuch* of the archdiocese in the mid-thirteenth century. Cf. Peter Acht, "Die erste Ordnung der Urkunden des Mainzer Erzstifts und Domkapitels," *Zeitschrift für bayerische Landesgeschichte* 33 (München, 1970) 40; K.H. Rexroth, "Der Stiftsscholaster Herward von Aschaffenburg und das Schulrecht von 976," *Aschaffenburger Jahrbuch* 4/1 (1957) 205ff. Present at this synod were the suffragan bishops of Speyer, Worms, Prague and Moravia: the first bishop of Prague had been consecrated in January 976; Moravia was a mission bishopric, without a definite seat as yet; see Wenner, *Rechtsbeziehungen* 146.

[324] *Vita Bernwardi cap. 18*, 767; Wenner, *Rechtsbeziehungen* 148-149; Hauck, *KGD* IV 20; Boye, "Synoden Deutschlands" 196; Böhmer-Will, *RAM* I 133; Hefele, *Conciliengeschichte* IV 656.

[325] Heidingsfelder, *Regg. Eichst.* I, Nr. 146; Hauck, *KGD* (1912) III 418ff. Among the items which must have been discussed at this provincial synod was the erection of the bishopric of Bamberg, an act performed later that year (27 October) at a national synod held at Frankfurt; cf. Philippi, *Osnabrück UB* I, Nr. 121; Heidingsfelder, op. cit. I 53, Nr. 147; Wenner, *Rechtsbeziehungen* 156.

[326] Hauck, *KGD* IV 7; Böhmer-Will, *RAM* I 148, Nr. 26 ("*plena synodus*").

[327] Boye, "Quellenkatalog" 76-77; Idem, "Synoden Deutschlands" 188, 195; Hinschius, *KR* III 484 note 3; *Vita Meinwerci* 145; *Vita Godehardi post* (c. 19) 206; Wenner, *Rechtsbeziehungen* 161.

[328] *Vita Meinwerci* 146-147, which includes the nineteen statutes enacted at the synod; Boye, "Quellenkatalog" 77; Idem, "Synoden Deutschlands" 195; Hauck, *KGD* IV 20 note 1, 38 note 4, and 84-85; Hinschius, *KR* III 484 note 2. The purpose of this synod, as with provincial synods in general, is found in the introduction to the statutes: "*Ego Aribo Moguntinae sedis archiepiscopus quamvis indignus cum ceteris fratribus nostris atque coepiscopis . . . synodum in Selegunstat condiximus . . ., quatenus com communi praedictorum fratrum consilio atque consensu multimodo divinorum officiorum atque synodalium legum componeretur dissensio, et disparilitas nostrarum singularium consuetudinum honesta consensione redigeretur in unum. Inconveniens quidem sancto illo conventu visum est, quod membra capiti discordarent, et illa diversitas in unius compagine corporis esset. Ideoque propter devitandas dissensiones communi decreto concilii haec capitula sancita sunt;*" cf. Wenner, *Rechtsbeziehungen* 162.

[329] Boye, "Quellenkatalog" 77-78; Hinschius, *KR* III 484 note 2; Hauck, *KGD* IV 20. Heidingsfelder, *Regg. Eichst.* I 20, Nr. 163, notes that it is not known whether this synod was actually held. Boye, "Synoden Deutschlands" 143, argues that although this is designated as a provincial synod for Mainz, it was in fact attended by the archbishops of Trier and Cologne, and the bishop of Metz, thus having the character of a national synod. See also Wenner, *Rechtsbeziehungen* 165-167, who holds it for probable that the synod did in fact convene.

1025 at Gandersheim[330] and again on 21 November at Mainz,[331], 21 September 1026 in Seligenstadt,[332] and Spring 1028 at Geisleben.[333] Many of these synods dealt with ongoing matters, such as the Gandersheim boundary dispute and the un-canonical marriage of the count of Hammerstein.[334] During the middle years of the eleventh century it is increasingly difficult to separate issues specific to the province of Mainz from those affecting the entire German realm.[335]

From the synod held 15-18 August 1071 at Mainz comes a set of decrees which testify of the legislative nature of late eleventh-century assemblies.[336] Then, once again a less complete record prevails: March 1073 at Erfurt,[337] October 1074 at Erfurt,[338] 1090,[339] and 1094 at Constanz.[340] Hauck maintains that provincial synods were all but dead by the

---

[330] Boye, "Synoden Deutschlands" 188, citing *Vita Godehardi post.* 187; Hinschius, *KR* III 484 note 2. Hauck, *KGD* IV 20, sees this a merely an episcopal court (*Sendgericht*), to which Wenner, *Rechtsbeziehungen* 169-170, offers convincing counter arguments; cf. especially p. 170 note 1.

[331] Hauck, *KGD* IV 20, and 123 note 3; *Codex Udalrici* 398, Nr. 226, and 408, Nr. 233; *RAM* I 282, Nr. 168; Wenner, *Rechtsbeziehungen* 170. The assembly held this same year at Grona is classified as a provincial synod in Boye, "Synoden Deutschlands" 140, citing *Vita Godehardi* 187, whereas on p. 188, he labels it a national synod.

[332] *Vita Meinwerci a. 1026* [95] 153; Boye, "Quellenkatalog" 79; Idem, "Synoden Deutschlands" 140-141, 188 (where he misplaces the synod in the year 1029), 232; Hinschius, *KR* III 484 note 2; Hauck, *KGD* IV 20; Wenner, *Rechtsbeziehungen* 170-173.

[333] *Vita Meinwerci* [99] 154; Boye, "Quellenkatalog" 80-81; Idem, "Synoden Deutschlands" 188, 196; Hinschius, *KR* III 484 note 2; Hauck, *KGD* IV 20 note 1; Wenner, *Rechtsbeziehungen* 176-177.

[334] See V. Bayer, "Zur Geschichte des Gandersheimer Streites," *Forschungen zur deutschen Geschichte* 16 (1877) 178ff,; W. Dersch, *Die Kirchenpolitik des Erzbischofs Aribo von Mainz (1021-1031)* (Marburg, 1899) 37ff.; D.v. Kessler, *Der Eheprozess Ottos und Irmingards von Hammerstein* (Berlin, 1923).

[335] See e.g., the assembly of some forty bishops which met at Mainz about the middle of October 1049. Called by Pope Leo IX, it was intended to deal with matters involving the Emperor Henry III; cf. Heidingsfelder, *Regg. Eichst.* I 69, Nr. 187; Hauck, *KGD* III 601 note 2. A reversal of this occurred at the synod held April/May 1085 at Mainz: under the direction of the archbishops of Mainz, Trier and Cologne, and attended by the bishops of Eichstätt, Verdun, Liège, Utrecht, Freising, Regensburg, Bamberg, Speyer, Konstanz, Lausanne, Augsburg, Prague, Hildesheim, Paderborn, Münster, and Minden, it declared the deposition of Pope Gregory VII; cf. Heidingsfelder, op. cit. I 88, Nr. 260.

[336] *Acta synodi Moguntinae*, in *Codex Udalrici* Nr. 37; Erhard, *Regg. hist. Westf.* I, Nr. 1126; Philippi, *UB Osnabrück* I Nr. 165; Heidingsfelder, *Regg. Eichst.* I Nr. 238; Ladewig, *Regg. Const.* I 63, Nrs. 493-497; *Lamberti mon. Hersfeld.* 185. See further, Meyer von Knonau, *Jahrbücher* II 78-80.

[337] Mansi, *Collectio* XX 53; Hinschius, *KR* III 486 note 4; Hefele, *Conciliengeschichte* IV 895; Böhmer-Will, *RAM* I 196, Nr. 76; Hauck, *KGD* IV 7.

[338] Böhmer-Will, *RAM* I 201, Nr. 103; Hauck, *KGD* IV 7.

[339] *Wirtemburg. UB* I 286, Nr. 239; Hauck, *KGD* IV 7.

[340] Hauck, *KGD* IV 9 note 3, and 84-85.

twelfth century, the few that were held being more proof of the institution's demise than its continuation.[341]   Boye, on the other hand, argues that while one cannot speak of a regular holding of provincial synods in the period 922-1059, they were frequent enough to have an effect upon the ecclesiastical life of the province; he senses that the institution remained intact and that frequent efforts were made to restore it to the position it originally had.   They were clearly seen as a part of the church structure.[342]

Known provincial synods for the twelfth century fall into several clusters and generally show the influence of specific prelates: e.g., ca. 1102 at Mainz and 1105/6 at Erfurt under Archbishop Ruthard (1089-1109);[343] 28 July 1118 at Fritzlar,[344] 18 October 1125 at Mainz,[345] 1127,[346] early June 1131 at Mainz at which Bishop Bruno of Strasbourg was charged with offenses by his subjects, and ended up relinquishing claims to the see of Strasbourg and returning to Bamberg,[347] and 18 October 1133 at Mainz under Adalbert I (1109-1137);[348] 20 March 1143,[349] 1148 at Erfurt,[350]

---

[341] *KGD* IV 20.

[342] "Synoden Deutschlands" 140.

[343] Boye, "Quellenkatalog" 69; Sudendorf, *Regestrum* II 116, Nr. 40; Hinschius, *KR* III 486 note 5, with additions by Hauck, *KGD* V 133 and IV 20, citing *Epist. Mogunt.* 376, Nr. 31 (*"in villa nostra"*).

[344] *Annales Patherbr.* 135-136; Philippi, *UB Osnabrück* I, Nr. 229; Erhard, *Regg. hist. Westf.* I, Nr. 1433.

[345] *Codex Udalrici*, Nrs. 226, 233; Hefele, *Conciliengeschichte* V 352; Böhmer-Will, *RAM* I 282, Nr. 168; Heidingsfelder, *Regg. Eichst.* I 105, Nr. 325.   The assembly dealt with the contested episcopal election at Würzburg and is placed by Hinschius, *KR* III 486 note 5, among the provincial synods; Boye, "Quellenkatalog" 78, sees this as a diocesan synod; Hauck, *KGD* IV 7 and 20 note 1, downgrades it yet further, arguing that it was an episcopal court, not a synod at all.   Writing after the fact, Gebhard referred to the assembly thusly: *"Iterum archiepiscopum adii, ipsius consilio concilio, quod in Moguntina ecclesia tunc temporis habuit, me una cum Eistetensi electo praesentavi, petens misericordiam vel iusticiam.   Et omnem obedientiam me ei et Moguntinae ecclesiae semper exhibuisse, ipsius testimonio in synodo comprobavi."* Cf. further, Wenner, *Rechtsbeziehungen* 169-170; Johannes Kippenberger, *Beyträge zur Geschichte des Erzbischofs Aribo von Mainz (1021-1031)* (Borna/Leipzig, 1909) 46f., 59f.

[346] Hauck, *KGD* IV 7; Böhmer-Will, *RAM* I 284, Nr. 186.

[347] *Annales S. Disibodi (a. 1131)* 24 (*"Concilium Moguntiae habitum, . . . ubi Bruno Argentinensis . . . super violentia, intrusione et consecratione impetitus . . ."*); Hauck, *KGD* IV 150; Heidingsfelder, *Regg. Eichst.* I 109, Nr. 339; Wentzcke, *Regg. Strassburg* I 316, Nr. 443.

[348] Hauck, *KGD* IV 170 note 8, citing Böhmer-Will, *RAM* I 298, Nr. 298; Heidingsfelder, *Regg. Eichst* I 109, Nr. 341; Schmidt, *UB Halb* I 141, Nr. 140; Dobenecker, *CdThur* I 269, Nr. 1284.   The papal legate Gerard presided over this synod.

[349] Hartzheim, *Concilia* III 349; Gudenus, *Cod. dipl.* I 135-143; Hauck, *KGD* IV 7 and 20; Idem, V 133; Böhmer-Will, *RAM* I 320, Nrs. 6-8; Goerz, *MRR* I, Nr. 2001; Ladewig, *Regg. Constant* I 97, Nr. 814; Weiss, "Konstanzer Bischöfe" 83.

[350] Mansi, *Collectio* XXI 749; *Wibaldi Epistolae* Nr. 178, in *Monumenta Corbeiensia*, vol.

16 May 1149 at Mainz,[351] and 1150 under Henry I (1142-1153);[352] 1154 at Mainz under Arnold of Selenhofen;[353] ca. 1171;[354] late May (before August) 1184 at Mainz,[355] 8 March 1190 at Erfurt,[356] 1191,[357] and May/June 1196 at Mainz under Conrad I (1183-1200).[358]

The record shows a much stronger tradition for the province of Mainz 1175-1200 than for Salzburg, but whereas six assemblies are recorded for the early thirteenth century under Eberhard of Salzburg, his counterpart in Mainz, Siegfried II of Eppstein (1200-1230), convened just one provincial synod before the Fourth Lateranum—in February 1209. Winkelmann and Böhmer-Will identified this synod on the basis of the rubric "*In concilio per nos apud Maguntiam celebrato mense Februario,*" contained in a charter

1 of Jaffé, *Bibliotheca* 298-299. Böhmer-Will, *RAM* I 341, sees this as a diocesan synod; Hinschius, *KR* III 486 note 5, considers it provincial, as does Hauck, *KGD* IV 20 and V 133. This letter, written by Archbishop Henry of Mainz to Abbot Wibald of Corbey refers to the action taken "*presentibus suffraganeis nostris Erfordie . . .*" Among those prelates specifically mentioned as being present were the Bishop Bernhard of Hildesheim and Abbot Henry of Hersfeld. The document further refers to a summons issued to Count Henry III of Käfernburg to make satisfaction "*Maguntiam ad sinodum nostram in proxima feria secunda post ascensionem Domini . . .*"

[351] The date for this synod is given in the report noted for the previous year. All previous lists of provincial synods have missed this.

[352] Böhmer-Will, *RAM* I 342, Nr. 121; Hinschius, *KR* III 486 note 5; Hauck, *KGD* IV 7.

[353] *Vita Arnoldi archiep.* 612: ". . . *auctoritate apostolica in Letare Jherusalem* [14 March] *totius sui metropolitanatus convocato concilio, manifestam hominum suspectionem, quantum potuit per se et . . . episcopos qui presentes et cooperatores erant, canonicis edictis et legibus a cleri eliminavit consortio aliaque quae ad domus dei decorem queque ad religionis studium caritatisque fervorem conducerent, modis omnibus conciliabat*"; Hinschius, *KR* III 487 note 1; Hauck, *KGD* IV 20 and V 133 note 1.

[354] Hartzheim, *Concilia* III 403 ("*in solemni synodo*"); Hauck, *KGD* IV 7.

[355] Heidingsfelder, *Regg. Eichst.* I 150, Nr. 471; cf. Böhmer-Will, *RAM* I 67ff., Nr. 121-168; Braun, *Bischöfe von Augsburg* II 162.

[356] Rosenfeld, *UB Naumburg* I, Nr. 359. That this was a provincial synod is inferred from the fact that witnessing the confirmation of relics acquired for the church of St. George at Ichtershausen by its prior Wolfram were Bishops Hubert of Havelberg and Berthold of Naumburg, the abbots of Saalfeld, Walkenried, St. Peter's in Erfurt, Reinhardsbrunnen, St. Pauline's Cell, Oldesleiben, Nuenstadt, and St. Georgenthal, Provost Arnold of the Mainz cathedral (who was at once the provost of Erfurt), the provost of Grecheburg, the dean of Hildesheim, the scholastic of Würzburg, the provosts of five collegiate churches, an archpriest, and two *magistri*—that is, two masters of the law. Such a collection of dignitaries was hardly necessary for the business referred to in the document.

[357] Hartzheim, *Concilia* III 790-791; Goerz, *MRR* II, Nr. 671; Gudenus, *Cdipl.* I 305; Hauck, *KGD* IV 7.

[358] The latter synod was missed in Hefele-Knöpfler, whereas Böhmer-Will, *RAM* II 106, Nr. 364, call it wrongly a diocesan synod: the document which tells of it was issued "*in generali Moguntina synodo, episcopis, abbatibus . . . approbantibus*"; the dating rubric also contains the phrase ". . . *in sancto synodo Moguntia . . .*" Cf. Finke, *Konzilienst.* 43 note 1; Acht, *Mainzer UB* II, Nr. 638; Hauck, *KGD* IV 7.

granted to the monastery at Eberbach. From this, it would seem that the purpose of the synod was to resolve a disputed tithe involving this Cistercian house. Winkelmann assumes that the synod had concluded by 20 February, since on that day Bishop Hartwig of Eichstätt and Abbot Kuno of Elwangen are documented at Nürnberg with Otto IV of Brunswick.[359] The set of decrees recently discovered by Peter Johanek in an Innsbruck manuscript and dated to the early thirteenth century may belong to this synod as well, in which case it had a clear pastoral purpose.[360] Since the archbishop placed his suffragans under obligation to ordain "that the following articles be strictly observed by their subordinates and that they charge each and every priest that they maintain these same articles in writing, and that they be read openly in every synod," it is evident that diocesan synods were an assumed regular practice by this particular metropolitan.

Such a statement notwithstanding, there is scarcely a trace of diocesan synodal activity for Mainz itself during the eleventh and twelfth centuries; perhaps provincial synods served a dual purpose where this archbishopric was concerned. On 6 October 1019 at Mainz, property was granted to the church of St. Dodard at Münchweiler;[361] at the "*plenaria synodus*" held in 1122 a controversy over a parish church was resolved;[362] and in 1127 the synod pronounced on a tithe matter.[363] Given the major political role

---

[359] *Phil. von Schw.* II, Exkurs VI (p. 484); Böhmer-Will, *RAM* II 140, Nr. 109; Rossel, *UB Eberbach* I 129, Nr. 65; Binterim, *Concilien* IV 388; Ussermann, *Episcopatus Wirceburg* 80; Hinschius, *KR* III 487 note 5, using Winkelmann, *loc. cit.* as his source.

[360] Innsbruck Stadtsbibliothek MS 16, 1ʳ. Peter Johanek, "Die Pariser Statuten des Bischofs Odo von Sully und die Anfänge der kirchlichen Statutengesetzgebung in Deutschland," *Proceedings of the Seventh International Congress of Medieval Canon Law* (Cambridge, 23-27 July 1984), ed. Peter Linehan, Monumenta Iuris Canonici, Series C: Subsidia, vol. 8 (Città del Vaticano, 1988) 332, suggests that the Innsbruck MS 16 was produced in a south German scriptorium (perhaps at the monastery of Kaisheim). Johanek places the undated set of statutes in the pontificate of Archbishop Siegfried II of Mainz (1200-1230) under whom three known synods were held—1209, 1221 and 1227, acknowledging, however, that this may not be all of them. The Innsbruck MS statutes draw heavily on the statutes issued at a Paris diocesan synod held under Bishop Eudes de Sully 1196/1208. Since these were well-known in the Curia by 1208 Johanek speculates that Siegfried of Mainz may have acquired a copy during his sojourn in Rome as a participant of the Fourth Lateran Council (p. 185); this would necessitate pushing the date of the Mainz synod at which they were published to after 1215, however, making the 1221 or 1227 provincial assemblies the logical candidates. But there are equally compelling reasons for associating these statutes with the Mainz synod of 1209, as we will argue below, and in Ch. Two.

[361] Boye, "Quellenkatalog" 75.

[362] Hartzheim, *Concilia* III 289; Hinschius, *KR* III 586 note 10, 587 note 2, and 586 note 7, where it is referred to as a "*generale concilium*."

[363] Hartzheim, *Concilia* III 300; Hinschius, *KR* III 587 note 2.

played by the primate of Germany, it is not surprising that Archbishop Conrad I delegated his authority to the dean of St. Severin at Erfurt who presided over a diocesan synod in that city in 1192.[364] Another synod held under Archbishop Conrad in 1196 declared that the *ministeriales* of the archbishopric could grant their allodial property to specific religious houses.[365] In the only recorded instance of a diocesan synod held during the pre-Lateran IV years of the pontificate of Archbishop Siegfried II of Eppstein (1200-1230) the cathedral provost, Conrad of Isenburg, and Gottfried, the cathedral dean, acting *vice episcopi* rendered a judgment at some time before September 1213.[366]

The suffragan bishoprics of Mainz also maintained synodal traditions, albeit each with its own peculiar pattern. The most striking picture in twelfth-century Germany is that found at Hildesheim and Halberstadt where frequent assemblies of the bishops with their clergy (and at times the laity as well) never went out of fashion. In Hildesheim, nineteen synods are recorded between 1125 and 1173, while eight more are documented for the two decades 1176-1198.[367] Bishops in the early thirteenth century maintained the practice despite the frequent upheavals occasioned by the civil war: 11 August 1201 (?), 1203, 21 October 1206 and again that same year at Goslar, 29 April 1208, 22 May 1209, 2 June and 10 October 1210, and 18 May 1212.[368]

Hildesheim synods were convened at specifically-designated times, usually on the Monday after *Laetare* (1146, 1160, 1176, 1184), or on the Wednesday after *Laetare* (1151). Those synods which were held in May or June convened on the Friday after Pentecost (e.g., 1209, 1210, 1212). There are at least two instances of semi-annual synods, and this practice is presumed to be the norm. Fall synods were summoned during the mid-twelfth century for the second Monday in October (1147, 1149, 1152). After 1185 only the late spring synod appears to have been used—no synods have the March date. While the usual venue for synods was Hildesheim,

---

[364] Dobenecker, *CdThur* II, Nr. 919.

[365] Hartzheim, *Concilia* III 463; Phillips, *Diöcesansynode* 175; Hinschius, *KR* III 587 note 1.

[366] Sauer, *Nassau UB* I, Nr. 335; Rossel, *Eberbach UB* I, Nr. 88.

[367] Cf. Hartzheim, *Concilia* III 322-323 (1131 *"generalis synodus"*), 362-363 (1149 *"generalis synodus"*), 415 (1178 *"publica synodus"*), 454 (1191 *"capitulum plenum"*); Janicke, *UB Hilds* I, Nrs. 239, 272, 316, 317, 373, 378, 428, 499, 517; Hinschius, *KR* III 586 notes 7, 8 and 11; Idem, 587 note 1; Hauck, *KGD* V 169 note 1; [ ] Volger, "Über die Daten der Synoden in der Diözese Hildesheim," *ZHV* 10 (1877) 402.

[368] Janicke, *UB Hilds* I, Nrs. 564, 580, 615, 616, 627, 635, 638, 654; Volger, "Daten der Synoden" 402; Hauck, *KGD* V 168-9 note 1, and IV 7 note 1.

those of March 1151 and 1206 met at Goslar, the second most important town in the diocese.[369]

Since the early ninth century the bishops of Halberstadt were regular attenders at Mainz provincial synods, and in accordance with the decrees of St. Boniface and the Carolingians, they may have held their own diocesan synods in the ninth and tenth centuries as well. The first documented assembly at Halberstadt was not until 1107/1109, however. Thereafter, the record reveals such frequency and regularity as to make it obvious that twelfth-century bishops built on a long-standing tradition: between 1114 and 1153 twenty-three synods are known. By the early twelfth century Maundy Thursday had become the fixed day for the spring assembly, and the Feast of St. Luke (18 October) served that in the fall. A third yearly synod, held on an unspecified day in May or June, is also noted on occasion.[370]

During the forty years which preceded the Fourth Lateranum, there is no evidence of a decline in Halberstadt synodal activity. Regardless of the bishop, assemblies were convened with the accustomed regularity: 28 May at Oschersleben and 29 November 1178 (the bishop was apparently away on St. Luke's day);[371] 11 July 1179;[372] 26 June 1180;[373] 20 May 1183

---

[369] Maring, *Diözesansynoden* 5-33.

[370] Hartzheim, *Concilia* III 280 (1120 *"publicum concilium"*), 281 (1121 *"publica synodus"*), 337 (1137 *"magna synodus"*), 356 (1147 *"synodus nostra"*), 365 (1150 *"plena synodus"*); Schmidt, *UB Halb* I, Nrs. 201, 205, 229-231, 242. Franz Winter, "Die Diözesansynoden des Halberstädter Sprengels im 12. Jahrhundert," *ZHV* 1 (1868), 251-286; 2 (1869) 78-90; 5 (1872) 423-435, adds greatly to our understanding of Halberstadt synods, to which Adolf Diestelkamp, "Zur Geschichte der Halberstädter Diözesansynoden," *Zeitschrift des Vereins für Kirchengeschichte der Provinz Sachsen* 27 (1931) 54-56, has added corrections. See further Binterim, *Concilien* IV 772; Phillips, *Diöcesansynode* 50; Hinschius, *KR* III 586 notes 8 and 11, 587 note 1; Hauck, *KGD* V 168 note 1. The document which Schmidt publishes, *UB Halb* I, Nr. 147, bears the date 16 April 1120 and contains a description of the rights and obligations of the provost-archdeacon of Kaltenborn. Therein is found the following threat of punishment: *"Et milites, qui annuatim bis ad sinodum maiorem Halberstadensem vel Caldenbornensem venire contempserint, tanquam putridum membrum ab ecclesia precidantur usque ad condignam satisfactionem."* This much-quoted charter has been used to argue that there were in fact two synods per year in the diocese of Halberstadt; cf. Hilling, "Gegenwart und Einfluss" 219, and those dependent on him: Maring, *Diözesansynoden* 23 note 5, Diestelkamp, *op.cit.* 55 note 16. Gescher, "Synodales" 395-397, argues persuasively, however, that this particular document is not referring to the episcopal *synodus* in which the bishop treats a variety of matters with the leading clergy and laymen of his diocese, but rather to the archidiaconal *Send* at Kaltenborn, which is contrasted with the *synodus maior* at Halberstadt—the greater Send—over which the bishop himself presides.

[371] Hartzheim, *Concilia* III 416 (*"publica synodus"*), 417-418 (*"publica synodus"*); Schmidt, *UB Halb* I, Nr. 282; Diestelkamp, "Halberst. Syn." 56; Phillips, *Diöcesansynode* 50, 52; Hinschius, *KR* III 586 note 8, 587 note 1, 588 note 7; Hauck, *KGD* V 168, note 1.

[372] Hartzheim, *Concilia* III 449; Schmidt, *UB Halb* I, Nr. 284; Phillips, *Diöcesansynode* 52; Diestelkamp, "Halberst. Syn." 56; Hauck, *KGD* V 168 note 1.

[373] Hauck, *KGD* V 168 note 1.

and at *two* other times that same year;[374] on Maundy Thursday and on 28 May 1184;[375] 19 July 1185;[376] on Maundy Thursday and 28 November 1186;[377] 1187;[378] 8-10 June 1189 at Halberstadt[379] and later that same year at Oschersleben;[380] 1190;[381] 1192;[382] 10 December/27 December 1194 (?);[383] 30 March (Maundy Thursday) and later in the summer 1195 at Gatersleben, and perhaps yet a third;[384] 1196(?);[385] 1197(?);[386] 1198;[387] 1199;[388] 28 May 1200;[389] 1202;[390] 1205(?);[391] 1211;[392] 1212;[393] 14 June 1214, which would have been the third synod of the year;[394] and 15 June 1215.[395]

With the exception of the summer synods which in the beginning were held at Gatersleben, after 1178 in Oschersleben and Wegleben, the synods

---

[374] Hartzheim, *Concilia* III 427; Schmidt, *UB Halb* I, Nr. 299; Phillips, *Diöcesansynode* 50; Diestelkamp, "Halberst. Syn." 56; Hinschius, *KR* III 587 note 1; Hauck, *KGD* V 168 note 1.

[375] Schmidt, *UB Halb* I, Nr. 305; Diestelkamp, "Halberst. Syn." 56; Hauck, *KGD* V 168 note 1.

[376] Schmidt, *UB Halb* I, Nr. 310; Diestelkamp, "Halberst. Syn." 56; Hauck, *KGD* V 168 note 1.

[377] Hartzheim, *Concilia* III 435 ("*plena synodus*"); Phillips, *Diöcesansynode* 50; Hinschius, *KR* III 586 note 9, 587 note 1; Hauck, *KGD* V 168 note 1.

[378] Winter, "Diözesansynoden" V 426.

[379] Hartzheim, *Concilia* III 448 ("*plena synodus*"); Phillips, *Diöcesansynode* 50; Schmidt, *UB Halb* I, Nr. 326; Diestelkamp, "Halberst. Syn." 56; Hinschius, *KR* III 586 note 9, 587 note 1.

[380] Hartzheim, *Concilia* III 448; Hauck, *KGD* V 169 note 1.

[381] Winter, "Diözesansynoden" V 427.

[382] Franz Peter Sonntag, *Das Kollegiatstift St. Marien zu Erfurt von 1117-1400*, Erfurter Theologische Studien 13 (Leipzig, 1962) 113, citing Alfred Overmann, ed., *Urkundenbuch der Erfurter Stifter und Klöster*, Teil I (706-1330), Geschichtsquellen der Provinz Sachsen (Magdeburg, 1926) I, Nr. 109.

[383] Winter, "Diözesansynoden" V 427; Hauck, *KGD* V 168 note 1.

[384] Winter, "Diözesansynoden" V 427; Hauck, *KGD* V 168 note 1.

[385] Hauck, *KGD* V 168 note 1.

[386] Hauck, *KGD* V 168 note 1.

[387] Winter, "Diözesansynoden" V 427.

[388] Hauck, *KGD* V 168 note 1.

[389] Hartzheim III 472-473 ("*generalis synodus*"); Phillips, *Diöcesansynode* 10, 50; Winter, "Diözesansynoden" V 427; Hinschius, *KR* III 586 note 7; Hauck, *KGD* V 168 note 1.

[390] Hauck, *KGD* V 168 note 1.

[391] Phillips, *Diöcesansynode* 52, citing Hartzheim, *Concilia* III 483.

[392] Hauck, *KGD* V 168 note 1.

[393] Schmidt, *UB Halb* I 421-422, Nr. 474; Hauck, *KGD* V 168 note 1.

[394] Schmidt, *UB Halb* I 425-426, Nr. 478; Diestelkamp, "Halberst. Syn." 55-56; Hauck, *KGD* IV 9 note 2 and V 168 note 1.

[395] Schmidt, *UB Halb* I 436, Nr. 489; Diestelkamp, "Halberst. Syn." 56; Hauck, *KGD* V 168 note 1.

were held in Halberstadt. Though generally presided over by the bishop himself, the summer synods of 1178, 1179, 1183, 1185, 1214, and 1215 were headed by the cathedral dean or provost. The overwhelming majority of references to synods contain juridical and/or administrative business. The assembly of 1128 demonstrates that they also had pastoral functions, however, a fact which can also be inferred from the sermon which the Cistercian abbot, Colquin of Sichem, delivered to the assembly in 1146, 1150, or 1151.[396] The most remarkable assembly was that of 1214, however, for on that occasion a trial by ordeal was conducted to determine the truth in a dispute over possessions between the monastery of St. Jacob and the Templars. A glowing iron, blessed by the bishop, was carried from the high altar through the nave of the cathedral to the altar of St. Mary by Prior Goswin of St. Jacob. Seeing their claims quashed by this appeal to a higher law, the Templars admitted their error and turned over the properties taken illegally.

The remaining suffragan bishoprics of Mainz show but sporadic synodal activity during the twelfth and early thirteenth centuries, indicating perhaps the influence of individual bishops rather than a strong local tradition. The Alsatian capital of Strasbourg records an assembly in early 992/fall 993,[397] but this clearly was not the first. While synods probably were held in Carolingian times as well, it is a document of the Saxon period which reveals that they were a long-standing tradition. In 1003 Bishop Werner received the imperial nunnery of St. Stephan as compensation for damages sustained during the civil war. Having taken possession, the prelate then convened a synod near the end of December 1004 in which the new relationships between the convent and the bishopric were announced. Among these was that in the future the abbess of St. Stephan was to enjoy a place of honor at diocesan synods (*"in conciliis episcopalibus"*) in the midst of the other abbesses, directly across from the bishop's chair, inasmuch as she held the *"secunda sedes civitatis."*[398]

Since the seating arrangement was hardly the primary object of the synodal deliberations, one may conclude that synods had been held for some time, and that well-developed procedures and specified places for those attending had been established. The participation of proctors from female

---

[396] Cf. Winter, "Diözesansynoden" II 81, citing Idem, *Die Cistercienser des nordöstlichen Deutschlands* (Gotha, 1868) I 74-75.

[397] Würdtwein, *Nova subs.* V 352-354. The document itself refers to an earlier synod. For a general discussion of Strasbourg synodalia, see Max Sdralek, "Die Strassburger Diözesansynoden," *Strassburger Theologische Studien* Bd. 2, Heft 1 (Strassburg, 1897) 1-9.

[398] Wiegand, *UB Strassburg* I 42, Nr. 51; Sdralek, "Strassburger Synoden" 4-5; Hauck, *KGD* IV 7 note 1.

religious houses, generally ignored by the canon law literature, has only been documented elsewhere for Münster and Osnabrück.[399] Such involvement of women should not seem unusual in a time when laymen also attended, however. Women's convents were the frequent object of business transactions and legislation at synods.

On 25 July 1035 Bishop William I (1029-1047) of Strasbourg consecrated the church at Burgheim and confirmed to it a tithe. He noted that at the next synod—"*in proximo suo generali concilio*"—of the diocese further action would be taken.[400] Later that same year (3 December) Bishop William participated in a major gathering of bishops at Limburg on the Lahn for the purpose of settling a dispute regarding the proper time for scheduling Advent; by its very nature, this was an extra-diocesan synod.[401] In 1041 Bishop William confirmed with his choirbishops (archdeacons) and the entire clergy of his church the decision of his synod regarding a grant by the noblewoman Bertha of Brandenberg to the monastery at Ebersheim, and the following year at yet another synod the possessions of that same monastery were confirmed.[402]

Like many other bishoprics, the independent synodal activity of Strasbourg became subordinated to the political issues of the Gregorian period. Thus, the only recorded synods attended by bishops Hermann (1047-1065), Werner II (1065-1077), Thiepald (1078-1082), Otto (1082/4-1100) and Cuno (1100-1123) were those summoned by the pope, his legates, the German emperors, or the archbishops of Mainz. E.g., Bishop Werner II was present at the synod held 15 August 1071 under the direction of Archbishop Siegfried I of Mainz, and in the presence of papal and imperial legates, for the purpose of investigating the election of Bishop Werner of Constanz.[403] Bishop Bruno, on the other hand, surrendered his episcopal chair at a Mainz synod held May/8 June 1131 in the presence of other bishops and a cardinal legate.[404]

At his own synod held in 1137 Bishop Gebhard (1131-1141) announced the establishment of a foundation of Augustinian canons at Ittenweiler by a

---

[399] See Heinrich Finke, "Die angebliche Fälschung der ältesten Münsterischen Synodalstatuten," *ZGAW* 54 (1891) Part I 162.

[400] Wentzcke, *Regg. Strassburg* I 273, Nr. 262.

[401] Wentzcke, *Regg. Strassburg* I 273, Nr. 265.

[402] Wentzcke, *Regg. Strassburg* I 274-275, Nrs. 268, 269. The existing documents are twelfth century forgeries which presumably are based on earlier records. See also, *Chron. Ebersh.* 442.

[403] Wentzcke, *Regg. Strassburg* I 281 Nr. 302; Ladewig, *Regg. Const.* I, Nr. 463.

[404] Wentzcke, *Regg. Strassburg* I 316, Nr. 443.

cathedral canon named Conrad.[405] His successor Burchard (1141-1162) held at least three synods: at some time before 26 October 1143 he announced that the abbot of Schwarzach had been granted exemption from the tax imposed upon those outsiders who came into the city of Strasbourg, the record of which states that "*Hec autem facta sunt in consistorio Argentinensi consentiente . . . ,*" to which were appended the names of numerous cathedral canons.[406] Between April/May 1145 he confirmed to the brothers of St. Thomas in Strasbourg a one-third tithe at St. Aurelian which had been granted by his predecessor Bishop Otto, after he had first read the document of conveyance at a diocesan synod where it was approved by all.[407] According to an entry in the registers of Bishop Burchard, "a few years before 1162" he presided at a diocesan synod where the parishioners in Dochedorf obtained the right of patronage over their own church against the claims of the abbot of Weissenburg.[408]

No synods are known for the pontificates of Bishops Rudolf (1163/4-1179) and Conrad I (1179-1180), but within months of the elevation of Henry I (1180/1-1190) this bishop-elect presided over a synod which adjudicated a dispute between Abbots Werner of Maursmünster and Henry of Moyenmoutier over property at St. Quirin.[409] Henry of Strasbourg also participated in two synods convened by his neighbor, Bishop Henry of Basel: the first, held between 1 December 1185 and 2 March 1187 confirmed the decision of Provost Frederick of St. Thomas in Strasbourg regarding a church in the diocese of Basel; the second, held on 2 March 1187, confirmed that same decision yet again.[410]

Two documents from the pontificate of Bishop Conrad II (1190-1202) appear to be the record of separate synods held in 1190 and on 1 April 1196, even though neither employs the actual word "synod" in the salutation or conclusion. The first attests that as an "*electus*" Conrad presided over a concord reached between the monks at Honau and the knight Garsilius of

---

[405] Wentzcke, *Regg. Strassburg* I 321, Nr. 461 ("*Sed ego gratia dei residens in synodo generali cupiensque cuncta digne deo gesta corroborari, . . .*"). Cf. also, Hauck, *KGD* IV 7, citing Wentzcke, "Ungedruckte Urkunden" 580, Nr. 2.

[406] Wentzcke, *Regg. Strassburg* I 329, Nr. 502; Würdtwein, *Nova subs.* VII 125; Sdralek, "Strassburger Synoden" 6.

[407] Wentzcke, *Regg. Strassburg* I 330, Nr. 508; Wiegand, *UB Strassburg* I 78, Nr. 97; Sdralek, "Strassburger Synoden" 8; Hauck, *KGD* IV 7 note 1. There was a large number of clergy who witnessed the document as well.

[408] Wentzcke, *Regg. Strassburg* I 339, Nr. 563, dated 1141/1160.

[409] Wentzcke, *Regg. Strassburg* I 349, Nr. 608; Bishop Henry was not consecrated until 25 July 1182 in Italy by the archbishop of Mainz.

[410] Wentzcke, *Regg. Strassburg* I 353-354, Nrs. 629, 630.

Berslett regarding the tithe at Nüvere and three other locations. This rather commonplace piece of business *"Actum est autem et publice promulgatum anno domini . . . assistentibus prelatis et canonicis maioris ecclesie, canonicis ecclesie sancti Thome et sancti Petri et laicis quam plurimis feliciter."*[411] The number of individuals assenting to this act far outweighed the importance of the act itself, leaving us to conclude that the real purpose of the assembly was that of a diocesan synod.

Equally compelling is the report which Bishop Conrad II sent to Pope Celestine III regarding a dispute between the abbot of Walburg and the abbot of Selz. Dated 1 April 1196 at Strasbourg, the report contains the formula: *"Acta sunt hec anno . . . in choro maiori Argentinensis ecclesie sub presentia abbatum, prepositorum, decanorum et aliorum honestorum virorum, tam laicorum quam clericorum, qui ad hoc vocati sunt, scilicet . . ."*[412] Thereupon follow the names of ten abbots, three provosts or priors, three archdeacons, many other cathedral canons, the dean of St. Thomas and several of the canons there, *"quorum consilio et aliorum sapientum preme . . . sententiam tulimus."* In other words, the bishop reached the decision with the assistance of the most prominent clerics and laymen of the diocese, i.e., in his diocesan synod.

At a synod held in 1201 at Strasbourg under the direction of the cathedral dean, one Walter fitz Walter publicly renounced his claims to the tithe at Harthausen against the monastery of Neubourg.[413] Possibly at this same synod, a complaint was brought against Abbot Peter of Neubourg by the *plebanus* Berthold of Berstein, also regarding the tithe at Harthausen; these were later dropped.[414] Having met challenges to Neuburg's rights, Abbot Peter secured confirmation thereof at the synod which met under the direction of Bishop Conrad himself in 1202.[415]

Though elected in 1202, Bishop Henry III of Strasbourg (1202-1223) was not consecrated until some time before 28 May 1207 by the archbishop of

---

[411] Wentzcke, *Regg. Strassburg* I 362, Nr. 660.

[412] Wentzcke, *Regg. Strassburg* I 366, Nr. 681.

[413] Würdtwein, *Nova subs.* X 198, Nr. 70; X 201 note "f"; Wiegand, *UB Strassburg* I 140; Wentzcke, *Regg. Strassburg* I, Nr. 714. See further, Luzian Pfleger, "Abt Peter von Neuburg im heiligen Forst, ein hervorragender Cistercienser an der Wende des 13. Jahrhunderts (1196-1214," *Cistercienser-Chronik* 16 Jg., Nr. 183 (May 1904) 137-138; Sdralek, "Strassburger Synode" 9-10; Hauck, *KGD* IV 7 note 1.

[414] Wentzcke, *Regg. Strassburg* I 380, Nr. 729; Hauck, *KGD* IV 7 sees the possibility of separate synods, though this seems unnecessary.

[415] Cf. Wentzcke, "Ungedruckte Urkk." 592, Nr. 12; Wentzcke, *Regg. Strassburg* I 380, Nr. 729 (*"Acta sunt . . . in presentia Cuonradi venerabilis Argentinensis episcopus et prelatorum eiusdem ecclesie . . ."*); Hauck, *KGD* IV 7 note 1.

Sens. On 6 November 1208 at Strasbourg a synod pronounced judgment in
a dispute between the abbot of Neuburg and Meffrid, the priest at Ober-
hofen, regarding the rights of patronage over the church at Donnen-
heim,[416] while on 4 November 1209 at Strasbourg a synodal decision
reached years earlier (1196) under Bishop Conrad II regarding the patronage
at Wittenheim was read aloud and confirmed once again.[417] A document
dated with just the year 1211 contains the record of an act of confirmation
which the bishop did *"in consistorio,"* suggesting that this too contains a
brief allusion to a diocesan synod which had just completed its work.[418]
Another synod in 1212 dealt once again with a dispute between the abbot of
Neuburg and another party, this time the priest at Ingweiler.[419]

The extant records thus reveal a rather vigorous diocesan synodal
tradition at Strasbourg on the eve of the Fourth Lateranum, even though
little evidence exists of concern shown for the pastoral aspects of church
life. Not until 1310 did a Strasbourg bishop compile a comprehensive set
of reform decrees for his diocese, utilizing statutes published at various
times by his predecessors.[420] The consequences of this apparent neglect
will be shown in the following chapter.

Mention of diocesan synods for Würzburg is more limited, consisting of
a few terse references to actions taken in connection with these assemblies.
A decree issued at Würzburg before 939 was included in Bishop Gundekar
of Eichstätt's (1057-1075) copy of the *Decretum*.[421] Although the bishop
of Würzburg, Adalbero of Lambach-Wels (1045-1090), was forced to
apologize at the Bamberg synod held 18 October 1052 for attacks against
the Bamberg church by his own clerics and to give assurances for the future
that the *bannus, iustitia* and *potestas* of the latter would be honored, there
is no record of his having held diocesan synods of his own.[422] At another
Bamberg synod held 13 April 1059, a list of nineteen proprietary and juris-

---

[416] Hessel, *Regg. Strassburg* II 6, Nr. 766; Würdtwein, *Nova subs.* X 235, Nr. 84; Pfleger,
"Abt Peter von Neuburg" 138.

[417] Hessel, *Regg. Strassburg* II 8, Nr. 776 (*"Acta 1209 . . . in synodo nostra . . . ,"*) and
with the *"communicato consilio"* of the entire Strasbourg clergy. Cf. also Wentzcke, *Regg.
Strassburg* I, Nr. 686.

[418] Hessel, *Regg. Strassburg* II 9, Nr. 780.

[419] Hessel, *Regg. Strassburg* II 11, Nr. 791; Würdtwein, *Nova subs.* X 266; Pfleger, "Abt
Peter von Neuburg" 138.

[420] Kehrberger, *Synodalstatuten* 38.

[421] Heidingsfelder, *Regg. Eichst.* I 77, Nr. 219.

[422] See Wendehorst, *Bistum Würzburg* 110; further, Guttenberg, *Regg. Bamb.* Nrs. 257,
258.

dictional claims against Bamberg, presented by the advocate of the bishopric of Würzburg, was heard and rejected.[423]

At a synod dated with the year 1115, Bishop Erlung of Würzburg (1105-1121) restored to freedom men who had been reduced to servitude.[424] Despite heavy service to the Empire, Bishop Embricho (1127-1146) also devoted his energies to the inner needs of his diocese. In addition to dividing his bishopric into archdeaconries and rural chapters, he convened several diocesan synods: 1128,[425] 1 May 1136,[426] 5 May 1137,[427] and 18 October 1144.[428] Under his successor, Gebhard of Henneberg (1150-1159) a single synod is recorded, that held in 1156.[429]

The pontificate of Bishop Herold (1165-1171) marks the first time since the days of Bishop Embricho that evidence for regularly-held diocesan synods is extant. Shortly after his accession he convened the clergy and laymen of his bishopric in an assembly.[430] A document dated 1167 and attested to by seven diocesan abbots probably records an action taken at a synod as well.[431] Another document preserved in Munich contains the protocol of a third synod held 21 October 1169 at Würzburg.[432] Bishop

---

[423] Wendehorst, *Bistum Würzburg* 110.

[424] *Mon. Boica* XXXVII 38, Nr. 76; Wendehorst, *Bistum Würzburg* 130; Hauck, *KGD* IV 7 note 1.

[425] Himmelstein, *Synodicon Herb.* 110; *Mon. Boica* XLV 6, Nr. 3; Wendehorst, *Bistum Würzburg* 145. In his synod the bishop proclaimed (*"recitata in sinodo"*) a grant of property to the monastery at Cella and received in exchange a house (*curia*) in Würzburg and a vineyard in Stenbach. See also, Julius Krieg, *Der Kampf der Bischöfe gegen die Archidiakone im Bistum Würzburg*, Kirchenrechtliche Abhandlungen 82 (Stuttgart, 1914) 16; Binterim, *Concilien* IV 215.

[426] Hartzheim, *Concilia* III 331-332; Phillips, *Diöcesansynode* 50; Hinschius, *KR* III 587 note 1; Hauck, *KGD* IV 7 note 1; Palazzini, *Dizionario* VI 172-173. Wendehorst, *Bistum Würzburg* 145, gives the reference for an unpublished document. The synod dealt with the establishment of a new parish.

[427] Hartzheim, *Concilia* III 335-336; *Mon. Boica* XLV 8, Nr. 4; Phillips, *Diöcesansynode* 50; Hinschius, *KR* III 588 note 7; Hauck, *KGD* IV 7 note 1; Palazzini, *Dizionario* VI 172-173; and Wendehorst, *Bistum Würzburg* 145. The bishop made a grant of property at Alolvesheim and resigned by Gerhard of Sulzebach to the monastery at Eberbach *"in sinodo nostra."*

[428] *Mon. Boica* XLV 13, Nr. 6; Wendehorst, *Bistum Würzburg* 145. The bishop permitted the monastery at Heilbronn to receive the tithe at Erlebach and Haselach in return for a grant of the parish church at Haselach to the bishopric *"in sinodo nostra."*

[429] *Mon. Boica* XLV 18, Nr. 10; Wendehorst, *Bistum Würzburg* 158. The synod dealt with the transfer of the parish church of Euskirchen to the monastery at Münchaurach.

[430] See Wendehorst, *Bistum Würzburg* 168, for references to archival sources.

[431] Binterim, *Concilien* IV 218; Wendehorst, *Bistum Würzburg* 168; Reimer, *Hess. UB* II/1, Nr. 101.

[432] Hartzheim, *Concilia* III 401: Bishop Herold of Würzburg proclaims (*"sub testimonio et presentia totius synodalis conventus"*) the grant of a tithe to Michelsberg. See also Phillips,

Reginhard of Abenberg (1171-1186) also held a synod in 1183,[433] while three are documented for the pontificate of his successor, Henry III of Berg (1191-1197): 1192,[434] 1194,[435] and 1197.[436] Whether multiple synods yearly ever became customary at Würzburg cannot be determined: a document of 1254 refers to but one: *"Singulis annis predicta statuta in synodo recitentur."*[437] The earliest set of diocesan synodal statutes dates from 1329.[438]

In the neighboring Franconian diocese of Bamberg the evidence is equally sparse. Although Bishop Eberhard I (1007-1040) was present at the provincial synod held at Seligenstadt on 21 September 1026,[439] not until the pontificate of Bishop Gunther (1057-1065) is there record of a diocesan synod. On 13 April 1059 the claims by the bishopric of Würzburg to the tithe at Neubruch in the diocese of Bamberg were successfully rejected. The matter remained a sore spot between the two churches for some time, however: in 1063 the Bambergers expressed complaints against the advocate of Würzburg (Count Eberhard) who apparently continued to oppress the inhabitants of Neubruch.[440] In the same synod (1059) Bishop Gunther threatened the slavic inhabitants of his bishopric with expulsion if they persisted in their disregard for the canonical prescriptions concerning the tithe and matrimony.[441]

Diöcesansynode 50; Hinschius, *KR* III 586 note 1; Palazzini, *Dizionario* VI 172-173; Wendehorst, *Bistum Würzburg* 168, citing Hermann Bloch, "Die Urkunden Heinrichs II. für Kloster Michelsberg zu Bamberg," *NA* 19 (1894) 659-661.

[433] Wendehorst, *Bistum Würzburg* 172.

[434] *Mon. Boica* XXXVII 146, Nr. 151; Hauck, *KGD* IV 7 note 1; Wendehorst, *Bistum Würzburg* 181. During the synod the bishop reprimanded a parish priest at Reicholzheim who had released his parishioners from the obligation to make a pilgrimage to the shrine of St. Kilian in Würzburg upon payment of money.

[435] Dobenecker, *CdThur* II, Nr. 964; Wendehorst, *Bistum Würzburg* 182. At the synod the bishop removed the chapel at Rothausen from the parish of Mellrichstadt and transferred it to the monastery Bildhausen.

[436] Bloch, "Urkunden für Kl. Michelsberg" 659, Nr. 2 (with date of 1194/1197): Bishop Henry III of Würzburg declares a compromise reached at his synod with Michelsberg regarding a tithe at Neubruch. Wendehorst, *Bistum Würzburg* 182, corrects this to 1197.

[437] *Mon. Boica* XXXVII 364, Nr. 323.

[438] Kehrberger, *Synodalstatuten* 107.

[439] For an extensive catalogue of sources for the bishops of Bamberg, see Guttenberg, *Bistum Bamberg*; for Eberhard at the synod of 1026, cf. p. 96.

[440] Hartzheim, *Concilia* III 126 and Mansi, *Collectio* XIX 883, both place the synod in the year 1058; Hinschius, *KR* III 587 note 3, sets it in 1057. Guttenberg, *Bistum Bamberg* I 104, citing *Epistolae Bambergenses*, in *Mon. Bambergensia*, vol. 5 of Jaffé, *Bibliotheca* 497, Nr. 8, dates it 1059.

[441] The bishop stated: *"Ego . . . propter multimodo meae ecclesiae negotia synodum universorum subiectorum tenui. Erat enim plebs huius episcopi, utpote ex maximine parte Slavonica, ritibus gentilium dedita, abhorrens a religione christiana, tam in cognatorum*

Under Bishop Rupert (1075-1102) two synods are recorded. In 1083 the "Peace of God" was proclaimed before a gathering of the diocesan clergy and laity,[442] while on 22 March 1087 the earlier decision that the tithe at Neubruch rightfully belonged to the church of Bamberg was published once more.[443] Based on these meager sources, we can also conclude that laymen still attended. There are no synodal decrees from this period; chroniclers generally do nothing more than mention the fact that a synod had taken place, without providing specifics.[444]

Bishop Otto I (1102-1139) held a synod in the crypt of St. Moritz' church in Bamberg at an unspecified time in 1134,[445] and another on 25 May 1137.[446] Thereafter, the record is silent until the pontificate of Bishop Timo (1196-1202) who convened a diocesan assembly on 16 September 1197.[447] According to the first extant synodal statutes published by Bishop Anton von Rotenhan in the 1430s, the Tuesday after Sunday *Exaudi* was the traditional day for synods. We cannot say to what extent this practice prevailed in the eleventh and twelfth centuries, however.[448]

The first known synod for the see of Constanz dates from October 864 under Bishop Salomo I;[449] thereafter, they are recorded for ca. 877 under Bishop Salomo II,[450] 919/934 under Bishop Noting,[451] 995 under Bishop

---

connubiis quam in decimationum contradictione decretis patrum omnino contraria."

[442] Guttenberg, *Bistum Bamberg* I 113.

[443] Hartzheim, *Concilia* III 206; *Epist. Bamberg.* 502, Nr. 10; Guttenberg, *Regg. Bamb.* Nr. 545. See also, Hinschius, *KR* III 589 note 3, Guttenberg, *Bistum Bamberg* I 113, and Wendehorst, *Bistum Würzburg* 110.

[444] Kehrberger, *Synodalstatuten* 37.

[445] Guttenberg, *Bistum Bamberg* I 129; Dobenecker, *CdThur* I, Nr. 1289.

[446] Guttenberg, *Bistum Bamberg* I 129; Binterim, *Concilien* IV 218; Phillips, *Diöcesansynode* 50 ("*Data et confirmata anno 1137. VIII. Kal. Junii. Feria III. in synodo Bambergensi, in praesentia cleri et populi*").

[447] Guttenberg, *Bistum Bamberg* I 162; Looshorn, *Bistum Bamberg* II 576. The business transacted involved ordering the monastery at Langheim to make compensation to the *plebanus* of Kronach, and of accepting the gift of a servant girl for the Bamberg church by a diocesan *ministerialis*.

[448] Cf. Kehrberger, *Synodalstatuten* 38. The notices which Binterim gives for additional synods at Bamberg in 1122, 1123, 1127, 1132, 1144, 1152 and 1154 require further authentication and study; cf. *Concilien* IV 215-218.

[449] Ladewig, *Regg. Const.* I, Nrs. 132-133. For a general discussion of synodal activity, see Karl Brehm, "Zur Geschichte der Konstanzer Diözesansynoden während des Mittelalters," *Diözesanarchiv von Schwaben* 22 (1904); Ursula-Renate Weiss, "Die Konstanzer Bischöfe im 12. Jahrhundert," *Konstanzer Geschichts- und Rechtsquellen* 20 (Sigmaringen, 1975) 159, 173.

[450] Ladewig, *Regg. Const.* I, Nrs. 161, 167; Brehm, "Konstanzer Synoden" 18. The synod appears to have come in the aftermath of a diocesan visitation.

[451] Ladewig, *Regg. Const.* I, Nr. 348; Brehm, "Konstanzer Synoden" 18; Hauck, *KGD* IV 7, citing *Ex Miraculis S. Marci* [ca. 930] 451: "*Tunc episcopus hoc audiens, in omnibus rebus*

Gebhard II,[452] and spring 1033 under Bishop Warmann.[453] The phrase *"tempore synodi"* of the St. Gall *Annales* speaks not only for the regular celebration of autumn synods at Constanz, but also for the actual holding of one by Bishop Eberhard I in October 1043 in the presence of the Emperor Henry III who presided over a large assembly of princes in Constanz.[454] Gebhard III is known to have held at least three assemblies of his clergy, on 1 April 1086,[455] before 8 April 1094,[456] and on 21 October 1105.[457] The middle synod reminds us that this was the age of Gregorian reform ideas, in that it issued a decree forbidding members of the diocese to attend services conducted by simoniacal or reprobate clerics. Changes were also made in the length of time to be used for celebrating Easter and Pentecost within the diocese. The third synod was the occasion for proclaiming a *Landfriede* until Pentecost 1106.

Evidence for the twelfth century does not reveal a vigorous synodal tradition, however. In 1127, shortly before his death, Bishop Ulrich of Dillingen assembled his diocesan clergy in a synod.[458] The next probable synod did not occur until 1143, under Bishop Hermann I of Arbon.[459] This same prelate announced the grant of lands at *Ahe* (Ach) to his episcopal church in 1158 by two laymen *"pro remedio animarum suarum suorumque parentum,"* the purpose of which was to augment the *"communem praebendam"* of the bishopric. Witnessing this transfer which *"facta sunt hec in choro Constanciensi"* were a large number of the cathedral canons whose presence at the synod is thus documented.[460] At yet another synod held 20 October 1171 under Bishop Otto the monastery at Weissenau had con-

---

suae voluntate satagere spopondit. Postea vero in sua synodo iussit publice predicare, quod . . ."

[452] Ladewig, *Regg. Const.* I, Nr. 403; Brehm, "Konstanzer Synoden" 18.

[453] Boye, "Quellenkatalog" 80-81; Ladewig, *Regg. Const.* I, Nr. 442; Phillips, *Diöcesansynode* 50; Brehm, "Konstanzer Synoden" 18.

[454] Boye, "Synoden Deutschlands" 235; Idem, "Quellenkatalog" 82; Ladewig, *Regg. Const.* I, Nr. 403. Whether regular autumn synods were the custom, as Brehm, "Konstanzer Synoden" 18 argues, cannot be proved.

[455] Ladewig, *Regg. Const.* I, Nrs. 531, 532; Brehm, "Konstanzer Synoden" 18; Hauck, *KGD* IV 7.

[456] Mansi, *Collectio* XX 795; Ladewig, *Regg. Const.* I, Nr. 571; Hinschius, *KR* III 587 note 4; Hauck, *KGD* IV 7, citing *Bern. chron.* 458; Brehm, "Konstanzer Synoden" 18.

[457] Ladewig, *Regg. Const.* I, Nr. 623; Brehm, "Konstanzer Synoden" 18.

[458] Ladewig, *Regg. Const.* I, Nrs. 754, 755; Meyer, *Thurgau UB* II 52, Nr. 21 (*"in publica residens synodo"*); Hauck, *KGD* IV 7; Brehm, "Konstanzer Synoden" 18.

[459] Ladewig, *Regg. Const.* I, Nr. 814; Brehm, "Konstanzer Synoden" 18.

[460] *Fürstenberg. UB* V 60-61, Nr. 96.

firmed all the rights and privileges bestowed upon it by his predecessors had done, especially the tithes.[461]

In April 1181 the emperor Frederick Barbarossa convened an assembly of princes at Constanz, among whom was Bishop Berthold (of Bussnang).[462] The prelate apparently used this occasion to conduct a synod for his diocesan clergy as well: a document dated at sometime after 1176 contains the decision of a diocesan synod at which the prelate confirmed to the monastery of Salem the possession of a swampy piece of land near Leustetten, on the basis of an earlier legal pronouncement made in the presence of the emperor, the claims of the *ministeriales* of Count Conrad of Heiligenberg notwithstanding.[463] A similar dispute between Abbot Dipert of St. Blaise (Sankt Blasien) and Henry, *plebanus* of Frichingen, over a one-third part of the tithe from Henry's parish church was decided in favor of the monastery.[464]

The succeeding bishop, Diethelm of Krenkingen, is credited with regarding his pastoral duties most seriously. During the first years of his pontificate he undertook an extended visitation of his diocese (presumably the present-day Swiss portion).[465] He also worked closely with the papacy in the supervision of the monasteries within his bishopric. A document dated 28 May 1199 makes known a judgment which was "*Actum coram nobis in choram Constantiensi . . .* ," regarding the monastery of St. Blaise and various tithe problems. Witnessing this event were numerous prominent members of the higher clergy of the diocese.[466] The document undoubted-

---

[461] *Wirtemburg. UB* II 167, Nr. 397 ("*Anno mclxxi . . . in generali capitulo hec facta sunt*").

[462] Weiss, "Konstanzer Bischöfe" 131; Prutz, *Friedrich I.* III 100.

[463] F. von Weech, "Codex Salemitanus. Urkundenbuch der Cistercienserabtei Salem," *ZGO* 35 (1883) 32-34 [Nr. 20] ("*Inde ventum est in synodum Constantiensem ubi Berhtoldus comes de Zolr etc. . . . Hoc factum est . . . et omni choro et aliis astantibus quam plurimis in eadem sinodo*"); Ladewig, *Regg. Const.* I 119, Nr. 1057; *Fürstenberg. UB* V 65, Nr. 104 (cf. note 3, where 1183 is suggested as the date for this synod; the emperor was also present in Constanz that year); Weiss, "Konstanzer Bischöfe" 131; Brehm, "Konstanzer Synoden" 18; Hauck, *KGD* IV 7.

[464] *Fürstenberg. UB* V, Nr. 110 ("*coram se, episcopo, in generali capitulo fecit*").

[465] Ladewig, *Regg. Const.* I 127, Nr. 1131; Meyer, *Thurgau UB* II 232, Nr. 64; Weiss, "Konstanzer Bischöfe" 173.

[466] *Wirtemburg. UB* II 331 Nr. 511. If such a rubric serves as an indicator for diocesan synods, an entire series of similar documents may require a re-assessment of synodal activity in Konstanz during the two decades which immediately preceded the Council of 1215: cf. Ladewig, *Regg. Const.* I, Nr. 1117 (1190 "*in choro Constantiensi*"), Nr. 1131 (4 Dec. 1192 "*in choro Constantiensi*"), Nr. 1133 (6 Dec 1193 "*in choro Const.*", Nr. 1160 (11 June 1199 "*in choro Const.*", Nr. 1179 (7 June 1202 "*in choro Const.*"), Nr. 1187 (27 June 1204 "*in choro Const.*"), Nr. 1216 (1206 "*in choro Const.*"), Nr. 1245 (1211 "*in choro Const.*"), Nr. 1248 (1212 "*in choro Const.*").

ly records a matter of business dealt with at an episcopal synod which was held in the choir of the cathedral at Constanz.

Although his visitation undoubtedly revealed matters of concern within his church, Bishop Diethelm was also directed to deal with problems by the pope himself.[467] It was perhaps in response to this command that he convened the synod which met on 6 April 1205. The documentary evidence for this assembly reveals only that a compromise was reached between the monastery at Schussenreid and the heirs of the lord of Wartenberg.[468] Given the context of Bishop Diethelm's episcopacy, however, there must have been matters of church discipline discussed as well.

The best evidence of this comes from a synod which Weiss places in 1206. Preserved in the decretals of Pope Gregory IX is the account of a priest who was tried and defrocked at a synod held at Constanz because he could not cleanse himself of the charge of incest (adultery with the wife of a relative). The matter apparently continued under papal delegates who confirmed the synod's judgment. In the meantime, the bishop died and the new bishop granted absolution. At the request of the accused, the pope then demanded a *retratio* of the synodal action and gave further instructions to the delegates.[469] This example shows that diocesan synods could and at times did concern themselves with the inner life of the church, but there is no indication that on the eve of the Fourth Lateran Council there was a clearly-defined standard of conduct within the diocese of Constanz. Apparently not until 1327 was a set of synodal statutes published for that purpose.[470]

Despite a tradition for holding diocesan synods on the first day of Holy Week and in mid-September which extended back to the pontificate of Bishop Ulrich (924-973),[471] and despite the fact that Augsburg bishops are

[467] Cf. Potthast, *Regesta* I 126, Nr. 1384; Weiss, "Konstanzer Bischöfe" 173.

[468] Ladewig, *Regg. Const.* I, Nr. 1197; *Wirtemburg. UB* II 349 Nr. 526; *Thurgau UB* II 274, Nr. 81 (*"Acta autem sunt hec in synodo Constantiensi coram omnibus publicata."*) Further, see Weiss, "Konstanzer Bischöfe" 159. April 7 was Maundy Thursday in 1205, the customary day for the spring synod.

[469] Cf. Migne *PL* CCXV, col. 1286; Greg IX decr. lib 5, tit 34, cap 15; taken over by Joseph Vochezer, *Geschichte des fürstlichen Hauses Waldburg in Schwaben* (Kempten, 1888) I 128; P. Trudpert Neugart, *Episcopatus Constantiensis alemannicus sub metropoli Moguntina*, vol. II ed. by Franz Joseph Monè (Friburgi Brisgoviae, 1803-1862) II 433. The *Corpus Iuris Canon.* II (ed. 1757) 708, places it in the year 1215; cf. discussion in Ladewig, *Regg. Const.* I 196. Further, Weiss, "Konstanzer Bischöfe" 173.

[470] Kehrberger, *Synodalstatuten* 83.

[471] Cf. *Vita Udalrici* 4, 392 (*"synodale colloquium"*), cited in Steiner, *Synodi August.* I Introduction to Sect. 4; Hauck, *KGD* IV 7. Zoepfl, *Bistum Augsburg* 69, asserts without documentation that Ulrich I held such synods every year according to the old canonical requirements. Hartzheim, *Concilia* III 1, contains the so-called *"sermo synodalis"* attributed

occasionally mentioned at general councils and provincial synods from 775 to 972, the first evidence for local synods thereafter comes from 23 November 1071. A document issued on that day bears record that Bishop Embrico had caused an oratory to be erected in honor of the Virgin Mary and St. Gertrude, an action taken ". . . *in presentia clericorum laicorumque . . .*" of his diocese—i.e., presumably at a diocesan synod.[472]

Under Bishop Walther two synods are recorded, the first held 21 September 1135[473] and a second which convened in 1151. In the latter year the cardinal-priest Octavian came to Augsburg in the company of the reforming prior at Reichersberg, Gerhoh, who may have made the legate aware of disciplinary problems which existed within the diocese. According to a report sent to the Curia, Bishop Otto of Freising was also present, as was an otherwise unidentified Bishop Emehard. Many of those clerics charged with maintaining concubines and committing fornication were suspended. Although the synod was under the direction of the papal legate and thus technically not diocesan in nature, Bishop Walther also used this highly ceremonial occasion to insure that his personal inheritance, which he had bestowed upon the cathedral chapter at Augsburg, would be non-alienable in perpetuity.[474]

On 17 September 1153 Bishop Conrad pronounced that in accordance with a decision reached "*in generali capitulo cum choro maioris ecclesiae ac VI . . . abbatibus ac XI regularibus praepositis ac innumera multitudine clericorum,*" the church at Ecchuia was not a daughter church of Eichach as Abbot Hezilo of St. Ulrich's monastery in Augsburg and Pfalzgrave Henry maintained, but was an independent mother church.[475] This example shows the diocesan synod functioning as an ecclesiastical court, adjudicating issues being contested between two parties. Other synods are recorded for 14 May 1196,[476] and 1211.[477] If such represents an accurate picture of twelfth-century practice, the alarming conditions noted in Ch.

---

to Bishop Ulrich; cf. Hinschius, *KR* III 588 note 1.

[472] Vock, *UB Augsburg* 5, Nr. 13.

[473] Hartzheim, *Concilia* III 329-330; Steiner, *Synodi August.* 71 ("*clero comprovinciali eodem tempore ad capitulum congregato*"); Hinschius, *KR* III 586; Zoepfl, *Bistum Augsburg* 129-130; Steichele, *Bistum Augsburg* II 612 note; Simonsfeld, *Jahrbücher* I 417 note; *AGHA* VI 810f. The recorded act of the synod was the confirmation of a cloister.

[474] *Isengrani Annales maiores* 313; cf. *MG Lib. de Lite* III 494-496; Zoepfl, *Bistum Augsburg* 132.

[475] Vock, *UB Augsburg* 12, Nr. 28. Hartzheim, *Concilia* III 376; Steiner, *Synodi August.* 71; and Hinschius, *KR* III 586 note 11, place the synod in the year 1154.

[476] *Wirtemburg. UB* II 316 Nr. 499 ("*Acta sunt . . . in sinodo nostra . . . et omnibus tam abbatibus quam prepositis aliusque prelatis necnon et clericis et laicis plurimis, qui prefatam traditionem tam sollempniter factam viderunt et audierunt*").

[477] Braun, *Bischöfe von Augsburg* 116.

Two at Augsburg at the beginning of the thirteenth century are clearly understandable. The earliest set of synodal statutes for Augsburg date from the year 1355, drawing from numerous thirteenth-century synods held in the province of Mainz, but apparently having no basis in an indigenous tradition of decrees.[478]

Diocesan synods at Speyer date to at least 1023.[479] Hartzheim has preserved the notice of a synod held in 1149 at which a grant was made to a religious house.[480] In 1176 an assembly of clergy and laymen was called a "*commune concilium*," a term found in other dioceses as well on occasion.[481] A document dated with just the year 1180 bears record of a dispute between the Cistercian monastery at Maulbronn and a priest at Germersheim regarding certain property which was resolved by Bishop Ulrich. Witnesses to this act were "*Henricus prepositus de domo, Arnoldus decanus, custos Adelbertus, prepositus Dietherus de sancto Widone, prepositus Johannes de sancto Germano, prepositus Conradus de sancta Trinitate, Busso Portinarius, Berewulfus et omnis synodus.*"[482] Thereafter, the record is silent until the beginning of the thirteenth century, however.

On 17/18 October 1202 Bishop Conrad of Speyer issued a charter "*in generali ac sollemni synodo*" which dealt with the incorporation of the parish church at Burgalben into the monastery of Wadgassen.[483] Among the obligations imposed upon the religious house was one which required the *plebani* (i.e., parish priests) of Burgalben to attend diocesan synods. This oblique reference to a concern for the *cura animarum* in his diocese is further substantiated by the fact that witnessing the act were the major

---

[478] Cf. Kehrberger, *Synodalstatuten* 107.

[479] Remling, *UB Speyer* I 25, Nr. 25. See Duggan, *Bishop and Chapter*, for an investigation of the shared power between the medieval bishop and his cathedral and collegiate chapters; for the role of diocesan synods, *op.cit.* 35.

[480] Hartzheim, *Concilia* III 362; Remling, *UB Speyer* I 96, Nr. 87 (". . . *in praesentia totius synodalis conventus*"); Hauck, *KGD* IV 7 note 1; Palazzini, *Dizionario* V 212-213; Duggan, *Bishop and Chapter* 35 note 96.

[481] Cf. "Urkunden über die bayerische Pfalz vom 12.—16. Jahrhundert," ed. Moné, *ZGO* 19 (1866) 167; Duggan, *Bishop and Chapter* 35 note 97.

[482] *Wirtemburg. UB* II 207 Nr. 421 ("*in synodali conventu . . . coram prepositis et decanis nostris ceterisque synodalibus personis, tam clericis quam laicis*"); Duggan, *Bishop and Chapter* 35 note 96. Provost John of St. Germain was the future archbishop of Trier, 1190-1212.

[483] "Kraichgauer Urkunden vom 12. bis 16. Jahrhunderts," ed. Moné, *ZGO* 13 (1860) 58, Nr. 2 ("*factum in generali ac sollemni synodo predicatum et publicatum*"); Beyer, *MRUB* II 240, Nr. 203; Duggan, *Bishop and Chapter* 35 note 97, citing Bienemann, *Conrad von Scharfenberg* 138. Among the witnesses was Abbot Peter of Neuburg whose affairs were often a matter of business at contemporary Strasbourg synods; cf. Pfleger, "Abt Peter von Neuburg" 140. Further, see comments of Hilling, "Geistlichen und Laien" 217, regarding the coupling of synodal attendance and the cure of souls.

ecclesiastical and secular figures of the bishopric of Speyer. Such an auspicious array of dignitaries would hardly have been necessary for an everyday juridical act.

Other assemblies were convened by this same bishop, though the nature is generally not pastoral—if one were to judge solely from the documentary evidence. A synod met at some unspecified time in 1206,[484] and another in 1211.[485] A document dated by Moné "before 15 April 1213" refers to action taken "*coram synodo Spirensi*" without the bishop. Presumably the cathedral dean presided in his absence, the cause of which is unknown. Although the bishop of Speyer, Conrad of Scharfenberg, acquired the additional bishopric of Metz and the imperial chancellorship in 1212—both of which may have made his presence in Speyer difficult to maintain, an examination of the witness list appended to the document leads us to conclude that the synod in question was held before the year 1207.[486] The final assembly recorded before the Fourth Lateranum was in 1213[487] and is referred to as "*generalis synodus nostra autumpnalis,*" suggesting the time of year which was customary for synods in the diocese of Speyer.

Though bordering on bishoprics of Westphalia and Saxony and to some extent reflecting conditions and trends of the province of Cologne, the diocese of Paderborn belonged to the province of Mainz. Like its neighbors Hildesheim and Halberstadt, it also showed an active synodal tradition, albeit less impressive than these two. Known synods of the twelfth century took place on 26 March 1103,[488] in 1173,[489] and on 6 April 1189 (the Wednesday after Palm Sunday),[490] but Hilling has argued that there were

---

[484] Würdtwein, *Nova subs.* XII 132, Nr. 45; Hauck, *KGD* IV 7; Mazetti, *Bischof Berngar* 15; Duggan, *Bishop and Chapter* 35 note 97, citing Bienemann, *Conrad von Scharfenberg* 141.

[485] Hartzheim, *Concilia* III 794; Würdtwein, *Nova subs.* I 170; Remling, *UB Speyer* I 167, Nr. 151; Hauck, *KGD* IV 7; Palazzini, *Dizionario* V 212-213; Mazetti, *Bischof Berngar* 15; and most recently, Duggan, *Bishop and Chapter* 35 note 96.

[486] "Kraichgauer Urkunden" 324, Nr. 38 ("*coram synodo Spirensi . . . quando in synado Spirensi super dicta causa sententia lata fuit, . . .*"). Moné dated the document "*vor dem 15. Apr. 1213*" because on that date Conrad of Neckarsteinach is documented as cathedral provost for the first time. More telling, however, is the appearance of the dean Albert in documents 1200-1207, and the replacement of the *portonarius* Albert, who is documented 1190-1207, by Conrad sometime in 1207.

[487] "Kraichgauer Urkunden" 323.

[488] Hartzheim, *Concilia* III 246; Wilmans, *Westf. UB Addit.* 27, Nr. 25 (1877); Hinschius, *KR* III 587 note 1; Hauck, *KGD* IV 7 note 1; Wilmans, "Paderborn Synode" 5; Palazzini, *Dizionario* III 278-279. The act recorded was the grant of property to a religious house.

[489] Erhard, *Regg. hist Westf.* II, Nr. 1991 (*UB* II 124, Nr. 368); Hauck, *KGD* IV 7 note 1; Hilling, "Paderborn Synode" 5.

[490] Hartzheim, *Concilia* III 448; Erhard, *Regg. hist. Westf.* II, Nr. 2235 (*UB* II 204, Nr. 490) ("*qui eo die ad synodum generalem convenerent*"); Hinschius, *KR* III 586 note 7; Hauck, *KGD* IV 7 note 1; Hilling, "Paderborn Synode" 5; Palazzini, *Dizionario* III 278-279.

other assemblies which show the characteristics of synods, even though the documents relating to them make no use of the term *synodus*. As was noted in the cases of Cologne, Münster and Osnabrück, there are other indicators which can and must be used in order to fully exploit the documentary evidence. Based on an analysis of witness lists, he has concluded that there were also Paderborn synods in 1136, 1142, and 1158.[491] That synods were held regularly in this diocese may be inferred from the obligation to attend faithfully which Bishop Bernhard imposed upon the abbot of the newly-founded monastery at Marienmünster in 1128.[492] Mention of *scabini* as being present at a synod in 1189 indicates that laymen occasionally attended as well.[493] Sometime between 1203 and 1215 Bishop Bernard of Paderborn issued a charter which indicates that the fall diocesan synod was held regularly at Orlinghausen.[494]

The well-documented synodal tradition for Eichstätt extends back to at least 893 at Monheim.[495] The *Sermo synodalis* of Bishop Gundekar (1057-1075) which was entered into the *Pontificale* demonstrates the importance laid upon the holding of diocesan synods by this reform-minded prelate of the eleventh century.[496] Twelfth-century synods are recorded for after 4 June 1137 at Eichstätt,[497] after March 1142 at Eichstätt,[498] 1183 at Eichstätt under Bishop Otto (1182-1196),[499] 1186 at Eichstätt,[500] 1188 at Eichstätt,[501] 1191(?) at Eichstätt,[502] and 1214/1216.[503] On 13 October 1210 Bishop Hartwig consecrated the cathedral at Eichstätt; thereafter synods were generally held from 13-16 October to commemorate that important event.[504]

---

[491] Erhard, *Regg. hist. Westf.* I, Nrs. 229, 242, 314; cf. Hilling, *Diözesansynoden* 19.

[492] Philippi, *UB Osnabrück* I, Nr. 196; Hilling, *Diözesansynoden* 15.

[493] Hilling, "Geistlichen und Laien" 225, citing Ehrhard, *Regg. hist. Westf. cod diplom.* II, Nr. 490.

[494] *Lippische Regg.* I 121, Nr. 132; *Westf. UB* IIIA, Nr. 23; see fuller discussion below, p. 258.

[495] *Mon. Boica* XLIX 4, Nr. 1 ("*cum affirmatione synodi nostri*"); Heidingsfelder, *Regg. Eichst.* I 34, Nr. 77.

[496] Heidingsfelder, *Regg. Eichst.* I 77, Nr. 219.

[497] Heidingsfelder, *Regg. Eichst.* I 110, Nr. 348.

[498] Heidingsfelder, *Regg. Eichst.* I 113, Nr. 359: the grant of a tithe was made to the abbey of Heilsbronn.

[499] Heidingsfelder, *Regg. Eichst.* I 148, Nr. 467: property was granted to the nuns at Monheim.

[500] Heidingsfelder, *Regg. Eichst.* I 151, Nr. 474.

[501] Heidingsfelder, *Regg. Eichst.* I 153, Nr. 481.

[502] Heidingsfelder, *Regg. Eichst.* I 157, Nrs. 492, 493, 494.

[503] Heidingsfelder, *Regg. Eichst.* I Nr. 577: the synod dealt with juridical matters.

[504] Heidingsfelder, *Regg. Eichst.* I, Nrs. 553-554; *Mon. Boica* XLIX 204, Nr. 133; 71, Nr. 35; *Pastoralblatt des Bistums Eichstätt* I (1854) 112, Nr. 5.

Despite its boasting of greatness in the tenth and eleventh centuries when it was a favored city of kings and the seat of prominent bishops, Worms became less significant during the course of the twelfth century and its prelates played increasingly minor roles. The synodal picture for this diocese is also quite sketchy and emerges relatively late: 1124,[505] 1174,[506] 1182,[507] 1196,[508] and again on 19 March 1197,[509] the bishops of Worms convened synods in their cathedral city. Thereafter, conditions presumably militated against other diocesan assemblies. As argued below in Ch. Two, the possibility of any synods at all during the pontificate of Lupold of Scheinfeld is so remote that all indications suggest a moribund synodal tradition in this diocese on the eve of the Council. Even the oblique reference by Pope Innocent III to the statutes which Cardinal-legate Guy Poré enacted for Worms in 1201 lacks the details to confirm that these were proclaimed at a synod.[510]

The dioceses of Chur, Verden, Prague, and Olmütz were on the periphery of the ecclesiastical province of Mainz and their relationship to the mainstream of church life is less well documented for the period before 1215. Both Prague and Olmütz were represented at the provincial synod held at Mainz in April 976,[511] yet there is no record of their own synodalia in the tenth and eleventh centuries.[512] Cosma of Prague mentions in his *Chronica Boemorum* that he and Andreas, as bishops-elect of Prague and Olmütz respectively, attended the imperial synod held at Mainz in 1103 where their elections were confirmed. He also makes note of the imperial synod held at Regensburg in 1109, but there is no specific mention thereafter of any synodal activity at the diocesan level in either Bohemia or

---

[505] Phillips, *Diöcesansynode* 50, citing Hartzheim, *Concilia* III 518.

[506] Goerz, *MRR* II 101, Nr. 357; Johannes Martin Kremer, *Genealogische Geschichte des alter ardennischen Geschlechts insbesondere des zu demselben gehörigen Hauses der ehemaligen Grafen zu Sarbrük* (Frankfurt & Leipzig, 1785) I 138, note 11; Franz Xaver Remling, *Urkundliche Geschichte der ehemaligen Abteien und Klöster im jetzigen Rheinbayern* (Neustadt/Haardt, 1836) I, Nr. 19; Binterim, *Concilien* IV 219 (*"Ab omnibus in nostra synodo iudicatum"*). The recorded act of the synod involved a grant to the monastery at Ramsen.

[507] Binterim, *Concilien* IV 219. At this synod various privileges belonging to the chapel at Cimbern were discussed; according to Binterim, this decision was appealed to the metropolitan synod at Mainz. I have found no corroborating sources.

[508] Hartzheim, *Concilia* III 464; Hinschius, *KR* III 587 note 1; Palazzini, *Dizionario* VI 170. The recorded act was the incorporation of a church.

[509] Goerz, *MRR* II 217, Nr. 792 (*"In publica sinodo Wormat."*); Baur, *Hess. UB* II 34, Nr. 20.

[510] Potthast, *Regesta* I, Nr. 1535, citing Theiner, *Vetera* I 61, Nr. 209. A similar mandate was sent to the canons at Mainz; cf. Ibid. I 61, Nr. 210.

[511] Stimming, *Mainzer UB* I 134, Nr. 219.

[512] Severus of Prague was present at the imperial synod held 25 October 1046 with Henry III; cf. Friedrich, *CdBoh* I 51, Nr. 49.

Moravia.[513]   One possibility comes from pontificate of Bishop Robert of
Olmütz in the early thirteenth century: a charter dated *vii Kal. Oct. 1208*
contains record of a transfer of two vills belonging to the bishopric to one
Stephan of Medlow, an act done ". . . *in presencia quam plurimum*
nobilium utriusque terre, approbante domino decano W. et universo convente
eiusdem ecclesie, . . . publice in capitulo Olomucensi . . ."[514]   The
description given of the body which approved this exchange is so similar to
that used for synods elsewhere at this time, that we may rightly conclude
that this too was a diocesan synod.   Otherwise, the existence of synods in
the Bohemian and Moravian churches must be argued by analogy and
common sense alone.[515]

The Province of Hamburg-Bremen

Though established as an archbishopric in 831 for the purpose of missioniz-
ing the Slavs, Hamburg lacked any suffragan bishoprics for well over a
century. Thus, the metropolitan authority of the archbishop had no concrete
basis. There are likewise no references to provincial synods before the mid-
eleventh century. The first evidence of such comes from the pontificate of
Archbishop Adalbert who apparently convened a series of synods between
1059 and 1062 for the purpose of publicly demonstrating his claims to

---

[513] Cf. *Cosmae Chron.* 103, 117.

[514] *CdMor* II, Nr. 41.

[515] See C. Höfler, *Prager Concilien in der vorhusitischen Periode* (Prag, 1862) xxviii: *„Es*
wäre jedoch eine ebenso irrige Auffassung zu glauben, dass die berühmte von Arnest gehaltene
Synode [1349] die erste sei, welche man in Böhmen gehalten hat, wie dass sie die einzige sei.
Nur die gänzliche Verkennung des eigentlich geistigen Wachsthumes, die diess in späteren
Jahrhunderten der Fall war, und die blinde Furcht vor Allem was eigenthümliches Leben in sich
schloss, in allem diesem Gefahr und Schaden witterte, konnte den früheren Zeiten eine so
grosse Trägheit zuschreiben, wie die, in welcher der Clerus des Mittelalters angeblich befangen
war.   Erzbischof Arnest erwähnt selbst in der Einleitung zu einen Provinzialstatuten, dass er
alle Synodalstatuten, welche von seinen Vorgängern oder von ihm selbst bisher erlassen worden
waren, so wie alle Provinzialconstitutionen der Mainzer Kirche damit aufhebe, inwieferne sie
sich auf die ganze böhmische Kirchenprovinz bezogen.   Nicht minder erklärte darin auch
Arnestus, dass die böhmischen Bischöfe jedes Jahr, wenn sie ihre Synoden hielten (cum suas
synodos celebrent), ihrem Clerus die genaue Beobachtung der an die Stelle der alten tretenden
Constitutionen aufs Eifrigste zur Pflicht machen sollten.   Wenn sich denn auch von den früheren
Synoden nur Weniges erhalten hat, so beweist doch auch dieses hinläglich, dass man in den
schwierigsten Zeiten—und in der That je schwieriger desto sicherer—kein wirksames Mittel
kannte, zwischen Haupt und Gliedern Eintracht und Verständniss zu erzeugen, Zucht und
Ordnung herzustellen, Missbräuche abzustellen, den Weg der Selbsthilfe zu entfernen und den
des Rechtes zu befestigen als Synoden. Man hat aber anzunehmen, dass schon vor Arnest jedes
Jahr zwei Synoden, die eine zu Sct. Vitus (15. Juni), die andere zu Sct. Lucas (18. Oct.)
gehalten wurden, in ähnlicher Weise wie dieses auch nach Arnestus regelmässig bis zur
Husitenzeit hervortritt."

ecclesiastical jurisdiction over the emerging Danish bishoprics. His plan failed, however, since the intended objects refused to attend his meetings. Shortly thereafter, the heathen Wends destroyed the fledgling bishoprics of Oldenburg, Ratzeburg and Mecklenburg. Thus, after 1103 when the Danish dioceses were transferred to the recently erected archbishopric of Lund, Hamburg found itself without any suffragans once more.[516]

Not until the time of Hartwig I of Stade (1148-1168) did local synods resume. Within months of his election and consecration he convened an assembly of his diocesan clergy at Bremen which lay west of the Elbe in a much less exposed position than Hamburg.[517] In order for provincial synods to have any meaning, however, he needed suffragan bishops; he thus undertook the immense task of restoring them. In 1149 he consecrated new bishops for Oldenburg and Mecklenburg, and in 1154 he re-established the bishopric of Ratzeburg. At the same time he tried to return Hamburg to the pre-eminence it had held vis-a-vis Bremen in the past.

In 1160 Hartwig established synodal regulations which were unique in the German church. With reference to the dangers of travelling the roads and rivers of the region, and out of consideration for the great distances involved in the province, he ordained that provincial synods for those living east of the Elbe—suffragans, prelates, clerics, nobles and other free-men—were to take place annually in Hamburg. General or diocesan synods, on the other hand, were to convene annually in Bremen. This solution allowed Bremen a place of honor while recognizing Hamburg as the metropolitan city of the province.[518] In spite of these regulations, however, there is no evidence of synods in the next two decades in either Hamburg or Bremen.[519]

During Lent (8 March/Sunday Laetare) 1187 Archbishop Hartwig II convened the clergy of the transalbine region in a diocesan synod held at Bremen which issued a regulation concerning the personal effects of deceased clergy.[520] A charter dated 1188, on the other hand, refers to business conducted "*in synodo autumpnali*," suggesting that the wording of

---

[516] Cf. Heinz Wolter, "Die Synodaltätigkeit der Erzbischöfe von Hamburg-Bremen bis zum Jahre 1223," *AHC* 22 (1990) 1-30.

[517] Cf. May, *REB*. I, Nr. 488.

[518] Hartzheim, *Concilia* IV 573; *Mecklenburg. UB* I 64-65, Nr. 70; Lappenberg, *Hamb. UB* I, Nr. 306 (". . . *ut in Hammenburgensi ecclesia semel in . . . anno cum suffraganeis, prelatis, clericis, nobilibus, liberis tantum Cisalbinus provincialis synodus, in Bremensi vero, sicut consuetum est, cum Transalbinus generalis synodus celebretur*").

[519] Cf. Hauck, *KGD* IV 8 and V 134, who argues that there were no recorded provincial synods during the twelfth century.

[520] May, *REB* I Nr. 626; the document is preserved in a seventeenth-century transcript of the *Manuale canonicum metropolitane ecclesie Bremensis*.

the 1160 document—"*suo tempore*"—meant twice yearly.[521]   Under Hartwig II, however, general synods could only be held intermittently. Owing
to the political complications which followed on the heals of Frederick
Barbarossa's death in 1189, he was forced to flee Germany for the greater
safety of England in 1190, remaining there about one year. Upon his return
he convened a diocesan synod in 1194.[522] Perhaps it was in this connection that the Bremen cathedral chapter complained to the pope concerning
Count Adolf of Schauenburg and others, that ". . . *comes ipse, clericos
eiusdem archiepiscopi ad eius sinodum sepius retat accedere.*"[523]

In 1206 Archbishop Hartwig confirmed an endowment made to the altar
of St. John the Evangelist in the Bremen cathedral by the cathedral chapter,
an act done in a diocesan synod which had been held during Lent at some
time previous: based on the known dates for those individuals mentioned
in the document, the synod probably occurred ca. 1197, perhaps during the
absence of the archbishop in the Holy Land; he was represented by his
suffragan, Bishop Dietrich of Lübeck.[524]

The limited references to diocesan synodal activity in Bremen under
Archbishop Hartwig II seem to show that they were held regularly, with
some interruptions in the early 1190s.   Provincial synods are another
matter, however.   The only known provincial synod held in Hamburg
between 1160 and 1223 occurred in 1201 when Hartwig presided over an
assemblage of clergy and laymen which included Bishop Isfrid of Ratzeburg, Provost Hermann of Bremen, Provost Hermann of Hamburg, Dean
Hilary of Hildesheim, Hermann the cellerarius at Verden, numerous Bremen
and Hamburg cathedral canons, and important lay dignitaries. The presence
of the latter confirms the fact that the practices noted in 1160 yet prevailed.[525]   One clear purpose of this synod was to show that Hamburg and
the territory east of the Elbe clearly belonged to the archdiocese and
province of Bremen. The moment of archiepiscopal glory was short-lived,
however, for in late 1201 the Danes took control of Hamburg. Hartwig's
death on 3 November 1207, the ensuing schismatic election which lingered

---

[521] May, *REB* I, Nr. 636; and Ehmnk, *Bremisches UB* I, Nr. 74. See also Hilling,
"Geistlichen und Laien" 217-218; Wolter, "Synodaltätigkeit" 17-19.

[522] May, *REB* I, Nr. 663.

[523] Cf. letter dated 1195 from Pope Celestine III to Count Adolf of Schauenburg and others,
Lappenberg, *Hamb. UB* I, Nr. 220; Hilling, "Geistlichen und Laien" 217.

[524] Ehmck, *Bremisches UB* I, Nr. 102, espec. notes 2-3; May, *REB* I, Nr. 715 (*"Nam
canonici de Wiltheshusen in generali sinodo nostra, que celebratur in media quadragesima,
coram Theodorico, venerabili fratre nostro Lubicense episcopo, vice nostra tunc presidente in
sinodo, . . ."*).

[525] Lappenberg, *Hamb. UB* I, Nr. 329; Hilling, "Geistlichen und Laien" 217; May, *REB*
I, Nr. 688; *Mecklenburg. UB* I, Nr. 170.

on into the second decade of the thirteenth century, and the Welf-Hohen-staufen struggle for political power which continued until the death of Otto IV, precluded there being any further provincial synods at Hamburg under the archbishop of Bremen until after the Fourth Lateran Council.

Diocesan synods for the Bremen suffragan bishoprics are scarcely known before 1215. The precarious nature of Ratzeburg has been noted above: founded ca. 1050 and destroyed in 1066 by an uprising of the Wends, it was re-established in 1154 by Duke Henry the Lion of Saxony and given a Premonstratensian bishop and cathedral chapter. Any tradition of synodal activity in that diocese was thus of most recent origin, if one in fact did exist at all.[526] Henry also transferred the diocesan seats of Mecklenburg and Oldenburg to Schwerin and Lübeck, respectively. On 1 February 1177 at Schwerin (*"Actum sunt . . . in generalis sinado Zwerin"*), Bishop Berno of Mecklenburg granted a tithe and other privileges to the monastery at Doberau.[527] Thereafter, the record is silent until after 1215, however.

On 12 May 1201 Bishop Dietrich of Lübeck confirmed the sale of the village (*Dorf*) Kührstorf by Count Adolf of Schauenburg to the monastery of St. John in the episcopal city. Witnessing this act was Bishop Brunward of Schwerin, two abbots, the provost and dean of the cathedral church at Lübeck, nine of the canons (*capitulares*) from the cathedral, and seven lay nobles.[528] Although no mention is made of a "*synodus*" in this document, the large number of prominent clergy and laymen present, and the manner in which the document declares the outcome of their deliberation, leave no doubt that a diocesan synod had just concluded at which this transaction took place. This assumption becomes all the more probable when we consider that in the same year (1201) Archbishop Hartwig II confirmed the transfer of Kührstorf at the above-noted provincial synod.[529]

The Province of Magdeburg

At a synod held under the presidency of the archbishop of Ravenna in October 968, the see of Magdeburg was elevated to a metropolitanate.[530]

---

[526] In general for Ratzeburg, cf. Bernhöft, *Ratzeburg* 1ff.

[527] *Mecklenburg. UB* I 118-119, Nr. 122.

[528] *CdLub* I 13-14, Nr. 9 (*"Acta sunt hec in vigilia pentecostes, in civitate Lubecensi, in choro maioris ecclesie, . . . sub multorum tam clericorum quam laicorum testimonio, et in sollempni die pentecostes, in facie tocius ecclesie, cleri et populi, in ambone, duorum Episcoporum, nostro videlicet et Zuerinensis, sollempni banno confirmata"*).

[529] *CdLub* 15-16, Nr. 10 (*"Acta sunt hec Hammenburg, publica nostra in synodo . . . , sub multorum tam clericorum quam laicorum testimonio . . ."*).

[530] Mansi, *Collectio* XVIII (1773) 501ff.; Heidingsfelder, *Regg. Eichst.* I 48, Nr. 131. In general for Magdeburg synods, cf. Claude, *Erzstift Magdeburg* II 137-138, 223-230.

Presumably, a tradition of diocesan synods already existed at this time, but
it is not until the pontificate of Archbishop Giselher near the end of the
tenth century that we learn details such assemblies. At some time between
summer 993 and winter 993/994 a monk at Nienburg named Siegfried, after
the death of his father, Margrave Hodo, left his monastery and returned to
secular life. Giselher and Abbot Ekkehard summoned him before the synod
at Magdeburg where Siegfried freed himself from his monastic vows with
the aid of twelve oath helpers.[531] The synod appears in this first reference
in one of its most important functions—as an ecclesiastical court. Since the
only participants were the archbishop and the abbot of Nienburg, however,
it is not certain whether this was a provincial or more probably a diocesan
synod.

Thietmar of Merseburg records a synod held in early spring 999 at
Magdeburg.[532] Presumably another synod took place in August 1004. On
the 8th day of the month Archbishop Tagino and all his suffragans were
present for the consecration of the buildings at the monastery at Nienburg;
from there they went to Merseburg with Emperor Henry II. At some point
before the consecration itself, the metropolitan may well have convened this
extraordinary assemblage of prelates into a provincial synod.[533] Thereafter, the sources are silent for over a century regarding provincial synodal
activity.

Sometime before 4 March 1135 the five suffragans, Abbot Arnold of
Berge, Priors Frederick of Bibra, Lambert of Neuwerk, and Wigger of Our
Lady, the cathedral provost, and other cathedral canons assembled before
Archbishop Conrad of Magdeburg in a provincial synod. Also documented
were the most prominent lay princes of the region, three additional *nobiles*,
and five *ministeriales*.[534] The circle of participants at future provincial
synods remained essentially the same. However, by the 1180s the number
of *nobiles* had decreased, while the number of those present from the
ministerial class had risen. A second synod held under Archbishop Conrad
is recorded for the year 1140.[535]

The long pontificate of his successor, Archbishop Wichmann, shows that
many synods were held. The frequency undoubtedly lies in an established
tradition: the provincial synod institutionalized the relationship between the

---

[531] Claude, *Erzbistum Magdeburg* II 224, citing *Thietmari Chron.* IV (cap. 60) 200.

[532] Boye, "Quellenkatalog" 69; Palazzini, *Dizionario* III 10-12, citing Mansi, *Collectio*
XIX, col. 236.

[533] Claude, *Erzbistum Magdeburg* II 224; *MGH Diplomata regum et imperatorum
Germaniae—Die Urkunden Heinrichs II* (Berlin, 1932f.) 83.

[534] Hartzheim, *Concilia* III 328; Israël, *UB Magd* Nr. 237; Claude, *Erzstift Magdeburg* II
224; Hauck, *KGD* IV 20 and V 134; Palazzini, *Dizionario* III 10-12.

[535] Hauck, *KGD* IV 20 and V 134.

archbishop and his five suffragans. Whether his predecessors did less is unknown. Nevertheless, on the basis of both direct references to synods and inferences it is possible to reconstruct the following list of synods: 29 May 1151 at Naumburg or Halle,[536] 24 January 1157 at Merseburg,[537] 31 January 1161,[538] 31 January 1163 at Magdeburg (referred to as a *capitulum*),[539] before 7 January 1166,[540] and 7 May 1171 (perhaps) at Naumburg.[541] In 1175, Wichmann presided over a synod at Halle-on-the-Saale at which the Wettin brothers, Otto of Meissen, Dedo of Groitzsch, Henry of Wettin, and Frederick of Brehna, petitioned for a Christian burial for a kinsman who had died in a tournament.[542] Further provincial synods were convened in 1178,[543] on 28 July 1181 at Lauterberg,[544] and 14 February 1182 at Halle.[545]

---

[536] See Israël, *UB Magd* Nr. 272. Claude, *Erzstift Magdeburg* II 225, adds this assembly to his provincial synod list based on the witnesses to the document.

[537] Israël, *UB Magd* Nr. 293 (*"Data Merseburch in generali concilio ibi celebrato"*). Cf. also Mansi, *Collectio* XXI 845; Hefele, *Conciliengeschichte* V 501; Hinschius, *KR* III 486 note 4, with date 1156; Hauck, *KGD* IV 20 and V 134, citing *Wib. ep.* 455 p. 586f.; Palazzini, *Dizionario* III 10-12. Claude, *Erzstift Magdeburg* II 138, 225 note 360, sees the rubric "general council" being employed to distinguish this from a diocesan synod. Among the issues treated was the Osnabrück tithe controversy, for which a final resolution was not yet found; cf. K.-U. von Jäschke, "'Studien zu Quellen und Geschichte des Osnabrücker Zehntstreites unter Heinrich IV,'" Teil 2, *Archiv für Diplomatik* 11/12 (1965/1966) 394.

[538] Israël, *UB Magd* Nrs. 303 (*"in publica sinodo"* and in the presence of *"tota ecclesia, que in eadem sinodo presens fuit"*), 307 (*"Actum . . . in capitulo Magdeburgensi"*). The synod dealt with matters pertaining to the diocese of Brandenburg, e.g., the recently established cathedral chapter. Cf. Claude, *Erzstift Magdeburg* II 226; Wentz/Schwineköper, *Erzbistum Magdeburg* 158; Curschmann, *Diözese Brandenburg* 121ff. and note 1.

[539] Israël, *UB Magd* Nr. 307; Gersdorf, *UB Meissen* xxii; Hauck, *KGD* IV 20, citing *UB Meissen* 57, Nr. 55; Claude, *Erzstift Magdeburg* II 138, 225.

[540] Israël, *UB Magd* Nr. 315A. Claude, *Erzstift Magdeburg* II 138 and 225 note 362, where he points out that since the bishops of Merseburg and Naumburg were absent, we cannot be certain whether this was a provincial synod.

[541] Israël, *UB Magd* Nrs. 334, 335; Claude, *Erzstift Magdeburg* II 138, 225; Wentz/-Schwineköper, *Erzbistum Magdeburg* 158.

[542] *Chron. Mont. sereni* (*a. 1175*) 155-156; the body was re-buried on 18 January 1176. Cf. also Mansi, *Collectio* XXII 167; Hinschius, *KR* III 487 note 5; Hauck, *KGD* IV 20 and V 134; Palazzini, *Dizionario* III 10-12; Claude, *Erzstift Magdeburg* II 138 and 225.

[543] Israël, *UB Magd* Nr. 357; Claude, *Erzstift Magdeburg* II 225. The bishops of Havelberg and Naumburg were not present.

[544] *CdSR* I/2 446; cf. Claude, *Erzstift Magdeburg* II 138, who notes that the document which all the Magdeburg suffragans attested was issued at Lauterberg, yet it is possible that the supposed synod met in Halle and that the participants moved from there to Lauterberg.

[545] Israël, *UB Magd* Nr. 379; Hauck, *KGD* IV 20, citing Mülverstedt, *RAMagd* I 686, Nr. 1652; Claude, *Erzstift Magdeburg* II 138 and 225, who notes that although the bishops of Brandenburg and Naumburg were absent, the cathedral provost of Naumburg did attend.

A charter issued 29 April 1186 at Halle by Bishop Eberhard of Merseburg in favor of the Naumburg cathedral provost, Dietrich, was witnessed by Archbishop Wichmann of Magdeburg, Provost Rogerus of Magdeburg, Provost Christian of Merseburg, Provost Henry of Glinde, and several other clerics. Such a gathering was disproportionate to the importance of the business transacted, suggesting that this transfer of property took place at the conclusion of a larger ecclesiastical assembly—the location at Halle points to a provincial synod.[546] A further possible synod is documented between September and December 1187: two documents issued by Archbishop Wichmann and Bishop Balderam of Brandenburg respectively attest to a grant made to the monastery at Gottesgnaden and to the confirmation of the possessions, rights and liberties of the monastery at Leitkau;[547] each was witnessed by a large group of bishops, abbots, priors and other prominent ecclesiastics from the province of Magdeburg, allowing the conclusion that the business of which the documents give a terse record was conducted at a provincial synod.

Abbot Widukind of Corvey issued a document in which he informed his chapter that at an assembly held 2 July 1191 at Gottesgnaden, Archbishop Wichmann, in the presence of Bishops Eberhard of Merseburg, Berthold of Naumburg, Alexius of Brandenburg, and Dietrich of Meissen, as well as numerous abbots and prelates of churches, had recognized the privileges and liberties of his monastery and had consecrated him with the assistance of his suffragans.[548] While the magnitude of this assembly might be explained alone in terms of the importance of Corvey among the monasteries of Saxony, it is more probable that a provincial synod preceded the consecration of the abbot.

Inasmuch as the document of 31 January 1161 (3?) has the note *"actum . . . in capitulo Magdeburgensi,"* it is assumed that at least some of the synods were convened in the chapter hall of the cathedral. The seating order at synods is known only from the fifteenth century, but it is probable that little had changed since earlier times. The bishops sat on both sides of the main altar, with the abbots, priors and prelates positioned between them. The cathedral canons sat in the choir chairs, while the parish priests and monks occupied the space between. Laymen were absent from such assemblies in the fifteenth century, but in the twelfth they stood or sat on

---

[546] Rosenfeld, *UB Naumburg* I, Nr. 335.

[547] Rosenfeld, *UB Naumburg* I, Nrs. 339, 340. Cf. also, Hauck, *KGD* IV 20, citing Krabbo, *Regg. MBr* 91, Nr. 458f.; Claude, *Erzstift Magdeburg* II 138, citing Israël, *UB Magd* Nr. 421.

[548] Rosenfeld, *UB Naumburg* I, Nr. 369; Claude, *Erzstift Magdeburg* II 138, 225; Franz Winter, "Erzbischof Wichmann von Magdeburg," *FDG* 13 (1873) 155.

the floor in the vacant spaces of the chamber. There are no known statutes which were enacted prior to 1200 at such provincial synods.[549]

In 1197, at a provincial synod held at Halle, Wichmann's successor, Archbishop Ludolf, acting in commission from the pope, investigated charges against Bishop Daniel of Prague.[550] The turmoil caused by the imperial schism after 1198, resulting in the excommunication of Ludolf by papal legates and in the overrunning of Magdeburg territory by the forces of both Philip of Swabia and Otto IV of Brunswick, account in large measure for the virtual disappearance of provincial assemblies during the years which immediately preceded the Fourth Lateranum. The only one of record was held on Ash Wednesday (18 April) 1207, the purposes of which were clearly ecclesiastical.[551] As noted in Ch. Two, however, there is inferential evidence of another provincial or diocesan synod held at the instigation of the papal legates Ugolino and Leo at some time between 15 September/30 November 1208. The decrees issued by them on that occasion are known only from the reference contained in a papal letter of 16 January 1209.[552]

Not all recorded Magdeburg provincial synods were convened in the same location: in addition to Magdeburg itself, Halle, Merseburg, Gottesgnaden, and possibly Naumburg and Nienburg were used. Meissen, Brandenburg, and Havelburg, on the other hand, were never selected, possibly because of their location on the periphery of the province. There is no definite day or date which can be identified as reserved for the holding of synods, yet they were quite obviously a regular occurrence unless interfered with by war. January appears to have been the preferred month, although several synods are recorded in the spring and summer; a fall synod was not customary. The matters of deliberation ranged from judicial questions to issues of Church practice and the consecration of churches and abbots. Whether matters of a pastoral nature were also discussed is difficult to say since there are no known statutes which were enacted at these synods prior to 1215. Their significance thus lies in the fact that at them the leading clergy and laymen of the Middle-Elbe region came together and had an opportunity to deal with pressing questions of both ecclesiastical and political nature.

---

[549] The oldest transmitted statutes for Magdeburg are from 8 May 1261; cf. Mansi, *Collectio* XXIV, col. 777-779; Claude, *Erzstift Magdeburg* II 227.

[550] *Continuatio Gerlaci abb. ad a 1197* 709, cited in Claude, *Erzstift Magdeburg* II 225-226.

[551] See below, Ch. Two.

[552] Mülverstedt, *RAMagd* II, Nr. 284; Potthast, *Regesta* I, Nr. 3614; Migne, *PL* CCXI, col. 1166.

The diocesan synods at Magdeburg were much less impressive affairs, yet they also represented a strong tradition prior to the Fourth Lateran Council. To them came the cathedral canons and the heads of collegiate churches and religious houses, as well as prominent laymen. The first documented assembly was during Lent (the week before Palm Sunday) 1107 at Halle, but the manner of expression allows us to conclude that what was happening was a common event.[553] The further references to diocesan synods allows us to speculate that most were held in the Lenten season: 1129 under Norbert of Xanten (?),[554] 29 March 1142,[555] after 15 February/before 1 September 1145,[556] 16 April 1147,[557] 15 January 1149,[558] 10 March 1156,[559] 18 October 1157 (?),[560] 19 May 1158 (?),[561] mid-March to mid-May and again on 20 November 1161,[562] 21 March 1163,[563] before

---

[553] Claude, *Erzstift Magdeburg* II 228, citing *Gesta archiep. Magd.* (cap. 13) 409: "*Anno igitur dominice incarnationis 1107, dum quadragesimali tempore Halle ex more haberet collequium synodale, inde Nienburg deveniens, ibidem dominicam palmarum celebravit.*"

[554] Hartzheim, *Concilia* III 342; Israël, *UB Magd* Nr. 247; Hauck, *KGD* IV 20 and V 134. Claude, *Erzstift Magdeburg* II 228 note 383, does not include it on his list of provincial synods, but rather on his "uncertain" list for diocesan synods.

[555] Israël, *UB Magd* Nr. 249; Claude, *Erzstift Magdeburg* II 228.

[556] Cf. Israël, *UB Magd* Nr. 258; Claude, *Erzstift Magdeburg* II 228 note 383, places this in the "unclear" category.

[557] Israël, *UB Magd* Nr. 261 ("*Data publice Magdeburch in sinodo*"); Claude, *Erzbistum Magdeburg* I 228 note 383. It is unclear whether *UB Magd* Nr. 262 was also issued at this synod.

[558] Israël, *UB Magd* Nr. 269; Claude, *Erzstift Magdeburg* II 228 note 384, argues that the date is better suited for a provincial synod, yet the witnesses mentioned are just the bishops of Brandenburg and Havelberg who frequently attended diocesan synods.

[559] Israël, *UB Magd* Nr. 283; Claude, *Erzstift Magdeburg* II 138 note 382.

[560] Winter, "EB Wichmann" 136, argues for one on this date inasmuch as *UB Magd* Nr. 294 was issued "*in facie totius sanctae Magdeburgensis ecclesiae.*" Claude, *Erzstift Magdeburg* II 138 and 228 note 383, recognizes the fact that this is one important indicator of a synod, but that it alone does not prove the existence of one.

[561] Winter, "EB Wichmann" 136, once again considers *UB Magd* Nr. 295 the record of a diocesan synod; Claude, *Erzstift Magdeburg* II 228, questions this on grounds that there were too few witnesses.

[562] Israël, *UB Magd* 378, Nr. 303 ("... *in publica sinodo Magdeburgensis*" and "... *tota ecclesia, que in eadem sinodo presens fuit*"); cf. Claude, *Erzstift Magdeburg* II 138, 229 note 387. Curschmann, *Diözese Brandenburg* 121 note 1, is not clear whether this and its sister synod were diocesan or provincial, yet in *UB Magd* Nr. 303 no suffragans are mentioned at all, while in *UB Magd* Nr. 304 only the bishops of Brandenburg and Havelberg, who usually attended diocesan synods, are mentioned as present.

[563] Israël, *UB Magd* Nr. 308 ("*in plena sinodo . . .*"); cf. Claude, *Erzstift Magdeburg* II 138, who is undecided whether this is a diocesan or a provincial synod.

1 September 1164,[564] 7 June 1168,[565] before September 1172,[566] 18 April 1176 ?,[567] and 6 June 1178.[568]

After about 1150 summer and autumn assemblies occur as well. According to the Magdeburg *Liber de consuetudines* which was compiled in the mid-thirteenth century, synods—and this probably means diocesan synods—were held on the Monday after Corpus Christi and St. Luke's day (18 October). Inasmuch as the first-mentioned feast was not introduced until the thirteenth century, it can only be the case of a recent setting of that particular date. The long-recognized practice of semi-annual assemblies was probably followed, however, and the Corpus Christi date merely replaced a less definite time in the early summer which had been observed previously. One may perhaps conclude that the practice of two synods per year was customary by 1215.[569]

A charter dated 1188 (before 1 September) declares that Archbishop Wichmann had granted to the city of Magdeburg the rights of town government, an act done *"concilio episcoporum, prelatorum et canonicorum ecclesie nostre burgraviique et aliorum fidelium nostrorum."*[570] Witnessing this act were Bishops Balderam of Brandenburg and Hupert of Havelberg, Abbot Sifrid of Hersfeld, various prelates of the Magdeburg church, provosts of collegiate churches, and many important nobles. The language of the document, the rank of those present, and the nature of the business itself make it clear that this was also the occasion of a synod, most probably diocesan.

It is notable that no synods were held at Halle after 1107, a fact possibly related to the sporadic nature of the record during the first half of the twelfth century. The disappearance of Halle as a venue may also have been connected with the grant of an archdeaconry to the prior of Neuwerk which made the personal appearance of the archbishop at that location somewhat superfluous.

The bishops of Brandenburg and Havelberg were frequently present at Magdeburg diocesan synods, a fact which may cause some of them to be

---

[564] Israël, *UB Magd* Nr. 309; Claude, *Erzstift Magdeburg* II 138, 228 note 383 ("uncertain").

[565] Israël, *UB Magd* Nr. 326; Claude, *Erzstift Magdeburg* II 138, 228-229.

[566] Israël, *UB Magd* Nr. 338; Claude, *Erzstift Magdeburg* II 138.

[567] Israël, *UB Magd* Nr. 347; Claude, *Erzstift Magdeburg* II 228 note 383, raise doubts concerning this, since important priors within the diocese were absent as witnesses.

[568] Israël, *UB Magd* Nr. 356; Claude, *Erzstift Magdeburg* II 138, 229.

[569] Cf. Claude, *Erzstift Magdeburg* II 226-229; further, G. Sello, "Domaltertümer," *MGbll* 26 (1891) 175.

[570] Cf. Rosenfeld, *UB Naumburg* I, Nr. 352; Israël, *UB Magd* I 421, Nr. 59; Dobenecker, *RdThur.* II, Nr. 808; Mülverstedt, *RAMagd* I, Nr. 1724; *CdSR* I/2, Nr. 540; Claude, *Erzstift Magdeburg* II 138.

mistaken for provincial assemblies. The failure to mention the attendance of the three southern bishops on these occasions will hardly have been an accident of the record, however. The appearance of Brandenburg and Havelberg is rather explained out of the precarious position of these two bishoprics: in contrast to the relatively well-established sees of Merseburg, Meissen, and Naumburg, they were in need of constant support from Magdeburg. The archbishop may even have convened a synod at Jüterborg on 29 April 1174, a somewhat singular event since that town lay within the bishopric of Brandenburg. Such could be accounted for, however, by the fact that Archbishop Wichmann was territorial lord over Jüterborg. The synod thus probably dealt with temporal as well as ecclesiastical matters.[571]

This dependency on Magdeburg by Brandenburg and Havelberg also explains why there is no discernable synod tradition for these dioceses before 1215. Naumburg on the other hand records assemblies ca. 1157,[572] 29 March 1195,[573] and 14 June 1199.[574] In the year 1174 the bishop of Merseburg released the vill Hilpertize from the payment of the tithe to the mother church and transferred that obligation to the monastery at Pegau ". . . *cum nostre synodi favore* . . ." The property remained a matter of contention between Merseburg and Pegau, however, as witnessed by a papal letter dated 13 July 1198 which implies that the dispute had been handled once again at a recent synod.[575]

The Functions of Synods

The preceding discussion of synodal activity in Germany prior to 1215 leaves no doubt that in many dioceses and provinces the practice of convening regular synods was still quite common on the eve of the Fourth Lateran Council. Those diocesan synods for which we have record were convened for a variety of purposes: the jurisdiction of the bishop in civil matters was at all times considerable and in certain periods such were

---

[571] Israël, *UB Magd* Nr. 343; Claude, *Magdeburg* II 229 and note 392. Witnesses to this document included the bishops of Brandenburg and Meissen, as well as the priors of St. Nicholas, St. Sebastian, Gottesgnaden, Neuwerk, Lauterberg—the same circle of individuals who normally attended Magdeburg diocesan synods. Curschmann, *Diözese Brandenburg* 279, 283, regards this as a diocesan synod for Brandenburg.

[572] Dobenecker, *RdThur* II, Nr. 166.

[573] Dobenecker, *RdThur* II, Nr. 975; Lepsius, *Hochstift Naumburg* Nr. 49; Rosenberg, *UB Naumburg* I, Nr. 384: Bishop Berthold II made known "*in synodo nostra*" the sale of the village Poleb to the monastery at Lausnitz.

[574] Dobenecker, *RdThur* II, Nr. 1097. The business recorded was the exchange of property.

[575] Kehr, *Merseburg UB* I, Nrs. 112, 140; Potthast, *Regesta* I, Nr. 327.

prominent in synodal records; all manner of litigation concerning ecclesiastical property and incomes came before him; it is also obvious that the bishop and his assembled clergy provided an important court of record which witnessed transactions between various parties and leant authority to the transfer of lands and churches to ecclesiastical corporations. By far the greatest number of documents which refer to diocesan synods in Germany before 1215 fall into these categories.

The older literature argues that while serving these other purposes as well, medieval synods were nonetheless primarily pastoral.[576] Such a concern seems clear in the command given about 1082/4 by Bishop Benno II of Osnabrück to the abbot of Iburg to come to the diocesan synods "*ut . . . quae ad animarum curam pertineant, cum ceteris fideliter decernat.*"[577] While the documents from the mid-eleventh till the early thirteenth century are generally silent about the pastoral activities of most bishops and therefore do not allow us to determine the impact of most synods on the inner life of the medieval church, the fact that they *should* make this their first priority is supported by the thirteenth-century canonist Hostiensis. Recognizing the mixed nature of diocesan synods, he nonetheless stressed the primacy of the *cura animarum*; most administrative, judicial or even legislative functions of the synod have a pastoral element. In canonistic theory, the synod was a recognized occasion for the bishop to correct the faith and morals of his subjects, as a follow-up to a visitation of his diocese, or in response to testimony given at the synod itself. By insisting that their clergy "should listen to the recital and exposition of the canons [issued at such assemblies] and even take away written copies from the synods, diocesans were combatting that ignorance of the faith and the law which constituted so grave a problem in the medieval Church."[578]

Hostiensis was writing in the aftermath of the Fourth Lateran Council, however, in the constitutions of which great emphasis was placed on the pastoral responsibilities of prelates. The Council's concerns were anticipated at the beginning of the thirteenth century in France at least by what Raymonde Foreville has called «*une orientation principale et décisive vers la pastorale sacramentelle à fondement théologique.*»[579] This new direction can be seen in the synodal statutes of Bishop Eudes de Sully issued for the diocese of Paris sometime between 1196 and 1208 as instructions for his

---

[576] Hinschius, *KR* III 587; Hilling, *Diözesansynoden* 46-51, and Maring, *Diözesansynoden* 68-71.

[577] Philippi, *UB Osnabrück* I, Nr. 196.

[578] See Cheney, *English Synodalia* 5-16, and for the quoted passage, 7-8.

[579] R. Foreville, "Les statuts synodaux et le renouveau pastoral du XIIIe siècle dans le Midi de la France," *Le crédo, la morale et l'Inquisition,* Cahiers de Fanjeux 6 (Toulouse, 1971) 119-150, espec. 120.

clergy. They dealt with practical matters, e.g., the administration of the sacraments—baptism, the Eucharist, confession, marriage, and unction—as well as with the rudiments of priestly conduct, clearly and concisely.[580]

Whether there was any congruity between Hostiensis' post-Council canonistic theory and the pre-Council practices in most of Germany is difficult to say. Hauck argues that there was very little of a pastoral nature in twelfth-century synods, buttressing this with the fact that he knew of only one twelfth-century reference to decrees passed to improve conditions in the German church—the synod of Arnold von Selenhofen at Mainz in 1154. The statutes themselves are missing, but a report survives in the *Vita Arnoldi* written shortly thereafter wherein we see the archbishop trying to reform the clergy, improve church services, and build piety; according to Hauck, Arnold apparently found no imitators among his contemporaries nor successors among the archbishops of Mainz for the next several decades. The very thing which previously had given synods their effectiveness (i.e., the concern for pastoral matters) now receded in favor of more temporal or administrative affairs.[581]

If, however, the synodal decrees of Innsbruck MS 16 were in fact published at the provincial synod of Mainz held in 1209, we have a strong indication that Bishop Eudes de Sully's influence was extending across the political frontier between France and Germany even before the great council of Innocent III. Two possibilities exist to explain this unique situation. Present in Paris during the pontificate of Bishop Eudes was a German cleric from the diocese of Mainz or Speyer, one *magister* Conrad. Referred to by contemporaries as a man learned in theology who taught at the schools of Paris,[582] Conrad could easily have obtained a copy of Eudes' statutes and

---

[580] Cf. Johanek, "Pariser Statuten" 327-328; L. Guizard, "Les statuts synodeaux d'Eudes de Sully et leur place dans l'histoire du droit canonique," *Revue historique de Droit Français et Etranger*, 4th Ser. 33, Nr. 4 (Paris, 1955) 632-633, attributes the spread of Eudes' statutes in part «*au caractère de nouveauté de certain textes, relatifs à la publication des bans du marriage ou à l'élévation de l'hostie à la messe.*»

[581] Cf. Hauck, *KGD* V 134, citing Idem, "Angebliche Statuten" 80ff. With reference to the diocese of Constanz, Kehrberger, *Synodalstatuten* 82, notes that there were synods long before there were any diocesan synodal statutes. One reason for that lengthy delay lies in the fact that the early synods were primarily administrative and legal business meetings. Not until the Fourth Lateran Council, he argues, did reform legislation become their central purpose. For the administrative/legal nature of early synods, cf. Phillips, *Diözesansynode* 54. Most recently, Johanek, "Synodalia" I 3, has questioned the notion that the holding of synods was an expression of a certain reform desire and that statutes were the result of conciliar procedures.

[582] Cf. *Chron. episc. Hildesheim.* 860: referring to Conrad's elevation to the bishop's chair at Hildesheim in 1221, the continuator of the chronicle remarked that this occurred ". . . *postquam Parisiis in divina pagina laudabiliter rexerat, et crucem contra Avienses praedicarat* . . ." The intellectual milieu of his Paris years is discussed in Pixton, "Konrad von

made them available to Archbishop Siegfried II of Mainz in anticipation of
the 1209 synod. As we will explain in further detail in Ch. Two, Siegfried
was under considerable pressure from the papacy to effect reforms within
his church, reforms made necessary by an extensive schism which had all
but destroyed the normal operations of the archdiocese. The second
possibility is that Siegfried II of Mainz himself obtained a copy of Bishop
Eudes' statutes during his exile in Rome in the years 1205-1208.[583]

The older view maintains that the paucity of published provincial or
diocesan statutes before 1215 suggests that most pastoral decrees were given
viva voce—by word of mouth. While it is no longer necessary to agree with
Hauck that Archbishop Arnold of Selenhofen in 1154 was the last German
prelate before the Fourth Lateran Council to attempt major reforms within
his church, Hauck's arguments can nevertheless be used with respect to the
decrees of the 1178 provincial synod at Salzburg: they are known to us
solely from oblique references to them in other sources, but at one time they
did exist. The fragment from the 1143 Salzburg synod extends further our
knowledge of twelfth-century legislation: the general reform of the entire
Salzburg church was tied into the establishment of chapters of canons
regular throughout the province.

Moreover, in at least three other instances sets of diocesan statutes are
still extant—those·of Toul in 1192, those which papal-legate Guy Poré
issued for Liège in 1203, and those of Utrecht from 1209. We will argue
in Ch. Two that the 1203 legatine statutes for Liège were also published just
previously at Worms and at Mainz, although copies of them in both
instances are lacking. Papal regulations for the cathedral canons at Magdeburg were likewise published at a diocesan synod in 1207, while in late
1208 a legatine synod at Magdeburg had issued decrees as well. The
statutes for Utrecht in 1209 were essentially the same as those also
published that same year at Cologne and Liège. The pessimistic view of
Hauck, Heydenreich, and Hilling that no new manuscripts containing
synodal decrees would likely be found thus needs to be revised.[584]

Reifenberg" 45-49. Heavily dependent on this is Irene Crusius, "Bischof Konrad II. von
Hildesheim: Wahl und Herkunft," *Institutionen, Kultur und Gesellschaft im Mittelalter—Fest-
schrift für Josef Fleckenstein zu seinem 65. Geburtstag*, ed. Lutz Fenske, Werner Rösener &
Thomas Zotz (Sigmaringen, 1984) 431-468.

[583] Cf. our discussion of this exile in Ch. Two below. That they were well-known in the
curia can be seen from the fact that in 1208 Innocent III recommended them to the church at
Athens as a model for ecclesiastical reform; cf. Johanek, "Pariser Statuten" 327, citing Odette
Pontal, ed., *Les statuts synodaux francais du XIIIe siècle* I: Les statuts de Paris et le synodal
de l'Ouest (XIIIe siècle), vol. 9 of Collection de documents inédits sur l'histoire de France
(Paris, 1971) 47.

[584] Hauck, *KGD* V 137 note 2; Johanne Heydenreich, "Zu den trierer Synodalstatuten des
13. Jahrhunderts," *ZSRG* KanAbt 56 (1936) 111; Hilling, *Diözesansynoden* 2.

Direct correlations between provincial and diocesan synods in the twelfth century are tenuous. We can only presume that the Mainz statutes of 1154 were read at Hildesheim in 1157 and at Paderborn in 1158; that the Salzburg statutes of 1143 were published at Gurk in 1146 or 1150, or that those of 1178 were published at the diocesan assemblies held at Gurk that same year and at Brixen in 1186;[585] or that the decrees issued at Mainz in 1209 were read and discussed at Hildesheim in May of that same year, at Eichstätt on 13 October 1210, at Halberstadt, Speyer, Strasbourg, and Augsburg in 1211, and at Strasbourg in 1212. The lack of information concerning both legislative and synodal activities in the other provinces prohibits further speculation.

It is equally impossible to determine which, if any, of the provincial synods or diocesan assemblies held shortly after general councils, such as that at Rheims in 1148 or Lateran III in 1179, published the constitutions given there. Hübner assumed that the statutes from Rheims were published at the provincial synod held at Salzburg in October 1150,[586], while other possibilities exist that the Lateran decrees were made known at the Münster diocesan synod of 1179, the Halberstadt synod of 26 June 1180, the Hildesheim and Constanz synods of 1181, the Magdeburg provincial synod of 28 July 1181, and the Cologne and Eichstätt diocesan synods of 1182 and 1183. Cheney suggests with some merit, however, that the practice of proclaiming the enactments of general Church councils at lower ecclesiastical levels may have ceased altogether, in which case Innocent III's decree was intended to revive it.[587] The following tables summarize the evidence for provincial synods during the twelfth century:

Table A: German Provincial Synods 1101-1160

PROVINCE	1100s	1110s	1120s	1130s	1140s	1150s
Bremen					1149	
Cologne	1110	1119		1132 1136 1138		1152
Magdeburg			1129	1135 1140		1151 1157

[585] Cf. Baur, "Brixner Synoden" 305, who assumes this for Brixen.
[586] "Provinzialsynoden" 198.
[587] *English Synodalia* 31.

PROVINCE	1100s	1110s	1120s	1130s	1140s	1150s
Mainz	1102 1105/6	1118	1125 1127	1131 1133	1143 1148 1149 1150	1154
Salzburg			1129	1137 1139	1143 1144 1146 1146 1146 1147 1150	1151 1153 1160
Trier				1132 1135 1135 1136		1152 1152 1157 1159

Table B: German Provincial Synods 1161-1215

PROVINCE	1160s	1170s	1180s	1190s	1200s
Bremen					1201
Cologne	1166		1186 1187		
Magdeburg	1161 1163 1166	1171 1175 1178	1181 1182 1186 1187	1191 1197	1207 1208
Mainz		1171	1184 1190	1191 1196	1209
Salzburg		1178 1180			1201 1202 1203 1204/7 1205 1209 1210
Trier	1161 1162 1163	1179	1187 1189		1214

The evidence of provincial synods for the century before Lateran IV seems at once impressive and disappointing—the former, because of the incontrovertible indication that this important organ of church government was still functioning in the early thirteenth century; the latter, because so little is known about the specifics of each province's practices. It is impossible to say whether the early regulations for provincial synods—requiring two yearly, summer and autumn—were ever generally observed. Certainly they were not common, although there is sporadic evidence in the provinces of Trier, Bremen, Magdeburg, and Mainz. Lateran IV was content with just one per year.

Twelfth and thirteenth-century canonists were agreed that the holding of diocesan synods was greatest among the duties of the bishop. Through his "power of jurisdiction" (*potestas iurisdictionis*) the bishop held supreme judicial, legislative, and governmental authority within his diocese. While in ecumenical and provincial councils, the bishops who participated contributed to the authority of the assembly's acts, the clergy who attended a diocesan synod under the presidency of the bishop were subject to his jurisdiction and formed merely a consultative body. The bishop could prescribe the matters for consideration and decide with whom he would consult. Those summoned were there to give him "due obedience and reverence," as stated by Innocent III in a letter of 31 December 1199 to the archbishop of Rossano.[588] Though the bishop generally presided in person, he could be represented at a synod by a general vicar or another bishop. The ability so to delegate his synodal authority derived from the bishop's role as ordinary and not from his consecration to the episcopal office. It thus followed that a bishop-elect might celebrate a diocesan synod, or that a synod might be convened *sede vacante* by the appropriate authority.

Writing in the 1160s, Master Stephen of Tournai had stated that from their election alone bishops

> are approved; from the confirmation of their election, they obtain power. For when the election has been confirmed, they can forbid the divine office and, for just cause, they can suspend clerics from their benefices. . . . However, they cannot remove orders from someone, since one cannot give what one has only from his consecration. For an elected official has the power of administration, but not the authority of dignity. . . .

---

[588] Cheney, *English Synodalia* 4 note 2, citing *Decretales* i. 33, 9 *"Quod super his"*; cf. Migne, *PL* CCXIV col. 823; Potthast, *Regesta* I, Nr. 919.

By the end of the twelfth century, papal practice reflected the decretist theory, accepting the judgment that an electus could not administer jurisdictional powers until his election had been confirmed. On the other hand, attempts by confirmed bishops-elect to discipline unruly clerics were upheld by the Curia against charges that as a mere *electus* they had no right to exercise this form of power.[589]

According to the canonists, there was no significant difference between the consecration of an archbishop and that of any other bishop. But, because the metropolitan was *more* than a bishop, there were particular powers—the *ius metropolicum*—pertaining to his office. His competence included the right to confirm elections of suffragans in his province and to consecrate them, the right to call provincial synods and to preside over them, and also general supervision and discipline within the province. Since the early Middle Ages the metropolitan's right to exercise these supraepiscopal powers was dependent upon his possession of the pallium. The definition of the significance of its bestowal was given by Pope Paschal II who appropriated a new term for the pallium—"the fullness of the episcopal office," stating that "before he has received the pallium the metropolitan is not allowed to consecrate a bishop or hold a synod."[590]

The significance of this doctrine for the present study lies in the fact that both before and after the Fourth Lateran Council many archbishops in Germany, whose loyalty to the *imperium* often conflicted with their obedience to the *sacerdotium*, were denied this ultimate symbol of their office and as a consequence were prohibited from convening provincial synods with their suffragans. Any attempt to reconstruct the synodal life of Germany during the period 900 to 1300 must take such factors into serious consideration. The often fragmentary nature of the lists of provincial synods thus seems to be a reflection of papal policy as much as of individual predispositions among the German archbishops.

---

[589] Migne, *PL* CCXIV, col. 823; Potthast, *Regesta* I, Nr. 919. Further, see Cheney, *English Synodalia* 1-4; Benson, *Bishop-Elect* 9, 91, 112; Hauck, *KGD* V 166.

[590] Cited in Benson, *Bishop-Elect* 169-170.

CHAPTER TWO

STATUS ECCLESIAE: THE GERMAN CHURCH IN THE
EARLY THIRTEENTH CENTURY

Haec dicit Dominus Deus: Vae pastoribus Israel, qui pascebant semetipsos:
nonne greges a pastoribus pascuntur? Lac comedebatis, et lanis operiebamini,
et quod crassum erat occidebatis: gregem autem meum non pascebatis.
(Ezekiel 34, 2-3)

[Episcopus Wormatiensis est] non pastor, . . . sed impostor, dissipator
et non dispensator, non defensor ecclesiae, sed offensor.
(Anonymous, ca. 1204)

The comprehensive nature of the constitutions published by the Fourth
Lateran Council reveals an awareness of deep-seated problems within the
fabric of the medieval Church. That Innocent III clearly perceived a
connection between the decline in Church order and the rise of religious
dissidence is indicated by the letters of commission given to the legates
which he sent into southern France in the early years of his pontificate, in
which he stressed that the development of the heresy of the Cathari was
above all attributable to the accumulation of ecclesiastical offices, to the
inactivity of the bishops—"those dumb hounds that cannot even bray," and
to the loosening of discipline among the clergy.[1] Languedoc was not alone
in being infected by religious heterodoxy, however. Northern Italy also
became a hotbed of activity, and evidence from German sources indicates
that well before the beginning of the thirteenth century, aberrant teachings
had also spread throughout the Rhineland.

The close proximity of Lorraine and the Rhineland to those regions in
France which were widely affected by Catharism made them especially
vulnerable to anti-Catholic and anti-sacerdotal movements at a very early
date. From 1143, when three heretics were burned at Bonn by the
command of Pfalzgrave Otto of Rheineck, until 1163 when Abbot Eckbert
of Schönau disputed with several others at Cologne, there is frequent
mention of Cathars in the sources of the Lower Rhine.[2] Shortly thereafter,

---

[1] Foreville, *Lateran I-IV* 278-9.
[2] *Ann. Brunwilar. (a. 1143)* 727. For a general discussion of twelfth-century Catharism, see Borst, *Die Katharer*; further, Kieckhefer, *Repression of Heresy* 12.

proponents of the forbidden dualism were also discovered at Mainz and Coblenz.[3]

By the latter part of the century the "purified ones" had been joined by the followers of other radical movements. In 1192, e.g., a synod held at Toul in the ecclesiastical province of Trier took harsh action against some professed Waldenses. Bishop Eudes of Vaudemont commanded the faithful to seize them and to bring them in chains before his tribunal.[4] Followers of Peter Waldo also appeared at Metz where large numbers of both men and women in the city itself and throughout the diocese were attracted to their teachings. These sectaries possessed French translations of several biblical writings, including the Gospels, the Epistles of Paul, the Psalms, and the Book of Job, from which they preached extensively in their secret meetings, offering their own interpretations. The Catholic priests who sought to correct them were ignored and their admonitions rejected, inasmuch as the dissidents claimed that only in their books could one find the true teachings of God. With a zeal unmatched by the clergy of the established Church, the heretic preachers spread the Waldensian doctrines ever wider throughout Lorraine.

The boldness of the heretics even reached the point where they verbally attacked Bishop Bertram of Metz himself. As he conducted services in the cathedral church one feast day in early 1199, he recognized two Waldensian preachers in the congregation and, pointing a finger at them, exclaimed: "These are the ones who were convicted of heresy in my presence at Montpellier and were driven from the city!" The accused were quick to respond: with them was a scholar who hurled insults at the bishop in the presence of all who had gathered for the Mass. As the men then left the cathedral, the crowd gathered about them and heard them expound their doctrines. The preachers found unexpected support from several patrician families who were upset with Bishop Bertram for having refused burial in hallowed ground to a relative of theirs who had been accused of usury. They thus took this occasion to stir up the populace even more against the prelate.

Before attempting to cut out this malignancy himself, Bertram first wrote to the pope, explaining the situation as he perceived it and mentioning by name some of the leading agitators. Innocent III responded to him and the cathedral chapter in a letter dated 12 December 1199, forbidding them to pass sentence before the Curia had learned more concerning those who had translated the Scriptures and had preached from those forbidden books.

---

[3] Cf. Ekbert of Schönau, *Sermones XIII contra Catharos*, in Migne, *PL* CVC, cols. 11-102; Roth, *Visionen und Briefe* 202-203.

[4] Hartzheim, *Concilia* III, 456; Hauck, *KGD* IV, 901; Pontal, *Liste des MSS* 431-432.

Bertram was commanded to ascertain who had produced the translations and for what purpose, and to assess the degree to which the innovations conformed to the doctrines of the Roman Church. He should then submit a thorough report to the Curia, upon which was to rest the decision concerning what action was to be taken.[5] In a separate letter dated the same day, the pontiff wrote to the burghers of Metz and admonished them with the aid of numerous passages of Scripture that they must reject the new teachings and hold fast to the true Catholic faith, lest they bring peril to their souls by continued espousal of such ideas.[6]

The bishop complied with the papal mandate and sent additional information in a second letter. He was unable to learn the identity of the translators, but he listed two of the preachers as a *presbyter* named Crispinus and his associate R[ ]. He noted that his warnings had had no effect, complaining to the pope that the truculent preachers claimed to obey God alone. They furthermore were said to have boasted that, should anyone attempt to destroy their books of Scripture, they would publicly renounce obedience to the bishop, the metropolitan, and the Roman pontiff.

Realizing the inability of the bishop of Metz to deal single handedly with such a threatening situation, Innocent III had also commissioned three Cistercian abbots to assist Bertram in the repression of the rebels. In a letter dated 9 December 1199 he directed the abbots of Cîteaux, Morimond and La Crête to proceed to Metz and, in the company of the prelate, to investigate the causes of the disturbance and the extent to which apostasy had spread in that diocese. They were also to command the sectaries to return to the bosom of the Church and then report their success. According to the near-contemporary Cistercian chronicler, Aubrey of Trois-Fontaines, the primary accomplishment of the commission lay in causing some of the vernacular books to be burned.[7] It is not known what else the abbots accomplished, however. Where Aubrey states that they eradicated the heresy, we should accept this cautiously, for when an abbot came to Metz in 1211 to preach the crusade against the Albigenses, the city broke out into disputes between those who supported such an action and some who had sympathies for the dissidents. It would therefore seem that antisacerdotal sentiments were still strong at Metz at that time, and a contemporary report affirms that they were even evident in 1221.[8]

[5] *Chron. Albrici (a. 1200)* 878; Potthast, *Regesta* I, Nr. 781; Migne, *PL* CCXIV, cols. 698-699; *Caesarii Dialogus* V 20; Grundmann, *Religiöse Bewegungen* 97-99.

[6] Migne, *PL* CCXIV, cols. 695-698; Potthast, *Regesta* I, Nr. 780.

[7] *Chron. Albrici* 878; see also Voigt, *Bischof Bertram von Metz* 119.

[8] *Chron. Albrici (a. 1211)* 892; Caesarius of Heisterbach, writing his *Dialogus* 1221/1222, noted at the conclusion of the discussion of the Waldensian movement under Bishop Bertram (V 20): "*Revera missi fuerant a spiritu erroris per quorum ora haereses Valdosianae ab uno*

Criticism of the German clergy did not come exclusively from religious heretics, however. Throughout the Middle Ages voices were heard from deep within the Church, censuring current practices and admonishing contemporaries to a higher level of religiosity. Early in the thirteenth century a well-trained and highly-perceptive Cistercian monk, Caesarius of Heisterbach, included a series of accounts about worldly canons and other secular clergy from the province of Cologne and surrounding regions of Germany in his *Dialogus miraculorum*.[9] He leaves little doubt that such individuals fell short of his standards of behavior and piety. There was, e.g., the unnamed young cathedral canon at Cologne who, after losing most of his clothing in gambling, appeared half-naked at the door of Heisterbach seeking admission as a novice. His plight evoked ridicule rather than sympathy among the sober monks, and his plea was met with a firm rejection. Caesarius further criticized the Cologne cathedral canon Albert of Brühl who entered Heisterbach as an old man and became known to him in his capacity as novice-master. The once-proud canon confessed that a book of eight pages would not suffice to list all his sins and errors: although he had preserved his chastity, he had been quite worldly and pampered, his special vice being ostentation in dress. While he was still quite young, his mother had become a nun at Abbess Hildegard's cloister Ruprechtsberg near·Bingen and had spent her days praying to God that Albert would forsake his erring ways; despite such intercession, however, the prodigal son became increasingly more notorious.

Yet another canon at Cologne aroused Caesarius' indignation in that he not only maintained a concubine, but also was reported as having absconded with the Host itself during the recitation of the Mass. A contemporary canon at St. Gereon in Cologne, named Werinbold, was a noble by birth and the possessor of numerous prebends. Yet, according to Caesarius he was so simple (i.e., poorly trained) that he could only count by pairs—a ham and a pair, a candle and a pair, etc. This lack of the essential education even to administer his offices left him defenseless against the wiles of others, and even his own servants took advantage of him.[10]

---

eorum sic dictae in eadem civitate sunt seminatae et necdum prorsus extinctae."

[9] Kaufmann, *Caesarius-Werken* 13-17, argues that Caesarius was born at Cologne and received his training early in life under *magister* Rudolf, scholastic at the cathedral school, and under Ensfrid, dean at St. Andreas. His conversion to the religious life occurred ca. 1198. A prolific writer, he made a catalogue of his works which contains thirty-six major and minor titles; cf. Schönbach, *Erzählungsliteratur* 4-45.

[10] *Dialogus* I 11; VII 55; IX 57; VII 7. For a general discussion of conditions within the Cologne church, see Kaufmann, *Caesarius von Heisterbach* 56-65, and also Ficker, *Engelbert der Heilige* 27 and 214, note 2.

In the moralistic view of Caesarius' day the ecclesiastical importance of secular canons had declined: cathedral and collegiate churches clearly belonged to the world—in sharp contrast to the cloisters, from which they were separated by a wide gap. Caesarius drew attention to a canon at Bonn, e.g., who "was pious and well-educated" and sat "in his cell . . . with the Apostle in his hand," while "certain of his fellow-canons kept hounds and sparrow-hawks, and filled the air with cries and shook the earth with the stamping of their feet." The contrast was intentional, and we may assume that in the author's eyes the former example of clerical behavior was the exception rather than the rule. He also claimed that an erstwhile canon at St. Andreas' in Cologne (but at length and to his credit a Cistercian monk!) reported that the clergy of that church "sit in the vestibule and speak against their brethren, and sit at night by the fire and become drunken."[11] Like laymen, however, repentant canons were pictured by Caesarius ending their days as monks, having taken solemn vows to begin a new life. Obviously, some did, thereby giving credence to this monastic perception of the ideal clerical state.[12] E.g., Abbot Gevhard of Heisterbach (1195-1208) had previously been a canon at St. Maria *ad gradus* in Cologne, filled with the vanities of the world. Once in jest, he had donned the Cistercian habit and participated in a religious celebration, only to be embarrassed by discovery. Shortly thereafter, to the astonishment of all, he left the canonate to become a novice at the Cistercian house of Himmerode. According to Caesarius he displayed such devotion there that he was chosen to become the second abbot at Heisterbach where he led the house in piety and discipline, trying through the deeds of a long life as a monk to expiate the deeds of his misbegotten youth.[13]

---

[11] *Caesarii Omasticon* I 143, Nr. 195; *Dialogus*, IV 119.

[12] The contemporary Austrian poet Walther von der Vogelweide gives a secular view of an ideal cleric, referring in several places to an *inclusus* or *Klausner* who represented a Christianity which was not counterfeit, nor contaminated by the lust for power and wealth. German scholars as early as Jacob Grimm sought to associate Walther's Klausner with a specific, historical personality who regarded the Roman hierarchy and the higher clergy as victims of a secularizing spirit. Julius Otto Opel, *Mîn guoter Klôsenaere* (Halle, 1860), argued for the identification of the Klausner with Conrad of Krosigk, the erstwhile bishop of Halberstadt who became a Cistercian monk in 1209. Such efforts have failed to withstand the criticism of more recent studies, however; see Gustav Nebe, "Conrad von Krosigk, Bischof von Halberstadt 1201-1209. Ein Lebensbild," *ZHV* 13 (1880) 209-227, espec. 223-225; Konrad Burdach, "Der gute Klausner Walthers von der Vogelweide als Typus unpolitischer christlicher Frömmigkeit," *Zeitschrift für deutsche Philologie* 60 (1935) 313-330, espec. 313-317. The most recent treatment of Conrad is by Alfred J. Andrea, "Conrad of Krosigk, Bishop of Halberstadt, Crusader and Monk of Sittichenbach: His Ecclesiastical Career, 1184-1225," *Analecta Cisterciensia* 43/1 (1987) 11-91; with reference to the *Klausner*, cf. 69-71.

[13] See *Dialogus* I 7.

Corroborating the view offered by Caesarius is a most remarkable description of Alsace at the beginning of the thirteenth century which was produced soon after 1295 at the Dominican convent at Colmar and apparently rests on earlier sources. While this work clearly shows the bias of the Friars Preachers who sensed the impact which their arrival had upon the religious and cultural life of the region, it may also serve to elucidate the conditions prevailing at Strasbourg and its environs at the commencement of Innocent III's pontificate. In a fashion quite alien to other contemporary works, it notes that

> About the year of the Lord 1200 there were few priests in Alsace, and one had to suffice to read the Mass in two villages, or in three or four small villages. For, many of the priests read two Masses almost daily—the first in one, and the second in another village; in a third they conducted devotionals, and if a funeral, a marriage, or a pilgrimage should arise, they read a third Mass there. Many priests possessed only limited training and were therefore seldom able to offer prudent counsel. Furthermore, virtually all of them had concubines; in fact, the peasants generally encouraged them to do so. For they said, 'A priest cannot be chaste; it is therefore better that he have only one wife, than that he entice and seduce all other women.' It was the practice for the clergy of foundations and for knights to seduce nuns from the nobility. . . . The secular clergy of the period were further wont to wear brightly-colored clothing. . . . Abbots and secular clergy took the possessions of the poor as security, believing that they did no wrong therein.[14]

That the conditions noted by Caesarius and the anonymous scribe at Colmar were not fabrications is substantiated by papal letters which expressed criticism of the German church and commanded those responsible for correcting abuses to accept that burden. On 1 July 1199, e.g., Innocent III commanded three clerics of the city of Erfurt to correct what was by now a very common abuse: the income intended for four canons at St. John's church in Erfurt had been divided among sixteen, thereby arousing complaints from the canons of that foundation. The papal representatives were ordered to correct that practice and to provide prebendaries at St. John's with sufficient incomes.[15]

Pluralism Among the German Clergy

Underlying this problem at Erfurt, Strasbourg, and elsewhere was the

---

[14] "Die Zustände des Elsasses im Beginn des 13. Jahrhunderts," *Annalen Kolmar* 123-135.

[15] Migne, *PL* CCXIV, col. 663; Potthast, *Regesta* I, Nr. 756; Overmann, *UB Erfurt* I, Nr. 128.

tendency of cathedral and collegiate churches to admit ever-increasing numbers of members without sufficient economic support. This was compounded by the practice of cathedral canons accumulating prebends in collegiate churches and of accepting the office of parish priest as well; being absent from the latter churches most of the time, these pluralists forced the remaining prebends and tithes to be divided among a larger number of canons, with vicars being appointed in order to have sufficient clerics to perform the essential functions of the church thus affected.

C. 13 of the Third Lateran Council's decrees (1179) had prohibited pluralism under penalty of losing what had been received, but the tendency continued unabated into the early thirteenth century, to which the following examples readily attest:

> *Berengar of Entringen*, who became bishop of Speyer in 1224, had been a cathedral canon there since ca. 1188; in ca. 1201 he appears as a subdeacon and canon at Strasbourg, in 1208 as archdeacon of Strasbourg, and in 1213 as cathedral cantor at Speyer.[16]
>
> *Conrad of Dahn*, who became bishop of Speyer in 1233, held the provostships of St. Andreas in Worms (since ca. 1198) and of the Holy Trinity in Speyer (since ca. 1214), the office of *custos* at St. Cyriak in Worms (since ca. 1197), that of *camerarius* in Speyer (in 1208/1209), and prebends as a canon in both dioceses.[17]
>
> *Conrad of Steinach* appears ca. 1206 as provost at Mosbach and therefore probably as a canon at Worms, 1209 as a cathedral canon at Speyer, and from 1211 until 1238 as cathedral provost at Speyer.[18]
>
> *Berthold of Neiffen*, who in 1217 became bishop of Brixen, held a canonate at Speyer since ca. 1202, since 1203 he appears as provost of St. Germanus in Speyer, in 1208 he became administrator of the bishopric of Trent; simultaneously he was a member of the Staufen chancery where 1212-1215 he appears as *regalis aule protonotarius* for Frederick II, being second only to the chancellor himself, Bishop Conrad of Speyer.[19]

---

[16] See *Wirtemburg. UB* II, Nr. 454 (1188); Wiegand, *UB Strassburg* I 122, Nrs. 150-151; Moné, "Kraichgauer Urkunden," *ZGO* 13 (1861) 322; Mazzetti, *Bischof Bernger* 5-12.

[17] See Schannat, *Hist. Episc. Wormat.* I 129; Remling, *UB Speyer* I 170, Nr. 154; Gudenus, *Sylloge* I 89, Nr. 37; Villinger, *St. Cyriakusstift* 76, Reg. 36; Gudenus, *Cod. dipl.* I 409; Bienemann, *Conrad von Scharfenberg* 128; Simon, *Stand und Herkunft* 25; Remling, *Bistum Speyer* I 461; Pixton, "Konrad von Reifenberg" 50 and note 39.

[18] See Gudenus, *Sylloge* I 69, Nr. 26; Würdtwein, *Nova subs.* X 255; *Wirtemburg. UB* III 419, Nr. 917.

[19] See Moné, "Urkunden über Lothringen," *ZGO* 13 (1861) 58; *Wirtemburg. UB* II 344, Nr. 522; Sparber, *Fürstbischöfe* 77; Böhmer-Ficker, *Regg. Imp.* V, Nrs. 6, 16, 52, 55-59, 61-

Siegfried II of Eppstein, who became archbishop of Mainz in 1200, held at the time of his elevation a prebend in the cathedral chapter at Mainz, the provostships of St. Gangolf (since ca. 1189) and St. Peter's (since ca. 1196) at Mainz, that of St. Martin's at Worms (since ca. 1194), those of Brünn (since ca. 1194) and Wyssehrad near Prague; the latter dignity also comprehended the office of chancellor of Bohemia.[20]

Arnold of Isenburg, who became archbishop of Trier in 1242, appears ca. 1210 as a canon and 1212 as *cellerarius* at Trier, ca. 1217 as an archdeacon at Trier and as provost of St. Gangolf in Mainz, a fact confirmed by a 1220 document in which Arnold appears as *Trevirensis archidiaconus et ecclesiae maioris in Magontia can[onicus]*.[21]

Conrad of Isenburg since ca. 1186 held a canonate at Mainz and the provostship of St. Bartholomew's at Frankfurt-on-the-Main; from 1195 until 1216 he was also the cathedral provost at Mainz.[22]

Henry of Saarbrücken, who became bishop of Worms in 1218, appears 1203 as provost of St. Peter's in Mainz and therefore also held a canonate there, in 1209 he is mentioned as provost of St. Maria *in campis*, in 1212 as provost of Neuhausen at Worms and as the cathedral dean of that church, 1216 as a canon at Mainz and as provost of St. Peter's in Worms, and in 1217 as cathedral provost at Worms.[23]

Conrad of Apolda appears ca. 1191 to ca. 1213 as provost of St. Maria *ad gradus* in Mainz and therefore also held a canonate in the cathedral chapter, from ca. 1192 until 1235 he also was the provost of St. Maria in Erfurt, and in 1200 he is mentioned as a canon at Halberstadt.[24]

Burchard of Wartberg appears ca. 1210 as a canon at Halberstadt and from 1213 until 1230 as provost at Jechaburg in Thuringia, by virtue of

---

63, 71, 73-74, 83, 90, 92, 97-99.

[20] See Böhmer-Will, *RAM* II 81, Nr. 222; Ibid. II xv; the most complete monograph on Siegfried is that of Lewin, *Siegfried II. von Eppstein*.

[21] Cf. Wampach, *UB Luxemburg* II 40. Nr. 29; Beyer, *MRUB* II 321, Nr. 286; Ibid. III 77, Nr. 76; Sauer, *Nassau UB* I, Nr. 345.

[22] See Acht, *Mainzer UB* II, Nr. 491; Conrad's predecessor as provost, Arnold, is last mentioned in a document dated simply 1196 (cf. Böhmer-Will, *RAM* II 164, Nr. 266).

[23] See Würdtwein, *Nova subs.* II 99; Böhmer-Will, *RAM* II 140, Nr. 108, and II 164, Nr. 266; Gudenus, *Cod. dipl.* I 421, Nr. 160; Glasschröder, *Pfälz. Urkk* Nr. 456; Gudenus, *Sylloge* 98, Nr. 40.

[24] Cf. Böhmer-Will, *RAM* II 87, Nr. 254; in 1213 Dietrich von Seelenhofen appears as provost at St. Maria *ad gradus* for the first time (cf. Baur, *Hess. UB* I, Nr. 89; Sonntag, *St. Marien zu Erfurt* 107; Dobenecker, *RdThur* III, Nr. 604a).

which he was also a cathedral canon at Mainz.[25]

Burchard of Woldenburg, who in 1235 became archbishop of Magdeburg, had been a canon at Hildesheim since ca. 1180, 1194-1232 he appears as provost of Petersbergstift near Goslar, 1202-1232 as provost of St. Blasius in Brunswick, and after 1212 as a cathedral canon at Magdeburg.[26]

Engelbert of Berg, who in 1216 became archbishop of Cologne, occupied the office of provost of St. George in Cologne after 1198, from 1199 that of cathedral provost and archdeacon of Cologne, from 1205 provost of St. Severin at Cologne, ca. 1205 provost at Deventer and at Züften; and from 1213 provost at St. Maria in Aachen.[27]

Dietrich of Altena, who in 1218 became bishop of Münster, possessed since 1199 the office of *custos* and a canonate at Cologne, since ca. 1199 that of provost at Soest and at Xanten (as the result of which he also held the title of *archidiaconus maior* for the archdiocese), and since 1207 the provostship at Münster.[28]

Rudolf de Ponte [Sr.] appears as a canon and archdeacon at Liège ca. 1200-1218; in 1208 he is also documented as a canon at Trier where, ca. 1217, he became an archdeacon. On 23 July 1218 he attested a document as both *Treverensis et Leodiensis archidiaconus.*[29]

Magister Rüdiger of Radeck, who became the first bishop of Chiemsee in 1215, possessed from ca. 1212 a canonate at Passau, the provostship at Zell, and the office of parish priest (*plebanus*) at Salzburghofen.[30]

Poppo of Andechs, who succeeded as bishop of Bamberg in 1237, occupied from ca. 1192 the provostship of St. Jacob's and a canonate at Bamberg, from ca. 1196 until 1215 the provostship at St. Stephan's, and from 1206 the cathedral provostship.[31]

---

[25] See Dobenecker, *RdThur* II, Nr. 1467; Böhmer-Will, *RAM* II 158, Nr. 220; Pixton, "Konrad von Reifenberg" 64.

[26] Cf. Pixton, "Konrad von Reifenberg" 78-79; Janicke, *UB Hilds* I, Nr. 506, 563; [ ] von Alten, "Zur Chronologie der Hildesheimer Bischöfe Siegfried I. und Conrad II. und der zu ihrer Zeit erscheinenden Hildesheimer Dompröpste," *ZVN* (1869) Anhang Nr. 12.

[27] See Ficker, *Engelbert der Heilige* 25-52; the cathedral provostship was contested until 1203 as noted below.

[28] See Krabbo, "Besetzung" 59.

[29] Cf. Beyer, *MRUB* II 279, Nr. 240; III 85, Nr. 85. For Rudolf's activities in the schismatic election at Liège, see below [p. 113].

[30] Cf. Kuhle, *Neubesetzung* 88.

[31] Cf. Looshorn, *Bistum Bamberg* I 606; II 564-577; Guttenberg, *Bistum Bamberg* 171-173.

A total picture of the extensive pluralistic practices of the early thirteenth century is impossible inasmuch as many ecclesiastical offices had less prestige attached to them than others, and they were therefore omitted from the list of dignities appended to clerics' names in the documents. The extent to which many cathedral clergy collected titles and incomes in their pursuit of power, influence, and wealth is clearly apparent, however. Those cathedral canons who were also archdeacons, and therefore had the responsibility for conducting visitations, were frequently unable to maintain residence requirements as well. The incongruence between precept and the practices of the dominant ecclesiastical figures in the various dioceses could not have gone unnoticed among those of lesser importance who would also have sought to enhance their standing through the accumulation of whatever prebends and incomes were available. Vicars might be appointed to fulfill ecclesiastical duties, but the meager incomes provided these men undoubtedly contributed to their lack of commitment to the task.

The papacy became aware of problems such as that in Erfurt in part through complaints sent to it by those parties who felt themselves injured or disadvantaged. For Caesarius of Heisterbach, much of the knowledge came as a result of his positions as novice-master and prior at his monastery which gave him countless opportunities to observe the state of clerical life throughout the Middle- and Lower-Rhine regions. As a dignitary at Heisterbach he also traveled widely and had occasion to converse with the hundreds of visitors and new religious who came to his house. In his view, the deplorable conditions which prevailed within the church of Cologne in particular, and the German church in general, were attributable to just one major cause—the archbishop himself, Adolf of Altena. Caesarius asserted that "after the death of Emperor Henry, [Adolf] offered the Empire up for sale, degraded himself with the poison of avarice, and thereby brought many to ruin." Applying to Adolf the words of Old Testament prophecy, he exclaimed, "Mourn, O Cologne, over the afflictions which thy bishop has caused, and over thine own sinfulness!"[32]

Caesarius' condemnation is shared by modern historians as well. The nineteenth-century scholar Julius Ficker remarked that "the name of Adolf of Altena should be mentioned first when those men are listed who bear the primary blame for the collapse of the power and unity of the Empire."[33] It was in fact this archbishop of Cologne who led the opposition against Emperor Henry VI's proposed hereditary kingdom in 1196, rejecting the election of the young Staufen heir, Frederick of Sicily. Upon Henry's death, the Staufen party elected his younger brother, Philip of Swabia, as

---

[32] *Dialogus* II 30; cited in Kaufmann, *Caesarius-Werken* 59.
[33] *Engelbert der Heilige* 20.

king on 8 March 1198 at Mühlhausen in Thuringia; the opponents, however, led by Adolf of Cologne, elevated Otto of Poitou (more often referred to as Otto of Brunswick), a younger son of Duke Henry the Lion of Saxony, 9 June 1198 at Cologne and bestowed the crown 12 July at Aachen. There thus was renewed the old Welf-Hohenstaufen conflict which was destined to wreak havoc upon the German state and the German church alike. The contemporary Swabian chronicler of Ursperg, Burchard, lamented that as a consequence of the throne controversy "hardly a bishopric, hardly an ecclesiastical dignity, or hardly even a parish church exists that has not been disputed."[34] Such an observation was essentially correct, inasmuch as the polarization of German society extended to within the numerous institutions of the Church; many of the problems to which the decrees of the Fourth Lateranum addressed themselves were thus either created or exacerbated during the German civil war.

The German Throne Controversy

As bitter as had been the struggle between the Hohenstaufen and the papacy under Frederick I and Henry VI, Pope Innocent III was slow in taking sides in the new throne controversy. An appeal to Rome by the Welf camp was nevertheless most welcome, inasmuch as it provided the papacy with the opportunity for putting into practice the theories of papal supremacy over the temporal affairs of Latin Christendom. For this reason it was also disturbing to learn that support for Otto IV among the German episcopacy was rapidly dwindling. During 1198 and 1199 all of the bishops in southern and central Germany allied themselves with the Staufen camp, and even many within Otto's North-German stronghold joined the opposition: included here were Archbishop Hartwig II of Bremen and Bishops Gardolf of Halberstadt, Gerhard of Osnabrück, and Hermann of Münster. Rumor had it that even Archbishop Adolf of Cologne was ready to defect.[35]

Characteristic of the German prelates of this time was Archbishop John of Trier. Serving as chancellor for Emperor Henry VI until the latter's death, John had held the provostship of St. Germanus in Speyer. In 1198 this ardent supporter of the Staufen political fortunes was elevated to the archbishopric and immediately found himself caught in the web of partisan issues. Shifting back and forth between Welf and Hohenstaufen camps, he tried desperately to placate the papacy, his clergy, the archiepiscopal

---

[34] *Chron. Ursperg.* 82. In general, our discussion of the German throne controversy follows that of Winkelmann, *Phil. von Schw.* II., as emended by Hauck, *KGD* IV 711-731, and Schwemer, *Innocent III.*

[35] *Chron. reg. Colon. (a. 1199)* 168.

ministeriales, and his own city. That he was not beyond reproach from his own clergy is evidenced by the directive given by Innocent III to Bishop Albert of Liège, Abbot Christian of St. Truijen and the provost of Maastricht, Dietrich of Ahr, about 1198 to investigate charges of misconduct brought against John by the cathedral dean, William of Salm. If they found him culpable, they were to suspend him publicly from his office and benefices alike. Nothing more is found in the records pertaining to this incident, and the fact that Dean William was witness to virtually all documents issued by the metropolitan thereafter suggests that he did not become estranged as a result of this complaint.[36] A harmonious relationship between the archbishop and the papacy was not the general course, however. Several times between 1198 and 1212 John of Trier bore the stigma of excommunication and his archdiocese suffered the deleterious effects of interdict.

To compound the papal worries about the lack of support for Otto IV, news reached Rome that Archbishop Conrad of Mainz, a man of impeccable character who enjoyed widespread respect, was seeking to resolve the throne controversy through his own good offices. As arch-chancellor of the Empire and as primate of the German church he had summoned an assembly to be held in July 1200 between Coblenz and Andernach on the Rhine, at which eight princes from each contesting camp would decide the issue. Representing Otto would be Archbishop Adolf of Cologne, the bishops of Münster, Liège, Utrecht, and Paderborn, the abbot of Corvey, and two lay princes; Philip's proctors were the archbishops of Trier and Salzburg, the bishops of Freising, Basel, and Strasbourg, and three lay princes.

Reports that the archbishop of Mainz was actually accomplishing his purpose disturbed the Curia. If successful, it would render moot the papal theory concerning disputed Imperial elections. Realizing the necessity of determining how the princes were to decide, Innocent was compelled to favor Otto publicly. He at once dispatched the acolyte Aegidius to Germany with the command that the princes elect Otto as king at the July 1200 assembly; for them to choose Philip would result in serious conflict with the Church. The papal plan misfired, however, inasmuch as the assembly never met. A second letter from Rome was likewise ignored.[37] Thus, it appeared that the issue of the German throne was not to be decided in Rome, but by the course of war.

---

[36] Potthast, *Regesta* I, Nr. 550; Volkert Pfaff, "Die deutschen Domkapitel und das Papsttum am Ende des 12. Jahrhunderts," *HJb* 93/1 (1973) 41. Corsten, "EB Johann I. von Trier" provides the most detailed general study of the pontificate of Archbishop John of Trier.

[37] Migne, *PL* CCXVI, col. 1019; Potthast, *Regesta* I, Nr. 1105.

Once he had shown support for Otto's party, Innocent III was obligated to labor further for a Welf victory. He tried not only to obtain money from the English king, Richard I, but more importantly to win over Philip II of France. For the latter purpose, he sent the legate Octavian, cardinal-bishop of Ostia, to the French court. Most of all, the pope sought to regain the support of those princes in Germany who had deserted Otto IV: e.g., Landgrave Hermann of Thuringia was threatened with excommunication and interdict, while Archbishop John of Trier was summoned to Rome under threat of suspension. Such measures had little impact, however, and the Welf party continued to disintegrate, while its Staufen antagonist gained strength; by October 1200 Bishop Dietrich of Utrecht had joined the Staufen faction, and even Otto's brother, Pfalzgrave Henry, had made peace with Philip.

One of the greatest obstacles to Otto of Brunswick's domination in northern Germany was the existence of a pro-Staufen archbishop at Magdeburg, Ludolf of Kroppenstedt. During the early years of the throne-controversy a veritable flood of papal letters was sent to this prelate, chastening, admonishing, and threatening him in an effort to bring about his acceptance of the Curia's candidate. Even a cursory reading of the sources and literature pertaining to the archbishopric and province of Magdeburg during this period reveals a church virtually overwhelmed with problems of order and discipline. These were largely the result that Magdeburg bore much of the brunt of the civil war, being a frequent target of Welfish attacks and the scene of Staufen countermeasures. Physical survival clearly took precedence over many ecclesiastical matters, prompting a letter from the pope in February 1200 which criticized the failure of that church to fill prebends according to the decrees of Lateran III, rather than allowing them to lie vacant for extended periods of time.[38]

Behind this letter lay the fact that the cathedral provost Roker had died in Syria in 1197, and during the two years where his office remained vacant, serious problems had developed. On 15 August 1198 Archbishop Ludolf's successor as cathedral dean, Henry of Glinde, was attacked and blinded by Gerhard of Querfurt. The malefactor was excommunicated, but his violent act was the cause for a further delay by the archbishop in filling the provost's office. Using his right of devolution, Innocent III in February 1200 named the Magdeburg cathedral canon and provost of St. Maria *ad gradus* in Mainz, Albrecht of Käfernberg, as the new provost. Albrecht was in Rome at the time and had personally campaigned for the appoint-

---

[38] Migne, *PL* CCXIV, col. 854; Potthast, *Regesta* I, Nr. 948. For a detailed discussion of conditions in Magdeburg during the throne controversy, see Kohlmann, *EB Ludolf* 30-69, and Silberborth, "EB Albrecht II." 50-66.

ment, but the Magdeburg cathedral chapter refused to accept it. The opposition may have stemmed from the fact that Albrecht's brothers-in-law were the lords of Querfurt, whose heinous crime against their dean had not yet been forgotten. The impasse continued for over a year, during which Innocent appointed a commission of Hildesheim clerics to execute his will, inasmuch as the archbishop appeared to have hindered it. At length Ludolf conceded the papal appointment, perhaps recognizing in Albrecht a talent which could benefit his church.[39]

Schismatic Elections at Liège and Mainz

Because most of the leading ecclesiastical figures in Germany favored Philip of Swabia in late 1200, the deaths of Bishop Albert II of Liège on 2 February 1200 and of Archbishop Conrad of Mainz on 20 October of that same year provided the Curia with significant opportunities to challenge the advantage. In both instances disputed elections ensued which drew the papacy into German affairs once more. In Liège three candidates were at first put forth: the former dean, Conrad of Urach; Archdeacon Henry of Jauche; and Provost Hugh of Pierrepont. Conrad at once withdrew and made his solemn profession at the Cistercian monastery of Villers in Brabant. Hugh, on the other hand, was given the regalia of his temporal office by Otto IV, prompting the supporters of Archdeacon Henry to appeal to Rome with the endorsement of King Philip. While welcoming the opportunity to decide an episcopal election in Germany, Innocent III was reluctant to rule against Hugh and Otto IV, even though their case had evident canonical defects. He therefore temporized until December 1200 when he summoned Hugh of Pierrepont to Rome where the latter was to present his case personally before the Curia.[40]

Meanwhile, the members of the cathedral chapter at Mainz had assembled in the late fall of 1200 to carry out a new election, only to have three members of their body protest that the presence of King Philip, who had hastened to Mainz upon hearing of Archbishop Conrad's death, compromised their freedom of action. Finding no support for their position, however, they left the city and took refuge at Bingen-on-the-Rhine. The election was then completed, with the unanimous vote falling upon Lupold

---

[39] *Chron. mont. ser.* 168; Potthast, *Regesta* I, Nr. 648, notes a letter dated 27 March 1199 in which Innocent III offers comfort to the blinded dean. According to Wentz/Schwineköper, *Erzbistum Magdeburg* 342, Henry of Glinde had sought the office of chancellor from Philip of Swabia, as Conrad of Querfurt, Gerhard's brother, fell under suspicion of treason. The date of the blinding makes this improbable, however; see further Kohlmann, *EB Ludolf* 30-39.

[40] *Chron. Albrici* 878; *Reineri Ann.* 655; Potthast, *Regesta* I, Nr. 1215; Kuhle, *Neubesetzung* 23.

of Scheinfeld, the bishop of Worms, who was immediately given the regalia. Lupold was a reliable supporter of King Philip, but a man totally lacking in any form of religiosity. Caesarius of Heisterbach called him a tyrant and bishop in name only, while Innocent III described him as a barbarian warrior, a plunderer of churches, and a total impostor.[41] The picture we have of Lupold is the antithesis of a shepherd: he was a man of unbridled passions for whom the civil war in Germany provided ample opportunity for pursuing his own and others' aims with the sword, rather than with the staff. His reputation was widespread, as evidenced by this verse written ca. 1210 by an anonymous Thuringian poet:

> *Bellicus Antistes pugnace cohorte Lupoldus,*
> *Imbelli movit bella cruenta Papae:*
> *Auxilio fretus regis quandoque Philippi;*
> *Qui lupus ante fuit, denique factus ovis.*[42]

The dissidents, who were in fact Siegfried of Eppstein and his relatives Werner and Philip of Bolanden, meanwhile had cast their votes for the provost of St. Gangolf and St. Peter's—Siegfried himself. In stark contrast to the image of Lupold is that given by the continuator of the *Gesta Treverorum* to describe the minority candidate—*"pauper et modicus."* Reacting quickly to this threat, Bishop-elect Lupold seized Bingen, thereby driving Siegfried to seek support from Otto IV who granted him the regalia as well. The Eppstein party also lodged an appeal at Rome, hoping through papal intervention to gain that which the canonical process had denied them.[43]

The decision by the papacy to resolve the schismatic episcopal elections was part of a more aggressive policy toward German affairs in general. Convinced of the validity of the doctrine of *plenitudo potestatis*, Innocent III was determined to influence the disputed throne question as well. Instead of a conclave under the leadership of the archbishop of Mainz, he envisioned one directed by his own personal representative who would ensure that the German princes unanimously recognize Otto IV as king; should they act contrary, the decision was to revert to the pope. According to Albert Hauck, the great scholar of the German church, the pontiff rarely

---

[41] The most detailed contemporary account of the schism at Mainz is found in the *Chron. Reinhardsbr.* 563-565; see also *Caesarii Dialogus* II 9; Hurter, *Innocenz III.* I 333, has assembled all that contemporaries had to say about Lupold. See also Georges Lacombe, *La vie et les oeuvres de Prévostin*, Bibliothèque thomiste 11 (Le Soulchoir, Belgium, 1927) 16-35.

[42] Cited in Bohmer-Will, *RAM* II xxx.

[43] See *Gesta Trev. cont. III* 391; Schwemer. *Innocent III.* 33-34.

ever planned a move more carefully.[44] Present at Rome in late 1200 was Guy Poré, a Frenchman by birth and the former abbot of Cîteaux, who had been sent in a commission to the Curia by England's erstwhile king, Richard I, to labor in behalf of the latter's nephew, Otto of Brunswick. Recognizing in this Cistercian monk an extraordinary talent, Innocent III elevated him to the cardinal-bishopric of Praeneste, one of the premier prelacies in the Roman church, and appointed him as a legate in matters pertaining to the Empire.[45]

The legate was given an ample supply of letters by the Curia, announcing his mission to the German prelates and princes and stating the powers which he was to enjoy. It was further proclaimed that Cardinal-bishop Guy was to be accompanied by the papal notary Philip and was to be supported in every possible way by Cardinal-legate Octavian, then laboring in France.[46] Already in Germany in advance of the legation was the acolyte Aegidius who had the responsibility of preparing the princes and prelates for the papal mission. Their task was to sense the feeling of the German princes and, if fairly certain that it would be well received, deliver to them a letter dated 1 March 1201, in which the papal position vis-a-vis the double election was clearly set forth: inasmuch as Innocent III had accepted Otto of Brunswick and had commanded it, they were simply to proclaim him king.[47] Avoiding southern Germany, the Staufen stronghold, Guy and Philip traveled by way of Montpellier to Troyes where on May 1201 they met Octavian and Aegidius, the latter of whom had probably just come from the Welf court. The result of this conference was that Octavian for the time being gave up plans for assisting in Germany, preferring instead to continue his negotiations with Philip Augustus, in the hope of winning the French court over to the Welf side.

Guy, Philip and Aegidius thus continued on to Liège, from where the cardinal-legate sent his two companions to Otto IV to obtain a renewal of the Welf's solemn promises of obedience to the Church, originally given at

---

[44] *KGD* IV 732.

[45] The mission of Guy Poré has been extensively treated by Winkelmann, *Phil. von Schw.* I 205-218; see also Hurter, *Innocenz III.* I 409-411, and Zimmermann, *Päpstl. Legationen* 32. Böhmer-Ficker, *Regg. Imp.* V/2, Nrs. 1515-1519, give the registers of extant documents pertaining to this legation. Contemporary references to it are found in the *Chron. Albrici* 418, and in *Caesarii Dialogus* VI 2; IX 51.

[46] See e.g., the letter issued between March and December 1200, empowering Guy to investigate the charges of crimes against Bishop-elect Hugh of Liège and to respond to the Curia by the second Sunday after Easter; Potthast, *Regesta* I, Nr. 1180. Cf. further the letter of 5 January 1201, announcing Guy to the German princes; Idem. Nrs. 1243-1245, printed in Migne, *PL* CCXVI, col. 1031. Letters of 1 March 1201 clarify the mission of the legate further for the German princes; cf. Potthast, *Regesta* I, Nrs. 1293, 1299.

[47] Potthast, *Regesta* I, Nr. 1293; Kempf, *NRI* Nr. 33.

the time of his election in June 1198. Only then would Guy be disposed to meet the throne contender personally and give him formal recognition as the sole legitimate German ruler. They accomplished that task in a mere three days, allowing Guy to meet Otto on 8 June at Aachen. Together they progressed to Cologne near the end of that same month.

The situation in Germany was hardly conducive to proclaiming a Welf victory, however. The party was without unity; its members even complained to the Curia about each other. Moreover, the Staufen faction refused to recognize the authority of the papal legates: its partisans rejected the pope's letters and would not admit his representatives into their cities. Thus, only a small number assembled in the Cologne cathedral on 3 July 1201 as Guy delivered to Otto IV and the princes the decree which Innocent III had drafted, recognizing the Welf candidate as king and commanding them to be obedient to him. Absent were all the Staufen supporters; even Archbishop-elect Siegfried of Mainz refused the summons to attend. Nevertheless, Guy proclaimed Otto king by the authority of his apostolic office, gave him the blessing, and pronounced the ban of excommunication against all who thereafter opposed him.[48]

Archbishop Ludolf of Magdeburg excused himself from the 3 July assembly at Cologne, claiming illness. In response to a second summons to attend a gathering of princes and prelates at Maastricht, he replied that the journey was too unsafe. The primary purpose of this second meeting was to repair a breach in the Ottonian party in Lorraine. There the declaration of 3 July was repeated and a marriage between Otto IV and the daughter of Duke Henry of Brabant was arranged.[49] It was here that a related matter was probably dealt with as well—the disputed election at Liège.

The solution presented some unique difficulties for the cardinal-legate. Bishop-elect Hugh of Liège had indeed responded to the papal command issued in December 1200 and had actually set out for Rome. His journey took him to Montpellier, but upon learning that the papal-legate was *en route* to northern Germany via the same city, he postponed his own departure for Rome and awaited Guy's arrival. The nature of their discussion is not known, but the results are very clear: instead of continuing on to the Curia, Hugh accompanied the cardinal northward again to Troyes, and thence to Liège where the latter awaited news from Otto IV. Once that primary reason for the legation had been discharged, the matter of the schism at Liège could be considered more fully.

---

[48] Böhmer-Ficker, *Regg. Imp.* V/2, Nr. 9971e.

[49] Ibid. V/ 2, Nr. 9975. See also Winkelmann, *Phil. von Schw.* I 221-222; Kohlmann, *EB Ludolf* 41.

The first issue was Hugh's failure to appear personally before the Roman Curia. Angered at this act of disobedience, Innocent III had suspended him and granted to his opponent, Henry of Jauche, the privilege of having one of his associates serve temporarily as the administrator of episcopal affairs in Liège. During their journey from Montpellier to Liège, however, Hugh had so ingratiated himself with the legate that in contradiction of the papal decree, Guy withdrew the administration of the *spiritualia* from Rudolf de Ponte and gave Hugh the certain assurance that the pope would confirm his election. A report of the entire handling of his legation was sent by the cardinal to Rome between 23 August and 30 September 1201, and although Innocent III was clearly upset with the legate's countermanding of his orders, and although Hugh's reputation was apparently not above reproach, the most important consideration was that the latter had supported Otto IV from the beginning.[50]   Thus, the pope accepted his representative's decision and the cause of Henry of Jauche was doomed.

Cardinal-legate Guy followed up the dismal showings at Cologne and Maastricht with yet a third summons to the prelates of Saxony.[51]   His primary target once more was Archbishop Ludolf of Magdeburg whom he tried to placate by agreeing to meet him halfway—at Corvey—on 23 August 1201. Again, however, the stubborn metropolitan failed to appear, and without him the legate's efforts to win the Saxon prelates over to Otto IV were quite futile. While the archbishop's political leanings undoubtedly made him unwilling to confront the legate in person, his absence could be excused by the almost simultaneous receipt of three new commissions which he sought to execute.

Foremost among them was the speedy resolution of a vacancy at Halberstadt. One individual upon whom the pronouncements of the legate at Cologne had made an especially profound impact was Bishop Gardulf of Halberstadt whose dual role as prince-bishop created within him a serious conflict of loyalties. Refusing to abandon Philip, he decided to go personally to Rome and to petition Innocent III either to withdraw from German internal affairs, or else to allow him to abdicate. Cardinal Guy gave him permission to do so, but while he was preparing to depart, Gardulf died on 21 August 1201. Although he seems to have stood alone among the bishops in his fear and concern at this time, showing that he awaited only ill from papal involvement in German matters, other contemporaries may also have shared that view: the continuator of the *Chronicon*

---

[50] Details of Guy's report are reflected in Innocent's letter written between October and 23 November 1201, in which he expressed displeasure with the Liège settlement; cf. Potthast, *Regesta* I, Nr. 1506; also Böhmer-Ficker, *Regg. Imp.* V/2, Nr. 9975.

[51] Kempf, *NRI* Nr. 73.

Halberstadensis maintained that Gardulf was brought down to his deathbed by his personal dilemma, destroyed by what the poet and political critic Walther von der Vogelweide called "the peril above all other perils."[52]

Because of a long-standing tradition, Archbishop Ludolf presided over the funeral and burial of Gardulf at the very time when the legate was expecting him at Corvey. He remained at Halberstadt long enough to influence the election of Conrad of Krosigk as bishop. The new prelate went at once to Halle where he received the regalia from Philip and was thereafter consecrated as a priest by the archbishop. Since Ludolf had apparently defied the legate's orders three times, and since the actions taken by him were in patent opposition to the cardinal's decrees made at Cologne on 3 July, Guy placed the Magdeburg metropolitan under the ban of excommunication. Archbishop Ludolf seemed totally unperturbed by the legatine actions taken against him. Before he even opened the letter containing the decision. he gathered his clergy together and appealed to Rome. He also continued to administer his office as if nothing had happened and remained loyal to Philip despite repeated threats. As Guy Porè shortly thereafter wrote to Innocent III, he had to admit that Otto IV was not so strong as those in Rome had supposed; neither were the German princes so subservient.[53]

While the Corvey assembly thus failed to accomplish its primary purpose with respect to Magdeburg, it nevertheless assured that another Saxon prelate was firmly within the Welf camp. In 1198 Conrad of Querfurt, the bishop of Hildesheim, accepted the postulation by the cathedral chapter of Würzburg to that wealthier see, yet without obtaining papal permission to do so. As the chancellor of King Philip, he became the target of both papal and Welf opposition. On 23 October 1198, an ardent supporter of the Welfs, Hartbert of Dalem, was elected by the Hildesheim chapter, but as late as 1 March 1201 he was still *electus*. During those two years the church of Hildesheim suffered untold damage as first the forces of Otto IV's brother, the Rhenish pfalzgrave Henry, and then those of Philip of Swabia overran its lands. Finally, Hartbert of Dalem received consecration at Corvey from Bishop Bernhard of Paderborn, acting under the direction of the cardinal-legate.[54]

During the months of adjudicating the schism at Liège and of attempting to win the Saxon bishops for Otto IV, Cardinal-legate Guy also turned his

---

[52] Bishop Gardulf's trial of loyalty, if not his faith, is described in detail in the *Gesta Halb.* 114-115. His views were shared by Caesarius of Heisterbach: ". . . *quod, magis, ut rei exitus probavit, imperii fuit divisio, quam confirmatio,*" cited in Winkelmann, *Phil. von Schw.* I 228.

[53] Winkelmann, *Phil. von Schw.* I 229-230.

[54] Kuhle, *Neubesetzung* 21.

attention to Mainz. The papacy had already shown its position vis-a-vis unapproved translations in the case of Conrad of Querfurt at Würzburg. It was a foregone conclusion that it would not alter its position with respect to Mainz. Lupold of Scheinfeld was unacceptable on other grounds as well, namely, that he was one of the most ardent supporters of the Staufen monarch whose dethroning Guy had been sent to effect. Innocent III had given the legate specific instructions in this matter—he was to determine whether Lupold, without being empowered by the pope to do so, had actually taken over the administration of the bishopric. If this be so, the cardinal was to reject him without delay.[55] Since knowledge of Lupold's investiture was not restricted to Germany, the outcome of the legatine inquiry and the consequences of the election at Mainz could be no surprise.

Following canonical procedures, Guy summoned both contenders to Bingen (in August 1201, prior to the Corvey assembly), to which spot Lupold refused to come since it lay within Siegfried of Eppstein's control. The inquest proceeded nonetheless, and upon learning that Lupold had indeed assumed administration of the temporalities of Mainz, Guy declared his election null and void. From the standpoint of canon law, Siegfried should have been treated in a similar fashion, since he had also forcibly assumed administration and had allowed himself to be invested with regalian rights by Otto IV without papal approval.

For the legate, however, it made a great difference whether investiture had been done by Philip or by Otto IV. The real reason that Siegfried II of Eppstein received confirmation of his election (before 26 September 1201) and permission to administer his archbishopric was because he supported the papal candidate in the throne controversy. Winkelmann contends that Siegfried had no better right to the office than did Lupold, yet he somewhat cynically notes that such an argument could have been constructed by the canonists in the Curia. Schwemer, on the other hand, claims that the argument was in fact formulated. Using a decree of Lateran III as the basis, Innocent III had devised a position which supported the rejection of Lupold and made the election of Siegfried the only one to be considered: the canons who had elected a *persona inhibita*—in this case an already-sitting bishop—by this very act lost their electoral rights; accordingly, only those three who voted for Siegfried—even though they were far short of the *maior et sanior pars*—had the legitimate voice.[56]

On 30 September 1201 Siegfried received consecration as a priest and then as bishop at Xanten under the hands of the legate.[57] His opponent

---

[55] Winkelmann, *Phil. von Schw.* I 223-224; Schwemer, *Innocent III.* 39-40.
[56] Schwemer, *Innocent III.* 46.
[57] *Ann. S. Ger. Colon.* 303 (ed. *Scr. rer. Germ.*).

was later banned because he refused to accept the decision reached at
Bingen. Thus, even though many of the legate's efforts to win support for
Otto IV had failed, he had, in his few months in Germany, managed to
resolve two important episcopal disputes in favor of the Welf faction. To
what extent they would remain so, however, could not have been foreseen.

In the nearby bishopric of Worms, the state of the church was clearly
affected by the Mainz schism. Since Bishop Lupold was not interested in
fulfilling his pastoral role, it fell to the indefatigable legate Guy to deal with
lapses in clerical discipline. We have no exact record of his activities, but
in November 1201 pope Innocent III directed the canons of that church to
receive humbly and to seek to observe inviolably the precepts which Guy
had established for them.[58] This letter presumably postdates Guy's visit
to Worms and was undoubtedly precipitated by reports that the clergy of
that diocese were unresponsive to the legate's decrees. While some of those
regulations may well have been directed at specific abuses unique to
Worms, it can be assumed that most were similar in tone and content to
those published a few months later for the clergy at Liège.

Some German prelates clearly failed to discharge their pastoral
responsibilities during the throne controversy, but there is evidence that
others made at least some effort to control their churches. In 1201
Archbishop Hartwig of Bremen convened a provincial synod, the specifics
of which are discussed in Ch. One, above.[59] Whatever reforming efforts
it may have proposed will have been negated by the capture of the
archbishop by Otto IV in early January 1202 and by the on-going struggle
for political advantage in northern Germany. It is significant that there are
no other synods recorded at Bremen during the next dozen years before
Lateran IV, the reasons for which will be discussed below. Other bishops
were prevented by both the general disorder and by the contumacy of their
clergy from making full use of synodal assemblies. For example, within a
short time of his accession, Archbishop Eberhard II of Salzburg secured
from pope Innocent III a bull which commanded all his suffragan bishops
to attend the yearly synods.[60] The implication is that Eberhard had been
previously unsuccessful in compelling such attendance and had at length
turned to the papacy for reinforcement of his metropolitan rights. When,
in fact, the archbishop convened synods during the next fourteen years,
support for them was minimal at best.[61]

[58] Theiner, *Vetera* II 61, Nrs. 209, 210; Potthast, *Regesta* I, Nrs. 1535, 1536.
[59] May, *REB* Nr. 688; Lappenberg, *Hamb. UB* I, Nr. 329; *Mecklenburg UB* I, Nr. 170;
see also above, Ch. One, p. 76.
[60] Potthast, *Regesta* I, Nr. 1251; von Meiller, *RAS* Nr. 8; Muchar, *Steiermark* V 34-35,
42-45.
[61] See Ch. One, pp. 31-32.

The success which Cardinal-legate Guy experienced in 1201 was not lost on other bishops and princes of Germany in the immediately following months. In early January 1202 (as noted above) Archbishop Hartwig of Bremen's resistance was broken as the result of his capture by Otto IV himself. Archbishop Ludolf of Magdeburg, who rejected all efforts by the legate in 1201 and early 1202 to reach an accommodation, refusing to meet with Guy under any circumstances, had also capitulated by the end of the latter year. By whom or where he received absolution is not known, but he even promised obedience to Rome in matters pertaining to the Empire, at least to the extent that he interpreted that position.[62] On the Lower Rhine, the last episcopal opponent of Otto, Bishop Dietrich of Utrecht, was also won over. More significant was the fact that in northern Saxony Bishop Conrad of Halberstadt found it necessary to soften his opposition.

Although he had acquiesced in the election of the pro-Staufen Conrad of Krosigk, Cardinal Guy was incensed by the fact that the bishop-elect of Halberstadt was invested by Philip and consecrated by the archbishop of Magdeburg 1 January 1202 (i.e., at a time when Ludolf stood under the ban). A peaceful man by nature, Conrad was summoned to Cologne by the legate, and upon his refusal to do so was summarily excommunicated. Conrad countered by taking up the cross on 7 April 1202 and departing for the Holy Land on 1 May. His journey took him to Zara and eventually to Constantinople where he witnessed the overthrow of the Greek monarchy by the Latin forces. Following the fulfillment of his vow in Palestine, he served briefly as bishop of Acre and then began his return home by way of Rome. While Conrad may thus have resolved his own personal dilemma for several years, his refusal to abandon the Staufen camp aroused antagonism among neighboring princes. He left the administration of his see to fellow prelates during his absence, but they were unable to carry out that trust effectively. Members of the Welf party broke into the bishopric shortly after his departure and spread havoc and suffering among its inhabitants.[63]

Even more important than the quelling of episcopal opposition in Saxony was the fact that Archbishop Adolf of Cologne, despite earlier rumors, remained steadfast—in part due to a papal admonition sent in the spring of 1202.[64] On 10 April 1202 Legate Guy summoned Bishop-elect Hugh of Liège to Cologne where the latter cleared himself of all charges of unsuitability by means of an oath of purification, aided by six ecclesiastical

[62] Hauck, *KGD* IV 737.

[63] Winkelmann, *Phil. von Schw.* I 248; for further on Conrad of Krosigk, see Pixton, "Anwerbung" 167-178.

[64] Migne, *PL* CCXVI, col. 1073; Potthast, *Regesta* I, Nr. 1658; Kempf, *NRI* Nr. 63.

compurgators; with this final obstacle removed, Hugh was confirmed by the legate and on Sunday, 21 April 1202, consecrated at Cologne. Shortly thereafter, the new prelate was personally conducted by the cardinal-bishop of Praeneste into Liège and formally installed on his throne. Despite the reluctance by Archdeacon Rudolf and other partisans of Henry of Jauche to accept the outcome, opposition to the new bishop generally subsided and in 1204 Henry was compensated with several substantial prebends. To further conciliate the Henrican faction, the Curia also honored a request from the legate that the considerable expenses incurred by their candidate in Rome be dismissed without payment.[65]

Two years of intense political maneuvering within the bishopric of Liège had exacerbated conditions among the clergy of that see, and the correction of such may have been on the agenda of the synod which Bishop Hugh convened at Pentecost 1202, just a few weeks after his entry into Liège.[66] It was presumably at the invitation of the bishop that Cardinal-legate Guy issued reform statutes for the church at Liège a year later.[67] The problems and abuses mentioned were specific to this church, but they must also have reflected ecclesiastical conditions in much of Germany at this time. The *vita communis*, which was ordained in the Rule of Bishop Chrodegang of Metz in 763 and reconfirmed in the statutes of the Council of Aachen in 816, had begun to loosen at Liège during the second half of the eleventh century. By ca. 1100, cathedral canons enjoyed personal servants and individual households. The several episcopal schisms of the twelfth century further weakened the corporate nature of the cathedral chapter: although the documents refer to the daily use of the refectory in the latter part of the century, this practice can only have applied to a portion of the chapter. The burning and destruction of the cathedral in 1185 must have completed the ruination of the *vita communis*. The institution of archdeacons also worked against its success: as representatives of the clerical estate, they quickly created a life-style which ran counter to the Aachen Rule. Thus, in 1203 Cardinal-legate Guy commanded the cathedral canons at Liège to cease sleeping outside the chapter dormitory without permission of the dean;

---

[65] *Reineri Ann.* 656-657; Winkelmann, *Phil. von Schw.* I 223; Kuhle, *Neubesetzung* 24.

[66] *Reineri Ann.* (a. 1202) 656: *"Episcopus ordines sollempnes in pentechoste fecit, et synodum celebravit."*

[67] Martène, *Collectio* 24; Binterin, *Concilien* IV 453-458; and Bormans, *Cartulaire* I 132, Nr. 84 (who places the document after October 1203): *"Cum ex officio legationis nobis iniuncte in ecclesiis infra legationem nostram constitutis que invenerimus resecanda resecare et plantanda plantare teneamur, ad Leodiensem ecclesiam accedentes ibi quedam vidimus et audivimus que digna emendatione videbantur. Unde habito consilio venerabilis fratris H. episcopi Leodiensis et eiusdem ecclesie capituli et aliorum prudentium, sic de dicta ecclesia dignum duximus ordinare, ea que bene et competenter in ea statuta invenimus approbantes."*

henceforth only those with a special reason could obtain permission from the dean to be absent for a period of up to three weeks. Longer absences had to be approved by the cathedral chapter itself.

The cardinal-legate furthermore ordained that six prebends were to be reserved for persons with the priestly consecration who were also to observe the residence requirement strictly and themselves celebrate the Mass, suggesting that, similar to upper clergy elsewhere, the canons at Liège were increasingly reluctant to accept the higher grades of consecration and the obligations incumbent upon them. Until 1213 the documents make use of the canons' forenames only, while appending the office and occasionally the grade of consecration. Thereafter, family names appear, indicating that great emphasis was now being placed on noble descent: a document dated 1178 was attested by twenty-three of the cathedral chapter's fifty-nine members, all of whom are listed according to the degree of consecration—nine *presbyteri*, three *diaconi*, and eleven *subdiaconi*. Henceforth, the sacramental nature of the canons retreats behind the administrative titles. It is to be assumed that the cathedral dean held the priestly consecration, but the same did not always hold true for the other eight archdeacons. In 1200 only six *presbyteri* can be positively identified: since two of them were archdeacons whose duties often took them away from the cathedral church, the acute shortage of priests implied in the legatine decrees becomes quite obvious.

In a modest attempt to curtail pluralism, the scholastic was prohibited from occupying the office of cantor as well, and vice versa. The cardinal-legate also directed the cathedral dean to be satisfied with his dignity alone, and not to seek after other offices as well, a decree clearly aimed at maintaining discipline at a higher level. The specific circumstances which prompted this are somewhat vague: attached to the cathedral chapter of Saint Lambert were several *canonici minores*, who had originally resided at the church of Notre-Dame-aux-fonts at Liège; although not a collegiate church, but parochial, Notre-Dame-aux-fonts had stood under an abbot appointed by the bishop. As a result of great abuses, Dean Walther of Liège, as abbot, had reformed this church in 1200, creating ten prebends out of the existing properties and incomes. In agreement with Bishop Hugh and the papal-legate, he also transferred the ten canons at Notre-Dame to St. Lambert where they became known as the *canonici sancti Materni*. Since Walther of Ravenstein still appears as *abbas s. Marie* in a document of December 1203, it is obvious that the legatine restriction against him had nothing to do with that office. He also is addressed as such until his death in 1209. Walther also appears for the first time as an archdeacon in December 1203, leaving open the question of whether his pursuit of this office prompted the decree.[68]

There were also the usual prohibitions against usury, maintaining concubines, and improper tonsure. Thus, for Liège at least, the long process of effecting reform within the ranks of the clergy was given added impetus by the presence and action of a mighty papal legate, exercising those full powers with which Innocent III had invested him. But even this was insufficient to be of any lasting consequence. In 1204 Bishop Hugh presided over a synod of his clergy and prominent laymen, the record of which speaks of the resolution of a dispute between the monastery of Alne and one Hugh of Florennes concerning the use of some common pasturage. It may also have been at this same assembly that, in contravention of the legatine statutes proclaimed one year earlier, the cathedral canons at Liège divided chapter property into prebends.[69] Even more remarkable is that at some time between this synod and 1207, Guy of Poré confirmed this action. The reversal of the legate's policy has been seen as a move designed to see that his political aims were not thwarted; thus, ecclesiastical reform was sacrificed to temporal expediencies.[70]

Nor was continued resistance to reform the only problem with which the bishop of Liège was confronted. In 1203 he had learned that heretics, and more particularly Waldenses, had been discovered in his city. To combat them he ordered that all French and German Scriptures be confiscated throughout his diocese.[71] Years of abuse by an undisciplined clergy and the neglect of pastoral responsibilities by predecessors for whom such matters were clearly secondary had thus created a major trouble spot within the province of Cologne.

---

[68] Cf. Görres, *Lütticher DK* 9-25; Bormans, *Cartulaire* I, Nrs. 85, 88, 89, 100, 101.

[69] *Reineri Ann.* 657: "*Domnus Hugo episcopus et domnus Heinricus de Iacia post multas dissentiones in concordiam redeunt. Domnus Heinricus a debitus suis . . . absolvitur, et ei cum tribus praebendis archidiaconatus Brabantiae donatur, pacificatis secum omnibus sotiis suis tam clericis quam laicis. Canonici Sancti Lamberti possessiones ecclesiae, mediante cardinali et episcopo assentiente, inter se dividunt, et praepositum destituunt.*"

[70] Bormans, *Cartulaire* I, Nr. 95; Görres, *Lütticher DK* 10-11; Schwemer, *Innocent III.* 97-100. Hurter, *Innocenz III.* 354, note 117, incorrectly claims that Guy reunited the cathedral canons with his ordinances. The establishment of prebends and the creation of a *capitulum clausum* proves just the opposite. The absence of the canons at Liège became more acute with the passage of time. Papal decrees which demanded that incomes of the guilty be restricted, even withdrawn, were of no lasting value. Neither was the practice of enhancing those who did attend with so-called "presence monies." In 1250 the lack of those with higher degrees led to a calamity: the papal-legate Peter of Albano complained that the number of subdeacons and deacons was so low "*quod non possit ad maius altare per canonicos deserviri.*" He therefore ordained that six members of the cathedral chapter be consecrated to the grade of subdeacon and deacon in his presence.

[71] Fredericq, *Corpus doc. inq.* I 63, Nr. 63.

Engelbert of Berg and the Provostship of Cologne

While the impact of the legate at this time upon the church of Liège was apparently negligible, his presence in Cologne for an extended period of time during 1201-1202 did give him an opportunity to affect church life within that archdiocese beyond the regulation of the political situation. Since 1199 there had been a disputed succession to the provostship of the cathedral chapter, the second most powerful office in the church. Upon the death of Provost Ludwig on 6 May, two rival candidates sought the position: the first was Engelbert of Berg, the fifteen-year-old cathedral canon, provost of St. George of Cologne, and cousin to Archbishop Adolf of Altena; opposing him was one of the *priores* of Cologne who did not belong to the cathedral chapter, Dietrich of Hengebach, provost of the church of the Holy Apostles, already a man of mature years, pious, virtuous and learned.[72] Dietrich received fourteen votes from the older and more prominent cathedral canons, while Engelbert garnered twenty-four, mostly from the younger *capitulares*.

Neither candidate complied entirely with the requirements of canon law. Dietrich was not a member of the cathedral chapter, and only in those cases where a suitable candidate could not be found *de gremio capituli* was an outsider to be chosen. Engelbert was too young and had received no more than the consecration of minor orders at the time of the election; furthermore, since the office of provost also included that of archdeacon, he failed to meet the requirement of Lateran III which set the age for such dignities at twenty-five. Nevertheless, both parties appealed to Rome for a decision. On 3 November 1199 Innocent III commissioned the abbots of Laach, Himmerode and Heisterbach to investigate; if they found the parties ready to accept a decision, they were to render it and conclude the dispute.[73] Engelbert was reluctant to accept such a resolution, however. Thus, the issue was transferred to Rome where it was to be decided on 29 September 1200. Believing it to be in his best interests to accelerate the

---

[72] Unless otherwise stated, the general narrative of these events follows Ficker, *Engelbert der Heilige* 30-34. Until 1297 the archiepiscopal election in Cologne was the province of the cathedral chapter and the high dignitaries, or *priores*, of the archdiocese. This latter group was comprised of the provost and a few privileged deans of the collegiate chapters, plus a few prominent abbots. The usual order of pre-eminence among the *priores* was: the cathedral provost, the cathedral dean, and thereafter the provosts of St. Gereon, St. Severin, St. Cunibert, St. Andreas, the Holy Apostles, St. Maria *ad gradus*, and St. George; cf. Ficker, *op.cit.* 12-13, and Hansheinz Harzem, "Die 'Prioren' im mittelalterlichen Köln," (Dissertation Cologne, 1949) 12.

[73] Potthast, *Regesta* I, Nr. 857.

decision, Dietrich of Hengebach then persuaded the judges to move the date up to 13 May of that same year.

To present his case before the Curia, Dietrich sent a representative, but Engelbert went personally. Unfortunately for him, he was captured *en route* by Count William of Jülich with whom the church of St. George was in conflict. It was thus necessary for the papacy to set a new date for 25 March 1201. When neither Engelbert nor a representative appeared for this second hearing, the candidate was fined; nevertheless, Innocent III still was reluctant to decide the issue without letting each side present its case. He therefore commissioned the provosts of St. Gereon (Dietrich) and St. Severin (Hermann) at Cologne, and Dean Christian of Bonn to handle the resolution of the dispute in Germany.

Engelbert of Berg was still not satisfied: he rejected the commission, claiming that one of its members was related to his opponent, and once more appealed directly to Rome. The commission was undaunted, however, and declared Dietrich of Hengebach to be the lawful provost of Cologne. In the face of such opposition, Engelbert went personally to Rome once more where he obtained an audience with the pontiff. Since Archbishop Adolf's (Engelbert's cousin) relationship with Otto IV had begun to sag, Innocent was at pains to avoid a breach altogether. Fearing that such would occur should he now confirm the decision of his commission relative to the disputed provostship of Cologne, he dictated a new letter on 23 January 1202 to his legate in Germany, Guy Poré, instructing him to preside over yet another tribunal called to decide this now-thorny issue.[74]

It never got to that point, however. By early 1202 the clergy and people of the Cologne archdiocese had also become partisan, and when Engelbert returned to the archiepiscopal city from Rome at Pentecost (2 June), a tumult erupted. The papal-legate, then in Cologne, was unable to discharge his mandate; instead, he transferred the matter once more to Rome, obviously having all he could cope with in the schismatic episcopal elections of Liège and Mainz. Engelbert thus journeyed yet a third time to Rome, as did a representative of Dietrich of Hengebach, but after hearing both sides and counseling with the members of the Curia, Innocent declared both elections void. On 9 April 1203 he commissioned Guy of Praeneste and the abbots of Kappenberg and Scheda to direct the cathedral chapter to proceed with a new election. If the canons failed to do so within one month, the commission was empowered to select a cathedral provost themselves.[75] Having thus played politics with this office for almost four years, the papacy set up an election which assured Engelbert's success.

---

[74] Potthast, *Regesta* I, Nr. 1581; printed in Ficker, *Engelbert der Heilige* 301.
[75] Potthast, *Regesta* I, Nr. 1877.

Enjoying the majority of support within the cathedral chapter, he was undoubtedly elected by the canons without further opposition and appears as provost that same year. In so resolving the matter, the papacy avoided estranging Archbishop Adolf of Cologne at a time when his support for Otto IV was most urgently needed. As was true with Liège and Mainz, the canonical merits of the candidates were less important than the political advantage which one presented over the other.

While Adolf of Cologne was a necessary component in the papal coalition, there is no evidence that the Curia concerned itself that the man lacked any pastoral tendencies. Neither he nor his successors to 1215 made any apparent attempt at ecclesiastical reform, being too caught up in purely political considerations to worry about non-temporal matters within their church. The central place of the Cologne church in the German throne controversy made political survival the greatest imperative. Thus, it was the papal-legate, rather than the prelates, who may have had the greatest religious impact upon the archdiocese during this period. According to Caesarius of Heisterbach, Cardinal Guy attempted to enhance the liturgical aspects of services in the cathedral by means of various new additions.[76]

Prepositinus of Cremona—Scholastic at Mainz

With a papally appointed bishop virtually secure on the throne of Liège and the archbishopric of Cologne deeply indebted to Rome, the cardinal-legate turned once more to the Mainz dispute. Despite papal pronouncements of the previous year (1201) favoring Archbishop-elect Siegfried of Eppstein, the majority of the Mainz clergy held on to Bishop Lupold of Worms, and the burghers swore that they would never accept Siegfried as their head. In their fervor to reject the latter, they failed to consider that Lupold of Worms was totally unworthy of their support. It must have been an especially grievous thing in Rome that among the staunchest opponents to Siegfried was the esteemed scholastic at Mainz, Prepositinus of Cremona. The man enjoyed a wide reputation as a scholar and authority on canon law. It could not have been a matter of indifference to him that he represented the side which the Curia had declared invalid. Prepositinus had been the head of the delegation which Lupold established at the outset of the

---

[76] *Caesarii Dialogus* IX 51: *"Tempore schismatis inter Philippum et Ottonem, dominus Wido Cardinalis, aliquando Abbas Cisterciensis, cum missus fuisset Coloniam ad confirmandam Ottonis, bonam illic consuetudinem instituit. Praecepit enim ut ad elevationem hostiae omnis populus in ecclesia ad sonitum nolae veniam peteret, sicque usque as calicis benedictionem prostratus iaceret. Praecepit etiam ut quotiens corpus Domini deferendum esset ad infirmum, scholaris sive campanarius sacerdotem praecedens, per nolam illud proderet; sicque omnis populus tam in stratis quam in domibus Christum adoraret."*

dispute to justify his election in Rome, and he remained loyal throughout the years of controversy. He was notably vocal in his opposition to the decision which the pope had made in favor of Siegfried.[77]

In the ranks of the opposition the renewed cry went out that Innocent III was bent on destroying the Empire. In order to diminish the power of the papal decrees, false reports were circulated which were meant to confuse the Welf party and to reveal the pope as uncertain in his decisions. Among the most spectacular was a series of forged letters which were passed off as papal bulls. Even though there had been a consistent policy of support for Siegfried by the Curia and the legate since 1200, the letters which appeared in Germany in early 1202 had a totally different tone. Despite the presence of the legate, they gave powers to the bishops of Passau, Freising and Eichstätt (all of whom tenaciously supported Philip of Swabia) to deal with the Mainz controversy as judges-delegate. As unlikely as it would have been for Innocent III to countermand his own representative's actions and to name members of the imperial party to pass judgment over such a vital issue, the resolution of which was of the greatest moment for the German throne controversy, the bishops accepted the appointment as though they believed in the reality of the powers, and on the basis of such summoned Siegfried and Lupold to appear before them. Siegfried sent a copy of the summons to the pope who responded on 24 September 1202, denouncing the letters as forgeries and accusing the three bishops with failure to examine the content or form of the powers granted in them. There was little doubt that the pontiff was totally satisfied with the conduct of his legate as expressed in a letter to the archbishop of Cologne dated 5 April 1202.[78] He even augmented Guy's actions by demanding that a new election be held at Worms if Lupold continued in his disobedience. The pope also struck down the protest from Lupold's supporters in the Mainz cathedral chapter concerning the intrusion of the legate, and he declared blasphemous their claim that Guy had accepted a bribe, since it was directed against one of the pope's own representatives. Then, in a spirit of harsh rebuke, Innocent declared that if Guy, or the pope himself, should do something improper, the Mainz canons were nonetheless obligated to remain humble and submissive so as to protect the Church, rather than revealing it openly, which act would be to their own discredit.

---

[77] Innocent III makes mention of this opposition in the letter which confirmed the grant of the scholastery to another; see Potthast, *Regesta* I, Nr. 2044, Migne, *PL* CCXV, col. 205, and Würdtwein, *Nova subs*. II 100. For further discussion, see Schwemer, *Innocent III*. 47-48.

[78] See Winkelmann, *Phil. von Schw*. I 225-227 for the general narrative of events; Potthast, *Regesta* I, Nrs. 1731, 1658.

The dissidents also sent letters allegedly written by the cardinals expressing discontent with the pope as well. These letters caused Innocent to write a retort on 5 April 1203. The strength and resolve of the opposition shows as well in an encyclical which Innocent III wrote near the end of 1203, stating that his enemies had used an illness as an excuse to spread the rumor that he had died and that a successor had already been chosen.[79] On 3 October 1202 the pontiff also wrote that he had heard that the bishop of Speyer, disobedient and rebellious to his commands, had sought to hinder them by seizing two nuncios who were carrying out papal instructions: one was allegedly put in prison and was even threatened with hanging.[80]

Siegfried of Eppstein was not deceived, neither was he deterred, by these forged letters. On 21 March 1202, having obviously ignored the summons from the three Staufen bishops, he received the pallium personally in Rome at the hands of the pope. Many other contemporaries may have shared the view of the chronicler Burchard of Ursperg who commented that "in this matter the pope did not pronounce judgment, but committed an injustice." Even though there was not much that could be said against the rejection of Lupold, the installation of Siegfried in their eyes made a mockery of all canonical precepts. It did not escape the comprehension of contemporaries that the issue was never one of suitability for the office—in which case Siegfried was clearly better qualified than the brutal Lupold of Worms—but merely that of loyalty to Otto IV who was the papal candidate for the German throne. Whoever refused to recognize the Welf was not only rebelling against the legitimate king, but also committing a crime against the authority of the pope.[81]

Simultaneous with the papal investment of Siegfried was the pronouncement of the ban of excommunication against Lupold of Worms. The continued support of this reprobate bishop by King Philip prevented the return of peace to Mainz, however.[82] So long as Philip sustained Lupold, the latter would claim the allegiance of a sizeable number of the Mainz clergy, nobles, burghers and *ministeriales*. As late as 20-21 April 1204 the Roman pontiff was issuing sharp rebukes to the canons and *ministeriales* on

---

[79] Kempf, *NRI* Nr. 96.

[80] Potthast, *Regesta* I, Nr. 1738; Migne, *PL* CCXVI, col. 1078.

[81] Potthast, *Regesta* I, Nr. 1643; Winkelmann, *Phil. von Schw.* I 226-227, citing *Chron. Ursperg.* 368: "... *nam domnus papa, multis volens uti rationibus, cassata, electione omnium de Liupoldo, factam electionem, quae nullo iure subsistere poterat, confirmavit, sicut exprimit in sua decretali, quae sic incipit: 'Bonae memoriae'. . .*"

[82] Migne, *PL* CCXIV, col, 964; Potthast, *Regesta* I, Nr. 1647. On 27 October 1203 Innocent III gave a commission to Abbots Peter of Neubourg and Eberhard of Salem, instructing them to use every means possible to dissuade Philip from continuing his support for Lupold as archbishop of Mainz; cf. Potthast, *Regesta* I, Nr. 2007.

account of their rebellion against their legitimate prelate (Siegfried) and against the Roman Church.[83] Not for several more years, however, did Siegfried manage to assert control over his church with any degree of success.

The schism at Mainz undoubtedly exacerbated already serious problems of discipline among the clergy of the city, archdiocese and province. An anonymous critic complained that the cathedral canons loved to hunt more than to pray, to feed their dogs more than poor people, and to give themselves over totally to amusements.[84] That they concerned themselves with worldly matters is also suggested by the difficulty which the cathedral scholastic had in 1191 wrestling from them control over the incomes of their young relatives attending the school at Mainz: the canons had wanted the right to allocate the resources, giving out just enough to provide the for the necessities, while retaining for themselves whatever portion of the pupils' stipends was deemed surplus.[85]

These indications of considerable laxity among the clergy at Mainz about the time of the double election in 1200 help explain why a man such as Lupold of Scheinfeld would be acceptable to so many of the canons. In fact, the support which the vast majority of the Mainz *capitulares* gave to the bishop of Worms is an unhappy commentary on the degree of spiritual commitment in that church. This lack of discipline would present a serious challenge to any archbishop who might attempt to correct them, and the apparent victory of Siegfried II of Eppstein in 1202 in the political arena nevertheless left him with the ecclesiastical problems which prevailed there at that time. Such problems were not unknown to the Curia, for on 9 April 1203 Innocent III admonished Siegfried to devote himself diligently to his pastoral office, and in April 1204 he again wrote concerning the rebellion and obstinacy in the church of Mainz which refused to accept Siegfried as its head.[86] Continued disorder caused by the schism prevented his acting immediately upon that command, and not until early 1209 was Siegfried able to take positive steps to reform his clergy.

As noted above, one of those most opposed to Siegfried had been the cathedral scholastic, Prepositinus of Cremona, but by the time of the papal

---

[83] Migne, *PL* CCXV, cols. 336, 338; see also Potthast, *Regesta* I, Nrs. 2188, 2192.

[84] Martène, *Thes. nov.*, I, cols. 323-327, under the heading "*Epistola Anonymi ad clericos Moguntinenses,*" and dated "*circiter 1110.*" Binterim, *Concilien* III 334, places the letter in the year 1204, noting the strong resemblance of this description to that given by Caesarius of Heisterbach for Cologne.

[85] See Biskamp, *Mainzer DK* 31-38; Falck, *Mainz im Mittelalter* II 166.

[86] Migne, *PL* CCXV, col. 45; Potthast, *Regesta* I, Nr. 1880; Migne, *PL* CCXV, col. 336; Potthast, *Regesta* I, Nr. 2188. See also Binterim, *Concilien* III 338, citing Raynaldi, *Annales* I, Nr. 51.

letter of April 1204 he was no longer at Mainz. A letter of 12 December 1203 contains papal confirmation of *magister* Symeon, a clerk of Cardinal-legate Guy, as head of the cathedral school.[87] Having grown weary of the endless conflict in Germany, Prepositinus appears to have relinquished his office at the Mainz cathedral in favor of a position on the faculty of theology at Paris. The tragedy for Germany is that this significant intellect was removed from its schools at a most critical time. One can only speculate what impact he might have had, had he remained and trained a generation of scholars at Mainz. On the other hand, his contribution to the learned tradition of medieval Christendom may have been far less without the added stimulus to his mind by the Paris schools. From 1206-1210 he was chancellor of the university of Paris, perhaps the supreme achievement for a scholar in his day.[88]

Growing Support for the Welf Candidate

Meanwhile, during the early summer of 1202 further changes occurred which augured well for an eventual Welf victory. In the south German see of Augsburg Bishop Udalschalk died on 1 June and the cathedral chapter at once elected one of its members, the canon Hartwig, as a successor. Hartwig was not without canonical defects, however, since he reputedly was the son of a minor cleric and a novice nun. Canon law prohibited consecration in such cases, so Innocent III declared the election invalid. Due to the humble petitions of the cathedral chapter, the pressures of the times, and the usefulness of the candidate, however, the pontiff at length agreed to allow him to administer the bishopric until a full investigation could be made. A commission was given to the archbishop of Mainz (Siegfried of Eppstein), Bishop Conrad of Würzburg and Abbot Eberhard of Salem.[89] Since, however, the abbot was unable to respond to the appointment and the bishop was killed shortly thereafter, Archbishop

---

[87] Würdtwein, *Nova subs.* II 100; Migne, *PL* CCXV, col. 205; Potthast, *Regesta* I, Nr. 2044; Böhmer-Ficker, *Regg. Imp*. V/2 3, Nrs. 58, 65, 9986. Baier, *Päpstl. Provisionen* 63, concludes from this that *magister* Symeon was a cleric from Langres.

[88] For a detailed study of his life and works, see Lacombe, *Prévostin* vii-viii, 6-46; Idem, "Prepositinus Cancellarius Parisiensis," *The New Scholasticism* 1 (1927) 307-319. Lacombe notes (*Prévostin* vii) that Prepositinus shares with William of Auxerre the sole distinction among his contemporaries of being cited numerous times by both Aquinas and Albertus Magnus. His works were found in most major libraries in the thirteenth century and were copied until well into the fifteenth.

[89] Potthast, *Regesta* I, Nr. 1750. Conditions at Augsburg are discussed in detail in Winkelmann, *Phil. von Schw.* I 302; see also Zoepfl, *Bistum Augsburg* 156.

Siegfried alone, in the presence of the Cardinal-legate Guy, made the inquiry.

The conclusion was that Hartwig was entitled to the pope's grace; he was in fact a highly qualified person, yet capable of duplicity nonetheless. The legate and the archbishop had assured that pope that "he is a son of obedience and is prepared to obey the commands of the Church,"[90] resulting in the papal confirmation of the election on 31 October 1203. Despite that, Hartwig was still *electus* on 24 August 1204, having received consecration neither as bishop nor as a priest, probably because he feared to obtain it from Siegfried on account of Philip, or from Lupold (of Worms) because of Innocent III.[91]

The fact that Hartwig was not a *presbyter* at the time of the election is symptomatic of a shift in attitudes in the Augsburg diocese within the preceding few decades. In documents of the twelfth century which were attested by cathedral canons, the grade of consecration for almost every individual is given. From about 1200, however, the family name replaced it. Therein is mirrored the fact that, as in Liège as well, the liturgical duty no longer stood in the forefront of the chapter's interests. Entry into the chapter was due largely to other considerations, primarily that of enjoying the prebends. It also suggests that the chapter regarded it as important to have prominent personalities—names of good repute and prestige—in its midst.[92]

The fall of 1202 brought a serious dispute between Otto IV and Archbishop Adolf of Cologne which threatened to upset the papal-Welf coalition and caused grave concern in the Curia. Mention was made above of the sensitive negotiations carried on at the time relative to the provostship of Cologne. Though the reasons for the dispute are unclear, papal-legate Guy restored peace and preserved the alliance. At the same time he took decisive action against some recalcitrant west German bishops: Matthew of Toul was subjected to a disciplinary investigation by Cardinal-legate Guy and two Cistercian abbots from the diocese of Verdun; and Bishop Bertram of Metz, who was almost blind, was reprimanded for failing to accept

---

[90] The legatine report is referred to in the papal letter of confirmation: Migne, *PL* CCXV, col. 171; Potthast, *Regesta* I, Nr. 2008. The letter of 5 November 1203 is in Potthast, *Regesta* I, Nr. 2014.

[91] Winkelmann, *Phil. von Schw.* I 302.

[92] Leuze, *Augsburger DK* 6-9, 23-26, 39. Already in the mid-twelfth century there had been complaints about the high rate of absenteeism among the canons. Vicars are first referred to at Augsburg in 1220, and in 1246 they are called *socii chori*. Further complaints concerning canons who did not observe the residence obligation resume in 1250, but these seem to have been directed primarily against those who had been provided with a prebend by the pope or his legates.

assistance and was assigned a coadjutor by the legate as well.[93]   More important was the treatment of the vacillating Archbishop John of Trier.

On 11 October 1202 King Philip had concluded an agreement with the *ministeriales* of Trier and had placed the burghers of the metropolitan city under his protection. The clergy and laymen of the archdiocese vowed in return never to elect anyone as archbishop who was unfriendly to the Staufen dynasty.[94] The other horn of the dilemma emerged just days later when the cardinal-legate apparently proclaimed the archbishop's excommunication for failure to declare his unqualified support for Otto IV.[95] Sensing the peril of his position, John wrote a letter to the pope, asking for permission to abdicate. While this act is generally viewed as that of a weak and confused individual, it may well have been intended as a measure aimed at preventing the pontiff from confirming the legate's sentence against him.

Meanwhile, Innocent III had received news of Philip's alliance with Trier and had written a very sharp reprimand on 8 November 1202, threatening the prelate once more with excommunication if he failed to declare openly his support for Otto IV. When John's own letter arrived in Rome, the papal fury broke loose in full strength. On 16 November Innocent again drafted a letter to his legate Guy, rejecting John's offer to abdicate since that might lead to a new schism at Trier or to the election of a Staufen partisan, or even to a more vigorous and determined man.[96] The cardinal was directed to accept the abdication only if the proper man could be found to fill the vacancy, but since the chances of this were very slight in the pro-Staufen church of Trier, John had to remain. His passivity and irresoluteness were to be preferred to another's potential hostility. Innocent furthermore attempted to apply pressure on John which might force him to espouse the Welf cause. On 20 November 1202 he commanded Archbishop Adolf of Cologne to assume spiritual lordship in those areas of the Trier church where he already exercised temporal jurisdiction, and the following day he commanded the archbishop of Mainz (Siegfried) to proceed to Trier where he was to admonish the clergy and people to accept the will of the pope. Inasmuch as all these measures failed, however, the Roman pontiff sent a letter on 24 February 1203 to all German bishops and to the papal-legate to pronounce excommunication upon John in the event he failed

---

[93] Migne, *PL* CCXIV, cols. 963, 1103 (Potthast, *Regesta* I, Nrs. 1652, 1758.

[94] For a detailed discussion of these and subsequent events involving Trier, cf. Corsten, "EB Johann I. von Trier," 187-188; Hauck, *KGD* IV 738; Pixton, "Dietrich von Wied" (1974) 58-59.

[95] Schwemer, *Innocent III.* 50.

[96] Migne, *PL* CCXVI, cols. 1074, 1081-1082; Potthast, *Regesta* I, Nrs. 1753-1754, 1764.

to appear in Rome within six months.[97]   Archbishop John ultimately
capitulated, traveling to Rome in mid- or late 1203 where he was absolved
and reconciled with the Curia.

In southern Germany and Burgundy opposition to Otto IV was also
countered with summonses to appear in Rome. The promise of help from
King John of England further gave the papacy the feeling that its policies
were about to be crowned with success. To make matters worse for the
Staufen camp, Conrad of Querfurt, bishop of Würzburg and chancellor for
King Philip, broke openly with his monarch in November 1202 and aligned
himself with Otto IV. He had done so primarily for the purpose of
obtaining papal confirmation of his unauthorized transfer from Hildesheim
to Würzburg in 1198. His defection was all the more critical since he had
been at the very center of Staufen court activity for several years; furthermore, his bishopric opened the heart of Germany to Philip's enemies. With
surprising speed, Philip mobilized his Swabian vassals and drove deep into
Würzburg territory. Desperate for help, Conrad turned to the papacy; by
the time his appeal reached Rome, however, he was dead.

On the evening of 6 December 1202 while *en route* to the cathedral in
his own city, Bishop Conrad was fallen upon by two imperial *ministeriales*,
the brothers Henry and Bodo of Ravensburg, and brutally murdered. The
primary reason for their violent attack was that Conrad had tried to curtail
the taking of Church property by members of the ministerial class, but the
defection of the bishop to the Welf camp may have been equally as
important a factor. That King Philip was in no way saddened to see the
traitor at Würzburg gone is perhaps seen in the fact that although he came
quickly to the city and allowed the friends of Conrad to destroy the fortress
Ravensburg, he himself did nothing against them. In this policy he may
have been influenced by the imperial marshall, Henry of Kalden, who was
the maternal uncle of the assassins.[98]

Pope Innocent III was not as indifferent to the murder and the
murderers, however. On 23 January 1203 he sent letters to all German
clerics with instructions to pursue the Ravensburgers without surcease,
declaring them anathema in public and subjecting their lands to the
interdict.[99]   The two brothers managed to escape to Italy and at length
placed themselves at the pontiff's mercy. The penance imposed on them
was life-long and severe, and it was augmented by the declaration that they

---

[97] Kempf, *NRI* Nrs. 78, 83-84; Winkelmann, *Phil. von Schw.* I 554; Migne, *PL* CCXVI,
col. 1089; Potthast, *Regesta* I, Nrs. 1765, 1769, 1833.

[98] *Chron. mont. ser. (a. 1202)* 170; Münster, *Konrad von Querfurt* 49.

[99] Potthast, *Regesta* I, Nrs. 1813, 1814; documents printed in Migne, *PL* CCXIV, col.
1167; Migne, *PL* CCXVII, 97, Nr. 63 (see also Lappenberg, *Hamb. UB* I, Nr. 336).

were unfit to hold any fiefs of the Würzburg church in perpetuity.[100] The irony is that within eight years these same two men were playing a central role in Würzburg politics once again and almost succeeded in disposing of Bishop Conrad's second successor in much the same manner as they removed him.

The vengeance wreaked out upon the Ravensburg family was almost as violent as their own act and bespeaks an age of self-help and vendetta. The breakdown in public order as a result of the civil war gave rein to the most uncontrolled passions. One of the victims of the situation at Würzburg was Henry III of Ravensburg, son of one of the assassins, who was forced to abandon his canonate at Würzburg and to rely on benefactors elsewhere in the German church until his elevation in 1232 to the episcopacy of Eichstätt.[101] That there were such benefactors makes it all the more ironic that no one had much good to say about the slain Bishop Conrad; his death aroused little sorrow anywhere.

In the neighboring diocese of Bamberg, Bishop Timo died on 12 October 1202 and the cathedral chapter proceeded to elect Provost Conrad of Ergersheim who expired without consecration on 11 March 1203. Under the influence of King Philip who was holding forth in the region at the time, the cathedral chapter then elected its own provost, Ekbert of Andechs, as bishop. A member of the Swabian retinue, Bishop Diethelm of Constanz, at once consecrated him as *diaconus*.[102] Besides the obvious political reasons, Innocent III rejected Ekbert for canonical grounds as well: he was not yet thirty years of age, and Bishop Diethelm who consecrated him was anathema in the eyes of the Curia because he was a supporter of the equally-banned duke (King Philip) of Swabia. In order to obtain a dispensation, Ekbert went personally to Rome in the fall of 1203. His efforts to obtain recognition of his election were futile, but the issue became moot when Innocent III expressed a willingness to appoint him to be the bishop of Bamberg: the price was his sworn obedience to the papacy. Ekbert thus was consecrated as a priest by Cardinal-bishop Peter of Porto and as bishop by Innocent himself on 22 December 1203.[103] Having first sworn unconditional obedience to the see of St. Peter, he received the

---

[100] See papal letter dated 3 July 1203, written to the archbishop of Salzburg and his suffragans, directing them to prevent either the murderers themselves or their heirs from holding any fiefs of the Würzburg church; Migne, *PL* CCXV, col. 128; Potthast, *Regesta* I, Nr. 1958.

[101] Pixton, "Konrad von Reifenberg" 65-66; further details in Heidingsfelder, *Regg. Eichst.* I 203-204.

[102] Kist, *Erzbistum Bamberg* 44; Winkelmann, *Phil. von Schw.* I 304.

[103] Migne, *PL* CCXVII, Nrs. 89, 90; Potthast, *Regesta* I, Nrs. 2070, 2073.

pallium on Christmas Day. Time would quickly show, however, how meaningless that vow was to the new bishop of Bamberg.

The schism at Mainz also impacted the suffragan bishopric of Strasbourg. Upon the death of Bishop Conrad II on 29 May 1202, the cathedral canons assembled within the specified time and elected their provost, Henry of Vehringen, to be the new bishop. Henry was unable to obtain consecration from his metropolitan, however, and it was not until the spring of 1207 that he received such under the hands of the bishop of Sens. During those many years, provost Albert of Strasbourg represented the episcopal office, but the lengthy delay allowed the cathedral chapter to gain great power over against the bishop.[104] We can only wonder whether the conditions described in the Kolmar Annals as prevailing in Alsace at the commencement of the thirteenth century—lack of clerical discipline, concubinage, disregard for or inability to render proper *cura animarum*, etc.—were in any way dealt with at the synods which Bishop Henry II of Strasbourg convened between 1208 and 1212.[105]

With the reconciliation between Archbishop Ludolf of Magdeburg and the Curia near the end of 1202, the metropolitan was immediately given the task of investigating the selection of Archdeacon Dietrich of Merseburg as bishop. The Merseburg cathedral chapter had chosen this illegitimate son of a count of Wettin to be its head and had followed the prescribed canonical procedures in postulating him to the Curia on account of his *defectus*. The archbishop was commanded to determine whether the candidate was in fact suitable for the office, including the extend of his training. Given the papacy's concern to win support for Otto IV, the definition of an *idonea persona* must also have taken his political inclinations into consideration. As a result of Ludolf's report, a papal directive was issued 3 May 1203 to the cathedral chapter, that it present the bishop-elect to the archbishop for consecration as a priest and as bishop. The papal assumption that Ludolf of Magdeburg had in fact accepted Otto IV was erroneous, however. The archbishop never interpreted his promise of 1202 in this fashion. Being much closer to the situation, Cardinal-legate Guy threatened Ludolf once more with excommunication for failure to support the papal political position; he also countermanded the papal directives and ordained that Bishop-elect Dietrich be consecrated by Hartbert of Hildesheim, a man of unquestioned loyalty to Otto IV. Dietrich hesitated

---

[104] Wiegand, *UB Strassburg* I, Nr. 140 (excerpt); Sdralek, "Strassburg Synoden," 10; Wentzcke, "Ungedruckte Urkunden" 572-576; P. Reinhold, "Das Mainzer Schisma und die Konsecration des Strassburger Bischofs Heinrich von Veringen (1207)," *Strassburger Diözesanblatt*, Neue Folge 1 (Strassburg, 1914) 343.

[105] See Ch. One, pp. 60-61.

to respond to that order, however, revealing his own unwillingness to break from the Staufen party, and as a consequence he was excommunicated by the legate. A letter of 1 July 1204 reveals that he now wished to be absolved, and on 19 September of that year he at long last received consecration as bishop and assumed his full role.[106]

The legate meanwhile went beyond his written warnings in trying to force Magdeburg and Merseburg into the Welf camp. He joined forces in the Thuringian campaign against Philip and was present at the siege of Merseburg during August 1203. The beleaguered city had to purchase immunity from plundering with a large sum of money. Thereafter, the Welf army moved northward to the border of the archdiocese of Magdeburg with the intent of punishing the archbishop. The entire region, as earlier Thuringia had been, was given over to Bohemian troops to ravage. The inhabitants fled with their families and possessions across the Elbe River, abandoning their lands to the devastation of the invaders. Guy's hope of thereby bringing the archbishop into submission was in vain, however. Ludolf declared openly that the affairs of the Empire were no business of Rome, a show of defiance which the legate had not expected, especially from a man well past seventy years of age. He threatened Ludolf anew with excommunication for his breach of oath and called him a "crazy old man." Nevertheless, the archbishop stood his ground, appealed once more to the Curia and returned to his ravaged city. Guy eventually published a ban against Ludolf at Cologne, together with a renewed excommunication of the archbishop of Bremen.[107]

Upon hearing news of this action, Innocent III wrote Ludolf once more, giving him one month to capitulate or else he (the pope) would give the bishops of Minden, Verden and Hildesheim the commission to proclaim the papal ban in all the neighboring dioceses. He also instructed the Magdeburg cathedral chapter to avoid intercourse with the metropolitan and to renounce their obedience to him. The archbishop flaunted his disdain for this papal action by joining the Staufen campaign in Thuringia. Thus, on 1 July 1204 the pope wrote Bishop Hartbert of Hildesheim, telling him that if Ludolf, who had now been ceremoniously excommunicated, did not seek absolution within two months, he (Hartbert) was to consecrate Dietrich of Meissen in his place. When this extension also ran out, Hartbert executed the papal

---

[106] Potthast, *Regesta* I, Nr. 1894. See detailed discussion of these events in Kohlmann, *EB Ludolf* 47-50, and in Schwemer, *Innocent III.* 87.

[107] The reports given in *Chron. mont. ser.* 169, and in *Chron. reg. Colon.* 202, are reconciled by Kohlmann, *EB Ludolf* 49.

command on 19 December 1204 with the aid of several other Welf
bishops.[108]

   This stubborn opposition by the archbishop of Magdeburg thwarted the
papal plans in Germany and frustrated the efforts by Cardinal-bishop Guy
to establish Otto IV as the unquestioned ruler. It also reveals the inner
workings of the mind of a shrewd, politically-oriented metropolitan for
whom an oath to the supreme pontiff of the Church was not an inviolable
matter. Innocent's attempts to bind the German episcopacy to his policies
by means of sacred promises were thus temporary victories at best;
situations which necessitated the making of such oaths were quickly forgotten. As a result, the trend which seemed to bode ill for Philip during the
early part of 1203 had clearly shifted by the end of the year. Papal success
was ephemeral since it was based on covenants extorted from individuals
who had no reason to remain faithful any longer than was expedient.

   One of the more lasting gains for the papal-Welf party was the result of
a disputed episcopal election at Münster during the course of 1203. On 9
June Bishop Hermann II (of Katzenellenbogen) died in the Cistercian
monastery of Marienfeld which he had helped found and to which he had
fled in the last years, seeking asylum from the endless turmoil of German
politics. Fearing the growing power of the advocate of Münster, the count
of Tecklenburg, the older members of the cathedral chapter, assisted by the
ministeriales and burghers of the city, sought a candidate from yet a
stronger family. Thus it was that the episcopal office was initially offered
to Engelbert of Berg, the cathedral provost at Cologne, who declined in the
probable expectation that he would shortly succeed to the archbishopric
itself.[109] The anti-Tecklenburg faction in the Münster church, which
comprised a majority of the cathedral canons, then met again to select a new
bishop: fearing reprisals from their opponents, they bolted the doors of the
cathedral church and had the *ministeriales* stand guard. Their choice fell
upon the provost of Bremen, Otto of Oldenburg, scion of another powerful
Westphalian family with strong feelings against the house of Tecklenburg.
Upon learning of their exclusion from the election, the younger members
of the cathedral chapter and the noble faction headed by the count of
Tecklenburg met and chose their own bishop, Provost Frederick of
Klarholz, an illegitimate offspring of the comital family.

   The development of the schismatic situation at Münster prompted the
majority faction to appeal the case to the Cardinal-legate Guy during the fall

---

[108] *Chron. mont. ser.* 169-171 (with wrong year); Migne, *PL* CCXV, col. 396; see also
Schwemer, *Innocent III.* 87, and Kohlmann, *EB Ludolf* 50.

[109] The discussion of the disputed election at Münster follows the study by G. Tumbüldt,
"Die münsterische Bischofswahl des Jahres 1203," *WZGK* 3 (1884) 355-370.

of 1203. The legate summoned proctors to Cologne where, on the appointed day and in the presence of Provost Otto of Bremen, they declared that Otto had been elected by the prelates of the Münster church i.e., the provost, dean, cantor and *custos*, and by the overwhelming majority of the members of the chapter; they were joined by the *sanior pars* of the diocesan clergy, to whom the abbots of the entire bishopric belonged. They were likewise certain that all the proper requirements had been met, namely, in the correct location and without outside family influence. On the other hand, they pointed out that the provost of Klarholz had been elected by not a single prelate, but by only a few canons who, with one exception, were the youngest in the cathedral chapter. They also argued that there was evidence that lay relatives of these canons had influenced the outcome of their election, and that the election itself had been held at an improper location, outside the cathedral.

The Klarholz party objected that a compromise had been reached before the election between the *ministeriales* and the cathedral canons which was contrary to canonical practice, that eligible cathedral canons had been excluded from the election process, that the consent of the advocate and other nobles had not been obtained, and that the *ministeriales* and burghers had closed the doors of the cathedral church in order to prohibit such individuals from participating. Thus, they had to meet elsewhere. The minority party furthermore maintained that the date of the election had been moved up, to which the majority members replied that the vacancy had already exceeded eighteen weeks, causing serious threats of danger to the Münster church.

Unlike the disputed election at Liège where he seemed eager to play a major and decisive role, the legate declined to referee this case in which there were so many charges and counter-accusations; instead, he summoned both parties to appear before the Roman Curia on 14 March 1204 where the issue would be resolved. There may have been other reasons for his reluctance as well, however. The legate's actions tended to favor the provost of Klarholz: he seems to have remained quiet about Frederick's illegitimacy in his report to the papacy; the granting of more time through the transfer of jurisdiction likewise gave the latter hope that he might press his case before the Curia. Although Otto of Bremen clearly had the strength of canonical precepts on his side, his political loyalty to Otto IV of Brunswick was seriously suspect, while Frederick enjoyed the Welf's support.

As it turned out, however, only the representatives of the provost of Bremen appeared before the Curia. They assured the pope that the provost of Klarholz was not of legitimate birth, a fact known to his electors. After hearing the entire case, the pope declined to reach a decision without testimony from the opposing side as well. He therefore transferred the matter back to Germany where the final judgment was to be reached by a commission which he appointed in a letter dated 28 May 1204.[110] In it, Innocent commanded three clerics (Provost Bruno of Bonn, Provost Dietrich of St. Cunibert in Cologne and Abbot Heribert of Werden) to decide whether the canonical rules had been observed in the election, whether a suitable person had been elected, but above all whether the minority faction had been aware of Frederick's illegitimate birth; if so, they were to impose penalties on those canons, including the loss of the right of election. If a new election was deemed necessary, it was to be held within fifteen days, or else the right would devolve to the pope.

In contrast to the instructions given in earlier schismatic episcopal elections in Germany, the letter does not reveal the pope's feelings with respect to the political situation, yet he clearly kept that in mind. All three members of the commission were strong Welf supporters at this time, and the charge to determine the suitability of whomever had been elected gave them a great amount of leverage. Provost Bruno of Bonn became the archbishop of Cologne in 1205, following the break between Otto IV of Brunswick and Adolf of Altena. Dietrich of St. Cunibert, on the other hand, joined the mass defection of Cologne *priores* from the Welf camp.[111] Further details concerning the commission are not known, but it is to be assumed that it confirmed Otto of Oldenburg as bishop of Münster. Despite previous support from King Philip, Bishop-elect Otto was now willing to pledge loyalty to Otto IV from whom he also received the *temporalia*.

Peace and order did not come at once within the region of the Münster church, however. The continuator of the *Chronica regia Coloniensis* stated that "*Otto (episcopus) auxilio amicorum armis episcopium violenter obtinuit,*" suggesting that overall recognition was gained only with force of arms.[112] Part of the problem may still have lain with Provost Frederick of Klarholz. Possessed of an ambitious and intriguing nature, he turned from being rejected as bishop of Münster to seeking other high ecclesiastical dignities. In doing so, he prolonged the travail of the Münster church for another two decades.

As Abbot Widukind of Corvey gave his support to Frederick in 1203 for the bishop's chair in Münster, he could little have suspected that this same man would be the cause of disorder within his own house. Frederick had been rejected as an episcopal candidate largely because of his illegitimate

---

[110] Böhmer-Ficker, *Regg. Imp.* V/2, Nr. 5897; *Westf. UB* V 89.

[111] See Pixton, "Dietrich von Wied" (1974) 60-62. Further, cf. Winkelmann, *Phil. von Schw.* I 305; Pelster, *Stand und Herkunft* 70; Kuhle, *Neubesetzung* 50.

[112] *Chron. reg. Colon., cont. II* 173.

birth. Only after the pope in 1205, at the request of Otto IV, dispensed him from the *defectus natalium* and allowed his *rehabilitatio* did he receive the privilege of assuming greater dignities.[113]   Not for many years, however, did he receive those honors for which he so eagerly sought. Then, on the very eve of the Lateran Council, a group of rebellious monks at Corvey elected him as abbot in opposition to the majority candidate, Abbot Hugold of St. Michael's in Hildesheim. Despite Frederick's failure to win the approval of that majority as well, he clung to his pretensions for several years. Corvey, as well as the church at Klarholz, suffered enormous financial burdens as a result of this struggle.[114]   Frederick was excommunicated twice during the schism, and following further violent actions by members of his faction deposed from his provostship by a general chapter of his order.

The truculent nature of this man is revealed in the fact that even these measures did not stop his uncontrolled grasp for power. He next sought to avenge himself on his successor at Klarholz with the aid of equally vicious relatives. The failure of ecclesiastical censures to deal with such a man ultimately resulted in a request from Abbot Gervasius of Premontré that the pope allow the bishop of Münster, either directly or through the bishop of Osnabrück (in whose diocese Klarholz lay), to take armed military action against Frederick.[115]   The papal response is not known, but the agitation of two bishoprics for over two decades came to an abrupt end, suggesting that armed force may have been the ultimate solution to this case of blind ambition.

The Defection from Otto IV

The schismatic episcopal elections of the early thirteenth century tested the tenacity of a Frenchman who refused to acquiesce to the wishes of a German clergy which supported Philip of Swabia over against Otto IV. For over three years Guy Poré had shouldered an enormous task filled with very complex situations which tested his wisdom, patience, diplomatic skills, understanding of canon law, and commitment to the papal position. In the end, however, he failed to turn the German princes and episcopacy away from their deeply-rooted support for the Staufen dynasty. What victories he did achieve were phantoms which required his constant attention to

---

[113] Sindern, *Kloster Corvey* 10-11.

[114] On 28 November 1216 Pope Honorius III ordered a Cistercian abbot to undertake a visitation of Corvey, undoubtedly in connection with the confusion brought on by Provost Frederick's intrusion; cf. Potthast, *Regesta* I, Nr. 5373.

[115] Tumbüldt, "Münsterische Bischofswahl" 358; see also *Westf. UB* III, Nr. 196.

prevent backsliding and outright desertion. His election as archbishop of
Rheims in 1204 must therefore have appeared as a welcome relief to him.
The capricious and volatile German situation could be forgotten in his new
role as primate of France.

With his departure, disputed elections had to be resolved in some other
way than with the aid of a papally-appointed arbitrator. Thus, in 1204
when a schism developed at Ratzeburg between the canon Philip, *capellanus*
to the former bishop, and the provost Henry, the count of Orlamünde was
charged with being the referee.[116] He chose Philip who administered the
see until his death on 15 November 1215 *en route* to the Fourth Lateran
Council. Another commission of interest in the present context was that
given on 15 May 1204 to the abbot of Afflighem, *magister R*[ ] from the
church at Thenis (Tirlemont in Brabant) and *magister* Gilbert, a canon at
Utrecht, whose task it was to investigate charges that W[ ], the dean at
Utrecht, had forsaken the *vita regularis* for the *saecularis*.[117] The Dean
W[ ] in question was presumably Wilbrand of Oldenburg who later became
bishop of Utrecht, giving us an insight into the religious character of this
man. While there is record of a diocesan synod at Utrecht in 1205, no
indication is given that it dealt with matters of clerical discipline. Certainly
the recent investigation of their own dean must have been on the minds of
the cathedral clergy, however. Four year later, papal legates did in fact
issue decrees for correcting abuses at Utrecht.

Although the ultimate failure of the Papal-legate Guy's efforts in
Germany may have been only partially evident before his departure, it
became more pronounced as a massive defection from Otto IV commenced
during mid- and late- 1204. As in 1196-1198, the German prelates were
once again led by Archbishop Adolf I of Cologne. Whether Adolf
perceived, or was even concerned about, the damage done by his actions is
questionable. What is clear is that in time he recognized that the elevation
of Otto of Brunswick had endangered his own position in northern
Germany: the archbishopric of Cologne had profited greatly from the fall
of Duke Henry the Lion of Saxony, Otto IV's father, and the ascending
power of the Welfs now threatened Cologne's territorial lordship. Thus, in
November 1204, Adolf joined those secular princes such as Otto's brother
Henry, the pfalzgrave on the Rhine, Landgrave Hermann of Thuringia,
King Ottokar of Bohemia and Duke Henry of Brabant who had gone over
to the Staufen camp, alienating in the process the papacy and his own

---

[116] *Arnoldi Chron.* 241-242; Masch, *Bistums Ratzeburg* 106; M-Alpermann, *Stand und Herkunft* 96.

[117] Migne, *PL* CCXV, col 344; Potthast, *Regesta* I, Nr. 2209.

episcopal city.[118] The treason of the mightiest among Germany's princes and prelates was soon followed by those of the second rank: the bishops of Liège, Münster, Osnabrück, Paderborn and Strasbourg. As Philip was crowned for the second time at Aachen on 6 January 1205, there were present not only the Saxon bishops, but south German as well.[119] Alongside the ever-faithful Diethelm of Constanz and Conrad of Speyer were the newly elected bishops of Regensburg, Würzburg and Strasbourg.

The pope's greatest anger was vented against Adolf of Cologne to whose perfidy he responded by declaring the archbishop excommunicated (11 March 1205) and deposed (19 June 1205), directing the *priores* of the church to elect a new head and imposing an interdict over the archdiocese.[120] Most of the Cologne *priores* had by this time also abandoned Otto IV; thus, as Bruno of Sayn, the provost of the collegiate church of St. Cassius in Bonn and leader of the opposition against the domination of the Cologne archbishopric by the dynasties of Berg, Isenberg and Altena, was elected archbishop on 25 July 1205, it was to a large extent the act of the majority of the lesser clergy at Cologne. While the burghers also gave their consent, only three *priores*—the cathedral dean Conrad, Provost Dietrich of the church of the Holy Apostles, and the abbot of Deutz—recognized Bruno. The remainder, comprising the provosts of the cathedral (Engelbert of Berg) and most collegiate churches, together with the monasteries and their abbots, closed ranks behind the deposed Archbishop Adolf. Under no circumstances did Bruno's authority extend beyond the walls of the city of Cologne.

The contemporary continuator of the *Chronica regia Coloniensis* noted that in the aftermath of the election disorder and conflict raged throughout the diocese. Adolf's supporters ignored papal threats and refused to abandon him. Thus, each German king had his own archbishop of Cologne, and these in turn had clergy who were loyal to them alone. Churches were plundered, others were damaged by fire or turned into fortresses; possessions were seized; monks and nuns were hunted down; and priests obedient to papal commands were replaced by excommunicants.[121] Among those

---

[118] According to Caesarius of Heisterbach (*Dialogus* II 44), Adolf's defection was bought with 9000 Marks, an amount which helped erase the prelate's former debts. Wolfschläger, "Adolf I. von Köln" 71-74, notes, however, that the real cause for the desertion of the Welf camp was an attack on Adolf's archiepiscopal rights (including toll and coinage), and the resumption of the use of the title *dux Saxoniae* by Otto IV's brother Henry.

[119] Böhmer-Ficker, *Regg. Imp.* V/2, Nrs. 90, 91.

[120] Migne, *PL* CCXVI, col. 1121-1122; Potthast, *Regesta* I, Nrs. 2443, 2445. See also Schwemer, *Innocent III.* 111-115; Hüffer, "Denkstein und Schisma" 132-133.

[121] *Chron. reg. Colon.*, cont. II (a. 1205) 175; also cont. III 220-223. See also the anonymous *Dialogus cleri et laici*, in Böhmer, *Fontes* III 400-407; Wolfschläger, "Adolf I. von

canons at Cologne who reaped criticism from Caesarius of Heisterbach at this time was Gottfried, a cleric of St. Andreas who served as Archbishop Adolf's mint-master and disperser of monies, having used his office to amass a personal fortune himself.[122]   Innocent III also wrote regarding Adolf: "Would that he had never been born, this son of Belial, who has tumbled the church and the city of Cologne into destruction through his ignominious actions."[123]   The pope also ignored a protest against Adolf's deposition lodged by Provost Engelbert; his erstwhile ally had been rejected.

Such measures by the papacy had little effect upon the former archbishop, however.   Equally unsuccessful were the attempts to compel the other German prelates and princes back to Otto IV.   As Bruno of Sayn was consecrated as the new metropolitan of Cologne 6 June 1206 by Siegfried of Mainz, there was not one German bishop who came forth to assist the primate.   He had to enlist two English bishops as substitutes.   Overall there was strong, violent opposition to the pope and his new archprelate. Innocent nevertheless sought to strengthen Bruno's position by sending him a letter, directing him to punish disobedient clerics of his church by withdrawing their prebends.[124]   Bruno was hardly in a position to implement such a mandate, however, for he no sooner received consecration than he was taken captive and held by Philip of Swabia at the latter's fortress at Rothenburg-ob-der-Tauber.

The inability of Archbishop Bruno to function as ordinary explains why the cathedral canons in 1207 turned to the Curia with a complaint.   The church at Huckarde near Dortmund had become badly secularized: specifically it was charged that because the canons there did not observe the residence requirement, a "*grave scandalum*" had arisen among both the clergy and the people.   Since Huckarde was subordinate to the cathedral chapter in matters both spiritual and temporal—its provost being at once the cathedral scholastic—such problems might have been dealt with by the

Köln" 99-100; Röhrich, *Adolf I. von Köln* 68-79.   In March 1205 Innocent III wrote to the *priores* of Cologne, expressing pleasure that they had held fast to Otto and the hope that they would prevail upon Adolf to change his mind; cf. Migne, *PL* CCXVI, col. 1121; Potthast, *Regesta* I, Nr. 2443.   Ficker, *Engelbert der Heilige* 312, Beilage 6, prints a letter written by the clergy of Cologne to the pope concerning their great oppression from the supporters of Adolf, and asking him to use his influence in behalf of the imprisoned Bruno.

[122] *Caesarii Dialogus* XI 44, tells of the death of Gottfried who, shortly before, had a vision of himself stretched out on an anvil and pounded small as a coin with a hammer by the "*Judenbischof*" Jacob.

[123] Cited in Ficker, *Engelbert der Heilige* 36.

[124] *Chron. reg. Colon.*, cont. *II (a. 1206)* 179-180; also cont. *III (a. 1206)* 223-224, where the defection of most provosts, abbots and chapter canons and lesser clergy is attributed to the constant threat from Engelbert and his confederates.   Potthast, *Regesta* I, Nr. 2943, gives a précis of the papal letter which is printed in Ficker, *Engelbert der Heilige* 311.

chapter dignitaries. The situation was compounded by the fact that the cathedral scholastic, Oliver of Paderborn, was attending the schools of Paris and participating in the Albigensian crusade as a preacher at the time, presumably leaving his duties at Cologne and at Huckarde to be performed by a vicar. Innocent III in response sent a mandate to three Cologne clerics to set in order the affairs at Huckarde by enjoining the canons to return to their obligations or else lose the benefits from the altar.[125]

The widespread opposition to Otto IV throughout Germany since 1198 appears to have had a gradual effect upon the Roman pontiff who by 1204-1205 dared not execute the ban which he had threatened against all of Otto's enemies. In some instances he even showed himself conciliatory toward the bishops. Wolfger of Passau, e.g., who had always been a Staufen supporter, was given permission in June 1204 to accept election at Aquileia.[126] By January 1205 Archbishop Ludolf of Magdeburg was also concerned to make peace with the papacy. He could no longer count on the loyalty of his cathedral chapter, and Innocent III's threats had at last had an effect. One of the canons at Magdeburg, Rudolf of Ranis, had gone to Rome and had lodged a complaint against the archbishop before the Curia, stating that while Ludolf had been excommunicated he had celebrated divine services. Being weighed down with years and not wishing to die as an excommunicant, the prelate sent two clerics to Rome for the purpose of justifying his actions and of seeking absolution. On 25 May 1205 the pontiff gave the Bishops Ditmar of Minden and Rudolf of Verden, and Abbot Heribert of Werden the commission to absolve Ludolf after he vowed to obey the pope in all matters pertaining to the Empire. At the same time he was to certify before them whether he had in fact performed any rites after the publication of the ban. Ludolf's willingness to accept such a commission and to abide by its decision attests to his realization that, being near death, his oath would not damage Philip. It must also have occurred to Innocent that this was the case. Nevertheless, the public submission of so esteemed a rebel enhanced the position of the papacy: Ludolf was probably received back into the bosom of the Church by July 1205.[127] On 16 August of that same year he died, being almost eighty years of age.

Among the factors influencing Innocent's reconciliation with Ludolf was the thought that when the failing prelate died, it would then be an easier matter to secure the election of a pro-Welf archbishop. This possibility was clearly on his mind in June 1205 when Conrad of Krosigk, the crusading bishop of Halberstadt, visited Rome. The primary purpose of his audience

---

[125] Cardauns, *Konrad von Hostaden* 125, Anlage 1.

[126] Potthast, *Regesta* I, Nr. 2255.

[127] (Inn. Ep. VIII 77) Migne, *PL* CCXV 645; Kohlmann, *EB Ludolf* 53-55.

with the pope was to repair his own relationship with the pontiff, aggravated by Conrad's refusal to obey papal commands relative to Otto IV in 1202, but conditions in Magdeburg and Halberstadt must also have been discussed. Since there was an old custom which prescribed that the bishops of these two churches preside at the burials of their respective colleagues, it was evident that Conrad would shortly fulfill that role for his aged metropolitan Ludolf. The pope undoubtedly committed him to secure the election of a pro-Welf candidate at Magdeburg as well. Only thus can we explain why Innocent allowed Conrad to depart after declaring that he would remain personally loyal to Philip.[128]

The candidate whom the pope favored was Albrecht of Käfernburg, the cathedral provost at Magdeburg who had already enjoyed papal favor in being elevated to that position in 1200 over the opposition of the chapter. The preferment thus shown was not without further consequences. Since 1200 Albrecht had continued his studies at Bologna where his progress was no doubt followed with interest by the Curia. The papal plans for elevating Albrecht to the archbishopric are further substantiated by the fact that the chronicler mentions Conrad of Krosigk traveling home from Rome by way of Bologna. Since this was the normal route over the Alps, there was no reason to make special reference to it unless Conrad spent some time in that city. Having reached an agreement with Albrecht that the latter would indeed be loyal to the pope in the event of his election as archbishop, Conrad continued his journey to Halberstadt, arriving there on the very day that Ludolf of Magdeburg died.[129]

Albrecht of Käfernburg, a product of the Hildesheim cathedral school and of the universities of Paris and Bologna, was elected archbishop of Magdeburg by a majority of the cathedral canons under the influence of Bishop Conrad of Halberstadt shortly thereafter. Several *capitulares*, most particularly the scholastic Rudolf of Ranis, objected to this choice and lodged an appeal in Rome. This same Rudolf had opposed the appointment of Albrecht as provost in 1200; his dislike for the new prelate was thus several years old and had apparently not been altered during the intervening years.[130]

Unless Innocent III was deceived, we must be cautious about seeing Albrecht as a firm Staufen supporter at the time of the election. Nevertheless, soon thereafter he hurried to Philip of Swabia and received the regalia. Innocent wrote him on 25 February 1206, informing him that he

---

[128] Schwemer, *Innocent III.* 103-106.

[129] See *Chron. mont. Ser.* 172; instead of "*Colonie in scholis constitutus,*" the passage should read "*Bononie . . .*"

[130] Silberborth, "EB Albrecht II." 10.

had confirmed the election, but that due to an incautious act which he had committed (clearly the trip to Philip's court) he really deserved to be rejected. Albrecht was informed that he must conduct himself in such a way as to merit the full grace of the pope, a not too cryptic reference to the fact that the pontiff was withholding the pallium for the present.[131] The archbishop-elect traveled personally to Rome in the autumn of 1206 where he convinced Innocent of his loyalty. On the Saturday before Christmas (23 December) the pope consecrated him as a priest; the following day Albrecht received the episcopal blessing and was granted at once the pallium and other graces.[132]

During those months when he was seeking recognition of his own position as metropolitan of Magdeburg, Albrecht of Käfernburg also received a commission from the pope to deal with problems within his suffragan bishopric of Naumburg. Bishop Berthold II had resigned his office there due to incapability, but had requested an extension of time for the actual relinquishing of his position. Albrecht was commanded by the Roman pontiff to make certain that the prelate did so prior to 1 November 1206.[133] Berthold's successor, Engelhard, appears as bishop-elect of Naumburg before the end of 1206, although the fact that he was not yet a priest at the time of the election necessitated a papal dispensation. He is not mentioned as a cathedral canon at Naumburg, but he was apparently not unknown to King Philip who secured the election.[134] By this time the Staufen relationship to the papacy had reversed itself and the pope no longer opposed bishops who openly supported Philip against Otto IV.

Albrecht of Magdeburg's visit to Rome at the end of 1206 also provided him with the opportunity for informing the Curia in detail about the problems which existed within his church. The antagonism displayed toward him by certain members of the cathedral chapter was but a symptom of a larger problem of discipline throughout the archdiocese of Magdeburg. A letter dated 8 February 1207 informed the chapter that the pope had confirmed Albrecht's election and commanded their obedience to him. A fortnight later the pontiff established a commission comprising the abbot of Sichem (Sittichenbach), the scholastic of St. Sebastian and *magister* Arnold, the *plebanus* of St. John's in Magdeburg, to investigate the excesses of Albert, the provost at Hunoldsburg, and of Rudolf of Ranis, both of whom

---

[131] (Inn. Ep. IX 22) Migne, *PL* CCXV col. 812; Potthast, *Regesta* I, Nr. 2694; Mülverstedt, *RAMagd* II 106, Nr. 251; Schwemer, *Innocent III.* 107; Hauck, *KGD* IV 744.

[132] Mülverstedt, *RAMagd* II 111, Nr. 265.

[133] Mülverstedt, *RAMagd* II 107, Nr. 253; Potthast, *Regesta* I, Nr. 2752; Lepsius, *Hochstift Naumburg* I 269.

[134] Lepsius, *Hochstift Naumburg* I 63; M-Alpermann, *Stand und Herkunft* 34; Kuhle, *Neubesetzung* 61.

were cathedral canons and had been the leaders in the opposition to the election of Albrecht as archbishop.[135]

Conditions within the cathedral chapter at Magdeburg were still not beyond criticism, however. On 6 March 1207 the pope again issued regulations for it, restricting the practice of selling their private residences (*curias*) to persons outside their body. Two days later Innocent III also established a new commission of three clerics (Bishops Conrad of Halberstadt and Dietrich of Merseburg, and the abbot of St. Johannisberg in Magdeburg) who were to enjoin the Magdeburg cathedral chapter not to deny entrance into that body to qualified priests and other honest men.[136] The immediate cause for this command is not stated, but it was clearly connected with the opposition mounted within the cathedral chapter to the exercise of the papal right of devolution in January of that year when the Roman pontiff named the nephew of the duke of Poland to the position of cathedral provost at Magdeburg and commanded the cathedral chapter to grant him a prebend.[137]

Yet another case which trampled on the cathedral chapter's traditional right to select its own members involved a privilege granted to Archbishop Albrecht on 13 February 1207 to fill the vacancies created in the cathedral chapter when the pope annulled appointments made by his predecessor Ludolf during the period of his excommunication.[138] Using that privilege Albrecht granted to *magister* Gernand, a canon at St. Nicholas collegiate church in Magdeburg who supported him during the disputed archiepiscopal election, a prebend in the Magdeburg cathedral chapter and appointed him

---

[135] (Inn. Ep. IX 261) Migne, *PL* CCXV, col. 1093; Mülverstedt, *RAMagd* II 113, Nr. 270; Potthast, *Regesta* I, Nrs. 3004 (8 February 1207), citing Franz Winter, "Erzbischof Albrecht II. von Magdeburg bis zu seiner Erwählung und Bestätigung," *Mgbll* 4 (1869) 187-189. Further, Migne *PL* CCXV, col. 1101; Mülverstedt, *op.cit.* II 115, Nr. 275; Potthast, op.cit. Nr. 3014 (17 February 1207), citing Winter, *loc.cit.* 190. See also, Silberborth, "EB Albrecht II." 10; Wentz/Schwineköper, *Erzbistum Magdeburg* I/1 384. Rudolf of Ranis served as scholast for the Magdeburg cathedral school 1209-1223.

[136] Mülverstedt, *RAMagd* II 115, Nrs. 277, 278; Potthast, *Regesta* I, Nrs. 3033 (6 March 1207)), 3036 (8 March 1207); Migne, *PL* CCXV, col. 1108. Wentz/Schwineköper, *Erzbistum Magdeburg* I/1 114-115, argues that although family names are generally missing from lists of cathedral canons before 1200, the reconstruction of the cathedral chapter from other sources allows the conclusion that in general noble or at least free birth was a precondition for entrance into it. Claude, *Erzstift Magdeburg* II 220, assumes a cathedral chapter comprised overwhelmingly of nobility until into the fourteenth century.

[137] Mülverstedt, *RAMagd* II 112, Nrs. 267, 268; Wentz/Schwineköper, *Erzbistum Magdeburg* I/1 120. Not until 1212 did Otto function as cathedral provost.

[138] Mülverstedt, *RAMagd* II 114, Nr. 273.

as cathedral scholastic. This action had to be reinforced by numerous papal documents and mandates dated 10 March 1207, however.[139]

Shortly thereafter, on Ash Wednesday (18 April) 1207, Albrecht convoked a synod at Magdeburg where the abuses cited in the papal letters were undoubtedly dealt with.[140] Attending this synod were at least the three suffragans whom he would consecrate on Easter Sunday—Sigbodo of Havelberg, Baldwin of Brandenburg and Engelhard of Naumburg—and numerous nobles of the region. Unfortunately, reform of the clergy quickly became a secondary issue as a fire broke out and destroyed the cathedral and much of the city on Good Friday of that same week. Although the archbishop set out at once to draft plans for the rebuilding, taking advantage of the presence of his suffragan bishops, the resumption of strife in Germany after 1211 hampered reconstruction, and it was not until the mid-fourteenth century that the new cathedral was completed.

Contemporaneous with Albrecht of Magdeburg was the reform-minded bishop of Meissen, Dietrich II of Kittlitz (1191-1208) who recognized and often stated that neither he nor his cathedral canons were capable of "stamping out the weeds which threaten to choke the good seed in the garden of the Lord." He therefore invited others whose commitment to reform was strong to assist him in that task. In 1205 he established a chapter of Augustinian canons in the church of St. Afra on the fortified mountain near the city, giving it to the *cura animarum* in the city of Meissen and the surrounding area by incorporating into it the *Marktkirche*—the church of Our Lady.[141] The inhabitants of the fortress, the retinue of the margrave and all the soldiers with their families, as well as the servants of the cathedral canons, were made parishioners. In order to ensure that the canons of St. Afra would remain as little corrupted by the secular canons as possible, the bishop further ordained that the provost of this chapter be chosen from within the convent itself, or from some other of the same order, and that he be presented to the bishop and invested by him. Indicative of the role intended for this convent of canons-regular was

---

[139] Mülverstedt, *RAMagd* II 116-117, Nrs. 279-282.

[140] *Magdeburger Schöppenchronik* 131-132; *Chron. mont. Ser.* 173; *Chron. Reinhardsbr.* 571: "*Sed in ipso reditu dum in parasceue divina perageret, ex peccatis incolarum matrix ecclesia flammis ultricibus cum ruinosis parietibus inedicibiliter interiit et miserandum novo pontifici spectaculum strages illa vehementer dissoluta exhibuit [20 Apr.]. Ipse tamen pontifex iunctis sibi aliis episcopis Nuenborgensem et Brandenborgensem episcopos in dominica resurreccionis venerabiliter consecravit*"; *Gesta archiep. Magd.* 418-419; *Monum. Erphesf.* 204; *Gesta abb. Bergg.* ed. Holstein, *Mgbll* 5 (1870) 382; *Bothonis Chronica*, ed. Leibniz, *Scr. Brunsvicc.* III 356; Silberborth, "EB Albrecht II." 19.

[141] Rittenbach/Seifert, *Bischöfe von Meissen* 111-126; Gersdorf, *UB Meissen* II, 4, Nr. 147.

its being designated as an *ecclesia secundaria* and the special recognition accorded to the canons: in the choir and in processions, their provost was to enjoy a place among the cathedral canons and before the cathedral vicars; and, so as to make the services in St. Afra more festive, a school of twelve non-tonsured boys was to be established, who were to receive instruction in music, choral song, Latin grammar, writing and composition.

The following year he prefaced a charter with an expression of melancholy perhaps felt by many of his peers whose efforts at reform had met near insuperable obstacles: "Today the life of mankind is burdened with innumerable vices . . ." Exhibiting many of those vices were his own clergy; thus, on 13 December 1206 he issued a joint decree with the cathedral chapter that on the feast of St. Augustine a solemn office was to be said, and nine readings from Augustine were to be scheduled each year.[142] The reason for such an institution is made clear in the document itself: a monk named Ludger from the Cistercian house of Altzelle—very learned it was said—had come to Meissen and had granted to the cathedral a copy of *De Civitate Dei*, on the condition that the feast celebration be introduced. It seems probable that previous to this time Meissen did not possess an exemplar of the work which therefore remained unknown to many of the clerics. At a time when proper models of the religious life were difficult to find, it was a most fortuitous circumstance to receive the writings of the great bishop of Hippo, after which the canons and clerics of Meissen might pattern their lives.

Changes in human behavior could not come about overnight, however. Attitudes developed during a lifetime of undiscipline and neglect of canonical obligations would require more than episcopal legislation to be actualized. Within less than two years of his reforming acts, Bishop Dietrich II of Meissen lay dead and had been succeeded by a much less capable and vigorous individual, Bruno II of Borsendorf (1209-1228). Bruno was actually a compromise choice, inasmuch as there had been four candidates for the episcopal office; he was probably already quite old at the time of his election, and over the next two decades he aroused the displeasure of his cathedral clergy to the point where they pleaded with the papacy that he be replaced. On 30 June 1228 the pontiff authorized the archbishop of Magdeburg and the bishop of Brandenburg to insist that the

---

[142] Gersdorf, *UB Meissen* II, 1, Nr. 75: "*Cum innumeris vitorum maculis cotidie sordescat vita humana, in eo potissimum ut speramus divinae proximamus indulgentiae, si eis saltem obsequii aliquid impendimus, qui ecclesiam dei prae ceteris et exemplis erexerunt et doctrinis correxerunt.*"

bishop of Meissen resign his office, recognizing the fact that great damage to the church had already been done.[143]

Elsewhere in northern Germany Bishop Hartbert of Hildesheim also took advantage of the temporary lull in the political conflict to deal with pastoral matters within his diocese. In 1206 the parishioners of St. Jacob's in Goslar drove out their priest and chose another in his stead, hiding a document of 1160 which expressly gave that right to the bishop. Unwilling to countenance such a renegade, Hartbert convened a synod at Goslar that same year to deal with the matter.[144] Unfortunately for his own flock, however, Hartbert would find himself in the position of an outcast within five years, a condition which rendered him incapable of fulfilling his role as shepherd thereafter.

The German Bishops and Matters of Canon Law

One of the more interesting papal letters relative to Germany from the year 1206 is the response of Innocent III (dated 28 August) to two separate inquiries by Bishop Bertram of Metz regarding matters of canon law. To the question of whether a Jew needed to be rebaptized who, being close to death, had personally recited the baptismal formula and plunged himself into some water in the presence of just other Jews, the pontiff declared that this was essential (*"per tuas nobis literas intimasti, quod quidam Iudaeus, in mortis articulo constitutis, cum inter Iudaeos tantum exsisteret, in aquam se ipsum immersit, dicendo . . . Nunc autem quaeris, utrum idem Iudaeus, in devotione Christianae fidei perservans, debeat baptizari"*). A second matter involved the propriety of ordaining individuals who had married another's widow (*"an is qui mulierum, ab alio viro traductam, sed non cognitam, sibi matrimonialiter copulavit, valeat ad sacerdotium promoveri?"*)[145] After discussing some of the points relative to the impediment of bigamy, the pontiff gave the response: *"Unde is, qui mulierum ab alio viro ductam, sed minime cognitam, duxit uxorem, quia nec illa, nec ipse carnem suam divisit in plures, propter hoc impediri non debet, quin possit ad sacerdotium*

---

[143] Rittenbach/Seifert, *Bischöfe von Meissen* 128-129; M-Alpermann, *Stand und Herkunft* 54; Kuhle, *Neubesetzung* 73.

[144] Janicke, *UB Hilds* I 616; Maring, *Diözesansynoden* 71.

[145] (Epist. Inn. IX, 159) Migne, *PL* CCXV 985-986; Potthast, *Regesta* I, Nr. 2875. Both the first episcopal letter which informed the pope of the Jew's actions, and the second requesting advice, are lost. Cf. Albert Dresdner, Ludwig Lewinski and Julius Aronius, ed., *Regesten zur Geschichte der Juden im Fränkischen und Deutschen Reiche bis zum Jahre 1273* (Berlin, 1902) 163-164, Nr. 369.

promoveri."[146]   This interest in the subtleties of canon law had been part
of Bertram's life for over thirty years. Coming out of Saxony, he acquired
the *magister* title and was a member of the circle of Gerard Pucelle, the
English master who was connected with the short-lived canonist school at
Cologne.[147] That the issues were not purely academic, we may assume
from the context of the early thirteenth-century German church; that they
had universal significance is evident from the fact that they became part of
the decretal collection of Pope Gregory IX.[148]

    The state of the church in Lorraine, of which matters at Metz give but
small evidence, can also be seen in the neighboring diocese of Toul. The
thaw in relations between the papacy and Philip of Swabia is nowhere better
reflected than in the fact that between 1205 and 1207 papal opposition to
Bishop Matthew temporarily ceased. Matthew was the son of Frederick of
Bitsch and Ludmilla of Poland who had entered the Church as a child and
had held canonates at Toul and St. Die from age six. Later he become
provost at St. Die and archdeacon of Toul, having prevailed against
opposition to his election. His uncanonical life as bishop since 1197
aroused new concern, however, and while Cardinal-bishop Guy was yet in
Germany he had excommunicated the prelate of Toul. The specific grounds
for the action were perjury, squandering church property, performing
ecclesiastical functions while suspended, and notoriously maintaining a
lengthy liaison with a nun, by whom he fathered two sons and a daughter.
Such behavior notwithstanding, on 7 June 1205, Innocent III directed three
prominent clerics from Paris, *G. maior archidiaconus, magister R[ ]
poenitentiarius S. Victoris* and *magister R[obertus] de Curzon Noviomensis
canonicus*, to absolve Bishop Matthew from the chains of excommunication,
but to leave standing the sentence of suspension which Cardinal-legate Guy
had imposed upon him; they were also to appoint a suitable procurator who

---

[146] Cf. "Bigamy," in *Catholic Encyclopaedia* II (1908) 561; J. Vergier-Boimond, "Bigamie
(l'Irrégularité de)," *Dictionnaire de Droit Canonique*, ed. Raoul Naz (Paris, 1935ff.) II, cols.
853-888, espec. 879-881.

[147] For a general treatment of Bishop Bertram, see Voigt, *Bischof Bertram von Metz*. A
brief biography is given by Stephan Kuttner, "Bertram of Metz," *Traditio* 13 (1957) 501-505,
upon which G. Gerbenzon, "Bertram of Metz, author of 'Elegantius in iure diuino' (summa
Coloniensis)?," *Traditio* 21 (1965) 510-511, Johannes Fried, "Gerard Pucelle und Köln,"
ZSRG KanAbt 66 (1982) 125-135, and Gero Dolezalek, "Zur Datierung des Kommentars 'De
regulis iuris' von Bertrandus Metensis," *Ius Commune* XI (Frankfurt, 1984) 32-36, lean. I
have not seen *Bertrandus Metensis de regulis iuris*, a Severino Caprioli descriptus, Università
di Perugia, Pubblicazioni della Facoltà di Giurisprudenza 27 (Perugia, 1981).

[148] *Decretalium D. Gregorii Papae IX.*, in *Corpus Iuris Canonici*, ed. Aemilius Friedberg
(2nd ed.; Leipzig, 1879; repr. Graz, 1959) l.III.t.42 *De baptismo et eius effectu* c.4 (p. 646);
l.I.tit.21 *De bigamis non ordinandis* c. 5 (p. 147).

was to administer the affairs of the bishopric in the interim.[149] Somewhat later (1 February 1207) the pope compromised even further by mandating that the case against the bishop of Toul and his dean regarding their allowing the church there to deteriorate, their excommunication, perjury and various other canonical charges be terminated.[150] Although everyone knew that Matthew was a complete reprobate, totally unworthy of the episcopal office, the preference given him makes it obvious that Innocent himself cared nothing at the time for the *cura animarum*; rather, the cause of the resolution of this conflict lay alone in political considerations.

In reality, further papal opposition to Philip of Swabia was futile; Otto IV was not to be helped. The Welf defeat near Wasserberg on 27 August 1206 brought his kingdom to an end. He barely escaped his antagonist and retreated to Brunswick, while his ally, the Anti-archbishop Bruno of Cologne, was taken prisoner and held captive, first at Trifels-on-the-Rhine and later at Rothenburg-ob-der-Tauber. The other major beneficiary of Otto's support, Archbishop Siegfried of Mainz, fled to a temporary haven at the Cistercian abbey of Altenberg, but later left the Empire altogether and sought refuge in Rome, living near the church of Sta. Sabina where he also became cardinal-priest.[151]

Innocent III meanwhile called in the favor granted to Wolfger of Ellenbrechtskirchen in 1202 when he allowed the translation from Passau to Aquileia. To the patriarch was given the task of establishing peace between the Curia and Philip. In 1206 Wolfger at last succeeded in bringing the Staufen ruler to extend an offer, but the pontiff refused to accept the conditions. After Wasserberg, Philip also sent delegates to Rome; the archbishop of Magdeburg, traveling to the Curia in his own cause, likewise tried to establish new negotiations. Realizing that he could no longer deal with Philip of Swabia as though he were still just a duke and not the legitimate king, Innocent at length altered his relationship to him and created a special legation with powers to effect peace between all parties. Dispatched to Germany were Cardinal-bishop Ugolino of Ostia and Velletri,

---

[149] Morret, *Stand und Herkunft* 67; Potthast, *Regesta* I, Nr. 2534; Migne, *PL* CCXV, col. 659. The administration of the bishopric was assumed by Walther abbot of St. Urban as *procurator Tullensis episcopatus*. Robert of Curzon later was elevated to be cardinal-legate for France; cf. Zimmermann, *Päpstl. Legationen* 43; Hauck, *KGD* IV 719. *Richeri Gesta* 285-288, gives a contemporary account of Matthew's activities.

[150] (Reg. Inn. IX, 259) Migne *PL* CCXV, col. 1087; Potthast, *Regesta* I Nr. 2995, 2996; Hauck, *KGD* IV, 719, 738.

[151] *Chron. reg. Colon. cont. III* (a. 1206) 223-224; Idem. (a. 1208) 226; *Reineri Ann.* 203; Hauck, *KGD* IV 745; Winkelmann, *Phil. von Schw.* I 399, note 3. Kuttner/Garcia y Garcia, "New Eyewitness Account" 159 and note 151, see the title of cardinal-priest of S. Sabina as vacant from 1202 to 1216, inasmuch as Siegfried was never referred to as such by the papal chancery. Cf. also Hüffer, "Denkstein und Schisma" 137.

and Leo, cardinal-priest of S. Croce. Preparing the way for them was Wolfger of Aquileia who hastened to Strasbourg with the most welcome news, joining Philip at Pentecost (10 June 1207).[152]

Shortly thereafter, the legates themselves met Philip at Speyer and commenced the difficult process of reconciling him with the Curia. With the resolution of this question were connected two major ecclesiastical issues: the ultimate disposition of the contested successions at Mainz and Cologne. The legates sought the total and unqualified recognition of Siegfried of Eppstein in Mainz, which meant the simultaneous rejection of Lupold of Worms. With respect to Cologne, they not only labored to secure Philip's recognition of Bruno of Sayn who had already been confirmed as archbishop by Innocent III, but also to obtain the release of Bruno from captivity. Though they did not have the authority to reject Otto IV as German king and force his abdication, they were empowered to persuade him to abdicate voluntarily. At a large and festive assembly (*Hoftag*) held at Worms during August 1207 the ban of excommunication was lifted from Philip by the two legates and the establishment of cordial relations between the Staufen monarch and the papacy was effected. The promise of peace and an end of strife was ultimately contingent upon Otto IV's willingness to abdicate, however. Until that actually happened, Philip was opposed to releasing Bruno of Sayn. Never fully cognizant of political realities, Otto refused to relinquish his crown, even despite the offer of considerable bribes from the Staufen camp—e.g., Philip's daughter was held out as a wife for the erstwhile monarch. In November 1207 at Augsburg, at the insistence of the legates, Philip finally agreed to release the Cologne archbishop who returned with them to Rome early the following year to await a change in the political conditions within his see. As an act of conciliation toward the Cologne *priores*, the legates also released the former archbishop, Adolf of Altena, from the three-year-long ban of excommunication.[153]

Adolf also went to Rome where, to the dismay of Bruno, he personally pled his case before the Curia. Thus, the question of who should be recognized as the legitimate archbishop of Cologne remained unresolved. While the affairs of the archbishopric were administered in Bruno's name by the *archidiaconus maior*, the two prelates struggled against one another

---

[152] Ugolino, the future Pope Gregory IX, was probably Innocent's uncle, being also a count of Segni; cf. Winkelmann, *Phil. von Schw.* I 414-420; Schwemer, *Innocent III.* 117-121; Ernst Brem, *Gregor IX. bis zum Beginn seines Pontificates* (Heidelberg, 1911) 204; Zimmermann, *Päpstl. Legationen* 39, 62; Hauck, *KGD* IV 748-749.

[153] Winkelmann, *Phil. von Schw.* I 422-429; Schwemer, *Innocent III.* 122-125; Hauck, *KGD* IV 750-751.

before the papal judges for a clear title to the office.[154]   The papacy, however, seemed content to move very slowly on this particular issue, waiting to see in which direction the political winds in Germany would finally blow.

Despite the growing power of Philip in Germany, it was unthinkable to the Curia that Lupold of Scheinfeld might succeed in his attempts to obtain Mainz.   At the November 1207 assembly the legates also extracted from Philip the concession to depose Lupold as archbishop and to recognize Siegfried of Eppstein as essentially the lawful primate.   The Staufen ruler's willingness to acquiesce on that issue was not an indication that he regarded Siegfried as better suited for the position of primate of the German church, but merely a necessary step to make the final peace possible.   Accepting the inevitable, Lupold renounced his archiepiscopal title in the presence of the legates and was released from the ban; unresolved was the question of whether he must also abdicate as bishop of Worms.   Representatives of Siegfried were then given permission to administer *ad interim* the spiritualities, but not yet the temporal affairs of the archdiocese.[155]   Siegfried had to await the final disposition of his case in Rome, but given his position as a cardinal and the actions already taken, the outcome was assured.

The legates returned to Rome in February 1208, confident that they had moved the German throne controversy closer to a settlement.   Lacking the authorization to recognize Philip openly as king, they took delegates of the latter with them, hoping to arrange for Philip's imperial coronation which now seemed a foregone conclusion; Innocent III had apparently given in completely.   The papal court must have been a curious sight in early 1208 as a stream of Germans went over the Alps to find solutions to their problems: making frequent and impassioned appearances were the opposing archbishops of Cologne, Bruno of Sayn and Adolf of Berg, pleading with the Curia to recognize them as the legitimate prelate, yet failing in their attempts to speed up the papal deliberations; joining them was Archbishop Siegfried of Mainz whose uncompromising opposition to the Staufen party since 1200 had made it impossible for him to return to Germany so long as Philip of Swabia reigned; Lupold of Scheinfeld also appeared to make certain that he did not lose Worms as well; present also were the delegates of Philip and of Otto; and lastly, there were the representatives of the city of Mainz who sought a lifting of the interdict which their disobedience

---

[154] Joseph Löhr, *Die Verwaltung des kölnischen Grossarchidiakonats am Ausgang des Mittelalters*, Kirchenrechtliche Abhandlungen 59/60 (Stuttgart, 1909) 277-286, lists Dietrich of Altena, a first cousin of Adolf, as the provost of Xanten and as the *archidiaconus maior* for the archdiocese of Cologne since 1199.

[155] Winkelmann, *Phil. von Schw.* I 430-431; Hüffer, "Denkstein und Schisma" 139-141.

toward Siegfried had brought upon their heads. It was clear that the center of gravity for German public life had shifted to Rome for the time being.

Accepting the arrangements made to that point, Innocent re-established his legation to Germany in mid-1208, giving them all the necessary powers to grant final recognition to Philip. He also sent the delegation from the city of Mainz back home, instructing them to take up their case with the legates when the latter arrived. In letters dated 3 June to the prelates and clergy of Mainz, the pontiff stated that since the archbishop of Mainz had now received "*iura tam spiritualia quam temporalia*," they were obligated to obey him.[156]

The Assassination of Philip of Swabia

The matter of Cologne remained unresolved, perhaps in deference to the as-yet delicate relations with Philip, but a date was set for dealing with it. Before that new date arrived, however, Philip of Swabia was assassinated and the question of making peace between Welf and Staufen, between Adolf and Bruno, became suddenly quite moot. The mortal blows, which Innocent III regarded as an act of God, were struck within the bishop's palace at Bamberg to which the king had retired for some rest on the afternoon of 21 June 1208. The assassin was the Pfalzgrave Otto of Wittelsbach, but almost at once the rumor began to spread that the bishop of Bamberg, Ekbert of Andechs, and his brother were parties to the conspiracy. The alleged reason for the murder was that Philip was attempting to prevent a marriage between the niece of the bishop and Otto, and in desperation the thwarted magnate had struck down his adversary.[157]

The irony is that Ekbert was one of King Philip's staunchest supporters. Even after his oath to the pope in 1203, that he would remain faithful to Rome in all matters whatsoever, he refused to abandon the Staufen ruler and to recognize Otto IV as king. Thus, before the end of 1204 he had been excommunicated and remained under the ban of the Church for almost two full years. As late as March 1206, while seeking release from the ban, he was forced once again to renew his oath of obedience as a pre-condition.[158] Not until the dramatic reversals which forced the papacy to make peace with Philip in 1207 could Ekbert move about as part of the Staufen retinue without fear of papal censure. Although there was not a shred of

---

[156] (Epp. Inn. XI, 93 and 94) Migne, *PL* CCXV, cols. 1411-1412; Potthast, *Regesta* I, Nrs. 3431, 3432.

[157] Winkelmann, *Phil. von Schw.* I 464-466, 477; Hauck, *KGD* IV 752, calls this „*die schlimmste Untat, welche die deutsche Geschichte kennt, . . .*"

[158] Winkelmann, *Phil. von Schw.* I 410; see also the sources cited for Ekbert's biography in Guttenberg, *Bistum Bamberg* 164-170.

evidence of a conspiracy involving the bishop of Bamberg, it was widely believed and even Otto IV pronounced the ban of the Empire (*Reichsacht*) over the accused. In fear for his life, Ekbert fled to the court of his brother-in-law, the king of Hungary, through whose entreaties the pope at length agreed to establish a commission to investigate the charges in early 1209.[159]

While Ekbert of Bamberg was thus at pains to exculpate himself from the charges of complicity in the murder, Otto IV of Brunswick reasserted himself in Germany and won the support of the papacy and of the princes and prelates alike, without any appreciable opposition. The first letter written by him to Innocent III after Philip's death expressed the hope that Bruno of Sayn and Siegfried of Eppstein would soon return. The re-ascendancy of Otto strengthened the position of Bruno who had always been loyal to the Welf ruler, and when he returned to Cologne on 11 September 1208, all of Adolf's supporters received him ceremoniously and swore fealty.[160]

Somehow, the blind ambition of Adolf of Berg refused to accept all that had transpired; even while the clergy of Cologne were repairing their relationship with Archbishop Bruno, Adolf dispatched a cleric named Hermann to represent him once more in Rome. The pope refused a new hearing, as noted in a letter dated 23 October 1208, but he did promise Adolf that if he would bow to the papal will respecting Cologne, he would receive another bishopric.[161] Unfortunately for the badly divided archbishopric, Bruno of Sayn died on 2 November 1208, even before the pope's letter to Adolf arrived, and the latter's hopes were once more rekindled. Perhaps owing to the continued hatred against the Berg party within the Cologne church, no unity among the *priores* could be achieved at the election held shortly thereafter.

Otto IV heard of the election dispute at Cologne while holding court at Strasbourg. It was important enough to him that he wrote the *priores* and commanded them to wait until he arrived before they proceeded further. Entering Cologne on 20 December 1208, he informed them that he preferred the bishop of Cambrai, a former supporter, for the position. The electors protested that the man did not even know the language of the land and rejected the suggestion out of hand. Caesarius of Heisterbach relates that at this juncture Dean Hermann of Bonn, a man of great erudition and reputation among the *priores*, claimed that he had been instructed in a vision of the Blessed Virgin to elect the provost of the church of the Holy

---

[159] Potthast, *Regesta* I, Nr. 3617.

[160] *Chron. reg. Colon., cont. III (a. 1208)* 226; Hüffer, "Denkstein und Schisma," 142; Röhrich, *Adolf I. von Köln* 93-95; Binterim, *Concilien* IV 415-417.

[161] Potthast, *Regesta* I, Nr. 3523.

Apostles, Dietrich of Hengebach, instead.[162] This selection was in fact made on 22 December and won immediate approval from Otto IV: Dietrich had been the opponent of Engelbert of Berg in the controversy over the Cologne provostship from 1199 to 1203, and as one who had stood faithfully by the Welf ruler even during the darkest moments of the throne dispute, he was clearly more acceptable than the treacherous Adolf.[163]

Adolf and his faction refused to accept that decision, however, and once more sent an appeal to Rome. Innocent rejected this latest effort as well: he not only confirmed the election of Dietrich and sent him the pallium, but he also commanded Adolf to be content with an annual pension of 250 Marks.[164] Dietrich was consecrated on 24 May 1209 (the Sunday after Pentecost), and as an indication of the changed political state of Germany, all the suffragans of Cologne were present. There were so many in fact that a conflict even arose over who was to confer the blessing: Dietrich thus appointed Bishop Hugh of Liège.[165]

Adolf withdrew to the archiepiscopal fortress of Neuss, across the Rhine from Cologne. He does not appear to have given up his title as commanded by the pope: a cornerstone of the church of St. Quirinus laid there in 1209 refers to him as *archiepiscopus*. That same title is given him in a 1209 document issued by the count of Hückeswagen, a vassal of the counts of Berg. The so-called *Scheinsrolle* at Andernach as late as 1211 also is dated according to the pontifical years of Adolf as archbishop of Cologne, revealing that this town still recognized him as the legitimate prelate.[166] The thing which encouraged Adolf in his role as the pretender was that Dietrich of Hengebach quickly aroused enemies within his church. Whereas he had earlier been known as a pious and reasonable man, soon after his elevation he is said to have followed bad counsel: making no distinction between laymen and clergy, between monks and peasants, he oppressed all with unjust taxes and exactions.[167]

The indictment may not be without some basis, but one must consider the state of the archbishopric at the time. Cologne had been through ten

---

[162] *Caesarii Dialogus* VIII 40.

[163] See Knipping, *REK* III, Nrs. 4, 40, which record commissions given to Dietrich by Innocent III relative to punishment of Cologne canons who supported Adolf of Berg against Bruno of Sayn; cf. also Migne, *PL* CCXVI, col. 1155; Potthast, *Regesta* Nrs. 2577, 3412; Böhmer-Ficker, *Regg. Imp.* V 1093, Nr. 5932.

[164] Migne, *PL* CCXVI, col. 142; Potthast, *Regesta* I, Nr. 3819; *Reineri Ann.* 661; Hauck, *KGD* IV 754.

[165] *Chron. reg. Colon. cont. II (a. 1209)* 184; *cont. III (a. 1209)* 229; Hüffer, "Denkstein und Schisma" 143-146.

[166] Hüffer, "Denkstein und Schisma" 143-147; Lacomblet, *NRUB* II, Nr. 25.

[167] *Caesarii Dialogus* VII 40.

years of war and devastation—Archbishop Bruno had found it necessary at his accession to obtain a papal dispensation to retain the incomes from his previous prebends for a period of two years just to meet the needs of his new office.[168] Earlier problems were compounded by the breakdown of public order once relations between Innocent III and Otto IV began to disintegrate. The taxes were thus seen as necessary for building fortifications and repairing destroyed church property. The church at Cologne would thus continue to be torn by partisan politics for seven additional years beyond the election of Dietrich of Hengebach.

The controversy at Mainz was more easily resolved with the death of King Philip. Upon hearing that news, Siegfried of Eppstein rushed to Mainz where he also was received without opposition. With the final obstacle removed, he was at last able to assume his full role as archbishop, and in early 1209 (before 20 February) he convened a synod for the purpose of effecting clerical reform and repairing damage inflicted upon his church during nine years of schismatic struggles. Since Bishop-elect Otto of Würzburg was present and attested a document with two seals—one which bears the circumscription "*Wirceb. electus*" and another with *Wirceb. eccl. episcopus*," it is probable that he received consecration from his metropolitan at this time. Siegfried of Augsburg, who appears 11 January 1209 as *electus*, may also have received the episcopal blessing at this synod. That Werner of Staufen, the bishop-elect of Constanz since 1206, used this occasion to resign his office, as Winkelmann suggests, has been disproved, however.[169]

Pre-Lateran IV Reforms at Mainz

The purposes of this synod were both pastoral and juridical; the decrees bear a strong similarity to statutes of Paris, issued by Bishop Eudes de Sully in 1208.[170] They give us another rare view into the inner-life of the German church on the eve of the Fourth Lateranum, allowing us to see

---

[168] Migne, *PL* CCXV, col. 755; Potthast, *Regesta* I, Nr. 2632.

[169] The synod is missing in Hefele/Knöpfler, *Conciliengeschichte* V, but Wenck, *Hess. Landesgesch.* II 132, Nr. 94 and note, as well as Rossel, *UB Eberbach* I, Nrs. 64, 65, prove its reality. Winkelmann, *Phil. von Schw.* II 484—Anlage VI, refers to the actions taken with respect to Eberbach on the basis of the above references. Finke, *Konzilienst.* 42-43, declares that there are "no known decrees." Further references by H-Bréholles, *Hist. dipl.* I 404; Böhmer-Will, *RAM* II 140, Nr. 109, and Hauck, *KGD* IV 135, note 1. The statutes appear to be those found in Innsbruck, Universitätsbibliothek, MS. 16, fol. 1ʳ by Johanek, whose discussion is found in "Synodalia" I 34-35, and III 62. The complete Latin text of the statutes is given in Johanek, "Pariser Statuten" 345-347.

[170] See Ch. One, pp. 52-53, 85-86.

those matters which concerned a major ecclesiastical figure in 1209. By analogy we may surmise that other churches had similar problems:

[1] Let baptism be celebrated with the greatest reverence and prudence, and especially with discrimination and enunciation of the words, wherein rests the power of the Sacrament, namely, "I baptize thee in the name of the Father and of the Son and of the Holy Spirit."

[2] Moreover, let them teach the laity—as much the men as the women, that in necessity they ought to baptize their own children, provided the same form is preserved in their own tongue. Fathers and/or mothers, if the most extreme necessity demands, ought to baptize their own.

[5] Let the Eucharist, the fonts, the Chrism, and the Holy Oil be under lock and key because of witchcrafts.

[6] Let not the deacons and clergy of lesser orders venture to bear the Eucharist, save either in the absence of a priest or when necessity demands.

[7] When the priest visits the sick, let him see to it that a lamp is born before the Eucharist reverently with a bright flame, and let them be moved with the tinkling of a bell, and let the priest see to it that the laity, when they see them being carried out, bow down and show reverence to the Savior in prayer; moreover, let the priest chant seven psalms or, if the way be longer, let him chant fifteen offices.

[8] A priest ought not celebrate mass twice in one day, except in necessity.

[11] Let the priests reserve the greater [penances] for the greater [sins] in confession as, for instance, homicide, acts of sacrilege, sins against nature, incest as well as debauching of virgins, striking parents, broken vows, and other things of this sort.

[12] When imposing penances upon youth, let the priests take care, for the extent of the penance ought to be according to the extent of the sin and the ability of the confessor, otherwise let the lesser be required of them.

[13] In the case of theft, usury, robbery, and fraud let the priests especially take care lest they impose other penances, namely, the performance of masses and the giving of alms and other things before they make restitution, for such a sin is not forgiven unless what was taken has been restored.

[16] Let matrimony be celebrated with honor and reverence and in the presence of the congregation [church], not with laughter and jestingly, lest it be lightly esteemed, and before it is performed, on three Sabbaths or feast-days which are removed one from another, because with three edicts the priest must inquire of the people, under penalty of excommunication, concerning the legitimacy of the groom and the bride, in accordance with which they ought to be joined, and before the plighted troth, concerning the making of the marriage contract, except in the presence of the priest in a sacred place—namely, before the doors of the church—and in the presence of the people.

[19] Let every priest have a book, which is called a handbook, in which the order of performing extreme unction and baptism and any other ordinary office of this sort is [set out] according to the usage which is maintained in the cathedral church.

[22] Let no priest have a concubine in his own house.

[23] In like manner, let no priest dare to go to a spectacle, to attend a dancing show, to enter taverns for the sake of drinking, to run about through the towns in laymen's clothes, and let them not wear raiment improper to their order.

[26] Let archdeacons be given the charge that throughout their term of office, they personally see to it that the excesses of their subordinates are corrected and that books, chalices, platters, robes and altars used in church services are properly maintained. Woe unto them if these are found to be excessively soiled.

Here we see clearly that concern for pastoral matters in the which Bishop Eudes of Paris anticipated many of the decrees of Lateran IV. Similar concerns as these were recognized at synods held after the Council at Cologne and Trier, reflecting a change in the role of synods as perceived by some German churchmen. The immediate impact of these reform canons upon the church of Mainz was ephemeral at best, however: Siegfried II of Mainz was forced to flee his city again in 1211, following the excommunication of Otto IV; furthermore, his role in the election, coronation, and recognition of Frederick II of Staufen from 1212 until late 1215 precluded his devoting much time to ecclesiastical or pastoral matters prior to the Fourth Lateran Council. It may thus be concluded that on the eve of the Council the problems besetting the archbishopric and province of Mainz had found little serious attention.

Siegfried's antagonist for the archbishopric of Mainz, Bishop Lupold of Worms, realized the futility of his cause with the death of King Philip and therefore left Germany in 1208. Unlike Adolf of Altena whose family ties gave him great influence and support within the cathedral chapter at Cologne, Lupold had been heavily dependent upon royal patronage; with its collapse, he had little practical hope of ever asserting his claims to the archbishopric. Furthermore, he had formally resigned his shaky office in the presence of papal-legates, doing so as a condition of his being received back into full communion in the Church. Until the fall of Otto IV in 1211 he served Frederick II of Sicily as legate in Italy, avoiding any further condemnation from the papacy while indulging his predisposition for warfare. His actions since 1200 left his bishopric deeply in debt and his successors also had to depend on their former prebends as major sources of income.[171] There is thus little question that the church of Worms was without a legitimate pastor during this entire time, the consequences of which have been discussed above.

An anonymous writing of the third or fourth decade of the thirteenth century gives a dismal picture of life within the German church, but focuses

---

[171] Krabbo, *Besetzung* 54; Pressutti, *Regg. Hon. III*, I 739, and 1392, Nr. 2.

especially upon the prelate of Worms:

> Propter tot improperia   factum dampnantes proprium,
> Ducuntur penitentia   Treveris et Moguncia.
> Sed allegat Wormacia   statuti privilegium;
> Repagulantur ostia,   nulli patet hospicium
> Petenti necessaria.
> Videns ergo perniciem   fundator urbis variam
> Nec meram cleri faciem,   sed pictam superficiem
> wangionumque rabiem,   cuius per avariciam
> Gignit vorago maciem,   recte dixit Wormaciam
> Quasi vermium aciem.[172]

The problems which the throne controversy had created within the church of Worms had not been eliminated by the 1230s or even 1240s, suggesting just how deeply the neglect by Bishop Lupold had affected it.

Conflicts in Lorraine and Northern Germany

The resolution of the schism at Mainz brought an end to one of the longest episcopal disputes occasioned by the throne contest. Apart from this conflict, however, there were others which impacted upon church life, such as those between pro-French and pro-German parties in Lorraine, and those which were essentially between the supporters of great noble families in the various German regions. On 25 July 1208 Bishop Albert II (de Hirges) of Verdun died during a struggle with his burghers. The cathedral dean and the chapter set the election date for the eighth day after the burial and, without notifying those *capitulares* who were absent from the city, they proceeded with the election. The choice of those voting fell upon Robert of Grandpré, *primicerius* or provost of Verdun, against whose canonically-irregular election the canon Herbert appealed to Rome. The pope in turn summoned proctors of both sides to Rome where Herbert claimed that Robert had been chosen because he had agreed to pay the debts of the former bishop, that he had been sworn to secrecy over the matter by the cathedral chapter, and that, having done so, had been enthroned. He further

---

[172] Cf. Cambridge University Library, vol. 11, 78; edited by Eduard Winkelmann, in *Monatschrift für rheinisch-westfälische Geschichte* 4 (1878) 336-338, and cited in Böhmer-Will, *RAM*, II xxxi. See further, *Chron. Reinhardsbr.* 94: *"At vero de hoc suo tam tumultuoso hiatu, ut probavit postea rei eventus, Lupoldus extorpuit, quia nimirum inexecrabili infamia in diebus dominice passionis stuprum in virginibus, adulteria in matrimoniis quam plurima patravisse putatus est, atque in eum modum, qui prius belligerante lingua nubibus etiam insultare videbatur, incredibili confectus inopia, miserando tenore, prodito et impignorato reddituum suorum patrimonio, meticulosus et profugus labifuga compulsus est."*

contended that the *primicerius* was a poorly-trained man. And yet, despite these factors, Herbert complained, the archbishop of Trier (John I) had confirmed the election and consecrated Robert as bishop. The proctors of the cathedral chapter defended their actions on the grounds that the unrest in the city (which had in fact cost the former bishop his life), had necessitated that the election proceed quickly, allowing no time for the absentees to arrive.[173]

Innocent III thereupon established a commission of three cathedral clerics from Rheims to investigate the validity of the charges, despite Herbert's insistence that the Curia alone make the decision. They were instructed, however, that a deposition was in order only if the charge of *defectus competentis litteraturae* were proven, and this they were to determine. The documentation of this investigation is lacking, but the commission's decision was to depose Robert. When the latter refused to acknowledge this, he was also excommunicated. Their objectivity in the matter may be somewhat suspect, however, since Herbert was also dean at Rheims (a fact hardly unknown in the Curia). Although well advanced in years, Robert went to Rome in 1215 for a personal audience with the pope. Innocent III did in fact withhold confirmation of the commission's action, but he likewise refused to quash it. The pontiff did not live to see the end of the dispute, but his successor Honorius III remained just as adamant about refusing Robert the bishopric. He did, however, release Robert from the ban at the request of the cathedral chapter and grant him a pension. The latter died suddenly in 1217 before he actually abdicated.[174] During more than nine years of conflict over the bishopric, the established machinery for effecting reform and maintaining discipline within the diocese of Verdun was thus essentially inoperative.

As in the frontier region of Lorraine, so too in northern Germany episcopal elections reflected not only the partisan alignments of the Empire, but international politics as well. Archbishop Hartwig of Bremen died on 3 November 1207 and, in the election that followed (no earlier than March 1208), Bishop Waldemar of Schleswig was chosen and supported by the majority of the cathedral chapter and the *ministeriales*, while the cathedral provost, Burckard of Stumpenhausen, and a few others abstained. According to the constitution of the Bremen church, the cathedral chapter at Hamburg should also have had a voice in the election, but it was ignored on this occasion because that city and its church were under the control of

---

[173] See Potthast, *Regesta* I, Nr. 3657.

[174] *Gesta Vird.* 520 and 527; (Regg. Inn. XI, ep. 261) Migne, *PL* CCXV, col 1565-1568, and (XV, ep. 196) *PL* CCXVI, col. 723-725; Pressutti, *Regg. Hon. III* I 59, Nr. 335. Further, see Morret, *Stand und Herkunft* 108-109; Kuhle, *Neubesetzung* 69.

the Danish king. Bishop Waldemar (cousin and rival of the Danish king) was studying at Bologna at the time of the election and it was here that a cathedral canon from Bremen found him and informed him of the chapter's choice; together they traveled to Rome for confirmation. Waldemar also received support from King Philip who appealed to the Curia on his behalf, seeing the bishop as a useful ally in northern Germany.[175]

Meanwhile, the Hamburg cathedral chapter elected the dissenting provost of Bremen who was quickly invested by the king of Denmark and thereby became the latter's pawn in international politics. At the same time the Hamburg canons lodged an appeal with Rome, pointing out the irregularity of Waldemar's election and requesting that their candidate, Burckard, be confirmed by Innocent III. Thus, the pontiff was faced at once with an opportunity to exercise his plenary powers of jurisdiction yet another time in Germany, but also with a dilemma. The chances of Bishop Waldemar were irreparably damaged when he failed to remain in Rome until the matter was resolved, as demanded by the pope. In fact, so displeased was Innocent that he excommunicated the prelate and sent a directive to the Bremen cathedral chapter to conduct a new election within one month (after March 1208).[176] The death of King Philip removed all support for Waldemar, but the bishop of Schleswig quickly found an ally in Otto IV and he continued his opposition to Innocent III and the Bremen church as late as July 1209.[177]

The issue had become quite involved for the canons at Bremen: they had been commanded by the pope to conduct a new election, but they found themselves at odds with Bishop Waldemar of Schleswig, the canons at Hamburg, Otto IV, the Danish king and their own provost. Their challenge was that of finding a candidate whose resources and family ties were sufficient to compete with the pretender Waldemar, while at the same time assuaging the opposition of Hamburg, The choice finally fell upon Gerhard of Oldenburg, son of Count Henry I of Oldenburg-Wildeshausen and Salome, daughter of Count Gerhard of Gelders, who since 1190 had been bishop of Osnabrück. Gerhard's brother was Otto, since 1203 cathedral

---

[175] See *Arnoldi Chron. slav.* (cap. 10) 242; *Ann. Stad. (a. 1208)* 355; *Ann. Essenbec. (a. 1209)* 225. For details on the schism, cf. Georg Dehio, "Waldemar Bischof von Schleswig, Erzbischof von Bremen," *HZ* 30 (1873) 222-238; Krabbo, *Besetzung* 41-45; M-Alpermann, *Stand und Herkunft* 67-68; May, *REB* 164, 195-201.

[176] Kuhle, *Neubesetzung* 58.

[177] On 2 July 1209 Innocent III directed Otto IV to drive the apostate Waldemar and his accomplices from Bremen; the same day he issued a mandate to Bishops Otto of Münster and Gerhard of Osnabrück, and to the suffragans of Bremen, that they publish the ban of excommunication against Waldemar and his associates. See Potthast, *Regesta* I, Nrs. 3760, 3761; Lappenberg, *Hamb. UB* I, Nr. 377.

provost at Bremen and later bishop of Münster, and his sister was the mother of Burckard of Stumpenhausen, the choice of the Hamburg cathedral chapter to oppose Bishop Waldemar in 1208.[178] The selection seemed ideal: the vast wealth of the Oldenburg family—their far-reaching connections with other churches in northern Germany—was surely sufficient to end the pretenses of Bishop Waldemar; furthermore, the family ties with Burckard of Stumpenhausen would assure support of the choice from him and the Hamburg chapter.

Despite his lofty pronouncements concerning episcopal elections, Innocent III often compromised for political reasons as has been shown above. While he did not approve the immediate translation of Gerhard of Osnabrück to Bremen, he did allow him to retain the former bishopric until he had received the pallium as archbishop.[179] Such a move undoubtedly served to bring Gerhard into the camp of Frederick II once the papacy had withdrawn its support of the Welf monarchy. Burckard of Stumpenhausen, who had never been confirmed by the pope, resigned as archbishop-elect and was re-admitted as cathedral provost at Bremen. Waldemar of Schleswig, on the other hand, remained obdurate and amid shouts of joy from burghers and *ministeriales* he entered Bremen. His determination not to surrender the archbishopric was so intense that the Roman pontiff finally summoned the monastic orders and the peasants of the region to a crusade against him.[180] Regardless of such measures, however, Waldemar adhered to Otto IV until the latter's inglorious end, watching his own power in northern Germany decline commensurate to that of the erstwhile emperor. With Otto's death, Waldemar's grip over Bremen was finally broken and he fled as a humble penitent to Rome. In 1220 Pope Honorius III released him from the ban and allowed him to enter the Cistercian monastery at Loccum where he died in obscurity in 1235/1236.[181]

The schism at Bremen had tremendous negative effects on the state of the Church in that province. During the entire conflict the king of Denmark made frequent punishing raids into Bremen territory, leaving death and destruction in his wake.[182] The thorough disarray of political conditions throughout the province since 1208 helps account for the apparent failure of archbishops of Bremen to convoke synods or in other ways deal with mat-

---

[178] Pelster, *Stand und Herkunft* 70, 82.

[179] Philippi, *UB Osnabrück* II, Nr. 47 (30 October 1210); Lappenberg, *Hamb. UB* I, Nrs. 378, 382; Potthast, *Regesta* I, Nrs. 4115-4118. Gerhard retained Osnabrück until 1216; he died 1219; cf. *Westf. UB* V, Nr. 228.

[180] Lappenberg, *Hamb. UB* I, Nr. 397.

[181] Potthast, *Regesta* I, Nr. 6362 (24 September 1220).

[182] See Krabbo, *Ostdeutsche Bistümer* 13; Idem, *Besetzung* 61.

ters of ecclesiastical reform in the years immediately preceding the Fourth
Lateran Council.

In reality, there were very few actual opportunities for effecting changes
within the German church between 1198 and 1215. The civil war so
engaged the energies of princes and prelates alike that even those who might
have sought reform found it virtually impossible to do so. Churches
throughout the Empire suffered the most: e.g., Gerlach, the provost of the
Premonstratensian monastery Mühlhausen in Bohemia reported that a
monastery lying in Otto's territory also had extensive property in Staufen
regions; it was thus unable to draw any income from them during the entire
period of the throne dispute, losing in this manner over 3000 Marks in
revenue. On occasion, Philip appropriated church property, angering the
Cistercian and Premonstratensian orders alike. Thus, the demise of Philip
provided an opportunity to institute changes and correct abuses, and we
have noted above some instances of this very thing. Occasionally, however,
even greater problems arose, as the death of the Staufen ruler removed a
strong territorial authority from southern Germany. A Swabian ministerial,
e.g., plundered the monastery at Weissenau without fear of reprisal; Abbot
Eberhard of Salmansweiler (Salem), likewise in Swabia, was forced to pay
tribute in the form of grain, cheese, wine and even money to several robber
barons of his region.[183] The papal registers contain numerous entries of
special letters of protection extended to religious houses during these
unsettled times.[184]

Innocent III's Relations With Otto IV

The complete reversal of the political situation in Germany after June 1208
also forced the pontiff to begin anew to secure recognition of the church's
privileges throughout the Empire from Otto IV. With that intent he
announced on 4 December 1208 the sending of legates to confer with Otto.
Departing Rome between 21 January and 3 February 1209, the Cardinals
Ugolino and Leo found him at Hagenau or Speyer near the end of February
or early March, and on 22 March 1209, a document issued at Speyer
recognized their demands of him: Otto renounced the right of spoils,
recognized the papal states and the Sicilian fief, agreed to help suppress
heresy, and renounced all influence in episcopal elections.[185] After the

---

[183] Winkelmann, *Phil. von Schw.* I 468-473; *Chron. Salemit.*, in Moné, *Quellensammlung*
III 27.

[184] Cf. Potthast, *Regesta* I, Nrs. 4763, 4766, for Maulbrunn and Schönau respectively.

[185] Zimmermann, *Päpstl. Legationen* 40, 191; Winkelmann, *Phil. von Schw.* II 141-144;
Hauck, *KGD* IV 765.

Speyer deliberations the legates traveled northward into the province of Cologne for the purpose of carrying out yet another portion of their mandate from the pope: they were to help effect a reform of conditions in the German church. According to the continuator of the *Chronica regia* at Cologne,

> *singulas civitates tam Saxoniae [Saxony] quam Alemanniae [Swabia] visitantes et iusticiam undique ecclesiis facientes, post pascha [29 March 1209] Coloniam venerunt, ubi a Theoderico Coloniensi archielecto et universo clero cum gloria suscepti et cum magno honore per dies 15 sunt detenti.*[186]

Their arrival at Cologne can be placed in the last week of April, inasmuch as Reiner of Liège noted that they were still in the city on 12 May.

On the latter day, they issued decrees for the ordering of church life within the province, which were later proclaimed in a general synod held at Liège.[187] It seems probable that they would have been present for the consecration of the Archbishop Dietrich of Hengebach on 24 May as well. According to the author of *Continuatio II* of the *Chronica regia* at Cologne, Dietrich had invited all his suffragans to attend that celebration.[188] We may thus assume that Bishop Dietrich II of Utrecht was among those bishops who contested for the right to consecrate the metropolitan.

Later that same year Dietrich of Utrecht summoned his clergy to treat matters relating to the state of the church in his diocese.[189] Hauck argues that these decrees were not the product of a diocesan synod, but rather regulations merely agreed upon and accepted by the ecclesiastical foundations of the diocese.[190] Given their corrective nature, and given the fact that similar sets of statutes were proclaimed publicly at Cologne and Liège that same year, it seems probably that the Utrecht prelate would have chosen the solemnity of a diocesan synod for promulgating these. Censures were pronounced against those found guilty of committing violence against church property—more particularly local laymen—suggesting that the practices and abuses of the civil-war period had not suddenly ceased. The deleterious effects of the throne controversy and the preoccupation of many

---

[186] *Chron. reg. Colon., cont. III (a. 1209)* 229.

[187] *Reineri Ann.* 661: "*. . . qui per quindecim dies in Coloniae moram fecerunt, et tam episcopum quam personas Leodienses ad se vocantes, nova decreta dederunt feria tertia ante pentecostem [12 May], quae in generali synodo postea sunt recitata.*" See also Binterim, *Concilien* IV 263, 417-418;

[188] *Chron. reg. Colon. cont. II (a. 1209)* 184: "*In octava pentecostes Theodericus electus omnes suffraganeos episcopos Coloniam invitavit, quatinus eorum suffragio secundum scita canonum episcopalibus insigniis investiri debuisset.*" See also *cont. III* 229.

[189] Binterim, *Concilien* IV, 458.

[190] Hauck, *KGD* IV, 8 and 9 note 2.

German prelates with that issue is also reflected in those decrees which were issued for the clergy, namely, that all healthy canons fulfill their choir obligations, that no canon hold two benefices in the same church, and that cathedral canons not possess the office of parish priest as well. Should a canon prove completely disobedient, the dean and the cathedral chapter were to suspend him from office or, failing this, withdraw his prebend altogether.

The decrees of the Utrecht synod were undoubtedly essentially the same as those promulgated on 12 May 1209 at Cologne by the papal-legates, and the same again as those unspecified "*nova decreta*" referred to by Reiner as being published at the synod held at Liège in 1209. The latter assembly also would have dealt with the request by Reiner that a visitation of his monastery be undertaken, and that accusations against Abbot Heinrich of St. Jacob's be investigated. As a consequence, the latter was removed from office, having been found guilty of negligence and serious moral turpitude.[191] Another possible response to the legatine synod at Cologne during May 1209 was the diocesan assembly convoked by Bishop Conrad I of Minden (ca. 1209-1214).[192] The only extant document issued at that synod refers to juridical matters which scarcely required synodal action: a grant to the monastery at Nenndorf was rescinded. It would be congruent with other suffragan bishoprics of Cologne to assume that statutes similar to those read at Cologne, Liège and Utrecht were also published on this occasion.

From Cologne the legates journeyed to Würzburg where, in late May 1209, they presided over a large assembly of prelates and princes: by their apostolic authority they granted a dispensation for the marriage of Otto IV to Beatrix, daughter of King Philip, a matter complicated by the prohibition against consanguinity.[193] Having resolved that, they may also have dealt with the allegations against Ekbert of Bamberg. Innocent III had charged them with determining his complicity in the murder of Philip of Swabia: if the allegations were true, they were to depose him without delay;

---

[191] *Reineri Ann. (a. 1208) 661: "Hoc anno Reinerus praesentium dictator, peticione fratrum suorum, cum I. contra Heinricum abbatem Romam ivit, et literas inquisitionis ad Coloniensis personas attulit, quia apellatus non venit nec sufficientem responsalem misit. Praeterea alia paria litterarum ecclesie sue acquisivit. . . . (a. 1209) In epiphania Domini Reinerus praesentium dictator Coloniae fuit, litteras quas a summo pontifice acceperat, inquisitoribus praesentavit, et ut ad locum accederent ammonuit, et Deum solum prae oculis habentes, sicut domnus papa praeceperat, quae corrigenda erant corrigerent, et quod regulare et honestum esset statuerent. Qui diem peremtorium praefixerunt post dominicam feria 4. qua cantatur Oculi omnium. Set tunc non venerunt, arduis negotiis impediti. Set aliam diem praefixerunt, feria 6. post dominicam qua cantatur Iubilate. Sed nec tunc venerunt, quia iter eorum adventus duorum cardinalium qui Coloniam venerunt impedivit, . . ."*

[192] Hilling, *Diözesansynoden* 8; *Westf. UB* IV, Nr. 39; Ch. One, above, p. 23.

[193] Winkelmann, *Phil. von Schw.* II 155-163.

otherwise, he was to be protected as guiltless with all the means of the Church.

It says much for the baselessness of the accusations that Ekbert's opponents used every means possible to impede the investigation. They appealed at once from the legates to the pope, and as Innocent III set a date for a hearing before the Curia, only Ekbert appeared. At length, the pontiff gave a commission to Archbishop Siegfried II of Mainz, Bishop Otto of Würzburg, and the abbot of Fulda on 13 November 1209 to bring the inquiry to a conclusion within three months.[194] For unknown reasons it dragged on until 1211, however, but by then the political situation persuaded them to restore Ekbert formally to his see without delay.[195] Whether the mandate given to the archbishop of Mainz on 3 February 1213 to investigate charges against Ekbert was a resumption of the earlier process cannot be determined.[196] It is nonetheless noteworthy that Ekbert does not appear in any documents until 1215, first in one of his own on 20 May at Würzburg, and then as a witness at the coronation of Frederick II of Staufen at Aachen on 29 July.[197] We cannot determine whether he was suspended from office over a two-year period, but such an inference seems plausible. The papal legates also worked out the details and set the date for the imperial coronation on 4 October 1209 at Rome, after which they returned to the Curia. Their efforts during 1208/1209 had brought Otto IV to the pinnacle of power and acceptance throughout the Empire, and had also ensured that the resolution of the German throne controversy was an act of the papacy. An end to the civil war promised peace and the opportunity for

---

[194] Migne, *PL* CCXVI, col. 150; Potthast, *Regesta* I, Nr. 3842; Böhmer-Will, *RAM* II 142, Nr. 130. A letter dictated that same day to the emperor stated that there had been too great haste in implicating Eckbert in the assassination of King Philip, and that the three prelates had been instructed to restore to the bishop of Bamberg all things which had been taken from him while they were conducting their investigation into the veracity of the charges; cf. *RAM* II 142, Nr. 129.

[195] *Chron. reg. Colon. cont.* III *(a. 1211)* 232. See also Winkelmann, *Phil. von Schw.* II 478.

[196] (Reg. Inn. XV, ep. 225) Migne, *PL* CCXVI, col. 757; Potthast, *Regesta* I, Nr. 4671; Böhmer-Will, *RAM* II 155, Nr. 200. See also a similar letter of explanation to the King of Hungary, Eckbert's brother-in-law; *RAM* II 155, Nr. 199. The papal letter to the archbishop was not without a bit of reproach, however: Innocent stated that as an apostolic legate Siegfried had undoubtedly had good intentions when deposing numerous bishops, but that when the deposed prelate and the one appointed to take his place sought to work out the legal implications, he ought not to interfere, but instead send them at a predetermined time to Rome where they could have an audience with the pope *"qui constitutus in sede iustitiae, et omnibus in iustitia debitor."* In other words, the archbishop was more of an obstacle than a facilitator in such processes.

[197] H-Bréholles, *Hist. dipl.* I 401.

princes and prelates alike to devote time and energies to restoring prosperi-
ty, security and ecclesiastical discipline.

Indicative of this concern in papal circles is the letter which Innocent III
sent to Archbishop Albrecht of Magdeburg. Dated 16 January 1209, it
commanded this metropolitan to implement those things which the legates
Ugolino and Leo might ordain.[198]   During their first legation to Germany
these two cardinals had visited Magdeburg at some time between September
1207 (when they were present at Quedlinburg) and 30 November 1207
(when they appeared at Augsburg) during which they laid the cornerstone
for the cathedral church of St. Moritz.[199]   Their second venture into
Saxony presumably fell between 22 March 1209 (when they appeared with
Otto IV at Speyer) and their ceremonious entrance into Cologne which both
Reiner of St. Jacob's and the chronicler at Cologne recorded.[200]   We can
also assume that among that ecclesiastical business which the *Chronica regia*
states was conducted by the two legates during their visit to Saxony was the
progress of reform in the spirit of their recent legislation; that they
convened a synod of the Magdeburg province seems probable.

Also in 1209 the pope chastened Bishop Conrad of Regensburg in two
separate letters dated 18 April. Conrad of Frontenhausen had been provost
at Freising and a canon at Regensburg prior to his elevation to the
episcopacy in 1204. From Freising he brought the intellectual, political and
episcopal skills for which that church was famous. Until the death of Philip
of Swabia, he served as chancellor at the Staufen court. Clearly related to
his absences from the diocese was the development of conditions for which
the pope now censured him: Innocent urged Conrad to look after his flock,
lest he be reproached even more harshly. It had come to the attention of
Rome that the rural priests and some rural deans, who were supposed to set
the example and correct abuses in others, lived openly with concubines;
when they gathered for their yearly synods they hid this fact to the injury
of their souls and to the anger of the people. There were furthermore
ministeriales who claimed to be under no ecclesiastical authority, and
without fear of penalty committed adultery, incest and other sins. It was
also alleged that many men, women and children died without the benefit

---

[198] Migne, *PL* CCXVI, col. 1166; Potthast, *Regesta* I, Nr. 3614 (*"Quocirca fraternitatem
tuam rogandam duximus et monendam, per apostolica tibi scripta mandantes quatenus ad ea
feliciter promovenda quae venerabilis frater Hugolinus Ostiensis episcopus et dilectus filius Leo,
tituli Sanctae Crucis presbyter cardinalis, apostolicae sedis legati, tibi ex parte nostra
suggesserint diligens studium et operam efficacem impendas; . . ."*); Mülverstedt, *RAMagd* II
139, Nr. 331; Ch. One, above, p. 79.

[199] See Böhmer-Ficker, *Regg. Imp.* V/2, Nrs. 9987h, 9988a, 9988b, 9989a. See also,
Magdeburg Schöppenchronik 132.

[200] Böhmer-Ficker, *Regg. Imp.* V/2, Nrs. 9992g, 9992h, 9993a.

of confirmation since they were not in the habit of going to the bishop to receive this sacrament. Since Conrad was the head of the diocese and as such was bound to conduct visitations, and as the doctor must know the causes of disease among his patients, the pope commanded him with his apostolic authority to deal personally with the investigation and healing of the problems. The prelate was empowered to exact money from the churches of his diocese to help defray the cost of such a visitation.[201]

Such problems clearly suggested the need for episcopal action, yet they were only part of the problem. Presumably through the annual archidiaconal visitations the bishop had learned of a problem which was not unique to Regensburg, one for which he sought help from Rome. Many parish churches in the diocese had been given to cathedral and collegiate canons who drew the incomes, but used vicars for the performance of the *cura animarum* whom they personally appointed and paid. The vicars in turn claimed exemption from the jurisdiction of the archdeacons and rural deans, and they were disinclined to obey any type of correction; their accountability, they claimed, was solely to the one who hired them. The bishop therefore had asked the pope for permission to assume the powers of appointing the cures himself; Innocent responded on 18 April 1209 that he was unable to grant such a request, however, because of canonical restrictions. He therefore recommended that the bishop either place the cathedral canons under obligation to discharge the *cura animarum* personally or compel them by means of ecclesiastical censures to appoint capable and zealous vicars.[202]

Once Conrad was free from the obligations of the royal chancery, he appears to have given much energy to matters of reform within his diocese. The misuse of ecclesiastical disciplinary power manifested itself in a grotesque form in his diocese: if a cathedral canon believed that he had been injured in his rights and prerogatives by one of his brethren, he at once boycotted the divine services and others canonical obligations, and obtained papal authorization to impose an interdict on the cathedral church so that no services could be held there.[203] The entire bishopric thus suffered for the sins of a few. In response to an episcopal complaint sent to Rome, Innocent III issued a letter dated 23 October 1209, strongly denouncing this malicious practice and announcing to the cathedral canons that he had given to the

---

[201] Cf. Migne, *PL* CCXVI, col. 34; Potthast, *Regesta* I, Nr. 3707; Ried, *CdRatisb.* I 297, Nr. 314. See also Janner, *Regensburg* I, 252-257; Staber, *Regensburg* 38-39; Hauck, *KGD* IV 9.

[202] Migne, *PL* CCXVI, col. 35; Potthast, *Regesta* I, Nr. 3708; Ried, *CdRatisb.* I, Nr. 315; Janner, *Regensburg* I 256-257.

[203] Janner, *Regensburg* 257; Staber, *Regensburg* 39.

provost and dean of Salzburg the task of correcting it, even to the point of
issuing ecclesiastical censures.

While Conrad of Regensburg displayed concern for pastoral matters
within his own diocese, he made no effort to comply with demands by his
metropolitan that he attend provincial synods. He was, e.g., absent from
the assembly held 1 May 1209,[204] and he likewise was among those
comprovincial prelates absent from the provincial synod held one year later
at Werfen: of the suffragans of Salzburg, only Walter of Gurk attended.
An indication that Eberhard's synods may have been more politically
motivated than pastoral at this time is suggested by an admonition sent to
him shortly after the 1210 assembly that he conduct visitations of the
religious houses of his diocese.[205] A probable outcome of this charge was
a complaint by the metropolitan that the nuns on the island called Chiemsee
(i.e., Frauenchiemsee) had lapsed into an undisciplined life and were
deserving of suppression. Though the archbishop apparently already had his
eye on this unruly cloister's lands and incomes as the nucleus of a new
bishopric which he hoped to establish at Chiemsee, the mandate given by
the pope to the abbot of Melk and the provost of the church of the Holy
Cross (diocese of Augsburg) was somewhat different: he directed them to
determine whether it was possible to effect reform within the community of
Benedictine nuns and whether the nearby foundation of canons regular
would consent to being transformed into the new episcopal church.[206] In
the end, the new diocese was formed around Herrenchiemsee, not its sister
house.[207]

Despite efforts to hold frequent synods with his clergy, Eberhard of
Salzburg was not able to prevent the development of serious problems
within his church. According to Thomasin de Zirclaria, a contemporary
poet from Friuli, Cathar teachings had penetrated into Austrian regions by
ca. 1210-1215, with especial centers being Passau and Vienna.[208] The

---

[204] See Ch. One, p. 32.

[205] Potthast, *Regesta* I, Nr. 4056; Meiller, *RES* I 199, Nr. 128.

[206] Migne, *PL* CCXVI, col. 868; Potthast, *Regesta* I, Nr. 4768 (20 June 1213).

[207] See Urmser Berlière, "Innocent III et la Réorganisation des Monastères Bénédictins,"
Revue Bénédictine 32 (1920) 23-42, 144-159, espec. 30-31: «*En principe, le pape répugnait
à la suppression de monastères, car cette mesur était en opposition formelle avec l'intention
des fondateurs; en pratique, il voulait qu'on tentat des essais de restauration. . . . Le pape
avait raison; le monastère des bénédictines fut maintenu, et les chanoines-réguliers acceptèrent
de constituer dans leur église le chapitre du nouvel évêché (1215), sans rien abandonner de
leur constitution régulière et sans laisser amoindrir leurs droits.*»

[208] Thomasin's poem, written in 1215, praises Duke Leopold of Austria for taking such a
firm stand against the heretics; cf. "Der Wälsche Gast," ed. H. Rückert, *Bibliothek der
gesammten deutschen National-Litteratur* 30 (Quedlenberg-Leipzig, 1852) 344f., vv. 126843-9;
also *Contin. Claustro-neuberg. a. 1210* 621; Borst, *Katharer* 103-104, citing Hantsch, *Gesch.*

trade routes which followed the Danube facilitated the spread of heterodoxy beyond the Rhine, just as the Rhine had aided the movement of such ideas from Languedoc and Burgundy. The incongruence between the clergy and the ideal depicted in the Scriptures allowed the Cathars to find adherents among the flock of the Salzburg province, just as they had in those of Trier, Mainz, and Cologne.

The brief respite from the German throne controversy allowed prelates such as Conrad of Regensburg and Eberhard of Salzburg to look after internal matters of their dioceses and provinces. The papacy also used this opportunity to reconsider matters which had been compromised by the exigencies of earlier years, e.g., the case of Bishop Matthew of Toul. After numerous delays, during which the debauched reputation of Matthew spread even wider, Innocent III finally declared him deposed on 5 January 1210 and commanded the cathedral chapter at Toul *"ut personam idoneam sibi in pastorem canonice eligant, cum Maherus super dilapidatione ac periurio impetitus per sententiam ab ecclesia Tullensi amotus est."*[209] Aubrey of Trois Fontaines wrote that Matthew was *". . . nec nominandus episcopus, rerum ecclesie dilapidator conprobatus . . ."*[210]

The successor at Toul was Rainald of Senlis, son of the French royal butler and maternal grandson of Count Rainald II of Bar. Under the influence of the counts of Bar and the French king, Philip II, he became the first Frenchman to occupy the episcopal throne of Toul in almost three centuries and reflected yet another aspect of imperial bishops' elections. Bishop Rainald's pontificate could not have been peaceful given the truculence of the deposed bishop, Matthew, and his relatives, however. It came to an unhappy end in 1217 with Rainald's murder by Matthew's brother, the duke of Lorraine.[211] In all, the Roman Curia was engaged with the case of Matthew of Toul for more than fifteen years, during which

Oesterr. I 93; Havet, *L'Heresie et le Bras* 143-4, citing Ferdinand Frensdorff in *HGbll* 6 (1876) 107. About 1260/1266 an anonymous cleric in the diocese of Passau created a collection of writings directed against the Cathars based on existing literature which he hoped would serve those attempting to uphold the Catholic faith against its enemies; cf. Alexander Patschovsky, *Der Passauer Anonymous*, Schriften der Monumenta Germaniae Historica, vol. 22 (Stuttgart, 1968) 1-150, espec. 78-116.

[209] (Reg. Inn. XII, ep. 149) Migne, *PL* CCXVI, cols. 169-170; Potthast, *Regesta* I, Nr. 3875. On the same day the pope gave a mandate to a bishop, a Cistercian abbot and a Premonstratensian abbot to take charge of replacing the bishop at Toul if the cathedral chapter of that church did not exercise its prerogative within fifty days; cf. Potthast, op.cit. Nr. 3876. See further, *Richeri Gesta* 285-288; Thiery, *Toul* 204-204; Winkelmann, *Phil. von Schw.* I 262; Schwemer, *Innocent III.* 67; Krabbo, *Besetzung* 288; Kuhle, *Neubesetzung* 74-75; Morret, *Stand und Herkunft* 67; Tillmann, *Innocenz III.* 176.

[210] *(a. 1210)* 891.

[211] Kuhle, *Neubesetzung* 74-75.

time both the pontiff and his legates had to ignore complaints against the reprobate just so that further confusion might be prevented. The entire situation placed Innocent's apprehensions vis-a-vis many an unworthy member of the episcopacy in the proper perspective, but it reveals the extent to which Rome was also compromised by the need to consider political and human realities when seeking to achieve ecclesiastical ends.

The relative calm of the year 1209 was not a long-term condition, however. Despite public announcements, Innocent III was never fully satisfied with the thought of Otto as emperor. Those misgivings were borne out when, contrary to his promise, the Welf sought to extend his control over southern Italy and Sicily in the months subsequent to his coronation as emperor. On 18 November 1210 the pontiff therefore found it necessary to place his own creation under excommunication; the following February he summoned the German princes to elect a successor.[212] Willy-nilly, the pope set in motion a new round of civil wars which would continue to affect adversely the already deeply-suffering German church.

Among the first prelates to break with Otto were the archbishops of Mainz, Trier, and Magdeburg who called Frederick of Sicily to come to Germany to claim the throne denied him since the death of his father in 1197.[213] Siegfried II of Mainz also received the papal mandate to publish the excommunication of Otto IV in Germany, an act carried out at the June 1211 assembly of princes and prelates at Bamberg, where he had come in the matter of Bishop Ekbert. The primate of the German church urged all other bishops to do the same.[214]

Opposition to a Staufen king went to work at once, however. Otto IV's brother, the Rhenish Pfalzgrave Henry, and his friends in Germany urged his speedy return from Sicily, and in the meantime they sought to halt the movement of desertion. Henry overran the archbishopric of Mainz, forcing Siegfried to flee to Thuringia where he remained until November of that same year.[215] Lotharingian nobles also assisted in ravaging the lands belonging to Otto's enemies.

The Archiepiscopal Schism at Cologne

While there were many prelates who remained loyal to Otto IV after the

---

[212] Potthast, *Regesta* I, between Nrs. 4134 and 4135; Röhrich, *Adolf I. von Köln* 96; Ficker, *Engelbert der Heilige* 49; *Ryccardus de San Germano* 334.

[213] Cf. *Gesta Trev. cont. III* 391: *"Unde post aliquot annos convenerunt apud Confluentiam Treverensis et Moguntinensis archiepiscopi et Spirensis episcopus Conradus . . . videre de statu regni; et missum est pro puero Friderico rege Sicilie, . . ."*

[214] Winkelmann, *Phil. von Schw.* II 274; Zimmermann, *Päpstl. Legationen* 191.

[215] *Chron. reg. Colon. cont. III (a. 1211)* 232; Winkelmann, *Phil. von Schw.* II 280.

proclamation of the papal ban, none was more important than the archbishop of Cologne who, with his episcopal city and the Low Countries, refused to obey the papal command. The two short years since the accession of Dietrich of Hengebach had restored a semblance of order and stability to the archbishopric of Cologne. As noted above, however, Dietrich's handling of affairs had not been good enough for his critics. Caesarius of Heisterbach complained that he extorted money and resorted to violence: according to reports which the prior of Heisterbach had received, the archiepiscopal fortress which Dietrich had caused to be erected on the Godesberg (south of Bonn) in 1210 had been financed with money forcibly taken from Jews.[216] The most reprehensible act, however, was his imprisonment of the peace-loving suffragan bishop, Otto of Münster, first at Cologne and then at Kaiserswerth under close watch, because the latter had withdrawn his support from the Emperor Otto IV.[217]

The task of dealing with the recalcitrant metropolitan of Cologne fell once again to the archbishop of Mainz, who also had the burden of confronting other prelates, clerics, princes, and towns who refused to submit to the papal will and renounce allegiance to the deposed ruler. The ban was first published by Siegfried II about March 1212, but Dietrich remained unbowed. During Lent of that year he took military action against his enemies, pillaging their lands with savage fury. He even turned against his own clergy who had refused to disobey the pope, and in a gesture of contempt for the papal decree against himself, he celebrated Mass during Holy Week and on Maundy Thursday consecrated the Holy Chrism. For this, he was declared deposed in April. The city of Cologne likewise found cause to regret its position, being placed under an interdict by the archbishop-legate of Mainz.[218]

Ever lurking in the shadows it seems, Adolf of Altena appeared once more in Cologne following Dietrich's deposition. As relations with Otto IV had begun to sour, Innocent III had altered his position toward Adolf: on 12 November 1210, six days before Otto's excommunication was published, the pontiff sent the erstwhile archbishop a letter in which the current state of affairs was reviewed and Adolf was praised for accepting his fate after 1208. Since he had not lost the episcopal consecration, but merely his office, Adolf was now given permission to wear the episcopal vestments (with the exception of the pallium), to celebrate the Mass, and with the sufferance of the bishops or abbots in whose dioceses or abbeys he might

---

[216] *Caesarii Dialogus* VII 40, 46; Kaufmann, *Caesarius* 60.

[217] Binterim, *Concilien* IV 410-411.

[218] *Caesarii Cat. archiep. Colon.* 346, 352; Böhmer-Ficker, *Regg. Imp.* V/2, Nr. 10729a; Böhmer-Will, *RAM* II, 183; Röhrich, *Adolf I. von Köln* 97; Krabbo, *Besetzung* 20.

be, to ordain clerics or monks to minor orders and to consecrate vestments
or holy vessels. He was also given permission to accept any ecclesiastical
office which might be granted him, except the episcopal, for which he must
have special papal approval.[219]

The reascendancy of the Staufen dynasty and the misfortunes of
Archbishop Dietrich of Cologne gave Adolf reason to hope that he might
actually regain his former office. He came to Cologne on the day before
Ascension (1 May 1212) with the claim that he had been reinstated by the
pope and that Dietrich had been deposed of office and prebends. While the
latter was certainly true, there is no evidence that his first assertion has any
validity. Nevertheless, he demanded obedience from the clergy on the basis
of papal authority. One must consider this account in the *Chronica regia*
and the claims of Adolf as based on some fact. Other contemporaries all
agree that the entire clergy of Cologne expressed support for him on 2 May,
and that Archbishop Siegfried of Mainz placed his former arch-enemy in
Dietrich's stead.[220]

It is nearly incomprehensible that the clergy of Cologne, even after the
many long years of turmoil which had been the result primarily of Adolf's
blind ambition and total lack of religious sensibilities, should continue to
show support for him and desire that he become their head once more. As
was true in Mainz where the canons accepted Lupold of Worms in his
attempts to claim the archbishop's chair, however, the actions of the
Cologne clergy speak louder than any text concerning their own level of
religiosity. Even more remarkable was the fact that although Siegfried of
Mainz failed to sense any unanimous support for Adolf among clergy and
laity alike, he nevertheless in his role as legate recognized him as archbishop and installed him in the highest dignity of the Cologne church. A new
election probably took place, details of which are lacking. Dietrich of Hengebach fled first to Otto IV at Nürnberg (documented there on 11 May
1212) and then to Rome where he sought to appeal Siegfried's decision.

The deposed archbishop had no success at all before the Roman Curia.
He experienced humiliation at the hands of avaricious lawyers and officials,
a fact which must have appeared to some contemporaries as divine
retribution. Caesarius of Heisterbach frequently comes back to the idea that
if Dietrich had used the good counsel of the *priores* of Cologne rather than

---

[219] Migne, *PL* CCXVI, col. 346; Potthast, *Regesta* I, Nr. 4131.

[220] *Chron. reg. Col. cont. III (a. 1212)* 233; *Reineri Ann. (a. 1212)* 664; *Caesarii Vita
Engelberti* I 3; *Caesarii Dialogus* VII 40; Knipping, *REK* III 21, Nr. 108; Krabbo, *Besetzung*
20; Wolfschläger, *Adolf I.* 107. See also detailed discussion in Hüffer, "Denkstein und
Schisma" 149-150.

that of his secular advisers, he would still be the archbishop. The Cistercian prior compared him during his stay in Rome to the poor Lazarus of the Gospels who pled in vain for a crumb of bread from the table of the rich—that is, Dietrich sought sound advice from Roman lawyers who charged exorbitant prices for their services. Caesarius noted that even the acquaintance of some of the cardinals was of no value to the beleaguered ex-prelate: as he offered one five Marks if he would say a good word in his behalf in the Curia, the cardinal is said to have replied: "For five Marks I would not even lift a foot."[221] Caesarius' account is still couched in moralistic terms, yet the germ is clearly accurate. In May 1213 Dietrich had to borrow 625 Marks from Roman merchants in order to meet his expenses as a litigant before the Curia; later on, additional sums of 700 and 200 Marks were also borrowed, but all without results. The Curia prolonged making any response to him at all.[222]

While the selection of Adolf of Berg may have been popular among many of the leading clergy and *priores* of the Rhineland capital, it fared no better in the Curia than did the deposed Dietrich. Innocent III quashed the appointment which Adolf made of a follower as *plebanus* of St. Christopher, a church dependent on St. Gereon at Cologne which had remained loyal to Dietrich. A tumult arose over the issue, but Adolf lost. The pope stated in a letter of commission for resolving this dispute that Adolf, the *quondam* archbishop, claimed to be reinstated by the papal-legate; the entire wording and tone of this missive show that the pontiff did not really accept such, however.[223] Regardless of how Adolf was reinstated, Innocent could still refer to the clause in the letter of 12 November 1210 which stated that the former archbishop must receive his approval in order to accept a bishopric. Thus, although the pope allowed Adolf to administer the temporal affairs of Cologne until early 1216, he withheld confirmation, consecration and the pallium. Both he and Dietrich ultimately had to be content with pensions. For all practical purposes, Cologne was without a functioning spiritual head not only from 1212 until 1216,[224] but also for most of the entire period since 1198.

The confusion of this situation can be seen in the dating formulae found in various documents. In the already-mentioned *Scheinsrolle* of Andernach appears for the year 1212, as Dietrich was deposed, a document on which

---

[221] *Caesarii Dialogus*, II 27; Hüffer, "Denkstein und Schisma" 151-152.

[222] Lacomblet, *NRUB* II, Nr. 47.

[223] Hüffer, "Denkstein und Schisma" 152.

[224] *Caesarii Cat. archiep. Col.* 352; Krabbo, *Besetzung* 21; Röhrich, *Adolf I.* 98; Hüffer, "Denkstein und Schisma" 153.

the rubric "*temporibus Thirrici Coloniensis archiepiscopi*" had been written over; the very next membrane is dated "*temporibus, quando Adolphus et Tirricus pro archiepiscopatu Coloniensi litigabant.*" A charter of Count Gottfried II of Arnsberg dated 23 November 1214 contains the addition: "*sub scismate Romani imperii durante werra archiepiscopatus Coloniensis.*" As Frederick II was crowned at Aachen on 25 July 1215, there was no archbishop of Cologne to perform this traditional rite and the archbishop of Mainz, who had deposed both Dietrich and Adolf, stood in his stead. That same year the Andernach *Scheinsrolle* contains a document dated "*regnante Friderico rege, in shismate Coloniensis episcopatus.*"[225]

The historians of the time—Caesarius of Heisterbach, the continuator of the *Chronica regia*, Christian of Mainz, the Ursperg chronicler Burchard, Arnold of Lübeck, and others—all develop a picture which agrees completely with that of the poet Walther von der Vogelweide relative to the general destruction which had prevailed during the German throne controversy of 1198-1212. For fourteen years armies moved through the Rhineland leaving Bonn, Remagen, Andernach and numerous villages in ashes. Countless bands of robbers roamed about, but the Bohemian troops of King Philip were the worst: according to the Heisterbach sources, they plundered that monastery and drove the monks off.[226] Without direction and pressure from their superiors, the young cathedral canons at Cologne amused themselves with hunting and games—if not worse, and they seldom visited the choir to fulfill their obligations there. Elsewhere in the archdiocese the clergy often hesitated to accept the responsibilities of their office, postponing consecration as deacons or priests until absolutely required for elevation to a higher dignity. At times, some dignities were left unfilled because no one wished to accept the clerical duties attached to them; especially was this true of the offices of sub-dean and choir-bishop: because they were so poorly endowed and thus provided no advantage to the incumbent, they were little sought after. Not until ca. 1217, when Archbishop Engelbert ordained that at least eight members of the cathedral chapter were to have priestly consecration, was this situation properly addressed. He also stipulated on 1 August 1220 that henceforth the position of parish priest at Lützenkirchen was to be combined with that of a sub-deacon in the cathedral chapter.[227]

Apart from the cathedral chapter at Cologne, Caesarius of Heisterbach was most biting in his criticism of the collegiate church of St. Cassius at

---

[225] Hüffer, "Denkstein und Schisma" 153.

[226] Cf. Kaufmann, *Caesarius* 14-15.

[227] See Ficker, *Engelbert der Heilige* 26-27; Lacomblet, *NRUB* II 48, Nr. 86.

Bonn, second only to the cathedral church in prestige within the archdiocese. His awareness of conditions there may in part be explained by the close proximity of Heisterbach to that town, but there were other sources as well: the dean of Bonn from 1194-1203, one Christian, resigned his dignity there and died as a novice at Heisterbach; from this *quondam decanus Christianus* Caesarius heard some of the tales incorporated into the *Dialogus*. There was, e.g., the unnamed canon who, together with his fellows, liked to visit certain reprobate nuns at the cloister Dietkirchen.[228] Frequent complaints were also heard against the failure of the canons at Bonn to observe residence and to participate in the Divine Office: a statute from 1156/1158 stressed the obligation for all holders of major prebends to attend choir services.[229] That the problem was not eliminated permanently is revealed by the fact that in 1228 the conferring of certain prebends and incomes was limited to resident canons.[230] Reports of abuses at Bonn even reached Rome, for in April 1212 Innocent III commanded the provost, *custos*, and scholastic at Münster to conduct an inquiry into charges that one *F[ ]*, a canon at Bonn, had committed simony in acquiring the provostship there.[231]

This papal missive seems incorrectly to give the name of the provost in 1212 as beginning with "*F*," however. Documents of the Cologne archdiocese show that Henry of Müllenark held that office 1211-1225; it is thus likely that it is he against whom the charges of simony were brought. The fact that he retained his office suggests that he was cleared, but the instance is not without further interest. Inasmuch as he was the new leader of the anti-Berg/Altena/Isenberg faction among the *priores* of Cologne, becoming archbishop in 1225, one can only surmise that the initial complaint against Henry came from within the Berg party and was intended to embarrass or eliminate a potential rival to the cathedral provost Engelbert of Berg, should the throne of Cologne become available.[232]

Among other bishops who refused to abandon Otto IV in 1211 were Hartbert of Hildesheim and Frederick of Halberstadt. They especially aroused the anger of Innocent III as they joined Otto VI in the summer of 1212 in a punitive attack against the rebel Landgrave Hermann of Thuringia. As a result of this, the pope issued letters in June 1213, directing that

---

[228] *Caesarii Dialogus* VIII 52.
[229] Knipping, *REK* II, Nr. 658.
[230] Dietrich Höroldt, *Das Stift St. Cassius zu Bonn*, Bonner Geschichtsblätter 11 (Bonn, 1957) Urk. 35.
[231] Migne, *PL* CCXVI, col. 568; Potthast, *Regesta* I, Nr. 4436.
[232] Höroldt, *St. Cassius zu Bonn* 207.

the *excessi* of Hartbert be investigated and that, if found to be true, a new man be elected as bishop.[233] That Hartbert did not capitulate—but instead died on 21 March 1216 under the ban of excommunication—suggests that he was both disinterested and incapable of fulfilling his pastoral role during the final one-third of his pontificate. It is ironic that this man who had served the papacy faithfully during the struggle between Philip and Otto should be cut off from the Church because he could not accept the altered political realities after 1211. It is obvious that his strongest ties were to the Welf dynasty, rather than to the Roman pontiff.

The clerics empowered by the pope to deal with Bishop Hartbert also received another mandate at the same time concerning the removal of Bishop Frederick of Halberstadt "*a regimine Halberstadensis ecclesiae perpetuo*" as well.[234] They were furthermore instructed to supervise the election of a "*persona idonea*" to fill the office. Frederick II of Kirchberg had been elected in 1208 to replace Bishop Conrad of Krosigk who had suddenly resigned his office, released his clergy from obedience to himself, and entered this Cistercian monastery at Sichem. Conrad had never felt comfortable in the episcopal office and, after his return from the pilgrimage to the Holy Land, had found the discord of the throne controversy too much for his disposition. Although Innocent III must have been made aware of such feelings during his interview with Conrad in 1205, he was nonetheless outraged upon hearing of this overt act of disobedience and summoned both Conrad and his new abbot to Rome. In the end, the monastic vows were honored, however, and Conrad was allowed to seek peace within the cloistered walls at Sichem. The conflict of allegiances caught up with Conrad's successor, Frederick, and the papal agents began their process to remove him from office. Unlike Hartbert of Hildesheim, however, Frederick renounced his support for the deposed Welf ruler and escaped the ultimate censure of the Church.

Friction Between Mainz and Würzburg

During the four to five years following the assassination of the imperial chancellor, Bishop Conrad of Würzburg, in 1202 the episcopal seat was occupied by Henry IV (*Caseus*) of Hessberg who was probably elected in

---

[233] Migne, *PL* CCXVI, col. 871; Potthast, *Regesta* I, Nr. 4748. The Hildesheim church was also placed under an interdict which the cathedral chapter appealed. Otto IV demanded that the chapter resume services, creating the other horn of their dilemma. Though the papacy lifted the ban on church services, the excommunication was upheld; cf. Janicke, *UB Hilds* I, Nrs. 656, 665-666; Krabbo, *Besetzung* 19; Bertram, *Bistum Hildesheim* 216.

[234] Migne, *PL* CCXVI, col. 872; Potthast, *Regesta* I, Nr. 4747.

December 1202 in the presence of King Philip. It appears, however, that he never received papal confirmation or consecration, due to his support for the Staufen claimant and his hostile attitude toward the murderers of his predecessor.[235] The death of Bishop Henry in 1207 brought to Würzburg a man who favored Otto IV of Brunswick as German king, a position made immeasurably more easy following Philip's death in June 1208. The first four years of Otto of Lobdeburg's pontificate witnessed conditions in Würzburg quite conducive to dealing with matters of a pastoral nature, but that was all upset by the prelate's refusal to abandon Otto IV once the latter had fallen from papal grace.

Punishment for rebellion in this instance was not merely excommunication, but deposition as well. On 6 June 1213 Innocent III directed Archbishop Siegfried II of Mainz in his capacity as an apostolic legate for Germany to depose Otto of Würzburg publicly and to secure the election of a bishop favorable to Rome and willing to support Frederick II of Staufen. The deposition proceeded as ordered, but the legate's choice as bishop reflected the same lack of acute political and spiritual sense which had been shown in his recognition of Adolf of Altena as archbishop of Cologne in 1212. Since the 1202 assassination of Bishop Conrad of Würzburg, the son of one of the murderers, a cathedral canon at Würzburg named Henry of Ravensburg, had resided at Mainz under the patronage of Archbishop Siegfried and held a prebend in the Mainz cathedral chapter and the office of provost at Bingen. The papal letter of 6 June 1213 reveals that the archbishop was especially well disposed toward Henry, but the reasons remain unclear.[236] Nevertheless, at some time before 3 February 1214 Otto of Lobdeburg was deposed and Henry of Ravensburg installed as bishop of Würzburg by Siegfried II of Mainz as metropolitan and papal-legate.[237]

Unlike Archbishop Dietrich of Cologne who went to Rome to plead his case, Bishop Otto remained in Germany to bring about his own restoration. Rather than placing his trust in the effectiveness and equity of canonical processes, he resorted to the arm of flesh. Into the picture there now

---

[235] Wendehorst, *Bistum Würzburg* 201-203.

[236] Potthast, *Regesta* I, Nr. 4746. See Wendehorst, *Bistum Würzburg* 204-207, for details of Otto's life to 1215.

[237] *Chron. mont. Ser.* 170: "*Cum Otto epus Herbipol. sicut et ceteri episcopi excommunicato imperatori oppositus esset, illi [the Ravensburgers] collectis in civitate armatis pluribus episcopum expulerunt, invenem quendam, ecclesiae ipsius canonicum, alterius ipsorum filium, pro eo auctoritate imperatoris instituentes.*" See also the discussion of these events in Winkelmann, *Phil. von Schw.* II 303; Herberhold, *Otto von Lobdeburg* 70. For details concerning Henry of Ravensburg, cf. Pixton, "Konrad von Reifenberg" 65-66 and note 113, and Heidingsfelder, *Regg. Eichst.* I 203-204.

returned the Ravensburg brothers, Henry and Bodo—the father and uncle of
Provost Henry of Bingen and the assassins of Conrad of Querfurt—together
with followers and associates whose hatred for the Lobdeburg family was
intense.   With unsheathed weapons they drove the ex-bishop and his
partisans from the city.   Otto managed to rally enough vassals of the
bishopric to win it back, however, and then he turned on the Ravensburgers
on their home ground, driving them from the diocese without any provisions
at all.[238]

Otto consolidated his victory over the Ravensburg faction by obtaining
absolution from his sentence of excommunication at the hands of Archbishop Albrecht of Magdeburg, likewise a standing papal legate in Germany,
and by switching his allegiance to Frederick II.[239]   In spite of this,
Archbishop Siegfried of Mainz continued to labor for the recognition of his
protégé Henry of Ravensburg, with the end result that bad feelings prevailed
between himself and his suffragan bishop of Würzburg until Otto's death in
December 1223.   Not until the Fourth Lateran Council were the legal
questions arising out of the schism at Würzburg resolved.[240]   And even
after that momentous assembly the bishop of Würzburg was excused from
attending provincial synods convened by his metropolitan, as expressed in
a papal communication.[241]   We may conclude therefore that for most of
the period immediately preceding the Council the bishopric of Würzburg
was in a state of confusion and disorder, thereby providing the setting for
many of the clerical abuses existing at the time.

Other comprovincial bishops of Mainz had concerns of their own at this
time.   Mention was made above of the conditions in the diocese of
Strasbourg at the commencement of the thirteenth century and of the delays
involved in securing the consecration of Henry II of Vehringen as bishop
(1202-1207).   Such factors as these may have created the milieu in which
heresy developed, for the *Annales Marbacenses* record that about the year
1212 nearly eighty heretics were burned at the stake, presumably as a
consequence of a diocesan visitation or synod.   Whether Caesarius of Heis-

---

[238] Krabbo, *Besetzung* 21.

[239] For the legation of Albrecht of Magdeburg, see Winkelmann, *Phil. von Schw.* II 305,
note 2.

[240] Cf. Krabbo, *Besetzung* 21; *Mon. Boica* XXXVII, Nr. 190; Böhmer-Will, *RAM* II 163,
Nr. 259.

[241] Papal dispensations from attendance at Mainz provincial synods were obtained 4 August
1218 and 11 October 1225; cf. Potthast, *Regesta* I, Nrs. 5886, 7492.

terbach's reference to ten persons burned for religious aberrations at the same city relates to this occasion or some later one cannot be determined.[242]

A sign of the changing attitude of Pope Innocent III toward those bishops who had supported the Staufen cause throughout the throne controversy and who were now even more essential as allies in the papal efforts to bring an end to the Welf monarchy is seen in the events which followed the death of Bishop Bertram of Metz on 6 April 1212. As in other Lotharingian bishoprics, this see was divided between pro-German and pro-French factions. The French party put forth the candidacy of Guillaume de Joinville, while the German majority postulated Bishop Conrad of Speyer. Given the political ramifications, Innocent approved the latter, even allowing Conrad to retain Speyer while adding Metz. Control of the left bank of the Rhine and of Upper Lorraine by one Staufen bishop was of strategic value to the pope and to Frederick II who had named Conrad to be his chancellor. Thus, until his death in 1224, Conrad of Scharfenberg held both bishoprics in obvious contradiction to canonical decrees.[243] That he thereby had less time for the pastoral responsibilities of those offices seems to have been of little concern in 1212.

Within months of Conrad's accession there, a papal letter was sent to the dean and chapter of St. Theobald at Metz, giving them power to pronounce anathema upon any cathedral canon who attempted to acquire a prebend in St. Theobald's as well.[244] Was Bishop Conrad perhaps trying to reward partisans? A further indication of the deterioration of pastoral concerns in the diocese during the recent civil war comes from a letter dated 19 January 1213 in which the Roman pontiff directed three canons at Metz to use ecclesiastical censures in compelling the patrons of the church at *Possessa* to provide more generously for the priest who had the *cura animarum* attached to it.[245]

While Innocent III was busy dealing with those bishops who refused to obey his command to abandon the ungrateful Otto IV, Welf partisans inflicted heavy punishment upon those who did comply. Among the most violent was Duke Henry of Brabant who wreaked havoc upon the city and diocese of Liège: churches and monasteries were plundered, sanctuaries

---

[242] *Ann. Marbac. (a. 1215)* 174: *"Ante tempora huyus concilii [i.e., Lateran IV] ferre triennio . . . heretici qui perverso dogmate lamenter seducunt . . .";* *Caesarii Dialogus* III 17. Havet, *L'heresie et le Bras* 143-144, citing Migne, *PL* CCXV 576), notes that Innocent III wrote the bishop concerning the expurgation of one Reimbold in this connection; cf. Potthast, *Regesta* I, Nr. 4358.

[243] See Kuhle, *Neubesetzung* 83; Bienemann, *Konrad von Scharfenberg* 56.

[244] Migne, *PL* CCXVII, 219, Nr. 174; Potthast, *Regesta* I, Nr. 4624.

[245] Migne, *PL* CCXVI, col. 746; Potthast, *Regesta* I, Nr. 4658.

were desecrated, and the consecrated Host was scattered. Bishop Hugh
himself was driven from the city and forced to find refuge at Huy. Shortly
after Ascension Day 1212 he convened a synod of his clergy and other
laymen for the purpose of dealing with the abuses of the duke. After the
list of crimes against the church had been read aloud, the ban of excommunication was pronounced over Duke Henry and all his cohorts, and an
interdict was declared throughout the diocese for the period of one year.[246]
It is probable that the legatine statutes of 1203 and 1209 were also re-read
at this time, reminding the clergy of their obligations with respect to
discipline.

Among the points of contention between the bishop and his clergy was
the apparent withholding of certain sums of money which he was obligated
to pay the cathedral canons on Maundy Thursday (*cena Domini*) each year.
The dispute reached the point where a complaint was lodged with the Curia,
charging the prelate with negligence, abuse of his powers, and counterfeiting, and other improprieties. On 20 December 1211 the pope commissioned
Deans Engelbert of St. George and Dietrich St. Cunibert, and the scholastic
at St. Severin in Cologne to investigate the charges and resolve the
dispute.[247]   A further issue related undoubtedly to *c*. 1 of the statutes
issued by Cardinal-legate Guy in 1203. At that time it had been stipulated
that all canons who did not have special permission to do otherwise must
maintain residence; those who ignored this were to be deprived of their

---

[246] *Reineri Ann.* 664: "*Sinodus Hoii celebratur, tota Leodiensis ecclesia lamentatur, organa
deponit et silet. Inter episcopum et ducem treugae dantur usque ad octavos sancti Johannis
baptiste.*" See further, *Chron. Albrici* 893; Binterim, *Concilien* IV 434; Winkelmann, *Phil.
von Schw.* II 304.

[247] Cf. *Reineri Ann.* (a. 1210) 663: "*Sedito magna est orta inter episcopum et clericos
maioris ecclesie pro diversis causis, et moneta, et maxime pro beneficio cenae quam idem
episcopus volebat eis quasi de iure subtraerer. Propter hoc et his similia deposuit organa sua
de communi consilio Leodiensis ecclesia. Iniciatum est hoc silentium sabbato post ascensionem
Domini, et pertractum est usque ad festum sancti Andree apostoli . . .*"; Bormans, *Cartulaire*
I, Nr. 105: "*Dilectus filius G. canonicus sancti Johannis, nuncius dilectorum filiorum
prepositi, decani et capituli ecclesie Leodensis, in nostra presentia constitutus, adversus
venerabilem fratrum nostrum Leodiensem episcopum diversa proposuit genera questionum,
videlicet quod cum idem episcopus teneatur apud cathedralem ecclesiam in cena Domini
conficere sollempniter ex iniuncto sibi officio crisma sanctum, ac tam ipsis quam universis
Leodiensis civitatis ecclesiarum canonicis quandam pecunie quantitatem de consuetudine ipsius
ecclesie approbata prebende nomine ministrare, nisi forte ipsum causa rationabili ab huiusmodi
excusaret, . . .*" The practice of distributing money to the canons is described by Aegidius of
Orval thusly: "*In coena autem Domini debent omnes ecclesiae venire ad caenam delebrandum,
quam episcopus sive absens, sive praesens, olatis, et nebulis et pomis, et vino debet conficere.
Si autem presens fuerit, debet ecclesiae S^d Lamberti triginta solidos probatae monetae dare,
et unicuiquam ecclesiae quindecim solidos*"; cited by Görres, *Lütticher DK* 28, from *Aegidius
Aureavall.* (ed. Chapeauville) I 312.

incomes.[248] Shortly thereafter, however, the cardinal must have modified this position, allowing those who were absent from their obligations in the choir etc. at Liège to collect one Mark annually. The continued abuse of this privilege by some cathedral canons eventually drove the more conscientious one to seek a remedy, and in 1214 they approached Archbishop Siegfried of Mainz, at that time himself a papal-legate, as the primate of the German church accompanied Frederick of Hohenstaufen on his march through the Rhineland. From him they gained a reversal of Guy's statute.[249]

Upon the death of Bishop Dietrich II (of Are) on 5/6 December 1212 in Utrecht the counts of Holland and Gelders, Archbishop Adolf of Cologne, and the bishops of Münster and Osnabrück gathered at Utrecht for the new election. The cathedral chapter found it impossible to remain independent under such circumstances and it therefore transferred its electoral rights to the archbishop. Adolf nominated Provost Otto of Xanten, brother of Count Gerhard of Gelders and brother-in-law of Count William of Holland, both of whom were ardent Staufen supporters. There can be no doubt that the Staufen camp was determined to secure this important North German see, strategic as it was for the ultimate overthrow of Otto IV. The contemporary chronicles are quick to point out that Provost Otto was a man of great political acumen and therefore well suited for the secular role of a bishop, but his ecclesiastical functions were apparently less important to those who both elected him and wrote of him: he was only eighteen years of age, far short of the canonical age of thirty.

---

[248] ". . . residentes canonici assidui sint in dormitorio nec possint iacere extra dormitorium nisi de licentia decani; transgressor vero arbitrio decani et consilio capituli puniatur; si quis rebellis inveniatur, stipendio suo privetur et communione fratrum usque ad dignam emendationem."

[249] The statute of Cardinal-legate Guy has not been preserved; it is known to us only from reference to it in the letter written by Archbishop Siegfried II of Mainz to the pope, dated 30 August 1214 at Maastricht; see Bormans, Cartulaire I, Nr. 112: "Capitulum sancti Lamberti Leodiensis nobis insinuare curavit quod olim per venerabilem fratrem nostrum Prenestinum episcopum tunc apostolice Sedis legatum in ecclesia ipsa talis fuit ordinatio procurata, quod absens canonicus per annum de stipendio suo perciperet marcam unam; ex quo facto ecclesie dampnum grave ac dispendium generatur, paucis presentialiter existentibus in eadem. Propter quod idem capitulum nobis humiliter supplicavit ut huiusmodi ordinationem indebitam dignaremur auctoritate legationis qua fungimur irritare. Nos igitur iustis eorum postulationibus sicut decens est et vigor equitatis exposcit exauditionis animum inclinantes, maxime cum per legem dissolvi mereatur quod statuitur contra illam, ordinationem premissam utpote iuri dissonam ipso legationis qua fungimur officio irritam omnino decernimus et inanem, statuentes ut si quis canonicorum preter licentiam decani vel ecclesie absens a stipendio suspensus fuerit, nichil percipiat et ecclesia illa tam in stipendiis quam servitio canonicorum iuxta communem aliarum ecclesiarum consuetudinem disponatur." Böhmer-Will, RAM II 162, Nr. 252, places the document in 1215, but the previous year is more probable.

There were thus three canonical impediments to this election: 1) the election was clearly not free from lay interference; 2) Otto of Gelders had a *defectus aetatis*; and 3) as a result of this, he should have been postulated to the Curia, rather than being elected. Normally the punishment for such errors was the quashing of the election and the withholding of episcopal incomes for a period of three years. Yet, although these facts were known in Rome, no word of protest was heard from that quarter, an obvious indication that the papacy also considered it expedient to have a pro-Staufen prelate in Utrecht without delay. Otto administered his bishopric for two and one-half years without problems and only in 1215 did he journey to Rome to obtain a dispensation from the *defectus*. He died *en route* on 27 March, never having received consecration.[250]   The healthy state of ecclesiastical life and clerical discipline during the three years of this pontificate must therefore also be in doubt.

The Election of Archbishop Dietrich II of Trier

Yet another episcopal election occurred in late 1212, that of Dietrich II of Wied, archbishop of Trier (1212-1242). His predecessor, John, had been obliged in 1211 to take up residence in Coblenz due to the pro-Welf orientation of the burghers, and the new election came at a time when that position had not yet been abandoned. Thus, for over two years Dietrich II was unable to have access to his own city and cathedral. In January 1215, under pressure from Frederick II, the townspeople accepted the hopelessness of the Welf monarchy and reconciled themselves with their prelate.[251] The following month, Archbishop Dietrich commenced what appears as one of the most comprehensive and ambitious reform programs by any single German prelate of this era. The first step in that program was to impose tighter restrictions upon the canons of his cathedral because he noted that,

> . . . directing the mind's eye toward the body of the church of Trier, we sorrowingly say that we find in her a languid head—to wit, the principal church of Trier. Indeed, although the number of canons in it is many, nevertheless an officiator is seldom to be found in the choir. For each and every one has followed his own desires, going about as he pleases, and neglecting the obligation of the choir.[252]

---

[250] *Gesta Traiect.* 409-411; *Ann. Stad.* 355; Krabbo, *Besetzung* 42-43; Pelster, *Stand und Herkunft* 51; Kuhle, *Neubesetzung* 84-89.

[251] Bohmer-Ficker, *Regg. Imp.* V/1, Nr. 755; Pixton, "Dietrich von Wied" (1974) 67.

[252] Günther, *CdRhM* II, Nr. 28; Beyer, *MRUB* III Nr. 29: ". . . *nos dirigentes mentis oculos ad corpus ecclesie Trevirensis, quod dolentes dicimus, inveniemus in ea caput languidum, maiorem videlicet ecclesiam Trevirensem. Sane cum in ea canonicorum multus sit*

In short, clerical absenteeism had become so acute at Trier as to impair seriously the normal and essential functions of the cathedral church.

Although the responsibility for correcting such abuses customarily rested upon the shoulders of the cathedral dean and the scholastic, Archbishop Dietrich declared that these two chapter officials had been ineffective "because the experiment of the division into prebends which had been recently carried out withstood [the corrective efforts] completely." The prelate had therefore felt compelled to intervene and to use his authority as ordinary to effectuate a satisfactory solution. By virtue of this power, it was ordained that,

> . . . for the honor of God and the emendation of the choir, it is universally ordained by us and by the entire chapter in a prudent decree, that, following the most pious institution of our predecessor in blessed memory, Lord Poppo, the refectory which he adopted in his own day and which has a [yearly] duration of a few months, shall be held to good effect for the entire year by our ordinance.

Clerical discipline was therefore to be strengthened through the requirement that the cathedral canons eat their meals at a common table each day, a practice which would, it was hoped, curtail both absenteeism and the neglect of choir service incumbent upon the canonical offices. Such a reform measure would serve "to recall those who are absent back to the church, reinvigorate those who are present, and coerce those who are negligent." Archbishop Dietrich cited the *"periculum divisionis, que nuper facta fuerat in prebendis"* as the major factor in the thwarting of the reforming efforts of the dean and scholastic. The exact date for such a *divisio in praebendis* cannot be determined accurately, but it occurred some time after 1037.[253] Since that time, individualistic pursuits on the part of many of the cathedral canons had eroded the corporate spirit and had hampered the essential functions and duties of the chapter. In an attempt to strengthen discipline among his clergy, the prelate therefore intended to re-establish a common table for them, following the example of his predecessor Poppo (1016-1047). Unlike that previous reform attempt, however, Archbishop Dietrich's *mensa communis* was intended to last the entire year, with the exception of the season of the annual wine-harvest. Stiff penalties for unexcused absences were imposed as well.

---

numerus, rarus tamen in choro inveniebatur operarius. Singuli enim sua desideria sequeban-tur, ambulantes in voluntatibus suis et chori debitum negligentes." See also, Binterim, *Concilien* IV 398-399; Pixton, "Reformprogramm" 12-23.

[253] Boshof, *Erzstift Trier im Mittelalter* 10-14; Jacobi, "EB Poppo von Trier" 21.

The immediate predecessor of Dietrich II, Archbishop John I, also had made a modest attempt to restore the communal character of the cathedral chapter at Trier. As the conditions attached to a grant to the chapter of two parish churches (Perl and Ochtendung), he had ordained that the canons come to Mass on three set days of the year and that thereafter they eat a common meal. Whoever missed either the Mass or the common meal should lose his share of income from the two churches.[254] It is clear from this rather simple act that John realized the extent to which economic factors were those most likely to motivate his clergy to perform spiritual tasks.

The above-mentioned conditions at Trier allow the conclusion that, when Archbishop Dietrich II reached a solution to the problem of discipline and absenteeism with his cathedral chapter, the canons there had not been accustomed to eating together at all frequently, perhaps just on special feast days such as those three stipulated by Archbishop John. The sixteen *capitulares* (those canons who enjoyed the full rights of *stallum in choro et votum in capitulo* lived in their own residences which surrounded the cathedral, enjoyed the fruits and responsibilities of individual prebends, and normally ate their meals apart from their brethren. The principal community tie which remained was their obligation to perform daily choir service in the cathedral. Archbishop Dietrich now proposed the strengthen that bond, and at the same time enforce the canonical requirement of presence, by abolishing the established practice of private, individual dining and re-instituting the common table.

The resumption of the common refectory placed renewed responsibilities upon the shoulders of the chapter *cellerarius*. For some time his duties had been to see that the canons received their allotted share of refectory income to use as they saw fit, and to provide board for the lesser clergy and students attached to the cathedral. Now, however, he not only had to provide for the daily menu, but also to ensure that the canons supported the upkeep of the table in the prescribed manner. Such a stewardship demanded someone who would support the archbishop's program, even in the face of possible opposition from the other canons. It is therefore not without significance that, at the time when the *mensa communis* was scheduled for re-introduction at Trier, the *cellerarius* was the prelate's young nephew, Arnold of Isenburg.[255]

It has been suggested that there were additional aspects to the archbishop's reforms as well. Jacob Marx maintained that the construction of an ambulatory between the cathedral and the adjacent church of the Blessed Virgin Mary at about this time as intended by the prelate to allow his clergy

---

[254] *Gesta Trev.* 396; Beyer, *MRUB* II, Nr. 181; Corsten, "EB Johann I. von Trier" 138.
[255] Cf. Pixton, "Reformprogramm" 16.

to stroll and to go to services apart from the public view and worldly distractions. Such an assertion is certainly consistent with what else we know of Dietrich's reform program and personality, but that he should also have restored a *dormitorium commune* for his cathedral clergy, as Marx contends, is most improbable.[256] Such a radical step would undoubtedly have evoked considerable opposition from the cathedral canons, evidence of which is totally lacking in the sources.

It is significant that Dietrich of Wied, the son of a Rhenish count, should have tried to reform a cathedral chapter comprised of the younger sons of the Lotharingian nobility. Like himself, they had been drawn into the Church as canons, mainly because it afforded them a livelihood. Generally excluded from the family patrimony due to accident of birth, they found a suitable alternative in the accumulation of clerical prebends and offices. Dietrich had been a member of the cathedral chapter before 1212, and by the vote of the canons he had been elevated to the archbishop's chair. He could hardly have been realistic in his expectation that reform would be either enthusiastically received or of long duration among such men. Another seeming paradox is that like many of his canons, Dietrich of Wied had also held prebends and offices outside the cathedral chapter while yet a canon there himself. Between 1190 and 1212 he was a canon, and since ca. 1194 provost, of the collegiate church at Rees (archdiocese of Cologne), and between 1196 and 1212 he held the provostship in the collegiate church of St. Cunibert in Cologne. Significantly, while provost of the latter church, he had conferred upon the chapter members the administration of prebends, a right which theretofore had been exclusively his own.[257] In other words, he had done the very thing which in 1215 he cited as the major cause of the disciplinary problems at Trier—he had allowed the canons at St. Cunibert to divide the chapter property into individual prebends which they thenceforth administered independently.

The reasons for this rather complete turnabout in precept and practice may lie in the great difference between a canon and an archbishop. As provost of St. Cunibert, Dietrich of Wied had been one of those leading Cologne *priores* who refused to abandon Archbishop Adolf in 1205, refused to obey the papal commands to support Bruno of Sayn, and refused to recognize Dietrich of Hengebach after 1208.[258] Yet, upon assuming the mantle of a prelate he became a model of obedience to papal commands. Thirteenth-century English literature compares this sort of transformation to

[256] Marx, *Erzstift Trier* II/2, 29-31.

[257] Cf. Knipping, *REK* II, Nrs. 1360, 1488; Beyer, *MRUB* II, Nr. 149; Ennen, *Quellen* II, Nr. 93.

[258] Cf. Pixton, "Dietrich von Wied" (1974) 60-61.

that which turned Matthew the Publican into Matthew the Apostle of the Lord Jesus Christ, and suggested that such changes were indeed expected of those who took up the miter and staff.[259]   Dietrich of Wied was yet another example of this metamorphosis.

   Despite Archbishop Dietrich's stated belief that the principal cause of the problem of absenteeism and growing secularism at Trier had been the division of chapter property into individual prebends, clerical discipline had also been greatly affected by the civil war in Germany. Archbishop John's frequent excommunications and the interdicts which were imposed upon the city and archdiocese undoubtedly weakened the power of the prelate to control his own clergy, and the influence of the clergy over the laity. The impact of any attempts at reform in Trier was destined to be inconsequential so long as the throne controversy hampered the functioning of the archbishop throughout his diocese. Only after the ascendance of Frederick II of Staufen was order restored to Trier, and one of the first public acts by Archbishop Dietrich II upon his return there in early 1215 was to attempt to re-impose discipline upon a clergy long accustomed to little or no control. His actions must have found considerable support in the papal letter of invitation to the Lateran Council which had been in circulation since 19 April 1213, and in which was clearly stated that matters pertaining to chapters were to be dealt with in the Council's sessions. Time would show how little in the way of reform had actually been accomplished by the end of Dietrich's quite lengthy pontificate, however.

On the Eve of the Fourth Lateran Council

The bull of convocation to the Council, *Vineam domini Sabaoth*, stipulated that in the over two years before the assembly convened, men of experience were to inquire in all regions of Christendom into those matters which required apostolic attention. Bishops and archbishops obviously bore the responsibility for preparing their clergy for the Council. Whether additional expectations were placed on the shoulders of the standing legates for Germany—Archbishop Siegfried II of Mainz and Archbishop Albrecht of Magdeburg—as Binterim suggests, cannot be determined.[260]   In the latter case, it would have been most difficult inasmuch as he had been defeated in battle by Otto IV of Brunswick on 11 June 1213. The cathedral provost and many others of the church dignitaries were captured and the archbishop had to flee for his own safety. Lacking any organized opposition, the erstwhile emperor ravaged the land around Magdeburg. As Albrecht sought

---

[259] Cf. Gibbs/Lang, *Bishops and Reform* 17-19.
[260] *Concilien* IV 266.

to return to his city, he was captured by a Welf partisan, Frederick of Kare, on 24 June; six days later he was rescued by loyal forces under the leadership of the Magdeburg burgrave. Then came the army of Frederick II of Staufen. Drawn primarily from Bohemia and Moravia, these unruly forces made little distinction between friend and enemy. When the Welf siege was finally lifted in November 1213, the city and archdiocese of Magdeburg lay devastated.[261]

From the foregoing discussion, a complex picture emerges with respect to the German church on the eve of the Fourth Lateran Council. There existed side-by-side prelates with considerable and obvious concern for pastoral and ecclesiastical responsibilities, and those totally lacking any. In spite of committed bishops, however, all levels of the German clergy were adversely affected by the political turbulence of the period 1198-1214, causing as it did numerous schisms and exacerbating already serious problems of discipline. Most of the German churches appear to have had difficulty with absenteeism, a situation which not even the appointment of vicars had corrected satisfactorily. Equally alarming was the growing tendency for canons to avoid higher grades of consecration, being reluctant to accept the greater expectations which were attached to these offices. Scattered though it is, the evidence suggests considerable heretical activity in Germany at this time, indicating a failure on the part of the established Church to meet the spiritual needs of a changing and more critical society. Although the degree to which aberrant religious beliefs and behavior had insinuated themselves into German society was apparently much less at this point than in Languedoc, a growing lack of respect for and obedience to the Roman Catholic clergy was nevertheless clearly manifest.

It was certainly not difficult for critics of the German church at the beginning of the thirteenth century to find examples of abuse and undisciplined behavior. Our perception of cathedral chapters and other ecclesiastical foundations cannot be drawn from negative instances alone, however: the same general conditions which fostered license among many of the canons at Cologne also helped produce outstanding churchmen such as Adolf of Tecklenburg who came to be regarded as a saint during his own lifetime, Bishop Oliver of Paderborn who in 1225 was elevated to the cardinalate, and Archbishop Dietrich II of Trier, one of the strongest advocates for clerical reform during the first half of the thirteenth century. It must therefore be borne in mind that most of the cathedral and collegiate clergy of Germany were not monks. Except for those bishoprics where canons-regular had been introduced into the cathedral churches (as at Ratzeburg, Brandenburg, Salzburg, Gurk, Seckau, etc.), they were secular

---

[261] Silberborth, "EB Albrecht II." 53-55.

in its literal meaning. Most of them had been determined for the clerical life at an early age by their families, expecting the institutions of the cathedral, collegiate or parish church to provide them with an education and a living, since the overwhelming majority of them were the younger sons of the local nobility and prominent burghers.

Major churches at the beginning of the thirteenth century administered vast resources and the existence of individual prebends in most of them allowed canons to live rather independent of external constraints. Even the *vita communis*, where it still prevailed, did not try to make canons into a monastic community, for they could own private property and many of them had their own dwellings.[262] They were merely obligated to fulfill certain minimum expectations attached to their prebends and offices: to live lives of sobriety and propriety, to maintain residence, and to satisfy their *raison d'etre*—that is, perform choir service.

Thus, in 1215 conditions at all levels of church life within the German ecclesiastical provinces demanded reform in relation to ideal expectations. The never-easy task of maintaining proper discipline within the orders of the regular clergy and the ranks of the secular clergy had been immeasurable compounded by the civil war which pitted suffragans against their metropolitans, diocesan clergy and townspeople against their prelates, and critics of the *status quo* against its advocates. The insinuation of lay matters into the fabric and function of the Church manifested itself in far more than just disputed elections; dynastic politics, international struggles, the growing exclusiveness of episcopal elections in favor of the cathedral clergy and at the expense of laymen, especially diocesan *ministeriales*, likewise exacerbated religious problems to the point that in several German bishoprics ecclesiastical order broke down entirely for years at a time.

Just as in the secular world the feudal obligations incumbent upon fiefs were becoming less important than the acquisition of the benefices themselves, so too in the world of cathedral and collegiate canons the obligations connected with prebends and canonates were generally being ignored or circumvented in the early thirteenth century, becoming subordinate to the accumulation of clerical incomes and offices. The multiplication of feudal ties led ultimately to the commutation of feudal service into money payments—the substitution of a cash nexus for a personal one—resulting in some cases in the strengthening of central authority. But the proliferation of prebends on the part of the canons had led to the use of vicars and to the general decay of clerical discipline. Pluralism and absenteeism were twin problems plaguing virtually all dioceses, but especially those in the western

---

[262] Charles Dereine, "Chanoines," *DHGE* 12 (Paris, 1953) 353-405; also Heyen, *Sankt Paulin zu Trier* 98-102.

regions of Germany. Diocesan, provincial and legatine synods attempted to deal with these and related matters of reform during the period 1198 to 1215, but there is little to indicate that their impact was profound. The impression one has is that of "hit-and-miss," sporadic and incomplete, frustrated at every turn by deteriorating and chaotic political conditions. A General Council, at which all bishops and dignitaries of both secular and regular foundations would be placed under strict obligation to address abuses was thus perceived as the best available point from which to commence fundamental reform within the Church.

CHAPTER THREE

THE GERMAN EPISCOPACY 1215-1245 AND THE TRANSMISSION OF THE FOURTH LATERAN DECREES

*Fili hominis, speculatorem dedi te domui Israel; et audies de ore
meo verbum, et annuntiabis eis ex me.*
(Ezekiel 3,7)

*In eminenti specula nos dominus constituere voluit, ut defectus ecclesiastice
discipline perspicacius intueri possimus in subditis, et ea, que digna
correctione viderimus, emendare debeamus in melius ad
profectum subditorum et gloriam altissime majestatis.*
(Archbishop Dietrich II of Trier, a. 1215)

The entire tone of Innocent III's letters and decrees from the Fourth Lateran Council makes it clear that the metropolitans and bishops were to be the primary agents through whom the regeneration of clerical discipline and the tightening of doctrinal conformity were to be accomplished. Thus, except for the two bishops in each province who were permitted to remain at home in order to administer to pastoral matters, all other members of the episcopacy were expected to be in attendance at the Council.[1] Most narrative sources state that some four hundred-twelve prelates were actually present, whereas a Zurich codex lists four hundred-four.[2]

---

[1] Migne, *PL* CCXVI, col. 324: *"Credentes igitur hoc salutare propositum ab illa descendere a quo est datum optimum et omne donum perfectum, universitati vestrae per apostolica scripta praecipiendo mandamus quatenus vos taliter praeparetis quod a praesenti Dominicae Incarnationis millesimo ducentisimo decimo tertio anno usque as duos annos et dimidum, praefixus vobis pro termino Kalendis Novembris, nostro vos conspectui praesentetis cum modestia et cautela, ita quod in vestra provincia unus vel duo de suffraganeis valeant episcopi remanere pro Christianitatis ministeriis exercendis, et tam illi quam alii qui canonica forte praepeditione detenti personaliter venire nequiverint, idoneos pro se dirigant responsales, personarum, et evectionem mediocritate servata quam Lateranense concilium definivit, ut nullus omnino plures, quivis autem pauciores secum adducere possit; . . ."* Register in Potthast, *Regesta* I, Nr. 4707.

[2] Cf. *Ann. Salisb.* 780; *Chron. Ursperg.* 378; *Chron. mont. ser.* 186; *Reineri Ann.* 674; *Gesta Leod. Abbr.* 135; *Ann. Admunt.* 595; *Chron. Magni Presb.* 527. Zurich, Zentralbibliothek MS Car. C.148, fol. 46ʳ. For a discussion of the MS, cf. Achille Luchaire, "Un document retrouvé," *Journal des Savants,* N.S. 3 (October 1905), 557-568; Jacob Werner, "Die Teilnehmerliste des Laterankonzils (1215)," *NA* 31 (1906) 577-592; Tangl, *Teilnehmer* 221-222; Hermann Krabbo, "Die deutschen Bischöfe auf dem vierten Laterankonzil 1215," *Quellen und Forschungen aus italienischen Archiven und Bibliotheken* 10 (1907) 275-300; Foreville, *Lateran I-IV* 450-462; *Rubricella in Reg. Vat. 8A,* ed. A. Theiner, *Vetera*

A closer look at the German participants reveals that for many of them the visit to Rome was for purposes in addition to receiving the pontiff's reform program, however.³ Foremost among them was Archbishop Siegfried II of Mainz, since 1211 or early 1212 one of two standing papal legates for Germany. He had a vital interest in the Council due to plans by King Ottokar of Bohemia to erect an archbishopric in Prague, a matter which the Curia was then considering.⁴ Undoubtedly there in the same regard were Bishop Robert of Olmütz and Bishop-elect Andreas of Prague. Although elected in 1214, Andreas of Guttenstein had not suffered himself to be consecrated by Siegfried of Mainz, lest such an act be construed as recognition of the latter's metropolitan rights over Prague; he therefore went to the Council as *electus* and received consecration there on 22 November from the pope himself.⁵

Equally embroiled in a dispute with his metropolitan was Bishop Otto of Würzburg. Tension between the two men had centered on the 1213 excommunication and deposition of Otto by Siegfried acting as papal legate: as noted in Ch. Two, the former had refused to abandon Emperor Otto IV and soon found Siegfried supporting an anti-bishop, Henry of Ravensburg, for his see. Also at issue was the right to consecrate the abbot of Camberg, a prerogative claimed by both Mainz and Würzburg. Bishop Otto's excommunication had been reversed by Archbishop Albrecht of Magdeburg who also served as a standing legate in Germany. Siegfried of Mainz thus went to Rome hoping to obtain papal confirmation of his actions and papal support for his claims. Innocent III ultimately appointed Cardinal-legate Ugolino of Ostia and Velletri to referee the dispute while both antagonists were still in Rome; to the disappointment of, Archbishop Siegfried, the

---

monumenta Slavorum meridionalium historiam illustrantia (Rome, 1864) I 63, Nr. 14. Kuttner and Garcia y Garcia, "A New Eyewitness Account" 118, suggest that this MS corresponds to Nr. 162 in the lost Register of Innocent III's eighteenth year: "*clxii. Item quoddam inuentarium de synode (sic) celebrata*"; cf. Vatican Archives, Indice, fol. 13ᵛ Nr. 234.

³ Binterim, *Concilien* IV 267, states that it is not known which bishops were present from the provinces of Mainz, Cologne or Saxony; fear of Otto IV undoubtedly kept many of them home. Heinrich Wolter, on the other hand, says that all attended the Council; cf. *Chronik von Bremen*, in Heinrich Meibom, ed., *Rerum Germanicarum*, Tom II: *Historicos Germanicos* (Helmæstadii, 1688) 56.

⁴ Cf. Krabbo, "Die deutschen Bischöfe" 281-282. Siegfried's familiarity with the Curia dated to the years of his Roman exile (1206-1208), which we have noted in Chapter II. His mandate as a standing legate for Germany probably expired at the Council; cf. Zimmermann, *Päpstliche Legationen* 69.

⁵ Cf. Frind, *Bischöfe von Prag* 51-53; *Canonicorum Prag. Cont. Cosmae* 170: "*1215 Andreas ordinatus in episcopum Pragensem Romae in die sanctae Caeciliae. Concilium Romae celebratur.*" See also, Krabbo, "Die deutschen Bischöfe" 283-284.

German primate, the issue was decided on 10 February 1216 in favor of the bishop of Würzburg.[6]

Among the other suffragans of Mainz present at the Council were Ekbert of Bamberg whose irregular election of 1203 had nevertheless been confirmed by the pope, thereby placing the prelate in papal debt. We have noted above that he was also suspected of complicity in the 1208 murder of Philip of Swabia, but had been absolved of that through the mediation of his brother-in-law, the king of Hungary. Suspicion continued to follow him, however, and in early 1213 Innocent III had directed the archbishop of Mainz to investigate charges brought against Ekbert. The latter thus attended the Council for the purpose of establishing better relations with the papacy. Also in attendance were Bishops Arnold of Chur and Conrad of Constanz.[7]

Absent from the province of Mainz were Bishops Siegfried of Augsburg who was occasionally at the German royal court during the winter of 1215/1216 and may therefore have helped administer affairs of state, Hartwich of Eichstätt, Frederick of Halberstadt who remained loyal to Otto IV until January 1215 and stayed home for the probable reason of defending his territories against the Welf (he also appears to have taken the cross in 1215 with his brother Gerhard and was perhaps putting his affairs in order with the intent of departing for the Holy Land the following year), Hartbert of Hildesheim who not only refused to abandon Otto IV but was also gravely ill in late 1215, Bernhard of Paderborn, Conrad of Speyer and Metz who was the imperial chancellor and therefore had to remain behind to direct the government, Henry of Strasbourg who was also frequently at court and may therefore have been part of the administration, Iso of Verden, and Lupold of Worms who, since 1215, had been Frederick II's legate for Italy and his representative in Sicily.[8]

---

[6] Böhmer-Will, *RAM* II, 163, Nr. 259; *Monumenta Boica* XXXVII, I 197; *Wirtemburg UB* III 40; Ussermann, *Episc. Wirceb.* 82; Krabbo, "Die deutschen Bischöfe" 284; Winkelmann, *Phil. von Schw.* II 303-304; Krabbo, *Besetzung* 20-21 note 3.

[7] Krabbo, "Die deutschen Bischöfe" 282-283; Bishop Conrad of Constanz' presence is further attested by a document which he issued ". . .*publice Rome ap. S.Agathen a.i.d. 1215, 17 .kal.ian., presid. sacros. Romane eccl. Innoc. III, a. pont. 18., pontif. nri. a. 6*"; cf. Ladewig, *Regg. Const.* I, Nr. 1299, and the further clarification by Paul Ladewig, "Anwesenheit Bischof Konrads II. von Konstanz in Rom im Jahre 1215," in *ZGO*, N.F. 3 (1888) 374-376.

[8] Krabbo, "Die deutschen Bischöfe" 285; Idem, *Ostdeutsche Bistümer* 19. Bishop Hartbert of Hildesheim died 21 March 1216 under the ban of excommunication. For the presence of the bishops of Augsburg and Strasbourg at the royal court, cf. Böhmer-Ficker, *Regg. Imp.* V, Nrs. 837, 842, 850. Papal uncertainty with respect to Lupold's intentions in Italy during 1215 is discussed by Tillmann, *Innocenz III.* 501a.

The province of Cologne was poorly represented. The schism in the metropolitan church itself had left the archiepiscopal chair without an occupant. The deposed Dietrich of Hengebach, who had been excommunicated in 1212, appeared in Rome in November 1215 hoping to be restored, but he was not permitted to participate in the Council. Only Bishop Hugh of Liège and Bishop Conrad of Minden took active part.[9] Absent were Bishops Otto of Münster who had been a prisoner of Otto IV from February 1214 until July 1215 and therefore remained at home to repair damages to his bishopric, Gerhard of Osnabrück who was among the strongest opponents to Otto IV and whose presence in northern Germany was still required, and Otto II of Utrecht who had just received the regalia of his office in May 1215 and may have regarded a second trip to Rome in the same year as too much of a financial burden for his church.[10] Perhaps he too felt the need to defend his lands against the Welf forces.

Leading the delegation from the province of Trier was Archbishop Dietrich II who, throughout his pontificate, exhibited a firm commitment to ecclesiastical reform and thus must have welcomed the program which Innocent III proposed. Since his election in late November/early December 1212 he had been almost totally pre-occupied with securing the German throne for Frederick II and, although he had received the pallium sometime in early 1213, he had not as yet journeyed to Rome for a personal confirmation by the pope as required. Thus, this occasion was most opportune for that purpose as well.[11] Accompanying him were Matthew of Lorraine, the *quondam* bishop of Toul whose non-exemplary life has been discussed above and who doubtless sought a reversal of his deposition, and Robert of Verdun who was hopeful that the Curia could also be moved to repent of plans to depose him.[12] Absent was Bishop Conrad of Metz and Speyer, the imperial chancellor.

At the time of the Council, the archbishop of Salzburg was involved in a struggle with Bishop Henry of Gurk who sought independence from his

---

[9] *Chron. reg. Colon.* 237; *Aegidii Aureaevall.* 119; Binterim, *Concilien* IV 419. Krabbo, "Die deutschen Bischöfe" 286

[10] The first trip to Rome in 1215 had been undertaken by Bishop-elect Otto I who had been elected in 1212 as an eighteen-year old. He sought a dispensation from the canonical requirement of age thirty, but died 27 March *en route* to the Curia; cf. Krabbo, "Die deutschen Bischöfe" 287, and our discussion above in CHAPTER TWO.

[11] Krabbo, "Die deutschen Bischöfe" 288. For Dietrich II's activities 1212-1215, cf. Pixton, "Dietrich of Wied" (1972) 160-165. Dietrich of Trier was a witness for Frederick II at Speyer on 11 October 1215, from where he would have set out for Rome; cf. H-Bréholles, *Hist. dipl.* I, 428.

[12] For a thorough discussion of this matter at Verdun, cf. Kuhle, *Neubesetzung* 69, where a complete bibliography of relevant sources is also found; see further, Krabbo, "Die deutschen Bischöfe" 288-9.

metropolitan as a prince under the Empire. Since the bishop of Gurk was already vicar for the province, Archbishop Eberhard planned to erect a new bishopric at Chiemsee with the intent of splitting the vicarial power between Gurk and the new see. Both prelates attended the Council—the archbishop to further his plans, the bishop to thwart them—, and although the Council approved the new bishopric, it quashed the proposed division of the vicariate. So intent was Bishop Henry on defending his rights that he borrowed sixty Marks of silver against eight hides of land, and also obtained loans from Bolognese bankers. The debts remained for years.[13] Accompanying the archbishop was Rüdiger of Radeck, the Salzburg cathedral canon who was Eberhard's hand-picked candidate for the new bishopric.[14]

Also involved in controversy was the bishopric of Passau. Since the late twelfth century the dukes of Austria had been pushing for the erection of a bishopric in their territory—at Vienna. The German throne controversy interrupted those plans, demanding most of the time and energy of the Babenberg dynasty, but by 1207 the Staufen ascendancy had allowed a resumption of ducal efforts. Duke Leopold VI wrote of his intentions to Innocent III as early as 1207,[15] but Bishop Manegold of Passau vigorously opposed them, since they meant a reduction of his episcopal authority in Austria. With the death of King Philip in mid-1208 the entire matter became stalemated; only upon the accession of Frederick II of Staufen in 1212 did the duke press his plans once more. Presumably present, either as a member of the Passau delegation or as a lawyer in the papal Curia, was Albert Behaim who, acting as a papal legate, had a profound impact on Germany in the late 1230s.[16]

The Babenberg scheme was greatly enhanced by the death of Bishop Manegold on 10 June 1215 at Vienna. Leopold saw in this an opportunity to secure the election of a more favorable prelate, inasmuch as, if the cathedral chapter wished to gather round the dead bishop, it would have to submit to his influence in the choice of a successor. Shortly thereafter the election was held—far from Passau—in Styria, out of which emerged Ulrich, a cathedral canon at Passau, who also headed the ducal chancery. Ulrich was opposed both by a majority of the cathedral canons and the populace of the city of Passau, requiring intervention from the pope and the king to quell the resistance. Not until 1216 did Ulrich receive priestly consecration from the archbishop, and thereafter the episcopal blessing.

---

[13] Obersteiner, *Bischöfe von Gurk* 81; Jaksch, *MC* I 453, 473; Krabbo, *Ostdeutsche Bistümer* 102 note 52; Idem, "Die deutschen Bischöfe" 290-291.

[14] Fuchs, *Besetzung* 68.

[15] See papal letter to the bishop of Passau dated 14 April 1207; Potthast, *Regesta* I, Nr. 3085.

[16] Fuchs, *Besetzung* 68.

Bishop-elect Ulrich thus went to the Council in order to receive papal support for his election and also to further the wishes of his ducal benefactor.[17]

The remaining suffragan of Salzburg attending the Council was Conrad of Brixen whose motives are unknown to us. Absent were Bishops Otto II of Freising and Conrad IV of Regensburg, the latter of whom was often at the court of Frederick II of Staufen and presumably had some governmental function during this time.[18]

From the province of Bremen the suffragan bishops of Lübeck, Ratzeburg, and Schwerin set out on the long journey to Rome despite the meager resources of their respective churches. Their primary objective was undoubtedly that of protesting the concession of their sees to the king of Denmark near the end of 1214 by King Frederick II, an action which had deprived them of their status as imperial princes. The aging Philip of Ratzeburg took ill in northern Italy, however, and died 14 November 1215 at Verona. His two companions meanwhile continued on to the Council, only to see their efforts in vain, as Innocent III confirmed the agreement in May 1216.[19] Archbishop-elect Gerhard, whose struggle for the chair of Bremen has been discussed above, remained at home, above all to protect his interests against both Otto IV and Bishop Waldemar of Schleswig, the rival claimant to his see.

The second standing legate for Germany since early 1212 was Archbishop Albrecht of Magdeburg who may have used the opportunity of the Council to seek resolution of a dispute between his church and the bishopric of Kamin: Magdeburg claimed metropolitan rights over Kamin, as did Gnesen, whereas Kamin desired to be exempt. It must be seen as a personal triumph for Albrecht that shortly after the Council Innocent III commanded Bishop Siegwin of Kamin to recognize Magdeburg as his metropolitan.[20] Accompanying the archbishop to Rome were Bishops Baldwin of Brandenburg and Sigbodo of Havelberg who both perhaps sought

---

[17] Krabbo, "Babenberger Landeskirche" 21-27; Idem, "Die deutschen Bischöfe" 291; Oswald, *Passau DK* 69f.; Herta Hageneder, "Die Beziehungen der Babenberger zur Kurie in der ersten Hälfte des 13. Jahrhunderts," *MIÖG* 75 (1967) 1-29. Concerning Ulrich himself, cf. Heinrich Fichtenau, "Die Kanzlei der letzten Babenberger," *MIÖG* 56 (1948) 256ff.

[18] See Krabbo, "Die deutschen Bischöfe" 291, citing Böhmer-Ficker, *Regg. Imp.* V, Nrs. 828, 829, 839, 840, 850, 852.

[19] See Böhmer-Ficker, *Regg. Imp.* V, Nr. 773; *Heinrici Chron. Lyv.* 291: "*Episcopus autem Raceburgensis cum episcopo Estiensi Theoderico festinans ad concilium Romanum, cum peregrinis euntibus in Theuthoniam mari se committens, . . .* "; Potthast, *Regesta* I, Nr. 5110; Krabbo, "Die deutschen Bischöfe" 291-292.

[20] Potthast, *Regesta* I, Nr. 5061; Krabbo, "Die deutschen Bischöfe" 293, notes that Albrecht was also the cardinal priest of SS. Nereus and Achilleus, yet Foreville, *Lateran I-IV* 456-457, cautions that in the list of cardinal priests present at the council neither Siegfried of Mainz nor Albrecht of Magdeburg is mentioned.

papal aid in strengthening their position over against Margrave Albrecht of Brandenburg who still supported Otto IV and posed a serious threat to the Brandenburg diocese. Absent were Bishops Bruno of Meissen and Engelhard of Naumburg. The see of Merseburg had been vacant since the death of Bishop Dietrich on 12 October 1215, and a successor was not elected until early 1216.

Also present were the patriarch of Aquileia and the bishops of Basel, Cambrai, Estonia, Riga, and Trent, but, although these six sees lay within the political boundaries of the Empire and their occupants were imperial princes, they were part of ecclesiastical provinces which lay predominantly outside of Germany and thus will not be included in this study. Rather, we are concerned with the twenty-one imperial-German archbishops and bishops in attendance, and another twenty-one sees which were unrepresented by their respective heads. By comparison, there were fifteen prelates present from England, Scotland, and Wales (and eighteen absent), seventeen in attendance from Ireland (and thirteen absent), twenty-three attending from Spain and Portugal (and twenty who remained away), seventy-six present from France, Provence, and Burgundy (and thirty-four absent), and one hundred twenty-four present from Italian dioceses.[21] Despite the civil war which had ravaged Germany since 1198, episcopal representation from that realm at the Council was thus quite comparable to that from more stable regions of Latin Christendom.

Although it was the prelates upon whom the greatest responsibility for reform was to rest, Innocent III had also demanded that monastic dignitaries and representatives from other ecclesiastical bodies be present at the Council. Such proctors are much less-well documented. Chronicles suggest that the total number was between 600 and 900, but the most common figure is *"ultra 800."*[22] How many of these came from Germany cannot be determined with any degree of exactness, but an approximation is at least possible. We know that Abbots Werner of Waussor (Benedictine; diocese of Liège),[23] Eudes of St. Laurence (Benedictine; Liège),[24] Christian of St. Truijen (Benedictine; Liège),[25] Siegfried of Pegau(Benedictine; Merseburg),[26] Ludeger of Altzelle (Cistercian; Meissen),[27] Eberhard of

---

[21] Cf. Werner, "Teilnehmerliste" 587; Foreville, *Lateran I-IV*, 458; Gibbs/Lang, *Bishops and Reform* 106-107. The number of bishoprics in each region is derived from Bonifacius Gams, *Series Episcoporum Ecclesiae Catholicae* (Ratisbon, 1873).

[22] E.g., *Ann. Salisb.* 780; *Reineri Ann.* 674; *Hermanni Altah.* 387.

[23] *Hist. Walciod.* 539; Tangl, *Teilnehmer* 230.

[24] *Historia monasterii S. Laurentii*, in Martène, *Collectio* IV, 1097.

[25] *Gesta abb. Trud.* 393.

[26] *Chron. mont. ser.* 186.

[27] *Chron. montis Ser.* 186; Tangl, *Teilnehmer* 230.

Salem (Cistercian; Constanz), Ulrich of Stein (Benedictine; Constanz), and Dietrich of Kreuzlingen (Augustinian Canons; Constanz)[28] were present, as were the priors Reiner of St. Jacob (Benedictine; Liège),[29] Dietrich of Lauterberg (Augustinian Canons; Magdeburg), William of Tzschillen (Premonstratensian Canons; Magdeburg),[30] Andreas of Kappenberg (Premonstratensian Canons; Münster) who possibly represented the bishop as well,[31] Wilbrand of Käfernburg, provost of the collegiate church of Saints Nicholas and Peter (Magdeburg), Anno of Biesenrode, the *cellerarius* at Magdeburg cathedral and H[ ] a cathedral canon,[32] *magister* Oliver and several *priores* from the archdiocese of Cologne,[33] an anonymous monk

[28] All three were witnesses at Rome to the document of Bishop Conrad of Constanz issued 16 December 1215 regarding a dispute between the church of St. John in Turtal and the Knights Hospitalers; cf. Ladewig, *Regg. Const.* I Nr. 1299. For Eberhard of Salem as a papally-appointed crusade-preacher, cf. Pixton, "Anwerbung" 167-188.

[29] *Reineri Ann.* 673-674; Binterim, *Concilien* IV 267. Based on Reiner's account, there were actually several prominent clerics from the diocese of Liège who made preparations to attend the Council: "*Annus 1215. . . . Septembri mense preparant se omnes prelati ecclesie, qui ad concilium disposuerunt ire. Feria 6. post festum sancti Lamberti [18 Sept.] exivit a nobis Renerus presentium dictator, procurator ecclesie nostre intravit Romam Simonis et Jude [28 Oct.] mansitque ibi usque Prisce [18 Jan.], rediitque in festo Matthie [25 Feb. 1216].*"

[30] Several clerics from the archdiocese of Magdeburg went to Rome at the time of the Council for the purpose of presenting before the Curia the two sides of a disputed election at Lauterberg. Both claimants undoubtedly had their supporters; cf. *Chron. mont. ser.* 185: "*Heinricus cum litteris archiepiscopi causam suam pape significantibus Romam profectus, iudices contra prepositum impetravit. Eo tempore indicto ab Innocencio papa Rome generali concilio, universi ecclesiarum prelati ad profeccionem se parabant. Prepositus vero, sicut et plerique alii, concilium prevenire cupiens, ut commodior et copia fieret sua negocia promovendi, cum a iudicibus Heinrici citatus fuisset, appellavit et copiosa sumpta pecunia Romam profectus est. . . . Tempore quo prepositus Romam proficisci parabat et cum eo Willehelmus Cillenensis prepositus, . . .*"; Tangl, *Teilnehmer* 230.

[31] Cf. *Westf. UB* III, Nr. 92, which records the grant of a house lying adjacent to the convent of Kappenberg to that same foundation by bishop Otto I of Münster; the charter is dated ". . . *anno dominice incarnationis M°CC°XV. quando dominus Innocentius generale concilium Rome celebravit, cui interfuit Andreas prepositus [scilicet Capenbergensis].*"

[32] Cf. the letter addressed to the provost (without name) by Innocent III which is included in the *Chron. mont. ser.* 186; Potthast, *Regesta* I, Nr. 5007. His identity is provided by Wentz/Schwineköper, *Erzbistum Magdeburg* I/1 315; he was half-brother to Archbishop Albrecht, and himself became archbishop in 1235. For biographical details on Anno, see Wentz/Schineköper, *op.cit.* I/1 400; the identity of H[ ] appears to be Heinrich of Plaue who is documented as a canon at Magdeburg from 1208; cf. Wentz/Schwineköper, *op. cit.* 467-468.

[33] *Reineri Ann.* 674: "*Multitudo signatorum, quid in concilio de eis fuerit dispositum, adventum magistri Oliveri vivifice crucis legati expectantium. Redeunte autem predicto magistro a sacro consilio, . . .*" Further, cf. Hermann Hoogeweg, "Der Kölner Domscholaster Oliver als Kreuzprediger 1214-1217," *WZGK* 7 (1888) 265. That other *priores* from Cologne were also present is deduced from the account found in the *Chron. reg. Colon.* (Annales Colonienses Maximi) 828: "*Tidericus igitur Coloniensis archiepiscopus diu ibidem demoratus, cum officii sui restitutionem minime inpetrare posset, priores ecclesiae acceptis a papa litteris*"

from Aulesberg (Cistercian; Mainz),[34] and at least seven clerics from the
diocese of Constanz.[35] A tradition preserved in the seventeenth-century
Fürstenberg chronicle places Abbot Berthold of Thennenbach (dioc.
Constanz) there as well.[36]

We have argued elsewhere that several prominent German clerics were
also in attendance, namely those who had been appointed by Innocent III to
direct recruitment of German crusaders: *magister* John, scholastic at
Xanten; Otto, the cathedral provost at Salzburg; and several Cistercian and
Premonstratensian abbots and monks—Peter of Neubourg (Cistercian;
diocese of Strasbourg), Daniel of Schönau (Cistercian; Worms), Frederick
and Conrad of Sichem (Cistercian; Halberstadt), Bruno of Rommersdorf
(Premonstratensian; Trier), and Walther of Villers-en-Brabant (Cistercian;
Liège).[37] It is also probable that Abbot Ulrich of St. Gall, who went to
Rome in the summer of 1215, remained for the Council.[38]

Given the total number of over 800 abbots, priors, and chapter representatives from throughout the Latin West who attended, it is reasonable to
assume that (as was true with the bishops) the greatest proportion came
from Italy and Languedoc, with fewer from Germany, northern France,
Iberia, Hungary, England, and Scandinavia. Not all German dioceses
would have had the sizeable showing documented for Constanz, Liège, and
Magdeburg. We may surmise that a significant number of religious

---

*alium eligere iussi sunt. Qui Coloniam redeuntes, et secunda feria post dominicam Invocavit
me in ecclesia beati Petri convenientes, . . ."*

[34] Giessen Universitätsbibliothek MS 1105, fol. 47ra-58vb; cf. detailed discussion of the
author in Kuttner/Garcia y Garcia, "A New Eyewitness Account" 115-123.

[35]Ladewig, *Regg. Const.* Nr. 1299: among the clerical witnesses to Bishop Conrad's
charter of 16 December 1215 at Rome were "*Vlricus custos Constant., Liutold. de Rotenlein
eiusdem eccl. canon., H. prepos. de Bvrren, Albert pleban. de Wile, Burchard. pleb. in
Bischoffingen, Berthold. Const. archid., Eberhardus plebanus de Horne, . . .*"

[36] *Fürstenberg. UB* I 79-80, Nr. 127, citing the manuscript *Chronik: "Berthold, Graff von
Vrach, Conradi Bruder, Abbt zu Thennenbach, ziehet nach Rom auffs Lateranenische
Concilium, hilfft neben anderen den Franciscaner Orden bestättigen vnnd hertzog Bertholden
von Zäringen, seiner Mutter Bruder, wegen seines Gottlosen . . . (Lücke) in den gaistlichen
Bann thun."* Johann Daniel Schöpflin, *Historia Zaringo Badensis* V (Carolsruhe, 1763ff.) 143,
cites an excerpt from a *Vita b. Hugonis* which notes: "*Idem Abbas (Bertholdus) veniens a
curia Romana.*" Siegmund Riezler, the editor of vol. I of the *Fürstenberg. UB*, concludes that
the Council provided Abbot Berthold with the opportunity of being with his more prominent
brother, Abbot Conrad of Clairvaux, who in 1217 became abbot of Cîteaux and in 1219
cardinal-bishop of Porto and S. Rufina; see also *Fürstenberg. UB* I 82, Nr. 135, which cites
a letter of 14 March 1217 from Honorius III to Abbot Conrad: "*Cum nuper in generali
concilio ad sedem apostolicam venientes essetis in foelicis recordationis Innocentii papae et
praedecessoris nostri praesentia constituti, . . .*"

[37] Pixton, "Anwerbung" 167-185.

[38] Cf. *Conr. de Fab.* 171.

dignitaries and chapter officials did not attend on account of illness, threat to their property by Otto IV or some other belligerent lay noble, or disputes with their prelates. The substantial cost which such an undertaking involved explains why most of the smaller corporations did not send proctors, however. There were approximately 1254 monasteries, priories, and chapters of canons regular within the six German ecclesiastical provinces under consideration in 1215. In addition, an estimated 230 cathedral, collegiate, and canoness-chapters flourished at the same time.[39] Thus, even if the thirty-eight or so clerics already accounted for had been joined by another ten to twenty others, fewer than three percent of the German religious houses, foundations, and chapters were directly represented at the Council.

In their study of the English bishops and thirteenth-century reform, Gibbs and Lang contended that only the attending bishops actually received individual copies of the Lateran constitutions and other documents which had been prepared beforehand by curial scribes.[40] Kuttner and Garcia y Garcia have argued, on the other hand, that other participants were given the decrees as well.[41] There seems to be inferential evidence in the case of Germany that the latter view is correct: several bishoprics whose prelates were not present nevertheless acquired the conciliar statutes by means of one or more of the monastic or secular clergy from that diocese. To have restricted the copies of the decrees exclusively to attending bishops would have seriously impaired the papal program of universal reform throughout the Church. Accordingly, at least twenty-one, and more probably twenty-nine or more[42] sets of the Council's decrees and muniments were transmitted back to Germany by the prelates and the forty to fifty other clerics returning in late 1215/early 1216. Among the extant thirteenth-century manuscripts of the Lateran IV constitutions are presumably several which were carried back by German participants.[43]

---

[39] These figures are based on the lists found in Hauck, *KGD* II 817-830; III 1011-1040; IV 975-1030; corrections and additions have been made on the basis of Cottineau, *Répertoire*, 2 vols., and the *Germania Benedictina* II (Bayern), V (Baden-Württemburg) and VI (Niedersachsen-Norddeutschland).

[40] Gibbs/Lang, *Bishops and Reform* 105-113.

[41] Kuttner/Garcia y Garcia, "A New Eyewitness Account" 164.

[42] The larger figure includes the possible representatives of absent bishops, such as the prior of Kappenberg for the bishop of Münster.

[43] Admont Stiftsbibliothek MS 22, fol. 245-6; Bamberg Stadtsbibliothek MS Can. 19; Bamberg Stadtsbibliothek MS Can. 20 (P.II.7), fol. 63v-70v; Bamberg Stadtsbibliothek MS Can. 23; Bamberg Stadtsbibliothek MS Patr. 132 (Q.VI.42), fol. 81-109v; Frankfurt MS 28; Fulda Landesbibliothek MS D.6; Fulda Landesbibliothek MS D.14, fol. 128-144v; Giessen Universitätsbibliothek MS 1105, fol. 47ra-58vb; Graz MS 374; Graz MS III, 106; Graz MS III, 138, fol. 233-246; Kassel Landesbibliothek MS Jur. 11 (w/o pag.); Koblenz Staatsarchiv

The major concern facing Innocent III and his successors with respect to the Fourth Lateranum was that of inducing the prelates and other ecclesiastical dignitaries to publish and implement the reform decrees within the spheres of their respective stewardships. Nowhere was this a greater challenge than in Germany where temporal and spiritual functions constantly competed for the interests and energies of the episcopacy. The nature of this dual role, and the reputation which it bestowed upon the German bishops is well summarized in a tale related by Caesarius of Heisterbach:

> A certain cleric from Paris declared some years ago that he would believe everything except that any German bishop could attain salvation. Why did he judge the German bishops more harshly than those from England, France, Lombardy, or Tuscany? Because almost all German prelates bore both swords at once—the spiritual and the temporal—, because they judged over life and death, engaged in wars, and concerned themselves more with the payment of their soldiers than with the salvation of the souls with which they had been entrusted. And yet, there were exceptions: for although the archbishops of Cologne were at once princes of the Church and dukes, several of them, such as Bruno, Heribert, and Anno, were able to attain saintliness.[44]

Such thoughts as these were clearly a product of their time and reflect the bias against secular clergy which is a common theme in Cistercian writings. As we have seen in the previous chapter, however, there is a strong element of truth in them as well, and the political uncertainties in Germany after the untimely death of Henry VI of Staufen in 1197 placed a premium on men of ability in temporal affairs. That bishops might also possess spiritual qualities appears to have been a lesser consideration for most contemporaries. The irony is that it was upon the shoulders of these prelates that so much rested if the regeneration of the Church according to the vision of Innocent III was to be realized.

During the period 1215-1245 one hundred twenty-eight men sat as confirmed and consecrated bishops or metropolitans in the six provinces of Bremen, Cologne, Magdeburg, Mainz, Salzburg, and Trier. The following table provides a brief summary of that group of prelates:

Bestand 162 Nr. 1401/3, fol. 129-136; Leipzig MS 968; Marburg MS C.2; Munich Staatsbibliothek MS lat. 3879; Munich Staatsbibliothek MS lat. 5822, fol. 164ᵇ-179; Munich Staatsbibliothek MS lat. 9596, fol. 255-291; Prague University Library MS xxiii.E.59 (according to Lobkowitz MS 439), fol. 1-23ᵛ; Vienna MS 2149; Vienna MS 2183; Zurich Zentralbibliothek MS C.148.

[44]*Caesarius Dialogus* II 27; cited by Ficker, *Engelbert der Heilige* 89-90, and by Hauck, "Geistlich. Territorien" 647.

Table C: The German Episcopacy 1215-1245

BISHOPRIC	YEARS	TRAINING	CHANCERY	ORDER	CLASS
MAINZ					
1. Siegfried II of Eppstein	1200-30	Mainz	C[1]		N[2]
2. Siegfried III of Eppstein	1230-49	Mainz			N
AUGSBURG					
3. Siegfried III of Rechberg	1209-27	Augsburg			M
4. Siboto of Seefeld	1227-47	Augsburg			N
BAMBERG					
5. Ekbert of Andechs	1203-37	Bamberg			N
6. *mag.* Henry of Catania	1242-57	Bamberg/ Bologna	N & C[3]		M
CHUR					
7. Arnold II of Matsch	1210-21	Strasbourg			N
8. Rudolf II of Güttingen	1223-26	Constanz		B[5]	N
9. Berthold of Helfenstein	1226-33	Constanz			N
10. Ulrich IV of Kyburg	1233-37	Strasbourg/ Constanz	C[4]		N
11. Volcnand of Neuenburg	1238-51	Chur			M
CONSTANZ					
12. Conrad of Tegernfeld	1209-33	Constanz			N
13. Henry I of Tanne	1233-48	Constanz	P[6]		N

[1] N = Notary; P = Protonotarius; C = Chancellor. Siegfried of Eppstein was chancellor for the kingdom of Bohemia.

[2] M = Ministerial; N = Noble; B = Bourgeois; ? = Unknown Origin.

[3] For Frederick II of Staufen.

[4] For Henry (VII) of Staufen.

[5] B = Benedictine; C = Cistercian. Rudolf II of Güttingen was the abbot of St. Gall.

[6] For Frederick II and Henry (VII).

BISHOPRIC	YEARS	TRAINING	CHANCERY	ORDER	CLASS
EICHSTÄTT					
14. Hartwich of Dolnstein	1195-1223	Eichstätt			N
15. Frederick I of Huwenstat	1223-25	Eichstätt			N
16. Henry I of Zeuppelingen	1225-28	Augsburg/ Eichstätt			M
17. Henry II of Tischingen	1229-32	Eichstätt			M
18. Henry III of Ravensburg	1232-37	Würzburg			M
19. Frederick II of Parsberg	1237-46	Eichstätt/ Freising			M
HALBERSTADT					
20. Frederick II of Kirchberg	1209-36	Halberstadt			N
21. Ludolf of Schladen	1236-41	Halberstadt			N
22. Meinhard of Kranichfeld	1241-53	Halberstadt			N
HILDESHEIM					
23. Hartbert of Dalem	1201-16	Hildesheim			N
24. Siegfried of Lichtenberg	1216-21	Hildesheim		B	N
25. *mag.* Conrad	1221-46	Mainz/ Paris			?
OLMÜTZ					
26. Robert of England	1202-40	N. France?		C	?
27. Bruno of Holstein	1245-81	Lübeck/ Magdeburg			N
PADERBORN					
28. Bernhard II of Ösede	1203-23	Paderborn			N
29. *magister* Oliver	1223-25	Paderborn/ Cologne/ Paris			B
30. Wilbrand of Oldenburg	1225-27	Hildesheim			N
31. Bernhard IV of Lippe	1228-47	Paderborn			N

BISHOPRIC	YEARS	TRAINING	CHANCERY	ORDER	CLASS
PRAGUE					
32. *magister* Andreas of Guttenstein	1214-24	Prague			N
33. Peregrin	1224-25	Prague			?
34. John II	1227-36	Prague			?
35. *mag.* Bernhard	1236-39	Prague			?
36. Nicholas of Riesenberg	1240-58	Prague			N
SPEYER					
37. Conrad of Scharfenberg	1200-24	Speyer	C[1]		M
38. Berengar of Entringen	1224-32	Speyer			N
39. Conrad IV of Dahn	1233-36	Worms/ Speyer/ Paris			M
40. Conrad V of Eberstein	1237-45	Speyer			N
STRASBOURG					
41. Henry II of Veringen	1202-23	Strasbourg			N
42. Berthold of Teck	1223-44	Strasbourg			N
43. Henry III of Stahleck	1245-60	Strasbourg/ Mainz			N
VERDEN					
44. Iso of Wölpe	1205-31	Verden/ Hildesheim			N
45. Luder of Borg	1231-51	Verden			M
WORMS					
46. Lupold of Scheinfeld	1196- 1217	Worms			N
47. Henry III of Saarbrücken	1217-34	Mainz			N
48. Landolf of Hoheneck	1234-47	Worms			M
WÜRZBURG					
49. Otto of Lobdeburg	1207-23	Würzburg			N
50. Dietrich of Hohenburg	1223-25	Würzburg			M
51. Hermann I of Lobdeburg	1225-54	Würzburg/ Bamberg			N

[1] For Frederick II of Staufen.

BISHOPRIC	YEARS	TRAINING	CHANCERY	ORDER	CLASS
TRIER					
52. Dietrich II of Wied	1212-42	Cologne/ Trier			N
53. Arnold of Isenburg	1242-59	Trier/ Mainz			N
METZ					
Conrad of Scharfenberg	1212-24	[See under Speyer]			
54. Jean d'Aspremont	1224-38	Metz/ Verdun			N
55. Jacques of Lorraine	1239-60	Trier/ Liège			N
TOUL					
56. Rainald of Senlis	1210-17	Toul?			N
57. Eudes II of Sorcy	1219-28	Toul?			N
58. Garin	1228-30	Toul		B	?
59. Roger of Marcey	1230-52	Verdun/ Liège			N
VERDUN					
60. Robert of Grandpré	1208-17	Verdun			N
Jean d'Aspremont	1217-24	[see under Metz]			
61. Rudolf of Thourotte	1225-45	Laon			N
COLOGNE					
62. Engelbert of Berg	1216-25	Cologne			N
63. Henry of Müllenark	1225-37	Bonn/ Cologne			N
64. Conrad of Hochstaden	1238-61	Cologne			N
LIÈGE					
65. Hugh of Pierrepont	1200-29	Liège			N
66. Jean II d'Aps (Eppes)	1229-38	Liège			N
67. Robert of Thourotte	1240-46	Laon/ Langres?			N
MINDEN					
68. Conrad I of Rüdenberg	1210-36	Minden			N
69. William I of Diepholz	1237-42	Minden			N
70. John of Diepholz	1242-53	Bremen			N

BISHOPRIC	YEARS	TRAINING	CHANCERY	ORDER	CLASS

MÜNSTER
71. Otto I of
    Oldenburg-
    Wildeshausen
	1203-18	Bremen/
		Bonn
					N

72. Dietrich III of Isenberg	1219-26	Cologne			N
73. Ludolf of Holte	1227-47	Münster			N
OSNABRÜCK 74. Gerhard of Oldenburg	1193- 1216	Bremen/ Osnabrück			N
75. Adolf of Tecklenburg	1216-24	Cologne		C	N
76. Otto I of Herbst	1226-27	Osnabrück?			N
77. Conrad of Veltberg	1227-39	Hildesheim			N
78. Engelbert I of Isenberg	1239-50	Cologne/ Münster			N
UTRECHT 79. Otto II of Lippe	1215-27	Utrecht			N
Wilbrand of Oldenburg	1227-33	[see Pader- born]			
80. Otto III of Holland	1234-49	Utrecht			N
SALZBURG 81. Eberhard II of Regensberg	1200-46	Constanz/ Augsburg/ Bologna			M
BRIXEN 82. Conrad of Rodank	1200-16	Brixen			M
83. Berthold of Neiffen	1216-24	Speyer	P[1]		N
84. Henry III of Tüfers	1224-39	Aquileia?			N
CHIEMSEE 85. Rüdiger of Radeck	1215-33	Salzburg			N
86. Albert I	1235-52	Salzburg			?

[1] For Frederick II of Staufen.

BISHOPRIC	YEARS	TRAINING	CHANCERY	ORDER	CLASS
FREISING					
87. Otto II of Berg	1184-1220	Passau			N
88. Gerold of Waldeck	1220-30	Freising			M
89. Conrad I of Tölz	1231-58	Freising			N
GURK					
90. Henry of Pettau	1214-17	Salzburg			M
91. Udalschalk	1217-20	Gurk			?
92. Ulrich of Ortenburg	1221-53	Salzburg/ Passau?			N
LAVANT					
93. Ulrich of Haus	1226-46	Salzburg?			?
PASSAU					
94. Ulrich II of Berg	1215-21	Passau	C[1]		?
95. Gebhard of Plain	1222-32	Passau			N
Rüdiger of Radeck	1233-49	[see Chiemsee]			
REGENSBURG					
96. Conrad IV of Frontenhausen	1204-26	Regensburg/ Freising			N
97. Siegfried the Rheingraf	1227-46	Mainz			N
SECKAU					
98. Carl I	1218-30	Salzburg			?
99. Henry I	1231-43	Salzburg			B
mag. Ulrich I of Sengenberg	1244-56, 1265-66	Bamberg			M
BREMEN					
100. Gerhard I of Oldenburg	1210-19	Bremen			N
101. Gerhard II of Lippe	1219-59	Paderborn			N
LÜBECK-OLDENBURG					
102. Berthold	1210-30	Lübeck			?
103. John of Lübeck	1230-47	Lübeck			B

[1] For Duke Leopold of Austria.

BISHOPRIC	YEARS	TRAINING	CHANCERY	ORDER	CLASS
RATZEBURG					
104. Henry	1215-28	Ratzeburg			?
105. Gottschalk	1228-35	Ratzeburg			M
106. Peter	1236	Ratzeburg			M
107. Ludolf	1236-50	Ratzeburg			M
SCHWERIN/ MECKLEN- BURG					
108. Brunward	1192-1238	Schwerin	C		M
109. Frederick of Schwerin	1238-39	Hildesheim			N
110. Dietrich	1239-47	Schwerin			M
MAGDEBURG					
111. Albrecht of Käfernberg	1205-32	Hildesheim/ Paris/ Bologna			N
112. Wilbrand of Käfernberg	1235-53	Magdeburg			N
HAVELBERG					
113. Siboto of Stendal	1206-19	Stendal?			M
114. William	1219-44	Havelberg			?
115. Henry of Kerkow	1245-71	Stendal			M
MEISSEN					
116. Bruno II of Borsendorf	1209-28	Meissen			N
117. Henry I	1230-40	?			?
118. Conrad	1240-58	Magdeburg			?
MERSEBURG					
119. Ekkehard Rabel	1215-40	Merseburg			M
120. Rudolf of Webau	1240-44	Merseburg			?
121. Henry I of Warin	1244-65	Merseburg			N
NAUMBURG					
122. Engelhard	1206-42	?			?
123. Dietrich of Meissen	1242-72	Naumburg			N

BISHOPRIC	YEARS	TRAINING	CHANCERY	ORDER	CLASS
BRANDENBURG					
124. Baldwin	1205-16	Branden-burg			?
125. Siegfried II of Wanzleben	1216-21	Branden-burg			N
126. Gernand	1222-41	Magdeburg			B
127. Ruotger of Kerkow?	1241-49	Branden-burg			M

Seventy-nine of these men can be determined as coming from the upper nobility, twenty-five from the lower nobility (ministerial), and twenty-two from bourgeois or unknown origins. Some of them were thoroughly brutal men, such as Lupold of Worms whom we encountered in Ch.Two. Gebhard of Plain, bishop of Passau (1222-1232), was accused of slaying one of his own cathedral canons,[45] only to be exonerated after he had resigned his episcopal office; two brothers, Dietrich and Engelbert of Isenberg, 1219-1226 as bishop of Münster and 1224-1226 as *electus* of Osnabrück respectively, actually conspired in the perfidious assassination of their own cousin, Archbishop Engelbert of Cologne, and were deposed in 1226.[46] Others, though not vicious, nevertheless had their personal vices.

Some bishops were just incompetent, unable to cope with problems as complex as those temporal and spiritual matters which pertained to a thirteenth-century German bishopric. In 1228, for example, a seventy-year-old monk named Garin was elected bishop of Toul. Although he declined the office, he was commanded to accept the miter by his metropolitan, Archbishop Dietrich II of Trier. Personal sanctity along was insufficient qualification for a demanding episcopal office, however, and after a brief but clearly traumatic pontificate, Garin secured papal permission in 1230 to resign and withdrew to his cell where he soon died.[47] A similar instance occurred at Hildesheim where, in 1216, the cathedral chapter elected a former member, Siegfried of Lichtenberg, now a monk at Fulda, to be bishop. Less than five years later Honorius III directed two German clerics to accept Siegfried's resignation and to make provision for a pension, stating that

---

[45] Binterim, *Concilien* IV 279; Dopsch, *Geschichte Salzburgs* I 335.

[46] Cf. Wolfgang Kleist, "Der Tod des Erzbischofs Engelbert von Köln: eine kritische Studie," *ZGAW* 75/1 (1917) 182-249.

[47] *Chron. Albrici* 922; Morret, *Stand und Herkunft* 70; Pixton, "Dietrich of Wied" (1972) 158-159.

Our venerable brother S. bishop of Hildesheim has implored us many times through his letters to intercede in his behalf—fearing that he is unable to exercise his pastoral office on account of the burden of excessive age, and that he might injure those over whom he has been set, since he cannot be beneficial to them—that we might concede to his wish that the license of the pastoral office be removed from him.

While age may well have been a factor, it was charges of negligence and gross incompetence which actually brought the commission to Hildesheim. In May or June 1221, Bishop Siegfried gave an accounting of his steward-ship, claiming that he had not alienated church property contrary to canonical strictures. A papal missive one year later contradicted this, however, indicating that the Curia had come to understand that the former bishop of Hildesheim had not only committed the alleged act of alienation, but had also burdened his church with debts. Even the pension of one hundred Marks yearly which Siegfried had established for himself from diocesan resources was deemed extravagant and ordered reduced, so that his successor would not have to pay for someone else's debts.[48]

German Bishops and the Schools

The new bishop of Hildesheim, in whose behalf Honorius III wrote the above-cited letter, was representative of another group of German prelates noted for their integrity, ability, and erudition. He was *magister* Conrad, reputed to have taught theology at Paris and to have preached against the Albigenses before 1209, previously dean at Speyer (1209-1216) and cathedral scholastic at Mainz (1216-1221), former member of Honorius III's penitentiary, a crusade-preacher in Germany under both Innocent III and Honorius III, reformer of the monasteries in the province of Mainz, and in 1220 overseer of all crusader recruitment activities throughout Germany.[49] Equally imposing was Albrecht of Käfernberg who had been trained at Hildesheim, Paris, and Bologna, and had been chosen to occupy the archiepiscopal chair at Magdeburg in 1205 largely on account of his reputation as an erudite man.[50] Despite the obvious advantages to an ambitious cleric, however, we can presently identify only nine of the one hundred twenty-seven bishops who sat between 1215 and 1245 who are

---

[48] Hoogeweg, *UB Hilds* II, Nr. 49. Raynaldi, *Annales* I, Nr. 1 *ad anno* 1221; Pressutti, *Regg. Hon. III* I, Nr. 3032.

[49] Cf. Pixton, "Konrad von Reifenberg" 43-81, with corrections offered by Crusius, "Bischof Konrad II. von Hildesheim" 431-468.

[50] Silberborth, "EB Albrecht II." 9-10; Winter, "EB Albrecht II." 183-190; Kuhle, *Neubesetzung* 55.

known to have studied at Paris or Northern France, Padua, or Bologna, and presumably to have received advanced training in theology and/or canon law.[51]

Unlike contemporary French and English bishops who have left their imprint upon the intellectual traditions of Western civilization, few German prelates of the thirteenth century were outstanding men of letters. One of the best-known was *magister* Oliver, author of the much-cited *Historia Damiatina* and an important correspondence, who was elected bishop of Paderborn in 1223. He never actually served in the office, however, being first embroiled in an election dispute and thereafter elevated to the cardinalate.[52] Extant are a few scattered works, such as the *Legatio in Armeniam et iter in terram sanctam*, written about 1211 by Wilbrand of Oldenburg, a Hildesheim cathedral canon who was elected bishop of Paderborn in 1225 and transferred to Utrecht in 1227,[53] and a Middle-High German versification of the Latin Barlaam legend (16,704 lines), which tells of an ideal monasticism, written by Otto II of Freising (1184-1220).[54]

---

[51] *Magister* Conrad, bishop of Hildesheim 1221-46 (Paris); *magister* Oliver, bishop of Paderborn 1223-25 (Paris); Conrad IV of Dahn, bishop of Speyer 1233-36 (Paris); Eberhard II of Regensberg, archbishop of Salzburg 1200-1246 (Bologna); Albrecht of Käfernberg, archbishop of Magdeburg 1205-32 (Paris, Bologna); *magister* Henry of Catania, bishop of Bamberg 1242-1257 (Bologna). Both Rudolf of Thourotte, bishop of Verdun 1225-1245, and Robert of Thourotte, bishop of Liège 1240-1246, were trained at Laon where presumably strong intellectual traditions still prevailed. Traditions point to Northern France as the area where Bishop Robert of Olmütz was trained. In contrast, Gibbs/Lang, *Bishops and Reform* 25-52, 192-194, have identified eighteen English prelates who sat 1216-1245 and who bore the title *magister* as evidence of university training.

[52] Wilhelm Junkmann, "Magister Oliverius Scholasticus, Bischof von Paderborn, Kardinalbischof von S. Sabina und der Kreuzzug von Damiette," *Katholische Zeitschrift für Erziehung und Unterricht* 1 (Köln-Düsseldorf, 1851) 99-129, 205-230; Hoogeweg, "Der Kölner Domscholaster Oliver" 235-270; Hoogeweg, "Die Paderborner Bischofswahl vom Jahre 1223," *ZGAW* 46(1883) 92-109; Hoogeweg, "Eine neue Schrift des Kölner Domscholasters Oliver," *NA* (1890) 186-192; Reinhold Röhricht, "Die Briefe des Kölner Scholastikus Oliver," *WZGK* 10 (1891) 161-208; Hoogeweg, *Schriften Oliverus*.

[53] Ed. Leo Allatius (Cöln, 1653). More recent editions by Johann Christian Moritz Laurent, *Itinerarium Terrae Santae—Wilbrands von Oldenburg Reise Nach Palästina und Kleinasien* (Hamburg, 1859) and *Peregrinatores medii aevi quatuor* (Lipsiae, 1864). Schaten, *Annales Paderbor.* I 711, notes: "*Quippe a parentibus, uti Henricus Pantaleon scribit de viris illustribus Germaniae, a prima aetate ad studia literarum traductus ob ingenii felicitatem in omni scientiarum genere et virtutum cultu mirifice inter aequales semper excellent,*" with respect to Wilbrand.

[54] Ed. by Adolf Perdisch as *Der Laubacher Barlaam, Eine Dichtung des Bischofs Otto II. von Freising* (1184-1220), Bibliothek des Literatur-Vereins von Stuttgart, vol. 260 (Tübingen, 1913) 1-574; R. Birkner, "Bischof Otto II. von Freising, der erste deutsche Barlaamdichter," *Wissenschaftliche Festgabe zum zwölfhundertjährigen Jubiläum des heiligen Korbinian*, ed. J. Schlecht (Freising, 1924) 285-298; Wattenbach-Schmale, *DGQ* 253.

Bishop Conrad of Hildesheim (1221-1246) was the author of a letter-book which dates from 1219/1226 and reveals that the *ars dictandi* had reached a high level of execution under his influence. Otherwise, there is no literary evidence of this erudite master of the Paris schools.[55]

Bishop Robert of Olmütz was something of an anomaly, however, being an Englishman according to surviving traditions. Where he received his training is unknown, but his literary works suggest northern France. So far as they are preserved, they deal with the topics of confession and scriptural exegesis, but he also authored a commentary on the *Cantica Canticarum*. A later tradition refers to him as *"clericus literatus multi scienti pollens."*[56] In all, the three decades of 1215-1245 saw three Cistercians and three Benedictines occupy episcopal chairs in Germany. Only after the First Council of Lyons did members of the mendicant orders obtain German episcopates, indicative of their growing importance in thirteenth-century society in general;[57] by contrast, between 1245 and 1274 only one other Benedictine and one Cistercian did so. Three cathedral chapters (Salzburg, Gurk, and Seckau) were filled with Augustinian canons and four (Havelberg, Brandenburg, Olmütz and Ratzeburg) were comprised of Premonstratensian canons. While it would be natural to assume that the monk- (or canons-regular) bishops were more committed to reform than their counterparts drawn from the secular clergy, we have noted above that at least two of these religious were totally ineffective as prelates.

Most of the German bishops fell between the extremes presented in the foregoing discussion. Though less savage, perhaps, than Lupold of Worms, more competent than Garin of Toul or Siegfried of Hildesheim, they were also less committed to principles of reform than the Cistercian, Premonstratensian, or Augustinian bishops. Although we cannot be certain about the intellectual and spiritual preparation of most of the bishops, a reconstruction of the cathedral chapters for this period reveals that only thirty of the one hundred twenty-seven were not chosen *"de gremio capituli"*—from within

---

[55] According to Böhmer, *Fontes*, lxxi, this *Missivbuch* was used in the compiling of the Scheid's, *Origines Guelficae* III (1750/xx) 678-687 under the rubric of *"diplomatarium Hildesheimensium Manuscriptum,"* and by Schannat in *Vindemiae Literariae* (Fuldae, 1723) 194ff. as *"Codex Manuscriptum Moguntinium."* Sudendorf also published it in *Regestrum* I (1849). See also Volger, "Daten" 402.

[56] Cf. J. Loserth, "Das Granum catalogi praesulum Moraviae," *AÖG* 88 (1892) 77; Berthold Bretholz, "Die Compilatio super Cantica canticarum. Ein unbekanntes Werk des Olmützer Bischofs Robert," *Zeitschrift des deutschen Vereins für Geschichte* 10 (1906) 191-197.

[57] See Williel R. Thomson, *Friars in the Cathedral: The First Franciscan Bishops 1226-1261* (Toronto, 1975) 41-57. For the larger picture of the Franciscan impact on Germany, see John B. Freed, *The Friars and German Society in the Thirteenth Century* (Cambridge, Mass., 1977).

the cathedral chapter. The majority were predominantly the younger sons of the local or regional German nobility who were elevated to the episcopacy after having received the customary schooling and experience in chapter and episcopal administration within their own churches.

The picture presented by the cathedral school at Bamberg at the beginning of the thirteenth century, while in many ways apparently unique, may nonetheless have been characteristic of others throughout the realm. About the year 1100, when Bamberg was the favorite city of the Salian emperors of Germany, its cathedral school stood at the pinnacle of its glory: from it emerged men prepared for service in both the church and the Empire, trained *"in litterarum scientia, in rerum agendarum pericia, in honestate morum, in gratia discretionum."*[58]   Bamberg's curriculum stressed grammar and rhetoric, however, and as the value of dialectic and logic became recognized, candidates for ecclesiastical or imperial preferment found it necessary to go to the schools of Rheims or Paris.   In the process, Bamberg lost its standing among the great schools of medieval Europe: while changes in emphasis were being made in French and Italian schools, Bamberg remained conservative, being satisfied with that which had brought it fame in the past.

The school at Bamberg nevertheless continued to train men for careers in the church: fifteen bishops of the twelfth century (not including those who sat in Bamberg itself) are known to have studied there.[59]   Yet, by about 1200 that training lagged behind what was available elsewhere.   The provost of the Bamberg cathedral, Berthold of Andechs, was elected archbishop of Kalocza (Hungary) thanks to the influence of his sister, the queen of Hungary.   Innocent III established a commission headed by the archbishop of Salzburg to determine whether the candidate was suitable for such a high office: they were to ascertain whether his training, if not exceptional, was at least adequate, and whether he was at least close to the canonical age for the position.   The archbishop *"asserens se reperisse illum textum expedite legentem et interpretantem eiusdem verba suo idiomate competenter, et apte preterea de constructione grammatica responden-*

---

[58] *Codex Udalrici* 305, Nr. 172, cited in Johannes Fried, "Die Bamberger Domschule und die Rezeption von Frühscholastik und Rechtswissenschaft in ihrem Umkreis bis zum Ende der Stauferzeit," *Vorträge und Forschungen* 30 (1986) 166-170.

[59] Frederick of Cologne, † 1131; Erlung of Würzburg, † 1121; Egilbert of Aquileia, later of Bamberg, † 1146; Burchard (Bucco) II of Worms, † 1149; Rugger of Worms (anti-bishop), † 1125; Bruno of Strasbourg, † 1165; Arnold II of Speyer, † 1126; Adalbero of Trier, † 1152; Eberhard I of Salzburg, † 1164; Wichmann of Zeitz, later of Magdeburg, † 1192; Adelpret of Trent, † 1172; Henry of Würzburg, † 1165; Otto II, elect of Brixen, then of Bamberg, † 1196; Reinhard of Würzburg, † 1186; Henry III of Würzburg, † 1197. See Fried, "Bamberger Domschule" 174.

tem"—he gave Berthold good marks on reading and translating a Latin text, and on grammatical construction. Nevertheless, the pope rejected him: not only was he too young at twenty-five years of age, but *"nec in iure canonico nec in divino eloquio vel tenuiter commendatum"*—he was not trained in either canon law or theology.[60] For the next several years Berthold studied at Vicenza under men trained at Bologna, succeeding in his pursuit of the Hungarian archbishopric and eventually transferring to the patriarchate of Aquileia.

The professional shortcomings of Berthold of Andechs may be representative of his contemporaries as well, most of whom were members of the high-nobility for whom high church offices were regarded as proprietary rights. The majority of German bishops during the first half of the thirteenth century were "home grown." Hildesheim produced six bishops who sat between 1216 and 1245,[61] but their training was presumably as conservative as that found at Bamberg. Anselm, the biographer of Archbishop Adelbert II of Mainz who received his clerical training at Hildesheim in the early twelfth century, notes that *"tempore iungere, casibus addere verba solebat, scribere prosam"*—that is, he was schooled in the rules of grammar.[62] Given Bishop Conrad II's background, things were likely to have changed little as late as the 1240s.

---

[60] See (Reg. Inn. X, 39) Migne, *PL* CCXV cols. 1132-1134, citing col. 1133B; further, Fried, "Bamberger Domschule" 178-180.

[61] A glimpse into the intellectual world of the Hildesheim cathedral chapter at the beginning of the thirteenth century is found in Winkelmann, *Phil. von Schw.*, II, Erläuterungen X: "Magister Gervasius von Tilbury und Magister Johannes Marcus von Hildesheim." The authorship of a late twelfth-century letter-collection found in MS 350 (Codex Veterocellensis/Altenzelle) of the Universitätsbibliothek in Leipzig forms the basis of a lively scholarly exchange between Wilhelm Berges and Hans-Jürgen Rieckenberg, "Eilbertus und Johann Gallicus. Ein Beitrag zur Kunst- und Sozialgeschichte des 12. Jahrhunderts," *Nachrichten* (Göttingen, 1951) Nr. 2, and Richard Drögereit, "Eilbertus und Johannes Gallicus," *Niedersächsisches Jahrbuch für Landesgeschichte* 24 (1952) 144-160; see also Wilhelm Berges and Hans-Jürgen Rieckenberg, "Eilbertus und Johannes Gallicus. Bemerkungen zu einer Rezension," *Niedersächs. Jb. f. LG* 25 (1953) 132-141, to which Drögereit replied Ibid. 142-154. More recently, the historical value of the letter-collection has been treated in Ferdinand Opll, "Beiträge zur historischen Auswertung der jüngeren Hildesheimer Briefsammlung," *DA* 33 (1977) 473-500. A further indication of intellectual life within the Hildesheim church ca. 1200 is found in the unpublished manuscript, "Das geistige Leben am Hofe Kaiser Otto IV. von Braunschweig," by Hans Martin Schaller, being the text of an address delivered on 3 July 1974 to a meeting of the Ausseninstitut der Technischen Universität Braunschweig.

[62] Fried, "Bamberger Domschule" 168 note 31, 171; J.S. Robinson, "The 'Colores Rhetorici' in the Investiture Contest," *Traditio* 32 (1976) 209-238; J.R. Williams, "The Cathedral School of Reims in the Time of Master Alberic, 1118-1136," *Traditio* 20 (1964) 93-114; J. Ehlers, "Verfassungs- und sozialgeschichtliche Studien zum Bildungsgang Erzbischof Adalberts II. von Mainz," *Rheinische Vierteljahrsblätter* 42 (1978) 161-184.

The central position of Cologne in the political and ecclesiastical life of Germany may also be seen in the fact that serious efforts were made to establish a prestigious cathedral school there in the second half of the twelfth century. Among the circle of friends whom John of Salisbury knew in Paris in the early years of the reign of King Henry II of England was Gerard Pucelle.[63] This native of England became a teacher at Paris at some time before 1156 and counted among his pupils Lucas of Hungary (who became bishop of Erlau), Walter Map, Ralph Nigel, and Master Richard, a relative of John of Salisbury. During Becket's exile in France, Pucelle was also a member of the archbishop's *familia*. At the height of the controversy over Canterbury (1165/1166), Pucelle announced his intentions of leaving for Germany, to which his friends recoiled in amazement, if not horror. Not only were the Germans regarded as schismatics in ecclesiastical matters, but as less refined than their French and English contemporaries.[64] Although Pucelle appears to have acquired several prebends in Germany, the most important was that of *magister scholarum* at the Cologne cathedral. Both Archbishop Rainald of Dassel († 1167) and his successor Philip of Heinsberg (1167-1191) had been trained in France, at Paris and at Rheims respectively. Pucelle remained in the Rhenish capital perhaps a year, after which he voluntarily resigned his prebend and returned to France. In 1179 or 1180, however, he returned to Cologne where he resumed his duties as scholastic at the cathedral until he was appointed to the see of Coventry in late 1182/early 1183.[65]

Pucelle's presence at Cologne may account for the fact that during the late 1160s and early 1170s numerous canonistic works were composed there: the evidence suggests the existence of a short-lived canon law school with close ties to the French schools.[66] During his lengthy absence,

---

[63] See Stephan Kuttner and Eleanor Rathbone, "Anglo-Norman Canonists of the Twelfth Century," *Traditio* 7 (1949/1951) 279-358, espec. 296-303; Johannes Fried, "Gerard Pucelle und Köln," *ZSRG* KanAbt. 99 (1982) 125-135. Unaware of the identity of the *Gerardus magister scolarum* who appears in Cologne documents from 1166-1180 is Goswin Frenken, "Der Kölner Domschule im Mittelalter," *Der Dom zu Köln. Festschrift zur Feier der 50. Wiederkehr seiner Vollendung am 15. Oktober 1880*, ed. Erich Kuphal (Köln, 1930) 248, 256. Friedrich Wilhelm Oediger, "Die niederrheinischen Schulen vor dem Aufkommen der Gymnasien," *Düsseldorfer Jahrbuch* 43 (1941) 75-124, and Idem., *Vom Leben am Niederrhein. Aufsätze aus dem Bereich des alten Erzbistums Köln* (1973) 354, accepts the identification of Master Gerard with Gerard Pucelle.

[64] See W.J. Millor, S.J., and C.N.L. Brooke, eds. *The Letters of John of Salisbury*, vol. II: The Later Letters (1163-1180), Oxford Medieval Texts (1979) 68, Nr. 158.

[65] See the letter dated 15 March 1178 from Pope Alexander III to Archbishop Christian I of Mainz who had interceded for Pucelle, asking that his German prebends be restored to him; *Epist. Mogunt.* Nr. 59.

[66] Kuttner/Rathbone, "Anglo-Norman Canonists" 298-301. Fried, "Gerard Pucelle und

however, the archbishop had appointed a new scholastic, *magister* Rudolf. Among Rudolf's pupils were Caesarius of Heisterbach, the later collector of anecdotes and biographer of both Engelbert of Berg and St. Elizabeth of Thuringia, and the young son of Frederick Barbarossa, the future Philip of Swabia.[67] According to Caesarius, Rudolf was somewhat acquainted with school law, and he was the recipient of two papal decretals (from Clement III and from Celestine III).[68] The quality of the man's intellect may perhaps be inferred from the fact that when Gerard Pucelle returned to Cologne in 1179/1180, Rudolf apparently made room for him by himself leaving his post for Paris where he taught several years.[69] Only after Pucelle's departure for Coventry did Rudolf resume his role as head of the cathedral school in Cologne.

Although Fried acknowledges the difficulty in assessing directly the impact which Gerard Pucelle had upon the church of Cologne, his appointment as scholastic of the cathedral school is symptomatic of a fundamental change. Previously, scholastics had attended the schools of France as the exception; with him, however, the practice commenced of selecting learned men, trained in canon law, as such. Following Gerard came the above-mentioned Rudolf who in turn was followed by the famous crusade-preacher Oliver, who ultimately became a cardinal in the Church. In the other foundations in the city of Cologne the knowledge of canon law increased as well, as evidenced by *magister* Bertram, a canon at St. Gereon who may be the author of a *Summa Colonienses* and other canonistic tracts,[70] whose appointment as archbishop of Bremen Gerard Pucelle tried in vain to promote at the Third Lateran Council in 1179.[71] Bertram

Köln" 132-133, notes 36-37, suggests the possibility that the three Gratian MSS of the late twelfth/early thirteenth century found in the Cologne Dombibliothek may in some way be connected with Gerard's influence. MS 127, in fact, dates from the time of Gerard's presence in Cologne, having been produced in the scriptorium of Great St. Martin.

[67] See Caesarius, *Dialogus* I 32, 38, 46, 196, 352; II 181; IV 26; IX 22. Philip's training is noted in *Hugonis Chronici cont. Weingartensis, MGH SS* XXI 478, line 38: "*Philippum . . . cuidam scolastico Coloniensi in clericum educandum commisit.*"

[68] See Fried, "Gerard Pucelle und Köln" 131 note 31.

[69] See Caesarius, *Dialogus* I 46: speaking of the Cologne cathedral canon Philip of Otterberg (later abbot of the Cistercian monastery at Ottenberg, d. 1225), Caesarius noted: "*Abbas Philippus de Ottirburg . . . Rudolphum eiusdem (sc. maioris) ecclesie scolasticum Parisiis legentem audivit.*"

[70] See Kuttner/Rathbone, "Anglo-Norman Canonists" 303; Winfried Stelzner, "Die *Summa Monacensis (Summa 'Inperatorie maiertati'* und der Neustifter Propst Konrad von Albeck," *MIÖG* 88 (1980) 94-112, espec. 95; Kuttner, "Bertram of Metz," 501-505; Gerbenzon, "Bertram of Metz" 510-511.

[71] Cf. Fried, "Gerard Pucelle und Köln" 134-135; Kuttner/Rathbone, "Anglo-Norman Canonists" 303. According to the *Annales Stadenses a. 1178-1179* (pp. 348-349), Gerard Pucelle praised Bertram as "*scientia decoratum, liberalibus artibus instructum, utriusque*

eventually succeeded to the bishopric of Metz where he served until his death in April 1212.[72] His continued interest in the subtle aspects of canon law can be inferred from the queries sent to Innocent III, the responses to which became part of the decretal collection of Pope Gregory IX.[73]

From among those young clerics trained at Cologne in the 1190s and early 1200s emerged eight who sat as prelates between 1215 and 1245. Of these, none had a greater impact on the religious life of his diocese and province during the first half of the thirteenth century than Archbishop Dietrich II of Trier whose erudition and familiarity with canon law has attracted the attention of medieval and modern commentators alike.[74] Dietrich's long-time confrère as both a canon at Cologne and as an archbishop was Engelbert of Berg, of whom contemporaries spoke less generously. Caesarius of Heisterbach reacted to the news of Engelbert's brutal assassination in November 1225 by inserting a brief tribute to him in his forty-third Sunday homily. Yet, amid the praise, Caesarius also spoke with great candor:

> Inasmuch as he was both a bishop and a duke, he devoted himself less to the former and descended much more often to the latter, so that one of our monks said to him, 'My lord, you are a good duke, but not a good bishop.'[75]

In the *Vita Engelberti* which Caesarius began writing soon thereafter, he makes a related unflattering comment:

> The holy Archbishop Engelbert . . . was less inclined toward the grace of preaching or expounding the Scriptures or the clerical way of life, and the eyes of many therefore became dim when they looked at the externals of his life, . . . As the oh-so-unhappy news of his death spread, many who knew of

---

testamenti pagina eruditum, decretorum legumque industria peritum virum . . ."

[72] Here again Betram was commended for his learning; cf. *Gesta episcoporum Metensium* (p. 546): *". . . et tam divinae quam humane legis egregie peritum."*

[73] Cf. Ch. Two, pp. 141-142.

[74] The anonymous author of the *Vita Theoderici* which formed part of the *Gesta Treverorum*, 398, wrote: *"Successit autem. . .Theodericus,. . .anno Domini 1212, qui et ipse, cum esset prudentie magne, paci et quieti magis quam bellis operam dedit."* Another continuator of the *Gesta Treverorum*, writing ca. 1260 referred to Dietrich of Wied and his nephew Arnold of Isenburg thusly: *"Viris religiosis, humilibus et devotis se tamquam pastores benigni tractabiles in omnibus offerebant et eos affectu ferventi fovebant, rebellibus et iniquis totis viribus strennue resistentes, quod multis papet evidentibus documentis. Plures virtutes et memorabilia opera dicti duo archiepiscopi perfecerunt, que non sunt propter fastidium legentium presentibus annotata, quorum memoria apud homines in eternum permaneat et anime apud Deum perpetuo requiescant in pace!"*; Ibid. 414. For the assessment of Archbishop Dietrich's legal expertise by Gottfried Kentenich, cf. p. 417, below.

[75] Homily XLIII in Hilka, *Die Wundergeschichten des Caesarius von Heisterbach* I: Einleitung, Exempla und Auszüge aus den Predigten des Caesarius von Heisterbach, 153-154, Nr. 220.

his worldly activities doubted whether he could merit salvation, saying, "O woe, now he has lost both body and soul.[76]

Engelbert was a politician in clerical robes, and despite attempts by modern admirers to make him into something else, his performance as a shepherd of the Cologne church left much to be desired.

Both Archbishop Albrecht of Käfernberg in Magdeburg and Archbishop Eberhard II of Regensberg in Salzburg were Bologna-trained men whose knowledge of canon law must have been considerable by contemporary German standards. According to the Magdeburg *Schöppenchronik*, Albrecht's preparation for advanced studies in law was acquired at the cathedral school in Hildesheim. After he had finished his studies there, he obtained a prebend in the Magdeburg cathedral chapter through the influence of Conrad of Querfurt, the chancellor of King Philip of Swabia, who had belonged to that body since 1182.[77] As a canon at Magdeburg Albrecht, the son of a comital family, came in close contact with a man of lesser social standing, Ludolf of Kroppenstedt, who had received his primary training at the cathedral school in Halberstadt, but had subsequently been sent to Paris by Archbishop Wichmann where he remained several years and became a friend and fellow-student of Thomas Becket. After Ludolf's return from Paris about 1168, Wichmann secured for him a position within the cathedral chapter at Magdeburg.[78] Following Wichmann's death in August 1192, Ludolf became archbishop of Magdeburg.

Under Archbishops Wichmann and Ludolf the persons responsible for instruction of young clerics in the cathedral school were the *magistri scholarum* Dietrich (fl. 1171),[79] John (fl. 1166-1182),[80] Henry of Glinde

---

[76] Prologue to Book III, in Fritz Zschaeck, ed., *Leben, Leiden und Wunder des heiligen Engelbert, Erzbischofs von Köln*, in *Die Wundergeschichten des Caesarius von Heisterbach* III/2 282.

[77] For the details of Albrecht's life prior to his elevation as archbishop, see Wentz/Schwineköper, *Erzbistum Magdeburg* I/1 117, 313; further, Silberborth, "EB Albrecht II." 111; Claude, *Erzbistum Magdeburg* II 223. Conditions within the cathedral school at Magdeburg in the late twelfth/early thirteenth century are discussed by H. Holstein, "Die Domscholaster von Magdeburg," *MGbll* 22 (1887) 297-303.

[78] Mülverstedt, *RAMagd* I Nr. 1481. For the critical details of Lupold's life as a cathedral canon at Magdeburg, see Wentz/Schwineköper, *Erzbistum Magdeburg* I/1 340-341.

[79] Mülverstedt, *RAMagd* I, Nr. 1508. Wentz/Schwineköper, *Erzbistum Magdeburg* I/1 341, note that a teaching responsibility was attached to Ludolf's prebend in the cathedral chapter, even though he is not mentioned as the *scholasticus*; see also, Alexander Budinszky, *Die Universität Paris und die Fremden an derselben im Mittelalter. Ein Beitrag zur Geschichte dieser hohen Schule* (Berlin, 1876) 150. Claude, *Erzstift Magdeburg* II 223, states that while the names of most Magdeburg scholastics of the twelfth century are known, we are almost totally uninformed concerning their scholarly activities.

[80] Mülverstedt, *RAMagd* I, Nrs. 1519, 1530, 1619, 1620; Wentz/Schwineköper, *Erzbistum Magdeburg* I/1 383.

(fl. 1185),[81] and Hermann of Landsberg (fl. 1196-ca. 1207).[82] It was the latter who supported Albrecht of Käfernberg for the vacated office of cathedral provost in 1200; as a canon of perhaps twenty-five years of age, Albrecht had undoubtedly shown his intellectual and administrative potential.[83] In 1205, despite opposition from within the cathedral chapter, Albrecht also became archbishop of Magdeburg.

Albrecht's influence on his cathedral school undoubtedly affected the intellectual and spiritual life of his province, yet despite his own training at Bologna jurisprudence played little role in Magdeburg's curriculum.[84] In 1207 he appointed *magister* Gernand as scholastic, in part as a reward for the latter's support during the dispute over the archiepiscopal office, in part because of his reputation as a learned man.[85] Trained as a theologian and logician, he was particularly noted as an expert publicist whose writings were used as models for others.[86] Gernand's skills as a judge and

---

[81] Mülverstedt, *RAMagd* I, Nrs. 1684, 1686, 1688, 1689, 1690, 1692, 1693, 1695; Wentz/Schwineköper, *Erzbistum Magdeburg* I/1 383, 341-342.

[82] Mülverstedt, *RAMagd* II Nr. 61; Wentz/Schwineköper, *Erzbistum Magdeburg* I/1 383-384.

[83] Specht, *Unterrichtswesen* 354, is incorrect in several respects when he states: "*So wurde der Graf Adalbert von Hallermünde, der im Jahre 1205 den erzbischöflichen Stuhl in Magdeburg bestieg, als er noch canonicus scholaris war, vom Domscholaster Hermann von Landsberg an die hohe Schule zu Paris gesandt.*" Albrecht apparently attended the schools in Paris at some point between 1192 and 1200, but his days as *canonicus scholaris* were spent in Hildesheim, not Magdeburg; cf. Wentz/Schwineköper, *Erzbistum Magdeburg* I/1 117; Mülverstedt, *RAMagd* II 96, Nr. 220.

[84] Wentz/Schwineköper, *Erzbistum Magdeburg* 116-117, citing Thietmar of Merseburg as their source, claim that the cathedral school at Magdeburg was excellent, providing a better education than was generally available. This generalization may only be applicable to the eleventh century, however. For the place of jurisprudence, see E. Rosenstock, *Ostfalens Rechtsliteratur unter Friedrich II.* (Weimar, 1912) 143, 116-117, who notes that there was a noticeable French influence in the cathedral school at the beginning of the thirteenth century.

[85] For the major details of Gernand's career as a cathedral canon at Magdeburg, see Wentz/Schwineköper, *Erzstift Magdeburg* I/1 384, 343-344. Innocent III confirmed this appointment on 10 March 1207; cf. Mülverstedt, *RAMagd* II, Nr. 279-282, referring to "*intuitu quoque probitatis et litteraturae tuae.*" Further discussion of Gernand's relationship to Albrecht of Magdeburg is in Winter, "EB Albrecht II." 192; Silberborth, "EB Albrecht II." 185, 194.

[86] The Saxon *Summa prosarum dictaminis* which was collected from his lectures, exists in two MSS, Munich Staatsbibliothek clm 9683 from Oberaltaich (13th c.), fol. 63, and Vienna Hofbibliothek MS 2516 (14th c.), fol. 1-34 rb; cf. Rosenstock, *Rechtsliteratur* 4-5; further, L. Rockinger, "Briefsteller und Formelbücher des elften bis vierzehnten Jahrhunderts," *Quellen und Eröterungen zur bayerischen und deutschen Geschichte* IX (München, 1863) 201-346; also, Wattenbach, *Deutschlands GQ* II 319. The compiler, whom Rosenstock (op.cit. 66) sees as *Conradus scholasticus Budesinensis* who flourished at Magdeburg from 1236, styles himself "*moderni usus et magistrorum qui suis temporibus egregie dictaverunt, maxime venerabilis*

diplomat undoubtedly won over his brethren in the cathedral chapter: in 1212 he received the dignity of cathedral dean, an office he held until 1221 when he was appointed by Pope Honorius III (with the full support of Archbishop Albrecht) to be bishop of Brandenburg. He filled this office for twenty years, during which time he was often used as an arbitrator in disputes, combining his theological training with a profound juridical sense. Besides Gernand, three other prelates who sat between 1215 and 1245 were Magdeburg-educated.

Unlike Bamberg's cathedral library which remained intact into modern times, that of Magdeburg suffered from the ravages of time and human action. It is nevertheless possible to reconstruct it to some extent, and this reconstruction confirms the impression that at least until Gernand's death the primacy of grammar and logic over other areas of study was assured at Magdeburg. The only juristic MS which can be proved for the diocese of Magdeburg as late as the 1230s is the *Summa Lipsiensis*, a copy of a work dating from the 1170s which was made at Halle in 1239.[87] At a later date (but still in the thirteenth century) a copy of the *Liber extra* and of the *Decretum* with glosses are also provable.[88]

By contrast, the cathedral library ca. 1200 contained the *Summa* of William of Auxerre, the work of Peter the Chanter, the sermons of the Paris chancellor Philip, and French copies of the glosses on the Psalms by Peter Lombard.[89] A cleric at Magdeburg dedicated a poem about Duke Ernest in Latin verse to Archbishop Albrecht II, using as his literary model Walter of Chatillon's *Alexandreis*.[90] In sum, French intellectual influence

---

patris et domini Gernandi Brandenburgensis episcopi sedulus imitator . . ."

[87] *"Anno MCCXXXIX Theodericus scriptor civis Hallensis . . ."* The source for the *Summa Lipsiensis* is determined by Heinrich Singer, *Die Summa decretorum des Magister Rufinus* (Paderborn, 1902) 167 of Introduction; see however, Emil Friedberg, *Die Canones-Sammlungen zwischen Gratian und Bernhard von Pavia* (Leipzig, 1887) 115-129, who argues for an Italian provenance. The thirteenth century work is in the Bibliotheca Albertina Lipsiensis MS 975, fol. 116-153. See further Rosenstock, *Rechtsliteratur* 116-117; Rudolf Helssig, *Katalog der juristischen Handschriften der Universitäts-Bibliothek zu Leipzig* (Leipzig, 1905) 126f. For the MSS which formed part of the Magdeburg cathedral library, see Valentin Rose, *Verzeichniss der lateinischen Handschriften der königlichen Bibliothek zu Berlin* (Berlin, 1893f.) XIII/2, Nrs. 305, 356, 386, 389, 397, 398, 402, 445 (all before 1300), 618, 624 (after 1300).

[88] Rosenstock, *Rechtsliteratur* 118.

[89] Rose, *Berliner Handschriften* XII/2 218, 220, 232; cf. also 305, 356, 386, 397, 398, 402, 445.; Rosenstock, *Rechtsliteratur* 143.

[90] Rosenstock, *Rechtsliteratur* 143; Karl Bartsch, *Herzog Ernst* (Wien, 1869) lxxii; Arthur Fuckel, "Der Ernestus des Odo von Magdeburg und sein Verhältnis zu den übrigen älteren Bearbeitungen der Saga vom Herzog Ernst" (Dissertation Marburg, 1895) 3; Silberborth, "EB Albrecht II." 225.

was far stronger than that of Italy in Magdeburg at the start of the thirteenth century, with literary interests far surpassing those of jurisprudence.

This lack of interest in either the study or collection of juristic works in Magdeburg was not necessarily characteristic of the times, however. The cathedral library at Halberstadt contained a large number of such MSS from the thirteenth century.[91] Whereas Magdeburg shows evidence of but one copy of the *Decretum* from the 1200s, at Halberstadt there were several, as well as a major collection of pre-Gregorian canonistic literature. All this is attributable to the fact that the last great representative of the older level of legal studies lived at Halberstadt for three decades, where he also taught.

Johannes Zemecke (*Teutonicus*) is documented as a cathedral canon at Halberstadt from 1212-1245.[92] He had studied at Bologna and had remained there as an independent legal writer; before 1215 he completed his gloss on the *Decretales*, the *Ordinaria*, which served as the model for Accursius. In it was made the last comprehensive use of the *Corpus Iuris Civilis* as an aid in the study of canon law. That the cathedral at Halberstadt also used Johannes' talents may be inferred from the fact that in addition to the office of *camerarius* he also held that of *scholasticus*. Johannes' use of a library for his works was obvious. Hints of the Halberstadt resources come from two thirteenth century codices given to the Universitäts-Bibliothek at Halle by Pernice in 1824: both contain among other items the *Compilatio prima decretalium*; one also included at the bottom margin the *Summa decretalium* of Bernard of Pavia; the other has room left for this, suggesting that (as in other MSS elsewhere) it was intended to included with it.[93]

Beyond this the MSS contain three separate sets of glosses for this collection of decretals, all dating from ca. 1200. Schulte regarded these as the most important ones known to him, and suggested that they were part of the materials which Johannes acquired in Italy; they made their way to Halberstadt 1200/1216.[94] We can assume that the three Halberstadt-trained bishops who sat 1215-1245 had access to these juristic materials, but the impact thereof cannot be determined.

---

[91] Rosenstock, *Rechtsliteratur* 117, citing Ye folio 34, 36, 41, 52, 63, 51, 80; Ye quarto 6.

[92] Johann Friedrich von Schulte, *ZSRG* KanAbt 16 (1895) 107ff.; Schmidt, *ZHV* 22 (1880) 9ff.; E. Seckel, *Historische Vierteljahrschrift* 10 (1894) 78.

[93] Rosenstock, *Rechtsliteratur* 118-119; Johann Friedrich von Schulte, *Literatur-Geschichte der Compilationes antiquae*, Sitzungsberichte der österreichischen Akademie der Wissenschaft 66 (Wien, 1870) 601, Nr. 1; Idem, *ZSRG* 16 (1895) 125, Nr. 57.

[94] Rosenstock, *Rechtsliteratur* 119.

The forty-six years during which Eberhard II of Salzburg presided over his archdiocese and province left an indelible imprint on the life of his clergy as well, and the five Salzburg canons whom he appointed as bishops in Chiemsee, Gurk, Lavant, and Seckau must have perpetuated many of his notions. Peter Classen has shown that southern Germany (and particularly the Salzburg ecclesiastical province) was the main region within the German-language area where the writings of the oldest school of Scholasticism—that of Anselm of Laon and William of Champeaux—were received.[95] During the course of the twelfth century, the writings of Peter Abelard, Hugh of St. Victor, Gilbert de la Porré and Peter Lombard also became known to a rather small layer of especially open theologians at monasteries and foundations belonging to the reform-orders of Cîteaux and Prémontré; occasionally one of the older Benedictine houses was receptive as well.[96]

Alongside theology developed an interest in jurisprudence and philosophy, the study of which was facilitated by the greater familiarity with Aristotle and scholastic methodology. The zeal with which Eberhard II set about to exploit every episcopal and metropolitan prerogative from the onset of his pontificate suggests a confidence in his position vis-a-vis the secular and regular clergy of his province which the study of the law certainly provided. As bishop of Brixen Eberhard had gone to Bologna for the purpose of studying canon law, but when Innocent III learned of his enthusiasm for secular (i.e., Roman) law, he ordered him home.[97]

Mainz not only trained all of its own prelates, but also at least five other bishops who served between 1216 and 1245.[98] At the beginning of

---

[95] "Zur Geschichte der Frühscholastik in Österreich und Bayern," *MIÖG* 67 (1959) 249-277. As early as 1130 Gerhoh of Reichersberg complained about the *"magistri per totam Franciam scholas regentes"* whose teachings were also attracting attention in southeastern Germany; cf. *MGH Lib. de lite* III 235.

[96] Eberhard I of Salzburg (d. 1164), who may have studied in France himself, made a gift of Peter Lombard's two major exegetical works—the commentaries on Paul and the Psalms—to the monastery at Admont (cod. Admont 36 and 52); cf. Classen, "Frühscholastik" 251, 267.

[97] Dopsch, *Geschichte Salzburgs* I 308; *Die Register Innozenz' III.*, I. Pontifikatsjahr 1198/99, bearb. von Othmar Hageneder und A. Haidacher, Publikationen der österr. Kulturinstituts in Rom II/1 (Graz-Köln, 1964) 209f., Nr. 144.

[98] Innocent IV referred to Siegfried III of Eppstein as *"vir scientia praeditus morum honestate decorus et consilii auctoritate praeclarus"*; cf. Fink, *Siegfried III.* 8. Siegfried himself said that he had been nourished since early childhood on the milk of the church at Mainz: *"Cum igitur ecclesia Maguntina nos ab infantia nostra lacte suo nutriverit et demum multis honoribus in ea prehabitis licet immeritis ad pontificatus apicem cum divina favente gratia sublimarit"*; cf. Gudenus, *CdMogunt.* I, 480; also Böhmer-Will, *RAM* II, xxxii. While the obvious allusion is to the income from prebends which Siegfried enjoyed, it is also probable that his intellectual training was obtained in the cathedral school as well. For further discussion of the Mainz cathedral school in the Middle Ages, see Falck, *Mainz im Mittelalter*

the 1180s a short-lived canonist school flourished at Mainz under Sicard of Cremona.[99] The latter may also have been responsible for attracting Prepositinus of Cremona who assumed direction of the cathedral school at Mainz in 1194, but this talented man abandoned that strife-torn city for the greater security of Paris at the height of the archiepiscopal schism which followed Conrad's death. Archbishop Siegfried II eventually secured the talents of a local product, the Parisian master, Conrad of Reifenberg, who headed the cathedral school from 1216 until 1221.[100] Thereafter those appointed to the office of scholastic at Mainz appear to have enjoyed at best a regional reputation.

The Diplomat Bishops

While Siegfried II of Mainz demonstrated considerable astuteness in the choice of the head of his cathedral school, he frequently displayed less prudence in other important decisions. We have noted above his lack of sound judgment when confirming suffragan bishops and exercising his role as papal legate. This same trait was manifest at the Fourth Lateranum, as witnessed in person by the anonymous monk from Aulesberg. Near the end of the final session (30 November) the matter of the barons' insurrection against King John of England was considered. The sentence of excommunication was read and the submission of John to the pope and the receipt of the kingdom of England as a papal fief were also explicitly made known. At this point, Archbishop Siegfried II of Mainz as primate of the German church and as the imperial archchancellor rose to protest this apparent violation of Hohenstaufen political claims. Despite a papal warning to be seated and silent, the impetuous prelate proclaimed once more that England was a fief of the Empire. A second caution proved ineffective and for a third time Siegfried asserted the imperial argument. The German primate's outburst antagonized the pope who had just finished praising John of England for having received his realm as a fief of the Roman church. Before the assembled fathers of Latin Christendom, the pontiff raised his hand, indicating silence, and addressed Siegfried in an annoyed tone: "If you will listen to me for now, I will hereafter listen to you!"[101] Having

---

163-167; Biskamp, *Mainzer DK* 31-38; Lacombe, *Prévostin* 14-25; Georg Wilhelm Sante, "Siegfried II. von Eppstein, Erzbischof von Mainz," *Nassauische Lebensbilder* 1 (Wiesbaden, 1940) 1-16; Franz Falk, "Die ehemalige Dombibliothek zu Mainz, ihre Entstehung und Schicksal," *Beihefte zur Centralblätter für Bibliothekswesen* 19 (Leipzig, 1897) 1-139.

[99] Stelzner, *Gelehrtes Recht* 91

[100] Cf. Pixton, "Konrad von Reifenberg" 43-49, 57-58.

[101] Cf. the account by the Giessen Anonymous, in Kuttner/Garcia y Garcia, "A New Eyewitness Account" 128, 158-161: *"Quia uero illud regnum Anglie ad imperatoriam, ut*

embarrassed himself and his monarch, the archbishop of Mainz at last became subdued and allowed the session to proceed to its conclusion.

Siegfried of Eppstein had been provost at Vyssehrad in Bohemia prior to becoming archbishop, and as such had served as chancellor of that realm as well. His closeness to the Bohemian king must have been a factor in the latter's plans to elevate Prague to the position of a metropolitanate, but the Mainz prelate resisted that idea despite papal pressure. In this instance his reasons were clearly not pastoral, but political, revealing his concern over a diminution of his province and a weakening of his power in the eastern portion of the Empire. Similar hopes lay behind efforts by Duke Leopold of Austria to secure the election of his *protonotarius* Ulrich as bishop of Passau in 1215, seeing the new prelate as a useful tool in the erection of a bishopric in Vienna.[102] Another *magister* Ulrich, who appears 3 March 1233 as a notary of Duke Frederick II of Austria and 1241-1243 as *protonotarius*, was nominated by the duke in 1244 to be bishop of Seckau for the same reasons.[103] The efforts by the dukes of Austria were frustrated until the latter thirteenth century, however.

Not the least characteristic of the diplomat-bishops was Conrad of Scharfenberg, bishop of Speyer and Metz and imperial chancellor for Frederick II until 1224. Under him a so-called "diplomat school" developed at Speyer, out of which several later prelates emerged. One of these was Berthold of Neiffen who served as bishop of Brixen 1216-1224: between 1212 and 1215 he was *regalis aule protonotarius* for Frederick II.[104] Succeeding him in that office 1217-1233 was the cathedral canon

dicitur, pertinet potestatem, ne ius suum in hoc principes imperii in posterum amittant, surgens pre ceteris Sifridus, sancte Moguntine sedis archiepiscopus, dictum regnum quod Romanorum imperatori et principibus Alimanie de iure attineret asserere et probare conabatur. Cui dominus papa, hoc considerato eleuata manu silentium indicens ut ab incepto sermone desisteret, et taliter contra ipsum locutus est: 'Audias me modo, posthac audiam te.' Et sic dictus archiepiscopus tamquam promptus obedientie filius, et decuit et oportuit, contra uoluntatem patris et domini surrexerit."

[102] See Hageneder, "Beziehungen der Babenberger" 2-3; for details on Ulrich himself, see Fichtenau, "Die Kanzlei der letzten Babenberger" 256ff.

[103] Krabbo, "Babenberger Landeskirche," 33; Hageneder, "Beziehungen der Babenberger" 3-5.

[104] Böhmer-Ficker, *Regg. Imp.* V, Nrs. 670b, 671, 683, 690, 692, 697, 698, 699, 705, 706, 837, 852, 855, 859, 874, 12441, 12516, 14658; Richard Fester, ed., *Regesten der Markgrafen von Baden und Hochberg 1050-1515* I (Innsbruck, 1900) Nr. 4380. For a discussion of Speyer as the training ground for well-qualified diplomatic personnel, cf. Böhmer, *Fontes* II 156 and note 1; also Siegmund Herzberg-Fränkel, "Geschichte der deutschen Reichskanzlei," *MIÖG*, Ergänzungsband 1 (Graz, 1885) 285; further, Bienemann, *Conrad von Scharfenberg* 127-132; Peter Acht, *Studien zum Urkundenwesen der Speyerer Bischöfe im 12. und Anfang des 13. Jahrhunderts* (Speyer in seinem Verhältnis zur Reichskanzlei) (Berlin, 1936) 43-47; further, idem., *Die Cancellaria in Metz. Eine Kanzlei- und*

at Constanz, Henry I of Tanne, who thereafter became bishop of Constanz (1233-1248).[105] Assuming the direction of the chancery 1233-1242 was Henry I of Catania, since before 1232 a notary there, and after 1242 bishop of Bamberg.[106] By far the most notable bishop to emerge from the training at Speyer was Conrad II of Hildesheim whose role as dean of the Speyer cathedral chapter 1209-1216 added yet another dimension to his remarkable personality.[107]

The experiences of these men as members of ducal, royal, or imperial chanceries helped them prepare for the intricacies of their political roles as bishops, brought them into intimate contact with the great secular princes of their day, and thereby paved the way for their appointment (or election) as sympathetic prelates of the Church, but did not as a rule develop those spiritual talents and sensibilities which the reform movement set in motion by Innocent III so urgently needed. The assessment of Conrad of Scharfenberg by a modern biographer, that "he felt more at home in affairs of state than in the duties of his ecclesiastical office,"[108] may thus apply equally to others as well. The notable exception here was Bishop Conrad II of Hildesheim whose exceptional talents in the temporal sphere have tended to overshadow his ecclesiastical accomplishments in the eyes of modern scholars.[109] Viewed collectively, the German episcopacy presents a very mixed picture of spiritual and intellectual leadership during the thirteenth century. One is reminded of Albert Hauck's critique that

> the German episcopacy was just as destitute of significant ecclesiastical personalities in the second half of the thirteenth century as in the first. In this regard, Engelbert II or Siegfried of Cologne cannot be ranked above Engelbert I or Conrad of Hostaden. Likewise, Werner and Gerhard of Mainz distinguish themselves little from their predecessors Sigfrid II and Sigfrid III. For all

---

Schreibschule um die Wende des 12. Jahrhunderts, Schriften des wissenschaftlichen Instituts der Elsass-Lothringer im Reich an der Universität Frankfurt, Neue Folge Nr. 25 (Frankfurt, 1940) 72-77.

[105] The details of Henry of Tanne's early career are summarized in Ladewig, *Regg. Const.* Nr. 1444.

[106] Krenzer, *Heinrich I. von Bilversheim* 9-15; Looshorn, *Bistum Bamberg* II 739-743.

[107] Cf. Pixton, "Konrad von Reifenberg" 49-54.

[108] Eduard Winkelmann, "Konrad III. von Scharfenberg," *Allgemeine Deutsche Biographie* 16 (Leipzig, 1882) 620-621.

[109] Cf. Hermann von Hoogeweg, "Bischof Konrad von Reifenberg als Reichsfürst," *ZVN* 64 (1899) 238-265. The need for a more comprehensive biography on Conrad was pointed out by Wilhelm Maurer, "Zum Verständnis der heiligen Elisabeth von Thüringen," *Zeitschrift für Kirchengeschichte* 65 (1953/4) 20 note 13; this appeal was repeated by Dieter Rüdebusch, *Der Anteil Niedersachsens an den Kreuzzügen und Heidenfahrten*, Quellen und Darstellungen zur Geschichte Niedersachsens, vol. 80 (1972) 63 note 5. The studies by Pixton, "Konrad von Reifenberg," and Crusius, "Bischof Konrad II.," focus only on the career of Conrad to 1221.

these prelates, political objectives had precedence over ecclesiastical. And it was nowhere otherwise than in the two great archbishoprics.[110]

We must also bear in mind, however, that the acceleration of spiritual and temporal conflicts in the Middle Ages had the consequence that in the biographies of the bishops the political struggles and reverses, acquisitions and losses, stand out so predominantly, and only occasionally are found reports concerning their ecclesiastical activities and the inner life of the diocese. That which attracted attention and disturbed, or affected in a positive way, larger circles of people was written down by the chronicler; he had no presentiment of how much more significant for future generations communications about the quiet effects of the Church would have been. Present-day experience may well be analogous to that of thirteenth-century Germany, since newspapers, weekly news-magazines, and electronic media contain far more of the sordid, sensational, and negative aspects of modern life than of that which is edifying, positive, and in accord with current laws and standards of behavior.

There were in fact several men of outstanding intellectual and spiritual abilities who rose above the norms of their age. The lacunae in the annals and chronicles of the thirteenth century with respect to pastoral activities for many of them is clearly a reflection of contemporary value judgments. The complete disappointment expressed by Hauck is thus, in our estimation, not fully warranted. While there are in fact relatively few indications of pastoral activities as compared with the temporal involvements of the German episcopacy in extant sources for the period under study, it will be the task and intent of subsequent chapters to find and interpret that evidence, and to reveal the contours of ecclesiastical institutions and governing principles at work. One would hope that evidence of "the inner life of the diocese" can still be found.

[110] *KGD* V/1 132.

CHAPTER FOUR

IMPLEMENTING THE DECREES OF THE COUNCIL: 1216-1223

Vos ergo audite parabolam seminantis. . . . *Qui autem seminatus est*
in spinis, hic est, qui verbum audit, et sollicitudo saeculi istius,
et fallacia divitiarum, suffocat verbum, et sine fructa efficitur.
(Evangelium secundum Matthaeum 13, 18-22)

Fidelis agricolae officium hoc exposcit, quod agrum sibi a patrefamilias
commissum spinis succrescentibus radicitus evulsis ad producendos
uberiores fructus fertiliorem reddere laboret, ne simul exortae
spinae semen suffocare valeant et ne ipsius agricolae possint
ullatenus evacuare labores. Hinc est quod cum simus cultores argi
dominici et religionem, quam forte in nobismet ipsis non habemus,
amplecti in aliis teneamur, ut quod per nostram absentiam
negligitur, eorum precibus et suffragio compleatur, . . .
(Bishop Dietrich II of Meissen, a. 1205)

Innocent III was a visionary to the extent that he believed the legislation of
the Fourth Lateran Council would cure the ills of the Church, yet he also
had the legist's skepticism regarding human volition, realizing that not all
bishops would enthusiastically enforce the program which he had presented.
He was thus determined from the outset to go beyond the episcopacy as the
agents of implementing the provisions of the Council, dispatching at once
legates to the various reaches of Latin Christendom. To Germany in early
1216 came Cardinal-priest Peter de Sasso (Saxonis), *tituli S. Pudentianae*;
the specific mandates given him are among those lost portions of Innocent
III's registers, yet they most certainly contained instructions relating to the
crusade decree *Ad liberandum*, to the reform of monasteries, and to the
ordering of affairs in the Empire, including the resolution of the
long-standing schism at Cologne.[1]

---

[1] Böhmer-Ficker, *Regg. Imp.* V/2, Nr. 9995a; Zimmermann, *Päpstl. Legationen* 45. The
departure of Peter from Rome was after 7 March 1216, on which date he witnessed a papal
privilege for Leubus; cf. Potthast, *Regesta* I, Nr. 464. Binterim, *Concilien* IV 276-277,
incorrectly attributes the comment in *Reineri Ann.* 674: "*Redeunte autem predicto magistro*
a sacro consilio, litteras quas a domino papa acceperat exsecutoribus suis distribuit, . . ." to
Peter; rather, this passage refers to the "*adventum magistri Oliveri vivifice crucis legati*" whose
litteras must have included copies of the crusade decree *Ad liberandum* and the papal authorization to collect the half tithe. Peter became archbishop of Lund in 1224 and died in 1228; cf.
Annales Ryensis, MGH SS XVI 406-407. Further discussion of him in Winkelmann, *Phil. von*
Schw. II 432; Hurter, *Innocenz III.* II 717.

At the diet which Emperor Frederick II held at Würzburg on 3 May 1216, the legate Peter confirmed the recently-elected Engelbert of Berg as archbishop of Cologne, paving the way for the immediate conferral of the regalia by the king.[2] The cardinal-legate later came to Cologne itself, where his presence leant support to Engelbert's efforts to restore archiepiscopal authority which had been so badly eroded during the three previous pontificates. Peter also took action against the chapter of St. Maria *ad gradus* which had refused to accept into its midst as a canon the son of a burgher to whom he had granted a prebend.[3] From Cologne Peter traveled up the Rhine where, on 10 September 1216, he issued a charter at Coblenz, confirming the decision by the abbess and nuns at Villich to limit the size of their house, in order that the resources not be overextended.[4] The direction of his itinerary during the summer of 1216 seems to preclude any personal influence of his upon a general chapter held 28 July 1216 at Constanz for the Irish monks in Germany.[5] Nor can we find direct evidence that he attempted to implement the reform constitutions of the Council in those portions of the provinces of Mainz, Cologne, and Trier where he sojourned.

Indications of Peter's involvement in the collection of the half-tithe imposed upon the clergy of the Latin Church for the length of three years as a means of raising funds to be used in the impending crusade are somewhat clearer, however. Shortly after the conclusion of the Council, a papal encyclical had been sent to the various German provinces, designating the already appointed crusade preachers to act as collection agents for the half-tithe as well.[6] During his travels through Germany Peter de Sasso

---

[2] *En route* to the Würzburg assembly, Peter attested a grant of property by the duke of Bavaria to the monastery at Indersdorf for the belated interment of the remains of Pfalzgrave Otto of Wittelsbach, the assassin of King Philip; present with him was Archbishop Eberhard of Salzburg who would then have accompanied him to the diet; see Böhmer-Ficker, *Regg. Imp.* V/2, Nr. 9995b; Winkelmann, *Phil. von Schw.* I 477 and II 432; further, *Rubrice lit. pont. a. XIX nr. 124ff.*, in Theiner, *Vetera* I 67.

[3] Böhmer-Ficker, *Regg. Imp.* V/2, Nr. 9995d; *Caesarii Dialogus* VI 28.

[4] Böhmer-Ficker, *Regg. Imp.* V/2, Nr. 9996; Winkelmann, *Acta Imp. inedita* I 474.

[5] In 1185 Pope Lucius III had directed that the heads of the Irish monasteries (*Schottenklöster*) in Germany come once each year to Regensburg. At the Fourth Lateranum, however, the interval was changed to once every three years, consistent with *c.* 12 of the constitutions, and the German houses were given the privilege of establishing their own congregation. The general chapters of the Irish monks were under the leadership of the abbot of St. Jacob's in Regensburg, who was also the general visitor of the German houses; cf. *Germania Benedictina* V 359; II 248

[6] Potthast, *Regesta* I, Nr. 5048: for the province of Cologne were named Oliver of Paderborn, John of Xanten, and Hermann of Bonn, who were to be assisted by John, a canon at Nivelles, and Arnold, a cleric at Münster; for Trier, Abbot Walther of Villers, Abbot Bruno of Rommersdorf, Conrad of Marburg, and two *subdelegati*, Blialdus and Deodatus, were ap-

must have learned of the opposition to the impost from a variety of directions, an opposition given poetic expression in the lyrics of Walther von der Vogelweide:[7]

> Tell me, Lord Collection Box,
> Did the pope send you here
> In order that you might sit in judgment and make us Germans poor?
> I wager that the silver [you collect] will be of little help in the Holy Land;
> The papal hand seldom distributes a great hoard of wealth.
> Lord Collection Box, you have been sent here to cause great damage,
> And to show us Germans to be fools.

Thus, when the cardinal-priest conferred with Abbot Eberhard of Salem at Salzburg on 3 November 1216, it was clearly for reasons in addition to the mere confirmation of a grant made to the latter's monastery by the bishop of Constanz.[8] As a papally-designated crusade preacher and collection agent for the province of Mainz, Eberhard would have traveled to Salzburg for the primary purpose of discussing those responsibilities. The opportunity presented itself for obtaining confirmation of the grant of property as well.

Admonitions by the pope to the archbishop of Mainz, written shortly after this meeting, indicate that support for the tax was less than enthusiastic

---

pointed; for Magdeburg and Bremen, Conrad of Krosigk, John of Xanten, and Conrad of Marburg. There are no printed copies of the letter for the provinces of Mainz or Salzburg; we assume, nevertheless, that the main preachers received this task. An isolated letter exists for the bishopric of Liège in which the agents are mentioned as the abbot of Floreffe, the prior of Louvain, the *plebanus* of St. Christopher at Liège and the canons Peter and Adam of St. Lambert's in Liège; cf. Böhmer, *Acta Imp. inedita* II 638; Potthast, *Regesta* I, Nr. 5050; Pixton, "Anwerbung" 167-174; Powell, *Anatomy of a Crusade* 31 note 21, citing Reinhold Röhricht, *Regesta Regni Hierosolymitani* (Oeniponti, 1893) II 58, for another German preacher, Theobald.

[7] *Sagt an, her Stoc,*
   hat iuch der babest her gesendet,
   dazr in richet und uns Tiutschen ermet unde pfendet?
   . . . ich waen des silbers wenic kumet ze helfe in gottes lant;
   grôzen hort zerteilet selten pfaffen hant.
   hêr Stoc, ir sît ûf schaden her gesant,
   daz, ir ûz tiutschen liuten toerinne unde narren.

See Friedrich Maurer, *Die politischen Lieder Walthers von der Vogelweide* (1972) 80 (Unmutston Strophe); Konrad Burdach, "Der Kampf Walthers von der Vogelweide gegen Innocenz III. und das vierte lateranische Konzil," *ZKG* 55 (1936) 470; Pixton, "Anwerbung" 183.

[8] Böhmer-Ficker, *Regg. Imp.* V/2, Nr. 9997; Winkelmann, *Acta Imp. inedita* I 474; Weech, *Cod. dipl. Salem.* I 138.

within that province.[9] Although no copy of such letters survives for the Salzburg province, we may assume that the chief preachers—Bishop Conrad of Regensburg and Provost Albert of Salzburg[10]—, either personally or through *subdelegati*, had also made an attempt at discharging this papal mandate. The clergy of this province undoubtedly were in no more sympathy with the imposition than their brethren elsewhere. The half-tithe would thus have been an important item to be discussed by the archbishop and his suffragan bishops of Passau, Freising, Gurk, and Chiemsee at the provincial synod convened during the latter part of 1216.[11]

The Salzburg Provincial Synod—1216

Given the fact that Archbishop Eberhard had accompanied the legate Peter from Indersdorf to Würzburg in May 1216 and that Peter attested at Salzburg on 3 November 1216, we may assume that the two had had numerous conversations concerning this impost; though the records are silent, it is not improbable that Peter was somehow involved in presenting this topic at the Salzburg synod. Hübner's argument that the synod was convened in late September rests on a document dated 24 September 1216; if the main group of participants did not arrive until several days later, however, Peter may well have been able to attend and by virtue of his apostolic authority to have imposed the obligation of the twentieth upon the assembled clergy.

---

[9] Potthast, *Regesta* I, Nr. 5363 (21 November 1216); Würdtwein, *Nova subs.* III 49, contains a letter which commands the archbishop and his suffragans to be prepared to deliver the collected sums over to the collectors by the feast of All Saints the following year. A further letter was sent on 28 February 1217 to the same effect; cf. Potthast, *Regesta* I, Nr. 5477; Würdtwein, *Nova subs.* III 43.

[10] For these two men as crusade-preachers, cf. Pixton, "Anwerbung" 171-183.

[11] *Ann. Salisb.* 780: "*Concilium provinciale a domino Eberhardo Salzpurch celebratur, cui interfuerunt Pataviensis, Frisingensis, Gurcensis, Chymensis episcopi. Ratisponensis vero propter seditionem sue civitatis interesse non poterat, sed praepositum, decanum, scolasticum maioris ecclesie pro se misit.*" See also, *Ann. Shir.* 632. Whereas Meiller, *RAS* 211, Nr. 177, places the synod in early 1216, Hübner, "Provinzialsynoden" 188-202, argues for late September, since on 24 September 1216 the bishop of Chiemsee and the abbots of Admont, Michelbeuern and Seon, the prior of Maria-Saal, the *plebani* of Mühldorf, Burghausen, Laufen and Taxenbach were witnesses for the Archbishop. We may also assume the presence of laymen, both *nobiles* and *ministeriales*, who attended Salzburg synods until well into the thirteenth century. See further, Obersteiner, *Gurk* 81, citing Jaksch, *MC* I 457; Dalham, *Concil. Salisb.* 96; Alphons Lhotsky, *Oesterreichische Historiographie* (München, 1962) 201-202.

Lateran IV had decreed that at each yearly provincial synod the decrees of
the General Council were to be read.[12] There can be no doubt that this
was done at this first provincial gathering at Salzburg; Eberhard attended the
sessions in Rome and he returned with a complete set of the constitutions
and other related documents from Lateran IV. The contemporary continuator of the *Annales S. Rudperti Salisburgenses* included in them the brief
notice for the year 1215 that

> *1215. . . . Universalis synodus celebratur est Rome, in qua fuerunt episcopi
> 412. Inter quos extiterunt Constantinopolitanus, Iherosolimitanus patriarche;
> primates autem et metropolitani 71; abbates et priores ultra 800. In ipsa
> synodo Kymensis episcopatus intituitur, et ad ipsam sedem Ruodigerus primus
> episcopus ordinatur.*[13]

As early as 1863 Eduard Winkelmann noted that essentially this same
account is found in numerous narratives written during the thirteenth century
in Germany, Italy, France, and England.[14] It is now understood that at,

---

[12] Lateran IV, *c.* 6: "*Sicut olim a sanctis patribus noscitur institutum, metropolitani
singulis annis cum suis suffraganeis provincialia non omittant concilia celebrare, in quibus de
corregendis excessibus et moribus reformandis, praesertim in clero, diligentem habeant cum
Dei timore tractatum, canonicas regulas et maxime quae statuta sunt in hoc generali concilio
relegentes, ut eas faciant observari, debitam poenam transgressoribus infligendo. Ut autem
id valeat efficacius adimpleri, per singulas dioeseses statuant idoneas personas, providas
videlicet et honestas, quae per totum annum simpliciter et de plano, absque ulla iurisdictione
sollicite invertigent, quae correctione vel reformatione sint digna, et ea fideliter perferant ad
metropolitanum et suffraganeos et alios in concilio subsequenti, ut super his et aliis, prout
utilitati et honestati congruerit, provida deliberatione procedant; et quae statuerint, faciant
observari, publicantes ea in episcopalibus synodis, annuatimper singulas dioeseses celebrandis.
Quisquis autem hoc salutare statutum neglexerit adimplere, a suis beneficiis et executione officii
suspendatur, donec per superioris arbitrium eius relaxetur.*" Implications of this are discussed
by Hübner, "Provinzialsynoden" 201, and Binterim, *Concilien* IV 270.

[13] *Ann. Salisb.* 780; According to Wattenbach-Schmale, *DGQ* 192-193, 224-227, the
Salzburg annals were originally derived from those of Admont in Styria, becoming independent
between 1181 and 1197; they survive in manuscripts of the fourteenth and fifteenth centuries.

[14] Winkelmann, *Kaiser Friedrich II.* 105; Mansi, *Collectio* XXII 954-1086; Raynaldi, *Ann.
eccles.* (a. 1215); *Ann. Herbipol.* 12; *Alb. Stad.* 356; *Reineri Ann.* 674; *Ann. Marbac.* 173;
Chron. Ursperg. 156-157; *Richeri Gesta* 4 (cap. 1). Winkelmann's statement was challenged
by Potthast, *Regesta* I, Nr. 437, but he reasserted and amplified his views in *Phil. von Schw.*
II 513. The complete text reads: "*Anno ab incarnatione verbi 1215. Celebrata est sancta
universalis synodus Romae in ecclesia Salvatoris, quae Constantiniana vocatur, mense
Novembri, presidente domno Innocentio papa tertio, pontificatus eius 18. anno. In qua fuerunt
episcopi 412. Inter quod extiterunt de principuis patriarchis duo, videlicet Constantinopolitanus et Hierosolimitanus; Antiochus autem, gravi languore detentus, venire non potuit, sed
misit pro se vicarium, Antheradensem episcopum; Alexandrinus vero, sub Sarracenorum
dominio constitutus, fecit quod potuit, mittens pro se diaconum, suum germanum. Primates
autem et metropolitani 71. Ceterum abbates et priores ultra octingentos, archiepiscoporum*

or near, the end of the Council an official or quasi-official summary or protocol was distributed to those in attendance, quite possibly together with the constitutions themselves. This argument is strengthened by the not infrequent occurrence of the protocol with extant manuscripts of the decrees.[15] Thus, within weeks after November 1215 some twenty-one or more copies of all the major documents distributed at the Council had been transmitted back to Germany and were housed in the repositories of the cathedral churches (and possibly in the libraries of several major exempt monasteries as well). From these documents the first generation of annalists and chroniclers (including the canon-historian at St. Rupert's in Salzburg) after the Council derived many of their details of the assembly; from the annalistic notations concerning the Council, we in turn can better assess the extent to which the Council was known at an early date.

In a document issued on 11 November 1216 by Duke Leopold of Austria, we find record of the resolution of a dispute over a tithe between the monasteries of Heiligenkreuz and Melk by means of a *compositio*, a process detailed in *c*. 55 of Lateran IV.[16] Presumably the duke or a member of his chancery had attended the provincial synod just weeks before and had appropriated the latest canonical procedures in his own dealings. Even before the provincial synod, however, clerics in the Salzburg province had become aware of the latest canon law practices. On 27 July 1216, three clerics from the diocese of Passau sat as papal *iudices delegati* in a dispute between the cathedral chapter at Salzburg and Pfalzgrave Rapoto of Krayburg: the pfalzgrave had erected a toll-station near Hallerbrück (west of Salzburg) to the disadvantage of the canons. On the appointed day a *nuntius* of the pfalzgrave appeared and proclaimed that although he was empowered to represent his principal he would not recognize the authority of the judges; furthermore, the venue was suspect, he claimed. He therefore lodged an appeal and departed *contumaciter*, before a decision had been reached. The judges thereupon heard arguments from the cathedral chapter that the appeal should be quashed, a motion which they accepted: Rapoto was excommunicated. At this point the archbishop interceded, in-

---

vero et episcoporum, abbatum et priorum et capitulorum absentium non fuit certus numerus comprehensus. Legatorum vero regis Siciliae in Romanorum imperatorum electi, imperatoris Constantinopolitani, regis Franciae, regis Angliae, regis Ungariae, regis Hierosolimitani, regis Cipri, regis Arragoniae necnon et aliorum principium et magnatus, civitatum aliorumque locorum ingens fuit multitudo."

[15] E.g., Giessen Universitätsbibliothek MS 1105, fol. 47ra-58vb.

[16] *UB Babenb.* II, Nr. 203: *"De his vero possessionibus, quas post supradictum Lateranense concilium acquisierint, decimas ex integro iuxta eiusdem concilii statutum solvent."* See also Stelzner, *Gelehrtes Recht* 206.

sisting that the pfalzgrave have time to make restitution before the ban went into effect.[17]

Stelzner sees this as the earliest example of the use of several elements in Roman/canon law procedure in Germany, including the use of a procurator in legal processes, the granting of powers to the procurator, and the appeal.[18] It demonstrates the amazing speed with which certain aspects of the Council's legislation were appropriated. Various details of the final resolution may have been worked out at the provincial synod which met shortly thereafter. There were also other matters—administrative in nature— which needed attention as well, and in this respect this particular provincial synod demonstrates in very detailed fashion the diverse functions which this single institution was called upon to perform.

The Salzburg chronicler noted that the bishop of Chiemsee was one of the suffragans who attended the provincial synod in 1216. At the end of his abbreviated version of protocol from the Fourth Lateranum he also preserved a local tradition concerning the erection of the bishopric of Chiemsee, an item found in none of the other German sources outside the province of Salzburg. Archbishop Eberhard had originally sought to dissolve the cloister Frauenchiemsee (Frauenwörth) in order to rid his church of a community of undisciplined nuns, but at the same time provide an endowment for a new bishopric. A papally-appointed commission (in 1209) had apparently recommended otherwise, however; rather than dissolving this Benedictine house, the pope approved the establishment around the Augustinian canons' foundation of Herrenchiemsee. Confirmation of that action had been given at the Council. Details of boundaries and the endowment with properties, churches and other rights and prerogatives were dealt with at the provincial synod, although many matters were not resolved until 1218.[19]

At the Council Innocent III had stressed the active role of prelates throughout the Latin church in effecting reform of both clergy and laity. Having first buttressed his own plans with the publication of the papal constitutions, Archbishop Eberhard next undertook the correction of abuses

---

[17] Hauthaler, *SUB* III 202-203, Nrs. 693, 693b; Meiller, *RAS* 527, Nr. 75; Stelzner, *Gelehrtes Recht* 90-92.

[18] See also Hageneder, *Geistliche Gerichtsbarkeit* 109ff.; further, Gaines Post, "'Sufficient Instructions', 'Reference Back', and Limited Mandates," in "Plena Potestas and Consent in Medieval Assemblies. A Study in Romano-Canonical Procedure and the Rise of Representation," *Traditio* 1 (1943) 383-407.

[19] Cf. Hübner, "Provinzialsynoden" 204, citing Meiller, *RAS* 209, Nr. 166; 210, Nr. 172ff.; 215, Nr. 197; 528, Nr. 82. See further discussion in Widmann, *Geschichte Salzburgs* I 340-341; Wilhelmine Seidenschnur, "Die Salzburger Eigenbistümer in ihrer reichs-, kirchen- und landesrechtlichen Stellung," *ZSRG* KanAbt 9 (1919) 177-287, espec. 186-199.

within his own church. Although certain aspects of these measures have long been known,[20] until recently it had been assumed that no protocol or transcript of this synod had survived, nor that any decrees published at it were extant. In 1977, however, Professor Peter Johanek of Würzburg identified a codex from the Benedictine abbey at Ebersberg preserved at Munich as containing the canons of Archbishop Eberhard's 1216 synod. The provincial statutes, which exist in only one known exemplar, perhaps came into being in conjunction with the synod itself, and after the return of the monastic delegate (the abbot?) they were bound together with copies of Gregory the Great's *Moralia in Job* and the decrees of the Council into a codex at Ebersberg;[21] together they comprised a rather unique "handbook" for bishops, although their use as such is not known.[22]

The general disorder which prevailed in Germany from 1198 until 1215 undoubtedly provided the impetus for those synodal provisions which dealt with punishments for, and protections against, lay attacks on church property.[23] The more immediate cause was undoubtedly the long-standing

---

[20] Hartzheim, *Concilia* III (1763), was unaware of it, but Hansiz, *Germania Sacra* II 322, and following him Mansi, *Collectio* XXII, col. 1103-1104, and Dalham, *Concil. Salisb.* 94, cite the letter of Honorius III which confirms the actions taken at the synod; cf. Potthast, *Regesta* I 496, Nr. 5635. Meiller, *RAS* 215, Nr. 195, gives the references to this synod found in the primary sources, as well as a list of the great synodal collections which include it. The synod is discussed in Hefele-Leclercq, *Conciles* V/2 1399; Gruber, "Eberhard II."; Binterim, *Concilien* IV 442-444; Hübner, "Provinzialsynoden" 201-204; Hauck, *KGD* V 135 note 2.

[21] Munich Staatsbibliothek clm 5822, f. 179ᵛ-180ʳ.

[22] See Johanek, "Synodalia" I 51-52, 89.

[23] "*[1] Prohibemus districte nequis episcoporum, vel aliorum prelatorum, vel clericorum inferiorum dignitatum, alicui excommunicato communionem audeat dare vel etiam communicare aliusquam satisfecerit competenter. Si quis autem hoc contempserit observare, et si spiecopus est, sit suspensus, donec se sedis apostolice conspectui representet.*

[2] Item, si quis parrochianus in parrochia sui pastoris deliquerit, et [ ] potestatem habeat ille pastor sufficienter eum ammonitum sententia excommunicationis studeat innodare. Quam sententiam omnes episcopi illius provincie et pastores, ipsis ab excommunicatore proprio intimatam, non differant executioni mandare, facientes eum districtius evitare.

[3] Item, si quis parrochianus alterius in altera parrochia constitutus deliquerit, potestatem habeat ille pastor racione delicti eum excommunicandi, et illam excommunicationem proprio pastori denunciet executioni mandandam, certo nomine designato, quod nomen vel nomina excommunicatorum omnibus diebus festivis recitentur coram plebe, et ab omnibus devitentur omni excusatione remota.

[4] Et si potestas fuerit malefactor, terram suam faciat interdicto subiacere, donec de sua absolutione per literas excommunicatoris constiterit manifeste.

[5] Si quis autem prelatorum vel clericorum convictus fuerit hoc ne fecisse, ipso iure sit suspensus donec satisfecerit competenter.

[6] Item si quis res ecclesiasticorum vel clericorum decedentium tempore vitae vel mortis rapere presumpserit, alicuius iuris pretexta, tamquam sacrilegus ab omnibus reputetur, nec absoluatur nisi a proprio episcopo satisfactione premissa, ita tamen ut compositio quam sancti canones sacrilegis statuerunt, exacta totaliter, illis quibus debetur secundum statuta canonum

conflict between the Salzburg cathedral chapter and Pfalzgrave Rapoto of Krayburg. A further consequence of this dispute may have been the grant of the archiepiscopal power of the ban (*Banngewalt*) to the cathedral chapter near the end of 1216, a measure aimed at better protecting the Salzburg church against her enemies.[24] Dopsch suggests that this move was aimed at giving the cathedral chapter greater power for its central role in reforming the canons regular of the province.[25]

In 1209 Innocent III had written Bishop Conrad IV of Regensburg regarding abuses in the appointing vicars for parish churches, with the result that the cure of souls suffered.[26] This appears to have been the direct cause behind the provincial statute of 1216 which required that vicars be approved by the bishop or the archdeacon, and that they be capable individuals.[27] A similar concern for the *cura animarum* undoubtedly lay behind a further statute which was aimed at the practice whereby certain abbots and priors of his province had appointed monks and canons regular to serve as priests in baptismal- and parish churches which were not fully and legally incorporated into their foundations. These clerics had reputedly done damage to both the cure of souls and to the clerical reputation through their undisciplined lives. Supported by *cc*. 30 and 61 of the Lateran IV constitutions, the archbishop had, with the concurrence of the bishops and other learned men in the synod, ordained that the heads of monasteries could only appoint ordained priests to such churches, and that these were answerable to the bishops for the *cura animarum*.[28] This specific statute

---

tribuatur."

[24] Cf. Hübner, "Provinzialsynoden" 203; Meiller, *RAS* 212, Nrs. 181, 182; Janner, *Regensburg* 289 (citing Meiller, *RAS* 527, Nrs. 73, 75).

[25] *Geschichte Salzburgs* I 329.

[26] Potthast, *Regesta* I, Nr. 3708; see pp. 160-162.

[27] "[ ] *Item nullus vicariis in ecclesiis constituatur, nisi presentatur episcopo vel archidiacono; si notus fuerit aut honestus, et provide, nec deiciatur nisi primo illis consultis.*"

[28] Lateran IV, *c*. 30: "*Grave nimis est et absurdum, quod quidem praelati ecclesiarum, cum possint viros idoneos ad ecclesiastica beneficia promovere, assumere non verentur indignos, quibus nec morum honestas nec literarum scientia suffragatur, carnalitatis sequentes affectum, non iudicium rationis. Unde quanta ecclesiis damna proveniant, nemo sabae mentis ignorat. Volentes igitur huic morbo mederi, praecipimus ut, praetermissis indignis, assumant idoneos, qui Deo et ecclesiis velint et valeant gratum impendere famulatum fiatque de hoc in provinciali concilio diligens inquisitio annuatim, ita quod qui post primam et secundam correctionem fuerit repertus culpabilis, a conferendis beneficiis per ipsum concilium suspendatur, instituta in eodem concilio persona provida et honesta, quae suppleat suspensi defectum in beneficiis conferendis; et hoc ipsum circa capitula quae in his deliquerint, observetur. Metropolitani vero delictum superioris iudicio relinquatur ex parte concilii nuncandum. Ut autem haec salubris provisio pleniorem consequatur effectum, huiusmodi suspensionis sententia praeter Romani pontificis auctoritatem aut proprii patriarchae minime relaxetur, ut in hoc quoque quatuor patriarchales sedes specialiter honorentur.*"

was given papal confirmation in a letter from Honorius III dated 14 December 1217.[29]

Among the missing portions of the decrees of this synod as preserved in MS 5822 at Munich were one or more sections which addressed the responsibilities of diocesan bishops and provincial clergy vis-a-vis archiepiscopal visitations. Since the very start of his own pontificate Archbishop Eberhard II had met stiff opposition and he had complained in 1201 to the pope that the regular clergy in particular failed to keep their obligations toward him during visitations—specifically they withheld the prescribed *procurationes*. A similar complaint prompted a papal bull dated 29 July 1210.[30] The prelate therefore sought to reinforce his own decree(s) of 1216 by obtaining papal confirmation of them. On 11 December 1217 Pope Honorius III granted this request, commanding all bishops, abbots, priors,

Lateran IV, *c. 61*: "*In Lateranensi concilio [scilicet, Lat. III, c. 10] noscitur fuisse prohibitum, ne quilibet regulares ecclesias seu decimas sine consensu episcoporum de manu praesumant recipere laicali nec excommunicatos vel nominatum interdictos admittant aliquatenus ad divina. Nos autem id fortius inhibentes, transgressores condigna curabimus animadversione puniri statuentes nihilominus quatenus in ecclesiis, quae ad ipsos pleno iure non pertinent, iuxta eiusdem statuta concilii episcopis instituendos presbyteros repraesentent, ut illis de plebis cura respondeant; ipsis vero pro rebus temporalibus rationem exhineant competentem. Institutos vero removere non audeant episcopis inconsultis; sane adicimus, ut illos repraesentare procurent, quos vel conversatio reddit notos vel commendat probabile testimonium praelatorum.*"

Salzburg 1216, *[14]* "*Item nullus monachorum vel regularium constituatur ad regulam ecclesiarum; si quodlibet monasterium in parochiis ad se pleno pertinentibus iure presentet episcopo clericum vel clericos seculares vel vice eorum archidiaconis, perpetuos vicarios constituendos, quibus tamen de ecclesiis predictis relinquatur, quod si ipsis et propriis [illegible].*" See further, Janner, *Regensburg* 289; Johanek, "Synodalia" I 89.

[29] Potthast, *Regesta* I 496, Nr. 5635; Meiler, *RAS* 214, Nr. 195; Pressutti, *Regg. Hon. III* I, Nr. 923; Hauthaler, *SUB* III 231-232, Nr. 717a: ". . . *cum quidam abbates et praepositi regulares tuae provinciae in ecclesiis baptismalibus et parrochialibus non plene pertinentibus ad eosdem instituissent contra Lateranensis statuta concilii monachos et canonicos regulares, qui viventes irregulariter multa illicita committebant in salutis suae dispendium, opprobrium ordinis et scandalum plurimorum, tu, volens morbo huic congruum remedium adhibere, de suffraganeorum tuorum ac aliorum virorum prudentium consilio in plena synodo provide ordinasti; ut abbates et praepositi regulares in talibus ecclesiis dioecesanis episcopis presbyteros repraesentent, qui eisdem episcopis de plebis cura respondeant, eis vero de rebus temporalibus rationem exhibeant competentem, prout in concilio Lateranensi statutum et nuper in generale exstitit innovatum.*"

[30] Meiller, *RAS* 170, Nr. 8 (1201): ". . . *cum iuxta canonicas sanctiones ad corrigendos excessus et vitia resecanda venerabilis frater noster* . . . *Salzburgensis archiepiscopis vobis et aliis provinciae suae praelatis ascitis singulis annis debeat concilium celebrare* . . . *quatinus, cum ab eodem archiepiscopo causa celebrandi concilium iuxta canonicas sanctiones fueritis requisiti, ipsius praesentiam adeatis.*" Further discussion in Janner, *Regensburg* I 289; Hübner, "Provinzialsynoden" 203. For the 1210 bull from Innocent III, cf. Meiller, *RAS* 199, Nr. 128.

and prelates of the province to receive the visitations of Archbishop
Eberhard with the respect due his office, to obey his ordinances, and to
support him in his efforts to improve discipline throughout the region of his
stewardship, insofar as such actions did not violate their own privileges.[31]

The contemporary account of this synod by an anonymous cathedral
canon at Salzburg (the continuator of the *Annales S. Rudperti*) states that
"the prelates of the monasteries from throughout the entire province, being
contumaciously absent, were excommunicated by the lord metropolitan in
this council, which sentence the lord pope Honorius III confirmed."[32] The
issues on which they broke with their metropolitan are clear: in the matter
of the appointment of religious or canons regular as parish priests they
regarded the archbishop's efforts as serious infringements on their
traditional right to appoint whomever they wished to their own incorporated
churches, but above all as an attempt to prohibit instituting conventuals as
parish priests and vicars altogether. They furthermore must have suspected
that the bishops would attempt to control the *temporalia* as well, and to
demand an accounting from the monastic *plebani* for them.[33]

The intransigence of the majority of Salzburg provincial abbots and
priors in 1216 was a not-unexpected consequence of the centralizing
tendencies of this archbishop and prelates elsewhere in general, and it was
indicative of how far the rift between themselves and their prelate had
spread. It was quite clearly the knowledge of the Lateran IV decrees and
their usefulness in the archbishop's attempts to tighten control over religious
houses which prompted the monastic dignitaries to boycott the 1216 synod.
That some of these same monastic dignitaries may have been among the 800
or more who attended the Lateran Council is quite probable, but the
majority of them must have learned of this potential threat to their position
and privileges after the Council by means of oral communication. This
reaction at Salzburg in 1216 again illustrates the speed with which some of
the decrees of the Council became common knowledge to those groups

---

[31] Hauthaler, *SUB* III, Nr. 717a; Potthast, *Regesta* I, Nrs. 5632; Pressutti, *Regg. Hon. III*
I, Nr. 914; Meiller, *RAS* 214, Nr. 194: ". . . *quatinus, cum ex rationabili causa provinciam
ipsam (Salisburgensem) eum (archiepiscopum) visitare contingerit, vos cum honore debito
recipientes eundem in hiis, quae ad officium suum pertinent, ei, sicut convenit, intendatis, ut
ipso suas et vobis vestras partes laudabiliter adimplentibus ecclesie vestre spiritualibus et
temporalibus auctore domino proficiant incrementis et nos eius sollicitudem et vestram
devotionem debeamus merito commendare.*" See Juritsch, *Babenberger* 435-437, for a
discussion of conditions in the province at this time.

[32] *Ann. Salisb.* 780: "*In quo concilio praelati monasteriorum totius provinciae
contumaciter absentes a domino Metropolitano sunt excommunicati, quam sententiam dominus
Honorius papa tertius confirmavit.*" See also, *Chron. Magni presb.* 527; *Ann. Shir.* 632. On
the reluctance of the Styrian monasteries, cf. Meiller, *RAS* 485, Nr. 22.

[33] See Hübner, "Provinzialsynoden" 202-203.

which were most affected by them; it also demonstrates how quickly some ecclesiastical leaders in Germany appropriated the general principles of canon law to the specific requirements of their own situations. Just as the pope supported the archbishop over-against his suffragan bishops in the matter of visitations, so too he confirmed Eberhard II's efforts to extend greater control over the conventuals of his province.

The synod also addressed such issues as the abuse of the rights of advocacy,[34] instability among religious,[35] protection for clerics against excommunicated laymen,[36] and the discipline of consecrated clerics who had lapsed back into lay life.[37] In this respect it clearly fulfilled the role of such assemblies as prescribed by the Fourth Lateran Council. If the synod was in any way typical of provincial gatherings elsewhere in thirteenth-century Germany, we may reasonably conclude that others from which we possess just the record of some administrative or juridical act served pastoral needs as well.

On 4 February 1217 Pope Honorius III wrote Archbishop Eberhard regarding a schismatic abbot's election at the Benedictine house of St. Lamprecht in Carinthia: the previous year, one faction had supported the monk Wolfger, while the other backed Prior Waltfried of Maria-Hof. Waltfried was probably one of the instigators of the earlier revolt (1210) against the archbishop during a visitation, and when the opposition party

---

[34] "*[8] Item si quis laicus ratione advocatione, si in rebus ecclesiae, dotibus et honoribus, plus usurpaverit accipere quam antique consentudo ratione permiserit, excommunicetur ab illo qui presidet ecclesiae viduare, donec ablata restituat et de dampno caveat in futurum.*

[9] Si qua ecclesia privilegia habeat quae advocatione contineatur certa iura, statuimus quod ipso iure contra ea faciens sit excommunicatus, et ab omnibus vitetur, qui superius dictam volverit effugere ulcionem."

[35] "*[12] Item si qua puella in monasterio per annos xii^{cim} vel amplius permanserit in habitu monachali, ipsa in eadem ecclesia perpetuo permaneat, et si exiens assumpserit vitam laicalem ad monasterium per censuram ecclesiasticam redire compellatur.*

[13] Item si monachus vel regularis canonicus per annos xii^{cim} permanserit, permaneat perpetuo."

[36] "*[10] Ut autem facilius quilibet clericorum excommunicatum ab ipso vel ab alio audeat publicare vel etiam devitare provido consilio, statuimus quatenus quilibet episcoporum in suo burgo, in civitate domum vel domos constituat in quibus recipiatur de ecclesiis suis profugos, vel eiectos potencia laicorum et ipsis faciant competenter provideri, reservatis duabus ecclesiis ad hoc opus pietatis, secundum qualitatem ecclesiarum, numero ordinato, quarum pensione ad hoc opus pietatis recepta. Illis personis efficacius possit provideri, et si regulares fuerint prelato episcopo provideat, subditis in aliis ecclesiis collocatis.*"

[37] "*[11] Item precipimus omnibus episcopis in Salzburgensi diocesi constitutis, ut omnes qui subdiaconatus vel diaconatus ordinem susceperunt et vitam militantes laicalem duxerint, et matrimonia contaxerint, ut ad clericatum redeantur habitu et tonsura, dissoluto matrimonio; vel postea inito nunciato moneatur diligentius et inducatus, et si necesse fuerit per censuram ecclesiasticam compellere non omittatur.*"

objected vigorously to Wolfger's consecration by the archbishop, Eberhard
had imposed the ban. At this, Waltfried turned to Rome for help. The
pontiff's orders to the metropolitan were to restore Waltfried *"sine delatione
libertati."* [38] Eberhard's delay in responding to the papal directive prompted another bull on 1 September 1217, in which Honorius commanded him
to remove Wolfger (*Wolcherus*) at once and to relax the sentence of
excommunication which he had laid upon the subdeacon and other monks
of the same house, inasmuch as the monastery claimed to be accountable
directly to the Roman See. [39]

Both the letter sent to Eberhard in September 1217 and that sent on 11
December 1217 to Abbot Rudolf of Kremsmünster and the priors of St.
Florian and Mattsee [40] refer to the fact that action was taken against the
rebellious monks at a synod. [41] Use of the term *plena synodus* and mention
of a decision reached with the counsel of the suffragans of Salzburg identify
this as a provincial synod. Since the disputed election took place in 1216
it is reasonable to conclude that the synod in question was also that of 1216,
in which case we have yet another piece of evidence for the diversity of
issues handled at that assembly. The schism at St. Lamprecht's was still
undecided in early July 1218. [42]

One of the few monastic dignitaries who did not boycott the 1216 synod
was Abbot Gottfried II of Admont, the foremost Benedictine house in
Styria, with close ties to the metropolitan church. Copies of important

---

[38] Pressutti, *Regg. Hon. III* I, Nr. 309.

[39] Rodenberg, *MG Ep. s. XIII* I, Nr. 32; Pressutti, *Regg. Hon. III* I, Nr. 762.

[40] Rodenberg, *MG Ep. s. XIII* I, Nr. 39; Pressutti, *Regg. Hon. III* I, Nr. 915.

[41] (1 September 1217): *". . . tu, . . . eum [scilicet Walterum] in ecclesia capi tyrannica
feritate fecisti, et in carcerem retrudi graviter vulneratum, ecclesia ipsa equis et rebus aliis
spoliata, ut sic saltem a iuris sui prosecutione desistere cogeretur; quo etiam sic detento pro
corrigendis eius excessibus, quos insinuasti esse varios et multiplices, tacito quod detineretur
in vinculis, apostolicas litteras impetrasti, ut earum occasione desevires liberius in eundem.
Porro cum idem procuratorem suum ad tuam synodum destinasset, contradicturum ne causa
pendente prefatum Wolcherum benediceres in abbatem, tu nichilominus post appellationem ab
ipso procuratore legitime interpositam illum, lite adhuc existente sub iudice, in abbatem
benedicere presumpsisti, et in procuratorem iamdictum nulla monitione premissa
excommunicationis sententiam promulgare, faciens ipsum de synodo turpiter eici, et a
servientibus tuis, licet esset subdiaconus, inhoneste tractari."* (11 December 1217): *"Set idem
canonicam fugiens ultionem contra eundem archiepiscopum se armavit, et ipsius ecclesie locum
eminentem ascendens fecit eum per suos satellites sagittari, quare predictus archiepiscopus,
cum alias impudentem pertinaciam suam non posset corripere, ipsum capi faciens et custodie
mancipari, postmodum de consilio suffraganeorum suorum in plena synodo in eum depositionis
sententiam promulgavit; . . ."*

[42] Pressutti, *Regg. Hon. III* I, Nr. 1493. See also Helmut J. Mezler-Andelberg, "Zur
älteren Geschichte der Abtei St. Lambrecht," *Carinthia* I (1961) 534-571, espec. 566ff.;
further, Stelzner, *Gelehrtes Recht* 92-93.

archiepiscopal and papal documents (and presumably the synodal statutes of 1216 and the Lateran decrees of 1215) would also have been preserved at Admont.[43] An interest in canonistic had existed here since the second half of the twelfth century; during the 1160s and 1170s, e.g., Admont monks made copies of various works of the Bolognese school.[44] By the early 1200s at the latest Admont also had its own complete copy of Gratian's *Decretum*.[45] While the abbot himself may have been a factor behind these acquisitions,[46] it is also significant that documents of 1210 identify one *magister Hainricus monachus* as a *"legista"*.[47] Presumably, he had acquired advanced training in Roman or canon law in the Italian schools which lay so close at hand. Near the end of the 1220s another Admont monk studying at Padua apparently made copies of various canonist works which he brought back to his house.[48]

Given his apparent obedience to, or support for, the reform programs of Innocent III and Eberhard II, it may have been at the instigation of Abbot Gottfried II that the brief notations concerning the Fourth Lateran Council were included in the *Annales Admontenses*, which served as the source for numerous other records established elsewhere in the province.[49] Clearly the monks at Admont had heard the papal constitutions and the archiepiscopal decrees read at the synod of 1216 itself, or within their cloistered walls upon the return of their abbot from Salzburg. Moreover, the interests of

---

[43] Cf. Franz Martin, "Zwei Salzburger Briefsammlungen des 12. Jahrhunderts," *MIÖG* 42 (1927) 313-315, and Zatschek, *Urkundenlehre* 124, 145, cited in Friedrich Kempf, "Das Rommersdorfer Briefbuch des 13. Jahrhunderts," *MIÖG*, Erg.-Band 12 (1933) 562; Dopsch, *Geschichte Salzburgs* I 1270 note 305.

[44] Admont Cod. 23 and 43; Stelzner, *Gelehrtes Recht* 21-22.

[45] Admont Cod. 48, written in Italy ca. 1200; cf. Stelzner, *Gelehrtes Recht* 24.

[46] Abbot Gottfried's own familiarity with canon law procedures may be implied from the commission he received, along with Prior Stephan of Admont and Archdeacon Henry of Gruscharn) in 1220 to act as a *iudex delegatus* in a tithe controversy between the abbot of Garsten and the *plebanus* at Wartberg, the Passau archdeacon and cathedral canon; cf. *UBLOE* II 623, Nr. 424.

[47] Cf. Zahn, *UB Steiermark* II 162, Nr. 106; 172, Nr. 115; Stelzner, *Gelehrtes Recht* 16, 148.

[48] Admont Stiftsbibliothek Cod. 22, containing *Compilatio I, Compilatio II, Compilatio III* with the glosses of Johannes Teutonicus and Tancred, *Compilatio IV*, and a fragment of the *Constititiones* of Lateran IV (c. 69 to conclusion). See Stelzner, *Gelehrtes Recht* 201-203; Kuttner, *Repertorium* 375; Antonio Garcia y Garcia, "El Concilio IV de Latran (1215) y Sus Comentarios," *Traditio* 14 (1958) 484.

[49] *Continuatio Admunt.* 592: [Codices A] *"1215. . . . Synodus celebrata est apud ecclesiam sancti Johannis Rome"*; [Codices B] *"1215. Domnus Innocentius papa synodum maximam Rome celebravit, et circa finem eiusdem anni moritur."* Whereas the protocol refers to the *"ecclesia Salvatoris, quae Constantiniana vocatur, . . ."*, the Admont redaction uses the more popular designation of *"ecclesia sancti Johannis."* In this respect it also deviates from the standard practice of those chronicles which depend upon the protocol.

some monks had brought them into direct contact with the canonistic writings of Vincentius Hispanus and Johannes Teutonicus during the decade of the 1220s as well.

Synodal Activity at Trier

Whereas there is both annalistic, and documentary verification of the 1216 provincial synod and of the transmission of the constitutions of the Fourth Lateranum at Salzburg, the record for Archbishop Eberhard's five metropolitan contemporaries is much less certain. Nevertheless, there is sufficient evidence to conclude that the publication and implementation of the Lateran IV decrees occurred (at least to some extent) within all provinces before 1224. This is especially clear with respect to Trier. Binterim states that "we must assume that Dietrich [II] followed the charge to hold yearly provincial synods, especially because he was in great favor with Frederick II and claimed first position in all meetings."[50] The logic here is unclear: it would have made far more sense to say that Archbishop Dietrich II obeyed the injunctions of Lateran IV because he was an ardent supporter of papal programs. As in other instances, however, Binterim appears to have gone beyond his sources in his interpretation. We have noted in Ch. Two the most ambitious reform program which Dietrich of Trier set in motion on the very eve of the Council. This metropolitan also had a long synodal tradition to draw on, and it is totally consistent with his actions of early 1215 that he would have acted at once to exploit the momentum given by the legislation of Innocent III in order to further his own pastoral and ecclesiastical ends. It is thus probable that at about the same time as Eberhard II was convening a synod for the province of Salzburg, Dietrich II of Trier summoned his suffragans and other ecclesiastical leaders for the purpose of publishing the decrees which he had recently received in Rome.

Support for this contention comes from an important collection of letters and other documents which was prepared under the direction of Bruno of Braunsberg, abbot of Rommersdorf (1214-after 1233), one of two papally-designated crusade preachers for the province of Trier.[51] Along with the papal mandates to Bruno himself were included the papal encyclical *Vineam*

---

[50] Binterim, *Concilien* IV 400: „*In denselben Generalconcilium wird auch Kap. 6 den Erzbischöfen aufgegeben, gemäss Vorschrift der canonischen Satzungen, alle Jahre ein Provincialconcilium zu halten, und man muss glauben, dass Theoderich diese Weisung befolgt habe, besonders da er bei dem Kaiser Friedrich in grosser Gunst stand, und bei allen Versammlungen den ersten Platz behauptete.*"

[51] Cf. Staatsarchiv Koblenz, MS Best. 162, Nr. 1401 (formerly Best. 201, A VII 1 Nr. 124), fol. 1b-28a. For Bruno as crusade preacher, cf. Pixton, "Anwerbung" 167, 175-6.

domini Sabaoth, a nearly complete set of the canons of the Fourth Lateranum, the decree *Ad Liberandum*, and a copy of the Council's protocol. Abbot Bruno obtained most of his materials ca. 1216 from the archiepiscopal treasury at Trier, confirming the fact that at the time of our presumed synod a set of the decrees was to be found there.[52] The immediate publication of the decrees by the archbishop to the leading clergy of the archdiocese would have greatly facilitated the task given to Abbot Bruno with respect to the impending crusade (e.g., collecting the half-tithe, etc.). Despite the fact that from his accession in December 1212 until 1220 when the Emperor Frederick II left Germany for his Sicilian kingdom, the metropolitan of Trier was perpetually engaged in securing the succession and recognition of the young Staufen ruler, he would not have lost the opportunity to publish the legislation which he had received at the Council.

Such a publication, and particularly of those decrees of the Fourth Lateranum which reiterated the responsibilities of bishops to reform their clergy, would have aided Dietrich's efforts in that regard. The introductory words to the decree issued in February 1215 regarding the re-establishment of the *mensa communis* in his cathedral chapter make it clear that he considered the cathedral chapter as the example which other collegiate churches should emulate.[53] It cannot have come as a surprise therefore when, in the spring of 1216 after his return from Rome, the archbishop began a renewal of the common table in the collegiate church of St. Simeon at Trier.[54] This bold move was without question reinforced by the papal constitutions which his clergy may have heard at a diocesan synod in the spring of 1216, but which became universally known throughout his province after the fall provincial synod. The following year, another major collegiate church—that of St. Florin at Coblenz—saw the reintroduction of the *mensa communis* as well,[55] and in 1227 the second leading church of

---

[52] Kempf, "Rommersdorfer Briefbuch" 563. The arrangement of the canons in the codex suggests that they were copied in a very short period of time by several different hands, each producing a sheet which was later assembled into a set, lacking only canons 12, 14, and 16.

[53] Beyer, *MRUB* III, Nr.29.

[54] Beyer, *MRUB* III 60, Nr. 57; cf. also Marx, *Erztstift Trier* IV 92; II/2 92.

[55] Beyer, *MRUB* III, Nr. 63 (10 March 1217). That diocesan synods were regarded as regular occurrences may be inferred from the text of this document: "*Idem etiam decanus cum eodem vicario in synodo presidebit, curam animarum populi gerendo, excessus corrigendo ceteraque prout expedire videbitur ordinando et nomine ecclesie archidiaconorum iura suis temporibus persolvendo. Vicarius vero ille perpetuus ad synodum Treverim et ad capitula archidiaconi suis temporibus procedet.*" Such a synod may have been the assembly in 1217 at which the archbishop "*communicato consilio praelatorum nostrorum, nobilium et ministerialium*" granted a wood and a mill near Altrich to the monastery Himmerode: witnessing this rather ordinary transfer were two abbots, all five archdeacons of the archdiocese of Trier, two other members of the cathedral chapter, two nobles and eight archiepiscopal *ministeriales*; cf.

the archdiocese, St. Paulin's at Trier, was also reformed in the spirit of 1215.[56]

The success of these reform measures is difficult to determine: there are indications that the common table was still in use at St. Florin's in 1249, but the documents are silent with respect to St. Simeon's.[57] Despite the obvious advantages at St. Paulin's, it is also probable that the attempt there failed. The archbishop had expected that the prestige and influence which he as the former provost and his brother as the current provost enjoyed in that collegiate church would work to the advantage of improved discipline. Within a year of the reform, however, Meffried of Wied was dead and a new provost had been appointed at St.Paulin, a certain Rudolf de Ponte [Jr.]. The cathedral provost of Trier, Rudolf de Ponte [Sr.], died at approximately the same time and was succeeded by the archbishop's nephew, Arnold of Isenburg. In order to secure the uncontested succession of Arnold, however, the prelate appears to have been forced to placate the most serious rival for the office, namely, the younger Rudolf de Ponte, an act which included granting to Rudolf the provostship at St. Paulin. With this concession may have gone all hope of re-instituting the *mensa communis* in that collegiate church.[58]

It has been argued that despite opposition, the archbishop was strong enough to re-establish the common table in the cathedral chapter.[59] In reality, extant documents suggest that as late as 1220 attempts to restore this institution on a permanent basis had been marginally successful at best. In the period from 1217 to 1219 the cathedral church was given several further endowments, the purpose of which was to strengthen the *mensa communis*.[60] Despite such, however, a papal letter of 2 May 1220, written to the cathedral chapter at Trier, indicates that the common table was still struggling for stability some five years after its establishment.[61] Three further documents from the period 1228-1239 indicate that the refectory was still receiving grants from various sources, but it cannot be stated with certainty that this income supported a common table for the cathedral

---

Beyer, *MRUB* III 72-73, Nr. 71.

[56] Goerz, *MRR* II, Nr. 1824 (27 November 1227).

[57] Beyer, *MRUB* III, Nr. 320.

[58] See Pixton, "Reformprogramm" 17-19; Heyen, *St. Paulin von Trier* 101-2, 582-583.

[59] Pellens, *Dietrich II. von Wied* 39.

[60] Beyer, *MRUB* III, Nrs. 64, 98, 108, 113, 113a, 113b, 113c, 160.

[61] Beyer, *MRUB* III, Nr. 131: "*Sane cum vos, sicut ex vestra relatione didicimus, tenues habentes redditus, servare hospitalitatem et commune tenere refectorium commode non possetis, bone memorie Treverensis archiepiscopus et venerabilis frater noster successor ipsius, vobis in hospitalitatis et communis refectionis vestre subsidium ecclesias St. Marie, S. Gervasi, de Perle, de Clottene, et de Guntereven cum pertinentiis suis de ipsarum patronorum assensu, prelatis intuitu contulerunt.*"

canons.[62] The residence obligation which the archbishop sought to enforce with the 1215 statute had to be strengthened by further legislation given at a synod in 1238. At the time of Dietrich's death four years later, there is no sign of the *mensa communis* whatever.[63] We may therefore conclude that, after several years of great effort, this reforming experiment was abandoned and the prelate returned to enforcing clerical discipline by means of more traditional methods.

The lack of sufficient funds for the refectory at Trier cannot be considered the primary reason for the failure of a vigorous reform program, however. The real problem appears to have been hidden by the canons' subterfuge. The needs of the refectory would have been greatly reduced had there been a more receptive spirit toward other facets of the *vita communis* within the cathedral chapter. After 1215 the canons at Trier continued to accumulate additional prebends and offices outside their chapter. They also claimed the right to hold the most important offices under the archbishop: five canons (including the provost, dean, and the *magister scholarum*) were at once archdeacons and bore major ecclesiastical responsibilities. Considering the size of the archdeaconates,[64] these men must have been absent from Trier often and for extended periods of time. It was thus not only difficult to control the behavior of the archdeacons, but their example of non-residence, especially that of the dean who was obligated to maintain such, exacerbated problems of maintaining the presence requirements for the other eleven *capitulares*.

Such considerations undoubtedly caused Archbishop Dietrich to effect several changes in the administrative personnel of his diocese. The cathedral dean, William of Salm, had occupied that office since 1192, and from about 1200 he was also the archdeacon of Longuyon. He is last mentioned as an archdeacon in August 1214, after which he acted solely in his capacity as dean until his death in 1224.[65] It seems clear that the

---

[62] Beyer, *MRUB* III, Nrs. 348, 368, 633.

[63] See the letter written by the cathedral chapter to Countess Irmensindis of Luxemburg, complaining that she had withheld incomes from their corporation; Bastgen, *Trierer DK* 19-20; Idem., "Eine Beschwerdeschrift des Trierer Domkapitels an die Gräfin Ermesinde von Luxemburg (1242)," *Trierisches Archiv* 15 (1909) 82. Since the "*distribucio redditum refectorii fieret inter presentes in choro*," the reason for its being withheld lay in the fact that the canons had not been fulfilling their obligations.

[64] Whereas the medieval archbishoprics of Cologne and Trier each had five archdeacons, the bishoprics of northern Germany had many more: Paderborn (9), Minden (12), Osnabrück (13), Bremen (14), Verden (20), Münster (31), Hildesheim (34), and Halberstadt (38); see Hubert Bastgen, "Die Entstehung der Trierer Archidiakonate," *Trierisches Archiv* 10 (1907) 5, note 1.

[65] Beyer, *MRUB* II, Nr. 126 (1192); Goffinet, *Cartulaire d'Orval* Nr. 117 (1214); Beyer, *MRUB* III, Nr. 238 (1224). See also Pixton, "Reformprogramm" 20-21. Four documents,

emphasis which the Fourth Lateran Council's decrees placed upon the *cura animarum* encouraged the archbishop to separate the office of cathedral dean from that of archdeacon, thereby enabling the dean to carry out his responsibilities for discipline within the cathedral chapter and archdiocese of Trier without the additional burdens of archiepiscopal administration. Most important was that now the dean could abide by the obligation of residence. This same policy was followed with respect to subsequent deans during the remainder of Dietrich II's pontificate.[66]

The other chapter dignitary charged with the improvement of canonical discipline at Trier was the *magister scholarum*. His most important task lay in the training and education of the young clerics who attended the cathedral school or waited to receive an established prebend in the chapter. A study of this school at the beginning of the thirteenth century reveals that it was in general decline—a far cry from its more glorious predecessor of the eleventh and early twelfth centuries.[67] It is thus significant to note that when the *magister scholarum* Othwin died in 1217, the archbishop separated his scholastic office from that of archdeacon, so that his successor might also devote his full time and energies to the duties of his office as head of the school.[68] *C.* 11 of the Lateran IV constitutions had stipulated that the metropolitan church ought to have a theologian who should teach the clergy whatever pertained to the *cura animarum*. In none of the documents which bear Othwin's name as a witness or agent of some business transaction does he ever appear with the academic title of *magister*. Significantly, the new

which were issued between 28 July 1216 and 18 April 1217, refer to Friedrich of Blankenheim as the archdeacon of Longuyon, whereas the subsequent archdeacon of Longuyon was Jacob of Lorraine; see Beyer, *MRUB* III, Nrs. 50, 67, 75, 156. Jacob of Lorraine appears for the first time as the archdeacon of Longuyon in a document which was issued in 1223; cf. *MRUB* III, Nr. 124. Since the other four archdeaconates remained occupied, it is obvious that William of Salm had been removed from the archidiaconal office.

[66] A document issued on 21 March 1225 mentions Werner as dean; Beyer, *MRUB* III, Nr. 242. In 1227 another William appears as dean; op.cit., Nr. 315. And in the year in which the archbishop died, a certain Werricus is mentioned as dean at Trier; Rodenberg, *MG Ep. s. XIII* II, Nr. 41. It is not possible to determine the family origins of these three deans, which leads to the assumption that they were not members of the prominent nobility whose sons regularly used their family names when they witnessed documents.

[67] See Gottfried Kentenich, "Die Trierer Domschule im Mittelalter," *Trierer Heimatbuch* (Trier, 1925) 177-192.

[68] In addition to the prebends which Othwin held in the cathedral chapter, he acquired the provostship at Carden (ca. 1200) and at Pfalzel (1212); Beyer, *MRUB* II, Nrs. 181, 283. After 1201 he appears frequently as *magister scholarum* in the documents; Beyer, *MRUB* II, Nrs. 191, 199, 296; III, Nr. 77. John of Rüggen, who had been archdeacon of Dietkirchen since 1210, appears as the archdeacon of Carden in a document of 23 July 1218; Beyer, *MRUB* III, Nr. 85. His position at Dietkirchen was assumed in 1217 by the archbishop's nephew, Arnold of Isenburg; Beyer, *MRUB* III, Nr. 76.

head of the school appointed by the archbishop in 1217 was a product of the schools—*magister* Ditmar, whose appointment may be seen as direct compliance with the Lateran decree.[69]

We have noted that Archbishop Dietrich's predecessor, John I, instituted the office of *officialis domini archiepiscopi* or *officialis curie Treverensis*.[70] Such a position first appears in the twelfth century at Rheims and was introduced into Germany by way of Trier.[71] Totally dependent on the prelate, this highly-trained specialist in canon law had the task of representing the archbishop (bishop) in juridical matters to an extent greater than the latter could do personally; having nothing to do with administrative concerns, he was able to assert greater influence in the sphere of ecclesiastical jurisdiction.[72] While the position was apparently established prior to 1212, it was only in the aftermath of Lateran IV that its impact began to be felt: the first known *officialis* appears in 1221, and his growing significance at this time seems clearly connected with other reform efforts by Archbishop Dietrich II. Even though the original intention may not have been to create a counterpoise to the growing power and independence of the archdeacons at Trier, the net result was clearly that. By 1242 serious tension had developed between these representatives of the old power structure and this newcomer.

---

[69] Beyer, *MRUB* III, Nr. 138. Ditmar appears for the first time as a member of the cathedral chapter in 1210; Wampach, *UB Luxemburg* II, Nr. 29. He is mentioned as *magister* for the first time in 1212; Beyer, *MRUB* III, Nr. 1, from which we may conclude that he probably received his training in the schools before he came to Trier.

[70] Cf. Corsten, "EB Johann I. of Trier" 133-134. The basis for Corsten's contention is a document dated 1258 which refers to the fact that "*temporibus venerabilium patrum pie memorie dominorum Johannis et Theoderici archiepiscoporum Trever. scimus et intelleximus observatum, et ipsos archidiaconos ecclesie Trevir. in huius iuris possessione extisse*"; cf. Beyer, *MRUB* III 1042, Nr. 1437. The archdeacons Simon of Franchimont and Henry of Bolanden are here claiming exemption from the jurisdiction of the archiepiscopal *officialis*, based on practices which prevailed before the insitution of this position in the archiepiscopal administration. According to Corsten, the first known *officialis* was the cathedral dean William. As we have argued above, William had in fact been released ca. 1216 from his decanal office, though he may well have then continued in the office of *officialis;* the documents give us no help whatsoever.

[71] Louis Carlen, "Zum Offizialat von Sitten im Mittelalter," *ZSRG* KanAbt 46 (1960) 221-222, dates the appearance of an *officialis* at Mainz to 1209; Franz Gescher, "Das älteste kölnische Offizialatsstatut (1306-1331)," *ZSRG* KanAbt 14 (1925) 478, notes one at Liège in 1204 and again in 1214. See also, Hans Foerster, "Die Organisation des erzbischöflichen Offizialatsgerichts zu Köln bis auf Hermann von Wied," *ZSRG* KanAbt 11 (1921) 254-255.

[72] Michel, *Gerichtsbarkeit und Verwaltung* 17-19; Feine, *Kirchliche Rechtsgeschichte* I 170, 305. In the resolution of the conflict between the abbey of St. Mary at Trier and Regina, the widow of the *ministeralis* Gerlach of Güls, the cathedral scholastic and *officialis* at Trier, Thymar, showed a knowledge of the newer canon/Roman law procedures, including the use of procurators; cf. Beyer, *MRUB* III, 377-379, Nr. 485.

At some unspecified time prior to 1238 Archbishop Dietrich II of Trier had spoken out against the careless treatment of the consecrated Host, the Holy Chrism, and the baptismal font, implementing *c.* 20 of the Lateran IV constitutions.[73] There are three additional references in the decrees of 1238 to previous occasions when the archbishop had inveighed against clerical and/or lay abuses : e.g., *c.* 2 (1238) indicates that he had *frequenter* decreed that in parishes where known robbers or oppressors of the clergy were wont to reside, all of the spiritual weapons of the church—interdict and excommunication—should be used to combat them;[74] and *c.* 22 (1238) dealt with restrictions giving aid to clerics engaged in military activities.[75] *C.* 26 (1238) sought to control the abuses associated with the appointment of vicars to fulfill various clerical obligations, noting that the incomes attached to church positions were not intended for the benefit of any single individual, but rather for the entire clerical estate. As was surely true for the provincial synod held in 1216 at Salzburg, this particular regulation drew support from *c.* 32 of the Lateran constitutions and demonstrates once again how general Church law was appropriated for specific local situations.[76] The conditions and abuses cited in these canons were

---

[73] Mansi, *Collectio* XXIII 482 (c. 27): *"Sicut saepe praecipimus, sic iterum praecipientes innovamus, ut Corpus Domini, sanctum oleum infirmorum, et fores sacri baptismatis sub diligenti sint custodia et clausum cum sacra Eucharistia, nec eant ad infirmum sine lumine et campana."* The wording of the Lateran IV decree is: *"Statuimus ut in cunctis ecclesiis chrisma et eucharistia sub fideli custodia clavibus adhibitis conserventur, ne possit ad illa temeraria manus extendi, ad aliqua horribilia vel nefaria exercenda. Si vero is ad quem spectat custodia, ea incaute reliquerit, tribus mensibus ab officio suspendatur, et si per eius incuriam aliquid nefandum inde contigerit, graviori subiaceat ultioni."* The corresponding Mainz statute from 1209 (?) is much more terse: (c. 5) *"Eucharistia, fontes, crisma, oleum sub sera sint propter sortilegia."*

[74] C. 2 (1238): *"Quam frequenter praecipimus, quod si quis ad locum aliquam praedam locorum ecclesiasticorum vel personarum ecclesiasticarum, vel personas eorum duxerit, per totam illam parochiam cessetur a divinis, dum ibi praeda et praedo aut praedae emtor fuerit. Si autem in ipsa parochia conventus fuerit, clausis januis et exclusis ipsius parochiae parochianis, divina ibi celebrentur submissa voce; ita quod foris audiri non possint. Si quis autem parochianorum decesserit, sepeliatur in atrio sine officio missae, et cum sola tantum commendatione, exceptis paedone, emtore, receptatore, vel fautoribus eorumdem ; vel si consumta fuerit praeda, sententiae praedictae serventur, si de praemissis constiterit vel per evidentiam facti, vel per iuramentum, quod his spoliati, si honesta fuerit persona: si quis autem circa haec emerserit, in iudicio iudicis relinquator. Sacerdotes locorum quibus de praemissis constiterit, statim sententias praedictas observent et faciant observari."*

[75] Trier (1238) c. 22: *"Cum statum sit, ut clerici, ministri, vel baillivi vel justitiarii laicorum auxilium ab ecclesia, si capti fuerint, non habeant; adjicimus quod si prius admonitus non cessaverit, ecclesiasticis beneficiis spolientur."*

[76] Trier (1238) c. 26: *"Cum alias institutum sit, quod vicariis competens portio debeat assignari, adjicimus, ut si iidem vicarii minorem acceperint et acceptaverint portionem, nihilominus actionem habeant ad petendam competentem, cum hoc inductum sit personae non*

clearly the outgrowth of disorders arising during the throne controversy and civil war; it would have been important to this metropolitan that they be corrected at the earliest possible opportunity. Since the 1238 statutes drew on earlier pronouncements by Archbishop Dietrich II of Trier, a provincial synod shortly after the Fourth Lateran Council is a reasonable supposition; certainly it would have filled a pressing need.

On 21 March 1217 Pope Honorius III wrote the abbot of St. Hubertus in the diocese of Liège, and the deans of St. John's and St. Martin's of the same bishopric, giving them the commission to make peace between Count William of Holland and Count Ludwig of Los who had become locked in a bitter struggle resulting from William's abduction of Ludwig's wife and his over-running of Ludwig's territory (*"super raptu Adae uxoris ipsius comitis"*).[77] The exact time when this act of violence had occurred is unknown, but it was presumably the previous year since, in the meantime, the archbishop of Trier, upon complaint from Count Ludwig, had imposed a sentence of excommunication and interdict upon the count of Holland and his supporters. On 22 March 1217 the Roman pontiff directed a second letter to the Abbot of St. Hubertus and his two associates, enjoining them to impose ecclesiastical penalties upon those clerics in the lands of Count William and his collaborators who had disregarded the ban pronounced by the metropolitan of Trier. In a companion letter he directed these same three clerics to observe the sentences themselves.[78] Late in 1218 the pope

---

in favorem; sed in favorem totius ordinis clericalis."

Lateran IV, c. 32: *"Exstirpandae consuetudinis vitium in quibusdam partibus inolevit, quod scilicet patroni ecclesiarum parochialium et aliae quaedam personae, proventus ipsarum sibi penitus vendicantes, presbyteris earundem servitiis deputatis relinquunt adeo exiguam portionem, ut ex ea congrue nequeant sustentari. Nam ut pro certo didicimus, in quibusdam regionibus parochiales presbyteri pro sua sustentatione non obtinent nisi quartum quartae, id est sextamdecimam decimarum. Unde fit ut in his regionibus pene nullus inveniatur sacerdos parochialis, qui vel modicam habeat peritiam literarum. Cum igitur os bovis alligari non debeat triturantis, sed qui altari servit vivere debeat de altari, statuimus ut, consuetudine qualibet episcopi vel patroni seu cuiusque alterius non obstante, portio presbyteris ipsis sufficiens assignetur. Qui vero parochialem habet ecclesiam, non per vicarium ser per seipsum illi deserviat in ordine, quem ipsius ecclesiae cura requirit, nisi forte praebendae vel dignitati parochialis ecclesia sit annexa; in quo casu concedimus, ut is qui talem habeat praebendam vel dignitatem, cum oporteat eum in maiori ecclesia deservire, in ipsa parochiali ecclesia idoneum et perpetuum studeat habere vicarium canonice institutum, qui ut praedictum est congruentem habeat de ipsis ecclesiae proventibus, libere alii conferenda, qui velit et possit, quod praedictum est, adimplere. Illud autem penitus interdicimus, ne quis in fraudem de proventibus ecclesiae, quae curam proprii sacerdotis debet habere, pensionem alii quasi pro beneficio conferre praesumat."*

[77] Pressutti, *Regg. Hon. III* I, Nr. 453.

[78] Rodenberg, *MG Ep. s. XIII* I, Nrs. 23, 24; Pressutti, *Regg. Hon. III* I, Nr. 456: ". . . in nobilem virum W. de Hollandia et fautores ipsius Traiectensis et Leodiensis diocesum et*

wrote the archbishop of Trier, commanding him to relax the ban of excommunication against Abbot Heribert of Werden who, at the request of *magister* Oliver, the scholastic at Cologne and the crusade-preacher, had absolved the count of Holland.[79] At the time of this latter action, the count was one of the leaders of the German forces engaged in the assault of the Egyptian city of Damietta; his co-leader was brother to the archbishop of Trier, Count George of Wied.[80]

The impending departure of the crusaders from the province of Trier in 1216, the need to raise sufficient money by means of the half-tithe on the clergy through the preaching efforts of Abbot Bruno and his colleagues, and the pronouncement of the ban of excommunication against the count of Holland by the archbishop of Trier acting as a papal agent, all point to the probability of a provincial synod that year. The dating of such a synod presents few problems. There is occasional evidence from the twelfth century that both spring and autumnal synods were held.[81] The above-mentioned synod of 1238 was convened on 21 September. If, by the thirteenth century, the winter/spring session had been discontinued in favor of the single late summer/early autumn one, a mid-August to mid-October date for such a gathering in 1216 is fully consistent with known practice and seems altogether plausible. The question of which suffragan bishops might have attended is a different matter, however. As noted in Ch. Three, Robert of Grandpré, bishop of Verdun, attended the Lateran Council and received the documents distributed there. Yet, charges of incompetence by members of his cathedral chapter must have affected his activities in 1216; refusing to step down despite ineptness associated with old age, he was eventually excommunicated by Cardinal-priest Peter de Sasso sometime late in 1216.[82]

---

terras eorum venerabilis frater noster Treverensis archiepiscopus auctoritate apostolica exigente iustitia promulgavit, . . ." See also the directive given once again to these three papal agents on 23 August 1217 concerning the excuses given by the count of Holland before the archbishop with regards to his observing the terms of the peace accord; Pressutti, *op.cit.* I, Nr. 735; Potthast, *Regesta* I, Nr. 5653 (without date).

[79] Rodenberg, *MG Ep. s. XIII* I, Nr. 81 (4 December 1218); Pressutti, *Regg. Hon. III* I, Nr. 1723.

[80] Cf. Röhricht, *Deutscher im Heiligen Lande* 118.

[81] E.g., the 1157 gathering is referred to as "*in synodo autumnali*", while in 1187 the spring synod was held 15 February (Sunday *Invocavit*) at Mouzon; the assembly which convened that autumn at Trier, however, appears to have been a diocesan synod. Other known dates for provincial synods include 18 January 1152 at Metz, 16 August 1152, and 11 March 1159.

[82] See letter of Honorius III dated 13 February 1217; Pressutti, *Regg. Hon. III* 79; Böhmer-Ficker, *Regg. Imp.* V/2, Nr. 9995e, and Winkelmann, *Phil. von Schw.* II 433, note 7. Further, Heydenreich, *Metropolitangewalt* 56; Calmet, *Hist. de Lorr.* II Preuv. 61. C. 28 of

Cardinal Peter's itinerary for 1216 can be reconstructed with only partial success: he appeared at Würzburg on 3 May, was thereafter in Cologne, and by 10 September at Coblenz. It is most unlikely that his entrance into and travel through the archdiocese of Trier was without the knowledge and occasional accompaniment of the archbishop: Dietrich II of Trier was himself at Coblenz on 28 July 1216,[83] but his whereabouts thereafter in the year cannot be placed. Nevertheless, the excommunication of Bishop Robert of Verdun would clearly have been done with the approval and participation of his metropolitan, and the provincial synod which we have proposed for this year would have been the ideal venue for such an important act. Given our speculations concerning Peter's connection with the Salzburg provincial synod held within a few days of 24 September 1216, it is reasonable to conclude that the presumed synod for the province of Trier took place between 5 and 15 September.

Robert of Verdun probably did not attend this synod; Honorius III, in a letter dated 13 February 1217, referred to the fact that he had lifted the ban over Robert as the latter personally resigned his office at Rome.[84] Robert's death that same year cleared the way for an uncontested election. The choice fell on a man not yet thirty years of age, however, and Jean (I) d'Apremont's efforts to obtain his confirmation presumably extended the delay in publishing the Council's decrees to the clergy of Verdun until the early 1220s, and another provincial synod of 1222 may have been the catalyst for bringing this about.[85]

The personal presence of the bishop of Metz at a provincial synod held in early September 1216 likewise is doubtful, but for rather different reasons. From 1212 until his death in 1224 Conrad of Scharfenberg served as imperial chancellor for Frederick II, but he also simultaneously occupied the episcopal chairs at Speyer and Metz. The former responsibilities demanded almost his full time at the Hohenstaufen court and allowed him little for ecclesiastical or pastoral activities. As a special privilege, Innocent III had also granted him extensive rights in October 1212 which provided him with a very independent position vis-a-vis the archbishop of Trier.[86]

---

the Lateran IV constitutions had made it clear that prelates who announced their intentions to abdicate, and then refused, were to be compelled to do so. Though not exactly intended for situations such as that which existed at Verdun, this conciliar decree nonetheless leant weight to the legate's efforts to replace an incompetent bishop with one who could function properly.

[83] Beyer, *MRUB* III, Nr. 50.

[84] Pressutti, *Regg. Hon. III* I, Nr. 335; Winkelmann, *Phil. von Schw.* II 433.

[85] In November 1218 he was still "*electus.*" Not until December 1219 is he first documented as an approved bishop; cf. Morret, *Stand und Herkunft* 109; Heydenreich, *Metropolitangewalt* 56; Clouet, *Histoire Ecclésiastique* II 366 note 2 and note 4.

[86] Among the most important privileges was that the archbishop of Trier could not depose

We can assume, however, that representatives of the bishop would have attended the synod. Bishop Conrad of Metz and Speyer was himself not present at Rome in November 1215 either. Thus, it was perhaps similar delegates who carried the documents of Lateran IV back to his church for publication and implementation. Whether knowledge of Innocent III's decrees came to the prelate directly from the Council or indirectly through his metropolitan, there are clear indications that actual implementation of specific decrees had begun at Speyer by 1219.[87] This being the case, can we assume a similar *terminus ante quem* for Metz? There is compelling evidence that by 1220 at the latest efforts had been made in this regard.

We cannot be certain that the bishop of Toul attended the synod either, yet there is one small hint that he did. The schism created by the activities of the deposed Bishop Matthew undoubtedly agitated things to the point where all the energies of Rainald of Senlis were consumed in merely preserving his office. In 1217 he was brutally murdered by partisans of Matthew while conducting an episcopal visitation.[88] The impulse to do so may well have come from his metropolitan in 1216 when, having read the constitutions of the Council, the archbishop challenged his suffragans to carry out their respective responsibilities vis-a-vis their clergy. Rainald's death precipitated a schismatic election, causing both parties to appeal to Honorius III for a decision. One "*electus*" withdrew at length; the victor, Gerhard, count of Vaudemont, died the year after his election without receiving consecration.[89] Thus, although Bishop Rainald had probably intended to follow up his visitation with a diocesan synod at which the problems of his bishopric could be viewed against the background of the recent conciliar and provincial legislation, he was unable to do so, and the badly-torn status of the church at Toul in 1217 is an almost certain indication that no effort was or indeed could be made there to implement the decrees of Lateran IV in any reasonable time after the Council. Only with

---

or excommunicate him without papal approval; this in effect released Conrad from most obligations owed by suffragans to their metropolitan; cf. Bienemann, *Conrad von Scharfenberg* 56-57; Migne, *PL* III, 709; Potthast, *Regesta* I, Nr. 4610. Conrad's itinerary given in Bienemann 157 argues against any possible participation in a synod at Trier in September/October 1216.

[87] See below p. 256.

[88] On 13 November 1217 Pope Honorius III commanded Garin, the abbot of St. Evre *poenitentiarius Tullensis*, to dispense the benefit of absolution to Duke Theobald of Lorraine, nephew of the deposed Bishop Matthew, who had been vindicated of any complicity in the assassination; see Rodenberg, *MG Ep. s. XIII* I, Nr. 38; Potthast, *Regesta* I, Nr. 5619; Pressutti, *Regg. Hon. III* I, Nr. 870.

[89] Calmet, *Hist. eccles.* II 154; Heydenreich, *Metropolitangewalt* 57; *Chron. Albrici* 907: "*electus moritur*"; Diegel, *Bischofswahlen* 50.

the election of Eudes II de Sorcy in early 1219 did such an opportunity present itself.

The exact date of the new prelate's consecration is unknown, but it was presumably just before 4 May 1219, on which date the archbishop of Trier appeared with him as a witness to a document issued by Duke Theobald of Lorraine.[90] Bishop Eudes, who had been cathedral cantor at Toul before his elevation, undoubtedly received a vigorous charge from his metropolitan concerning the implementation of the Council's decrees within his diocese. His bishopric had suffered great financial hardships over the past several years, a fact which had prompted Pope Honorius III to grant Eudes' predecessor the privilege of retaining his cathedral prebends for a period of five years.[91] Presumably, Eudes enjoyed that boon as well. The presence of the archbishop at Toul in the spring of 1219 must have given the new prelate considerable leverage over against his own clergy whose schismatic behavior during the previous decade and more had reflected a church badly in need of correction. A provincial synod at this time is not an unlikely event, though the attendance of such by the other suffragans cannot be documented.

In contrast to the Dominican Jean de Mailly who gives little evidence that the statutes of Lateran IV were widely known in the diocese of Metz, another Dominican—the anonymous author of the *Vita Theoderici*—writing at almost the same time, noted that numerous attempts were made to implement *c.* 50 of the Lateran IV constitutions (*de visitationibus*) within the province of Trier for a number of years, but that by the time of his writing (ca. 1250) this practice had fallen into desuetude.[92] One such visitation was that which Pope Honorius III mandated 30 March 1218 to the Benedictine abbots (Jacob) of St. Matthias at Trier and (Garin) of St. Evre at Toul, and to the Cistercian abbots (Eustacius) of Himmerode and (Peter?) of Weiler-Bettnach in the dioceses of Trier and Metz respectively, for the monasteries in the province of Trier; since many of the religious houses had

---

[90] The *Chron. Albrici* 907, notes tersely: "*Gerardus Metensis primicerius, frater comitis Hugonis de Waudani Monte, in episcopum Tullensem electus moritur; et cantor Odo in episcopum promovetur.*" See also Heydenreich, *Metropolitangewalt* 57, citing a manuscript *Histoire de Metz* by Benoit, p. 439.

[91] Pressutti, *Regg. Hon. III* I, Nrs. 871, 872, 1099; Krabbo, *Besetzung* 54-55, note 2.

[92] *Gesta Trev.* 399: "*Factum est concilium generale apud Lateranum sub Innocentio papa anno Domini 1215, cui eciam interfuit Theodericus archiepiscopus; in quo concilio amputati sunt tres gradus consanguinitatis in matrimonio contrahendo; et statutum fuit ibi, ut de triennio in triennium haberentur capitula in singulis provinciis ad reformationem monasteriorum diversorum ordinum et visitationes fierunt; quod aliquot annis servatum, postmodum ivit in dissuetudinem. Fecit in concilio dominus papa sermonem, sumpto hoc themate: Desiderio desideravi hoc pascha manducare vobiscum, antequam patiar. Et mortuus est Innocentius papa eodem anno non evoluto. Fuit autem concilium mense Novembri.*"

fallen into both spiritual and temporal decline, the visitors were charged with the task of correcting and reforming all things which appeared in need of such.[93] That the visitation had the full approval of the metropolitan may be implied from the biographer's phrasing of his account, but the short-lived success of such measures also implies growing opposition to repeated inspections.

The continuator of the *Gesta Treverorum* also made mention that the archbishop had been present at the Council where "*amputati sunt tres gradus consanguinitatis in matrimonio contrahendo* (Lateran IV, *c.* 12)," and that "*Fecit in concilio dominus papa sermonem, sumpto hoc themate: Desiderio desideravi hoc pascha manducare vobiscum, antequam patiar.*" Apart from the account given by an anonymous monk from the archdiocese of Mainz in 1216, this is the earliest reference in any German source to the sermon which Innocent III delivered at the opening session of the Council on 11 November 1215. A copy of that sermon was among the documents which Archbishop Dietrich carried on his return from the Council and may have served his biographer roughly three decades later. The well-informed nature of the Trier account clearly points to direct use of the constitutions.[94]

Traces of Synodal Activity at Mainz

Whereas the contours of Archbishop Dietrich II of Trier's response to Lateran IV legislation immediately following the Council are quite easily recognized, evidence of similar activities by his neighbor, Archbishop Siegfried II of Mainz, is less discernable. This is singular, inasmuch as a strong synodal tradition existed at Mainz and Siegfried of Eppstein himself is known to have convened synods in 1209, 1213, 1221, and 1227. There is, however, once again inferential evidence that a provincial synod was held in late 1218: on 4 August 1218 Pope Honorius III granted to Bishop Otto of Würzburg exemption from personal attendance at synods summoned by his metropolitan, allowing him to send in his stead suitable representatives from his church. Given the previous record of animosity between Otto of Würzburg and Siegfried of Mainz, such a privilege was apparently issued in response to an urgent appeal by the suffragan bishop who had just been summoned to a provincial assembly.[95]

---

[93] Potthast, *Regesta* I, Nr. 5740; Pressutti, *Regg. Hon. III* I, Nr. 1202; Manrique, *Ann. Cisterc.* IV 62, and espec. 143: "*Etsi curiam pastoralis . . . quae in temporalibus et spiritualibus plurimum sunt collapse, iuxta decretum in concilio generali factum.*"

[94] See Wattenbach-Schmale, *DGQ* 351

[95] Würdtwein, *Nova subs.* III 83; Potthast, *Regesta* I, Nr. 5886; Pressutti, *Regg. Hon. III* I, Nr. 1570; Krabbo, *Besetzung* 21 note 3; Wendehorst, *Bistum Würzburg* 208. Binterim,

Yet another hint is buried in a letter which Pope Honorius III sent to Bishop
Andreas of Prague 2 April 1218.   Andreas was residing in Rome at the
time, having left his bishopric in late 1216 in the wake of a major dispute
with King Ottokar of Bohemia.   In the spring of 1217 the prelate imposed
an interdict and forbade all burials within his diocese.   Over time, however,
numerous members of the Bohemian clergy abandoned their bishop and
went over to the side of the Premyslid ruler.   Thus it was that during a
personal audience with the pontiff, Andreas had proposed having the
archbishop of Mainz excommunicate in the provincial synod all clerics who
had accepted, or in the future accepted benefices from the hands of a
layman, contrary to the ecclesiastical practices of the Prague church.
Honorius' letter approved the idea,[96] but the further ramifications thereof
are unknown.   Nevertheless, the request by Bishop Andreas and the
response by the pope give the distinct impression that provincial synods
were such a regular occurrence, that any infractions of the canonical rules
governing the Bohemian church could be dealt with at such an assembly in
the immediate future.

Assuming that such a synod was indeed convened in 1218 and/or 1219,
the primary purpose will have been the publication of the Lateran constitutions and the crusade decree *Ad liberandum* which the archbishop had
personally brought back from the Council.   Given the Council's emphasis
on the *cura animarum*, we may presume that those statutes which we have
associated with the 1209 provincial synod at Mainz were also presented once
again.   The crusade provisions were further bolstered by two papal letters
(dated 21 November 1216 and 28 February 1217) which commanded
obedience, particularly to the half-tithe which had been imposed on the
clergy, and instructed that these monies be transferred to the agents who had
been designated for that purpose.[97]   A third letter dated 4 January 1219 sug-

---

Concilien IV 342, states that no one mentions that Siegfried published the Council's decrees
upon his return, or that he summoned his suffragans to a synod, as was the case with the
archbishops of Trier and Salzburg; who can doubt it, however?

[96] Friedrich, *CdBoh* II 164, Nr. 177:   "*Cum, sicut in nostra proposuisti presencia
constitutus, concilium Maguntinum subiecerit excommunicacionum sentenciis clericos Pragensis
diocesis, qui deinceps de manu laica sine tuo vel successorum tuorum assensu iuxta pravam
eiusdem diocesis consuetudinem ecclesiastica receperint beneficia, vel sic recepta infra duos
menses post dictam sentenciam in tuis vel successorum tuorum manibus non ducerent
resignanda: nos tuis precibus inclinati, cum per hoc, sicut asseris, pravam eiusdem diocesis
consuetudinem predictum voluerit concilium aboleri, factum huismodi auctoritate apostolica
duximus approbandum.*"

[97] Würdtwein, *Nova subs.* III 49, 43; Potthast, *Regesta* I, Nrs. 5363, 5477; Pressutti, *Regg.
Hon. III* I, Nrs. 110, 381.

gests that the subsidy still had not been collected in full within Siegfried's province.[98]

Among those who may have accompanied the archbishop to Rome in 1215 was an anonymous cleric—most probably a monk from the Cistercian house at Aulesberg in Hesse—who, on the 17th day of March 1216, wrote a letter from Rome to his superiors in Germany, providing an eye-witness account of the proceedings of the Fourth Lateranum, many details of which are found in no other contemporary source. In the fourteenth or fifteenth century, the letter was bound into a codex at the Cistercian monastery at Haina in Hesse, to which the White Monks of Aulesberg had transferred in 1221, together with an early-thirteenth century copy of the constitutions of the Council, a portion of Innocent's initial sermon to the assembled body on 11 November 1215 (*Desiderio desideravi*), the papal bull of convocation (*Vineam domini Sabaoth*), and a copy of the protocol.[99] The editors of the letter contend that it was the so-called Giessen Anonymous who brought back to Germany copies of the muniments of the Council which were later bound in the same codex as his letter of March 1216. While this is certainly possible, it is equally plausible that the documents relating to Lateran IV were acquired by Aulesberg/Haina at some later date—copies of originals acquired by the archbishop of Mainz, produced as an accompaniment to the Giessen Anonymous letter.

Whatever the original provenance of the Giessen Anonymous' documents, it is obvious that early thirteenth-century clerics in the province of Mainz had access to the major papal letters relating to Lateran IV, as well as to a set of the decrees which the archbishop had published. Apart from the Giessen Anonymous, the contemporary literary sources from Hesse are silent on the matter of the Council,[100] but Thuringian chronicles confirm

---

[98] Würdtwein, *Nova subs.* III 76; Potthast, *Regesta* I, Nr. 5959; Pressutti, *Regg. Hon. III* I, Nr. 1783.

[99] Kuttner/Garcia y Garcia, "A New Eyewitness Account" 115-164, especially 119-120.

[100] E.g., the *Chronicon Moguntinum*, begun about 1253 by a priest named Christian residing at Mainz, drew on some annals which are now lost for the years 1208-1247, and although he went to some length to discuss the problems which befell the church at Mainz during the archiepiscopal schism and the throne controversy, he omitted any reference at all to the Council and its reform program aimed at re-invigorating clerical discipline and religious life. The silence of this source should not be construed as evidence that information about the Council was lacking at the time Christian wrote, however, but rather as an indication that the Fourth Lateranum simply did not interest him within the context of his work. According to Potthast, *Repertorium* III 248, the author was Archbishop Christian (1249-1251), who wrote the account ca. 1252 after he stepped down. Cornelius Will, "Über den Verfasser des Chronicon Moguntinum (liber de calamitate ecclesiae Moguntinae)," *HJb* 2 (1881) 335-387, argues that the author was not Archbishop Christian, but rather the auxiliary bishop Christian of Livonia, which Wattenbach-Schmale, *DGQ* 138-139, accepts.

the fact that the legislation of Innocent III had been officially and extensively proclaimed throughout the archdiocese.   About the year 1276 the *Chronica S. Petri Erfordensis moderna* were begun at Erfurt, and in the fourteenth century a chronicle was written at the Benedictine monastery of Reinhardsbrunn, not far from Erfurt.   For the years 1209-1215 both incorporated the text of a lost *Historiae* of Reinhardsbrunn, written ca. 1217.[101] The author of the *Historiae* was quite correctly informed on several details of the Fourth Lateranum, leaving little doubt that he possessed actual copies of its major muniments.   Although it is possible that the scribe, or some member of his house, had attended the Council personally, as Benedictines they would probably not have received individual copies at that time.   Rather, they were subject to the ecclesiastical control of the archbishop and would have been given the constitutions at his instigation.   It is therefore reasonable to conclude that the representatives of Reinhardsbrunn, or of the prominent collegiate churches of Erfurt, received knowledge of Innocent's decrees at the 1218 synod held at Mainz. Archbishop Siegfried's copy of those decrees or another preserved at Erfurt appear to have served as the basis for the *Historiae Reinhardsbrunnenses*.

From these lost *Historiae*, some sixty years after the event, another scribe at Erfurt excerpted into the *Chronica S. Petri*.[102]   This account is less dependent upon the protocol than other German sources, yet the scribe was clearly aware of this document.   He also reveals a familiarity with the bull of convocation (*Vineam domini Sabaoth*) and with details of actions taken in the various sessions, such as the confirmation of the election of Frederick II as the German king and the resolution of the civil war in England.   He likewise refers to the opening sermon of Innocent III on 11

---

[101] Wattenbach-Schmale, *DGQ* 411-412.

[102] *MGH SS rer. Germ.* II 213: "*m.cc.xv. Innocencius papa, ut vires ecclesie metiretur, ad cunctas orbis partes, eciam remociores, apostolica accintus magnanimitate dirigit apices preceptivos, firmiter edicens, ut, quisquis archiepiscoporum, episcoporum, abbatum, prepositorum atque quorumcumque ecclesiarum prelatorum ad concilium generale in festo sanctorum omnium Lateranis celebrandum excitus non occurat, per censuram ecclesiasticam apostolico se feriendum ense non ambigat. Ecce sagena Petri per mare magnum et spaciosum manibus expansa, pusillos cum magnis exhinbens, trahit milia milium; tamen et si velis archiepiscopos recensere, eorum numero sitas cum diligenti eciam calculatione non queat computari. Denique sub pressura multitudinis episcopi, abbates et quam plures alii novissimum in concilio spiritum exalaverunt, non pape, sed Deo redditur racionem de cunctis, que in hac vita gesserunt. Ibi facta primum exhortacione in sermone polito de fide, spe et caritate disseruit, deinde Fridericum augustum futurum imperatorem publice declaravit, cuique ecclesie sua iura esse servanda innotuit, regem Anglie et reges alios suo apostolatui subiciens, instituta edidit ecclesiarum. His et aliis modis suum terminavit concilium, estimans sui precium laboris, si pro cunctis suis participibus tam copiosam cleri multitudinem ad sui presenciam apostolatus evocasset.*"

November and the death of one of the participants. The source for such details was clearly an eye-witness, undoubtedly someone who attended the Council as a member of the Mainz delegation.

About the year 1261 an anonymous Franciscan friar at Erfurt began the *Chronica minor auctore Minorita Erphordensi*, a work which was completed rather quickly and re-issued in subsequent recensions in 1265, 1267/8, and 1272.[103] From this it is clear that the scribe had access to a considerable collection of materials which made his task easier, including items pertaining to the Fourth Lateran Council. Unlike previously-discussed accounts, however, his finds the constitutions enacted by Innocent III in 1215 scattered among other items related to the latter's pontificate.[104] Rather than an actual copy of the constitutions and other muniments of the Council, it therefore appears that the author of this portion of the *Chronica minor* at Erfurt made use of the *Decretales* of Pope Gregory IX or the *Compilatio quarta* of Johannes Teutonicus wherein were found the decretals of Innocent III. The materials available to the writer of the *Historia Reinhardsbrunnenses* may thus have been long since replaced by the more

---

[103] Wattenbach-Schmale, *DKQ* 409; Potthast, *Repertorium* III 329.

[104] *Cron. minor Erph.* 644-649: "*Hic fecit plurimas decretales. . . . Hic papa constituit, ut ultra quartum gradum consanguinitatis licite contrahatur matrimonium [Lateran IV, c. 50; Decretal. Greg. IX. l.IV, tit.14, c.8]. . . . Extra. de electione: Venerabilem [Lateran IV, c. 23; Decretal. Greg. IX. l.I, tit.6, c.34]. . . . Iste papa Innocensius III statuit, ut in omni Christianorum provincia notabiliter distinguatur habitus Judeorum in utroque sexu [Lateran IV, c. 68; Decretal. Greg. IX. l. V, tit.6, c.15]. Constituit eciam, et nullus clericus habeat plura beneficia ecclesiastica vel duas dignitates absque dispensacione sedis apostolice [Lateran IV, c. 29; Decretal. Greg. IX. l.III, tit.6, c.18]. . . . Hic papa Innocencius eciam constituit, ut quilibet adultus ad minis semel in anno plebano suo confiteatur et ad minis in pascha percipiat corpus Domini, nisi de consilio eius abstineat; et constituit, quod confessor nulla racione prodat peccatum confitentis. Extra. de penitenciis: Omnis utriusque [Lateran IV, c. 21; Decretal. Greg. IX. l. V, tit.38, c.12]. . . . Hic papa eciam constituit, ut prelati subditos clericos suos seu presbiteros exactionibus gravare non presumant et visitantes parrochias et ecclesias evectionum numerum non excedant, ita quod episcopu XX vel XXX habeant [ministros], archidiaconi V vel VII, decani sive archipresbiteri II, et quod sine canibus venaticis et avibus proficiscantur, ne graventur ecclesie nimietate expensarum. Extra. de censibus: Cum apostolus [Lateran IV, c. 33, drawing on Lateran III, c. 4; Decretal. Greg. IX. l. III, tit.39, c.6]. . . . Et constituit, ut in ecclesiis doctores et studium gramatice habeantur, et quod metropolitana ecclesia magistrum habeat, qui legat in theologica facultate, et quod illi in expensis provideatur [Lateran IV, c. 11; Decretal. Greg. IX. l. V, tit.5, c.4]. . . . Hic papa Innocencius III. pontificatus sui anno 18, anno vero Domini 1214. in Lateranensi palacio plurimum sollempne et isti mundo generale concilium celebravit in festo omnium sanctorum. Ibi prelatorum et aliorum multitudo maxima congregata fuit. In quo ipse papa multas constituciones edidit, et inter alias de passagio et cruce signandis in subsidium Terre Sancte maxime mentem posuit, et per ecclesiam universalem orationes ante Agnus Dei in missa pro Terra Santa instituit, videlicet psalmum Deus venerunt gentes cum precibus et collecta Deus qui admirabili providentia.*"

current canonistic collections when the Franciscan scribe set himself to his task. Because of the importance which Erfurt enjoyed within the eastern reaches of the archdiocese of Mainz,[105] the availability of the Lateran IV decrees for the clergy of Thuringia from the time of the 1218 provincial synod cannot be questioned.

As noted above with respect to Salzburg and Trier, the constitutions of the Council laid the responsibility for effecting reform among the clergy on the shoulders of the episcopacy. It may thus have been in connection with this presumed 1218 provincial synod that Archbishop Siegfried II appointed his cathedral scholastic, *magister* Conrad—the former dean at Speyer, to conduct visitations of the province in direct compliance with *cc.* 6 and 12. That Conrad's efforts met fierce opposition in some quarters, not unlike that encountered by his Salzburg counterparts, is revealed by a letter of Honorius III dated 20 February 1220 in which *magister* Solomon of Würzburg and two other clerics were commanded to execute the penalties imposed by Conrad on certain adulterous priests of the province.[106] Although details are lacking, it appears that some of the more truculent clerics had raised objections to Conrad's investigations, claiming that he had no authorization to do so. Conrad in turn had placed them under the ban of excommunication, which they still ignored. Solomon and his colleagues were assured that the visitations were approved and that the penalties were to be carried out.

The impact of the provincial synod held in 1218 at Mainz upon the comprovincial bishops is not altogether clear. It is certain that the bishop of Constanz was present at Rome in 1215 where he received the acts of the Council, and that he convened a synod shortly after his return, where the decrees of Innocent III would have been publicly proclaimed.[107] Another synod held 26 March 1221 at Constanz resolved a dispute between the abbot

[105] On the intellectual position of Erfurt, see Gray Cowan Boyce, "Erfurt Schools and Scholars in the Thirteenth Century," *Speculum* 24/1 (1949) 1-18.

[106] Horoy, *Honorius III opera* Nr. 83; Potthast, *Regesta* I, Nr. 6196; Sudendorf, *Regestrum* III 53, Nr. 35; Pressutti, *Regg. Hon. III* Nr. 2336; Pixton "Konrad von Reifenberg" 71-72.

[107] Ladewig, *Regg. Const.* I, Nr. 1299; cf. Nr. 1435: while yet at Rome in the days following the Council in 1215, Bishop Conrad of Constanz acted as referee in a dispute between the monastery of St. John in Turtal and the Hospitallers at Bubikon. His decision was publicly announced and accepted at the first diocesan synod held after his return from the Council. At the next synod, which the scribe states was held "*processu vero temporis,*" the abbot of St. John proclaimed that he had purchased property in several locations with the money received in the settlement with the Hospitallers. The wording of the account suggests that synods were frequent events under Bishop Conrad, and there is no reason to assume that the first one held after his return was other than in 1216. See also Brehm, "Konstanzer Synoden" 18-19; Hauck, *KGD* IV 7 note 1.

and monks of Salem and the monastery of St. Georgien in the Black Forest
(Silva Negra) over a chapel at Schönau: St. Georgien claimed that it was
a mother church, not filiated to the church at Herzogenenweiler (which in
turn was subject to Salem) as Salem maintained. According to the
testimonies given before the synod, the claims of Salem were upheld.[108]
Present at both synods presumably was Abbot Ulrich of St. Gall who on 7
April 1217 received papal permission to wear the miter and annulus,
symbols of the episcopal office, on account of his probity and devotion.
The indulgence granted him the right to use them in all processions and
synods, and especially on feast days.[109]

The annals and chronicles of the period also attest that the proceedings
of Lateran IV had become widely known within the diocese at an early
date. About the year 1229/1230 the former prior of the Premonstratensian
convent of Ursperg in Swabia, Burchard, began to compile his *Chronicon
Urspergensium* which reveals a familiarity with canon law, making frequent
references to Gratian, Irenaeus, and the decretal collection of Peter of
Benevento. It has been suggested that he had perhaps studied canon and/or
Roman law at Bologna before assuming the provostship at Ursperg in 1215.
As the latter, he was presumably present at the Lateran Council and quite
certainly in attendance at the synods held thereafter by the bishop of
Constanz and the archbishop of Mainz. That Burchard was interested in the
Council and had direct access to its muniments is shown from his inclusion
of the letter of convocation (*Vineam domini Sabaoth*) and the complete
protocol in his chronicle.[110] Given his acquaintance with and interest in
canon law, however, it is puzzling that he did not mention any of the
constitutions. Nevertheless, 1229/1230 can be accepted as the *terminus ante
quem* for the general familiarization with the decrees of Lateran IV within
the diocese of Constanz, a process which had begun with the diocesan synod
of 1216.

Also within that diocese lay the Benedictine abbey of Engelsberg where,
between 1223 and 1241, a monk commenced a *Continuatio* of the *Annales*
which until about 1175 had been kept at St. Blaise. Among his entries is

---

[108] *Fürstenberg. UB* V 86, Nr. 128 (*"Siquidem hec sententia data fuit in generali capitulo
nostro"*).

[109] Rodenberg, *MG Ep. s. XIII* I, Nr. 25; Potthast, *Regesta* I, Nr. 5512; Pressutti, *Regg.
Hon. III* I, Nr. 480.

[110] *Burchardi Chron.* 105 (*Vineam Domini Sabaoth*), 111: *"Anno ab incarnatione verbi
MCCXV. Celebrata est sancta universalis synodus Rome in ecclesia Salvatoris, que
Constantiniana vocatur mense Novembri, . . ."* Discussion of authorship in O. Abel, "Die
Ursperger Chronik," *NA* XI (1858) 76-115; Georg Gronau, "Die Ursperger Chronik und Ihr
Verfasser" (Dissertation Berlin, 1890) 5-87; Wattenbach-Schmale, *DGQ* 115-117; Potthast,
Repertorium II 609.

an abbreviated version of the protocol,[111] which leaves uncertain the matter of whether he had direct access to the documents of the Council. What little he conveys could have been extracted from the more complete *Chronicon Urspergensium* being maintained not far away, but his inclusion of the Council's notice in his record suggests that this great event and its actions had become known to the members of his house.

Not all contemporary writers in the diocese of Constanz felt compelled to make mention of the Council, however. About the year 1215, for example, a Premonstratensian canon named Walther at the convent of St. Peter in Marchtal began to write a history of his foundation in which no reference is made to Lateran IV. Such an omission is clearly understandable, given the specific purpose of the work, but it suggests that the contemporary abbot of Marchtal had not personally attended the Council: elsewhere in Germany such a notation was of obvious importance to religious houses, since the Council was the most significant and spectacular ecclesiastical event of its day; participation in it by some local dignitary was certainly worth mention in the annals and chronicles.[112] The same observation can be made with respect to the history of the Benedictine monastery of St. Gall, completed in 1232 by Conrad de Fabaria, a monk at that house and priest at St. Othmar's church. His *Casus S. Galli continuatio tertia* covers the period 1203-1232 and, although it mentions the fact that Abbot Ulrich of St. Gall went to Rome several times between 1212 and 1216 in behalf of Otto IV—most recently in June 1215, it is silent about any role he might have played in negotiations during the Council.[113] And yet, it seems most likely that Abbot Ulrich would have been there. Given the Council's legislation which affected conventuals (such a the triennial general chapters) and placed restrictions upon their involvement in the *cura animarum*, it is furthermore puzzling that Conrad's own personal interests did not produce some notation about it in his history.

Bishop Hartbert of Hildesheim, on the other hand, did not attend the Council, inasmuch as he had been excommunicated for his continued support of the deposed Emperor Otto IV. Following Hartbert's death on 21 March 1216, the Benedictine monk from Fulda and former cathedral canon

---

[111] *Annales S. Blasii* 280: "*1215. Domnus Innocentius papa III. habuit Rome in Lateranensi ecclesia concilium, cui interfuerunt 415 episcopi, abbates et alii prelati 800.*" See Wattenbach-Schmale, *DGQ* 320; Pl. Teuner, "Die ältesten Jahrbücher Engelbergs," *Geschichtsfreund* 8 (1852) 101-113; Ferdinand Güterbock, *Engelbergs Gründung und Erste Blüte 1120-1223* (Zürich,1948) 75-80.

[112] *MGH SS* XXIV 662-683; Wattenbach-Schmale, *DGQ* 309.

[113] *MGH SS* II 165-183; Böhmer, *Fontes* II (1849) lxxi; Wattenbach-Schmale, *DGQ* 289; Potthast, *Repertorium* III 608;. G. Meyer von Knonau, *Mitteilungen von St. Gallen* 17 (1879) 133-252.

at Hildesheim, Siegfried of Lichtenberg, assumed the episcopal chair. In spite of the general incompetence which led to his resignation in 1221, there is evidence that he at least made some effort to hold synods and to publish the decrees of the Council: in 1216 the Cistercian monastery at Wöltingerode sought a papal exemption from synodal attendance, suggesting that the new bishop had recently tried to compel such despite the general dispensation granted previously to the entire Order. A synod in 1216 would certainly have presented the legislation of Lateran IV to the Hildesheim diocesan clergy. Perhaps it was in response to the constitutions of Innocent III that in 1216 the cathedral *cellerarius* at Hildesheim, Burchard, established a prebend at the nearby Kreuzkirche, the occupant of which was obligated to celebrate the Mass and to participate in the choir service. We are on firmer ground with 1220, however, when this same prelate convened a synod just months before stepping down from his office.[114] Without knowing just how the documents of the Council had been obtained, we may nonetheless conclude that their contents were made known to the Hildesheim church between 1216 and 1220.

On 30 April 1218 Pope Honorius III confirmed the request made by Bishop Henry of Strasbourg with respect to *c.* 57 of the Lateran IV constitutions concerning the use of the interdict, in order to protect his church in the event the Hospitallers and other members of his diocese acted contrary to the decrees *"quia non sunt bulla sedis apostolice roborata."*[115] In 1219 Bishop Henry once again wrote the pope, this time seeking relief from the crusade tax, claiming that too many other problems which had arisen since the Lateranum required his prior attention.[116] On 13 February 1220 Pope Honorius III wrote the clergy and people of the Alsatian see, confirming that for the sum of 200 Marks he had exempted them from the crusade half-tithe, *"quod a tempore dicti concilii guerris continuis regionis afflicti graviter et oppressi ac alias rapinas et incendiis multipliciter lacessiti tantam sterilitatem in anno sustinuere praesenti, quod vitam inopem deducentes vix possint de tot calamitatibus respirare."*[117] The statutes and other documents distributed at the Council were thus certainly known in the Strasbourg diocese before this time, even though Bishop Henry had not been present in Rome in 1215 to receive them. Some unnamed agent(s) of the Curia had made the Strasbourg population at least aware of the provisions of the decree *Ad liberandum.* The obvious persons were Abbot Peter of

---

[114] Janicke, *UB Hilds* I, Nrs. 685, 690, 751.

[115] Hessel, *Regg. Strassburg* II 20, Nr. 839; Hefele, *Conciliengeschichte* V 897.

[116] Hessel, *Regg. Strassburg* II 23, Nr. 852.

[117] Würdtwein, *Nova subs.* XIII 243; Potthast, *Regesta* I, Nr. 6193; Pressutti, *Regg. Hon. III* I, Nr. 2329.

Neubourg and those other papally-designated crusade-preachers for the ecclesiastical province of Mainz. But, Abbot Peter probably also attended the Council and may have been the channel through whom the complete set of decrees came into the hands of the bishop. If Bishop Henry attended the 1218 provincial synod, he was undoubtedly made aware of the papal admonitions to Archbishop Siegfried as well. Thus, although there is no direct reference to a diocesan synod at Strasbourg until 1227/1229,[118] there can be no doubt that by 1218/1219 at the latest the clergy of this diocese were aware of the statutes of Lateran IV, whether as the result of a recent episcopal assembly, of publication at the provincial level, or of systematic agitation by papally-appointed crusade-preachers and subsidy collectors.

About the year 1240 an anonymous scribe at Abbot Peter's Alsatian monastery of Neubourg began a continuation of the *Annales Marbacenses* which contains a rather extensive account of the Fourth Lateranum, including almost verbatim the protocol.[119] His possession of this actual document (or a copy) seems all the more probable given his former abbot's presumed role in the transmission of the Council's muniments back to Strasbourg in 1216, and if copies of the protocol were available to various religious houses, it is equally valid to assume the accessibility of the constitutions as well.

In stark contrast to the extended account of the Council found in the annals of Marbach/Neubourg, the *Annales Sancti Trudperti*, maintained at the Benedictine house of St. Trudpert in the Münsterthal (southern Black Forest) state briefly: *"1215. Hoc anno factum est Romanum concilium sub Innocentio papa."*[120] Dating from the second half of the thirteenth century

---

[118] See below, pp. 358-359.

[119] *Ann. Marbac.* 173-174. Böhmer, *Fontes* II (1849) lxix, claimed that the annals were written at Neuburg ca. 1186-1194, and continued there to 1238; R. Wilmans, "Das Chronicon Marbacense, sonst Annales Argentinenses genannt, und sein Verhältnis zu den übrigen Geschichtsquellen des Elsasses," *Archiv* 11 (1858) 115-139, argues against Böhmer, *Fontes* II 96-111, that the text for the years 1162-1238 inclusive is by one hand, rejecting the notion that a *continuatio* to the original work was written at Neubourg. The introduction to the edition of the Annals published in 1907 in the *MGH Scriptores rerum Germanicarum* xiii, draws on a further half-century of debate in stating that the *Continuatio* for the years 1213-1238 was written at Neuburg to which the responsibility for maintaining the Annals had been transferred 1226/1236. Wattenbach/Schmale, *DGQ* 120, sees three stages: 1) written ca. 1194-1200 by Provost Friedrich of St. Thomas who was chaplain of Henry VI and also served Philip of Swabia; 2) the continuation after 1201, which was later augmented to 1208, and was written at Marbach after 1230; 3) from there the work passed to Neuburg where it was glossed and near the end of the 1240s made part of the present codex. See also *Dictionnaire des Auteurs Cisterciens* M-O (1978) 564, which notes that controversy centers over the possibility that Peter is himself the continuator of the *Annales Marbacenses*.

[120] *MGH SS* XVII 293.

and covering the period 593-1246, these annals are purportedly independent of other sources from the late twelfth century. But, their close similarity to the *Annales Zwifaltenses* points to a common source for both.[121] The latter, maintained at Zwiefalten near Weissenburg, in the diocese of Constanz, contain the terse statement: "*1216. Concilium Romae claro iam canone pollet,*"[122] and may date from the first half of the thirteenth century.

At the time of the Council one of the most important protégés of Bishop Conrad of Metz and Speyer occupied the office of cathedral dean at Speyer. As such, he was the cathedral dignitary most responsible for maintaining discipline among the canons. But this *magister* Conrad had also been appointed as a crusade preacher for the province of Mainz in 1213, and in this role he was a probable participant at the Council.[123] To him may be traced whatever copies of the statutes were available to the dioceses of Metz and Speyer after 1216. That the statutes were in fact known within the bishopric of Speyer almost at once is attested by an episcopal charter issued on 23 August 1219 for the collegiate church of St. Germanus in the city of Speyer itself, establishing a school for the training of young boys in response to Lateran IV's *c.* 11.[124]

---

[121] Wattenbach-Schmale, *DGQ* 328.

[122] *MGH SS* X 58, line 15. Cf. Wattenbach-Schmale, *DGQ* 314 (citing E. Schneider, *Die Zweifeltner Annalen und Ortliebs Chronik* (1889); also *Württ. GQ* 3 (1889) 7-22); Potthast, *Repertorium* II 353.

[123] Pixton, "Anwerbung" 167, 171, 185; Idem, "Konrad von Reifenberg" 71-72.

[124] Moné, *ZGO* 1 (1850) 270-271, Nr. 5: "*Confirmantis assensum inveniri decet in his precipue faciliorem, que constituta in alicuius ecclesie statum fuerint meliorem. . . . ita ut prebenda scole et scola perpetualiter annexa sit prebende, sic ut qui in eandem successerit prebendam, gratis, exceptis minoribus munusculis, quae in consuetudine habentur, doceat scolares, et hoc in propria persona, nisi forte de gratia capituli adjutorem obtineat, et tam diu sit in percipiendo, quam diu fuit in docendo, nisi molestia egritudinis excusetur, in quo casu vicem suam, si cronica fuerit egritudo, peraliam personam ad consilium capituli assumendam supplebit. His ita propositis supplicaverunt, ut super premissis assensum nostrum simul et favorem ipsis exhibere dignaremur.*"

Lateran IV, *c.* 11: "*Quia nonnullis propter inopiam et legendi studium et opportunitas proficiendi subtrahitur, in Lateranensi concilio pia fuit institutione provisum, ut 'per unamquamque cathedralem ecclesiam magistro, qui clericos eiusdem ecclesiae aliosque scholares pauperes gratis instrueret, aliquod competens beneficium praeberetur, quo et docentis relevaretur necessitas et via pateret discentibus ad doctrinam'. Verum quoniam in multis ecclesiis id minime observatur, nos praedictum roborantes statutum, adicimus ut no solum in qualibet cathedrali ecclesia sed etiam in aliis, quarum sufficere poterunt facultates, constituatur magister idoneus a praelatos, cum capitulo seu maiori ac saniori parte capituli eligendus, qui clericos ecclesiarum ipsarum et aliarum gratis in grammaticae facultate ac aliis instruat iuxta posse. Sane metropolitana ecclesia theologum nihilominus habeat, qui sacerdotes et alios in sacra pagina doceat et in his praesertim informet, quae ad curam animarum spectare noscuntur. . .*" The connection between the Lateran IV decree and the establishment of the

Speyer charters reveal only limited use of the synod in the twelfth century, yet, almost from the time of Conrad of Scharfenberg's accession in 1200 there is a steady stream of synodal evidence and synods must have been regarded as regular and normal gatherings on the eve of the Council.[125] Since 1212, however, Conrad had held two bishoprics and was imperial chancellor for Frederick II. While he clearly had little time for the pastoral demands of those offices, it is congruent with pre-Council practice to assume that the statutes of Lateran IV, evidence of the implementation of which is clear by 1219, were published at some unrecorded diocesan synod held shortly before that time. The simultaneous administration of Speyer and Metz by Conrad of Scharfenberg, the constant companion of the Hohenstaufen kings until his death in 1224, is reflected in the annalistic traditions maintained by these two bishoprics during the thirteenth century. The brief notice found in the *Annales Spirenses* which cover the period 1184-1259 and were probably written during the decade of the 1250s suggests some acquaintance with the documents which Dean Conrad brought back to Speyer from Rome, but the orientation of the account is noteworthy, since it reveals a perception that the recognition of Frederick II was the most important aspect of the Council.[126] The otherwise quite customary citing of the protocol was not done by the Speyer scribe, however.

---

school at St. Germanus is suggested by Specht, *Unterrichtswesen* 335. Related to the strengthening of the schools in Speyer is another document dated 1226 which records the establishment of an endowment by a certain devout widow named Petrissa, from which bread was to be purchased for the poor scholars attending the cathedral school; cf. Moné, "Brotstiftung für arme Schüler im Dom zu Speier," *ZGO* 2 (1851) 136-138. Moné notes that in the thirteenth century there were numerous complaints in the region of the Upper Rhine regarding travelling students. He suggests that the creation of this endowment was an attempt to tie such young clerics to the ecclesiastical structure in order to wean them away from their vagabond lifestyle. That these itinerant scholars often embraced a life which had an adverse effect upon younger clerics is perhaps generally known, but a specific piece of evidence may be pertinent in this respect. Preserved in the Hofbibliothek at Karlsruhe, MS Reichenau Nr. 109, is what appears to be a copy of a thirteenth-century synodal statute: "*Quoniam virus haereticae pravitatis partibus Alemanniae, nescimus a quo fonte latenter infusum, nostris heu temporibus se usque adeo dilitavit . . . Quia vagi scholares, qui vulgo Curhardini vocantur, deo abhominabilem vitam ducunt, divinum officium invertunt, unde etiam laici scaldalizantur, monachis dant apostatandi materiam, quippe quos de claustris suis recedentes et alibi in seculo receptaculum non invenientes ipsi in suum recipiunt consortium: statuit haec sancta synodus prohibendo, ne quis clericus eos recipiat vel aliquid det eisdem; quod si fecerit, a superiori suo suspensus acriter corrigatur. nullus etiam scolaris recipiatur in chorum et scolas frequentans.*" The date of the synod is unknown, yet the period 1219-1226 provides a most suitable context.

[125] Cf. pp. 68-69.

[126] *Ann. Spir.* 80-85: "*Anno domini 1215 coronatus est rex Fridericus Aquisgrani. Eodem anno celebratum fuit concilium Rome a papa Innocente III, et confirmatus est rex Fridericus in regno Romano.*" See also Wattenbach-Schmale, *DGQ* 128.

There are no annalistic sources which help establish the *terminus ante quem*
for the publication of the constitutions of the Council in the bishopric of
Chur. Despite this, however, and without any indication that a synod had
been held, it is clear that the bishop of Chur took steps in early 1219
towards implementing the Council's decrees which he had received
personally in 1215. If he attended the provincial synod posited for Mainz
in 1218 their importance would have been stressed once more in his
presence. It was presumably in response to such assemblies that in April
1219 the prelate approved the establishment of a collegiate church at Misox
by one Henry of Sax: the six canons who comprised the chapter there were
given responsibility for administering all of the parish churches in the Misox
valley, a move seen as intended to bring greater uniformity to the *cura
animarum* of this region.[127]

We have noted earlier that at some time between 1203/1215 Bishop
Bernhard of Paderborn announced that some property at Kachtenhofen
which produced eighteen *denarii* annually and which belonged to the
custodia of the cathedral church had been transferred to the monks at
Waddenhart (Marienfeld) by the cathedral *custos C.* for a rent of two and
one-half *solidos*, which was to paid annually in the fall "*cum Orlinchusen
synodus celebratur, in cuius ecclesia parochia hec bona sita sunt.*"[128] In
1219 the agreement was renegotiated, reflecting perhaps rising values or
greater need for money on the part of the Paderborn cathedral chapter:
Bishop Bernhard announced that the *custos* Volrad had re-conferred the
property at Kachtenhusen on Marienfeld for a sum of three *solidi* which was
to be paid in heavy Paderborn coin at the annual fall synod at Orlinghausen.[129] As with several other suffragan bishoprics of Mainz, 1219 thus
represents the logical *terminus ante quem* for the publication of the Lateran
IV constitutions at Paderborn.

Although no known representatives of Halberstadt were present at Rome
in 1215, the Cistercian monk and *quondam episcopus Halberstadensis*,
Conrad of Krosigk, undoubtedly was. We have noted in Ch. Three that, as
a papally-designated crusade preacher, he had definite reasons for being at
the Council. He was thus the probable means of transmitting the decrees
back to Halberstadt where they were publicly proclaimed on 18 October
1216, in 1218, or 1220.[130] Conrad's role as transmitter is even more

---

[127] Affentranger, *Chur* 127: „*Die Bestimmungen des vierten Laterankonzils fanden auch
im Bistum Chur teilweise ihre Verwirklichung.*"

[128] *Lippische Regg.* I 121, Nr. 132; *Westf. UB* IIIA, Nr. 23.

[129] *Lippische Regg.* I 130, Nr. 151; *Westf. UB* IIIA, Nr. 141.

[130] Hauck, *KGD* V 168 note 1, gives 1215 (corrected by Dobenecker, *RdThur* II, Nr. 1697
(German translation in Gottfried August Benedict Wolff, *Chronik des Klosters Pforta nach
urkundlichen Nachrichten. Von der Gründung 1223 (bis zur Gründung der Schule 1543)* I

certain with respect to the neighboring bishopric of Naumburg. Not only did he have the responsibility of implementing the provisions of the crusading decree *Ad liberandum* within the province of Magdeburg, but he also was appointed acting bishop at Naumburg for the incumbent Engelhard who had taken up the cross. In October 1217 the latter is mentioned with the German forces at Acre, while on the 9th of that same month Conrad of Krosigk presided over a synod for the diocese of Naumburg. Inasmuch as Engelhard had not attended the Council himself, any assembly which he might have held with his clergy before his departure was most likely preoccupied with that concern; it is thus probable that Conrad's synod was the first occasion on which the clergy of Naumburg had received an official publication of the decrees.[131]

A similar argument can be made for the bishopric of Merseburg. Bishop Ekkehard was not personally present at Rome in 1215, but the following year, as also in 1217 and 1218, he convened synods, the records of which contain mention of juridical activities only.[132] There can be little doubt, however, that the constitutions of the Council were also published at one or more of these synods, since the Benedictine abbot, Siegfried of Pegau, must have returned with copies of them. Given Abbot Siegfried's presence at the Council and his presumed role in transmitting its decrees to the clergy of the diocese of Merseburg, it is surprising that no contemporary scribe at his house took up pen to make note of that in the *Annales Pegavienses*, however. Not until ca. 1280, after almost ninety years of inactivity, did someone resume entries for the years 1191-1227. Included in these is a short variation of the protocol of the Council and a notation that the latter was called *"principaliter propter subsidium terre sancte, . . ."*[133]   While

---

(Leipzig, 1843) 309f.), 1218 and 1220; cf. Schmidt, *UB Halb* I, Nrs. 503, 521; Hartzheim, *Concilia* III 504 (under date of 1219); Phillips, *Diözesansynode* 52. The recorded synodal acts involved the confirmation of property purchased by the collegiate church of Notre Dame in Halberstadt, and the resolution of a dispute between the foundation at Gernrode and two brothers regarding the office of *Truchsess*.

[131] Dobenecker, *RdThur* II, Nr. 1765; also Lepsius, *Hochstift Naumburg* 66; Krabbo, *Besetzung* 88. The synod dealt with the founding of the monastery Eisenberg by the Margrave of Meissen, but also gave attention to attacks against the diocese by the Thuringian *ministeriales*.

[132] Cf. *UB Merseburg* I, Nrs. 162-164. The recorded issues respectively were (1216) a conflict between the monastery Pforta and the knight Rüdiger of Lössen concerning fishing rights in the Luppe, Morluppe and the Pustenitzsee which was decided in favor of the monastery, (1217) the confirmation of a grant to the monastery Altzelle by Count Friedrich of Brehna, regarding ten hides in the vills of Glasau and Militz, and possessions in Ranstädt, and (1218) the confirmation to Altzelle the grant from Margrave Dietrich of Meissen of the vill Ranstädt and ten hides each in the vills of Glasau and Militz.

[133] Böhmer, *Fontes* II 314; *MGH SS* XVI 234-270; Wattenbach-Schmale, *DGQ* 414-418.

the current view is that the Pegau annalist extracted most of his material directly from the chronicle of Martin of Troppau, this notation suggests equally well that those charged with implementing the provisions of *Ad liberandum* within the diocese of Merseburg—namely, Conrad of Krosigk and others, had done so to such an extent that the clergy more than two generations later still remembered those activities.[134]

Bishop Hugh of Liège

Present with Abbot Siegfried of Pegau at the Council was Bishop Hugh of Liège who received a copy of the decrees to publish before his clergy. Hugh made a pilgrimage to the shrine of St. James at Campostella at the conclusion of the assembly, returning to his diocese and city several months later. During 1217 he convened a synod of his clergy at which Innocent's decrees were undoubtedly read.[135] It may have been on this occasion as well that the bishop ordained that children should be confirmed from age seven on, and that only adults need attend confession,[136] thus implementing directly *c*. 21 of Lateran IV (*Omnis utriusque sexus*) into the religious practices of his diocese.

Attending the synod which Bishop Hugh summoned was Abbot Waselin of the Benedictine house of St. Jacob in Liège who, because of something which hindered the bishop himself, pronounced the final blessing. Also present may have been one or more of the religious who had accompanied the prelate to Rome and who, between ca. 1216 and 1251, wrote detailed accounts of the assembly. Prominent among them was Reiner, since 1197 prior of St. Jacob's, who maintained *Annales* for the period 1194-1230

---

[134] The primary responsibility for preaching the crusade in northeastern Germany was given in April 1213 to *quondam episcopus* Conrad of Krosigk and Abbot Friedrich of Sichem. The former bishop is said to have recruited in Halle on the Saale, and his presence at the court of Frederick II at Eger on 10 June 1214 may have served a similar purpose. The efforts of Abbot Friedrich are virtually unknown, and the increased activity of John of Xanten in the provinces of Bremen and Magdeburg after 1216 allow the conclusion that Friedrich was no longer serving. Conrad of Marburg, mentioned in 1218 as "*predicator Maguntinensis et Misnensis diocesium*", also joined the efforts of Conrad of Krosigk and John of Xanten. Although the preaching activities of many decreased following the death of Pope Innocent III in July 1216, Conrad of Krosigk and Conrad of Marburg are said to have kept up their activities in northern Germany. For a detailed discussion and primary sources, cf. Pixton, "Anwerbung" 166-191.

[135] *Reineri Ann.* 674-676: ". . . *Ad memoriam futurorum scribimus, quod Waselinus abbas Sancti Jacobi benedixit sanctam sinodum, episcopo absente, cum tali quali debuit reverentia et sollemnitate.*" See also Binterim, *Concilien* IV 435. From the location of this reference among the items attributed to the year 1217, the synod seems to have been in mid- or late-summer.

[136] Browe, *Pflichtkommunion* 153; *MGH Concil* II (cap. 2) 807; a 1288 synod raised the age to twelve (cf. Mansi, *Collectio* XXIV 899).

contemporaneously with the events described. It was thus soon after the Council that he inserted the protocol almost verbatim into his record, undoubtedly using as his source that copy received by Bishop Hugh. Having personally witnessed the events of the Council, Reiner was also able to expand upon that terse account, noting that "the first day [i.e., the first session] was on the Feast of Saint Martin, the second on the 12th *kalends* of December, the third on the Feast of Saint Andrew; then was concluded this holy and catholic synod."[137] Reiner also included the announcement of the crusade provisions by Innocent III during the first session on 11 November, the excommunication of the English barons, and the action taken against Otto IV of Brunswick.[138] Any who read Reiner's annals would have been made quite aware of many aspects of the Council. The rather sizeable number of clerics from the diocese of Liège known to have been present in November 1215 would also have served to spread knowledge of Innocent's decrees beyond what was accomplished by the bishop's publication of them at his synod.

Shortly after 1236, the Cistercian monk Aubrey at Trois-Fontaines in the diocese of Châlons-sur-Marne completed a universal chronicle, drawing from several sources and providing considerable detail concerning events in the diocese of Liège. Similar to Reiner, he had access to the protocol of Lateran IV which he also cited verbatim, but, immediately following the

---

[137] *Reineri Ann.* 673-674: "*Celebrata est sancta universalis synodus in ecclesia sancti Salvatoris que Constantiniana vocatur, mense Novembri presidente domno Innocentio tercio papa, pontificatus eius octavo decimo anno. In qua fuerunt episcopi 412, inter quos extiterunt de precipuis patriarche duo, Constantinoplitanus et Jerosolemitanus; Antiochenus autem gravi languore detentus venire non potuit, sed misit pro se vicarium Antetadenum episcopum; Alexandrinus vero sub Sarracenorum dominio constitutus, fecit quod potuit, mittens pro se diaconum germanum suum. Primates autem metropolitani 71, ceterum abbates et priores ultra octigentos; archiepiscoporum vero, episcoporum, abbatum, priorum . . . non fuit certus numerus comprehensus; legatorum vero regis Sicilie in Romanorum imperatorem electi, imperatoris Constantinopolitani, regis Francie, regis Hungarie, regis Jerosolimitani, regis Cipri, regis Arragonum, necnon et aliorum principum magnatum et civitatum, et aliorum etiam locorum affuit multitudo. Prima dies sinodi fuit in festo sancti Martini, secunda 12. Kalendae Decembris, tercia dies in festo S. Andree; completa est sancta et universalis sinodus.*"

[138] *Reineri Ann.* 674 [lines 39-41]: "*Propter hanc violentiam tota Anglia sub interdicto ponitur a domno papa, qui omnes barones Anglie et fautores eorum excommunicavit in generali concilio, tunc quia idem rex signatus erat, tunc quia ipsum regnum ei resignaverat et ab ipso tributaliter receperat.*" [lines 45-46] "*Ottonem vero generali consilio excommunicatum et destitutum renuntiavit, . . .*" [lines 48-54]: "*Iste [Innocentius tertius] etiam generale consilium precedenti anno in Laterani celebravit, sicut lector in eodem anno invenire poteris. Ipse etiam fere totum mundum tam per se quam per executores suos zelo fidei accendit et ad signandum induxit, et viam euntium generali consilio ordinavit, et de propria substantia 30 milia librarum et 6 milia marcarum signatis assignavit, exceptis navibus et galeis quas Romanis et vicinis civitatibus preparavit; seque in propria persona tempore profectionis iterum in Sicilia promisit . . .*"

concluding statement of that report (". . . *ingens affuit multitudo*"), he
appended the line: "And these are the statutes of this great council, seventy
in number, briefly noted." After enumerating *cc.* 1-17, that is, the two
doctrinal decrees and the first fifteen reform constitutions, he broke off with
the remark: ". . . and many others until the seventieth."[139] There can
be no doubt that Aubrey had at least a summary of the constitutions before
him when he wrote, an item which a short trip to Châlons or even Liège
would have secured. His account is one of the most extensive of any
contemporary produced from within or near the region of the medieval
German church and demonstrates beyond reasonable doubt that the decrees
of Lateran IV were known to areas of Brabant and Champagne by
1230/1240 at the latest. The primary credit for this clearly belongs to
Bishop Hugh and his synod of 1217.

Between 1247 and 1251, another Cistercian monk, Aegidius of Orval
(Aureavallis in the diocese of Liège) produced the *Gesta episcoporum
Leodensium* which included an account of Bishop Hugh. While it may have
borrowed from Reiner, it is more likely that it cited directly from the
protocol which Hugh brought back from Rome. Breaking off after the line
"*In qua fuerunt episcopi 412*" of that document, Aegidius added his own
comment that "among them was Bishop Hugh of Liège. But, leaving that
which was enacted in the same council, let us return to our history of
Liège."[140] Thus, although Aegidius felt disposed to exclude the business
of the Council from this account, it is obvious that at the time he wrote, the
tradition at Liège which preserved the memory of the bishop's presence
there was still strong. This is even more apparent from the *Gesta
episcoporum Leodensium abbreviata* which Aegidius wrote about the same
time. The account derives in part from the general protocol of 1215 and
from the bull of convocation issued in 1213 (*Vineam domini Sabaoth*), but
it also includes details which are found in no other German source and

---

[139] *Chron. Albrici* 903: "*Et hec sunt capitula huius magni concilii numero 70 breviter
annotata.*" ". . . *sequuntur et alia multa usque ad 70.*" The contention by R. Wilmans,
"Über die Chronik Alberich's," *NA* 10 (1849) 175-223, that Aubrey was a monk at
Neumoustier near Huy in the diocese of Liège, rather than at Troisfontaines in the diocese of
Châlons has not found general acceptance; see P. Kassian Haid, "Ein Kleiner Beitrag zur
Kenntnis Alberichs von Troisfontaines und dessen Chronik," *Cistercienser-Chronik*, 20 Jg., Nr.
236 (1908) 289-290; Potthast, *Repertorium* II 167; and Kuttner and Garcia y Garcia, "A New
Eyewitness Account" 163.

[140] *Aegidii Aureaevall.* 119: "*Anno gratie 1215, tempore Innocentii tertii, celebrata est
sancta universalis synodus in ecclesia sancti Salvatoris que Constantiniana vocatur, mense
Novembri, presidente Innocentio papa tercio, pontificatus autem eius 18. anno. In qua fuerunt
episcopi 412, inter quos fuit Hugo Leodiensis episcopus. Sed quid in eodem concilio actum sit
relinquentes, ad nostram Leodensem historiam revertamur.*" See also Potthast, *Repertorium*
II 132; Wattenbach, *DGQ* II (6th ed., 1894) 147, 424, 462.

therefore must represent a local and independent historical tradition.[141] The otherwise unspecified source from which details concerning Bishop Hugh were drawn appears to have been a *Vita Hugonis* written by the bishop himself, from which chroniclers in and around Liège drew so many of their details relating to the Council.[142]

At roughly the same time as Aegidius was making his notations, another anonymous scribe wrote the *Continuatio* to the *Historia Walciodorensis Monasterii* (Waussor/Waulsort, a Benedictine house in the diocese of Liège) which once again shows a familiarity with the protocol of 1215 (whether direct or by extraction from some nearby chronicle), but it confounds the number of patriarchs and metropolitans given as present in that document (70) with the number of abbots, priors, etc. (800) to produce the figure 700 for the total number of monastic and chapter dignitaries present. The *Historia* also incorporates local tradition as well, which had preserved the fact that Abbot Werner of Waussor had personally attended the Council.[143] That fact alone assures us that the monks of this house were well aware of the legislation promulgated at that assembly and explains the inclusion of some mention of Lateran IV in the *Historia*.

The same can be said for the great Benedictine house of St. Truijen (St. Trond) where the anonymous author of the *Continuatio tertia* of the *Gesta abbatum Trudonensium* included an oblique reference to the protocol, but drew on the locally-preserved tradition that Abbot Christian was among the

---

[141] *Gesta Leod. Abb.* 134: *"1215. . . . Anno eodem papa Innocentius tertius decimo octavo anno celebrat concilium, ubi fuerunt quadringenti et duodecim episcopi, nuncii quinque regum et alii quamplurimi nuncii. Ibi quatuor ordines sunt instituti, scilicet Predicatorum, Minorum, Trinitas et Scolarum. Ibi fuerunt tres dies synodi, Prima die synodi Hugo Leodensis fertur sedisse inter prelatos in habitu laicali quasi comes in mantello et tunica scarlata, capellum viride habens in capite. Secunda die tanquam dux in cappa manicata viridi. Tercia die sicut episcopus mitratus. Et hec fecit, quia papa convocaverat omnes principes seculares et personas ecclesiasticas tribus annis ante. De hoc themate papa predicavit: Desiderio desideravi etc. Quidam episcopus Romanus visitavit Hugonem episcopum, cuius orationibus commendavit se et suam plebam. Cui Hugo inquisivit: 'Quantus est vester populus?' Cui episcopus: 'Domine, habeo circa mille viros in mea dyocesi.' Cui Hugo: 'Et ego habeo plus quam centum milia.' Et episcopus subiunxit: 'Domine, habeant prandium vestrum et orationes vestras, quia nimis habetis agere.' Papa contulit Hugoni episcopo lachrimam Salvatoris et iuncturam beati Pauli. Hic autem visitavit sanctum Jacobum, quia hoc voverat pro prelio de stepes."*

[142] See Friedrich Franz, "Die Chronica Pontificum Leodiensium. Eine verlorene Quellenschrift des XIII. Jahrhunderts" (Dissertation Strasbourg, 1882) 1-59.

[143] *Hist. Walciod.* 539 (line 5): *"Ipse [i.e., abbas Werner de Waussor] interfuit concilio Lateranensi, quod celebravit dominus Innocentius papa cum septingentis patriarchis, archiepiscopis et episcopis necnon et multis ecclesiasticis personis diversorum ordinum . . ."* Potthast, *Repertorium* I 617; Wattenbach, *DGQ* (6th ed., 1894) 154.

"*ultra 800*" monastic and chapter dignitaries who attended the Council.[144]
That fact, and the succession of *magister* John of Xanten as abbot of
St. Truijen in 1222, leaves no doubt that the religious of this house were
well acquainted with the statutes of the Council from the earliest possible
date. John had been a papally-appointed crusade-preacher 1213-1221, had
probably attended the Fourth Lateranum personally, and must have
possessed at least some of the major documents distributed there.[145]

St. Truijen lay in the Dutch-speaking regions of the diocese of Liège
which bordered on the see of Utrecht. Sometime during early 1217 Bishop
Otto II of Utrecht presided over a synod at which his vassal, Henry of
Smithuizen, surrendered the right of patronage over the church at Steen-
deren [Stenre] which he had held as a fief; the bishop thereupon granted this
property to the Premonstratensian convent at Bethlehem. The witness list
for the charter issued on this occasion makes it clear that laymen still
attended Utrecht synods at this time.[146] Serious problems with some of
those laymen may also have been on the synod's agenda. Lack of success
by the prelate resulted in a request for papal assistance, however. On 5
July 1218 Pope Honorius III commissioned the provost of Münster and the
deans of the cathedral and the collegiate church of St. Lüdeger in Münster
to put an end to certain acts of violence which were being committed against
the cathedral canons and other clergy in the diocese of Utrecht.[147]

The occasion of the synod must undoubtedly have been utilized for the
purpose of publishing the constitutions of Lateran IV as well, yet the fact
that Bishop Otto was not present at Rome in 1215 leaves the manner of their
transmission to Utrecht uncertain. That those provisions of the Council
relating to the impending crusade were commonly known is certain,
inasmuch as *magister* Oliver, the scholastic at Cologne, *magister* John of
Xanten and several other colleagues had been agitating all regions of the
Cologne province since 1213, enlisting the support of the laymen and clergy
alike in this grandiose undertaking. In the months following the Council

---

[144] *Gesta abb. Trudon. (continuatio III)* 393: "*Indic. Anno Domini 1215 ac anno
prelationis eiusdem 23. Innocentius papa tercius Lateranense consilium celebrat, ubi inter
ceteros ecclesiarum prelatos Christianus huius loci abbas vocatus interfuit.*"

[145] For John as a crusade-preacher, see Pixton, "Anwerbung" 174; further, *Caesarii
Dialogus* VII 23; Piot, *Cartulaire de St. Trond* 181, Nr. 145 (letter of Bishop Hugh of Liège
to John, then dean at Aachen, bearing date of 1222, informing him of his election as abbot of
St. Truijen and challenging him to reform it); Knipping, *REK* III, Nr. 392 (letter of Honorius
III to Archbishop Engelbert of Cologne, 19 August 1223, which mentions that John has become
abbot at St. Truijen); also H. Kesters, "Jan van Xanten, Kruistochprediker en abt van
Sint-Truiden," *Ons geestelijk erf* 28 (1954) 5-26.

[146] Sloet, *Oorkondenboek* 451, Nr. 446 ("*synodus episcopalis*"); Oppermann, "Untersuchungen" 261.

[147] *Westf. UB* III 67, Nr. 130; Potthast, *Regesta* I, Nr. 5856.

those same papal agents had been involved in collecting the half-tithe which Innocent III had imposed upon the clergy as well. Certainly this tax, which had been a major issue of the 1215 assembly at Rome, and the imminent departure of the bishop and many of the inhabitants of his diocese for the Holy Land were discussed at the synod.[148] It is thus surprising that those who maintained the annalistic tradition in the diocese of Utrecht found no reason to comment on either the Council or the prelate's pilgrimage to the Holy Land. Despite this silence, however, we may be certain that many of the clergy and laymen of this bishopric were aware of the details of Lateran IV from at least 1217, having been instructed in such by Bishop Otto II, by papally-appointed crusade preachers and tithe collectors, and by individuals from the neighboring diocese of Liège.

By the end of 1219 provincial synods had been held, and visitations conducted, in the provinces of Salzburg, Trier, and Mainz. The other three German metropolitan churches remain silent for the same period. It may be no mere coincidence, however, that the provinces of Cologne, Magdeburg and Bremen were the ones most adversely affected by the civil war of 1198-1215. Yet, despite the continued turmoil in northern Germany until the death of Otto of Brunswick in 1218, many of the numerous diocesan synods recorded for the years immediately following the Council were from that much-punished region. The occurrence of such diocesan gatherings suggests that the *constitutiones* of Lateran IV were published by bishops without even waiting for provincial introduction. Knowledge of the Council's decrees must also have spread quickly as the various individuals who were personally present related their experiences to others, and as papal agents traversed Germany in the business of the impending crusade. Some indication of the response to the half-tithe within the province of Magdeburg may be gained from the papal letter addressed to Archbishop Albrecht and his suffragans under date of 23 February 1218, in which they are accused of having done nothing at all![149]

---

[148] For Otto as a pilgrim, see Röhricht, *Deutscher im Heiligen Lande* 116, where sources are noted. The recruiting activities of the crusade preachers in Pixton, "Anwerbung" 175-191.

[149] Pressutti, *Regg. Hon. III* I, Nr. 1110; Rodenberg, *MG Ep. s. XIII* I, Nr. 49: "*Approbante generali concilio extitit ordinatum, ut omnes clerici, tam subditi quam prelati, vicesimam ecclesiasticorum proventuum usque ad triennium integre conferant in subsidium Terre Sancte, quibusdam dumtaxat religiosis exceptis ab hac prestatione merito eximendis, et hiis qui sunt illuc personaliter profecturi. Licet autem super modo ferendi ac distribuendi vicesimam ipsam vobis et aliis archiepiscopis ac episcopis dudum direxerimus scripta nostra, referentibus tamen multis audivimus, quod eadem nusquam est fere collecta. Unde super prudentia vestra non possumus non mirari, quod non habuistis super hoc aliam sollicitudinem tam pro vobis ipsis quam pro subditis vestris, cum non ignoretis constitutionem in ipso generali concilio factam contra illos qui fraudem in hoc scienter committerent, et fraudi lata negligentia comparetur. Cum igitur tempus immineat passagii generalis, fraternitati vestre per apostolica*

Resistance to the Crusade Half-Tithe

Financing the crusade by means of the half-tithe must have been a topic on the agenda when another Salzburg provincial synod convened in the fall of 1219. The three years stipulated by the decree *Ad liberandum* had by now elapsed, but the reproaches given many archbishops by Honorius III indicate that numerous delays had occurred.[150] The Salzburg annals do not make mention of this issue, yet a papal letter dated 25 March 1221 ordered the archbishop to deliver up those monies collected in his diocese.[151] Moreover, a Passau synod in 1220 dealt expressly with the half-tithe, indicating that the agitation of the clergy in that region had extended beyond the provincial synod by another year.[152] As was the case in 1216, the bishops of Regensburg and Brixen were absent from the Salzburg assembly.

Problems involving the rights of advocacy and patronage between the duke of Austria and the metropolitan of Salzburg resulting from the establishment of the bishopric of Seckau in 1218 must also have been dealt with.[153] Not until 1228 was this issue finally settled, however, when the

---

scripta precipiendo mandamus, quatinus singuli per vestras dioceses vicesimam ipsam diligentissime collegatis, ultra mare, secundum quod expressum est prioribus litteris quas super hoc vobis direximus, deferendam."

[150] Potthast, *Regesta* I 523, Nrs. 5956, 5959, to Bremen and Mainz respectively. In both instances the pontiff announced that he was sending Martin *cubicularius* and Johannes *marescalcus sui, militiae Templi et hospitalis Hierosolimitani fratres ad partes Alamanniae* to take charge of the collection.

[151] *Ann. Salisb.* 782: *"Concilium provinciale a domino Eberhardo arciepiscopo Salzpurch celebratur, cui interfuit Pataviensis, Frisingensis, Gurcensis, Chymensis, Sekowensis episcopi."* See also *Chron. Schir.* 632: *"1219. Hoc anno habita est synodus secunda Salzpurgae in maiori ecclesia sancti Routperti sub Eberhardo arciepiscopo"; Ann. Osterhov.* 543; *Hermanni Altah.* 387. Printed in Hartzheim, *Concilia* III 502 (510); Dalham, *Concil. Salisb.* 96; Meiller, *RAS* 222, Nr. 225. Mansi, *Collectio* XXII 1133-1136, cites this passage (as printed in Hansiz, *Germaniae Sacrae* II 324), and lists the following agenda items: I) *"In synodo Saltzburgensi deliberatum de decreto Concilii Lateranensis anno MCCXV ut omnes Clerici vigesimam partem Ecclesiasticorum proventuum conferant ad triennium in subsidium terrae sanctae, exceptis duntaxat religionis;* II) *Itemque de literis Apostolicis Innocentii III, quibus dabatur venia Clericis, proventus beneficiorum per triennium obligandi;* III) *Spondanus putat in eodem Provinciali Concilio constitutam fuisse Diocesin novam Seccoviensem, . . ."* Hefele-Leclercq, *Conciles* V/2 1428, and Binterim, *Concilien* IV 443, see this as the primary purpose of the synod. Further discussion in Hübner, "Provinzialsynoden" 204-205; Gruber, "Eberhard II."; Hauck, *KGD* V 135 note 2. The concluding date according to Meiller was after 24 September (when the bishops of Seckau and Chiemsee, and the abbots of Admont and Viktring, the cathedral provost and the cathedral dean were witnesses), yet before mid-October; cf. *RAS* 531, Nr. 91; 591, Nr. 92. The papal letter is in Pressutti, *Regg. Hon. III* I, Nr. 3207.

[152] See below, p. 268.

[153] Cf. Potthast, *Regesta* I, Nr. 5627. This letter dated 2 December 1217 indicates that Archbishop Eberhard had sent Provost Karl of Friesach to Rome to request the creation of a

boundaries and the extent of the endowment were agreed upon.[154] Ecclesiastical matters were also discussed, especially the neglect by the Augustinian canons in fulfilling their priestly duties, observing the fast, and adhering to other rules of their Order.[155] The degeneration of discipline among the canons-regular was a serious concern: Archbishop Conrad I had made them an important element in his church organization during his reform efforts in the mid-twelfth century. The disregard for their commitment to higher ideals than those found generally among the secular clergy had prompted action both at the Fourth Lateranum and at the 1216 provincial synod at Salzburg. Continued lack of discipline and obstinacy on the part of the Augustinian canons now demanded further action in 1219. Clearly connected with this synod was the commission given 3 April 1220 by Honorius III to the bishops of Chiemsee and Seckau, and to the Salzburg cathedral dean, Kuno, (all of whom were Augustinian canons themselves): with the approval of the archbishop, they were granted authority to excommunicate all canons-regular who refused to obey the statutes of the General Council and their general chapters.[156] Such a statement clearly presupposes the prior publication of the statutes, the fact of which Eberhard had undoubtedly communicated to the pope. This constant pressure from the archbishop to reform had the effect that in the years 1218-1224 no fewer than three general chapters of the Salzburg congregation of the Augustinian canons were held.[157] It is also significant that the site for these assemblies

new bishopric in Seckau because of the difficulties in properly conducting visitations, given the size of the archdiocese of Salzburg (*"quod Salzeburgensis diocesis usque adeo sit diffusa, quod eam non possit commode visitare"*). The pope appointed Bishops Otto of Freising, Berthold (*electus*) of Brixen, and Abbot Gottfried of Admont to conduct an investigation into the feasibility of such a proposal. Papal permission to erect the new bishopric was granted 22 June 1218; cf. Potthast, *Regesta* I, Nr. 5843; Pressutti, *Regg. Hon. III* I, Nr. 1461; Meiller, *RAS* 216, Nr. 203; Muchar, *Steiermark* V 79.

[154] Hübner, "Provinzialsynoden" 205; Meiller, *RAS* 216, Nr. 203; 217, Nr. 204ff.; 529, Nr. 84. See [ ] Ludger, "Die Erhebung des Stiftes Seckau zum Domstift," *Studien und Mitteilungen aus dem Benediktiner- und Zisterzienserorden* 10 (Salzburg/München, 1889); Seidenschnur, "Salzburger Eigenbistümer" 199-205; Dopsch, *Geschichte Salzburgs* I 329 and note 784.

[155] Hübner, "Provinzialsynoden" 204.

[156] Meiller, *RAS* 225, Nr. 241: "... *quod in ordine canonicorum regularium suae provinciae tam in divinis officiis, quam ieiunis et aliis observantiis tanta existat diversitas, quod confusionem in ducere videatur, quibusdam ex ipsis generalis statuta concilii et eorum communis capituli observare renitentibus* ..."; Potthast, *Regesta* I, 544, Nr. 6219; Hübner, "Provinzialsynoden" 204; Dopsch, *Geschichte Salzburgs* I 329. A reminder of this period of intense scrutiny of the canons-regular may be the fifteenth-century copy of *c.* 12 of the Lateran IV constitutions from the monastery at Indersdorf; see Munich Staatsbibliothek clm 7841, fol. 122-123: *Lateranse concilium pro ordine canonicorum regularium.*

[157] See Gilles Gérard Meersseman, "Die Reform der Salzburger Augustinerstifte (1218)

was always the archiepiscopal city itself, presumably so that Eberhard could better monitor their proceedings.

Despite considerable evidence of his efforts to implement the constitutions of Lateran IV and to reform the conventual clergy of his province, the collaboration of the suffragan bishops as a result of Eberhard's synods of 1216 and 1219 is less well defined. The only diocesan synod of which we have record in the aftermath of the provincial assemblies appears to be that one convened at Passau in 1220, at which the collection of the half-tithe according to the statute of Innocent III in the Lateran Council was addressed.[158]   Since Bishop Ulrich of Passau had taken the cross at Aachen in 1215, but had as yet left that vow unfulfilled, his synod of 1220 undoubtedly made known the provisions for his imminent departure as well. The following year he set out in the company of Duke Ludwig of Bavaria and joined the Christian forces in Egypt. The malaria-ridden Nile delta became his last earthly sphere of activity: he died at Damietta 30 October 1221.[159]

The Passau synod of 1220 must also have considered the reform decrees issued at Salzburg and at the Fourth Lateranum.[160]   Bishop Ulrich attended the Council and had received copies of the constitutions and other major documents. Hageneder's study of ecclesiastical judicial practices in Upper and Lower Austria shows how intense the reception of Roman and canon procedural law was in the diocese of Passau, while Stelzner's brilliant examination of canonist manuscripts dating from the twelfth and thirteenth century reveals an amazing picture of monks and canons regular throughout

eine Folge des IV. Laterankonzils (1215)," *Zeitschrift für schweizerische Kirchengeschichte* 48 (Fribourg, 1954) 81-95. The sixty-one statutes were found in a thirteenth-century manuscript preserved in the episcopal library at Maribor (Marburg) in Slovenia: MS Q 18, fol. 30^r-32^r; see also the brief description of the MS in Milko Cos, *Codices aetatis mediae manuscripti, qui in Slovenia reperiuntur* (Laibach, 1931) 192, Nr. 115.

[158] *Ann. Salisb.* 782: "*Capitulum cum multis clericis Patavie celebratum est a domino Ulrico episcopo, ubi aderant legati domini Apostolici pro vicesima parte omnium proventuum trium annorum secundum Innocentii III in concilio Lateranensi statutum.*" Cited in Hansiz, *Germaniae sacrae* I 365; Hartzheim, *Concilia* III 505; Binterim, *Concilien* IV 444; Schrödl, *Bistum Passau* 183; Hübner, "Passauer Synoden" 5-6; Hübner, "Provinzialsynoden" 201-205; Kerschbaumer, *St. Pölten* 190. The names of the *legati Apostolici* are not given. Presumably they were *Martin cubicularius* and *Johannes marescalcus suus, militiae Templi et hospitalis Hierosolimitani fratres* mentioned in Potthast, *Regesta* I, Nrs. 5956, 5959, as being sent to Germany by Honorius III to collect the half-tithe; cf. Würdtwein *Nova subs.* III 76; Lappenberg, *Hamb. UB* I 367, Nr. 421.

[159] Röhricht, *Deutscher im Heiligen Lande* 111.

[160] Both Hübner, "Passauer Synoden" 6, and Kerschbaumer, *Sankt Pölten* 190, assume this to be the case.

southeast Germany and Austria acquiring texts and learning the newest concepts in church law with amazing speed.[161]

No one illustrates this better that the Augustinian canon Altmann who had been trained at Freising, but also held a prebend at St. Florian in the diocese of Passau. About the year 1200 the first canonist is documented in the circle of Bishop Wolfger of Passau—the cathedral canon Henry who appears as *decretista*.[162] At some time between 1200 and 1204 Bishop Wolfger presided over a diocesan synod at which the *magistri decretalium* played a prominent role.[163] A document dated 1212 mentions an Albert *decretista* as well.[164] Undoubtedly these specialists in canon law comprised an important element within the church at Passau, and they formed a circle to which Altmann of St. Florian also belonged. In 1212 Altmann was elected provost of his foundation following the elevation of the previous provost, Ulrich, to be the head of the cathedral chapter in Salzburg. Several times during the next decade Altmann served a one of the *iudices delegati* appointed by the pope to bring disputes of various sorts to a resolution.[165] His primary importance, however, lies in the fact that he produced a major canonistic treatise, the *Ysagoge iuris*, an introduction into church law based on Gratian's *Decretum* and the *Decretales* which gives clear evidence that a copy of the constitutions of the Fourth Lateranum lay before him 1216/1220 as he wrote this work.[166]

That other diocesan clergy in Passau had become aware of those constitutions by the time Bishop Ulrich departed for the crusade seems beyond dispute as well. During the early thirteenth century there were several sets of annals and chronicles which were maintained within his diocese. By far the most extensive notations were made at the Benedictine abbey of Göttweig in Lower Austria where, beginning about the year 1208, the *Annales Gotwicenses* were resumed after over six decades of inactivity. Thus, the entry for the year 1215 is in all probability quite contemporaneous

---

[161] Cf. Hageneder, *Geistl. Gerichtsbarkeit*.

[162] *UBLOE* II 461, Nr. 316.

[163] *FRA* II 21 3, Nr. 2; Hageneder, *Geistl. Gerichtsbarkeit* 18-20.

[164] *UB Babenb.* I 184, Nr. 185.

[165] Cf. for example, Potthast, *Regesta* I, Nr. 6046: together with the abbot of Kremsmünster and the prior of Ardagger he was given the mandate to investigate the dispute between the abbot of Melk and the parish priests Ulrich of Traiskirchen and Henry of Mödling.

[166] St. Florian Cod. XI 720 (fol. 5ʳ, 5ʳ, 29ᵛ, 30ʳ, 12ᵛ, 24ᵛ, 45ᵛ, 55ʳ, 30ʳ): among the marginal glosses are the Council decrees *cc.* 23, 24, 29, 32, 33, 41, 50, 62, and 64 in full text which as *novellae* could not have been taken from the *Compilatio quarta* of Johannes Teutonicus; see here, Stelzner, *Gelehrtes Recht* 81-87, 207 and note 103. From the *Compilatio quarta* the following constitutions were presumably copied: *cc.* 18, 21, 51, 52 (fol. 51ʳ, 54ᵛ, 47ᵛ, 46ʳ).

with the events themselves.[167] The author of these lines was quite aware
of what transpired at the Council, having made reference to items found in
no other German sources, namely the condemnation in *c*. 2 of the teachings
of the Calabrian abbot Joachim of Fiore, and the details of internal problems
in the diocese of Passau. He was also aware of the actions taken concerning the patriarch of Jerusalem on 12 November following the first session
of the Council, an item only duplicated in the account by the Giessen
Anonymous. The Passau scribe is likewise only one of three in Germany
who make reference to deliberations concerning the vacant see of Constantinople. Above all, however, he noted that Innocent III "fortified the
church by means of certain new constitutions which are found among the
series canonicas scripturas."

Stelzner has identified Göttweig as one of numerous monastic centers
where canonistic interests had existed since at least the late twelfth
century.[168] It thus seems reasonable that the Göttweig continuator had
access to copies of several pertinent documents from the Council which
Bishop Ulrich had brought back to Passau, but the details of matters not
mentioned in the protocol suggest that the reporter possessed more than
mere second-hand information. It is probable that he himself, or someone
close to him at Göttweig, attended the Council as part of the Passau
delegation. He also seems fully aware of the fact that the constitutions of
Lateran IV were taken up into the decretal collections, such as that of
Johannes Teutonicus which appeared in 1216.

Another strong annalistic tradition in the diocese of Passau flourished at
the Benedictine abbey of Melk on the Danube in Lower Austria. It also
served as the basis for several other Austrian records. For the year 1215
the Melk *Annales* contain the brief notation that "in this year a great synod
was held under Innocent III, at which were present bishops from parts
beyond the seas; and he died this same year and Honorius succeeded
him."[169] Written after the death of Innocent III in mid-1216, this entry
nonetheless was contemporary with the events of the Council and contains

---

[167] *Ann. Gotwic.* 602: "*1215. Innocentius papa generale concilium Lateranis celebrat, ubi
heresim cuiusdam Joachym abbatis conf . . . luculento tractatu conroborat, quibusdam etiam
novis constitutionibus ecclesiam munivit, quarum series inter canonicas scripturas invenitur.
Iter quoque Hierosolimitanum consiliis et exhortationibus instituit. Item electio Ulrici
Pataviensis episcopi que Manegoldo decedente per discordiam celebrata fuerat, auditis hinc
inde . . . partibus ab ipso confirmatur. Intererat huic concilio patriarcha Constantinopolitanus
qui Romane ecclesie conciliis . . . retroactis temporibus interesse desierat.*"

[168] *Gelehrtes Recht* 60, 191-193: „*Aus alledem ist unverkennbar, dass Göttweig im 12.
Jahrhundert für die Pflege des gelehrten Rechts eine wichtige Rolle spielte.*"

[169] *Ann. Mellic.* 507: "*Hoc anno synodus magna facta est sub Innocencio III, etiam quod
de transmarinis partibus episcopi ibi affuerunt, et hoc anno moritur, et Honorius ei successit.*"
For the details of Melk's annalistic tradition, see Schmale, "Annalistik" 191.

a veiled allusion to the disputed succession at Constantinople; it is a hint at least that someone at Melk was more intimately acquainted with the fuller agenda of the Council as well.

Since 1133 Klosterneuburg in Lower Austria had been occupied by a community of Augustinian canons among whom were several whose interest in canonistic had resulted in the acquisition or production of Gratian's *Decretum* or commentaries on it.[170] Several recensions of the Melk annals were also maintained by this community, being expanded after 1177 and continued until at least 1224. Both codices of the *Continuatio secunda* and that of the *Continuatio tertia* contain notes relating to the Council.[171] The discrepancies between the Melk entry and the Klosterneuburg accounts point to an independent source for the notation on Lateran IV in the latter records. The wording of the Klosterneuburg annals follows the protocol much more closely and thus may derive from a copy of that document preserved at Passau or even Salzburg.

About the year 1213 the annalist (or annalists) at the Benedictine abbey of Garsten on the Enns in Upper Austria broke with the traditional sources of his information (Melk and Admont) and until 1256 wrote from independent knowledge and experience. Included in this period is a notice for 1215 which, although an obviously abbreviated account, clearly relies on the protocol of the Council rather than on Melk or Admont.[172] Since it refers explicitly to the church in which the Council was held in Rome, it cannot be a mere extraction from the *Annales S. Rudperti* or from any other records kept within the Salzburg province. Oblique though it may be, this entry suggests that shortly after the Council and the synods of 1216 and 1219 at Salzburg monks at Garsten were acquainted with at least some aspects of the constitutions and activities of the Lateran IV.

The continuator of Magnus of Reichersberg's annals for the period 1203-1222, on the other hand, borrowed predominantly from other Austrian sources, so that the notation for 1215 in his record is virtually identical to

---

[170] Stelzner, *Gelehrtes Recht* 60, 193, 196: various copies of the *Summa decretalis* of Paucapalea were available in the late twelfth century at Admont, St. Ruprecht's in Salzburg, and Klosterneuburg; at the beginning of the thirteenth century Klosterneuburg acquired a Gratian MS (probably Klosterneuburg Cod. 87 with the apparatus of Johannes Teutonicus which came into being shortly after 1215).

[171] *Ann. Mellic., Continuationes Claustroneoburgenses (secunda)* 622: [Codex scotorum] "*1215. . . . Synodus celebratus est apud ecclesiam Johannis Rome.*" [Codex B] "*1215. . . . Synodus celebrata est apud ecclesiam sancti Johannis Rome.*" *Continuatio tertia,* 635: "*1214. Synodus Rome facta est sub Innocentio papa apud ecclesiam sancti Johannis.*" For details on the *Annales,* see Schmale, "Annalistik" 192; Wattenbach-Schmale, *DGQ* 219.

[172] *Ann. Admunt.* 595: "*Innocentius III. papa in ecclesia Salvatoria que Constantiniana vocatur, sinodum, cum 412 episcopis celebravit.*" For the historiography, cf. Wattenbach-Schmale, *DGQ* 226.

that found in the *Annales S. Rudperti*. Similarly, Abbot Hermann of Niederaltaich (1242-1273), whose *Annales (Chronicon) Altahenses* were begun ca. 1250, makes only slight variations to the Salzburg account.[173] Again, the erection of the bishopric of Chiemsee was an issue of the Council which alone interested the Austria scribes. We have noted above that one of the extant thirteenth-century manuscripts of the Lateran IV constitutions was preserved at Oberaltaich, suggesting that Abbot Hermann may have had access to the entire set of documents distributed at the Council. Copies of these could have been obtained as a result of the provincial or diocesan synods conducted by Archbishop Eberhard and Bishop Ulrich immediately after Lateran IV, to which Hermann's predecessors—the abbots of Niederaltaich—and their counterparts at Oberaltaich would have been summoned.

Further evidence of widespread acquaintance with the acts of the Council is found in the *Annales* written at about the same time (ca. 1250) at the Benedictine house of Kremsmünster in Lower Austria.[174]   Although inexact with respect to the date of the Council (a marginal note places it between 1210 and 1221), these *Annales* show evidence of having had the constitutions as sources. The author is not only aware of actions taken relative to the mendicant orders (cf. *c*. 13), but he also possessed specific knowledge of *c*. 12 which called for triennial general chapters of all monastic orders. The emphasis which Archbishop Eberhard II placed upon these assemblies undoubtedly made most religious of the Salzburg province more aware of this decree than perhaps any other from Lateran IV. It has been argued that the annals of Kremsmünster borrowed heavily from those kept at Admont until ca. 1216.[175] While this may be accurate in a general

---

[173] *Chron. Magni presb.* 527: *"1215. . . . Universalis synodus celebrata est Rome sub Innocentio papa tercio. In qua fuerunt episcopi 412. . . . Ad quam sedem Rudigerus episcopus ordinatur."* Hermanni Altah. 387: *"1215. Manigoldus Pataviensis episcopus obiit; Vlricus eiusdem ecclesie canonicus succedit. Universalis synodus celebrata est Rome, in qua fuerunt episcopi 412. Inter quos extiterunt Constantinopolitanus, Ierosolimitanus patriarche; primates autem et metropolitani 71, abbates et priores ultra 800, presidente Innocentio papa tercio. In ipsa synodo Kymensis episcopatus intituitur; ad quem sedem Rudgerus primus episcopus ordinatur."* For discussion of both annals, cf. Schmale, "Annalistik" 180-188; Wattenbach-Schmale, *DGQ* 201-4; Josef Klose, *Das Urkundenwesen Abt Hermanns von Niederalteich (1242-1273, Seine Kanzlei und Schreibschule,* Münchener Historische Studien, Abteilung Geschichtliche Hilfswissenschaften, ed. Peter Acht, vol. 4 (1967) 1-12.

[174] *Hist. Cremifan.* 634: *"Huius tempore Innocencius papa III. habuit concilium Lateran. et fecit constitucionem: In singulis provinciis, etc. (post add.: et hoc ideo, quia tunc novi surrexerunt, in quibus plures viri et femine virtutem miracilis claruerunt, sancti Augustini et Benedicti professoribus graviter errantibus a patrum suorum preclarissimis institutis.) Item cepit ordo Predicatorum, qui per Honorius papam confirmatus 1216. Item ordo Minorum fratrum 12 . . ."*

[175] Wattenbach-Schmale, *DGQ* 214.

sense, the discrepancies in the accounts of the Fourth Lateranum make it clear that the Kremsmünster scribe had access either to a full set of Council documents, or to portions which had been extracted for circulation among the religious houses of the Passau diocese.

Heavily dependent upon the Kremsmünster annals are the *Bernhardi Cremifanensis Historiae* which cite almost verbatim the former's notation concerning the Council.[176] As was also true with the *Annales*, the use of the introductory words of *c*. 12 suggests that those who read this entry in the *Historiae* were fully acquainted with the actual canon and had felt the impact thereof through the vigorous reform programs of the archbishop of Salzburg.

One of the possible participants at the Council, but an apparent absentee at the 1216 provincial synod at Salzburg, was Abbot Conrad of Scheyern, the head of a Benedictine abbey in the diocese of Freising from ca. 1206 until 1225, who compiled the *Annales Shirenses* and included in them a brief statement concerning the Council.[177] This account was one of the earliest written in Germany after the conclusion of the Council and makes clear that the protocol was available in the diocese of Freising despite the bishop's absence in 1215. The two deviations from the standard text are somewhat curious, however, namely, the substitution of *Aquilegensis* for *Iherosolimitanus* among the patriarchs, and the use of the figure 807 for the number of abbots, prior, and chapter representatives present, instead of the customary *"ultra 800."* The figure 807 may in fact be more accurate, and an actual participant at the Council may have known that fact, but we cannot be certain. The reference to the patriarch of Aquileia appears to be a case of mental transfer, inasmuch as Wolfger of Ellenbrechtskirchen had previously been bishop of Passau and was undoubtedly well-known to the abbot of Scheyern. As we have noted in Ch. Three, Wolfger of Aquileia was indeed at the Council and Abbot Conrad may have accompanied him there. In any case, to anyone within the province of Salzburg, the mere mention of the office of patriarch would have brought the prestigious see of Aquileia first to mind.

---

[176] *Bernardi Cremif. Hist.* 672: *"Item Innocentius III. papa Lateranis concilium celebravit, ubi editit: In singulis provinciis, etc. Et hoc ideo, quia tunc novi ordines surrexerunt, in quibus plures utriusque sexus miraculis claruerunt, professoribus regularum sancti Augustini et beati Benedicti graviter errantibus a suorum patrum preclarissimis institutis."*

[177] *Ann. Shir.* 632: *"1215. Synodus habita est sollempniter Kal. Novembris ab Innocentio papa, cui interfuerunt 412 episcopi, cardinalis 72, abbates, praepositi, priores 807, patriarcha Constantinopolitanus et Aquilegensis."* See Wattenbach-Schmale, *DGQ* 256-8; Chevalier, *Repertoire* I 1019; Johann von Hefner, "Über den Mönch Conrad von Scheyern mit dem Beinamen Philosophus," *Oberbayerisches Archiv* 2 (1840) 155-180.

At least three other sets of annals were maintained within the diocese of Freising during the early thirteenth century which make mention of the Council of 1215. In the episcopal city itself, scribes at the monastery of St. Stephan apparently added regular notations to the *Annales Frisingenses*, making probable the contemporaneity of the remark: "*1215. Sinodus Rome facta est sub Innocentio pontifice III. episcoporum plus quam quadringentorum.*"[178] Though much abbreviated, the account ultimately derives from the Council protocol which Bishop Otto II must have received at the Salzburg synod of 1216. Use of the protocol for both the *Annales Shirenses* and the *Annales Frisingenses* before ca. 1220 suggests that Otto II also had a copy of the constitutions which he would have received at the provincial synods of 1216 or 1219 and which presumably he published before his death in 1220.

Until ca. 1227 the compilers of the *Annales* at the Premonstratensian monastery of Schäftlarn borrowed their materials from Ensdorf, but the latter, insofar as they have been preserved, make no reference to Lateran IV.[179] Thus, the brief report for 1215 at Schäftlarn must derive from some other source, though not necessarily the primary one: "*Concilium Rome sub Innocentio papa celebratur.*"[180] Schäftlarn was once again a community of canons regular in which an interest in canonistic flourished,[181] but a more complete picture of its library or scriptorium holdings ca. 1216/1220 seems impossible.

At some time during the first-third of the thirteenth century the constitutions of the Fourth Lateranum were bound together with the only extant copy of *Historia pontificum Romanorum* and other texts into a single MS volume at Zwettl.[182] This rather early text of the Council's decrees, a second version also preserved at Zwettl,[183] and a third complete text which comes from the Augustinian-canon foundation of St. Andrä on the Traisen and had close ties to Altmann of St. Florian[184] give yet further

---

[178] *Ann. S. Steph. Frising.* 55. See also Wattenbach-Schmale, *DGQ* 254.

[179] Cf. Wattenbach-Schmale, *DGQ* 251-255.

[180] *Ann. Scheftlar.* 388.

[181] Stelzner, *Gelehrtes Recht* 60.

[182] Zwettl Cod. 255, fol. 151ʳ-168ᵛ; cf. Joachim Rössl, in Karl Kubes & Joachim Rössl, *Stift Zwettl und seine Kunstschätze* (1979) 32, who notes that the various parts of Cod. 255 were clearly „*schon im 1. Drittel des 13. Jahrhunderts in Zwettl zu der vorliegenden Form vereint.*" Many important texts have remained all but unknown because their identification was too easy: the Zwettl Cod. 255, e.g., was listed in the *MSS Katalog* of Rössler (1891) simply as „Traktat über Gott und die Dreieinigkeit"; see Stelzner, *Gelehrtes Recht* 64, 189.

[183] Zwettl Cod. 106, fol. 94-108ᵛ; see also Stelzner, *Gelehrtes Recht* 189, 206; Trusen, *Gelehrten Rechts* 133f.

[184] *Sammelhandschrift* Cod. Vat. lat. 2692, fol. 75-93ᵛ. The provenance of this MS would still not be known but for reference in it to the texts of Altmann. It has been in the Vatican

evidence of the rapid and extensive transmission of this legislation following the provincial synod at Salzburg in 1216. Canons-regular from both Zwettl and St. Andrä served the papacy as *iudices delegati* under Honorius III; their interest in and complete familiarity with recent canonical decrees made them valuable servants of the Curia. The elevation of St. Andrä to the status of an episcopal church by Archbishop Eberhard in 1228 provides a possible reason for the copy of the constitutions being there.[185]

Preserved in the Bodmer Library at Cologny-Genève is a manuscript which is mentioned in a catalogue of the monastery at Tegernsee in Bavaria in 1483.[186] Bound together with the original MS of *Lampertus Hersfeldensis Vita s. Lulli Moguntini*, which dates from the eleventh century, is a collection of the *Canones (seu Decreta)* of the *Concilium Lateranense IV (a. 1215)*. Whether Tegernsee possessed this copy of the decrees in the first half of the thirteenth century cannot be determined. The terse and inaccurate remark found in *diaconus* Werner's *Annales Tegernseensis*: "*1209. Concilium Lateranense*",[187] a narrative regarded as contemporary to the events mentioned, suggests a later date for the entry, by a scribe who had limited information about the Fourth Lateranum.

Present in Rome in 1215, but absent from the 1216 synod at Salzburg, was Bishop Conrad of Brixen. The trip to the Lateran Council may well have been too strenuous for him, as he died late the following year. In fact, ill health was the reason given for his absence at Salzburg. Nevertheless, he brought with him from Rome copies of the constitutions and other pertinent documents. Although there is no direct evidence that he published the decrees before his death, a charter issued by Pope Gregory IX on 28 June 1230 may provide some insight into Bishop Conrad's efforts to effect changes in clerical life in the spirit of Lateran IV. The pontiff confirmed the institution of the provostship and four priests at the church of St. Mary at Brixen, who were under obligation to celebrate the Mass daily and

---

Library since at least the seventeenth century. Closer investigation with ultraviolet light has revealed the ownership mark on fol. 94ᵛ: "*Iste liber est mo[naster]ii S. Andree c[is] Trays[enam].*" See further discussion in Stelzner, *Gelehrtes Recht* 207-209.

[185] On the erection of a bishopric in Lavant, see M. Pagitz-Roscher, "Das Augustiner Chorherrenstift St. Andrä im Lavanttal," *Carinthia* I (1967) 297ff.

[186] Bibliotheca Bodmerensis Cod. 80; see Elisabeth Pellegrin, ed., *Bibliotheca Bodmeriana Catalogus*, V: Manuscrits Latins (Cologny-Genève, 1982) 148-153. The catalogue for books at Tegernsee was compiled by Ambrosius Schwarzenpeck in 1483; see Munich clm 1925, fol. 36ᵛ. The codex later became part of the private collection of the prince of Oettingen-Wallerstein at the castle Maihingen in Swabia; see Wilhelm Wattenbach, "Geschichtliche Handschriften der fürstlich Oettingen-Wallersteinschen Bibliothek in Maihingen," *NA* 7 (1881) 173-174, Nr. 10. It came to the Bodmer library in 1948.

[187] *Annales Wernheri Aliorumque Tegernseensis*, *MGH SS* XXIV 59; cf, further, Wattenbach-Schmale, *DGQ* 258-259; Potthast, *Repertorium* II 339.

perform other religious duties (*"qui quotidie ibi missarum solemnia et alia divina celebrent"*), an act done earlier by Bishop Conrad *"b[eata] mem[oria]."*[188]

Conrad II of Rodank-Rodeneck had been the provost of Neustift 1183/1185, later he held the office of cathedral provost at Gurk, and in 1200 he succeeded to the bishopric of Brixen on the heels of Eberhard of Regensberg who was translated to the metropolitanate of Salzburg.[189] Once again we find significant connections between individuals and collections of canonistic texts. Both Gurk and Neustift show evidence of an interest in the *Decretum* in the latter twelfth century. To Conrad of Albeck who likewise was associated with both Neustift and Gurk we owe a version of the *Summa Monacensis* compiled 1175/1178; he may also have been the channel through which various works of the French-Rhineland canonist school came to Neustift.[190]

Bishop Conrad's successor at Brixen was Berthold of Neiffen, *regalis aule protonotarius* for Frederick II of Staufen from 1212 until 1215, who had been elected bishop in late 1216/early 1217. Yet, although there is no evidence that his election was challenged by either the emperor or the pope, he remained bishop-elect for several years. He also had taken a crusade vow (perhaps with Frederick II at Aachen in July 1215 at the hands of *magister* Conrad of Speyer and *magister* John of Xanten). On 14 May 1218 Honorius III wrote Bishop Berthold and *"universis clericis tam civitatis quam diocesis Brixiensis"* that *"cum Brixiensis episcopus crucesignatus in procinctu sit itineris ut exequatur votum suum, mandat ut eidem assignent vicesimam pro subsidio Terrae Sanctae."*[191] The pontiff obviously believed that the personal involvement of the prelate in the crusade would give him added incentive to see that the half-tithe was collected promptly, and the assurance given the clergy of the bishopric that their contributions would directly support their bishop may have spurred on their generosity as well. Presumably there was a synod at which these details were handled, but the record is silent. At some time after 23 June 1218 Berthold began the fulfillment of his vow, joining the Christian forces engaged in the assault of Damietta in 1219.[192] He was thus unable to respond to Archbishop Eberhard's summons to the provincial synod that year, but would most certainly have sent proctors.

---

[188] Potthast, *Regesta* I, Nr. 8575.
[189] Sparber, *Fürstbischöfe* 73-75; Stelzner, *Gelehrtes Recht* 55.
[190] Stelzner, *Gelehrtes Recht* 191.
[191] Pressutti, *Regg. Hon. III* I, Nr. 1317.
[192] Röhricht, *Deutscher im Heiligen Lande* 101.

The anonymous scribe of the *Annales Brixenses*, which in one recension date from about 1250, noted tersely: *"1215. Hoc anno factum est concilium Lateranense per Innocentium papam, et ibi constitutum est eundi ultra mare."* [193] The matter of the crusade was a concern closely associated with the Council by a later generation, but this account may also rest upon documentary support, more particularly the decree *Ad liberandum* which participants at the Council received. This decree had even greater significance for the bishopric of Brixen, since the monies collected undoubtedly helped finance the peregrination of Bishop-elect Berthold of Neiffen . This fact, and the omission of this decree in most other annals of the Salzburg province, argues strongly for the independent nature of the Brixen account.

It cannot be determined whether the sparse notes for the period 880-1260 found in a manuscript from the former Benedictine monastery of Georgenberg in Tyrol, also within the diocese of Brixen, originated there. The British Museum has preserved the manuscript which dates from the thirteenth century and states: *"Anno domini m.cc.xv. Innocentius magnus Rome concilium celebravit."* [194] Although this source is silent concerning the publication of the Lateran IV decrees, we may nevertheless conclude from our discussion of the *Annales Brixenses* that the complete set of documents from the Council was available at Brixen from early 1216 and had been published before about 1250.

Perhaps it was the stress placed by *cc.* 17 and 20 of the Lateran IV decrees on the proper care of the Eucharist and other sacramental materials, and on the proper conduct by priests while officiating in their holy office, which prompted a letter from the bishop of Brixen to Pope Honorius III complaining that one *magister* Maurus, a priest at the church of St. Brigitta in Brixen, lacking the Host and the chalice on a certain day, had nevertheless celebrated the Mass using leavened bread and a wooden cup. The pope responded that *"propter hunc excessum"* the priest was to be deprived of his office and prebend *"in perpetuo."* [195] How representative such indifference to sacred things was of other German clergy we cannot say, but this sort of misbehavior was bound to come to light through use of the visitation prescribed by the Council.

---

[193] *Annales Brixiensis, MGH SS* XVIII 818; cf. Potthast, *Repertorium* II 257.

[194] *Annales montis S. Georgii, MGH SS* XXX 721; British Museum MS 18.344 (13th c. hand); Wattenbach-Schmale, *DGQ* 265.

[195] Potthast, *Regesta* I, Nr. 7825 (1216/1227 without closer dating): *"qui, cum quadam die hostiam et calicem non haberet, in pane fermentato et in scypho ligneo colemnia celebrarat . . ."*

Regensburg presents a different situation. Bishop Conrad IV attended neither the Council at Rome nor the provincial synods of 1216 and 1219. Representatives of his were present at the 1216 assembly, however, and presumably acquired a set of the constitutions at that time. There is, in spite of this, no reference to either Lateran IV or its decrees in the *Annales Pruveningensis*, compiled at the Benedictine abbey of Prüfening on the Danube near Regensburg during the decade of the 1270s, or in the *Notae Sancti Emmerani* which derive from various manuscripts produced at this important religious house. However, the *Annales Osterhovenses*, written at the Premonstratensian convent under Abbot Ulrich (1288-1313), do recall the Council.[196] It is possible that a synod was called in response to the papal letter of 26 September 1220 regarding arsonists in the diocese of Regensburg,[197] but firm evidence is lacking. The report of such depredations against church property was perhaps the result of an episcopal visitation conducted earlier in the year. As he had done in 1209/1210, Bishop Conrad also invited help in correcting problems within his diocese in 1221. Responding to that, Honorius III issued the command on 6 May 1221 to the abbots of St. Peter's in Salzburg and of Raitenhaslach, and to the prior at Berchtesgaden, *"ut monasteria monialium civitatis et dioecesis Ratisponensis visitent et reforment."*[198] Thus, although there are no explicit indications that Conrad published the constitutions of Lateran IV, the inferences that he did so, and that he attempted to effect changes within his church consistent with those decrees are clearly recognizable.

The diocese of Gurk offers several challenges for us in our efforts to determine when the legislation of Lateran IV became publicly known and accepted. Bishop Henry II, who was elected in 1214, attended the Council in November 1215 and apparently the provincial synod in late 1216, died on 7/8 September 1217.[199] His successor, Udalschalk, who attended the provincial synod in 1219, resigned his office in December 1220, due in part to his age, but also because of advancing blindness.[200] The view held by Hirn and Gruber, that Udalschalk stepped down in connection with a visita-

---

[196] *Annales Pruveningensis, MGH SS* XVII 607; *Notae Sancti Emmerani, MGH SS* XVII 574; *Ann. Osterhov.* 543: *"1215. . . . Universalis synodus celebrata est Rome in Laterano a domno Innocencio papa III, in qua fuerunt 412, etc. In ipsa synodo Chimensis episcopatus instituitur, ad quam sedem Ruedgerus primus episcopus ordinatur."* The dependence on the *Annales S. Rudperti Salisb.* is obvious. Cf. discussion of sources in Wattenbach-Schmale, *DGQ* 233-4, 251.

[197] Ried, *CdRatisb* I 326, Nr. 342; Potthast, *Regesta* I, Nr. 6370.

[198] Pressutti, *Regg. Hon. III* I, Nr. 3355 (*"Ad audientiam nostram . . ."*).

[199] Hauck, *KGD* I 966; Kuhle, *Besetzung* 86; Jaksch, *MC* I 346; Krabbo, *Ostdeutsche Bistümer* 101; Obersteiner 80.

[200] Hauthaler, *SUB* III, Nr. 759; Pressutti, *Regg. Hon. III* I, Nr. 2820; Hauck, *KGD* I 966; Jaksch, *MC* I 357, Nr. 469; Idem I 375, Nrs. 489-490.

tion of his diocese ordered by Archbishop Eberhard has not found wide support.[201]   Nevertheless, the growing incapacity of a suffragan bishop must have been a concern for the metropolitan at the 1219 assembly of prelates and at that which convened in November 1220 at Gars as well.[202] As late as 27 August 1223 the pope complained to Bishop Ulrich that his predecessors had not met their commitment to the financing of the crusade; he was ordered to do so without delay.[203]

The picture which emerges for the ecclesiastical province of Salzburg between 1216 and 1220 is thus quite well defined. There is no doubt that most, if not all, suffragans had begun to implement the decrees of the Fourth Lateranum, yet at the same time they appear to have resisted efforts by the archbishop to exploit that legislation in his own desire to strengthen his metropolitan authority. The extent to which Eberhard went in his efforts to effect changes can also be seen in the commission given on 3 April 1220 to Bishops Rüdiger of Chiemsee and Carl of Seckau, and to the dean of Salzburg: responding to a request from the metropolitan who had maintained "*quod in ordine canonicorum regularium suae provinciae yam in divinis officiis, quam ieiuniis et aliis observantis tanta existat diversitas, quod confusionem inducere videatur, quibusdam ex ipsis generalis statuta concilii et illa communis capituli observare renitentibus*," the pontiff directed that "*cum gravitate ac maturitate debita procedentes*" they ordain what should be standard.[204]

Once again we gain a glimpse into the process by which the constitutions of the Council were transformed into practices which governed the religious life of a German province. That these particular men should have been given such discretionary powers also reveals something of their knowledge and reputation in matters of canon law. At the same time, however, we must remember that both bishops had until recently been members of the Salzburg cathedral chapter and had been personally selected by Archbishop Eberhard for the newly-created bishoprics. Rüdiger of Radeck appears as *magister* 1212-1215, having acquired advanced training (at Bologna in canon

---

[201] Cf. J. Hirn, "Erzbischof Eberhards II. von Salzburg Beziehungen zu Kirche und Reich," *Jahresbericht des kaiserlichen Obergymnasiums in Krems* (1875); Gruber, "Eberhard II."; Dopsch, *Geschichte Salzburgs* I 323 note 721. See further the introductory comments to Jaksch, *MC* I, Nr. 494; Ch. Stöllinger, "Erzbischof Eberhard II. von Salzburg (1200-1246)," (Dissertation, Wien, 1972) 78.

[202] Hauthaler, *SUB* III, Nr. 758; the possibility that this was a provincial synod is voiced by Dopsch, *Geschichte Salzburgs* I 329 note 786, based on a consideration of those who attested the document.

[203] Pressutti, *Regg. Hon. III* II, Nr. 4544.

[204] Meiller, *RAS* 225, Nr. 241; Potthast, *Regesta* I, Nr. 6219; Pressutti, *Regg. Hon. III* I, Nr. 2380.

law?).[205]   Carl of Seckau was the archbishop's representative in Rome during the negotiations which helped establish his bishopric; his abilities were thus well-known to the papacy when, in 1220, he was directed to help correlate religious practices among the regular clergy of the Salzburg province.[206]

On 10 January 1222 Pope Honorius III commanded the suffragans of Salzburg that, in the event their archbishop summoned them to a synod, they were to obey him, and that they were also to receive him with honor during visitations.[207]   Such a visitation must have commenced immediately for on 4 February 1222 the Roman pontiff found it necessary to compensate for some of the misplaced zeal of the archiepiscopal visitors: to the cathedral canons of Gurk he granted the privilege of continuing their weekly practice of venerating the Blessed Virgin, despite the prohibition of such by the priors of Ranshoven and Reichersberg.[208]   One week earlier Honorius had also directed the *capitulares* at Gurk to observe the canonical statute which their bishop had decreed,[209]

A further aspect of this visitation involved the Styrian house of Benedictine monks at St. Lamprecht.   *C.* 33 of Lateran IV had ordained that *procurationes* demanded by prelates and archdeacons during visitations were to be granted only in those cases where they themselves conducted the visit, and that such visitors must show concern for not overburdening the religious communities by excessive demands or too large a retinue.   In St. Lamprecht's case, however, it was not as much economic as jurisdictional disagreements which underlay its antagonism.   As noted earlier, the monks at St. Lamprecht had claimed to be directly accountable to the Holy See, exempt from the ecclesiastical control of Salzburg.   Thus, when the archiepiscopal visitor, the archdeacon of Carinthia, appeared at their monastery and demanded to be allowed to discharge his commission, he was physically ejected.[210]   The prelate responded by excommunicating the abbot and monks and imposing an interdict on their monastery, but the problem itself remained unresolved.

---

[205] See Kuhle, *Neubesetzung* 88; Krabbo, *Ostdeutsche Bistümer* 107; Hauck, *KGD* IV 965-966.

[206] Krabbo, *Ostdeutsche Bistümer* 109.

[207] Hauthaler, *SUB* III, 300, Nr. 772; Meiller, *RAS* 229, Nr. 262; Potthast, *Regesta* I, Nr. 6760.

[208] Potthast, *Regesta* I, Nr. 6781; Meiller *RAS* 227, Nr. 251; Pressutti, *Regg. Hon. III* I, Nr. 3777; Hirn, *Kirchenrechtliche Verhältnisse* 47.

[209] Potthast, *Regesta* I, Nr. 6778; [ ] Ankershofen, "Urkundenregister," *AÖG* XXII (1869) 360, Nr. 788; Pressutti, *Regg. Hon. III* I, Nr. 3766.

[210] Potthast, *Regesta* I, Nr. 6767; Pressutti, *Regg. Hon. III* I, Nr. 3745; Meiller, *RAS* 229, Nr. 264; Cheney, *Visitations* 131.

On 22 January 1224 Pope Honorius III issued a commission to the bishop
of Chiemsee, to the abbot of Milstadt, and to the scholastic at Freising,
directing them to examine the claims of exemption by St. Lamprecht which
was based on a supposed privilege of Pope Paschal.[211] Eventually the
archbishop reached an agreement with St. Lamprecht: though he conceded
that he would pay the expenses himself if he appeared unannounced for a
visitation, he successfully asserted his right to conduct such a review of the
inner life of the monastery.[212]

Eberhard had also written the pope concerning another of the statutes of
the Fourth Lateranum (c. 11) which instructed metropolitans to establish
strong schools where priests and other clerics could be trained properly. On
7 February 1222 Honorius responded, noting that since his church consisted
of canons-regular, he was approving the archbishop's request that "*magistrum B. monachum monasterii de Hausen ad hoc officium assumat.*"[213]
The creation of the office of scholastic, together with that of cantor,
provided two important elements in the prelate's cathedral school, ensuring
that "the youth are not lacking in discipline or training."[214] Eventually,
the metropolitan appointed a Dominican friar to head his school.[215]

On 30 April 1223 Eberhard declared that he had exchanged the tithe-
properties at Cirkenz, Jaering and Sakkach, which he had previously granted
to his cathedral chapter, for others lying much closer to Salzburg and
therefore more easily accessible, on condition

> . . . *ut, cum canonicis hactenus cappae nudae et simplices darentur, de
> proventibus illarum curiarum de reliquo dentur subvestitae cum pellibus
> agnellinis, nec tamen de vestibus, quas antea recipere solebant a camerario,
> quicquam eis huius occasione commodi minuatur; et ipsi vice illius emolumenti
> post obitum nostrum ad altare, quod fundandum erit iuxta sepulturam nostram,
> ebdomadarium ad missam defunctorum continue habeant, cuius praebenda par
> sit praebendae cantoris.*[216]

---

[211] Pressutti, *Regg. Hon. III* II, Nr. 4703; Meiller, *RAS* 536, Nr. 102; Potthast, *Regesta*
I, Nr. 7147.

[212] Widmann, *Geschichte Salzburgs* 337-8; Meiller, *RAS* Nr. 266.

[213] Rodenberg, *MG Ep. s. XIII* I, Nr. 190: "*Ex parte siquidem tua fuit nobis humiliter
supplicatum, ut cum ecclesie tue, in qua canonici regulares existunt, velis iuxta constitutionem
concilii generalis de aliquo viro perito in facultate theologica providere, qui et ipsos docere
valeat et commisso tibi clero et populo ministrare pabulum verbi Dei, quia indecens videretur
personis religiosis personam adiungere vel potius preficere secularem, cum nequaquam in bove
ac asino sit arandum nec induenda sit vestis lino lanaque contexta, . . .*"

[214] Dopsch, *Geschichte Salzburgs* I 1080.

[215] Dopsch, *loc.cit.*

[216] Meiller, *RAS* 231, Nr. 270.

Thus, even without the setting of a synod he attempted to add this dress-requirement to the laws and regulations governing the conduct of his clergy.

Synodal Efforts in the Archdiocese of Cologne

The long pontificate of Archbishop Eberhard II of Salzburg was obviously a positive factor in any attempt at ecclesiastical reform. On the other hand, the archiepiscopal vacancy at Cologne in November 1215 and the twenty-six month delay between the election of Engelbert of Berg (29 February 1216) and his receipt of the pallium (after 24 April 1218) clearly affected the speed with which decrees of the Council were published within that province.[217] Copies of the major documents were carried back to Cologne by those *priores* of the archdiocese who had attended the Council, yet the continuator of the *Chronica regia Coloniensis*, writing ca. 1220, made no apparent use of either the protocol or the constitutions in compiling his record.[218] His knowledge of the actual dates on which the sessions of the Council commenced and ended, and the background to the election controversy at Constantinople are details (albeit somewhat garbled) mentioned in few other German accounts. The fact that he found nothing else worth noting among the numerous actions taken at the Council—and

---

[217] Engelbert was consecrated as archbishop on 24 September 1217 by Archbishop Dietrich II of Trier; cf. Knipping, *REK* III, Nr. 141, citing *Chronica regia Colon.* 213. On 24 April 1218 Pope Honorius informed Engelbert that he was sending the pallium by means of two clerics from Cologne to Archbishop Dietrich of Trier, from whom he could obtain it; cf. Potthast, *Regesta* I, Nr. 5761; Pressutti, *Regg. Hon. III* I, Nr. 1252; Knipping, *REK* III 37, Nr. 192. Given the cathedral scholastic Oliver's role as one of the most prominent crusade-preachers, there can be no doubt that assemblies had been held for recruitment and money-raising purposes. On 27 January 1217 Pope Honorius III addressed a letter to all those who had accepted the cross in the province of Cologne, giving them further instructions about their undertaking; cf. Ennen, *Quellen* II 65, Nr. 55; Potthast, *Regesta* I, Nr. 5435; Pressutti, *Regg. Hon. III* I, Nr. 284.

[218] *Chron. reg. Colon.*, cont. II (a. 1215) 194: "*In festo sancti Martini papa . . . celebravit in . . . exceptis abbatibus, prepositis, decanis aliisque ecclesiarum prelatis, quorum non erat numerus, exceptis clericis, monachis aliisque totius ordinis aut professionis viris, quorum multitudo computari non poterat*"; cont. III (a. 1215) 237: "*Eodem etiam anno papa Rome concilium habuit. Ubi tam de transmarinis partibus quam de cunctis christianorum finibus patriarchis, archiepiscopis, episcopis, abbatibus, prelatis ecclesiarum congregatis, in ecclesia sancti Iohannis baptistae concilium in festo sancti Martini inchoatum et usque ad festum sancti Andreae protractum; nichil dignum memoriae quod commendari possit ibi actum est, nisi quod orientalis ecclesie, quod antea inauditum fuit, se subditam Romanae ecclesiae exhibuit. Nam Constantinopoli duo in patriarchas electi Romam [ad concilium] venerunt et iudicio papae se submiserunt. Quos ambos consilio cardinalium deposuit, et tercium substituit et investivit et ad propriam sedem remisit.*"

absolutely nothing concerning the reforming aspects in sharp contrast to known eye-witnesses such as the Giessen Anonymous[219]—leads to the conclusion that he was not personally present, but rather relied on a second party's memory for details of the Council. We may perhaps conclude as well that the reform decrees had not as yet been published at Cologne when he wrote his account.

The occasion for that publication was most likely the provincial synod held at Cologne in 1220 and attended by the bishop of Liège and numerous *priores* of the archdiocese. A document dated that year, but without closer reference to time or place, attests that *"priorum Coloniensium sententia"*—that is, by a decision of the highest clergy of the archdiocese of Cologne—, the right of patronage which the collegiate church of St. Severin in Cologne claimed over the church in Werdohl had been granted to the monastery Flechdorf in Waldeck. The final clause in the charter states that *"acta sunt hec in provinciali concilio, venerabili domino Engelberto archiepiscopo presidente."*[220] A further reference to this same assembly is provided by Caesarius of Heisterbach who, writing in 1221, noted an incident which occurred *"anno praeterito"*: a young Jewess of Louvain had converted to Christianity and had entered the convent of Parc-aux-Dames near Crespy; at the entreaty of her bereaved parents, Bishop Hugh of Liège had demanded that the cloister deliver the girl into his hands; an appeal beyond the bishop apparently went to Cologne and, at the 1220 synod, Archbishop Engelbert commanded his suffragan to cease his recovery efforts and to leave the matter be.[221]

Supporting the archiepiscopal position in this issue was *c.* 70 of the Lateran decrees which stipulated that Jews who had received baptism were to be constrained by the prelates from returning to their former faith.[222]

---

[219] Cf. Kuttner/Garcia y Garcia, "A New Eyewitness Account" 135.

[220] *Westf. UB* IV 60, Nr. 87.

[221] *Caesarii Dialogus* II 25. Hartzheim, *Concilia* III 514, places the synod in 1222, as does Mansi, *Collectio* XXII, col. 1181-1182, Binterim, *Concilien* III 421, and Hefele-Leclercq, *Conciles* V/2 1436. Finke, *Konzilienst.* 47-48, corrects this to 1220 and equates it with the *Westf. UB* reference; Hauck, *KGD* V 135 note 3, accepts Finke's arguments. Ficker, *Engelbert der Heilige* 95 and 241 note 1, places the synod mentioned by Caesarius in the year 1219, another 1220 (cf. Ficker's "Regesta Engelberti", *op.cit.* Nr. 99, and others (cf. *Dialogus* V 21, VI 20, IX 52) the statutes of which have all been lost. Foerster, *Engelbert von Berg* 79, makes no distinction between the provincial synod of 1220 and the diocesan synod of 1221.

[222] Lateran IV, *c.* 70: *"Quidam, sicut accepimus, qui ad sacri undam baptismatis voluntarii accesserunt, veterem hominem omnino non exuunt, ut novum perfectius induant, cum prioris ritus reliquias retinentes, christianae religionis decorem tali commixtione confundant. Cum autem scriptum sit: maledictus homo qui terram duabis viis ingreditur, et indui vestis non debeat lino lanaque contexta, statuimus, ut tales per praelatos ecclesiasrum ab observantia veteris ritus omnimodo compescantur, ut quos christianae religioni liberae voluntatis arbitrium*

Since the bishop of Liège proved unwilling to prevent such from happening, Archbishop Engelbert imposed sentence on the case. This incident again demonstrates the manner in which the general principles of canon law contained in the constitutions of Lateran IV were implemented within the dioceses and provinces of the Church to meet specific situations. It also provides support for the conclusion that on this occasion in 1220 Archbishop Engelbert caused the entire set of constitutions from the Council to be publicly read before the Cologne provincial clergy as well.

A possible *terminus ante quem* for the synod and the formal introduction of the Council's decrees into the province of Cologne is provided by an archiepiscopal statute dated 1 August 1220, requiring at least eight canons in the cathedral chapter to have the priestly consecration.[223] As we noted in Ch. Two, disregard for such matters had become acute at Cologne during the early years of the thirteenth century—the result of the throne controversy and the neglect of pastoral matters by the archbishops themselves. The responsibility for reform which the constitutions of Lateran IV re-affirmed was clearly a motivating force in the enactment of this statute, and its implementation would have been a natural consequence of the most recent publication of Innocent III's decrees themselves.

Unlike the neighboring Rhenish provinces of Mainz and Trier for which we have explicit evidence that visitations of monasteries had also gone on since the Council, we must infer such with respect to Cologne. The abbot of Werden returned to his monastery in 1218 to find it badly in need of correction. We do not know of any role played in this regard by the archbishop, but on 4 December 1218 Pope Honorius III issued a charge to the abbots of Verden, Siegburg and Deutz to assist their brother at Werden in his efforts to reform his house.[224] Presumably as a consequence of the provincial synod in 1220, the pontiff issued a command to the archbishop of Cologne and his suffragans on 3 March 1221 that they not allow nuns' cloisters to accept more persons than their resources allowed, lest the ability of such establishments to perform their functions be diminished.[225]

A Presumed Provincial Synod for Magdeburg

On 30 August 1220 Archbishop Albrecht of Magdeburg, together with Bishops Engelhard of Naumburg, Ekkehard of Merseburg and Siegfried of

---

obtulit, salutoferae coactionis necessitas in eius observatione conservet; cum minus malum existat, viam Domini non agnoscere, quam post agnitam retroire."

[223] Lacomblet, *NRUB* II 48, Nr. 86. See also Ficker, *Engelbert der Heilige* 27.

[224] Pressutti, *Regg. Hon. III* I, Nr. 1724.

[225] Pressutti, *Regg. Hon. III* I, Nr. 3144 ("*Ad nostram noveritis . . .*").

Brandenburg issued a charter to Bishop Frederick and the cathedral dignitaries at Halberstadt, stipulating that they could grant an indulgence to all people from their dioceses who visited the Halberstadt cathedral on the day of the arrival of the relics of St. Moritz and the re-consecration of the episcopal church.[226] This assembly of prelates from the province of Magdeburg in the metropolitan city clearly had other business which the letter does not mention: Böhmer suggests the possibility of a provincial synod; Mülverstedt is silent on the matter.[227] Although there had been diocesan synods at Naumburg and Merseburg since the Lateranum, this appears to be the first occasion on which the archbishop and one or more suffragans had been together. The fact that three of the four were present on this occasion argues strongly for this being an assembly of considerable importance, the very sort of setting in which the metropolitan could fulfill his obligation of publishing the Council's statutes.

Given the training in canon law which Archbishop Albrecht had received at Paris and Bologna both before and after his elevation to the prelacy, and the fact that he was personally present at Rome in 1215, such a late date for an official introduction into his province of the constitutions seems unlikely. Yet, the unresolved political questions in northern Germany may in part account for the delay. That the constitutions which Albrecht received at the Council were known to his archdiocese by no later than this synod is suggested by the *Chronicon montis sereni*, compiled ca. 1227/1230 at Lauterberg, which includes the protocol of Lateran IV almost verbatim.[228]

Unexplained remains the apparent failure of the bishops of Havelberg and Brandenburg, both of whom were present at Rome, to convene synods between 1216 and 1220 for the purpose of publishing the constitutions. A

---

[226] Riedel, *CdBrand* I 8, Nr. 137; Böhmer-Ficker, *Regg. Imp.* V/2, Nr. 10867.

[227] Mülverstedt, *RAMagd* II, Nr. 600. A similar indulgence was granted to all the faithful in the diocese of Halberstadt on 2 June 1222; see Pressutti, *Regg. Hon. III* II, Nr. 4019.

[228] Cf. p. 186: "*Sinodus universalis Rome in ecclesia Salvatoris, que Constanciana vocatur, mense Novembri celebrata est, presidente Innocencio papa III, pontificatus eius anno 18, in qua fuerunt episcopi 412, inter quos erant patriarche duo, Constantinopolitanus et Jerosolimitanus. Antiochenus languore detentus, missit pro se vicarium Anteradensem episcopum. Alexandrinus sub Sarracenorum dominio constitutus, fecit quod potuit, mittens pro se diaconum germanum suum. Primates autem et metropolitani fuerunt 71, abbates et priores ultra octingentos. Absencium vero archiepiscoporum et episcoporum et abbatum et priorum non est numerus comprehensus. Legatorum vero, regis videlicet Sicilie in Romanorum imperatorem electi, imperatoris Constantinopolitani, regis Francie, regis Ungarie, regis Jerosolimitani, regis Cipri, regis Arragonensis nec non et aliorum principum et magnatorum et civitatum aliorumque locorum ingens affuit multitudo. Siffridus abbas Pegaviensis Heinrico de Rekkin Sereni Montis canonico expulso in concilio commissionem obtinuit, cuis exemplar hic inserere libuit pro testimonio veritatis.*" For details on the annalist, see Böhmer, *Fontes* I lxxi; Wattenbach-Schmale, *DGQ* 401.

search of the papal registers frequently reveals patterns, however, and the sudden appearance of references to three letters written within a three-week period to the collegiate church at Stendal in the diocese of Brandenburg suggests that some sort of agitation there had triggered complaints which the Curia had had to address. It is thus not improbable that at some time just previous to early June 1220 Stendal had been affected by several outside forces aimed at controlling its affairs. On 2 June, for example, the pope gave the commission to the scholastic, dean and canon Ludolf of the Magdeburg cathedral to investigate the complaint by the prior and chapter at Stendal that the archdeacon of Balsamen in the diocese of Halberstadt was demanding obedience from their churches.[229]   Two weeks later the pontiff granted an indulgence to Stendal "*ut nulli synodum in eorum ecclesia ipsis invitis liceat celebrare*" and the prohibition "*ne quis episcopus vel praelatus eos excommunicationi aut dictam ecclesiam praesumat subicere interdicto.*"[230]   Had the bishop of Brandenburg just attempted such an action? We are not told, but this suggests at least that there was some synodal activity in Brandenburg after all. Fearing retaliation from either the bishop of Brandenburg or the diocesan officials in Halberstadt, the chapter at Stendal further requested to be placed under the special protection of the Holy See, to which the pope agreed on 19 June 1220.[231]   All of the issues touching upon Stendal would have been logical for discussion at a provincial synod held at Magdeburg in late August that same year.

Although there is no indication that the letter was drafted in a diocesan synod, there is nonetheless a rather remarkable statement of the inner workings of a medieval diocese contained in the papal confirmation of possessions and privileges pertaining to the cathedral church at Branden-burg. The original declaration was written by Bishop Siegfried II of Wanzleben on 28 December 1216, just days after his election, confirmation and consecration, though the approbation by Gregory IX is dated 14 December 1233.[232]   Siegfried had been cathedral provost at Brandenburg.

---

[229] Riedel, *CdBrand* I/5 32, Nr. 24; Potthast, *Regesta* I, Nr. 6268; Pressutti, *Regg. Hon. III* I, Nr. 2479.

[230] Riedel, *CdBrand* I/5 32, Nr. 23; Potthast, *Regesta* I, Nr. 6273; Pressutti, *Regg. Hon. III* I, Nr. 2496.

[231] Potthast, *Regesta* I, Nr. 6274; Pressutti, *Regg. Hon. III* I, Nr. 2498.

[232] Potthast, *Regesta* I, Nr. 9341; Rodenberg, *MG Ep. s. XIII* I, Nr. 567. See also the discussion of dating the privilege in Curschmann, *Diözese Brandenburg* 369-371: Exkurs I. Although Bishop Baldwin died shortly after 16 November 1216, the fact that he was present with the archbishop of Brandenburg on that date suggests that he might have had the physical strength to convene a synod during the eleven months since the Council; cf. Mülverstedt, *RAMagd.* III 588, Nr. 338. We cannot conclude that he did so, however. Nor are the details of the joint appearance of the Magdeburg and Brandenburg prelates sufficient enough to allow the identification of this event with a provincial synod. The single known transaction was the

As such he had led the struggle to free episcopal elections from the domination of the margraves of Brandenburg. The declaration of the cathedral chapter's rights, written almost immediately after his own election, is a clear example of how quickly the precepts of the Fourth Lateranum were implemented. Supported by *cc.* 23, 24, 25, 26 and 28 of the Council, the Brandenburg cathedral chapter claimed the exclusive right to elect the bishop.[233] A further direct appeal to the Lateran constitutions is made in defining the pastoral role of the bishop: *"Correctiones quoque discipline regularis et morum reformationes eorundem canonicorum, que vires sui prepositi excesserint, iuxta antiquam et hactenus observatam consuetudinem et Lateranensis statuta concilii per nos et successores nostros nullo penitus interiecto appellationis obstaculo corrigantur."*[234]

Illustrative of the sort of problem with which the archbishop of Magdeburg and his suffragans had to contend is the mandate given Albrecht II on 21 July 1221, ordering him to require his own cathedral provost, Otto, nephew of the duke of Poland, to accept the higher grade of consecration as a deacon since he was also archdeacon over the city of Magdeburg and was daily involved in matters pertaining to the archidiaconal *Send.*[235] Otto had been granted *stallum in choro et locum in capitulo* by Pope Innocent III on 8 January 1207, at the same time he was given the provostship as the successor to Albrecht of Käfernburg,[236] and he had used this papal

confirmation of a privilege for the cloister at Lehnin.

[233] Cf. Rodenberg, *op.cit.* 462, line 37: *"Obeunte siquidem ipsius ecclesie antistite, in successore ipsius eligendo iuxta morem aliarum ecclesiarum cathedralium Saxonie ipsius ecclesie canonicos liberam habere decernimus electionem, nullusque eis invitis per surreptionem aliquam preponatur; set ille in ipsa ecclesia locum et officium pontificis obtineat, quem unanimi voluntate vel de consilio maioris et sanioris partis eiusdem ecclesie capituli de gremio ipsius ecclesie vel aliunde viderint eligendum. Alie vero conventuales ecclesie et plebani ipsius diocesis non se faciende electioni aliquatenus integere presumant, set consensum electioni canonice facte prebeant."* See also Krabbo, *Ostdeutsche Bistümer* 46-49; M-Alpermann, *Stand und Herkunft* 19; Wentz, *Bistum Brandenburg* 29.

[234] Rodenberg, *op.cit.* 461, line 2.

[235] Hertel, *UB Stadt Magdeburg* I 39-40, Nr. 81; Potthast, *Regesta* I, Nr. 6692: *"... um Otto maior propositus archidiaconatum civitatis habeat sue prepositure annexum et causas audiat cotidie sinodales, idem tam ab ipso quam a capitulo suo sepe commonitus ad diaconatus ordinem non accedit, tamquam ad hoc, eo quod est subdiaconus noster, compelli non possit nec ad ordinem superiorem assumi sine nostra licentia speciali. Nos igitur ordinandi eundem tibi licentiam concedentes fraternitati tue per apostolica scripta mandamus, quatinus, si est ita, ipsum, ut ad ordinem diaconatus accordat, ex parte nostra moncas et inducas eundem ad id, si necesse fuerit, per archdiaconatus subtractionem appellatione remota compellens."*

[236] Mülverstedt, *RAMagd* II 112, Nrs. 267, 268; Potthast, *Regesta* I, Nrs. 2963, 2964. For a detailed discussion of the cathedral provostship, see Eduard Stegmann, "Die Magdeburger Dompropstei," *MGbll* 68/69 (1933/1934). See also Wentz/Schwineköper, *Erzbistum Magdeburg* 118-120. The cathedral chapter had refused this provision, putting forth its own candidate, Walther of Arnstein, who held office until 1211/1212. The chapter apparently

provision to shield himself against demands both from the prelate and from his brethren in the chapter. The refusal of so influential an official of the cathedral chapter and the archiepiscopal administration to accept the higher expectations incumbent upon one with the higher degrees of consecration undoubtedly had a negative impact upon other clergy of the diocese and province. The hypocrisy of one who shied away from a life of discipline and commitment must also have been obvious to those whom he attempted to control through the authority granted him as an archdeacon of the bishopric.

The Province of Trier

As noted in connection with Magdeburg and its suffragan bishoprics in 1220, so too with respect to the ecclesiastical province of Trier during the second half of the year there is an unusual cluster of papal documents written in response to episcopal and other requests, suggesting that there had been ecclesiastical activity during late 1219 and early 1220. This activity in turn seems clearly related to archiepiscopal efforts to reform the churches of his province in the spirit of Lateran IV. On 24 July 1220, e.g., the pope wrote to the bishop and cathedral chapter at Toul, confirming an action taken by them previously, that of reducing the number of prebends at Toul from sixty to fifty.[237] Such a solution to the disparity between cathedral chapter resources and the number of individuals claiming support from those resources can be seen as an effort to properly support the canons in their ecclesiastical and sacramental obligations. These concerns must have been frustrated, however, for on 23 December of that same year Honorius III granted to the bishop of Toul permission to retain the incomes from all benefices which became vacant in his church over the next three years for a period of two years each, in order that he might pay off debts with which the bishopric was burdened.[238] To the cleric Nicholas at Toul the pope also granted permission to hold another prebend *"eius morum et scientiae meritis inspectis, . . ."*[239]

---

appealed to an old privilege from an earlier pope, according to which the cathedral canons at Magdeburg were entitled to wear sandals during the Mass and to exclude the reception of priests who had not been consecrated wearing them. On 8 March 1207 Innocent III obligated the cathedral chapter to receive other qualified priests and other honorable persons into its body who had no such consecration; cf. Mülverstedt, *op.cit.* 116, Nr. 278. The cathedral chapter at length conceded, and from 1212 Otto served as provost.

[237] Horoy, *Honorii III opera* III 485, Nr. 1; Pressutti, *Regg. Hon. III* I, Nr. 2576 (*"Cum a nobis . . ."*).

[238] Horoy, *Honorii III opera* III 617, Nr. 155; Pressutti, *Regg. Hon. III* I, Nr. 2915.

[239] Horoy, *Honorii III opera* III 616, Nr. 154; Pressutti, *Regg. Hon. III* I, Nr. 2916 (23

On 24 July 1220 the Roman pontiff issued a mandate to the abbots of St. Mansuy and St. Nabor, in the dioceses of Toul and Metz respectively, granting them authority to act as *"visitatores et correctatores"* for the monastery at Gorze. This commission was issued *"ad petitionem abbatis, donec a communi capitulo provinciae Treverensis de aliis visitatoribus sit provisum."*[240] The following year a broader mandate was issued to the Cistercian abbots of Himmerode and Caladia in the dioceses of Trier and Verdun respectively, *"ut monasteria monachorum Nigrorum Treverensis provinciae visitent et reforment, nullis litteris obstantibus inquisitionis vel visitationis pro abbate Gorziensi ad abbatem sancti Arnulfi vel ad abbatem sancti Naboris et ipsorum collegas a Sede Apostolica impetratis."*[241] It is ironic that one of the very houses from which the reforming impulses of the tenth and eleventh centuries emanated was by 1221 itself in desperate need of outside correction. This is in and of itself significant, however, for whereas the re-invigoration of church life in an earlier age began within the walls of Gorze and Cluny and Cîteaux and Prémontré, in the thirteenth century it was being imposed from above. These references to Gorze, despite their unhappy revelations regarding this once-dynamic house, nevertheless provide evidence that both visitations and general chapters were at work at this time, augmenting the efforts by the archbishop and his suffragans in their provincial and diocesan synods.

Between 26 November and 7 December 1220 Archbishop Dietrich II of Trier and Bishop John of Verdun are documented together at Trier conducting several matters of business: on 26 November the metropolitan presided at a judicial hearing in which an archiepiscopal *ministerialis* restored to the bishop property and jurisdictional powers which he had claimed for himself;[242] shortly thereafter the archbishop lent his seal to one of his *ministeriales* who had publicly recognized his feudal relationship to the bishop of Verdun for a fortress at Lemberg;[243] and on 7 December he proclaimed that the bishop had reached an accord in his presence with Count Gerlach of Veldenz regarding their feudal relationship as well.[244]

December 1220).

[240] Horoy, *Honorii III opera* III 486, Nr. 2; Pressutti, *Regg. Hon. III* I, Nr. 2578.

[241] Pressutti, *Regg. Hon. III* I, Nr. 3225 (*"Quia de monasteriorum . . ."*). See also Potthast, *Regesta* I, Nr. 6978 (with date 1223), and Manrique, *Ann. Cisterc.* IV 228.

[242] Hans-Walter Herrmann, ed., *Inventar der saarländischen Betreffe des Bestandes "Collection de Lorraine" in der Handschriftenabteilung der französischen Nationalbibliothek* (Saarbrücken, 1964) 244.

[243] Beyer, *MRUB* III 125, Nr. 137; Goerz, *MRR* II 406, Nr. 1497; Carl Pöhlmann, ed., *Regesten der Grafen von Zweibrücken*, Veröffentlichungen der pfälzischen Gesellschaft zur Förderung der Wissenschaften 42 (Speyer, 1962) Nr. 64.

[244] Herrmann, *Inventar* 243, citing a thirteenth-century cartulary of the bishopric of Verdun; Goerz, *RET* 34, citing a copy of the same at Coblenz.

Once again we have evidence of an extended set of inter-actions between these two prelates, in the midst of which there was ample opportunity and presumably the need as well to confer about the state of the Verdun church. Despite the lack of evidence that other suffragans were also present, this occasion may well have served the convening of a provincial synod.

Though issued at this very time and therefore too late to have had an impact on this particular provincial synod, three papal letters which were dictated on 4 December 1220 shed light on issues which may well have been discussed.   The first was a commission to the bishop, scholastic and a cathedral canon at Strasbourg, instructing them to investigate and resolve a dispute between the scholastic *I[acobus]* at Metz and *magister G.*, the cantor at Toul, regarding the position as head of Metz's cathedral school.[245] The second charter confirmed the recent statute adopted at Metz that canons who were absent from the cathedral church and thus failed to perform their obligations in the choir and elsewhere, were to be deprived of the incomes from their prebends, except they be on pilgrimage, undertaking studies at some distant school, or in possession of a license from the chapter.[246] Related to this was the confirmation of a grant made to the cathedral chapter by the abbot and convent at Gorze with the consent of the bishop of Metz: the incomes from the church at St. Quentin with its appurtenances were to be used for daily distribution among the *capitulares* who observed the canonical hours.[247]   A similar motive lay behind Bishop Conrad's grant of a toll-income to the cathedral chapter that same year.[248]

These measures taken at Metz reveal the influence of the archbishop of Trier whose efforts to restore the *vita communis* within his cathedral chapter since 1215, and to re-establish a more corporate spirit within several collegiate churches of his bishopric since early 1216, were clearly known to his suffragans.   Thus, although there is no explicit mention of Bishop Conrad of Metz convening a diocesan synod at this time, the nature of his undertakings strongly suggests that they were introduced within that setting. Supporting his somewhat limited efforts at reform were the constitutions of the Fourth Lateran Council which he would also have published by 1220.

---

[245] Pressutti, *Regg. Hon. III* I, Nr. 2822.

[246] Horoy, *Honorii III opera* III 584, Nr. 119; Pressutti, *Regg. Hon. III* I, Nr. 2825.

[247] Horoy, *Honorii III opera* III 584, Nr. 120; Pressutti, *Regg. Hon. III* I, Nr. 2826.

[248] Bienemann, *Conrad v. Scharf.* 163.   In 1183 Bishop Bertram of Metz had tried to control absenteeism by withholding income from the prebends of negligent canons: *"Tandem huic malo salubre providimus remedium cleri nostri communicato consilio ordinantes et multo rogatu fratrum loci illius nostra firmiter auctoritate statuentes, ut illis solis fratribus de cetero in toties dicta ecclesia s. Arnualis stipendium exhibeatur, qui ibi mansionarii fuerint et servitio ecclesie sedulo et devote vacaverint"*; cf. Beyer, *MRUB* II, Nr. 64; Goerz, *MRR* II, Nr. 500.

Evidence of this is scarcely to be found in the brief note in the *Chronicon universalis Mettensis*, attributed to the Dominican friar Jean de Mailly who died in 1250: "1214. A council at Rome under Pope Innocent, at which Emperor Otto was deposed."[249] Writing when he did, Jean may have been too far removed from the affairs of the Council to realize that his account was inaccurate: Otto IV of Brunswick had not been deposed at the Council, but rather in 1212, in consequence of his excommunication and intransigence. What did happen in 1215 was a refusal by the papacy to reconsider Otto's status and the confirmation of the election and coronation of Frederick II. The notation therefore appears to rest neither on a documentary basis, such as the protocol or a copy of the constitutions, nor on the clear recollection of eye-witnesses to the events, but rather on the hazy memory of the scribe or other individuals of the happenings of the period 1212-1215. As with the *Annales Spirenses* which show the influence of the imperial chancellor and his basically political interests, the Metz chronicle reveals a secular spirit—and for the same reason.

Factors Which Militated Against Synods at Bremen

The question of early publication of the Council's decrees within the province of Bremen is even more problematic. Binterim notes that Bremen (and Magdeburg) had generally capable shepherds in the thirteenth century, men who participated in person or through representatives at the Lateran Council and most imperial assemblies. He assumes therefore that they published the decrees of Lateran IV in their provinces and saw to their execution, although the chronicles tell us little.[250] Archbishop Gerhard I had in fact been absent in 1215 and, although two of his suffragans and presumably representatives of a third attended, there is no evidence of any other clergy from his province being present at the Lateranum. Yet, even if the archbishop obtained a copy of the statutes immediately upon the return of his suffragans, his failure to convoke a provincial synod in 1216, 1217 or 1218 may also have been the result that the pretender, Waldemar of Schleswig, had not yet conceded the see of Bremen to Gerhard and was even still engaged in belligerent actions against him.[251]

---

[249] *Chron. Mett.* : "*1214. Concilium Rome sub Innocentio papa, ubi Otto imperator deponitur.*"

[250] Binterim, *Concilien* IV 450.

[251] According to the *Ann. Stad.* 356, Gerhard I of Bremen held his ceremonial entrance into his archiepiscopal city in 1217, though the exact date is unrecorded; cf. May, *REB* I 205, Nr. 746. There is likewise no indication that either a provincial or diocesan synod was held in conjunction with this event.

It is thus uncertain to what extent the Bremen church hierarchy and clergy
were familiar with the decrees at an early date. Papally-appointed crusade-
preachers such as John of Xanten and the former bishop of Halberstadt,
Conrad of Krosigk, had been active in the province since 1213, and their
re-appearance after the Fourth Lateranum bearing copies of the decree *Ad
liberandum* undoubtedly brought this aspect of the Council to the attention
of clergy and laity wherever they went.[252] The papal admonition of 2
January 1219 was necessitated by the slow response of the Bremen province
to the half-tithe imposed on the clergy in 1215, however; the knights
Templars and Hospitallers whom Honorius III sent to direct the collection
in northern Germany undoubtedly were armed with further copies of *Ad
liberandum*.[253] Those same papal tithe-collectors would have arrived in
Bremen not long before the death of Archbishop Gerhard I on 14 August
1219. There is no evidence that the doctrinal and reform decrees of the
Council had been published in his province prior to his death. Yet, even
without the reinforcement which *c.* 29 of Lateran IV gave to efforts to curb
the insidious practices of pluralism, familiarity with *c. 13* of the decrees of
the Third Lateran Council should have caused concern over the permission
granted on 12 April 1218 for the cathedral dean at Bremen to hold
simultaneously a prebend at Münster,[254] and for the cathedral provost to
retain two other parish churches.[255]

Archbishop Gerhard's successor, Gerhard II of Lippe, was likewise
unable to convene a provincial synod for several years. Although he had
been consecrated soon after his election on 1 September 1219, he did not

---

[252] See Pixton, "Anwerbung" 178-179.

[253] Lappenberg, *Hamb. UB* I 367, Nr. 421; May, *REB* I 209, Nr. 759; Potthast, *Regesta*
I, Nr. 5956; Pressutti, *Regg. Hon. III* I, Nr. 1779.

[254] *Westf. UB*, III, Nr. 92 Add; Pressutti, *Regg. Hon. III* I, Nr. 1238; Rodenberg, *MG Ep.
s. XIII* I, Nr. 58; May, *REB* I 206, Nr. 749. See Lateran IV, *c.* 29: *"De multa providentia
fuit in Lateranensi concilio prohibitum, ut nullus diversas dignitates ecclesiasticas et plures
ecclesias parochiales reciperet contra sacrorum canonum instituta, alioquin et recipiens sic
receptum amitteret et largiendi potestate conferens privaretur. Quia vero propter praesump-
tiones et cupiditates quorundam, nullus hactenus fructus aut rarus de praedicto statuto provenit,
nos evidentius et expressius occurrere cupientes, praesenti decreto statuimus, ut quicumque
receperit aliquod beneficium habens curam animarum annexam, si prius tale beneficium
obtinebat, eo sit iure ipso privatus, et si forte illud retinere contenderit, alio etiam spolietur.
. . ."* According to a note in Ehmck, *UB Bremen* I 675, the dean at Bremen 1213-1222 was
Bernhard; *magister* Bernhard *Bremensis* appears as a cathedral canon at Münster 1213-1233,
and as the dean of Bremen in 1221. Dean Bernhard was a member of the family of the lords
of Lippe; in 1219 he was the leading cathedral canon at Bremen in efforts to secure the election
of his brother Gerhard as archbishop. The concession to Dean Bernhard may thus have been
an early indication of papal support for this dynasty in any future developments at Bremen.

[255] Pressutti, *Regg. Hon. III* I, Nr. 1238; Ehmck, *Bremisches UB* I 675, Nr. 273;
Rodenberg, *MG Ep. s. XIII* I, Nr. 57.

receive the pallium at once, due to a protest lodged against him in Rome by the provost of Hamburg. Owing to political considerations, the matter was prolonged until 5 January 1223 when Honorius III finally conferred the pallium.[256] This delay in receiving the fullness of his archiepiscopal authority may explain why, in 1220, the archbishop granted to the church at Hamburg the privilege of having the Chrism consecrated by one of the suffragan bishops of Bremen in case of necessity.[257] On the other hand, this move by the clergy at Hamburg also has the appearance of a calculated effort to reassert their independence vis-a-vis Bremen.

In January 1221 Archbishop Gerhard published an accord reached between himself and the Hamburg canons regarding the use of the title *"Episcopus Bremensis"* versus that of *"Episcopus Hammaburgensis."* He also agreed that, in accordance with a decision of Pope Innocent III, provincial synods in the future would be held in Bremen and in Hamburg, and that general synods and general chapters would be held at the appointed time in Hamburg as was customary.[258] Objection to this by the Bremen cathedral chapter led to papal mandate given between late July 1221 and late February 1222 to Prior Andreas of Kappenberg (who had been present at Lateran IV), Dean Hermann of St. Paul's and the scholastic Lutbert of St. Lüdeger's—all in the diocese of Münster—to conduct an investigation into the claims by Hamburg.[259] According to the report from the Bremen cathedral canons, Archbishop Adalbert at one time had called his suffragans in Denmark, Sweden and Norway to a provincial synod in Hamburg because of its favorable location; due to the destruction of this city, however, Adalbert's successors then convened synods in Bremen, a practice which the cathedral clergy at Hamburg now wished to reverse. Although Bremen had been the venue for synods for some forty years, the Hamburg chapter demanded that their city be restored to its former position as the site of synods, and that the metropolitan dignity be transferred back to their church. The papal commission was given the task of hearing the case and rendering a decision.

---

[256] Lappenberg, *Hamb. UB* I 404, Nr. 460; Potthast, *Regesta* I, Nrs. 6915, 6916; May, *REB* I 220, Nrs. 793, 794. The papal letter indicates that the pallium had been requested by four clerics sent to Rome in behalf of the archbishop of Bremen: the provosts of St. Marienberg and St. Anschar, and the *magistri* and cathedral canons at Bremen, Arnold and Alexander. The pallium was being sent via Bishop Adolf of Osnabrück who was authorized to accept Gerhard's oath of loyalty to the papacy. The prelate at Bremen was also admonished to look after the many needs of his badly-damaged church.

[257] May, *REB* I, Nr. 776. On 21 July 1222 Pope Honorius III confirmed the resolution of this dispute; cf. Potthast, *Regesta* I, Nr. 6878; Pressutti, *Regg. Hon. III* I, Nr. 4096.

[258] May, *REB* I 216-217, Nr. 778.

[259] Lappenberg, *Hamb. UB* I, Nr. 451; Potthast, *Regesta* I, Nr. 6751; May, *REB* I 218, Nr. 787.

Behind this inquiry lay the ongoing political struggle between the cathedral chapters of Hamburg and Bremen to assert their own pre-eminence over the other. The *Kirchenordnung* which Archbishop Hartwig had established in 1160 had dictated that provincial synods were to convene in Bremen, diocesan synods in Hamburg. The archiepiscopal schism during the previous decade and the delays in establishing Gerhard II with full powers gave the Hamburg canons opportunity to press their demands before the Curia. A related dispute was to be settled by the dean of the Holy Apostles and the provost and the canon, *magister A.*, at St. Maria *ad gradus* in Cologne who on 25 December 1221 were given the commission to inquire into the use of the title "*archiepiscopus Hammaburgensis*" by the archbishop of Bremen.[260]

At an unspecified time in 1222 the papal *iudices delegati* announced their decision, quashing the archbishop's earlier special accord with Hamburg.[261] Not until about Advent 1223, however, was Archbishop Gerhard II able to announce that the long-standing dispute between the church of Hamburg and Bremen had been resolved: Hamburg recognized that the title and archiepiscopal dignity belonged exclusively to the Bremen church; the archbishop was to convene provincial synods and general chapters (i.e., diocesan synods) as in the past; the clergy of churches in the Trans-Elbe region would only be called to Bremen for synods by a special *appellatio*.[262]

Given the limitations to archiepiscopal authority until early 1223, we can conclude that no provincial synods had been convened before that time for the purpose of publishing the constitutions of Lateran IV for the prelates and clergy of the Bremen church. The *terminus ante quem* was 1240, on the other hand, for in the latter year Abbot Albert of Stade resigned the office he had held for eight years and became a Minorite. At the same time he concluded his *Annales Stadenses*, using materials which had been collected by his monks over the space of his abbacy. Included in his notations was one concerning the Council, citing almost verbatim the protocol circulated in 1215. While it is possible that this information was extracted from other sets of annals, it is more probable that a copy of the protocol and the accompanying constitutions of the Council were available in Bremen and

---

[260] Lappenberg, *Hamb. UB* I 395, Nr. 449; Potthast, *Regesta* I, Nr. 6745; Pressutti, *Regg. Hon. III* I, Nr. 3660.

[261] May, *REB* I 220, Nr. 792; Lappenberg, *Hamb. UB* I, Nr. 459; Hoogeweg, *UB Hilds* II, Nr. 53.

[262] Lappenberg, *Hamb. UB* I, Nr. 468; May, *REB* I 222, Nr. 799.

that they had already been published prior to Albert's use of the summary in his annals.[263]

The inability of the archbishop to convene a provincial synod and to publish the Council's decrees before 1223 should not have hindered their becoming known with the suffragan bishoprics of Lübeck, Ratzeburg and Schwerin, however, inasmuch as those bishops had set out for Rome in the fall of 1215. Although Bishop Philip of Ratzeburg died *en route*, one need not assume that he was not accompanied by clerics from his diocese who continued on to the assembly and returned home with the constitutions. Likewise the prelates from Lübeck and Schwerin received the decrees. There were thus at least three sets of Lateran IV documents housed within the province shortly after the Council. The only evidence of a diocesan synod during this time comes from two charters issued 24 May 1217 by Bishop Henry of Ratzeburg *"in maiori sinado [sic] nosta . . ."* The first contains the report of an sentence pronounced by him *"et a clericis et a militibus et universis qui aderunt approbata"* concerning a dispute between the parishioners of Bergedorf and their priest; the second is the confirmation of grants made to that same church by one Count Albert.[264]

The Legation of Gregory of Crescentio

Even if that same synod published the decrees of the Council, word must have reached Rome that certain ecclesiastical matters required more than episcopal attention. On 31 December 1220 Pope Honorius III sent a letter to Bishop Henry of Ratzeburg, and to his colleagues in Schwerin, Lübeck, Olmütz, Prague, and Meissen, commanding them to receive with honor the Cardinal-legate Gregory of Crescentio, and to obey the ordinances which he enacted for their churches.[265] The details of this legation are sparse: it was instituted at the request of the kings of Sweden and Denmark for the purpose of resolving some political issues related to those two realms; but it also assumed the task of dealing with Church order in the reaches of

---

[263] *Ann. Stad.* 356; Böhmer, *Fontes* (1849) lxix; Potthast, *Repertorium* II 175; Wattenbach-Schmale, *DGQ* 423.

[264] *Mecklenburg. UB* I, Nr. 228, 233; Lappenberg, *Hamb. UB* 356, Nr. 154.

[265] Gersdorf, *UB Meissen* I, Nr. 91; *Mecklenburg. UB* I, Nr. 271; Friedrich, *CdBoh* II, Nr. 204; Böhmer-Ficker, *Regg. Imp.* V, Nr. 9997a; Potthast, *Regesta* I, Nr. 6459. The legate was given authority *"ut evellat et destruat, edificit atque plantet, prout queque secundum datam sibi a deo prudentiam viderit facienda."* The papal announcement sent two days earlier to King Ottokar commended Cardinal Deacon Gregory to him and explained that *"concesso sibi plene legatonis officio per omnes terras, que tue iurisdictionis existunt, ut extirpet nociva et planet salubria, prout queque secundum datam sibi a deo prudentiam viderit facienda"*; cf. Friedrich, *op.cit.* Nr. 203.

northern and eastern Christendom.[266] In the absence of evidence to the contrary, we may assume that the ordinances referred to by Honorius III were somehow related to or derived from the constitutions of the Fourth Lateranum which were thus published for the first time in some of these bishoprics through the efforts of this papal legate.

With respect to Prague, this was not the case, however. Bishop Andreas had returned from the Council in the summer of 1216. That he apparently held a synod and published the decrees seems probable from the sequence of events which followed. *Cc.* 45 and 46 of the Lateran constitutions dealt with the oppression of the Church by laymen, and they gave Andreas ammunition with which to attack the policies of King Ottokar of Bohemia.[267] The reaction of Ottokar and other lay nobles was vehement, forcing Andreas to flee the realm on 26 October of that same year and assume residence in Rome. A letter from Pope Honorius III to him, dated 12 March 1217, instructs him to deal swiftly with the miscreants:

> *Nolentes igitur per aliquorum contumaciam confundi ecclesie libertatem, presencium tibi auctoritate mandamus, quatenus iuxta officii tui debitum prefatos laicos, super premissis in tua diocesi contra clericos deliquintes, ut ab huiusmodi presumpcione desistant, monicione premissa, per censuram ecclesiasticam, appellacione remota, compescas; nichilominus studium adhibeas et operam efficacem, et statuti sacri concilii generalis ab omnibus inviolabiliter observentur.*[268]

Although the immediate target of this papal mandate was the Bohemian king and his nobles, it also seems clear that the pope expected all inhabitants of

---

[266] Cf. Zimmermann, *Päpstl. Legationen* 78; Anton Pokorny, *Die Wirksamkeit der Legaten des Pabstes Honorius III. Eine historische Studie*, Programmschrift der Niederösterreichischen Landes- Oberrealschule Krems (1886) 28. Binterim, *Concilien* IV 277, incorrectly associates the note in *Burchardi Chron.* (a. 1220) 114: *"Mittuntur legati in Franciam pro statutis concilii conservandis,"* with the legation of Gregory by omitting the words *"in Franciam."*

[267] Dudik, *Prag* 96-98, argues that it was the publication of the Lateran decrees at a diocesan synod in mid-summer/early fall 1216 which triggered a strong reaction from King Ottokar and forced Andreas to flee Bohemia. The objectionable constitution of Lateran IV was apparently c. 46: *"Adversus consules ac rectores civitatum et alios, qui ecclesias et viros ecclesiasticos talliis seu collectis et exactionibus aliis aggravare nituntur, volens immunitati ecclesiasticae Lateranense concilium providere, praesumptionem huiusmodi sub anathematis districtione prohibuit, transgressores et fautores eorum excommunicationi praecipiens subiacere, donec satisfactionem impendant competentem. . . ."* Bachmann, *Gesch. Böhmens* I 457, argues that Andreas waited until after the death of Pope Innocent III on 16 July 1216 before challenging King Ottokar's position over against the Bohemian church because of Innocent's tacit acceptance thereof. What Andreas appears to have demanded was a return to the state of independence enjoyed by his bishopric prior to the pontificate of Bishop Daniel II († 1215).

[268] Friedrich, *CdBoh* II, Nr. 138.

Ottokar's realm to be made aware of and observe the full range of conciliar decrees.

After repeated warnings which the king's officials ignored, Andreas on 10 April 1217 imposed an interdict upon his diocese which encompassed all of Bohemia.[269] King Ottokar and many of the Prague clergy thereupon turned to the pope who refused to hear their plea, charging that he had heard reports that in the realm of Bohemia clerics were being subjected to secular tribunals and even condemned to death, church tithes were being confiscated, and the church in general was being oppressed.[270] The Bohemian king meanwhile had approached Archbishop Siegfried II of Mainz, metropolitan for Bohemia and former chancellor of that realm, who once again displayed his complete lack of perception by lifting the ban on 29 May 1217.[271] Honorius III took up Andreas' cause, however, and over the next four years a steady stream of papal missives was directed at the archbishop, the king of Bohemia, and various other German prelates who were appointed as papal emissaries and negotiators.[272] By the time an accord was announced on 11 January 1221, the diocese of Prague had suffered the deleterious effects of interdict for more than four and one-half years, numerous clerics and laymen had been excommunicated, and ecclesiastical institutions had been weakened. Resolving the issues between the prelate and the king became a protracted affair, however, and Andreas died on 30 July 1223 at Rome.[273]

The actual steps taken by Cardinal-legate Gregory to restore normal church life to Bohemia are revealed in several letters sent to him from

---

[269] *Ann. Prag.* 121, has the proper sequence of events, whereas *Cont. Cosmae* 170, has Andreas pronouncing the interdict and then leaving Bohemia: *"1216. . . Eodem anno 4. Idus Aprilis Andreas posuit interdictum in Bohemia a divinis et a sepultura, deinde Romam declinavit."* Further discussion by Winkelmann, *Phil. von Schw.* II 452-453; Bachmann, *Gesch. Böhmens* I 457-465.

[270] See Friedrich, *CdBoh* II 128-130, Nr. 139 (mid-April 1217) for Ottokar's complaint; for Honorius' response, cf. Potthast, *Regesta* I, Nr. 5566 (22 June 1217).

[271] *Canonicorum Prag. Cont. Cosmae* 170: *"1217. 4. Kal. Junii archiepiscopus Magontinus Bohemiae interdictum relaxavit."* Archbishop Siegfried's letter of explanation to Andreas, dated late April 1217, is in Friedrich, *CdBoh.* II 130, Nr. 140. See also, Janner, *Regensburg* 293-294. Archbishop Siegfried of Mainz took the side of the king from the very outset of this dispute, in part because of his opposition to Andreas' plans to transform Prague into a metropolitanate; cf. Bachmann, *Gesch. Böhmens* I 458.

[272] Cf. Potthast, *Regesta* I, Nrs. 5582, 5612, 5705, 5706, 5707, 5714, 5729, 5737, 5790, 5916, 5935, 5939, 6102, 6111, 6215, 6346, 6457, 6479.

[273] *Canonicorum Prag. Cont. Cosmae* 171: *"1224. Andreas episcopus Pragensis Romae existens in exilio obiit."* Friedrich, *CdBoh* II, Nr. 260, corrects this entry to 1223, noting that Andreas' successor Peregrin appears as *episcopus Pragensis* on 1 October 1223 (cf. *op.cit.* Nr. 252).

Rome and in charters to which he was a signatory.[274] Attention must also have been given to ecclesiastical matters in Moravia. Bishop Robert had been commanded to make certain that the interdict imposed by Bishop Andreas over all the realm of Bohemia was observed by Cistercian and Premonstratensian houses of his diocese.[275] On 29 March 1218 Honorius III informed Robert that he had been suspended from office and prebends until he presented himself personally before the Curia to answer changes of ignoring the interdict and of celebrating Mass in Prague.[276] Excommunication apparently followed, but on 5 November 1218 Honorius informed the cathedral chapter and people of Moravia that Bishop Robert had humbled himself and had been re-instated.[277] All the more scandalous must have been the announcement made 18 January 1219 that the pope had given a commission to the Cistercian abbots of Zwettl and Ebrach, and to the prior of Zwettl, to investigate charges made against Bishop Robert by Abbot William of Siloe, that he had committed two acts of murder, had had carnal knowledge of two nuns and numerous other women, and had deflowered a virgin.[278]

Following his labors in Bohemia and Moravia, Cardinal-deacon Gregory turned northward into the province of Magdeburg where in December 1221 he visited Meissen. He was doubtless informed about conditions in the

---

[274] *Canonicorum Prag. Cont. Cosmae* 170: "*1221. Gregorius cardinalis a rege Prziemysl et ab universo clero honorifice susceptus, ecclesias aperuit et interdictum relaxavit.*" Letters of commission and instruction were given or sent to Gregory by the Curia on 4 January 1221 (Pressutti, *Regg. Hon. III* I 486, Nr. 2946; Böhmer-Ficker, *Regg. Imp.* V, Nr. 9997b), 23 January 1221 (Potthast, *Regesta* I, Nr. 6525; Böhmer-Ficker, *op.cit.* V, Nr. 9997c), 19 June 1221 (Potthast I, Nr. 6689; Friedrich, *CdBoh* II, Nr. 214; Böhmer-Ficker, *op.cit.* V, Nr. 9997e) and 11 February 1222 (Potthast, *op.cit.* I, Nr. 6790; Böhmer, *op.cit.* V, Nr. 9998a). Gregory presided over the great assembly of clerics and princes who gathered on 2 July 1221 at Rugelsdorf (*in monte Scach*/Berg Staatz) between Retz and Seefeld in Austria to witness the publication of *Litterae de pacis* between Ottokar and Andreas: Ottokar renewed the privileges and immunities of the Prague church in the presence of the cardinal, Bishop Robert of Olmütz, two other Slavic bishops, Duke Leopold of Austria and Styria, Poppo of Andechs, the cathedral provost at Bamberg, sixteen abbots, Prior Walter of Klosterneuburg, and various Bohemian nobles (cf. Friedrich, *op.cit.* II, Nrs. 216, 217). Further discussion in Bachmann, *Gesch. Böhmens* I 464.

[275] Potthast, *Regesta* I, Nr. 5729 (dated 4 March 1218). An earlier letter (dated 12 May 1217) urged Robert to see to it that the interdict was observed within the diocese of Prague and to urge the king and nobles to respect the liberty of the Church; cf. Friedrich, *CdBoh* II, Nr. 141. Yet other commands were sent on 4 March and 27 March 1218; cf. Friedrich, *op.cit.* II, Nrs. 157, 159.

[276] Boczek, *CdMor* II, Nr. 90; Friedrich, *CdBoh* II, Nr. 159; Potthast, *Regesta* I, Nr. 5737; Pressutti, *Regg. Hon. III* I 199, Nr. 1195; Rodenberg, *MG Ep. s. XIII* I 40, Nr. 54.

[277] Potthast, *Regesta* I, Nr. 5916.

[278] Boczek, *CdMor* II, Nr. 97; Friedrich; *CdBoh* II, Nr. 170; Potthast, *Regesta* I, Nr. 5964.

diocese and about the implementation of the Lateran decrees as well.[279] Although Bishop Bruno had not personally been at the Council, a leading abbot from his diocese, Lüdeger of Altzelle, did attend. Through the latter, the documents distributed to the participants presumably were brought back to Meissen for use in synods there. A thirteenth-century note in the historical record maintained at Altzelle—the *Annales Veterocellenses*—tersely states: "*1215. Concilium Innocentii pape III.*"[280] A marginal note, also from the thirteenth century, adds: "*Hic gloriosum Lateranense concilium celebravit, ubi multa notabilia sunt statuta.*" Though unhappily brief, this entry suggests that the clergy of the diocese had been made aware of the "*notabilia statuta*" by their prelate in the years since the Council. What further directives Cardinal Gregory may have given are not recorded, however.

One matter which certainly came to the legate's attention was an attack made against the aging Bishop Bruno of Meissen in 1221 by the sons of the lord of Mildenstein to avenge the loss of a case involving a disputed tithe.[281] On 29 January 1222 at Probstheida near Leipzig, the miscreants were ordered to appear with thirty others in sackcloth and ashes, and with scourges in their hands, before the synods of the bishops of Naumburg and Merseburg to confess their crime and to make full restitution. Since the Meissen church had been adversely affected even more than the others, they were to appear with fifty pledges in sackcloth, on Maundy Thursday (the traditional day for synods) during the recitation of the Holy Office.[282] A letter of Honorius III dated 31 March 1223 reveals that they did not obey this legatine command, for it announced the excommunication of the brothers to the entire province of Magdeburg, "inasmuch as their reprehensible deed has remained unatoned for to this day, and because they have not only refused to offer compensation to the bishop, but have in fact seized his property and that of his servants."[283]

These documents are most significant to our study in that they leave no doubt that synods were held regularly in the bishoprics of Naumburg, Merseburg, and Meissen. We have noted above the synods documented at Merseburg in 1216, 1217, and 1218, and the Naumburg assembly of 1217; apparently there were others—unrecorded—between then and 1222. The reference to a general tradition of regular yearly synods on Maundy

---

[279] Rittenbach, *Bischöfe von Meissen* 135; Gersdorf, *UB Meissen* II 4, Nr. 4; Böhmer-Ficker, *Regg. Imp.* V, Nr. 9998.

[280] *Ann. Veterocell.* 43; Chevalier, *Repertoire* (Topo-Bibliogr.) I 88.

[281] Cf. Gersdorf, *UB Meissen* I, Nr. 82.

[282] Gersdorf, *UB Meissen* I, Nr. 92; Rittenbach, *Bischöfe von Meissen* 130-134.

[283] Gersdorf, *UB Meissen* I 90, Nr. 97; Potthast, *Regesta* I, Nr. 6977; Pressutti, *Regg. Hon. III* II, Nr. 4272.

Thursday at Meissen assures us that the zeal for reform which Bishop Bruno displayed prior to the Council was carried over into the post-Lateran period as well. We may thus justifiably conclude that he (and his colleagues at Naumburg and Merseburg) had already published the constitutions at some synod previous to the legate's visit.

Cardinal-legate Gregory is recorded during the month of February 1222 at Wratislava, during March at Prague, and during April in Lübeck.[284] At the latter city on 17 April he granted to all who visited the cathedral church on the feast of the Beheading of St. John the Baptist a forty-day indulgence. There is no record of whether he conducted other ecclesiastical business. Such might be assumed, however, for the next documented venue for his legation was Schleswig where on 1 November he presided over a synod which issued a decree against certain inheritance practices.[285] On 22 November at Ratzeburg he issued another letter of indulgence in behalf of the cathedral church at Lübeck.[286] Further details of how he affected that diocese are also lacking.

Whilst a papally-appointed legate was directing various ecclesiastical matters along Germany's eastern and northern borders, other prelates assumed the initiative on their own. The year 1221 witnessed the first clearly recorded and identified diocesan synod at Trier since the Council. Given the rather aggressive reform measures undertaken by the archbishop since his return from the Council, it is probable that this diocesan synod dealt with more than just the resolution of a conflict between the collegiate church at Carden-on-the-Mosel and some parishioners at Machern over the small-tithe which the latter owed Carden.[287] If we are incorrect in associating the decrees repeated at the provincial synod of 1238 with that held in 1216, this diocesan synod would seem the most likely alternative. Especially is this true for the concern expressed by the archbishop for the vessels and elements of the Holy Sacraments, inasmuch as that same year (1221) the archbishop of Cologne dealt with a similar problem. At a diocesan synod Engelbert ordained that in all churches of the archdiocese the symbols of the sacraments be kept under lock and key, in order to prevent the frequent theft of the Consecrated Host by heretics.[288] Again, the conciliar underpinning for this was c. 20 of Lateran IV, but it may also

---

[284] Böhmer-Ficker, *Regg. Imp.* V, Nrs. 9999, 10000, 10001.

[285] Böhmer-Ficker, *Regg. Imp.* V, Nr. 10001b.

[286] Böhmer-Ficker, *Regg. Imp.* V, Nr. 10002; see also Nr. 10003.

[287] Goerz, *MRR* IV, Nachtrag 2, Nr. 2329.

[288] Binterim, *Concilien* IV 421; *Caesarii Dialogus* V 21, IX 52, VI 20; Finke, *Konzilienst.* 48, argues that the citations from Caesarius which Ficker, *Engelbert der Heilige* 96, uses to support his claim that Engelbert held numerous provincial assemblies, are in fact references to diocesan synods. See also Gescher, "Geschichte und Recht" 35-36.

reflect the influence of the statutes issued at the synod of Paris in 1208 by Bishop Eudes of Sully. The archprelate also placed prohibitions against the offering of hospitality to vagabonds (*vagantes*) who posed as clerics. Presumably, the archbishop also reminded his diocesan clergy of their obligations regarding the half-tithe imposed by the Fourth Lateranum, since Pope Honorius III had recently written him on the matter.[289]

On 25 August 1221 the abbots of Murbach and Neubourg and the count of Würth arranged a reconciliation between Frederick II and the bishop of Strasbourg. The agreement was referred to by Archbishop Siegfried II of Mainz and the suffragan bishops of Worms, Halberstadt, Augsburg, Chur, and Verden in an undated letter which was drafted "*in sancto concilio Moguntino nuper congregati,*" asking the emperor that he recognize the accord.[290] This assembly can only have been a provincial synod which was held shortly before 25 August 1221, at which the decrees of Lateran IV were read once again, but for which further details are lacking.

Siegfried of Augsburg had been absent from the Council in 1215, and there is no evidence of any clerics from his diocese being present at Rome who could have transmitted copies of the Council's documents back home. The year 1221 may be seen as the *terminus ante quem* for his receiving the constitutions of Lateran IV, however, inasmuch as by then two provincial synods had been held which would have proclaimed the decrees of Innocent III to all suffragans who were present. Just when those same decrees were published for the diocese of Augsburg therefore remains unknown. Bishop Siegfried is mentioned in a document of 30 April 1219 as a pilgrim, and he landed at Damietta in September 1219, suggesting that he had made preparations for this journey at a prior assembly of his clergy.[291] He was back at the royal court by November 1219.

Not until 1273 do we find positive evidence of a diocesan synod at Augsburg, but such a delay is totally incongruous with the pattern established elsewhere in the German church.[292] The *Annales Elwangen-*

---

[289] Pressutti, *Regg. Hon. III* I, Nr. 3509 (1221, without closer indication of month or day). Foerster, *Engelbert von Berg* 79, interprets the word "*vagantes*" in Caesarius to mean monks who refused to observe the rule of stability; Knipping, *REK* III 186, Nr. 551, argues that they were Cistercian *conversi*. Gescher, "Geschichte und Recht" 34-35, on the other hand, suggests that they were laymen who appropriated the tonsure and the monastic habit in order to move about under their protection while committing their misdeeds.

[290] Missing in Hefele-Knöpfler, *Conziliengeschichte*, the synod is noted in Johann Daniel Schöpflin, *Alsatia aevi Merovingici, Carolingici, Saxonici, Salici, Suevici diplomatica* I (Mannheim, 1775) 347; Winkelmann, *Acta imperii* I 483, Nr. 603; Böhmer-Will, *RAM* II 181, Nr. 408; Böhmer-Ficker, *Regg. Imp.* V, Nr. 3862; Hessel, *Regg. Strassburg* II, Nr. 870; Finke, *Konzilienst.* 49; Hauck, *KGD* V 135, note 1.

[291] Röhricht, *Deutscher im Heiligen Lande* 97; Zoepfl, *Bistum Augsburg* 165.

[292] Zoepfl, *Bistum Augsburg* 211-212.

ses, maintained by a Benedictine house in the diocese of Augsburg—at Elwangen in Württemburg, have notices to 1237 and are assumed to be contemporary to the events described. The brief notice found there regarding the Fourth Lateranum was later expanded with the aid of the equally contemporary *Annales Neresheimenses* into the record found in the *Chronicon Elwacense*.[293] We recognize once more the words of the protocol, but further knowledge of the Council appears to have been lacking. It is thus uncertain whether the same effort was expended in publishing the constitutions in Augsburg that had been noted in some of the neighboring dioceses. Significant may be the fact that the third scribe for the *Chronicon Ottenburanum*, which was compiled during the abbacy of Conrad (1193-1227), is totally silent on the matter of the Council.[294] As a Benedictine house, Ottenbeuern would have been obligated to send representatives to diocesan synods convened by the bishop of Augsburg, but the *Chronicon* offers no help in that regard.

Pluralism—A Universal Problem

Although the German prelates were generally charged with implementing the constitutions of Lateran IV, they occasionally found it necessary to deal with exceptions to those decrees granted by the papacy. We have noted in Ch. Three that pluralism was a serious problem on the eve of the Council. The tendency for pluralists to employ vicars in fulfilling the obligations incumbent upon them as the holders of multiple benefices had weakened the control of the diocesan administration over both properties and clerics. C. 29 of the Lateran IV decrees had placed strictures upon the granting of additional benefices where the *cura animarum* was involved. Yet, as early as the pontificate of Honorius III dispensations from these prohibitions were being granted. On 26 May 1218 an indulgence was granted to Dietrich, the cathedral provost at Cologne "*ut plura beneficia ecclesiastica pluresque dignitates, non obstante decreto concilii lateranensis, consequi possit.*"[295] A practice still quite rare in 1220 would become a major problem itself by mid-century.

Perhaps the most flagrant example of the contradictions between canonical precepts and the exigencies of German church life developed in

---

[293]*Ann. Elwang.* 20: "*1215. Concilium Innocentii papae III.*" *Ann. Nerresh.* 23: "*1215. Rome celebrata est synodus in ecclesia Salvatoria, que Constantiniana vocatur, sub Innocentio papa tertio, qui itinerant episcopi 412.*" *Chron. Elwac.* 37: "*1215. Concilium Innocentii papae tertii, in ecclesia Salvatoris que Constantiniana vocatur, cui concilio intererant 412.*" See Wattenbach-Schmale, *DGQ* 273-374; Potthast, *Repertorium* II 308.

[294] *MGH SS* XXIII 610-630; cf. Wattenbach-Schmale, *DGQ* 277.

[295] Pressutti, *Regg. Hon. III* I, Nr. 1378 ("*Qui bene meritos . . .*").

the aftermath of the death of Bishop Arnold II of Chur on 24 December 1221. A schismatic election produced two contenders: the cathedral canon Henry (III) of Rialt, and Albert of Güttingen, an unreformed pluralist who, in addition to holding a prebend in the cathedral chapter at Chur, had been a cathedral canon at Constanz since 1200 and at Augsburg since 1209, and was currently provost of the collegiate churches of St. Stephan in Constanz and of Sindelvingen.[296] The resolution of the dispute was transferred to the Curia, but before it could be heard there both contestants died (Albert before 13 May 1223, and Henry on 14 September 1223). The new election (before 23 February 1224 when he appears as *electus*) fell upon Albert's brother, Rudolf I of Güttingen, the abbot of St. Gall, who had supported the former financially in his bid for the bishop's mitre; he appears to have bought his own election so as not to lose altogether the money spent on Albert. In return for a payment of 300 Marks, he received papal permission to retain his abbacy for three years and also to receive the income from his deceased brother's prebend for six years. Conrad de Fabaria complained that in laboring for his brother's election, Abbot Rudolf put St. Gall in a bad financial situation. In late 1226 Honorius III apparently sent instructions to the monks at St. Gall to make preparations to elect a new abbot after the expiration of the three-year boon (February 1227). This letter probably prompted Rudolf to journey to Rome personally in order to seek an extension of the privilege. He died 17/18 September 1226 while there and was buried 19 September in the Lateran crypt by Cardinal-bishop Conrad of Urach. His ambitions left both St. Gall and Chur with huge debts.[297]

Bishop Conrad of Hildesheim

At the time of the Mainz provincial synod in 1221, it was known that the pope had granted permission to Raynaldo de Puzalia, a papal subdeacon and provost of St. Severin in Erfurt, to receive additional prebends to which the

---

[296] Cf. Affentranger, "Bischöfe von Chur" 135-147; Krabbo, *Besetzung* 81-83; Simon, *Stand und Herkunft* 42.

[297] *Conr. de Fabaria* 172-173. On 21 October 1229 Pope Gregory IX commissioned the bishop of Bologna to see to it that the monastery at St. Gall paid its debts to certain merchants of Rome and Siena; cf. Clavadetscher, *Cartularium Sangallense* III, Nr. 1167: ". . . *quod cum ipsi bone memorie . . . episcopo Curiensi, qui et abbas erat monasterii sancti Galli, quandam pecunie summam pro Curiensis ecclesie ac ipsius monasterii procurandis negotiis mutuassent certis loco et termino sibi reddendam, . . .*" According to a charter issued 25 May 1230, Abbot Conrad of St. Gall had reached an agreement with Ubertus Baccus of Siena, paying 500 Marks for the loans of 700 and 500 Marks incurred by his predecessor; cf. Clavadetscher, *op.cit.* Nr. 1175.

cure of souls was also attached. It was later announced that Raynaldo had received the provostship of the collegiate church of St. Bartholomew in Frankfurt. A similar concession was granted on 25 April 1227 to Gerbodo, cathedral provost at Mainz, allowing him to acquire the provostship of the collegiate church of St. Peter while retaining other benefices which he had held before the Council.[298] Thus, just as papal political policy before 1215 often undermined its ecclesiastical/spiritual goals, the practice of papal provisions served to negate some of the positive accomplishments of the post-Lateran period.

The bishop of Hildesheim was not present at the 1221 provincial synod at Mainz because on 31 June of that year Siegfried of Lichtenberg resigned his office amid charges of gross negligence and incompetence. His successor received consecration at Erfurt on 19 September 1221, undoubtedly at the hands of the archbishop of Mainz who had been a major force in his elevation. Within weeks of receiving the bishop's miter at Hildesheim, *magister* Conrad, formerly the cathedral scholastic at Mainz, summoned his clergy in a synod.[299] This dedicated servant of the papacy thus commenced the final and perhaps the most significant chapter in his eventful career, giving heed to the pope in whose closest company he had been as a papal penitentiary 1216-1221.

The following year Bishop Conrad of Hildesheim gathered his clergy once more to treat a matter of serious consequence to his church and all of Lower Saxony—the charges of heresy brought against one Henry Minnecke. This Premonstratensian canon had been elected prior of the Cistercian convent of Mariengarten at Neuwerk, near Goslar. Soon thereafter, he became suspected of teaching false doctrines and was given several warnings (possibly at diocesan synods) by Bishop Siegfried. The new prelate, Bishop Conrad, was much less inclined to tolerate such deviance, however: previous to becoming the dean at Speyer in 1209 and subsequently scholastic at Mainz in 1216, he had distinguished himself as a master of theology at Paris and had also participated in the preaching efforts against the Albigenses in Languedoc. Upon his succession as bishop, he therefore renewed the command for Minnecke to desist, only to find himself being publicly attacked in the prior's sermons.

To confront this truculence head-on, the bishop went personally to Neuwerk and, in the presence of the nuns and many of the leading clerics

---

[298] Potthast, *Regesta* I, Nrs. 6574, 7885; Würdtwein, *Nova subs.* IV 117, VI 1. For further details, cf. Pixton, "Konrad von Reifenberg" 60-61, 64.

[299] Hoogeweg, *UB Hilds* II, Nr. 21 (*"coram nobis in synodo nostra"*). For details of Conrad's election and confirmation, see Hoogeweg, "Bischof Konrad II." 238; Pixton, "Anwerbung" 166-191; Idem, "Konrad von Reifenberg" 72-81.

of his diocese, examined the orthodoxy of Henry himself. Discovering views on the Holy Spirit, the Blessed Virgin, the acceptance of Satan, and marriage which ran counter to the approved teachings of the Church, Conrad renewed his prohibition against preaching by Minnecke. When such mild remedies failed, however, the prelate, assisted by several Cistercian abbots, condemned the teachings and declared Minnecke deposed at a synod held 1222 at Hildesheim.[300] Conrad also instructed the convent at Neuwerk to elect a new prior, but the nuns were so committed to Henry that they refused to do so. In the face of such willful opposition, the prelate then turned to Rome for assistance. Having journeyed in the fall of 1222 to meet with the emperor in Italy, he also secured a letter from the pope dated 19 January 1223 which commanded all those involved in the Minnecke controversy to obey the bishop under penalty of excommunication. The nuns still were not cowed by this, however, and they in turn sent a letter of complaint against the bishop to both the Roman pontiff and the emperor. They charged Conrad with failing to honor imperial rights, in that he had unilaterally deposed the prior of a house which stood directly under the Empire.

Frederick II, having just recently reached a peaceful agreement with the papacy, was ill-disposed to get involved in an issue of alleged heresy. He therefore deferred a decision to the German bishops present at his court. These in turn gave support to their colleague, Bishop Conrad, who was also present; in a letter dated 12 March 1223 the prelates admonished the nuns at Neuwerk to obey their bishop and to cease their disturbances. Shortly thereafter (9 May), the pope also rendered a decision, going well beyond the judgment of Bishop Conrad: Honorius III gave the prelate authority to appoint a new prior at Neuwerk himself.[301] Conrad also received counsel from the bishops and cardinals present at the court of Frederick II at Ferentino to bring an end to the entire matter by seizing the author of the confusion and imprisoning him. Upon Conrad's return to Hildesheim, this was done. Even from prison, however, Minnecke refused to submit. He appealed to the pope and demanded that another hearing be granted. Thus, on 23 May 1224 Honorius III agreed to this petition, giving orders to his legate in Germany, Cardinal-bishop Conrad of Porto and S. Rufina, who fulfilled this mandate during the fall of that same year.[302]

---

[300] *Chron. mont. ser.* 199; Hartzheim, *Concilia* III 515 and 795-796; Hoogeweg, *UB Hilds* II, Nr. 59; Potthast, *Regesta* I, Nr. 7260; Maring, *Diözesansynoden* 72-75; Hefele-Leclercq, *Conciles* V/2 1444-5; Hoogeweg, "Bischof Konrad II." 256-260.

[301] Potthast, *Regesta* I, Nr. 7013; Sudendorf, *Regestrum* II 160-163, Nr. 75.

[302] Rodenberg, *MG Ep. s. XIII* I 238; Potthast, *Regesta* I, Nr. 7260; Winkelmann, *Friedrich II.* I 240-242.

Few of the synods recorded during this period had such extended issues, however. The notices for the assemblies held at Liège in 1222 and Osnabrück in 1223 attest to the fact that the synodal tradition was still vital, but their content is of little interest to us.[303] They may, however, have taken up those issues dealt with at the 1220 provincial synod at Cologne which were relevant to their own situation. On the other hand, the possibility of a synod at Verdun during June 1222 deserves attention, since if that is in fact the case it represents the first known diocesan assembly for that bishopric since the Council of 1215. Four documents, two without any date, one with just the year 1222, and another dated 13 June 1222, refer to an exchange of property which took place between the cloister of Mary Magdalene at Verdun and the monastery of St. Matthias at Trier, an act confirmed by Bishop Jean and by the cathedral chapter at Verdun.[304] The rather sizeable number of clergy participating in this exchange, either as principals or witnesses, suggests that the transaction occurred in a synodal setting, at which other matters were discussed as well.

Perhaps this diocesan synod was also the occasion on which Bishop Jean exercised the authority granted him on 21 December 1221 by Pope Honorius III, that he absolve those clerics of his diocese who had not yet paid their half-tithe for the crusade, or who, on account of other irregularities, had been excommunicated, all on condition that they pay their obligation in full.[305] Like their brethren elsewhere in Germany, the clergy in the diocese of Verdun seemed ill-disposed to surrendering part of their incomes for this papal enterprise, despite frequent reminders and threats of ecclesiastical sanctions.

The limited documentary evidence for Verdun is barely augmented by the *Annales S. Pauli Virdunensis* which exist in a thirteenth-century manuscript, but unfortunately contain few entries at all for the period of our interest: the third from last notation is dated 1215; the penultimate is dated 1249 and appears to have been written well after the fact. It thus seems probable that the entry for 1215 was also made years after the Council, stating briefly that "Frederick was consecrated king at Aachen, and a council was celebrated at Rome on the Kalends of November that same year by the lord Pope Innocent, to which he summoned the archbishops, bishops, and abbots of all Christendom."[306] While this account bears strong

---

[303] Hauck, *KGD* I 8, note 1, refers to synods at Osnabrück in 1223 (Philippi, *Osnabrück UB* II 112-114, Nrs. 153-154) and before 1224 (*loc.cit.* II 132, Nr. 177).

[304] Goerz, *MRR* II, Nrs. 1567-1570.

[305] Pressutti, *Regg. Hon. III* II, Nr. 3642.

[306] *Ann. S. Pauli Virdun.* 502: "*Fridericus Aquisgrani consecratus est in regem, et celebratum est concilium Rome Kalendas Novembris eodem anno a domino papa Innocentio, ad quod convocavit archiepiscopos episcopos abbates fere tocius christianitatis. . . .*"

similarity to that found in the neighboring *Annales Spirenses*, there are enough deviations to suspect that behind its terse lines lies the protocol of 1215. Beyond that, however, conclusions are not possible.

Less specific are the contemporary *Annales S. Vitoni Virdunensis* which were extended in their first recension to 1215 and note: "1216. A general council was convened at Rome, at which the Emperor Frederick took the crusading vow."[307] This reference to Frederick II's taking the cross at the Council is the result of confusion with the oath sworn at Aachen in July of that same year (1215) in the presence of the crusade-preachers Conrad of Speyer and John of Xanten, or a subsequent vow taken at Rome in 1220. The flattening of time suggests that the scribe was well-removed from the events themselves, relying on some faded memory rather than documents. Whatever the time at which the decrees of Lateran IV were introduced into the diocese of Verdun, by the 1250s there is little real awareness of them manifest in the annalistic traditions of the bishopric. It would be most enlightening to be able to analyze the synodal statutes attributed to Bishop Jean d'Aix who occupied the see of Verdun 1247-1252; the oldest known statutes for this bishopric, they are unfortunately lost.[308]

The papal privilege granted to the bishop of Toul in December 1220 became the center of an interpretational dispute between the prelate and his clergy, an argument which may have erupted during a diocesan synod early the following year as the bull was read. At issue was the precise meaning of the phrase "*beneficia suae dioecesis*" contained in the letter. For this reason Bishop Eudes requested a clarification from the Curia. On 11 January 1222 Honorius restated the privilege and sought to make explicit what had previously seemed unclear.[309] At the same time he issued a directive to the abbots of Derven and *Bellus locus*, and to the prior at Derven, houses in the dioceses of Châlons and Toul respectively, that in this dispute they not suffer the bishop to be defrauded.[310] Two days later the pontiff commanded the same agents to impose upon the clergy of the city and diocese of Toul the obligation to commit a one-fifteenth part of their annual incomes for the alleviation of the debts of the bishopric for a period of three years.[311] The issue itself became significant in the history of can-

---

[307] *Ann. S. Vitoni Virdun.* 527: "*1216. Convocatum est Rome generale concilium, et ubi cruce signatus est imperator Fridericus. . . .*" See also Potthast, *Repertorium* II 347.

[308] See Abbé Charles Aimond, "Les Anciens Synodes du Diocese de Verdun," *La Semaine Religieuse du Diocèse de Verdun* (1923) 42-44, citing N. Roussel, *Histoire écclésiastique et civile de Verdun* (édition revue; Bar-le-Duc, 1863-1864); Pontal, *Liste des MSS* 478-479.

[309] Horoy, *Honorii III opera* IV 70, Nr. 86; Pressutti, *Regg. Hon. III* II, Nr. 3711.

[310] Horoy, *Honorii III opera* IV 70, Nr. 87; Pressutti, *Regg. Hon. III* II, Nr. 3712.

[311] Pressutti, *Regg. Hon. III* II, Nr. 3721.

on law since the papal clarification was included in the decretal collection of Gregory IX in 1234.[312]

There are indications that during October 1222 and again in 1223 Archbishop Dietrich II of Trier held additional provincial synods with one or more of his suffragans. In the former year he was once again at Verdun where he witnessed the transfer of the fortress Lemberg to a *ministerialis* named William who was a vassal of the bishop of Verdun; the enfeoffment was made by the counts of Bleicastel and Zweibrücken.[313] Although these latter two magnates would have had no role to play at a provincial synod, it is nevertheless reasonable to conclude that the metropolitan convened such an assembly for the prelates and major abbots who were also present at this time.

A charter with just the year 1223 as the date attests that the archbishop had incorporated the parish church in Köllerthal into the monastery at Wadgassen, and that Count Simon of Saarbrücken had renounced the rights of patronage over the church. Witnessing this event were Bishop Jean of Verdun, the abbots of St. Eucharius (Matthias) and Metlach, and numerous dignitaries of the archbishopric of Trier.[314] As noted frequently above, such an assembly was not necessary for a mere incorporation—certainly not the presence of a suffragan bishop! Though Bishop Conrad of Metz was often in his episcopal city between March and September of that year, the surviving documents of his episcopacy offer no indication that he was in any way involved in these assemblies.[315] By late March 1224 he was dead.

One of the issues with which the synod may have dealt was contained in a letter dictated to the archbishop on 5 October 1223 by Pope Honorius III. The metropolitan was ordered to provide Richard, a cathedral canon at Verdun, with a suitable archdeaconate or provostship or similar ecclesiastical dignity within the province of Trier, inasmuch as it had been impossible for three previously-appointed *iudices delegati* to execute a grant made by the pope to the same cleric of one of the two archdeaconates which

---

[312] *Decretal. Gregorii IX. lib. 5. tit. 40. De verb. signific. c. 32*; see Friedberg, *Corp. Iur. Can.* II. lib. V. tit. XL. c. XXXII. p. 926: "*Tua nobis fraternitas intimavit, quod, quum tibi pro relevatione oneris debitorum, quo premeris, duxerimus indulgendum, ut fructus beneficiorum, quae interim in dioecesi tua vacare contigerit, tibi liceat biennio retinere, quidam, apostolicae gratiae privilegium sinistra interpretatione restringere molientes, asserunt, praebendas et maiora beneficia nequaquam beneficiorum nomine contineri, super quo interpretationem apostolicam postulasti. Nos igitur, interpretum huiusmodi sententiam reprobantes, auctoritate praesentium declaramus, quod in hoc casu praebendae ac alia beneficie generali beneficiorum nomine continentur.*"

[313] Herrmann, *Inventar* 245.

[314] Beyer, *MRUB* III, Nr. 222.

[315] See Bienemann, *Conrad v. Scharf.* Urkundenregister.

"*contra canonicas sanctiones obtinebat T. quondam primicerius ecclesiae Virdunensis . . .*"[316]

The dating of this synod is limited first of all by the papal letter of 5 October; a reasonable length of time would have been required for that missive to be delivered. Thus, late October would seem to be the earliest possible opportunity—the *terminus a quo*. As the *terminus ante quem* we may see 23 November 1223, on which day the archbishop of Trier conferred the fiefs of Arlon and Luxemburg, held of the archbishopric by Walram, duke of Limburg and count of Luxemburg, upon the latter's wife Ermengarde and their children.[317] This event, which must have attracted not only the archbishop of Trier but clergy and nobles from the Lotharingian bishoprics as well, was of major significance for the entire region: not only the dukes of Limburg and the counts of Luxemburg, but also the counts of Wied from whom Archbishop Dietrich II sprang, traced their lineage back to the counts of Ardennes who flourished in the tenth century. Members of this great family had been bishops of Metz, dukes of Bavaria, German empresses and counts of half a dozen hereditary territories which were created in the eleventh and twelfth centuries.[318]

The possessions of the counts of Luxemburg in 1223 were vast; next to the dukes of Lorraine, they were lords over the largest territory west of the Rhine which lay within the Empire. Estimates are that in the mid-twelfth century they controlled more than thirty fortresses, and near the end of the thirteenth century close to one hundred. The assemblage of those required to pay homage to the countess at this time alone must have been quite sizeable, and the fact that the lordships of Arlon and Luxemburg interfaced with the bishoprics of Lorraine and the archdiocese of Trier gave the four prelates of this province ample reason for being personally present, or at least represented on this occasion. It is thus altogether probable that at some time just prior to 23 November, the metropolitan of Trier met with his suffragans in a provincial synod.

Reform Efforts at Worms

Mention of a synod at Worms in 1223 also catches our attention, since it is the first one recorded in that bishopric since 1197.[319] We have noted in Ch. Two that the diocese of Worms was badly torn and financially ruined

---

[316] Pressutti, *Regg. Hon. III* II, Nr. 4515.

[317] Goerz, *MRR* II 438, Nr. 1618; Hontheim, *Hist. dipl.* I 699; Ernst, *Hist. de Limbourg* IV 17.

[318] Cf. genealogical/biographical summaries in Beyer, *MRUB* II lix-lxiii.

[319] Boos, *Wormser UB* I, Nr. 128 ("*universa synodus*"); presiding over the synod was the cathedral provost, not the bishop. For the earlier synods, see Ch. One, p. 71.

by this ambitious and brutal prelate, and his neglect of pastoral matters allowed severe problems to develop which even the decrees of Papal-legate Guy Poré could hardly have corrected. Although the synod of 1223 and its successor of 1224[320] dealt with the composition of disputes, testimony of which is found in the documents, it may also have been on these occasions that the constitutions of Lateran IV were first introduced into the diocese.

The bishop of Worms since 1217 was Henry of Saarbrücken, formerly a leading cleric within the archdiocese of Mainz and one fully acquainted with the synods of 1209, 1218, and 1221. Although no known proctors of the Worms church were in Rome during the Council, copies of the decrees of Innocent III were accessible at Mainz. Because of a challenge to his election by an absent cathedral canon, Bishop-elect Henry was not confirmed until after 10 July 1218; not before the latter part of that year was he therefore able to exercise the spiritual powers of his office.[321]

According to Schannat, Bishop Henry's efforts at reform were not without opposition. Some nuns went so far as to assault him physically on an occasion not otherwise specified.[322] The *moniales* in question were perhaps those of the Augustinian cloister Nonnenmünster, located just outside the city walls. Their obstinacy in the face of episcopal reform efforts led to complaints by the bishop before the Roman Curia. Finally, on 17 May 1233, Pope Gregory IX directed the archbishop of Mainz to fill the house with members of another established and recognized Order, inasmuch as the bishop of Worms had removed all the former occupants (*vitam ducentes multipliciter dissolutam*) and had dispersed them among the various convents of Augustinian canonesses in his diocese. The final solution came in 1236 when Cistercian nuns were introduced into the house.[323]

Other communities of nuns in Germany were likewise the target of reforming activities. E.g., on 19 May 1222 the Cistercian abbot of Sichem in the diocese of Halberstadt was given a papal mandate to visit the cloister

---

[320] Guden, *Sylloge* Nr. 59 ("*in sinodo*"); Hartzheim, *Concilia* III 517; Phillips, *Diözesansynode* 138.

[321] Pixton, "Konrad von Reifenberg" 60-61; Krabbo, *Besetzung* 53-57 und Urkunden-Anhang Nrs. 1-2; Pressutti, *Regg. Hon. III* I, Nr. 739; Potthast, *Regesta* I, Nr. 5867.

[322] Binterim, *Concilien* IV 278, citing Schannat, *Hist. Wormat.* 373.

[323] Potthast, *Regesta* I, Nrs. 9194, 10245; Auvray, *Registres de Gregoire IX* I, Nrs. 1306, 3336; Würdtwein, *Nova subs.* VI 35; Manrique, *Ann. Cist.* IV 534; Schannat, *Hist. Wormat.* II 119, Nr. 131; *Archiv für Hessische Geschichte* II 303. On 28 January 1239 Pope Gregory IX issued a mandate to Bishop Conrad of Hildesheim to investigate the situation at Nonnenmünster further: based on the papal letter of 1236 the bishop of Worms had evicted the Benedictine nuns and had commenced the process of bringing Cistercian replacements, despite the fact that the reprobate *moniales* had lodged an appeal with the Curia; Conrad was instructed to "*corrigenda et reformanda corrigat et reformet*"; cf. Auvray, *op.cit.* II, Nr. 4748.

of Heiligenthal and to effect an improvement in both temporal and spiritual matters.[324] This visitor was none other than Conrad of Krosigk whom we have encountered above as a man committed to the reform and regeneration of clerical life. This papal intervention in the diocese of Halberstadt suggests that the bishop had written the Curia concerning the problems at Heiligenstadt, having himself become aware of them as a result of a diocesan visitation. Because of the exempt status of Cistercian houses, however, the prelate was unable to take direct action himself in correcting the abuses. As a former bishop who still enjoyed the episcopal powers, the Cistercian Conrad of Krosigk was ideally suited for such a task.

Early in March 1223 Hartwich of Dolnstein, bishop of Eichstätt, died after a pontificate of almost thirty years. He did not attend the Council, nor do we possess any references to his clergy being present. He is documented just once between 20 June 1215 (at Ulm as a witness for Frederick II of Staufen) and 15 January 1219: on 28 August 1216 at Eichstätt he resolved a complex dispute involving tithes owed the monastery at Rebdorf.[325] It is thus probable that Hartwich was among those prelates and princes who accompanied King Andreas of Hungary on the crusade in 1217/1218.[326] As suggested with other prelates, he may well have convened his clergy in some sort of assembly in connection with his imminent departure in 1217, but we have no supporting evidence. His absence throughout the entire year of 1218 excludes the possibility that he attended the provincial synod held at Mainz late that year, yet he may well have been represented by members of the cathedral chapter who thus could have obtained copies of the Council's decrees for use in his own diocese. That they were known in Eichstätt by the time of his death is clear from the events which followed.

The election held shortly after Hartwich's burial was challenged and eventually ended up before the Curia. The details of this dispute are contained in a papal letter of commission issued to Bishop Siegfried of Augsburg, to Abbot Conrad III of Kaisheim in the diocese of Augsburg, and to the cathedral scholastic Henry of Zeupplingen at Augsburg on 13 June 1224, and reveal much about medieval German episcopal politics.[327] Pope Honorius III informed his *iudices delegati* that both the bishop-elect, the former cathedral *custos* at Eichstätt, Frederick of Huwenstat, and the cathedral provost, Henry, had appeared before the Curia in Rome. Henry, along with the cathedral provost Gottfried of Regensburg and an Eichstätt

---

[324] Potthast, *Regesta* I, Nr. 6834; Manrique, *Ann. Cist.* IV 450.

[325] Heidingsfelder, *Regg. Eichst.* Nr. 575.

[326] Röhricht, *Deutscher im Heiligen Lande* 102.

[327] Pressutti, *Regg. Hon. III* II, Nr. 5041; Heidingsfelder, *Regg. Eichst.* Nr. 607. For discussion of this election, see also Krabbo, *Besetzung* 96-98; Hauck, *KGD* IV 952-953; Heidingsfelder, *Regg. Eichst* 162-163, 187-188; Simon, *Stand und Herkunft* 52.

cathedral canon named Henry of Mur had given an account of the disputed
election and of an ealier papal commission headed by Abbot Albert of
Komburg. The bishop-elect had also given testimony concerning the course
of events: at the death of Bishop Hartwich, some fourteen of the forty-five
prebendarii of the Eichstätt church were not present in the city; of these,
four were more than six-days distant, one (Ulrich) was excommunicated,
and one (Henry) was suspended; the remaining eight were summoned back
so that they might participate in the new election, but they declined, three
being sick and the other five engaged in business which prevented their
immediate return; they all agreed, however, to accept the decision of the
majority of the chapter; of the thirty-one canons who were actually present,
thirteen had no voting rights; having failed by means of the *scrutinium* or
inspiratio to come to a choice regarding the successor, the eighteen present
and authorized canons appointed five of their number to represent them;
these five had elected Frederick, a decision accepted by all but the cathedral
provost Henry who was not present, and the suspended and excommunicated
Henry of Mur; the archbishop of Mainz had examined the election, found
it valid, and had confirmed it in the presence of Henry of Mur who
represented the cathedral provost; and although Frederick had also received
the regalia and had begun to administer the affairs of the diocese, provost
Henry had obtained letters of commission to the abbot of Komburg and his
fellow judges through falsely representing the situation in Rome; these had
declared Frederick's acts null and void.

Provost Henry reported events somewhat differently: after the death of
Bishop Hartwich and the burial of his body the following day, he (the
provost), Dean Siegfried, the scholastic Albert and those canons present on
the occasion had met behind the high altar in the cathedral to await word
from the episcopal advocate, Count Gebhard, regarding Hartwich's personal
property which Gebhard had confiscated upon the prelate's death; the count
had appeared with several of the *ministeriales* of the church and others, and
had demanded without saying a word about the property that a new election
take place immediately; the *electus* and his supporters proceeded to do this,
while he (the provost), pointed out that the *ministeriales* could not
participate in the election, and that those cathedral canons who were close
enough to return to the city needed to be summoned and given that
opportunity; the dean, whose prerogative it was to set the date for a new
election, ought to do so with that in mind; as the *electus*, the *ministeriales*
and his supporters demanded an immediate election, he (the provost)
removed himself from Eichstätt with Henry of Mur, and sent an appeal to
Rome; after their withdrawal, those remaining agreed to select five
cathedral canons and five *ministeriales* to represent them in the election
which was carried out in a tower chamber of the cathedral.

The provost continued in his statement before the Curia that, shortly after the ten men had commenced their deliberations, a spokesman for them returned to the larger body and announced that if the *custos* Frederick would agree to the confiscation of Bishop Hartwig's personal property, and to the loss of the right of the bishop of Eichstätt to appoint the provost at St. Walburg in that city, they were prepared to offer him the miter and staff; Frederick agreed and at once began to administer his office; four days after the election he received the regalia at Augsburg, despite the fact that the protesting cathedral provost (Henry) was present at the time, and despite the fact that it was known that Henry had lodged an appeal with Rome and with the archbishop of Mainz.

The bishop-elect protested before the pope and his judges that Henry had been excommunicated on two separate occasions on charges of *"crimen apostasie, defectus natalium"*, and *"periurium"*: he claimed that at the very time of the election Henry had been under the ban, and that the archbishop of Mainz had pronounced it once again following Henry's public protests. He therefore asked Honorius III to lift the earlier judgment against him, to require his opponents to pay the costs of litigation, and to remove any and all obstacles preventing his receiving consecration as *episcopus*.

The provost responded that the earlier excommunication had been declared invalid *auctoritate apostolica* and urged that the other requests of his antagonist be disregarded. He requested that since the previous election had been carried out with the participation of the laity, without waiting for the arrival of authorized voters, and since the elect had performed acts after receiving confirmation, the papacy quash the election and grant the exclusive privilege in this instance to him and his associates, since his opponents had acted *"contra formam generalis concilii"* and *ipso facto* had lost that right.

Honorius III, having first invalidated the pronouncements of the abbot of Komburg and his associates, gave the new commission the mandate to determine whether the allegations were true that the provost was under the ban of excommunication at the time of the election, or in any other was unentitled to participation therein; if this was in fact the case, they were authorized to command him to be silent on this matter for ever after, and they were to proceed with the consecration of the bishop-elect without any further delay. They were also required to investigate the validity of the provost's charges and to deal with things as the church canons required. We do not have any details concerning this second commission, but it appears that Frederick of Huwenstat's election was quashed. He never did receive consecration and his successor appears as early as 2 July 1225.[328]

---

[328] Heidingsfelder, *Regg. Eichst.* 193, Nr. 611

Ironically, his successor was Henry of Zeupplingen, a cathedral canon at Eichstätt and the scholastic at Augsburg, one of the three *iudices delegati* nominated to investigate his own election. We do not know whether Henry was chosen by Provost Henry and his supporters (as the provost had requested), whether he was elected by the full cathedral chapter at Eichstätt, or whether he benefitted from a papal provision.

This protracted situation at Eichstätt reveals several points which deserve our further attention. This was the first episcopal election at Eichstätt since the radical changes of a decade earlier which had essentially deprived laymen of any remaining influence in the process: we should not assume that the advocate of Eichstätt and the episcopal *ministeriales* were unaware of these changes, including those pronouncements made at the Fourth Lateran Council; Provost Henry specifically appealed to those decrees in his request that the election of his opponent be quashed. And yet, the archbishop of Mainz once again had confirmed a questionable election! One has to wonder just how much Siegfried of Mainz understood of the ramifications of the Council's legislation, or was he simply doing what seemed politically expedient?

The large number of absent canons from the cathedral chapter at the time of their prelate's death also illustrates the acuteness of the problem of absenteeism with which various German prelates sought to deal during the thirteenth century. The willingness of the five canons to concede their voting rights to the decision of the majority also indicates an apathy toward that responsibility: their present business (be it personal or on behalf of their church) was deemed more important than being present for the election of the man who would probably preside over their church for the next decade or more.

At some time in late March/early April 1223, having been barely confirmed by his metropolitan and invested with the *temporalia* of his office, Frederick of Huwenstadt convened what is referred to as the first synod of his pontificate—"*in prima sinodo nostra,*"[329] demonstrating the truth of contemporary canonist theory regarding the episcopal office: unlike archbishops-elect who could not convene provincial synods, bishops-elect held such authority by virtue of their election alone.[330] The primary issue, if one is to judge solely on the basis of extant documents, was a long-standing conflict over the chapel at Bachhausen as a filiation of the parish church at Weidenwang. An Eichstätt cathedral canon, Conrad of Phaffenhouen, who was also the *plebanus* at Weidenwang, put forth his claims, while the priest at Bachhausen, one Henry, asserted counter-claims

---

[329] Heidingsfelder, *Regg. Eichst.* 189, Nr. 604.
[330] See Ch. One, pp. 83-90.

and appealed his case to the Roman Curia. Inasmuch as the appeal did not contain specific grounds, the entire synod determined on the basis of the institutes of Innocent III that the appeal was to be disregarded. Conrad of Phaffenhouen further asserted that the issue had already been settled under Bishop Hartwich (perhaps at an unrecorded synod), upon which the assembled clergy pronounced that the previous decision was to stand.[331] C. 35 of the Lateran IV constitutions had provided detailed instructions on the very question of appeals, and this citing of it in 1223 makes it clear that a copy of those decrees was available in the diocese of Eichstätt at the time and that the leading clergy of that church were acquainted with them.[332] Once again we see the direct application of canon law precepts to specific cases in the operation of the medieval church.

Curbing Excesses in the Archdiocese of Cologne

During the latter part of 1224 or early 1225, Caesarius of Heisterbach

---

[331] Heidingsfelder, *Regg. Eichst.* 187-189, Nr. 604; *Mon. Boica* XXXXIX 75, Nr. 38: "*Notum sit omnibus Christi fidelibus, quod cum Bernhardus, olim in Widenwanc plebanus, longo tempore possederit capellam in Bachusen quiete et sine querela usque ad mortem, ita ut esset filia barrochie sue in Widenwanc, et magister Wernherus, Eistetensis scolasticus, successit in eadem barrochie ipsi Bernhardo et eodem iure possedit ibi pro filia capellam Bachusen, donec Ramungus miles olim de Svabahc movit ei litem super eadem capella Bachusen, ita ut ius patronatus ad ipsum pertineret. Coram antecessore nostro Hartwico, felicis memorie Eistetensi episcopo, legitime probatus fuit, prefatam capellam cum omnibus suis pertinenciis ad barrochiam in Widenwanc pertinere et filiam esse debere. Sed prefatus Ramungus, ob hoc a lite non desistens, prefatam capellam tam ipse, quam uxor eius contra iusticiam detinere presumentes, assignaverunt eam Heinrico sacerdoti Orlin cognominato, quem tamen antecessor noster numquam investivit. Precedente vero tempore et lite pendente, cum nos ad regimen Eistetensis ecclesie, licet immeriti, fuissemus electi, Cunradus de Phaffinhouen, Eistetensis canonicus, qui iam adeptus erat ipsam barrochiam in Widinwanc, prescriptam causam et eiusdem cause processum publice coram nobis in prima sinodo nostra proposuit, presente Heinrico prenominato sacerdote, qui etiam econtra allegans pro parte sua respondebat ea, que seivit et potuit, et eum in omnibus ei pacientem prebuimus audienciam, sedem Romanam appellavit. Sed quia et ante sentenciam nec ab aliquo gravamine nullisque certis causis expressis facta fuit illa appellacio, indicavit tota sinodus nostra secundum instituta domini pape Innocencii tercii tali appellacioni non esse deferendum.*"

[332] Lateran IV, c. 35: "*Ut debitus honor deferatur iudicibus et litigatoribus consulatur super laboribus et expensis, statuimus ut ubi quis coram iudice convenerit adversarium, ille ante sentenciam ad superiorem iudicem absque rationabili causa non provocet, sed coram illo suam iustitiam prosequatur, non obstante si dicat quod ad superiorem iudicem nuncium destinaverit, aut etiam literas impetraverit ab eodem, priusquam delegato fuerint assignatae. Cum autem ex rationabili causa putaverit appellandum, coram eodem iudice causa probabili appellationis exposita, tali videlicet quae si foret probata, deberet legitima reputari, superior de appellatione cognoscat, et si minus eum rationabiliter appellasse cognoverit, illum ad inferiorem remittat et in expensis alteri parti condemnet. Alioquin ipse procedat, salvis constitutionibus de maioribus causis ad sedem apostolicam perferendis.*"

completed his twenty-first Sunday homily, the only one which appears in
dialogue form; its subject was the pericope of the Good Shepherd.
Caesarius laments over the evils of his day, indicating that at times the cure
of souls had even been given over to minor children. In this context he
placed harsh words in the mouth of one of his novices:

> I have heard from a learned and pious man in whom was a zeal for righteous-
> ness, who stated at a Cologne synod: "How shall those guide others' souls
> who cannot as yet control their own drawers [i.e., who are not yet out of
> diapers]?"[333]

Although Caesarius utilized the literary device of the novice as his source,
it is probable that he himself heard that condemnation of existing practices
while attending the synod in question. Given the time when Caesarius
wrote his sermon, it is also probable that the synod was or recent nature.

The more exact date of the synod may perhaps be inferred from other
passages in this same homily. Caesarius was particularly critical of the lust
for money which had taken control of the archdeacons of Cologne, and he
stated:

> For this reason did the scholastic of Cologne, Oliver, say in his recent sermon
> in the presence of several archdeacons: "When the archdeacon conducts a
> visitation of his parishes and a priest cannot understand the 'believe in God,'
> i.e., the meaning of the preposition, he is immediately declared to be a
> heretic, but if he offers [the archdeacon] money, he becomes—sanctified
> [worthy of salvation]."[334]

The fact that the well-known Oliver had preached this before the archdeacons allows the conclusion that it occurred at a diocesan synod where the
latter belonged to the most important participants. Furthermore, if this
inference is correct, we may also be justified in assuming that it was Oliver

---

[333] *Hom.* II 97: *"Novitius: Unde quendam virum litteratum et religiosum, in quo zelus
iustitiae, in synodo Coloniensi audivi dicentum: 'Quomodo regerent animas, qui nondum
noverunt regere braccas suas?'"* See further discussion in Gescher, "Geschichte und Recht"
37-40, who cites a parallel example in the sermons of the French crusade-preacher Jacques de
Vitry; a partial translation thereof is in Th.F. Crane, *The Exempla or Illustrative Stories from
the Sermones vulgares of Jacques de Vitry*, Publications of the Folk-Lore Society 26 (London,
1890) 1, Nr. 1.

[334] *Hom.* II 97: *"Unde Oliverus, scholasticus Coloniensis, in sermone suo nuper
praesentibus quibusdam archidiaconis sic ait: 'Quando archidiaconus parochias suas visitat,
si sacerdos nescit credere in Deum, id est, virtutem praepositionis intelligere, statim haereticus
iudicatur. Dat pecuniam et santificatur.'"* Cf. Gescher, "Geschichte und Recht" 38-39 and
Notes, for a detailed discussion of the significance of the preposition "in" in the theological
arguments of the thirteenth century.

whom Caesarius cited as being critical of the under-aged clerics who were totally inadequate as pastors of the flock. We know from a reference found in Caesarius' *Dialogus miraculorum* that Oliver preached in Cologne on Ash Wednesday (8 March) 1223, having just returned from several years of activity as a crusade preacher and leader. Since the time for diocesan synods at Cologne later became fixed during the period of Lent, it is not unreasonable to conclude that Archbishop Engelbert of Cologne convened such a synod at this same time in 1223, and that among other items of church business the learned and persuasive scholastic of the Cologne cathedral, Oliver of Paderborn, delivered a sermon in which he criticised various unhappy practices then existing in the diocese.[335]

In October 1223 Archbishop Siegfried of Mainz convened a synod in the church of St. Maria at Erfurt. The location of this assembly suggests that it too was diocesan, but perhaps only for the Thuringian clergy. Binterim has pointed out that previously a dispute had existed between the archbishop and this region of his diocese, and that the prelates of churches in Erfurt and elsewhere in Thuringia had not been present at the earlier Mainz synods.[336] We have noted above, however, that the author of the *Historiae Reinhardsbrunnenses* was well informed of the Council and its statutes by ca. 1217/1218, allowing the conclusion that proctors of Erfurt churches had been in attendance at the provincial synod of Mainz held in 1218, and that the decrees of Lateran IV had been published throughout Thuringia as well. In addition to renewing familiarity with those decrees, the 1223 assembly at Erfurt adopted measures aimed at improving the worship practices within the archdiocese: it was ordained that every feast be celebrated with its own *laudes* in nine lections.[337]

By the end of 1223 synods had been held in at least five of the six German provinces and in as many as thirty separate dioceses, the primary purpose of which presumably was to publish the enactments of the General Council of 1215.[338] Our reconstruction of German synodalia 1216-1223

---

[335] Cf. Gescher, "Geschichte und Recht" 40. Finke, *Konzilienst.* 164, notes that the archbishopric of Cologne remains well behind others in the evidence of either provincial or diocesan synods in the thirteenth century; he attributes this to the political situation in Cologne which militated against provincial assemblies, however. By contrast, the archbishop of Tarragona in Spain held nine synods in the first eleven years after Lateran IV.

[336] Binterim, *Concilien* IV 345.

[337] *Chron. S. Petri Erford.* 226: "*MCCXXIII. Sifridus Moguntinus archiepiscopus habuit concilium Erphordien in ecclesia beate Marie et instituit, quod omne festum habens proprias laudes in novem lectionibus celebraretur*"; and based on this, *Ann. Erphord.* 80; Mansi, *Collectio* XXII, cols. 1205-1206; Supplem. I, 920; Hefele-Leclercq, *Conciles* V/2 1443-1444; Hauck, *KGD* IV 7-9, V 135 note 1.

[338] Jedin's remark, *Handbook of Church History* III/2 206-207, that there are no references to the introduction of the decrees of Lateran IV into Germany, thus needs revision.

is admittedly incomplete. As additional specialized studies by those more familiar with the peculiarities of diplomatics for each diocese and region appear, this will be expanded and further clarified. At the present time, however, clear evidence exists that some bishops actually utilized the principles of canon law embodied in the decrees to deal with specific problems within their churches. Chroniclers and annalists from virtually every region of Germany who were at all contemporary to the Council possessed some knowledge of it, and in several instances they included excerpts of the constitutions in their records. We may thus conclude that many of these writers had direct access to the constitutions which had been produced in the papal chancery and distributed to those prelates or their representatives who were in attendance at the Council. Lacking a large bureaucratic organization, Innocent III had to rely on existing machinery to implement his reform program. Given the human factors to which we have so often alluded, this process was fated to be erratic, incomplete, and inconsistent with the vision of an idealistic pope.

CHAPTER FIVE

IMPLEMENTING THE DECREES OF THE COUNCIL: 1224-1245

Ne pro defectu pastoris gregem dominicum lupus rapax invadat aut in facul-
tatibus suis ecclesia viduata grave dispendium patiatur, volentes in
hoc occurrere periculis animarum et ecclesiarum indemnitatibus
providere, statuimus ut ultra tres menses cathedralis vel
regularis ecclesia praelato non vacet, . . .
(Lateran IV. c. 23)

Electiones episcoporum, personarum et aliarum dignitatum tunc a sede
apostolica et legatus eius taliter sunt suspensae, ut contra voluntatem
eligentium is vel ille praeficeretur in qualibet dignitate, qui vel
cuius amici tunc videbantur sedi apostolicae plus favere.
(Chronicon Augustensis, a. 1239)

During the first eight years after the Fourth Lateran Council, various
German prelates made efforts to publish and implement the decrees of
Innocent III which were aimed at revitalizing the Church and correcting
abuses among the clergy. We have seen that there was by no means
universal commitment to such a program, be it for lack of a pastoral sense
of responsibility or other non-religious factors. Although the Roman pontiff
sent Cardinal-priest Peter de Sasso as his legate to Germany in early 1216,
the real burden of responsibility for executing the reform measures had
rested on the shoulders of the prelates. Opposition had been met on several
fronts: diocesan abbots and priors who resisted efforts by their ordinaries
to strengthen their control over conventuals; religious communities which
lacked the discipline to reform themselves, yet also resisted externally-ap-
plied correctives; individuals who had succumbed to the spirit of heresy or
anti-sacerdotalism and thereby posed a threat to the established order.

In 1224 the somewhat un-coordinated nature of the reform movement
became altered by the appearance of a mighty cardinal-bishop from the
papal Curia. Whether it was perceptible to the German episcopacy or not,
the center of gravity shifted to a point outside their circle, whence the
papacy tried to enforce those decrees of the Council deemed essential to the
Church. The year commenced as had previous ones, with bishops
conducting diocesan assemblies in the traditional manner. On 21 February
Pope Honorius III wrote to the provost and dean of the cathedral chapter at
Passau, instructing them "*ut praelatos et clericos Pataviensis dioecesis ad*
synodum ab episcopo Pataviensi in civitate Pataviensi vocatos, ad eam

accedere per censuram ecclesiasticam compellant."[1] This letter reveals two significant things, first, that the prelates of Passau had apparently held other synods since that recorded by the annalists for the year 1220, that these had been disappointing in terms of attendance, and that Bishop Gebhard now intended to hold yet another synod; second, that the bishop was attempting to appropriate for diocesan use a tactic employed by Archbishop Eberhard II of Salzburg on several occasions with respect to provincial assemblies: solicit papal support in commanding the appearance of clerics at synods.

A major issue for consideration at the Passau synod was the financial status of the bishopric. Elected in 1222 Gebhard of Plain had struggled to recover from the debts accrued by his predecessors. His appeal to Rome resulted in a letter written 22 February 1224 to the prelates of churches and the clergy throughout the diocese of Passau: Honorius III gave them the command to help relieve the burdens of the Passau church by means of a subsidy.[2] Bishop Gebhard's relationship with his clergy remained strained throughout his pontificate.

Archbishop Eberhard's insistence that his suffragans attend provincial synods had been challenged on several occasions during the first two decades of his pontificate. It was clearly in response to a request for papal assistance from him that Honorius III on 10 January 1222 ordered the comprovincial bishops of Salzburg to obey the summons to a new synod, should the archbishop convene one, and to receive him with honor during his visitations.[3] It thus seems clear that the metropolitan intended to announce another synod in the immediate future. The only record of such, however, is a reform statute for the monasteries belonging to the Orders of St. Benedict and St. Augustine, published at a provincial synod held in 1224, but now lost.[4]

Less controversial than the Passau synod perhaps was the customary spring assembly which Bishop Frederick of Halberstadt convened for his diocese on 25-26 March 1224 at Gatersleben: the recorded business was the

---

[1] Pressutti, *Regg. Hon. III* II, Nr. 4787 ("*Querelam venerabilis fratris . . .*").

[2] Pressutti, *Regg. Hon. III* II, Nr. 4803 ("*Stupida noscuntur esse . . .*").

[3] Potthast, *Regesta* I, Nr. 6760; Meiller, *RAS* 229, Nr. 262, with note that the papal letter had been petitioned by Eberhard himself.

[4] Janner, *Regensburg* 317; Jodok Stülz published the reform decree among various miscellanea as, "Notizen aus und über Ranshofen am In," *Notizenblatt zum Archiv für österreichische Geschichtsforschung* 4 (1854) 466, of which neither Dalham nor Hansiz give notice: "*Ad reformationem quoque ordinum Canonicorum regularium S. Augustini et St. Benedicti nostrae provinciae cura pastoralis officii attendentes sacro ordinante Concilio ordinamus praesidentes capitulis antedictis videlicet de Ordine S. Augustini canonicorum regularium dominum praepositum metropolitanae ecclesiae Salisburg., praepositum monasterii b. v. Mariae Neunburgensis pataviensis diocesis . . . quibus plenam concedimus facultatem citandi et evocandi per censuras et ecclesiasticos ad regularia scilicet capitula celebranda.*"

resolution of a dispute between Abbot Siegfried of Huysburg and the knight John of Lewenberg concerning the rights of advocacy over several hides of land in Asterendorp and Reinstadt. The visitation of the cloister of Cistercian nuns at Heiligenthal in 1222/1223 may also have been a matter of discussion.[5] Bishop Conrad of Minden convened a synod on 11 April 1224, his first recorded since Lateran IV. He had personally attended the Council and therefore possessed copies of the decrees and other muniments. Without further details, we may assume that the Lateran constitutions were published no later than 1224 for this diocese.[6] Apparently Bishop Dietrich III of Münster also convened a diocesan synod about this same time, at which he confirmed the sentence of excommunication which his *officialis et exactor*, Prior Herdric of Schildwolde, had pronounced upon Prior Emo and the Premonstratensian convent of Bloemhof/Witt-Werum (*Floridus Ortus*) in Frisia.[7]

The Legation of Cardinal-Bishop Conrad of Porto

That same month of April Pope Honorius III announced the appointment of Cardinal-bishop Conrad of Porto and S. Rufina as legate for Germany, giving him the primary responsibility for furthering the crusade effort.[8] Traveling by way of France, Conrad convened a synod at Paris on 5 May 1224, presided at the resolution of a conflict involving Count Theubalt of Champagne and the lords of Châtillon, and spent several days in Liège in late May/early June where he issued charters in favor of the monastery Val-des-Vierges and the church of St. Denis in Liège.[9] His visit undoubt-

---

[5] Binterim, *Concilien* IV 515; Phillips, *Diözesansynode* 50; Schmidt, *UB Halb* I 503, Nr. 565, with date 1224 (". . . *et alii quamplures in nostra sinodo existentes. . . in plena sinodo nostra publice Gatersleve*").

[6] *Westf. UB* IV 38, Nr. 142 ("*synodus generalis in coena domini*").

[7] *Emonis Chron.* 500: "*Anno eodem, anno inquam Domini, Herdricus prepositus de Skeldwalda, dum plena auctoritate episcopi fungeretur et nimis insolesceret, tum quia acepalus erat, tum quia diviciae ei affluebant, in quibus speravit, et precipue de brachio episcopi, quia dixit plane se non curare, quid universi religiosi sentirent, dummodo in gratia episcopi consisteret, motus est igitur prepositus et conventus Floridi Orti contra eum zelo Phinees, qui coeunti cum Madianitide non pepercit.*" See papal mandate to Bishop Ludolf that he relax he ban within eight days of receipt of the letter, charging that the sentence had been pronounced "*sine cause rationabili contra statuta concilii generalis auctoritate propria . . .*"); Potthast, *Regesta* I, Nr. 7218; *Westf. UB* III 108, Nr. 199. A second letter of the same date was sent to the priors of Ortus S. Mariae and Dokkum and to *magister I. de Novo ecclesia plebanus* granting them authority to relax the ban, should the bishop delay in doing so.

[8] Böhmer, *Regg. Imp.* V/2, Nrs. 6570, 6571, and p. 1523; Roth von Schreckenstein, "Urach" 334; Würdtwein, *Nova subs.* IV 125.

[9] Roth von Schreckenstein, "Urach" 336, questions the accuracy of *Reiner Ann.* 679, which has Conrad at Liège on Easter (14 April): "*Anno 1224. bissextili, pascali die 18 Kal. Maii.*"

edly recalled memories of his youth when he had been a canon at the cathedral church of St. Lambert. To what extent the abuses present then had been corrected by the legislation of Papal-legate Guy Poré and Bishop Hugh of Pierrepont cannot be determined. One matter which his old friend Bishop Hugh brought to his attention was the condition of the church of St. Adalbert at Aachen, where resources were being pushed beyond their limits. In an effort to correct this problem, the cardinal-legate ordained that the chapter be limited to fourteen canons.[10]

The appearance of the cardinal-bishop, who knew so well the conditions of the German church, had a profound effect upon synodal activity and reform efforts elsewhere in Germany as well. We have already noted the considerable effort put forth by some bishops since the Council to implement those decrees which they had received from Innocent III. Our record is fragmentary, however, and it cannot be assumed that all bishops had been diligent in eliminating the abuses which abounded in their dioceses. With a confidence born out of years of sitting in the highest councils of the Church, or of presiding over the hundreds of Cistercian houses of Latin Christendom and of knowing personally many of the men who now occupied sees in Germany, Conrad of Urach asserted his apostolic role in both the political and ecclesiastical affairs of the Empire.

On the Friday of Pentecost (7 June) he arrived in Cologne where, according to the continuator of the *Chronica regia*, he was received with great honor.[11] The crusade-preacher Oliver of Paderborn, coming from his labors in Frisia, sought him out there. From a letter which Oliver wrote near the end of May to those clerics charged with carrying on with recruitment efforts, it appears that the cardinal-legate had summoned a council or synod of bishops: in addition to the consideration of essentially political matters (primarily the capture of the Danish king by the count of

---

Domnus Conradus filius ducis de Cerenges [i.e. Zähringen], *quondam Sancti Lamberti canonicus, post Villariensis abbas, modo cardinalis episcopus legatus in Alemannia, Leodium veniens Vallem benedictam dedicat.*" Binterim, *Concilien* IV 277, follows Reiner in incorrectly identifying Conrad as the son of the duke of Zähringen. His mother was the sister of Duke Berthold V of Zähringen; his father, however, was Duke Egino the Bearded of Urach. In 1214 Conrad had been elected abbot of Clairvaux, and in 1217 he became abbot of Cîteaux and head of the Order.

[10] Potthast, *Regesta* I, Nr. 8897; Quix, *Cod. dipl. Aquens.* I/2 108, Nr. 154. Presumably this is one of those otherwise unspecified things which Binterim, *Concilien* IV 277, states were put in order at this time.

[11] *Chron. reg. Colon. Cont. IV (a. 1224)* 253. See also *Emonis Chron.* 499; Roth von Schreckenstein, "Urach" 340-341; Binterim, *Concilien* IV 277. According to Caesarius of Heisterbach, *Homiliae* III, ed. Johannes Andreas Coppenstein (Coloniae, 1615) 59, Cardinal-legate Conrad conducted a trial of an accused heretic while at Cologne; cf. Joseph Greven, "Die Entstehung der Vita Engelberti des Caesarius von Heisterbach," *ANrh* 102 (1918) 32.

Schwerin, the crusade and other ecclesiastical matters were to be discussed.[12] Although the council failed to materialize, Oliver undoubtedly met with the cardinal and discussed the progress of the recruiting. There was another matter which held Oliver's attention, however.

Among Oliver's fellow students at Paris was Emo, a man of great learning and religious commitment who had also studied at Orleans and Oxford. In 1224 this erudite man was serving as prior of Bloemhof near Groningen, a house of Premonstratensian canons lying within the diocese of Münster. In his capacity as a papally-appointed crusade-preacher since 1213, as scholastic of the Cologne cathedral, and as parish priest at Huckarde and other places, Oliver had had numerous opportunities for maintaining contact with his friend over the years. Moreover, as the above-cited letter indicated, he had just left the diocese of Münster as he journeyed to meet with Cardinal-bishop Conrad. He thus carried with him a plea for help in Emo's struggle against the heavy-handed behavior of the episcopal visitor, Provost Herdric of Schildwolde.[13]

We can only surmise that Emo's scholastic and/or legistic training had augmented his sense of outrage over such an abuse of authority, and when his open opposition to the extortions of the episcopal official led to his excommunication, he wrote an appeal to the cardinal-legate; as late as the June meeting with Oliver, however, the Cistercian legate had apparently not responded. Thus, Emo had also appealed to Rome. In a letter which Honorius III dictated to Bishop Dietrich of Münster on 8 April 1224, the latter was chastised for acting contrary to the statutes of the Fourth Lateran Council, and he was ordered to relax the ban of excommunication within

---

[12] Hermann Hoogeweg, ed., *Die Schriften des Kölner Scholasters, soäteren Bischofs von Paderborn und Kardinalbischof von S. Sabina Oliverus*, Bibliothek des Litterarischen Vereins in Stuttgart, vol. 202 (Tübingen, 1894) Einleitung xl-xli; Reinhold Röhricht, "Die Briefe des Kölner Scholasticus Oliver," *WZGK* 10 (1891) 207, Nr. 8: "*Ad concilium domini Portuensis episcopi, sedis apostolice legati, pro negotio crucis principaliter nos oportuit accedere. Ideoque, quia fidelitatem vestram et industriam experimento didicimus, negotiam crucis, quod nobis a summo pontifice commissum est, vobis tam in Groniga quam per totam Frisiam Monasteriensis dioecesis committimus in absentia nostra, sive in terra pacanda et armis deponensis, sive in causis signatorum.*"

[13] The abuses of the visitor are enumerated in a letter which Oliver wrote about 10 March 1224 to the abbot of Prémontré: "*Alteri illorum videlicet Emoni, abbati Floridi Horti, a clero et populo plenum testimonium modestie ac laudabilis vite perhibetur, reliquus Herdicus de Skeldwalda prepositus non solum apus populares, verum etiam a bonis et gravibus sufficienter infamatur. Officialis enim gerens nogocium excommunicat et absolvit, ecclesias claudit et aperit pro precio et, quod abominabilius est, baptismum parvulorum impedire nititur quibusdam ecclesiis crisma negando pro unius vel paucorum delicto, nisi pecunia crisma redimatur*"; see Röhricht, "Briefe Olivers" 207, Nr. 7.

eight days of receiving the communication.[14] The instructions found in *cc.*
8 (*De inquisitionibus*) and 47 (*De forma excommunicandi*) seem to be those,
in contradiction of which the bishop was accused of acting.

The human dynamics of this situation are themselves quite significant.
Dietrich of Isenberg had been chosen bishop of Münster in 1218 under the
strong influence of his cousin, Archbishop Engelbert of Cologne; previous
to the election he had been provost at the Cologne cathedral, an office in
which he had succeeded Engelbert in 1216.[15] Oliver and Dietrich had thus
served for over a decade together in the cathedral chapter at Cologne, and
the scholastic had witnessed the manipulation of that church by members of
the Berg-Isenberg-Altena family since the days of Archbishop Adolf I.
Given the sort of personality which Dietrich possessed, and which revealed
itself more fully the following year, it is not surprising that he confirmed
the actions of his official Herdric in 1224.

The papal order appears to have been ignored, for on 20 June 1224
Cardinal-bishop Conrad sent a letter from Zülpich to the bishop of Münster,
directing that the latter cease giving support to Herdric against Prior Emo.
From Bonn the following day, the legate again wrote, declaring that unless
the provost of Schildwolde obeyed the bishop he was to be excommunicated.[16] In the judicial hearing that followed, held before the *consules terrae
et iurati de Upstallesborne*, Bishop Dietrich III found it necessary to retract
the ban against Emo, whereupon the prior of Bloemhof rendered obedience
to the prelate. The dispute between Emo and Herdric was thus resolved;
on 23 May 1225 Bishop Dietrich consecrated Emo as abbot of his house.
Emo himself recorded the event with some elaboration.[17] His inclusion of

---

[14] Cited in *Emonis Chron.* 502: "*Dilecti filii prepositus et conventus Floridi Orti sua nobis
conquestione monstrarunt, quod tu in eos sine causa rationabili, nulla competenti monitione
premissa, contra statuta concilii generalis auctoritate propria excommunicationis sententiam
promulgasti. Ideoque fraternitati tue per apostolica scripta mandamus quod, si ita est, infra
octo dies post susceptionem presentium sententiam ipsam sine qualibet difficultate relaxes.*"
See also, Potthast, *Regesta* I, Nrs. 7218, 7219.

[15] Krabbo, *Besetzung* 59; *Westf. UB* III 133, Nrs. 123-125; Pelster, *Stand und Herkunft* 70-
71. Dietrich had also been provost of St. Patroklus in Soest and, as such, an archdeacon in
the Cologne church; he also held the provostship of St. Victor in Xanten.

[16] Roth von Schreckenstein, "Urach" 341; Böhmer-Ficker, *Regg. Imp.* V/2, Nrs. 10008,
10009.

[17] *Emonis Chron.* 508: "*Octavo quoque Kalend. Maii intravit domnus Theodericus tercius
Monasteriensis episcopus, et decimo Kalend. Iunii in ebdomada pentecostes apud Floridum
Ortum sicut amicus honorifice susceptus; et eodem die ecclesiam ipsius dedicavit. Eodem
quoque die Emo prepositus Floridi Orti per manus impositionem prefati venerabilis antitistis
ex miseratione divina, astantibus fratribus suis, nomen et officium abbatis suscepit, anno
conversionis eius 17, indictione 13., concurrente 2, epacta 9, anno pontificatus prefati
ponfificis 7, in ordine pontificum Monasteriensium vicesimi quinti, qui cepit anno gratie 1219.
et sedit annos 7. . . . Anno inquam gratie 1225, anno pontificatus domni Honorii pape tercii*

the Fourth Lateranum in his dating formula suggests that in his eyes at least the Council loomed large in contemporary history. Cryptic though it may be, the reference hints at an awareness of things not explicit in the text.

This entire affair reveals something about the reception of the decrees of the Fourth Lateranum as well. There is no evidence previous to 1224 that the bishops of Münster had convened diocesan synods for the purpose of publishing either the Council's constitutions or the decrees of the provincial synod of 1220. Bishop Otto I of Münster was not personally present in Rome in 1215; he is documented as a pilgrim in 1217 and died 6 March 1218 before Caesarea in Palestine.[18] It is therefore obvious that before his departure he would have had to make provisions for his absence, such as appointing a coadjutor, etc. Furthermore, the large numbers of warriors and clerics whom Oliver of Paderborn and his associates had recruited from the diocese of Münster, plus the necessity of ensuring that the half-tithe was properly forthcoming from the diocesan clergy—all of these factors make it highly probable that some sort of diocesan assembly (and presumably a synod) had been convened at some time during the first twelve to eighteen months after the Council; if such be a correct assumption, then we are equally entitled to assume that the constitutions of Lateran IV were publicly proclaimed at this time.

Those decrees would have been brought back to Münster by Andreas, the prior of the Premonstratensian convent of Kappenberg, who went as Bishop Otto's representative. We must also assume that those same constitutions were repeated in 1224 in conjunction with the excommunication of Prior Emo of Bloemhof. But the fact that Pope Honorius reprimanded Bishop Dietrich for acting contrary to the Council's statutes in this respect suggests that neither he nor his diocesan officials understood the implications of that legislation. If, on the other hand, the bishop knowingly went against the statutes of 1215, his disregard for the order of the Church is but further manifested. In either case, we seem to have an equally clear demonstration that Emo knew the rightness of his position, meaning that he was familiar with the Lateran decrees and made use of these new laws in seeking redress from Provost Herdric's abusive behavior.

Before he died in 1237, Emo compiled a chronicle which incorporates a great deal of primary source material. He clearly had access to letters and other documents as he wrote. The notices for 1214-1216 were apparently

---

10., *anno a concilio Lateranensi 13., prime presicationis magistri Oliveri 12, . . .*" A similarly long dating formula appears for the year 1230; cf. Idem 512: ". . . *annus ex quo capta est Iherusalem a Saladino 40, . . . tercie predicante magistro Oliveri 16, . . . annus 18. a conciio presidente Innocentio papa III, . . .*"

[18] Cf. Röhricht, *Deutscher im Heiligen Lande* 108.

written sometime after July 1216 (inasmuch as they refer to the death of Innocent III), but before 1222; there was thus little time-lag between event and record.[19] It is obvious that although Emo made slight changes in the wording, he had before him the actual documents (or extensive extracts) which his fellow Premonstratensian Andreas of Kappenberg had carried back to Münster. He not only cited from the bull of convocation (*Vineam domini Sabaoth*), but also from the protocol. Whereas the original document gives the location of the Council as "*ecclesia Lateranensis, quae Constantiniana vocatur*", Emo rendered it "*ecclesia Lateranensis, que Constantinopolitana dicitur.*" It is clearly the same church, a fact known well to Emo who spent over a month in Rome during 1212 conducting business for his house before the Curia: daily he attended Mass and witnessed the pope himself officiating in the cathedral of St. John Lateran. The number of bishops and abbots present finds agreement between Emo and the protocol, but whereas the latter merely states the time as being "*mense Novembri*", Emo is clear as to the date of the first session (11 November). This confirms our contention that he had access to first-hand information, undoubtedly obtained from Prior Andreas as well.

Given this concern for detail, it is noteworthy that Emo's chronicle says nothing about the purpose of the Council or about any of the decrees. At least there is nothing under the date 1215. Earlier, however, after treating the crusade in Spain in the year 1212, he wrote a notation for the following

---

[19] *Emonis Chron.* 475: "*Anno quoque 7. conversionis sue concilium Rome celebratur 3. Idus Novembris. Sic nanque scripsit domnus papa: Taliter vos preparetis, quod a presenti incarnationis 1213. anno usque ad duos annos et dimidium, prefixus vobis pro termino Kallendis Novembris. Que synodus congregata est in basilica Lateranensi, que Constantinopolitana dicitur, 412 episcoporum tam Latinorum quam Grecorum, et abbatum 800 et aliorum ecclesie prelatorum, prepositorum et decanorum, anno pontificatus domni Innocentii . . .*" The editor of the chronicle for the *MGH*, Ludwig Weiland, remarks (p. 475, notes 36-37) that the date 1213 found in the beginning is more correctly that of the papal bull *Vineam domini Sabaoth* which he believes Emo extracted from Burchard of Ursperg's chronicle where it was cited in full. Weiland also contends that Emo used Burchard for his account of the Council. Neither argument is convincing, however, inasmuch as it is probable that the protocol itself had been available in Münster since the return of Provost Andreas of Kappenberg in 1216. That the Ursperg chronicle could not have been used is further evident from the fact that Emo cites details of the Council and its decrees which are not found in Burchard's account at all. Since the papal bull of convocation was sent to all dioceses, it is also probable that a copy of *Vineam domini Sabaoth* was preserved at Münster and used by Emo. See also G. Gelhorn, *Die Chronik Emo's und Menko's von Floridus Hortus* (Danzig, 1878) 3-67; further comments in *NA2* 1 (1876) 199-200; 8 (1883) 378-380; N. Backmund, "Die mittelalterliche Geschichts-schreiber des Praemonstratenserordens," *Bibliotheca Analectorum Praemonstratensium* 10 (Averbode, 1972) 169-182.

year which bears consideration.[20] It is not likely that Emo thought that there were two separate Councils, one in 1213 and the other in 1215. He mistakenly substituted the date of the bull *Quia maior nunc* (1213), which announced the pending crusade and established preachers in the various provinces of Christendom, for that of the Council. He then noted under that incorrect date details which he had heard or read, as e.g., how many bishops were present and which decrees were published, but again he made a slight error in listing 413 prelates. His mention of the fact that the matters *"principaliter"* discussed at the Council pertained to the impending crusade suggests that he wrote the above notations shortly after the resumption of crusade-preaching activities in the province of Cologne by Oliver of Paderborn, John of Xanten, and others, but before he had actually seen or heard the reform decrees.

After he had already written these notations (after June 1216, since he refers to the death of Innocent III), he obtained the actual documents from the Council, including the protocol and the bull of convocation. Not wishing to erase what he had already entered in his chronicle, he appears to have put the addition in the margin, which a later copyist then inserted in the text, giving it the convoluted aspect which it now exhibits. Such an explanation accounts for the *"quoque"* between the two sets of notations as well.[21]

The Disputed Election at Paderborn—1223

Another issue undoubtedly discussed at Cologne, and a major reason for Oliver's appearance there, was the disputed episcopal election at Paderborn. On 28 March 1223 Bishop Bernhard of Paderborn had died and a majority of the cathedral canons had chosen Oliver—a man of international reputation and a product of their own cathedral school—to be their new head. Six canons, together with Abbot Albert of Abdinghof and the collegiate canons at Bussdorf who claimed a traditional right to participate in the election, objected to the choice, however, and declared themselves for Provost Henry of Bussdorf, a member of the influential, power-hungry and lawless dynasty of the lords of Brakel. Archbishop Siegfried II of Mainz,

---

[20] (a. 1213) 475: *"Post hanc gloriosam victoriam idem apostolicus orientali ecclesiae compassus, predicatores crucis per regna misit occidentis. Cor apponens ad liberationem terre sancte, orationes generales instituit, concilium indixit, quod celebravit in Lateransi basilica anno 1213. mense Novembri; cui interfuerunt 413 episcopi. Abbatum et aliorum prelatorum ecclesiae turba convenit, que dinumerari facile non poterat. Ubi principaliter ordinatum est de hiis, que ad subsidium terre sancte pertinenbant. Terminus etiam generalis expeditionis prefixus erat; infra quem idem summus pontifex obdormivit in Domino."*

[21] Gelhorn, *Die Chronik Emo's* 66-67.

in whose province Paderborn lay, confirmed Henry's election and the provost of Bussdorf received the regalia from Henry (VII). Oliver's efforts to gain recognition at Cologne did not bear immediate fruit, for on 19 August 1224 the papal-legate issued a decree forbidding either Oliver or Henry of Brakel from receiving the incomes of the bishopric of Paderborn. He also authorized the provost and dean at Paderborn to excommunicate any who acted contrariwise.[22] On 30 November 1224 Oliver is still mentioned as the cathedral scholastic at Cologne, and not until 7 April 1225 did Honorius III name him as bishop.[23]

The confusion at Paderborn makes impossible the assertion found in the older collections of synodal acts that Oliver convened a synod in 1224 at which all the decisions and ordinances of previous councils in his diocese were gathered into one codex.[24] Though Hartzheim and those dependent on him argue for the reality of such a collection as late as 1418, in all probability it never existed at all. Our extensive survey of twelfth-century synodalia has revealed a very meager record of any sort of legislation; even in those dioceses such as Passau and Salzburg where we have considerable evidence of canonistic activity in the first two decades of the thirteenth century, no such collection of local decrees was generated. It is thus totally inconsistent with other contemporaneous bishoprics to posit a substantial body of synodal statutes at Paderborn by 1224. Despite his great erudition, Oliver was more a theologian and historian than a legist.

The mistaken notion of the 1224 synod is thus explained by Finke as follows: a manuscript history found at Paderborn—the *Cosmodromium libri VI*—written by one Gobelinus Persona, states (*c. 4*) that "*Sub eo [Olivero] liber ecclesie Paderburnensis, qui regula dicitur, videtur esse innovatus, ut*

---

[22] See Hermann Hoogeweg, "Die Paderborner Bischofswahl vom Jahre 1223," *ZGAW* 46/2 (1883) 92-108; Idem, *Schriften Olivers* Einleitung xxxv-xlix; Krabbo, *Besetzung* 84-95; Wilhelm Thöne, "Soziologische Untersuchungen über die einstigen Edelherren von Brakel im Kreise Höxter i.W.," *Westfälische Zeitschrift* 93 (1937) 39-77, espec. 53-55.

[23] Cf. Finke, *Konzilienst.* 51. Already on 28 July Oliver appears at the court of Frederick II at San Germano, and in August he is referred to as the cardinal-bishop of Sabina. At best he held the office of bishop for four weeks, but more probably he never was other than bishop-elect at Paderborn.

[24] Hartzheim, *Concilia* III, 514-515: "*Synodus Paderbornensis 1224. Hic Episcopus Oliverius, facundissimus totius Germaniae Orator, et celeberrimus suae aetatis Theologus, non tantum populum Evangelii praeconio docuit, non tantum cruce signatos plurimos acquisivit; sed et synodo cleri congregata, superiorum Synodorum decreta (inde ab anno 777 vide Tomi I. nostri pag. 238) et laudabiles consuetudines sacrorum ac temporum in unum codicem collegit, ut in omnium manibus essent, et facile memoria comprehenderentur*" (citing Schaten, *Ann. Paderbor.* IX 1003), and noting that the collection was still in existence in 1418. Hefele-Knöpfler, *Konziliengeschichte* V 938, and Hefele-Leclerq, *Conciles* V/2 1447, accept it uncritically, as do Hinschius, *KR* III 592 note 1, Philipps, *Diözesansynoden* 65-66, and Palazzini, *Dizionario* III 278-279.

elici ex eodem, ubi ponitur ordinacio septimane paschalis et ubi ponitur dies sanctorum Prothi et Jacinthi." Yet another work, Eisengrein's *Catalogus testium veritatis*, published in 1565,[25] misunderstanding the passage about "*regula*", stated it thus: "*Oliverius . . . theologus profundus synodales constitutiones ex iure et patrum decretis sumptas colligens omni clero Paderbornensi, ut perfectius vitae institutum assumeret, scripto proposuit.*" Schaten, who compiled the *Annales Paderborensium* in 1774, then combined both references: according to him, the "*liber*" which Oliver caused to be written contained not only "*laudabiles consuetudines sacrorum ac temporum*" (Gobelinus), but also "*superiorum synodorum decreta*" (Eisengrein). Naturally he must admit that the book is lost, for he had never seen it! Schaten also turned Eisengrein's very implicit reference to a synod into a matter of fact. Thus, the synod at which the statutes of previous Paderborn assemblies were drawn together into a single compilation becomes an invention only.[26]

While the cardinal-legate was occupied with matters at Cologne, other German prelates were involved in the endless process of effecting change within their dioceses. The badly-deteriorated discipline at the Benedictine house of St. Burchard in Würzburg had become the object of concern not only for the general chapter for the province of Mainz which apparently met in 1222,[27] but also for the bishop. That both authorities had ordered a visitation and reformation of the house is revealed in a papal letter written 1 June 1224 to the abbots of St. Michael and *Bilitehius* in the dioceses of Bamberg and Würzburg respectively, and to the dean at Bamberg.[28] The episcopal visitation was undoubtedly ordered by Otto of Lobdeburg who died on 4 December 1223. He had been at the Council in 1215 and had returned with the constitutions and other muniments. He had absented himself from all provincial synods since 1218, however, and there is no explicit evidence that he himself had convened any diocesan synods. Nevertheless, his concern for St. Burchard gives a small hint that some sort of implementation of Innocent III's decrees had begun at Würzburg by late 1223.

Otto's successor, Dietrich of Hohenburg, appears already on 8 January 1224 as *episcopus*, indicating that the election and confirmation had been

[25] Wilhelm Eisengrein, *Catalogus testium veritatis locupletissimus* (Delingae, 1565).

[26] Finke, *Konzilienst.* 51

[27] Mersseman, "Salzburger Augustinerstifte" 83, citing Stephanus Hilpisch, *Geschichte des Benediktinischen Mönchtums* (Freiburg/Br., 1929) 238, lists general chapters for the Benedictines in the province of Mainz in 1222, 1224 and 1227. See also Urmser Berlière, "Les chapitres généraux de l'Ordre de S. Benoit," *Revue Bénédictine* 18 (1901) 374; Idem, 19 (1902) 38.

[28] Pressutti, *Regg. Hon. III* II, Nr. 5028.

without any serious opposition.[29] He died between 14 December 1224 and 25 February 1225, however, leaving him little opportunity for affecting the inner life of his church.[30] Dietrich in turn was followed by the nephew of Bishop Otto, Hermann of Lobdeburg, who presided over the see of Würzburg for almost thirty years. On him rested the responsibility of maintaining any semblance of reform within his diocese.

From the fourteenth century comes a manuscript of the *Annales Herbipolenses* which contain entries for the years 1125-1158, 1202-1204, and 1215. The earlier portion is a continuation of the *Chronicon Ekkehardi Uraugiensis*, but the relation of the Fourth Crusade is probably from an eye-witness. Likewise, the account of the Fourth Lateranum which cites verbatim the protocol given to Bishop Otto at the Council, appears to be contemporary.[31] It is thus reasonable to conclude that the decrees were available within the bishopric of Würzburg from the time of Bishop Otto's return from Rome and that the publication and initial implementation of them commenced soon thereafter.

The Condemnation of Henry Minnecke

Near the end of August, or in early September 1224, Cardinal-bishop Conrad, Archbishop Engelbert of Cologne, King Henry (VII), and numerous other prelates and princes left Cologne to travel northward to the region of the Elbe. Their main purpose was to arrange the release of King Waldemar of Denmark from captivity at the hands of the count of Schwerin. The deliberations took place at Bardewick in the diocese of Hildesheim, and it was there on 29 September that the cardinal presided over a special synod of bishops who heard charges of heresy brought against Prior Henry Minnecke by the bishop of Hildesheim. In the presence of the legate, the archbishop of Bremen, the bishops of Halberstadt, Naumburg, Merseburg, Minden, Münster, and Schwerin, the bishops-elect of Paderborn (Oliver) and Osnabrück, and others learned in the Holy Scriptures, the prelate of Hildesheim disputed with the prior of Neuwerk. Minnecke's false teachings were listed and the penalties which Bishop Conrad had imposed upon him were declared just by the papal representative. Since he refused to recant, Minnecke's fate was thus sealed.[32] At a diocesan synod held at

---

[29] Hauck, *KGD* IV 958; *Wirtemburg. UB* III 146, Nr. 669; Beyer, *MRUB* III 186, Nr. 224; Simon, *Stand und Herkunft* 60.

[30] Cf. *Wirtemburg. UB* III 157, Nr. 679; H-Bréholles, *Hist. dipl.* II 840.

[31] Wattenbach-Schmale, *DGQ*

[32] Hartzheim, *Concilia* III 795; cf. Böhmer-Ficker, *Regg. Imp.* V, Nr. 3941; Hauck, *KGD* V 136 note 3; Hefele-Leclercq, *Conciles* V/2 1445-6; Cologne was there but not mentioned at the council (cf. *Chron. Luneb.* = Eccard, *Corp. hist.* I, 1403); *Chron. reg. Colon. cont. III*

Hildesheim on 22 October 1224, the prior of Neuwerk was once more examined by the bishop in the presence of the legate, convicted of heresy, deposed from his office, degraded from his orders, and turned over to the secular authority for punishment. With all hope of a reversal in the decision lost, the Cistercian nuns at last accepted the authority of the bishop and his newly-appointed prior. For Henry Minnecke, the outcome was less happy, however: on 25 March 1225 he was burned at the stake as a heretic.[33]

From Hildesheim, Conrad of Porto led a large contingent of German prelates and secular princes to Toul, near the border between the Empire and the kingdom of France, where they were joined by King Henry (VII), the archbishops of Besançon, Trier and Mainz, and by yet other dignitaries.[34] At the same time, Louis VII of France had arrived at the nearby fortress of Vaucouleurs where, on 19 November, Louis tried unsuccessfully to arrange a marriage alliance with the Empire against England.[35] Two days later the legate issued the commission to Abbot John of St. Truijen regarding the visitation of the Benedictine monastery at Stablo (Stavelot-Malmedy) in the diocese of Liège.[36] Cardinal-legate Conrad's sojourn in

---

254; Roth von Schreckenstein, "Urach" 342-345; Sudendorf, *Regestrum* I 160-162; Winkelmann, *Phil. von Schw.* II 435-437.

[33] Conrad's report of the decision reached at Hildesheim is printed in Hartzheim, *Concilia* III 515-516, and Mansi, *Collectio* XXII 1211-1212. A summary of the major documents relating to the case is given by Winkelmann, *Friedrich II.* 414-417. The trial of Minnecke is noted in the *Chron. Erfurt.* 252. Further discussion in Hauck, *KGD* IV 767 note 3, V 136 note 3, and V 169 note 1; Hefele-Leclercq, *Conciles* V/2 1446; Binterim, *Concilien* IV 345-347; Phillips, *Diözesansynode* 50.

[34] *Chron. Albrici* 914: "*Domnus cardinalis Conradus, a Roma regressus et per imperium Alemannie constitutus legatus, Leodium venit ibique Vallem Benedictam ordinis Cisterciancis de novo fundatum circa pentecosten consecravit, deinde Tullum venit in octavis beati Martini cum Coloniensi et Moguntinensi archiepiscopis et cum imperatoris filio rege Henrico et maioribus Alemannie.*" See also Roth von Schreckenstein, "Urach" 346. On 17 November 1224 at Toul, Archbishop Dietrich II of Trier was witness along with the archbishops of Mainz and Besançon, the bishops of Strasbourg, Speyer, Liège, Metz, Cambrai and Toul, the abbot of Murbach, both dukes of Brabant (father and son), Duke Matthew of Lorraine, Duke Walram of Limburg, Margrave Diepold of Vohburg, Count Simon of Saarbrücken, and various other counts to Henry (VII)'s privilege for the abbey at Gemblours; cf. H-Bréholles, *Hist. dipl.* II 813; Goerz, *RET* 35; Idem, *MRR* II 445, Nr. 1650.

[35] Cf. *Chron. Albrici* 914: "*Rex quoque Francie Ludovicus cum suo colloquio et consilio fuit in eodem confinio, apud castrum Valliscoloris, et sequenti die utriusque regni consiliatores in unum convenientes congruum colloquium ad invicem habuerunt.*" H-Bréholles, *Hist. dipl.* II 811; Böhmer-Ficker, *Regg. Imp.* V/2, Nr. 10020a; Roth von Schreckenstein, "Urach" 346; Ficker, *Engelbert der Heilige* 126.

[36] Böhmer-Ficker, *Regg. Imp.* V/2, Nr. 10021; Piot, *Cartulaire* I 182; Roth von Schreckenstein, "Urach" 381; *Gesta abb. Trudon. cont. III (a. 1222)* 393. As early as 9 March 1222 Pope Honorius III had announced the commission given to the Cistercian abbot of Claustrum in the diocese of Trier and to the Premonstratensian abbot of Steinfeld in the

Liège in May/June 1224 or the assembly at Cologne must have brought to his awareness conditions requiring urgent attention at this house. The selection of Abbot John was not accidental, inasmuch as this former scholastic at Xanten and crusade-preacher who was well-known to the legate had been elected abbot of St. Truijen precisely because he enjoyed the reputation as an advocate of discipline; under his supervision that house is said to have experienced significant reform.[37] His impact upon Stablo deserves closer study.

Leaving Toul, the cardinal progressed on to Metz where, on 29 November 1224, he rendered a decision in a dispute between the abbot and Order of Prémontré on the one side, and the priors of Magdeburg, Lizeke, Brandenburg, Havelberg, Ratzeburg, and other Premonstratensian houses in Saxony on the other, concerning the subordination of the latter to the general chapter at Prémontré.[38] Since its inception, the Order had convened yearly general chapters to which all heads of monasteries were expected to come. The Saxon houses claimed a papal exemption, however, and had opposed efforts by both Abbot Hugh II of Prémontré (1172-1191) and Pope Urban III (1186/1187) to enforce attendance. Innocent III on at least two occasions (1198, 1208) had commanded that they comply with the decrees of their Order despite the dispensation.[39] This issue was at length resolved in 1224: while the Saxon houses conceded their subordination to Prémontré and the general chapter, they were nonetheless permitted to attend the latter every three years.

Conrad of Urach's departure from Toul had come at a time when Bishop Eudes de Sorcy was engaged in a heated dispute with Abbot Garin of the Benedictine monastery of St. Evre. Garin had been one of the papally-appointed visitors of the ecclesiastical province of Trier in 1218, and he was a man in whom the archbishop had great confidence. In late 1223 or early 1224, during a severe illness, he had taken the advice of an opponent within his house and had not only released all the monks from their vow of obedience to him, but had resigned his office as well. The illness had not

---

diocese of Cologne, that they were to commit the administration of Stablo into the hands of the abbot of Prüm for the purpose of effecting major reforms there, the fact of which he had given notice to the archbishops of Trier, Mainz and Cologne, and to the bishop of Metz; cf. Pressutti, *Regg. Hon. III* II, Nr. 3822.

[37] Cf. Pixton, "Anwerbung" 174; further references in Ch. Four, note 145. John's service was further rewarded (or his responsibilities further increased) when, on 14 February 1226, Cardinal-legate Conrad gave him permission to retain the abbacy of St. Truijen while assuming that at St. Heribert in Deutz as well; cf. Böhmer-Ficker, *Regg. Imp.* V, Nr. 10072.

[38] Mülverstedt, *RAMagd* II, 331-332, Nr. 718; Böhmer-Ficker, *Regg. Imp.* V/2, Nr. 10022; Roth von Schreckenstein, "Urach" 347.

[39] Hauck, *KGD* IV 381; *UB d. Kl. UL.Fr.* 58, Nr. 64; Potthast, *Regesta* I, Nr. 3583.

proved fatal, however, and on 7 May 1224 Pope Honorius directed Archbishop Dietrich of Trier to investigate the situation, and to restore order at St. Evre by rejecting Garin's resignation and nullifying his subsequent actions.[40]

Bishop Eudes of Toul had meanwhile appointed the monk Boso of Derven in Garin's stead, having accepted Garin's resignation. When the latter appealed his case to Rome, he was excommunicated. Honorius therefore established a commission of three clerics from Langres—the cantor, and the *magistri* P., archdeacon, and F. de Lenti, canon—to make a determination of the merits of each side in the dispute.[41] The outcome of that commission is unknown: although the ban imposed on Garin appears to have been lifted, the bishop refused to reinstate him in his office. This in turn had resulted in threats of excommunication against the bishop by his metropolitan.

Coincident with the visit to Toul by Cardinal-legate Conrad and the various German prelates in November 1224 Bishop Eudes had convened a synod at which the bishop of Porto had preached the crusade. During the synod Garin and some his fellow monks physically ejected Eudes from his throne. The prelate appealed to Rome, and on 4 and 7 December 1224 Honorius III issued mandates for three clerics from Châlons-sur-Marne, the archdeacons *magister* Jean Barat and R[ ], and the canon Richer: the first commissioned them to investigate the charges that the bishop had been threatened *iuris ordine praetermisso* by Archbishop Dietrich; the second directed them to call the disputing parties together and to inquire at length into the causes of the dispute; if they found the charges against Garin and his brethren to be valid, they were to excommunicate the monks publicly for their audacious actions.[42]

Surprisingly, Garin's reputation did not suffer at all during this dispute. He appears to have enjoyed the esteem of secular and regular clergy alike. Upon the death of Bishop Eudes in 1228, the cathedral chapter at Toul elected this seventy-year old monk to be the new prelate.[43] One is tempted to interpret this as a sign that the canons sought his leadership in reforming their church, but it may be that they simply hoped to avoid a schismatic election by casting their votes for a candidate acceptable to all parties.

---

[40] Potthast, *Regesta* I, Nr. 7683; Friedberg, *Corp. Iur. Can.* II. lib. I. tit. IX. c. XIV. p. 114; Pressutti, *Regg. Hon. III* II, Nr. 4970; Goerz, *MRR* II, Nr. 1793; Pixton, "Dietrich of Wied" (1972) 128.

[41] Pressutti, *Regg. Hon. III* II, Nr. 5067.

[42] Potthast, *Regesta* I, Nrs. 7327, 7328; Pressutti, *Regg. Hon. III* II, Nrs. 5199, 5208.

[43] *Chron. Albrici (a. 1228)* 922: "*Moritur episcopus Odo Tullensis, cui succedit abbas Garinus Sancti Apri, senex et emeritus*"; Morret, *Stand und Herkunft* 70; Pixton, "Dietrich of Wied" (1972) 128 note 99.

Reluctant to accept additional burdens in his frail condition, Garin nevertheless submitted to the pressure from the pope and Archbishop Dietrich, serving for a time as both bishop of Toul and abbot of St. Evre. In a matter of months, however, he renounced the bishopric and returned permanently to his monastery where he died in 1230.[44]

The synod held at Toul between 22 October and 19 November 1224 is the first evidence we have of such an assembly in the decade since Lateran IV. Bishop Rainald (de Senlis) had received copies of the muniments himself in 1215, but he was murdered in 1217 by the partisans of the deposed Matthew of Lorraine and his bishopric was embroiled in a schism until 1219. It is thus possible that no synods were held before 1224, at which time the constitutions of the Council and the provisions of the provincial synods at Trier would have been published.

One of those who would have attended a diocesan synod at Toul was the monk Richer who flourished ca. 1218-1264 at the Benedictine monastery of Senones in the Voges, and who wrote the *Gesta Senoniensis Ecclesiae*. As did so many of his contemporaries, he cited verbatim the protocol of Lateran IV, but he went beyond the record of most in relating other details of the Council, including the content of some of the decrees.[45] Unlike some accounts of the pope's sermon delivered on 11 November 1215, however, Richer's shows that he was familiar with more than just the title. His detailed description of *c.* 50 of the constitutions precludes the possibility that he simply borrowed his notations from an existing set of annals, such as those of Marbach/Neubourg, Aubrey of Trois Fontaines, or Aegidius of Orval. Being a Benedictine, Richer (or some predecessor) would have been obligated to attend diocesan synods convened by the bishops of Toul, or the provincial synods of Trier, at which the decrees of Innocent III had been

---

[44] *Chron. Albrici* 926: *"Apud Tullum episcopus Garinus se deposuit, et post multos qui fuerunt nominati factus est episcopus magister Rogerus primicerius Virdunensis, vir nobilis et litteratus"*; Pixton, "Dietrich of Wied" (1972) 129.

[45] *MGH SS* XXV, 255: *"In qua synodo dictus Innocentius papa sermonem proprio ore protulit, ita incipiens: Desiderio desideravi hoc pascha manducare vobiscum, antequam moriar. In quo sermone inter ceteros tratatus et disputationes [de] fidei conservatione, de statu ecclesiarum et personarum eas regentium liquide prosecutus, limpidius de obitu suo, et quod ei iam super hoc Deus signum fecerat in bonum, mirabiliter pertractavit. Et quod mirabilius est dictu, de matrimonio ita efficaciter disputavit, ut ipsos gradus contrahendi matrimonium potius usque ad quartum gradum debere restringere, quam in septimo gradu, in quo antiquitus constitutum erat, permaneret; asserens, quod pro intricata cognationis computatione minus provide contrahebant et divortia celebrabant. Unde idem papa conubia matrimonii extra quartum gradum tantum fieri decrevit. Et si in quinto gradu ex una parte et in tercio ex altera incti fuissent, precepit non separari; et alia multa indixit, quibus iurisperti adhuc utuntur. Et sic quilibet ad propria reversus est."* On Richer as historian, see Böhmer, *Fontes* (1849) lxxii; Potthast, *Repertorium* II 971.

published. It may be more than coincidence that the two German accounts which refer to the reduction in the number of prohibited degrees of consanguinity were produced in Trier and Toul, both lying within the same province and subject for over thirty years to the influence of Archbishop Dietrich II.

Whereas Garin of St. Evre enjoyed the reputation of a devout and disciplined Benedictine, another house of Black Monks within the diocese of Toul gave cause for deep concern. Cardinal-legate Conrad had written the Curia concerning the election of a new abbot at St. Mansuy who had not as yet taken his vows. On 5 March 1225, at a time when Conrad was already in Austria, Pope Honorius III directed him to compel all the monks at St. Mansuy to make their profession and then to proceed with a new election.[46] Such irregularities had undoubtedly come to the attention of the legate during his visit to Toul, either as a result of reports from a general chapter or communication from the bishop or archbishop. A more general mandate was given by Gregory IX on 30 March 1227, indicating perhaps that the situation at St. Mansuy was not unique.[47]

The cardinal-legate's involvement with the bishopric of Toul extended yet again to the bishop himself, however. Reports had reached Conrad of Porto that Eudes had actually appropriated some of the collected monies for his own purposes; moreover, he was accused of even embezzling funds derived from the commutation of crusade vows. The debts under which his bishopric labored were considerable and efforts had been made in the past to relieve the prelate of such by various measures. Perhaps it was some mean-spirited cleric of his church who had lodged the complaint with the legate in retaliation for his having to help alleviate the bishop's problem. Whatever the source, the result was that Bishop Eudes of Toul had been suspended and an interdict was imposed upon his church. On 28 May 1225 Pope Honorius III directed his legate in Germany to relax the suspension and interdict; in the meanwhile he was to give letters of commission to three clerics from Rheims who were to inquire into the charges against the bishop. If they were true, the *iudices delegati* were to compel the prelate to make full restitution.[48]

During his progression through the ecclesiastical province of Trier in late 1224, Cardinal-legate Conrad undoubtedly had extensive contact with Archbishop Dietrich. That metropolitan had had a busy year, being involved in the dispute and other problems at Toul, but with his other two

---

[46] Horoy, *Honorii III opera* IV 804, Nr. 104; Pressutti, *Regg. Hon. III* II, Nr. 5359 (*"Per litteras tuas. . ."*).

[47] Auvray, *Registres de Gregoire* IX I, Nr. 122.

[48] Horoy, *Honorii III opera* IV 864, Nr. 168; Pressutti, *Regg. Hon. III* II, Nr. 5513.

suffragan bishoprics as well. On 24 March Conrad of Scharfenberg, the imperial chancellor who for twelve years had held both the bishopric of Speyer and that of Metz, died,[49] necessitating a new election in both cathedral chapters. At Metz, the choice fell upon Jean d'Aspremont who, since 1217 had been bishop of Verdun; the pope approved the postulation and, by 23 July 1224, Jean had assumed his new office.[50] This in turn had necessitated a new election at Verdun.

Jean d'Aspremont showed great interest in securing the see of Verdun for his relative Rudolf of Thourotte, the cantor at Laon, and he agitated in Rudolf's behalf among the members of his former cathedral chapter. He succeeded in winning a majority of the votes, but a minority group supported *magister* Jean Barat, archdeacon of Châlons. Before the actual vote, the minority party lodged a protest against the eventual election of Rudolf, despite which, having in fact won the election, Rudolf received confirmation from the metropolitan of Trier and assumed the administration of his diocese. The candidate of the minority could not claim against his opponent that he had the *pars maior* in his favor, but he did argue that the *pars sanior* of the cathedral chapter supported him. The leader of this latter group, Archdeacon Henry, demanded that they undertake a *"collatio persone ad personam et zeli ad zelum."* Jean Barat attempted to pursue his weakly-based claims by means of a legal process in Rome, while he called on the strong arm of his friend, the count of Bar, to assert his claims within the diocese.[51]

These extreme measures by the opposition party ultimately led to a commission which Honorius III established under the direction of the bishop

---

[49] "Das Todtenbuch des Speier Domstifts," ed. Moné, *ZGO* 26 (1875) 425; Bienemann, *Conrad v. Scharf.* 101.

[50] *Chron. Alrici* 913: *"Mortuo Conrado Spirensi et Metensi episcopo, factus est Spirensis episcopus Berengarius eiusdem ecclesie decanus, episcopus autem Virdunensis Iohannes postulatus est Metis et concessus de permissione summi pontificis."* Jean appears for the first time as *episcopus Metensis* at the royal court on 23 July 1224; cf. Böhmer-Ficker, *Regg. Imp.* V, Nr. 3727. See also Krabbo, *Besetzung* 99-100; Morret, *Stand und Herkunft* 33-34; *MGH SS* X 528; Hauck, *KGD* IV 963.

[51] For details of the Verdun schism, cf. *Chron. Albrici* 913-915: *"[1225] Apud Virdunum in cathedra pontificali de voluntate et consilio Metensi episcopi Iohannis positus fuit consobrinus eius, cantor Radulfus Laudunensis, filius domni de Torota, appellantibus ad papam archidyacono Henrico Malapota, Montisfalconis preposito, cum aliis personis que erant in parte eius. Et huius cause ventilatio ultra annum processit eo quod pars appellantium innetebatur consilio et auxilio comito Barrensis. Sed cum captus fuisset idem comes ante natale Domini in Burgundia a Iohanne Cabilonensi, filio comitis Stephani, et ab Henrico Viennensi fratre Gegardi iam defuncti, tandem post suam redemptionem et reversionem cum eodem Radulfo pacem habuit et cum ipso Virdunum obsedit"*; further, Pressutti, *Regg. Hon. III* I, Nr. 5170; Krabbo, *Besetzung* 100-101. Archdeacon Jean of Châlons was one of the *iudices delegati* appointed in 1224 for the resolution of problems in Toul.

of Paris.[52]   When this commission exceeded its mandate, Rudolf complained to the Curia and a second one, under the presidency of the bishop of Strasbourg, replaced it.[53]   We are not informed concerning the further course of the process which eventually ended in Rudolf's favor. It took years, however, before the prelate could enter his own city which had become quite independent during the confusion of the schism.[54]

At some time between 24 March and 23 July 1224, the archbishop of Trier presided at the consecration of the new bishop of Metz, presumably assisted by his suffragans, the bishop of Toul and the bishop-elect of Verdun. The likely occasion for this was in May: on an unspecified day in May 1224 Archbishop Dietrich II of Trier attached his seal to a covenant between the bishop of Metz and the duke of Brabant against the count of Leiningen-Dachsburg.[55]   It seems most probable that the bishop-elect of Metz had first received episcopal consecration, after which various matters of a temporal nature, including the alliance, were handled. Perhaps it was at this assembly as well that the above-noted archiepiscopal confirmation of the election of Rudolf of Thourotte occurred. There is thus strong argument for construing this assembly as a provincial synod.

The problems at Verdun were clearly on the metropolitan's mind when the cardinal-legate visited his province in the fall of 1224. Three months later, while the cardinal was *en route* from St. Gall to Freising, a diocesan synod for Trier was convened at Coblenz. The only record of the synod is a document dated 22 February 1225 which speaks of a judgment given by Dean Richard, the *custos* Waldever and a canon H[ ] as "*iudices a domino papa constituti*" in a dispute between the collegiate church at Carden and the *ministeriales* of Mertlach regarding a tithe.[56]   This particular date had special significance in the diocese of Trier, being the feast of the *cathedra Petri apostoli*. Unlike many feastdays which were celebrated simply by variations in the Divine Office, the feast of St. Peter's chair was a *festa fori*—that is, one of the most important in the liturgical year, when most aspects of daily work and public activities were halted.[57]   Inasmuch as the cathedral at Trier was consecrated to St. Peter, the solemn commemoration

---

[52] Pressutti, *Regg. Hon. III* I, Nr. 5170 (22 November 1224).

[53] Potthast, *Regesta* I, Nr. 7512; Pressutti, *Regg. Hon. III* I, Nr. 5542 (1 July 1225). See also Krabbo, *Besetzung* 100-101.

[54] See Winkelmann, *Friedrich II.* 492ff.; Thiery, *Toul* 220.

[55] Goerz, *MRR* II 460, Nr. 1713.

[56] Beyer, *MRUB* III, Nr. 241

[57] Hermann Grotefend, *Handbuch des historischen Chronologie des deutschen Mittelalters und der Neuzeit* (Hannover, 1872) I 62; II 188. On this same day at Trier a *Schröffengericht* was held to adjudicate temporal issues involving burghers of the city; cf. Goerz, *MRR* II, Nr. 1699.

of this feast, with the importance drawn to the keys given to the chief apostle by Christ, served to re-affirm the role of the archbishop as the successor to the apostles. Twelfth-century evidence for Trier indicates that diocesan synods were not as yet held on fixed days. It is probable therefore that the custom of celebrating synods on the feast-day of St. Peter's Chair was commenced under Archbishop Dietrich II and can be viewed as a move aimed at strengthening his position with respect to his clergy.

Cardinal-bishop Conrad of Porto had meanwhile continued his travels. During the first days of 1225 he progressed over Hagenau to Ulm where he attended a *Hoftag* (diet) in January which dealt once again with marriage proposals for Henry (VII). Thence, he traveled by way of Constanz (29 January), St. Gall (16 February), and Freising (1 March) to the monastery of Heiligenkreuz in Austria (1 April) and at length to Graz (6 June). This six-month period between his appearance in Metz (29 November 1224) and his documentation in Graz reveals little of his actual efforts, either in behalf of the crusade or in matters relating to Church order and discipline. Allowing even ample time for travel and much-needed rest (Conrad was by now fifty-five years old or more), he must still have had opportunities for deliberating on the major ecclesiastical issues of his day. The fourteen documents which trace his actions during this half year were hardly the sole reasons for his meeting with prelates and princes.[58] There is no evidence that the bishops of Metz, Strasbourg, Constanz, Freising, or Passau, through all of whose dioceses he passed in his journey, convened synods as a result of his visit. Perhaps Conrad already had it in mind to summon a synod for all German bishops, such as that announced later that year for Cologne, preferring to treat matters of Church order in a single assembly, instead of in numerous diocesan or provincial ones. The conditions which he found in his travels were doubtless reflected in his subsequent legislation.

The Erection of the Bishopric of Lavant

During his sojourn in the ecclesiastical province of Salzburg the cardinal-legate undoubtedly heard further aspects of Archbishop Eberhard's plans to erect yet another *Eigenbistum* (proprietary bishopric). Pope Honorius III had written the metropolitan on 27 January 1224, praising him for the two new episcopacies which he already had established and for considering a third.[59] Four months after Conrad's recorded visit in Freising Bishop

---

[58] Cf. Roth von Schreckenstein, "Urach" 347-348; Böhmer-Ficker, *Regg. Imp.* V/2, Nrs. 10024, 10025, 10025a, 10026, 10027, 10027a, 10028, 10029, 10030, 10030a, 10031, 10032, 10032a, 10032b.

[59] Pressutti, *Regg. Hon. III* II, Nr. 4724. On the erection of the bishopric at Lavant, see

Gerold and the Cistercian abbot Eberhard of Salem were given the task of determining the feasibility of erecting a new bishopric around the recently-established church of St. Andrä in Lavant.[60] Communications from the cardinal were undoubtedly behind the establishment of this commission at this time. Just as the details in the erection of new bishoprics at Chiemsee and Seckau had been worked out at provincial synods held in 1216 and 1219, so too the erection of the bishopric at Lavant between 1225 and 1228 must have necessitated unrecorded provincial assemblies during this time as well.[61]

Any synod held for the province of Salzburg in 1225 must also have considered the growing problems within the bishopric of Brixen. On 1 January 1225 the pope had written Bishop Henry concerning a former abbot at the monastery of Schwarzach (*Aqua nigra*) within his diocese who, despite having been deposed by decree of the pontiff himself, had continued to cause commotion at the cloister and has even attacked several of the monks. The prelate was ordered to use every means possible in compelling the contumacious man to desist, invoking secular authority (i.e., the monastery's lay advocate) if necessary.[62] A week later Honorius III wrote Bishop Henry again, this time concerning heretics living within his city. He was given the responsibility of destroying their fortified houses, and he was directed not to absolve any of them from the ban of excommunication unless they had first presented themselves personally before the Curia.[63] That same day the pope also revoked a privilege which the bishop had granted to one of his cathedral canons because of favorable treatment which his kinsmen had given suspected heretics.[64] Yet another directive was sent to Bishop Henry on 15 July 1225, urging punishment for those who waged battle against faithful catholics in his city.[65]

Cradled in the Alps of South Tyrol, Brixen straddled the language frontier between German and Italian. Into its towns had come the ideas of

---

also Seidenschnur, "Salzburger Eigenbistümer" 205-207.

[60] Potthast, *Regesta* I, Nr. 7449; Meiller, *RAS* 235, Nr. 291; Pressutti, *Regg. Hon. III* II, Nr. 5557 (14 July 1225); Krabbo, *Ostdeutsche Bistümer* 106-107; Fuchs, *Besetzung* 35; Dopsch, *Geschichte Salzburgs* I 313, 321-326.

[61] The canonical regulations for the new bishopric were issued on 10 May 1228 (Meiller, *RAS* 241, Nr. 317); four days later, on Pentecost Sunday, at Straubing, Bishop Ulrich was consecrated by Archbishop Eberhard (cf. *Ann. Salisb.* 784). The setting was one often used for provincial synods, and the presence of other suffragans suggests that this too was a provincial synod.

[62] Pressutti, *Regg. Hon. III* II, Nr. 5248, with incorrect designation as *Albert*.

[63] Potthast, *Regesta* I, Nrs. 7346; Rodenberg, *MG Ep. s. XIII* I 189, Nrs. 264, 266; Pressutti, *Regg. Hon. III* II, Nr. 5262, with incorrect designation as *Albert*.

[64] Pressutti, *Regg. Hon. III* II, Nr. 5264, with incorrect designation as *Albert*.

[65] Rodenberg, *MG Ep. s. XIII* I 197, Nr. 275; Pressutti, *Regg. Hon. III* II, Nr. 5561.

Peter Waldo, borne by merchants and refugees from Lombardy. Over the next several years a veritable flood of papal letters maintained a steady agitation of the bishop of Brixen whose responses failed to eradicate the pernicious doctrines and their propagators.[66] Though the record is silent, we may speculate that one or more synods were convened within this diocese for the purpose of directing clerical attention on the problem.

Not only the bishop of Brixen, but the archbishop and the remaining suffragans as well were given the command by Honorius III on 15 May 1226 that when they were informed by visitors of the Order of St. Augustine in the province that abbots and priors ought to be removed from their offices on account of their sins, they were in no wise to neglect to proceed against them, regardless of who they were and the reputation of their houses.[67] This papal bull was no doubt prompted by an archiepiscopal request and gives clear indication that even after the flurry of activity during the first decade following the Council, Archbishop Eberhard had lost none of his determination to effect church reform. Unlike many of his contemporaries whose authority in that regard was pre-empted by papal-legates, Eberhard rarely had to contend with them, an indication perhaps that the Curia was generally satisfied with his efforts.

The Cardinal-Bishop in Bohemia and Saxony—1225

Following his stay at Graz in early June 1225 Cardinal-legate Conrad of Porto crossed into Bohemia where he is recorded on 26 June at Prague.[68] His primary reason was to resolve a dispute surrounding the new bishop of that city. As noted above, King Ottokar of Bohemia had quarreled with Bishop Andreas in 1216 over the issue of lay domination of the Bohemian church. The prelate had summoned a synod that year where he published the decrees of Lateran IV, but he had been forced to flee to Rome soon thereafter. He died in exile 30 July 1223. The Prague cathedral chapter quickly elected a successor, hoping to circumvent the papal claims to appoint a new prelate under such circumstances. The choice fell upon Peregrin, the provost of Melnik, to whom the archbishop of Mainz granted investiture. Pope Honorius III was displeased with these actions, however, and openly criticized the new bishop-elect as belonging to those clerics friendly to King Ottokar, whom Andreas had excommunicated. The pontiff therefore declared the election invalid and gave to Cardinal-legate Conrad

---

[66] See Rodenberg, *MG Ep. s. XIII* I, Nr. 275 (15 July 1225); Idem. I, Nr. 295 (6 May 1226).

[67] Pressutti, *Regg. Hon. III* II, Nr. 5937.

[68] Böhmer-Ficker, *Regg. Imp.* V/2, Nrs. 10033, 10033a, 10034.

the task of supervising a new one. It is to the legate's credit that he was able to persuade Peregrin to resign in return for a yearly pension of 150 Marks.[69]

The cardinal left Bohemia between 26 June, when he is last documented in Prague, and early August, when he appears in Meissen.[70] The Prague cathedral chapter apparently had not selected a new bishop at that time; the successor, Budislaus, first appears in 1226, but died 10 July of that same year without having really functioned in his office. Inasmuch as his death also occurred at Rome, the papacy assumed control over the election once more; Honorius III declared that representatives of the cathedral chapter were to present themselves before him at Rome and there conduct the election. Chosen by this delegation was the scholastic of Prague, *magister* John, albeit after the death of Honorius III. Pope Gregory IX therefore gave several Passau clerics the task of proving the worthiness of the candidate: John was approved and was consecrated 19 December 1227 by the archbishop of Mainz.[71] Given the almost constant contention during the latter years of Bishop Andreas' pontificate, and from his death in 1224 until the final resolution in 1227, it seems highly doubtful that any synods had been summoned in that diocese since the presumed assembly of 1216.

On 14 March 1225 Bishop Frederick of Halberstadt convened a synod at which a dispute between the cloister Marienthal and the parish priest Rudolf of Gatersleben was composed.[72] Later that same month another assembly which is also identified as a diocesan synod confirmed the grant by the landgrave of Thuringia to the newly-established cloister at Mehringen.[73] Some five months later, Cardinal-bishop Conrad of Porto arrived in the city where he remained for a fortnight. His way to Halberstadt had led over Halle-on-the-Saale where, on 15 August, he had dealt with several matters of Church order and discipline. At the nearby Premonstratensian convent of Lauterberg, the prior and his brethren were still at odds with one another. The situation was even worse at the Benedictine house of Riesa. Following the death of Prior John, at a time when Archbishop Albrecht of

---

[69] Roth von Schreckenstein, "Urach" 349-350; Krabbo, *Ostdeutsche Bistümer* 76-79.

[70] *Chron. mont. Sereni* 221; Böhmer-Ficker, *Regg. Imp.* V/2, Nr. 10035a; Roth von Schreckenstein, "Urach'" 350.

[71] Krabbo, *Ostdeutsche Bistümer* 77-79.

[72] Schmidt, *UB Halb* I, Nr. 569 (". . . *in plena synodo nostra . . .*"). Hauck, *KGD* V 168 note 1, recognizes that there were two synods in 1225.

[73] Schmidt, *UB Halb* I 506, Nr. 570 ("*actum Halb. per sentenciam in generali sinodo nostra, presentibus clericis et laicis infinitis*"). This is the synod placed by Hartzheim, *Concilia* III 515, in the year 1224; Hefele-Leclercq, *Conciles* V/2 1447, accepts the year 1224, then changes the date to 25 March, making this synod identical with the one found in *UB Halb* I, Nr. 565.

Magdeburg was in Italy as the imperial legate for Lombardy, the monks had elected a certain Albert, a cathedral canon at Meissen, who occupied the office for over one year without ecclesiastical confirmation. When the archbishop returned, he appointed to the same office the canon Alexander of Neuwerk near Halle, claiming that right since the monks at Riesa had failed to present a suitable person within the prescribed time period. Albert himself had turned to the legate for help, and while agreeing to hear the case, Conrad of Porto also insisted upon listening to the archbishop as well.

One of those who spoke out in favor of Albert was Bishop Ekkehard of Merseburg who brought serious charges of misconduct against Alexander. In fact, the entrance of Bishop Ekkehard into this controversy took it in an entirely new direction. During the legate's visit in Halle, he had heard numerous complaints against Prior Dietrich of Lauterberg, a cousin of the Merseburg prelate. Similar reports came from members of the cathedral chapter at Meissen who claimed to have heard it directly from Dietrich's own convent. Since the legate had deposed Provost Rudolf of St. John's during his visit in Halberstadt,[74] the opponents of Dietrich were hopeful that the cardinal-bishop as a just and incorruptible man would dispose of him in a similar fashion.

The issue of Lauterberg was not resolved before the legate's departure from Halberstadt about 31 August, but it was resumed in Magdeburg on 1 September. It was here that the bishop of Merseburg found the opportunity to talk with the cardinal about Riesa. The first solution proposed was to remove Dietrich of Lauterberg and appoint Albert to the position of prior at that house, thereby eliminating two problems at once—the complaints of the canons at Lauterberg and the disputed priorship at Riesa. Upon learning of the threat to his cousin, however, Bishop Ekkehard of Merseburg abandoned his former protégé Albert and threw his total support to Alexander. The concerns for reform were thus abandoned to family interests: Alexander did indeed receive Riesa, while Dietrich of Lauterberg retained his office.[75]

One should not forget that the pen which retold the events of this period was held by an outspoken opponent of Prior Dietrich. On the other hand, Bishop Ekkehard is revealed as a man of duplicity whose commitment to serious reform was superficial at best; he ended up endorsing a man whose life he had condemned only a few days earlier, in order that the high position of a close relative might be preserved. The convent of Lauterberg, moreover, was forced to accept as prior a man with whom it could no

---

[74] *Chron. mont. Sereni* 221; Böhmer-Ficker, *Regg. Imp.* V/2, Nr. 1037a. See also Mülverstedt, *RAMagd* II, Nr. 743; Hauck, *KGD* IV 799.

[75] Roth von Schreckenstein, "Urach" 350-352.

longer live in harmony. The financial situation of the canons was also adversely affected, for, as the cardinal-bishop demanded the normal provision of six Marks for his services, it had to pawn three silver incense burners.

While at Magdeburg on 1 September 1225, the cardinal became involved in a dispute with the half-brother of Archbishop Albrecht, Wilbrand of Käfernburg, provost of the collegiate churches of St. Nicholas at Magdeburg and Bibra, over Conrad's plans to commandeer a prebend at Bibra.[76] The power of the legate was clearly manifest over-against this man who was brought into submission and was forced to appear before the papal representative in sackcloth and ashes with a scourge in his hand. Magnanimously, Conrad forgave the provost's error. Later that same month, on 20 September, the cardinal consecrated Bishop-elect Hermann of Würzburg as a priest; on the following day Hermann received the episcopal blessing in the Magdeburg cathedral at the hands of the legate as well.[77] The early Mass on 22 September (the feast of St. Moritz) was an awesome ceremony: seven bishops—those of Estonia, Kamin, Havelberg, Brandenburg, Merseburg, Hildesheim, and Würzburg—, and as the eighth the archbishop of Magdeburg, read the eight lections, while the cardinal-legate read the ninth. To his *"Deus miseratur nostri et benedicti vobis,"* the bishops responded *"Amen."*[78]

Among the business dealt with at this Magdeburg synod was a dispute at the nun-cloister Quedlinburg between Abbess Sophia and the convent. Sophia, from the Danish royal house, had been attacked in the cloister itself by certain of her servitors and vassals. She was deposed and replaced by Bertrada of Krosigk, sister to the former bishop of Halberstadt, Conrad, who was now the Cistercian abbot of Sichem. On 26 September the cardinal legate rendered a decision with the advice of the archbishop and the bishops of Merseburg, Brandenburg, and Hildesheim. Despite the participation of the latter, the assembly was undoubtedly a provincial synod, the judgment of which was to retain Sophia and to compensate Bertrada. Though opposed by Halberstadt and the *ministeriales* of Quedlinburg, the decision remained.[79]

---

[76] See Wentz/Schwineköper, *Erzbistum Magdeburg* 315; Mülverstedt, *RAMagd* II, Nrs. 744-747.

[77] Mülverstedt, *RAMagd* II, Nr. 748.

[78] *Chron. mont. ser.* 222; Hartzheim, *Concilia* III 518-520; Roth von Schreckenstein, "Urach" 350-353; Binterim, *Concilien* IV 451, with date of 1224; Hefele-Leclercq, *Conciles* V/2 1447-1448; Hauck, *KGD* IV 799; Idem. V 136 note 3.

[79] Mülverstedt, *RAMagd* II, Nr. 749; Roth von Schreckenstein, "Urach" 353; Hefele-Leclercq, *Conciles* V/2 1447-1448. The bishop of Hildesheim was present in his capacity as a papally-appointed crusade-preacher. See the letter addressed to the archbishops of

In the last days of September 1225 Cardinal Conrad intended to go to Lauterberg on his way to Naumburg, but although the convent awaited him with great expectation, he never appeared. He had not forgotten the concerns of the canons, however. On 1 October from Naumburg he appointed a commission to conduct a visitation of Lauterberg, comprised of the bishops of Merseburg and Brandenburg, together with the abbot of Pforte. While the bishop of Merseburg went in person, the others sent surrogates. The visitation arrived on 21 October and conducted its office in a manner which outraged the chronicler: Prior Dietrich was allowed once more to retain his office and dignities, a man clearly unsuited for them in the eyes of the canons of his own convent. Nevertheless, the influence which his cousin Ekkehard enjoyed by virtue of the episcopal office preserved for Dietrich his position and thwarted the efforts at reform which had been attempted so often.[80]

The Assassination of Archbishop Engelbert of Cologne

On 3 October 1225 the legate was at Erfurt, *en route* to Cologne where he planned to celebrate a council with the princes of the German church. Those abuses which he had observed during his travels were undoubtedly to be dealt with comprehensively at that time. He had progressed only as far as Würzburg by 6 November, from where he published decrees relating to the correction of problems in the collegiate church of St. Anschar at Bremen.[81] It was probably on this occasion also that he issued a statute to the dean and cathedral chapter at Würzburg, prohibiting the transfer (and therefore alienation) of any gifts, residences, *curiae*, or other possessions to laymen or other persons by the canons.[82] Conrad's intentions were radically altered, however, for the very next day the archbishop of Cologne, Engelbert of Berg, without question the most powerful and influential German prelate of his day and the man appointed by Frederick II himself to serve as the imperial regent during the minority of Henry (VII), was brutally murdered by his cousin, the count of Isenberg. Upon receiving

Magdeburg and Bremen and their respective clergy written by the cardinal-legate and dated 31 August 1225 at Halberstadt; Mülverstedt, *op.cit.* II, Nr. 742.

[80] *Chron. mont. ser.* 223; Böhmer-Ficker, *Regg. Imp.* V/2, Nrs. 10047b, 10048; Roth von Schreckenstein, "Urach" 354.

[81] Ehmck, *Bremisches UB* I 161, Nr. 140; Böhmer-Ficker, *Regg. Imp.* V/2, Nr. 10051; Roth von Schreckenstein, "Urach" 354; Hauck, *KGD* IV 799.

[82] Statute confirmed by Gregory IX on 1 March 1232; cf. Potthast, *Regesta* I, Nr. 8885; *Mon. Boica* XXXVII, 249. The cause of this confirmation so many years after the actual promulgation of the statute is not known.

word of this heinous crime, the legate postponed the national assembly until 30 November and transferred the venue to Mainz.

The selection of Mainz as the site of the council undoubtedly was related to the position of the archbishop as the primate of the German church. It seems likely, however, that a provincial synod had already been summoned for about that same time. On 11 October 1225 Pope Honorius III wrote to Archbishop Siegfried, reproaching him for attempting to compel the bishop of Würzburg to attend synods convened by him, actions clearly in violation of the indulgence granted to Bishop Otto in 1218, and admonishing him to be "*contentus quod se tibi praesentet, cum eum a te vocari contigerit, per idoneos nuntios et sollempnes.*"[83] This papal letter undoubtedly was sent in response to an appeal of the summons by the bishop. It suggests that although the bishops of Würzburg had not attended any provincial synods personally during the ten years since the Fourth Lateran Council, they had been represented by members of their diocesan clergy.

The death of Bishop Otto of Lobdeburg in 1223 should have brought to an end the personal antagonisms which separated the church of Würzburg from the metropolitan church of Mainz. There should thus have been no real justification for Bishop Hermann's appeal of his summons to the provincial synod scheduled for late 1225. Despite the papal admonition, Archbishop Siegfried appears to have been intent on reversing what he regarded as a dangerous precedent. On 5 June 1226, Pope Honorius issued a mandate to the provost of the cathedral and to the provost and dean of St. Maria *ad gradus* in Cologne that they inquire into complaints by the archbishop and cathedral chapter at Mainz, to the effect that Bishop Hermann was attempting to remove himself from the metropolitan jurisdiction of Mainz by means of exemption from synodal attendance. If they found that the excuses offered were not valid, but frivolous only, they were to revoke the indulgence granted in 1218 to Hermann's predecessor.[84] The problems encountered by Archbishop Eberhard II of Salzburg in enforcing synodal attendance by his suffragans were thus being experienced in the province of Mainz as well.

The provincial synod called by Archbishop Siegfried II of Mainz for October/December 1225 thus became a legatine council intended for the ecclesiastical princes of the entire German realm. It actually commenced

---

[83] Rodenberg, *MG Ep. s. XIII* I, Nr. 285; Potthast, *Regesta* I, Nr. 7492; Würdtwein, *Nova subs.* IV, 131; Wendehorst, *Bistum Würzburg* 217.

[84] Würdtwein, *Nova subs.* IV 135; Potthast, *Regesta* I 653, Nr. 7583. The resolution of the dispute is unknown. Under Archbishop Siegfried III of Mainz, however, relations improved: the bishop of Würzburg is documented at both the provincial synod of July 1239 and that of 25/26 June 1243; cf. Böhmer-Ficker, *Regg. Imp.* V, Nr. 4403a; Mansi, *Collectio* XXIII 687-688; Wendehorst, *Bistum Würzburg* 217.

several days later than planned, being attended by a number of prelates who were returning from the marriage of Henry (VII) to Margaret of Austria at Nürnberg. Such a gathering of German bishops for the purpose of treating matters of an ecclesiastical or pastoral nature had not occurred since the Mainz synod of 1154, and it is for this reason that modern commentators have called it a "national council." The older editions of the legislation, e.g., Hartzheim, reproduce the council in two sessions, a *Concilium Germanicum* and a *Concilium Moguntinum*.[85] Binterim has shown, however, that it was a single council in several sessions which convened during the space of more than a week, called *Germanicum* because it brought together bishops from all over Germany, and not just from the province of Mainz.[86] The council had three concerns: a call to arms for the crusade, an investigation into the assassination of Archbishop Engelbert of Cologne, and the improvement of ecclesiastical discipline. Contemporary chroniclers were primarily interested in the second, however. Emo, the Premonstratensian abbot at Bloemhof, provides details which augment those of Caesarius of Heisterbach's biography of the slain archbishop. The dignitaries of the Cologne church displayed before the assembled prelates the blood-stained cloak and the hat which had been struck thrice with a sword, lamenting in biblical phrases, "Behold here, Jacob, the garment of thy son," to which the cardinal and the assembled crowd responded, "Woe is me, a wild animal has devoured him." In a solemn address, the papal-legate praised Engelbert, declaring him a martyr and urging other prelates to follow his example in the conduct of their office. With obvious reference to the dispute which had led to Engelbert's death, he noted that many other bishops had often enfeoffed their relatives with Church property without regard for their obligations of stewardship. He noted that they paid little heed when such relatives despoiled Church property or even squandered it away. Together with the bishops present, he then declared the ban of excommunication over Count Frederick of Isenberg and ordained that the censure be published in all provinces where his legatine authority carried—Mainz, Cologne, Trier, Bremen, and Magdeburg, to be read in all churches on each Sunday after the extinguishing of the candles.[87]

---

[85] Hartzheim, *Concilia* III, 520-523: *Concilium Germanicum 1225— contra simoniacos et concubinarios clericos celebratum*; Idem. 524: *Concilium Moguntinum*. See also *Gallia christ.* (1731) V, col. 483; Manrique, *Ann. Cisterc.* IV 278-286.

[86] Binterim, *Concilien* IV 465; Hefele-Leclercq, *Conciles* V/2 1448-1450; Hauck, *KGD* IV 767 note 3; V 136 note 3.

[87] Emo excerpted by Ficker, *Engelbert der Heilige* 353-6; Ficker, op.cit. 176, cites Caesarius of Heisterbach, *Vita* II, 13; Ficker, *Engelbert der Heilige* 267 note 4, states that the mid-December date is suggested by the document which Conrad of Urach issued 17 December in behalf of the monastery Eberbach at Mainz (published since Ficker's day in Rossel, *UB*

Excommunication was pronounced against the count's accomplices as well—any who with counsel or with actions participated in the murder, and also against all who had offered protection to, or had intercourse with, those banned. The *ministeriales* of Cologne had raised the guilty cry against all the Isenberg brothers and several other counts, but above all against Dietrich, bishop of Münster. This prelate had sent letters to Mainz protesting his innocence and demanding a time and place for a hearing. The bishop-elect of Osnabrück, Engelbert of Isenberg, was even brash enough to request consecration in a letter as well. In response, the legate informed the brothers that their case would be further considered at an assembly set for the feast of the Purification of Mary (2 February) 1226, summoning them to appear ready to defend themselves against charges of treason and murder.[88]

The matter of church discipline was taken up on 8/9 December at Mainz and resulted in the issuance of fourteen canons by the legate relative to grave abuses by the German clergy.[89] As noted above, Bishop Conrad of Porto had traveled extensively throughout the provinces of Trier, Cologne, Mainz, Salzburg, and Magdeburg during more than a year's stay in Germany, and he had had countless opportunities for observing conditions generally. The statutes are an unhappy testimony of clerical standards as perceived by a Cistercian cardinal. At the same time they leave little doubt that the reform of the Church which Innocent III had envisioned would come about as a result of the Fourth Lateran Council had made little progress in Germany. Many clerics in the towns and countryside had concubines and had willed their prebends to them and their mutual children.[90] Others, though excommunicated, continued to serve in office; some merely officiated in the presence of excommunicates. Many clerical offices were rented out to lay occupants, a practice regarded as simony and harshly condemned. Other matters pertaining to the curtailment of worldly

---

Eberbach I, Nr. 390).

[88] Böhmer-Ficker, *Regg. Imp.* V/2, Nr. 10054a; Roth von Schreckenstein, "Urach" 355-356.

[89] Winkelmann, *Friedrich II.* 256 note 2, refers to the then unedited and unused decrees of the council which are found on a parchment at Brussels, according to *Archiv* 7 (1848) 832. The codex 4° has heading: "*Concilia provincilia Coloniensia ab a. 1225 usque ad a. 1423.*" The first listed is that of 1225: "*Concilium habitum tempore Honorii III. in Alemania per Conradum cardinalem et episcopum.*"

[90] There is an obvious direct connection between this legatine statute for all of Germany and the specific order given to the cathedral canons at Würzburg; cf. Potthast, *Regesta* I, Nr. 8885 (papal confirmation of 1 March 1232).

lust and carnal depravity among a significant portion of the German clergy were also dealt with.[91]

The decrees of 1225 draw on earlier conciliar legislation: e.g., c. 14 (*Ut clericorum mores*) of Lateran IV provided the general basis for the cardinal-legate's c. 1,[92] whereas c. 9 drew on c. 17 of the Third Lateran Council of 1179 (*in quibusdam locis fundatores ecclesiarum aut heredes*).[93] The 1225 statutes were ordered to be published in provincial and diocesan synods each year (c. 14), reaffirming c. 6 of Lateran IV. On 22 November 1226, Pope Honorius III commanded the archbishop of Bremen to use those decrees of the cardinal-legate in disciplinary action against the former provost of Reepsholt (one S[ibodo]) and other canons of Bremen on account of simony and various clerical lapses.[94] We may infer from this that copies of the legatine statutes were distributed at the national synod and that within a year they were available generally throughout the realm. That the legatine legislation was also known in the diocese of Liège seems evident from the fact that the anonymous compiler of the *Chronica Villariensis Monasterii*, writing about 1250/1260, included verbatim all of c. 13 in his account.[95] Later synods at Mainz restated Conrad's decrees as well: in 1310 they became part of the Mainz synodal collection and thus had an effect in that province until the end of the Middle Ages.[96]

The 1225 *Concilium Germanicum* was of especial importance because it demonstrated that Conrad of Porto was intent on continuing the ideas of Innocent III relative to the purpose of synods. Few people in the Roman Curia at the time could have understood the German church to the extent

[91] Hauck, *KGD* V 137 note 1; Hefele-Leclercq, *Conciles* V/2 1449; Binterim, *Concilien* III 348, 465.

[92] Hauck, *KGD* IV 6 note 7.

[93] Hauck, *KGD* IV 40 note 1.

[94] May, *REB* I, Nr. 828; Ehmck, *Bremisches UB* I, Nrs. 330, 336; Pressutti, *Regg. Hon. III* II, Nrs. 6062, 6200, 6072, 6148; Potthast, *Regesta* II, Nrs. 2098 (Nr. 7615a-26161), 7657a-26127.

[95] [*C. 9 (de Conrado abbate nono)*] 198: "*Comque strennue officium legationis perageret, Maguntiam devenit, ibique celebrato solempni concilio, edidit hoc decretum: Licet contra refrenandos insidialores pudicitie sanctarum virginum pene gravissime sint statute tam canonice quam legales, quidam, laxatis voluptatis habenis, in lacum miserie et in lutum fecis se immergunt, ut obliti salutis eterne, normam honestatis temerantes, earum pudiciam interpolare presumant; contra quos terminum rigoris opponimus, statuentes, ut, quicumque pudicitiam monialium cuiuscumque habitus ansu sacrilego sollicitare presumpserit, ab officio, si clericus fuerit, si laicus, a perceptione corporis Domini se noverit suspensum. Qui vero sacrilegum carnis commercium cum talibus habuerit, ipso facto excommunicationis sententia se noverit innodatum, monialis vero seu canonica, que huiusmodi crimen flagitiosum perpettraverit, ulterius ad officium aliquod in monasterio nullatenus admittatur, sed in signum iniquitatis sue ultima tam in claustro remaneant quam in choro.*"

[96] Hauck, *KGD* V 136-137.

that he did, inasmuch as he was the same man who had been elected by a faction of the cathedral chapter at Liège to be bishop in 1200, before withdrawing to the life of a Cistercian monk at Villers-en-Brabant. By 1209 he was prior of that house; in 1211 he was elected abbot. His reputation as an ardent reformer and as a rigorous administrator led to his elevation as abbot of Clairvaux in 1214, and in 1216 he became abbot of Cîteaux and general of his Order. From this vantage point, he was able to see the larger picture of the medieval Church and to enact legislation aimed at correcting abuses. Unlike the situation in 1215 where Innocent III distributed his decrees and commanded that the prelates enforce them, Conrad was now present among the bishops and archbishops and could demand compliance with his and the Council's constitutions by means of his apostolic authority. By insisting that his statutes be read in both provincial and diocesan synods yearly, he sought to ensure that such assemblies would remain primarily concerned with pastoral matters and not degenerate into mere administrative and judicial occasions.

There seems to have been a certain ambivalence regarding them in Rome, however. On 8 March 1227, just ten days before he died, Honorius III granted power to Archbishop Siegfried of Mainz to absolve any clerics who had been excommunicated by himself or by papal legates on account of their having maintained concubines, and who, while under the ban, had celebrated the Mass, provided that they petitioned for such absolution.[97] This policy of conciliation seems to have been quickly overturned by Pope Gregory IX who on 20 June 1227 commissioned *magister* Conrad of Marburg, *praedicator verbi Dei*, to compel parish priests and others in holy orders throughout Germany to put aside their concubines as ordained by Conrad of Porto, or else suffer ecclesiastical censure.[98]

During the final week of Advent (22 December) 1225, Bishop Ekkehard of Merseburg confirmed the emancipation of the new church in Oelzsch and the purchase of a hide of land in Dallschütz as compensation for the church at Dallschütz ". . . *in sinodo nostra* . . ."[99] Like so many other assemblies of the period, this act is the only evidence of the synod which has been recorded, yet there can be little doubt that the prelate also published the cardinal's decrees of just two weeks earlier. In spite of Ekkehard's behavior in the matter of the Lauterberg priorship, he could hardly have risked ignoring the legate's mandate with him still so close at hand.

Conrad of Porto in fact spent Christmas in Cologne; thence, in mid-January 1226, he traveled northward into the regions of Xanten and

[97] Pressutti, *Regg. Hon. III* II, Nr. 6277.
[98] Potthast, *Regesta* I 687, Nr. 7946; Auvray, *Registres de Gregoire IX* I, Nr. 113.
[99] *Merseburg UB* I, 157, Nr. 192.

Utrecht in the interest of the crusade.[100] On the appointed day for judging those accused in the assassination of Archbishop Engelbert (2/3 February), he and some nine bishops assembled in the dining hall of the episcopal residence at Liège where, after he had given the blessing, he ordered the spectators to vacate the chamber. Those who were disobedient he threatened with the ban. It then came to a heated tumult, sparked by the charges against the bishop of Münster made by the *ministeriales* of Cologne and the equally-vociferous denials of complicity from the Münster *ministeriales*. The following day, by means of a ruse, the clergy met alone and reached a verdict. The archbishop of Trier praised his fallen friend Engelbert, as spokesman for the bishops. Then, due to a lack of solid evidence against the bishops of Münster and Osnabrück, they were allowed to clear themselves by means of compurgation. The bishops who were supposed to do this reneged, however. Under the circumstances, the only choice was to suspend the accused prelates until the pope decided the issue himself. The legate meanwhile named the bishop of Paderborn administrator of both bishoprics in spiritual affairs; Bishop Wilbrand also took temporal control of Osnabrück, and with the count of Gelders administered the *temporalia* of Münster as well.[101]

Both accused prelates set out for Rome where they hoped to receive a different verdict. The pope, however, confirmed the legatine decision and by 30 June 1226 rumors were spreading throughout Germany that the pontiff had deposed the two Isenbergers. The trauma of being accused of complicity in the assassination of the archbishop proved too much for Bishop Dietrich of Münster: having failed to convince either the synod at Liège or the Roman Curia of his innocence, he died shortly thereafter on 18/22 July.

There were thus two episcopal elections within the province of Cologne during the second half of 1226. At Münster the choice fell upon Ludolf of Holte, a canon in the cathedral and provost in Frisia.[102] Emo of Bloem-hof, who was personally present at the hearings held at Liège, says nothing

---

[100] Böhmer-Ficker, *Regg. Imp.* V/2, Nrs. 10056a- 10067a.

[101] The primary sources for the synod are *Emonis Chron.* 510; *Chron. Albrici (a. 1226)* 917; *Reiner. Ann. (a. 1225)* 679; *Vita Engelb.* 322. See further, Mansi, *Collectio* XXIII, col. 11 seq.; Hartzheim, *Concilia* III 524-526; Harduin, *Acta Concil.* VII, col. 142; *Westf. UB* III, Nr. 220; Hauck, *KGD* IV 767 note 3; 798-799; Idem V 136 note 3; Binterim, *Concilien* III 426; Hefele-Leclercq, *Conciles* V/2 1450; Roth von Schreckenstein, "Urach" 357-359. Those archbishops or bishops present were Gerhard II of Bremen, Iso of Verden, Conrad I of Minden, Otto II of Utrecht, Conrad of Hildesheim, Dietrich of Münster, Engelbert I of Osnabrück, Hugh of Liège, and Dietrich II of Trier.

[102] Krabbo, *Besetzung* 111; *Westf. UB* III, Nrs. 69, 91, 200, 208; Pelster, *Stand und Herkunft* 71.

at all about the details of Ludolf's succession. At Osnabrück the cathedral canons selected Otto who died on 6 April 1227; he in turn was succeeded by a cathedral canon from Hildesheim, Conrad of Veltberg.[103] Consecration for bishops-elect Ludolf and Otto presumably came before or in conjunction with the great celebration held at Cologne on 20 September 1226 as Henry of Müllenark, formerly provost at Bonn, was consecrated as archbishop of Cologne by Dietrich II of Trier.[104] Presumably on this occasion or in November of that same year when the new metropolitan convened an assembly of bishops in his city to deal with the purgation of those accused of conspiracy in the assassination of his predecessor, the legatine decrees of 1225 would also have been proclaimed. If, as Binterim claims, this latter assembly was a probable provincial synod, it is the only one known for the eleven-year pontificate of Archbishop Henry.[105]

For the new prelate at Münster establishing a strong synodal tradition appears to have been an important matter. During the first year of his pontificate he presided over a diocesan synod which issued a judgment concerning the rights and obligations of rent-paying peasants.[106] The decision had an authoritative significance, being renewed in Münster and also used in Paderborn in 1262 as the basis for a similar statute.[107] During the remainder of the thirteenth century the synods at Münster became fixed on two dates, the Monday after the feast of Saints Gereon and

---

[103] Pelster, *Stand und Herkunft* 83; Krabbo, *Besetzung* 111.

[104] *Chron. reg. Colon. cont. IV (a. 1226)* 258: *"Ipso anno Henricus Coloniensis electus in archiepiscopum a Treverensi archiepiscopo Colonie in vigilia Mathei apostoli cum magna sollemnitate consecratur, presentibus omnibus suffrageis suis, necnon et Iacobo Aconensi et Hermanno Lealensi episcopis."*

[105] Binterim, *Concilien* III 430; *Chron. reg. Colon. cont. IV (a. 1226)* 259: *"Qui [scil. archiep. Colon.] in festo Martini, sequenti scilicet die, anno sequenti, qua corpus lacerum glorioso archiepiscopi Colonie est receptum, quamque idem episcopus advivens pro forma conpositionis agenda ipsi prefixerat, Colonie presentatus est, et tercia die facta confessione et proditis complicibus huius facti, extra muros civitatis in rota positus, super modicam piramidem est elevatus. Postea convenientibus episcopis et nobilibus terre, vasallis Sancti Patri, nobiles quidam, qui pro huiusmodi interfectione suspecti habebantur, licet difficulter, ab archiepiscopo et prioribus Coloniensibus ad expurgationem obiecti criminis sunt admissi."* On the charge given by the new archbishop on the day of his consecration to the Cistercian monk Caesarius of Heisterbach regarding the writing of a hagiographic *Vita* which would serve as the foundation of efforts to secure canonization for Engelbert as a martyr, see my forthcoming article, "Engelbert or Elizabeth: Candidates for Beatification in the Thirteenth Century," *Sewanee Medieval Studies* (1994).

[106] *Westf. UB* III, Nr. 235: 1227 (*"Gerlago de Dingethe sancti Marie decano, in cuius factum est synodo"*). Sometime between 1226 and 1248 a synod was held which a later Dean Friedrich recalled: *". . . quod in nostra synodo episcopali presidente pie memorie Ludolpho episcopo nostro, . . ."*; cf. *Westf. UB* III, Nr. 232. Perhaps they are one and the same. See also Bierbaum, *Diözesansynode* 383-384; Finke, "Münster Synode" 162.

[107] *Westf. UB* IV, Nr. 916.

Victor (10 October) and the fourth Sunday of Lent. Most of the recorded synods dealt with juridical matters, and the documents reveal that by the end of the century the bishop did not even attend such assemblies himself.[108]

At some unidentified time (presumably in early 1226) the cardinal-bishop of Porto also addressed issues relating to the clergy in the archdiocese of Bremen. The surviving record hereof is contained in a letter dated 22 November 1226 in which Pope Honorius III commanded Archbishop Gerhard to carry out the investigation into charges of "*symonia et aliis diversis criminibus*" against Sibodo, the provost of Reepsholt, and other cathedral canons at Bremen, which the legate Conrad had given him.[109] The prelate's lassitude in enforcing canonical strictures is perhaps symptomatic of his entire pontificate, however. Eight months later a new pope, Gregory IX, issued a sharp reprimand to Gerhard, claiming that he had received complaints from members of the Bremen parish that there was within the city of Bremen but one parish church, with a very large and widely scattered congregation; moreover, the parish priest (*plebanus*) had but two assistants in a situation where ten could hardly do the work, so that the individual members of the parish (and especially the sick) could not be cared for properly and many died without the benefits of the Eucharist or Penance, resulting in great consternation among the people. The pontiff therefore ordered that the city of Bremen be divided into three separate parishes, each with its own parish priest, and that appropriate regulations be given for the ordering of church life.[110]

---

[108] *Westf. UB* III, Nrs. 232, 235, 672, 688, 761, 830, 850, 868, 928, 988, 1223, 1401, 1501, 1507, 1540, 1566. Caspar Franc. Krabbe, *Statuta Synodalia Monasteriensis* (Münster, 1849) 5, begins his list with Bishop Eberhard (1275-1301). See also Finke, "Münster Synode" 161-165, who notes that all later reform decrees refer back to his.

[109] Ehmck, *Bremisches UB* I 679, Nr. 330; May, *REB* I 229, Nr. 828; Pressutti, *Regg. Hon. III* II, Nr. 6062. The investigation against Sibodo became a protracted affair: during his stay in Bremen in 1230 Cardinal-legate Otto had appointed the Dominican prior for the province and the dean and scholastic at Bremen's cathedral church to conduct a visitation, during which the provost at Reepsholt had appealed to the Curia; after investigation there, the pope sent instructions on 4 June 1233 to the bishop and scholastic at Hildesheim for execution; cf. Auvray, *Registres de Gregoire IX* I, Nr. 1365. Owing to the many other tasks which Bishop Conrad of Hildesheim had been given (crusade-preaching etc.), he had been unable to conclude the business with respect to Reepsholt, and had returned the matter to Rome. Thus, on 9 June 1235 Pope Gregory IX issued a new mandate to three provosts from the diocese of Paderborn; cf. Auvray, op.cit. I, Nr. 2621. The expenses incurred by the provost of Reepsholt during the long process were the subject of the commission which Gregory gave on 1 July 1236 to the provosts of the cathedral and of St. Martin at Münster, and to the scholastic at St. Martin; cf. Auvray, *op.cit.* I, Nr. 3221.

[110] May, *REB* I 231, Nr. 839; Ehmck, *Bremisches UB* I, Nr. 144; Potthast, *Regesta* I, Nr. 7983. At the very time when this complaint from the parishioners in Bremen was being presented at Rome and the papal response was being prepared, Archbishop Gerhard of Bremen

In addition to presiding at the consecration of his neighboring archprelate at Cologne in 1226, Archbishop Dietrich II of Trier attended to matters within his own province. At an unspecified time that same year, he was present with Bishop Jean of Metz at Toul as an accord was reached between Count Henry of Bar and the cathedral chapter of Toul, in which the count promised protection against all men save the bishops of Metz and Verdun.[111] We may assume that the un-mentioned bishop of Toul was also present, and that the occasion was that of a provincial synod. Undoubtedly the disturbances caused by the schismatic episcopal election at Verdun the previous year were still being felt and efforts by prelates to establish and maintain amicable relations with the major secular powers of Lorraine were important. Once again, however, the state of the four churches in the province would have been on the synodal agenda as well.

Papal Exceptions to the Lateran IV Decrees

Characteristic of situations found perhaps in other German cathedral churches was that addressed in a mandate given to *G[uido] archidiacono et magistro [ ] subthesaurario Tullensi et F. canonico de Vico Metensis diocesis* on 21 May 1226 by Pope Honorius III. Although the Curia had already sent letters to the chapter at Metz with the command that they provide one *B. pauperi clerico*, a man who had served *fideliter et devote* in their church since childhood with a canonate and a prebend, certain of their number had nominated "*magister R[ogerus] scolasticus et camerarius Virdunensem . . . qui licet primiceriatum, archidiaconatum, scolastriam et camerariam in ipsa Virdunensi ecclesia et in Treverensi praebendam obtinet . . .*", all the while the poor cleric *B.* was still waiting in hopes of acquiring a permanent position within the cathedral chapter.[112] We have noted that in the period immediately preceding the Fourth Lateran Council the acquisition of large numbers of prebends by individual German clerics had militated against the sort of discipline and commitment to spiritual duties which were part of the image projected for those who would be disciples of Christ and servants of God. The Council had legislated against pluralism with respect to the *cura animarum*, restating the decrees of Lateran III on the subject. This papal directive clearly indicates, however, that some ten

---

was participating in the battle against King Waldemar II of Denmark, suggesting that politics, and not the cure of souls, was his first priority; cf. May, *REB* I 231, Nr. 838, citing primary sources. That the archbishop did in fact respond to the papal directive is revealed by *REB* I 232-233, Nrs. 845-846 (dated 1228/1229).

[111] Heydenreich, *Metropolitangewalt* 110 note 193, citing manuscript *Histoire de Metz* by Benoit, p. 441; Tabouillet, *Hist. de Metz* II 432.

[112] Pressutti, *Regg. Hon. III* II, Nr. 5950.

years after Innocent III's decree, a very successful pluralist at Verdun was finding further benefices and prebends at Metz and even within the archiepiscopal church at Trier. The *iudices delegati* were therefore instructed to make provision for a benefice for *B.* at Metz, and to assign to him a canonate and a prebend in the cathedral chapter: *B.* was in other words to have full rights, including *"stallum in choro et votum in capitulo."* It would appear from this example that the aristocratic character of the cathedral chapter at Metz, and similarly at many other German sees, was being challenged.

The papacy's willingness to set aside canonical sanctions against pluralism can also be seen in another case involving the church at Toul. A cleric *"Tullensi, in iure canonico competenter instructo"* had requested with his bishop's support permission from Pope Honorius III to acquire yet another benefice. The latter's death had left the matter incomplete, and on 6 April 1227 Gregory IX granted an indulgence for the cleric to obtain additional ecclesiastical benefices producing a yearly income of up to twenty-five Marks.[113] Three months later the pope instructed the bishop of Toul to confer a prebend in the cathedral church upon a cleric named Peter who had served the prelate faithfully in various capacities and had exposed himself to numerous dangers in the process, provided that Peter was willing and able to maintain residence as required by the cathedral chapter.[114]

Similar provisions were made in behalf of clerics in the dioceses of Utrecht, [115] Osnabrück,[116] Strasbourg,[117] Trier,[118] Mainz,[119] Magdeburg,[120] and Würzburg.[121] That such dispensations clearly lay within the purview of the Roman pontiff can also be seen in the commission given on

---

[113] Auvray, *Registres de Gregoire IX* I, Nr. 121.

[114] Auvray, *op.cit.* I, Nr. 126 (dated 9 June 1227).

[115] Auvray, *op.cit.* I, Nr. 199 (22 June 1227).

[116] Auvray, *op.cit.* I, Nr. 273 (*"Johanni, thesaurario ecclesiae S. Johannis Osnaburgensis concedit, ut, praeter illa beneficia quae nunc obtinet, adhuc unum beneficium, si illi canonice offeratur, constitutione non obstante concilii generalis, recipere libere valeat."*)

[117] Auvray, *op.cit.* I, Nr. 297 (10 May 1229).

[118] Auvray, *op.cit.* I, Nr. 369: Archbishop Dietrich was ordered to investigate the merits of one Dudo de Cruce, a cleric of the bishop of Metz, and if warranted dispense him from the *"defectus natalium"* so that, if he should be considered for the office of bishop, he could accept it.

[119] Potthast, *Regesta* I, Nr. 8551; Auvray, *Registres de Gregoire IX* I, Nr. 452 (11 May 1230): *". . . non obstante constitutione concilii generalis."*

[120] Auvray, *Registres de Gregoire IX* I, Nr. 490 (13 September 1230): the archbishop was instructed to find a canonate in the conventual churches of the city, with the exception of the cathedral, for *magister Johannes physicus.*

[121] Auvray, *op.cit.* I, Nr. 554.

11 December 1232 to the bishop, *thesaurarius*, and the canon G. at Osnabrück to take action against the canon C. of the collegiate church of St. Andreas in Cologne: despite the fact that he supported himself with the church at Dhorenspic and with numerous other benefices without the dispensation of the apostolic see, he had been brazen enough to acquire yet another church at Lüdinghausen *"post generale concilium"*; Bishop Conrad and his associates were ordered to allow the canon at St. Andreas to retain the last acquisition, but the other benefices were to be conferred on other suitable individuals.[122]

An issue which would also have come up at a provincial synod held at Toul in 1226 was that of the disputed provostship at the collegiate church of St. Mary Magdalene at Verdun. The two contesting clerics were *Guillelmus de Tirangulo et R. Virdunensis canonicus*. If this canon *R.* is the same person as the scholastic Roger d'Ostenge de Marcey noted previously, we have but further indication of this totally unbridled ambition at work. On 26 January 1227 the Roman pontiff appointed a commission consisting of the scholastic of St. Paulin at Trier, the canon Hugo at Burgen and *magister* G. Goyn, the latter two of whom were canons at Rheims, to investigate and resolve the situation.[123] The schism was compounded by the fact that the first candidate had been elected by the provost and members of the chapter, while the second had been appointed by the archbishop. The metropolitan's reasons for involvement are not known; presumably he could justify preferment of a pluralist over his rival, however.

The following month the pontiff granted to Bishop Eudes of Toul power to remove from their ecclesiastical benefices and churches priests and clerics of his diocese who had immediately followed their own fathers in such positions and offices, contrary to *sanctiones canonicas*; he was also admonished to exercise his obligation to remove *sacerdotes concubinarios* from their offices.[124] The most recent injunctions against such practices would have been the legatine council held at Mainz in 1225, along with any restatement of those statutes at the Trier provincial synod in 1226. Lateran IV had also legislated against these, however, in which case we see at Toul a specific instance where Innocent's constitutions were to be applied.[125]

---

[122] Auvray, *op.cit.* I, Nr. 995.

[123] Horoy, *Honorii III opera* V 183, Nr. 53; Pressutti, *Regg. Hon. III* II, Nr. 6199.

[124] Horoy, *Honorii III opera* V 182, Nr. 52; Pressutti, *Regg. Hon. III* II, Nr. 6256.

[125] Lateran IV, *c.* 31: *"Ad abolendam pessimam quae in plerisque inolevit ecclesiis corruptelam, firmiter prohibemus, ne canonicorum filii, maxime spurii, canonici fiant in saecularibus ecclesiis, in quibus instituti sunt patres; et si fuerit contra praesumptum, decernimus non valere. Qui vero tales ut dictum est, canonicare praesumpserint, a suis beneficiis suspendantur."*

An Alleged Provincial Synod at Trier—1227

Clearly the most controversial provincial synod mentioned in the great collections of Martène, Hartzheim, Mansi, and others is that allegedly held at Trier in 1227.[126] The seventeen canons were contained in a fourteenth-century codex found in the Benedictine abbey of St. Matthias near Trier. According to a note appended to the statutes, the synod was held in the "*ecclesia Stae. Mariae maioris Treveris.*" At first flush they seem to be what they claim. Very soon, however, traces of the Second Council of Lyons (1274) appear; Martène questioned the dating for this reason.[127] Both Hartzheim and Mansi, on the other hand, accepted their authenticity. The editor of the *Statuta synodalia archidiocesis Trevirensis*, J.J. Blattau, raised the issue of the excerpts from Lyons II in his commentary to the "Trier 1227" statutes, and suggested that a scribal error had changed what should have been 1277 into 1227.[128] Despite previous caveats, however, Hefele-Knöpfler accepted it uncritically,[129] as did Jakob Marx, the contributor to Herder's *Kirchenlexikon*.[130] More recent scholars (among them Hauck,[131] Arens,[132] and Heydenreich)[133] have pointed out the problems involved in regarding the "1227" statutes as genuine. The general consensus now is that they were enacted in 1277, drawing upon the

---

[126] Trier Stadtbibliothek MS 1731; cf. Georg Heinrich Pertz, "Handschriften der Stadtbibliothek zu Trier," *Archiv* 2 (1843) 605. Printed in Martène, *Collectio* VII 107ff.; Hartzheim, *Concilia* III 526-535 "*ex Codice Ms. Pergameno Abbatiae Benedictinae S. Matthiae prope Treveros*"; Mansi, *Collectio* XXIII 26-38. At the end of the manuscript is the inscription "*Celebratum est hoc Concilium in Ecclesia Stae. Mariae majoris Treveris, a Venerabili Domino Trevirensi Archi-Episcopo praesentibus Provincialibus Episcopos et Provinciae Praelatis. Anno Dni mccxxvii Kal. Martii Explicit.*" Hartzheim indicates (p. 526) that the existence of this codex was brought to his attention by Rev. D. Dh'ame of the abbey of St. Matthias, noting however that the recent edition of the *Gesta Trevirorum* by Johann Nikolas Hontheim (*Prodromus Trevericus*) did not make mention of the synod of 1227.

[127] Martène, *Thesaur. Anecdot* IV 158, believed that the Codex had three distinct parts: 1) that which contained statutes derived from Lyons II; 2) that which contained statutes from "Trier 1227"; and 3) Liber Instructionum ad clerum compositus per venerabilem dominum G. Durand episcopum Mimatensem.

[128] J.J. Blattau, *Statuta synodalia archidiocesis Trevirensis* I (Trier, 1844) 14ff.

[129] *Konziliengeschichte* V 944-950; see also Hefele-Leclercq, *Conciles* V/2 1454ff.

[130] J. Marx, "Synoden-Trier," *Kirchenlexikon*, ed. Wetzer & Welte (2nd ed. Freiburg i. Br.; Herder Verlag, 1907) XII 14-22, sees the decrees as a "*Pastoral in nuce*" written to instruct the clergy in the cure of souls; he regards the synod as diocesan rather than provincial.

[131] Hauck, *KGD* IV 9-10 note 6, argues that based on internal evidence the statutes probably belong to the last quarter of the thirteenth century.

[132] Arens, "Datierung" 85-104, considers 1277 to be the best date, though he does not exclude the possibility of an "*Urtext*" from 1227.

[133] Johanne Heydenreich, "Zu den Trierer Synodalstatuten des 13. Jahrhunderts," *ZSRG* KanAbt 25 (1936) 478-484.

legislation of an undated French synod of about 1200, Mainz 1233, and Lyons II.[134]

Hartzheim records another synod for 1227 which appears to be authentic—that held at Mainz. The major issue, based on surviving evidence, was the prohibition against lay advocates inheriting church lands.[135] To an extent, this position was supported by c. 44 of the Lateran IV constitutions which forbade the alienation of ecclesiastical properties without the legitimate consent of the respective prelates. The problem of lay encroachment on Church property was undoubtedly common during the uncertainties of 1198-1215 and required years to correct. We may also speculate that the papal privilege granted on 8 March 1227 to the archbishop regarding clerics with concubines found execution at this time. This synod is also significant in that it was the last one summoned by Archbishop Siegfried II who had presided over his church for nearly thirty eventful years. His legacy to his successors was a somewhat ambiguous one: on the one hand there is the evidence of a vigorous effort to enforce discipline within his archbishopric and province, to use both provincial and diocesan synods as instruments of reform, and to assert his role as primate of the German church and a major figure in the political affairs of the Empire; on the other hand there is the unmistakable pattern of poor judgment which caused him to rush headlong into confirming suffragans prematurely, quarrelling with suffragans to the detriment of church life throughout his province, and antagonizing the Curia. Nevertheless he was an extremely durable sort of prelate who accommodated himself to three different kings or emperors, three successive popes, and a host of papal legates who periodically pre-empted him as the titular head of the German ecclesiastical structure.

Whereas the archbishop of Mainz had the weight of position on his side, the sitting German prelate most trusted by the Curia was Bishop Conrad II of Hildesheim. During the first decade of the thirteenth century he had served the pope as a preacher against the heretics in Languedoc, during the second decade as a crusade-preached and collector of the half-tithe imposed by Lateran IV, and during the 1220s he was again summoned to use his extraordinary talents in the cause of the Holy Land.[136] On 4 June 1227

---

[134] See Pellens, *Dietrich II. von Wied* 21; Johanek, "Odo von Sully" 336-341.

[135] Hartzheim, *Concilia* IV 615; Hauck, *KGD* V 135 note 1, claims that it is not certain whether this was a diocesan or provincial assembly.

[136] See Rodenberg, *MG Ep. s. XIII* I, Nr. 244; Hermann Hoogeweg, "Die Kreuzpredigt des Jahres 1224 in Deutschland mit besonderer Rücksicht auf die Erzdözese Köln," *Deutsche Zeitschrift für Geschichtswissenschaft* 4 (1890) 57-58; Pixton, "Anwerbung" 190.

Conrad also convened a synod, the only record of which speaks of a grant of properties to the monastery of St. Godehard by the bishop.[137]

Both the prelate and his clergy would have been aware of another matter, however, which probably had been undertaken at the request of Bishop Conrad. During the visit to Hildesheim by the papal-legate Conrad, the latter's *capellanus*, a canon at St. Moritz in Hildesheim named Rodulfus, had been charged with preaching the crusade. He also undertook the task of reforming certain "*miserrimus mulieres, quae in lutum ceciderant.*" His efforts had won the women away from their sinful ways and resulted in the creation of a religious house for their temporal and spiritual support. The work must have been completed just prior to the synod convened by Bishop Conrad, for on 8 June 1227 Pope Gregory IX wrote to Rodulfus, congratulating him on his success; that same day letters were sent to various prelates in Germany, informing them of the situation and urging their support of the newly-established community.[138]

The bishop of Halberstadt, Frederick II of Kirchberg, meanwhile held synods with his clergy in 1226,[139] on 29 November 1227 (probably due to the fact that he was away from his city on the feast of St. Luke),[140] and on 18 February 1228.[141] Given the close co-operation between the bishops of Halberstadt and Hildesheim, and the cardinal legate, we can assume that the decrees of Conrad of Porto, issued at the national synod at Mainz in 1225, were promulgated at such synods as well.

Sometime between 1227 and 1229 Bishop Berthold of Strasbourg summoned the first recorded synod in his diocese since the Lateran Council. Given the tradition of synods at Strasbourg prior to the Council, it is probable that the troubles of the throne controversy had disrupted the practice. The issue for which we have surviving record was that raised by a baptized Jew who had separated from his un-baptized wife, and who sought to gain custody of their fourteen-year-old son who had remained with his mother, so that the lad could be raised in the Christian faith. The legal

---

[137] Hartzheim, *Concilia* III 536; Hoogeweg, *UB Hilds.* II, Nrs. 223-224 ("*in plenaria synodo*"); Hauck, *KGD* V 169 note 1.

[138] Auvray, *Registres de Gregoire IX* I, Nrs. 110-112; Rodenberg, *MG ep. XIII s.* I, Nrs. 356-358; Potthast, *Regesta* I, Nr. 7926.

[139] Schmidt, *UB Halb* I 522, Nr. 585 ("*in nostra synodo*"); the surviving record deals with the composition of a conflict.

[140] Schmidt, *UB Halb* I 534, Nr. 598 ("*hac facta recognitione publica nos de sententia synodali banno nostro episcopali ecclesie . . .*").

[141] Schmidt, *UB Halb* I 543, Nr. 604 ("*ad nostram sinodum, que erat vj feria post Invocavit, . . . ipsa sinodo, cui tunc vice nostra maior presedit prepositus, . . .*"). Hauck, *KGD* V 168 note 1, remarks that diocesan synods were probably no less frequent in the thirteenth and fourteenth centuries than they were in the eleventh and twelfth, using Halberstadt as an example.

ramifications of the custody battle had been dealt with at a diocesan synod, but the outcome there appears to have been ambiguous since the bishop then sent the matter to the pope for final resolution; in the meantime, he had assumed guardianship of the boy. On 16 May 1229 Pope Gregory IX responded that because the boy was subject to the authority of his father, to whose family he belonged and not to that of his mother, he ought not remain with persons who might threaten his salvation or even seek to take his life. Thus, despite his tender years, the boy should be given to his father.[142]

Generally speaking, the documentary evidence for synods held in Germany during the years 1228-1230 does not reveal anything of great interest. We have already noted above that, with the departure of Cardinal-legate Conrad of Porto in early 1226, those synods which have been recorded become once more dry administrative and/or judicial assemblies. The one notable exception was that held in 1228 at Bamberg, inasmuch as it is the first one recorded for that bishopric since the Council. Bishop Ekbert of Bamberg had been in Rome in November 1215 and had received the constitutions which were distributed. His energies immediately thereafter appear to have been occupied in making preparations for the crusade, and although he may have held a synod in that connection before his departure, we have no record of such; in October 1217 he is documented at Acre, in the company of his brother-in-law, King Andreas of Hungary, and numerous other German pilgrims.[143] Ekbert still sat as bishop in 1228, and it may thus have been on this occasion that the constitutions of the Fourth Lateranum were introduced to his church.[144] In any case, this year may clearly be regarded as the *terminus ante quem* for the reception of the Lateran decrees within the Bamberg church.

During the synod, discussion centered on the right of individuals to convey church property. The center of the dispute was Berthold (Boppo)

---

[142] Hartzheim, *Concilia* III 536; Phillips, *Diözesansynode* 138 (with date of 1230); Auvray, *Registres de Gregoire IX* I, Nr. 298; Potthast, *Regesta* I, Nr. 8399 ("*ex litteris tuis accepimus, perlatam fuisse ad synodam tuam huiusmodi quaestionem, quod quidam videlicet de Iudaicae coecitatis errore ad Christum . . . adductus, uxore sua in Iudaismo relicta, in iudicio postulavit instanter, ut eorum filius quadriennis assignaretur eidem ad fidem catholicam quam ipse susceperat perducendus. . . .*") The letter was taken up into the *Decretales* of Gregory IX (*lib.3. tit.33 de conv. infid. c. 2*). See also Binterim, *Concilien* IV 354; Hessel, *Regg. Strassburg* II 53, Nr. 947; Aronius, *Regg. der Juden* 196, Nr. 445.

[143] Cf. Röhricht, *Deutscher im Heiligen Lande* 98.

[144] The original document from the episcopal archives is now in Munich Hauptstaatsarchiv clm 2721; printed in Paul Oesterreicher, *Denkwürdigkeiten der fränkischen Geschichte, mit besonderer Rücksicht auf das Fürstentum Bamberg* III (Bamberg, 1832ff.) 22. See also Looshorn, *Bistum Bamberg* II 645; Krenzer, *Heinrich von Bilverstein* 17; Guttenberg, *Bistum Bamberg* 169.

of Andechs, provost of the Bamberg cathedral and also of the collegiate church of St. Jacob. This same man had been elected archbishop of Kalocza in Hungary in 1206, but had failed to receive confirmation from Pope Innocent III and had returned to Bamberg.[145] This "career" cleric who had studied canon law for a time in Italy argued that he could grant the church at Trubach to whomever he desired. The parish priest at Buchil, one Conrad, challenged this and declared that the church at Trubach belonged to the "true shepherd of Buchil (himself!)" and produced witnesses to support his claim. Realizing the weakness of his assertions, Boppo waxed angry, threw his miter at the feet of the bishop, and exclaimed: "Let whoever wants it have the church, if I cannot grant it according to my own desires!" The priest Conrad then picked up the discarded miter and was confirmed by the synod in his rights.

We have also noted above the struggles associated with maintaining some semblance of the *vita communis* at Trier from the tenth century until 1220. Elsewhere, similar problems were experienced: only the vigorous efforts of the bishops of Paderborn 1051-1223 had prevented its total dissolution there as well. In 1227 the cathedral chapter petitioned Bishop Wilbrand to abolish the common life, but he refused. Yet, the next bishop, Bernhard of Lippe (1228-1247), did so in the very first year of his pontificate.[146] This capitulation to pressures from within his church suggests that this may have been a condition of his election. In doing so, however, he lost one of the last effective controls over his clergy and opened the door for further relaxation of ecclesiastical expectations.

On 30 June 1228 Pope Gregory IX extended to Archbishop Albrecht of Magdeburg and Gernand of Brandenburg the commission to effect the resignation of the see of Meissen by Bishop Bruno who had sat there for nineteen years. *C*. 28 of the constitutions of Lateran IV had declared that

> *Quidam licentiam cedendi cum instantia postulantes, ea obtenta, cedere praetermittunt. Sed cum in postulatione cessionis huiusmodi aut ecclesiarum commoda quibus praesunt aut salutem videantur proprium attendisse, quorum neutrum suasionibus aliquorum quaerentium quae sunt sua, seu etiam levitate qualibet volumus impediri, ad cedendum eos decernimus compellendos.*

Consistent with those principles, the pontiff noted that "*[episcopus] adeo in diebus suis processisse dicatur, quod propter aetatis senescentis in ipso defectum Misnensis ecclesia iam graviter est collapsa . . .*"[147] The papal

---

[145] See above, Ch. Three, pp. 206-207; also Guttenberg, *Bistum Bamberg* 171-172.

[146] Maria Hanneken, "Die ständische Zusammensetzung des Paderborner Domkapitels im Mittelalter," *Westfälische Zeitschrift* 90/2 (1934) 80.

[147] Gersdorf, *UB Meissen* II/1 98, Nr. 107; Potthast, *Regesta* I, Nr. 8223.

directive was ultimately in response to a request from the cathedral chapter at Meissen during the winter of 1227/1228, but it is not unreasonable to speculate that a more recent report from the archbishop had triggered the commission at this time. Presumably in late spring 1228 the metropolitan had convened a provincial synod, on the agenda of which was the state of the Meissen church. Based on a decision reached there, some agent of Magdeburg had hastened to Rome for reinforcement. On 31 October 1228 at Halle the aged bishop renounced his office through representatives who appeared before Bishop Gernand.[148]

We are not fully aware of the role played by the archbishop in this drama, but we may be certain that the proper management of the dioceses within his province was a major concern. That Bishop Gernand of Brandenburg enjoyed his fullest confidence may be seen in the fact that while Albrecht was in Italy on imperial business, Gernand acted *vice archiepiscopi* in the administering of the archdiocese.[149] Perhaps it was at this same provincial synod that Archbishop Albrecht renewed the call given at the Fourth Lateranum for more regular and effective use of the episcopal visitation. Responding to that mandate, Bishop Engelhard of Naumburg conducted a visitation of all non-exempt monasteries and cloisters in his diocese, a fact we learn from a letter sent on 6 September 1228 to the abbot and convent of Bosau: acknowledging that it was within his stewardship as bishop to strengthen that which contributed to the saving of souls, while eliminating that which fostered decay, the prelate noted how much emphasis the archbishop of Magdeburg had placed on episcopal visitations of dioceses, thereby eliminating evils, uprooting thorns and thistles, and cultivating the lily of chastity and all else which brought honor to the life of the clergy.[150] The imagery of the garden which appears in many episcopal documents of this period should not disguise the fact that serious lapses of clerical discipline were evident.

A similar motivation lay behind the mandate sent to Bishop Gebhard of Passau on 13 June 1228 by Pope Gregory IX to correct the monks and nuns, both secular and regular, as well as the other clergy of his diocese. Drawing specific attention to *c*. 30 of the Lateran IV decrees, he admonished Gebhard to give heed that the prelates and heads of such houses left able men to look after parishioners, inasmuch as they themselves were frequently required in ecclesiastical business elsewhere.[151] We are not

---

[148] Gersdorf, *UB Meissen* II/1 98, Nrs. 108, 109; Krabbo, *Ostdeutsche Bistümer* 63; Rittenbach, *Meissen* 137-138; M-Alpermann, *Stand und Herkunft* 54.

[149] Krabbo, *Ostdeutsche Bistümer* 47-51; M-Alpermann, *Stand und Herkunft* 20-21.

[150] Lepsius, *Hochstift Naumburg* 72; Schötting-Kreys, *Dipl.* II 440.

[151] *Mon. Boica* XXVIII/2 151; Potthast, *Regesta* I, Nr. 8208: "*Cum autem prelati ecclesiarum sepe propter occupationes alias non sufficiant ministrare populo verbum Dei et*

told just how the prelate went about fulfilling this papal mandate, but his
efforts were met with resistance from within his own cathedral chapter and
from the clergy in the Austrian portion of his diocese. That same year he
placed the truculent clerics under the ban of excommunication. Following
a personal visit to Rome, he extended the ban to virtually all of his clergy.

Acting as papal *iudices delegati* the abbot and prior of Zwettl lifted the
ban on the cathedral chapter near the end of 1229; the Austrian clerics,
however, remained suspended and were summoned before the Curia. The
dispute moved to a higher level with the murder of the cathedral canon,
Eberhard of Jahenstorff, one of the most bitter opponents of Bishop
Gebhard. Immediately suspicion fell on the prelate, and Albert Behaim, an
archdeacon at Passau, demanded that Rome take up legal proceedings
against him.[152]   Soon thereafter representatives of the cathedral chapter
appeared in Rome bearing the bloody head of the slain canon.[153]   Before
a decision could be reached, however, Gebhard journeyed to the Curia once
more, offering the pope his resignation as bishop of Passau; Gregory IX
accepted this near the end of August 1232. The investigation which the
pope had ordered had meanwhile concluded, without in any way implicating
the beleaguered prelate.[154]   A mandate given on 11 May 1235 to the
abbots of Heiligenkreuz and Camp instructed them to conduct a visitation
of a venerable old monastery in the diocese of Passau where a monk had
admitted some laymen during the main meal of the day, who proceeded to
inflict physical punishment to certain of the brothers with drawn swords,
and then increased their calumny by invading the private chambers of the
abbot and driving him therefrom.[155]

---

statutum ob hoc fuerit in generali concilio, ut ad sancte predicationis officium salubriter viri
assumantur idonei potentes in opere ac sermone, qui plebes solicite visitantes eas verbo
edificent et exemplo, aliquos de clericis tue diocesis tibi associare procures, qui tibi
cooperatores et coadiutores, in quibus convenit existentes, tam verbo predicationis quam
visitationis officii tibi suffragium convenienter impendant, ut tua et ipsorum sollicitudine muri
Jerusalem et templum domini reparentur."   See also commentary of Kerschbaumer, *Sankt*
Pölten 190.

[152] Fuchs, *Besetzung* 66; Schreitwein, *Ep. Pataviensis* in Adrian Rauch, *Rerum Austriaca-*
rum Scriptores II (Wien, 1793/1794) 499; see also Kerschbaumer, *St. Pölten* 190-191. Ludwig
Heinrich Krick, *Das ehemalige Domstift und die ehemaligen Kollegiatstifte des Bistums Passau*
(Passau, 1922) 21, provides sketchy biographical details for Eberhard; his brother, the
Minnesänger *magister* Albert of Jahenstorff, went on crusade in 1189 with Frederick
Barbarossa.

[153] *Ann. Altah.* 391.

[154] Auvray, *Registres de Gregoire IX* I 526, Nr. 858 (29 August 1232); Dopsch, *Geschichte*
Salzburgs I 335.

[155] Potthast, *Regesta* I, Nr. 9900; cf. Manrique, *Ann. Cist.* IV 511.

Also within the province of Salzburg the bishop of Regensburg took steps to deal with problems of several sorts. Perhaps as a result of an episcopal inquisition into acts of violence and arson against church property, the prelate had imposed the ban of excommunication upon several individuals in his diocese. These in turn had laid their case before the Curia, and on 10 March 1228 Pope Gregory IX directed the prelate to absolve "*incendiarios suae diocesis et civitatis ab excommunicationis sententia . . . cum multi eorum ad sedem apostolicam propter varia impedimenta venire non possint.*"[156] Bishop Siegfried received a different sort of papal response two years later, however. Once again we may presume that an episcopal visitation had revealed widespread concubinage among the religious and secular clergy of his diocese. On the authority of the decrees issued by Cardinal-legate Conrad of Porto in 1225, he excommunicated the guilty priests and expelled the women from their residences. Some of those affected by this censure must have appealed their case to Rome, for on 3 July 1230 Gregory dictated a letter to the prelate, cautioning him to proceed very slowly in absolving any clerics from the ban, lest they hasten to resume their illicit relations with their former companions.[157]

Bishop Siegfried of Regensburg had acquired his office in 1227, the result of a schismatic election which occurred upon the death of Conrad IV of Frontenhausen. The *ministeriales* and a minority of the cathedral chapter had chosen the cathedral provost Gottfried as bishop, while the majority candidate was Abbot Berthold of St. Emmeran, the most prestigious Benedictine house in the diocese—"*vir per omnia venerando et industrio.*" Despite his unclear title to the episcopal office, Gottfried rewarded his supporters with grants from the patrimony of his church.[158] As the result of a protest from other members of the cathedral chapter, the pontiff

---

[156] Ried, *CdRatisb* I 349, Nr. 366; Potthast, *Regesta* I, Nr. 8141.

[157] Potthast, *Regesta* I 736, Nr. 8580; Ried, *CdRatisp* I 364, Nr. 380: "*A nobis suppliciter postulasti, ut cum in clericos concubinarios civitatis et diocesis Ratisbonensis generalem excommunicationis sententiam promulgaris, et quidam ex ipsis, qui eandem incurrentes sententiam per simplicitatem et iuris ignorantiam divina officia postmodum celebrantes, ad mandatum tuum sint redire parati, dignaremus misericorditer agere cum eisdem, nos igitur confidentes de fraternitatis tue prudentia, et tibi facientes gratiam specialem, presentium tibi auctoritate concedimus, ut sufficienti cautione recepta, quod non resumant dimissas focarias, et habere alias non presumant, iniuncta quoque ipsis penitentia competenti, eaque peracta, cum eis valeas dispensare, prout saluti eorum videris expedire; eis vero, quos scienter in contemptum ecclesiastice discipline tibi constiterit celebrasse divina, per biennium ab officii executione suspensis, postmodum, si bone fuerit conversationis et vite dispensare super hoc poteris cum eisdem.*"

[158] Krabbo, *Besetzung* 112-116; Georg Ratzinger, *Historisch-politische Blätter für das katholische Deutschland* 64 (München, 1869) 356; Idem, *Forschungen zur bayrischen Geschichte* (Kempten, 1898) 107.

summoned proctors to Rome where they elected the cathedral cantor at Mainz, Siegfried, from the family of the Rheingrafen, who was then at Rome—a *"vir scientia, vita, et fama praeclarus."* Gregory IX quickly confirmed this and notified the *ministeriales* and city officials thereof (10 June 1227).[159] Siegfried received consecration at the pope's hands at Anagni. Provost Gottfried and his supporters were deprived of their benefices and their place in the choir, under penalty of excommunication until they had personally appeared before the Curia in Rome.[160]

In 1230 Bishop Siegfried of Regensburg, one of the most ardent supporters of the Staufen dynasty in Germany, was appointed imperial chancellor, an office which he held until his death in 1246.[161] Under those circumstances he was absent from his diocese most of the time and had very little impact on the spiritual life of his church.[162] There is no record of synods at Regensburg after 1230, though the incomplete nature of the evidence does not rule such out altogether. Nevertheless, Janner regards him as one of the best bishops Regensburg had during the medieval period.[163]

Lay attacks against clerics and church property also was an issue at this time in the diocese of Freising. Bishop Gerold had been elected in 1220, but his supercilious and extravagant life had driven his bishopric deeply into debt. His cathedral chapter had complained to Pope Honorius III about his alienation of church property and his undisciplined ways. No sooner had Gregory IX assumed the papal throne than he addressed the problems in Freising. On 27 April 1227 he commanded the bishop of Eichstätt and the abbots of Aldersbach and Salem to inform him in detail about conditions,

---

[159] Ried, *CdRatisb* I 349, Nr. 367; Potthast, *Regesta* I, Nrs. 7927, 7955; Auvray, *Registres de Gregoire IX* I, Nr. 106. The possible influence of the archbishop of Mainz is seen in the fact that Siegfried was his cousin.

[160] *Notae S. Emmerammi, MGH SS* XVII 574, 575

[161] Harry Bresslau, *Handbuch der Urkundenlehre für Deutschland und Italien* I (Leipzig, 1889) 421.

[162] Staber, *Regensburg* 42-45.

[163] Janner, *Regensburg* 330-415: „*Für die Diöcese war er ein guter Bischof; gute Sitte und Disciplin aufrecht zu erhalten, oder sie wieder herzustellen, ist sein stetes Bemühmen, und dass auch die Wissenschaft zu seiner Zeit hoch geschätzt wurde, zeigt die grosse Anzahl Graduirter, die sich unter den Domcanonikern finden. Die Klöster und klösterlichen Institute erfreuten sich seines Beistandes, seiner steten Hilfeleistung, seiner ordnenden, kirchlich organisirenden Aufsicht. In dieser Thätigkeit ist Sigfried über alles Lob erhaben. Würden die kirchenpolitischen Verhältnisse dem Bischof gestattet haben, sein volles Augenmerk auf die Diöcesanangelegenheiten zu richten, so würden auch in dieser Hinsicht nur die vorzüglichsten Resultate zu verzeichnen sein. Unbedingt muss Sigfried unter die besten Bischöfe der Diöcese Regensburg gezählt werden.*"

and that they summon Gerold to appear in Rome within four months.[164] He appears to have submitted to those orders, inasmuch as he continued to function in his office for an additional three years. Nevertheless, his apparent indifference to ecclesiastical or religious matters may explain why lay encroachments against his church became more violent, and why there is no record of diocesan synods for Freising throughout the duration of his episcopacy.

The violence done to the church and canons at Berchtesgaden by various laymen of the diocese appears to have been treated without any involvement from the prelate.[165] On the other hand, Bishop Gerold seems to have taken action against those who committed acts of arson against church property: on 1 July 1228 the pope granted him permission to absolve those whom he had excommunicated and to see to the restoration of those buildings destroyed by fire in the city and diocese.[166] Perhaps at least the bishop had held an inquest into the brigandage. In the end, however, it was too little and too late: Gerold of Freising was forced to resign his office in August 1230.[167]

At some time prior to 20 June 1229 the Benedictine nuns' abbey of St. Julia in the diocese of Brixen received a visitation from three Dominican brothers who had been commissioned to perform that task.[168] The lengthy list of regulations imposed by the visitors had apparently been ignored, for on the above-noted date Pope Gregory IX issued an injunction to the abbess and the convent that they be observed *inviolabiliter*. Contact with the business of the outside world was restricted, both through prohibitions against leaving the cloister without license from the abbess, and through specifying those who could be received within its walls.[169] Various provisions were made for maintaining the order of the house as well: silence was to be observed in the cloister, in the oratory, the dormitory, and the refectory; meals were not to be eaten outside the refectory; disobedient

---

[164] Böhmer-Ficker, *Regg. Imp.* V/2, Nr. 6692; Potthast, *Regesta* I, Nr. 7887; Auvray, *Registres de Gregoire IX* I, Nr. 52; Fuchs, *Besetzung* 44.

[165] See Potthast, *Regesta* I, Nrs. 8179 (27 April 1228), 8185 (2 May 1228), 8192 (10 May 1228).

[166] Potthast, *Regesta* I, Nr. 8226: "*Ex parte tua . . . indulgimus facultatem absolvendi eos, qui de civitate ac diocesi Frisingensi incendium commiserunt, ac convertendi mulctas in reparationem ecclesiae et civitatis per ignem devastatae.*"

[167] Fuchs, *Besetzung* 45-46.

[168] Auvray, *Registres de Gregoire IX* I, Nr. 316.

[169] "*Intra claustrum aliquam personam, et specialiter milites, clericos aut dominas non recipiat abbatissa, nisi esset episcopus, abbas, vel prior, aut alia religiosa et honesta persona, que causa predicationis ad plus ter in anno veniret; vel nisi sacerdos existeret, qui causa dandi penitentiam et faciendi que circa infirmam debent fieri, ad ipsam accederet, tanta infirmitate gravatam quod ad parlatorium ire non posset; . . .*"

nuns were to be excommunicated and separated from the community of the others.

In February 1229 and again in February 1230 diocesan synods were held in Trier which dealt with such banal issues as the incorporation of parish churches into larger foundations and the confirming of the sale of a house at Trier. The first assembly was hardly for that single incorporation, however, and those present as witnesses—the provost and dean of the Trier cathedral chapter, the former of whom was also an archdeacon, two additional archdeacons, eleven other cathedral canons, and the abbots of St. Maximin, St. Matthias, St. Maria, and St. Martin—undoubtedly heard the words pertaining to the *cura animarum* which the document preserves.[170] In compliance with *c.* 12 of the Lateran IV decrees, a provincial general chapter of the Benedictine Order was also held at Trier in 1230. Presiding were the abbots of St. Mattheis at Trier and St. Evre at Toul,[171] assisted by the Cistercian abbots of Himmerode (archdiocese of Trier) and Werschweiler (diocese of Metz). As was the case with the regulations issued for the convent of St. Julia the previous year, the statutes issued by this chapter may reflect conditions found throughout the German church at this time.[172]

---

[170] Beyer, *MRUB* III, Nrs. 339 (February 1228/9), 368 (24 February 1229/30). Our study of known Trier synods reveals that most were held on or near the feast of *Cathedra Petri apostoli* (22 February). Since the Trier cathedral was dedicated to St. Peter, this major feast day—a *festum fori*—was clearly a special day in the Trier church and one on which a synod under the presidency of the archbishop would assert anew his apostolic power. It would thus seem most likely that the assembly of 1228/1229 was a diocesan one: "*ut ad presentationem abbatis et conventus, qui ibidem fuerunt pro tempore, vicarius perpetuus honeste conversationis, qui ecclesie sibi commisse preesse valeat et prodesse, ibidem secundum quod canonicum instituatur. Cui etiam tantum de ipsius ecclesie redditibus volumus assignari, ut iura nobis et archidiaconi loci debita non subtrahantur et ipse ibidem commode et honeste sustentetur, qui etiam vicarius ad synodum episcopalem et archidiaconi consimili lege subiectionis in omnibus cum aliis vicariis perpetuis venire teneatur.*" See also Nr. 340, with date February 1228/1229, issued by the dean and provost of the cathedral chapter, this document, which testifies of the grant of a house in Trier to a burgher of the city, was witnessed by seventeen members of the cathedral chapter who had undoubtedly been present at the diocesan synod.

[171] Because of the imprecise nature of the documents, it is not known whether the abbot of St. Evre was Garin, *quondam episcopus Tullensis*, or his successor. Given the prominent role of this house under Garin, the designation of its abbot to act as one of the presiding officials at the general chapter is understandable. The abbot of St. Mattheis, the most prominent Benedictine house in the archdiocese of Trier, was Jacob (1211-1257) from the ducal house of Lorraine; see W.K. Prinz von Isenburg, *Stammtafeln zur Geschichte der europäischen Staaten* (1956) II 6, and Pellens, *Dietrich II. von Wied* 28.

[172] Hontheim, *Hist. Trev. dipl.* I 704-705, Nr. 469; Calmet, *Hist. eccles.* II 444; and Blattau, *Statuta syn. Trev.* I 31, place the general chapter in the year 1230. According to Urmser Berlière, who cites Calmet as his source, "Les chapitres généraux," *Mélanges d'histoire bénédictine*, IVᵉ série (Maredsous, 1902) 62, it occurred in 1218. This incorrect date

St. Benedict had intended his Rule to be but the beginning in the life of a monk, declaring that it was satisfied with the minimum expectations.[173] Certainly portions of that work would have been read before the assembled Black Monks, but there were further matters which the visitors to the monasteries would have stressed, and these deserve closer examination. The first provision was that a permanent doorkeeper be appointed in each house to watch over the cloister entrance, lest ingress and egress occur without proper authorization and supervision.[174] Although this issue is also dealt with in the Rule, its placement at the head of the list in 1230 gives some indication of its neglect.

With the exception of during Lent morning meals should consist of a porridge or gruel, eaten with a main dish of five eggs or a moderate portion of cheese until satisfied; for the evening repast herbs or fruit were prescribed, along with a main dish of eggs or cheese.[175] During Lent there was less to eat. The absence of bread in the diet seems noteworthy.

In an amplification of the Rule a head covering and a choir-mantle of black were prescribed.[176] St. Benedict had stipulated that the brothers be given clothing suited for the location and climate of the house; they should not be concerned about color or style of the clothing, making do with whatever was available and inexpensive in their respective areas. The four abbots also issued regulations regarding shoes, trousers and hair.[177] The obvious concern here was to prevent religious from imitating the practices of the secular clergy, but above all of the laity. Conditions noted ca. 1200

---

was taken over in Stephanus Hilpisch, *Geschichte des Benediktinischen Mönchtums* (Freiburg/Br., 1929) 241, and Philibert Schmitz, *Histoire de l'ordre de St. Benoit* (Maredsous, 1948) III 96. Pius Schmieder, *Die Benediktiner-Odensreform im 13. und 14. Jahrhundert* (Linz, 1867) 5-6, 27, is unaware of this general chapter, asserting that for Germany at this time not the slightest trace of chapters for the Orders can be found. For a recent discussion of the general chapter, see Pellens, *Dietrich II. von Wied* 26-28.

[173] Cf. E. Pfiffner, *Die Regel des heiligen Benedikt* (Einsiedeln-Zürich, 1947) 128f.

[174] "... *ut in qualibet ecclessia conventuali ad introitum claustri janitor sedules habeatur, ne horis incompetentibus cuidam egrediendi vel ingrediendi claustrum concedatur libertas.*"

[175] "*Tempore, quo bis comeditur, in mane pulmentum pro tempore convenienter apparatum et generali, scilicet quinque ova, vel pars casei ad suffientiam apte moderata; in sero herbae vel fructus, pitantia etiam ovorum et casei, prout prior providerit, ministrentur. Tempore vero jejuni, duo pulmenta cocta cum pitantia pro tempore convenienti ministrentur.*"

[176] "*Pileos et capas alterius quam nigri coloris non ferant.*"

[177] "*Vestimenta et calceamenta nec nimis curta, nec nimis longa habeantur. . . .Tonsura ita fiat, ut vix aures a crinibus tangantur, et corona solito fiat amplior. Calceamenta rotunda fiant et non notabilia. Secundum regulam sancti Benedicti monachi semper vestiti et cincti dormiant, et secundum consuetudinem nunquam sine caligis. . . . In Adventu Domini nonnisi semel concedatur rasura barbae et coronae. A pascha usque ad idus Septembris, a quindena in quindenam fiat, et tum usque ad pascha per tres septimanas fiat. Caligae fiant regulares, hoc est sine pedulibus.*"

in Ch. Two above were thus still prevalent in 1230. Of particular interest is the proscription against riding without express permission from the abbot.[178]

Clearly the memory of the situation at St. Mansuy in 1225 lay behind the decree of 1230 that no monk could be exempted from the discipline of the cloister, nor could he enjoy rights and privileges within the monastic community without having first made full profession.[179] Various provisions were made for disobedient monks, including exclusion from the Divine Office, excommunication, transfer to another location, and even punishment by secular authority.[180] In perhaps the harshest measure of all, the abbots also declared that each year on the fifth Sunday before Easter all monks possessing private property were to be excommunicated along with their collaborators; similar actions were to be taken against those who robbed and burned monastic buildings.[181]

Consistent with statutes given by Cardinal-legate Conrad in 1225 at Mainz, the general chapter at Trier renewed its commitment to celibacy, ordaining that no secular female could live within the confines of the cloister.[182] The regulations of 1230 were thus aimed at specific abuses found in the fourteen or more Benedictine houses lying within the archdiocese of Trier and in those additional abbeys, priories and cells scattered throughout the province.

The Legation of Otto, Cardinal-Deacon of S. Nicolai

Aegidius of Orval records a synod held by the bishop of Liège in 1229 at which a cleric claimed to have received private revelation to the effect that if the bishop did not retract one of his synodal statutes he faced imminent

---

[178] *"Sine abbatis licentia et ecclesiae utilitate nullus equitet."*

[179] *"Inhibetur authoritate totius capituli, ut nullus monachorum a disciplina emancipetur vel ponatur in ordine maiorem, nisi facta prius prefessione."*

[180] *"Statuimus etiam, ut monachus abbati vel ei, qui praesidet capitulo, rebellis et inobediens excommunicetur. Quod si non cito se correxerit, quandiu in conventu fuerit, a divinis cessetur. Si autem nec ita se emendaverit, fratres simul cum abbate ipsum ejiciant, et si opus fuerit, saeculari manu amoveatur. Si autem ejectus, postea redire voluerit, recipiatur, transmittendus in alium locum, quousque obedientia et humilitas satis valeant comprobari."*

[181] *"Item praecipitur, ut annuatim feria quinta ante pascha fiat excommunicatio solemniter in proprietarios, conspiratores, fures, et incendiarios."*

[182] *"Infra ambitum claustri nulla mulier, nisi tantae authoritatis fuerit, quod facile non possit excludi, admittabur; exceptis diebus solemnibus et processionibus, et sepulturis et anniversariis. . . . Item communi consensu diffinitum est, ut infra ambitum monasterii nulla saecularis mulier cohabitationem habeat, nec soror, nec conversa saecularem habeat ancillam."*

death.[183]   The nature of the bishop's decrees is unknown, but the often-hostile attitude of certain members of the cathedral chapter at Liège towards any sort of reform measure can be inferred from the violent reaction which a legatine visit to the city the following year precipitated.   That visit and numerous others were planned by the Curia during the months while the various independent synods were being held and corrective measures being taken in Germany; the intent was to assume tighter control over the German church by means of a papal legate.   In February 1229 the legation of Otto Candida, *titula S. Nicolai in carcere Tulliano diaconus cardinalis* was announced.[184]   The primary purpose of his mission was to bring about the fall of Frederick II and his son Henry (VII), a move which the papacy regarded as essential since Frederick had crossed the northern border of his Sicilian kingdom in 1229 and aroused fears in Rome concerning the safety of the papal states.   The missives which came out of the Curia were disguised to focus on ecclesiastical matters and on the continued resolution of issues involving the Danish realm, however.

By March 1229 Otto had reached the Flemish frontier of the Empire.   It was reported that he desired to proceed on to Denmark from Valenciennes, but since he had already set the dates for several synods in Germany, King Henry suspected that his real intent was to stir up the clergy against the emperor.   Henry therefore forbade any ecclesiastical assemblies and refused passage through Germany to the legate.   Instead of taking a ship from Flanders to Denmark as he did later on, Otto remained at Valenciennes for a period of four months.   The only reason for this could have been his belief that he could observe the German situation better from there.   During those months he followed closely the course of German events and the major personalities in public life.   He also sought to establish connections with and among the leading princes and prelates, at the same time trying to identify someone willing to be anti-king.   In this latter pursuit, he ultimately failed: two of the strongest candidates, the duke of Bavaria and Otto of

---

[183] *Aegidii Aureavall.* 121:   "*Anno domni Hugonis ultimo personaliter ipse sanctam synodum celebrare instituit decretumque in ea veteranis sancivit Legie privilegiis contrarium. Cuidam autem persone per spiritum innotuit, Domino revelante, prefatum intra anni circulum migraturum antistitem, si non quod promulgaverat quantocius irritaret.*"

[184] In general, see Winkelmann, *Friedrich II.* II 65-74, 228-229. Zimmermann, *Päpstl. Legationen* 107-108, notes that the letters of appointment and announcement are no longer extant, yet his impending arrival is suggested in a papal letter written 5 February 1229 to Archbishop Heinrich of Cologne, granting a petition that no one except a "*legatus a suo latere destinatus*" was authorized to pronounce the sentence of suspension or excommunication in his territory without a special mandate of the apostolic see; cf. Potthast, *Regesta* I, Nr. 8333; Ennen, *Quellen* II, Nr. 1227 (incorrectly attributed to 1227).

Brunswick, were defeated and rejected by the princes respectively. With this, the legate's chief purpose in coming to Germany was thwarted.

Cardinal Otto was unable to create a party among the German bishops not only because of their loyalty to Frederick II and his house, but also because they were unhappy with the ecclesiastical policies of the legate. They did not countenance his favoring of the new orders, nor were they supportive of his reforms which were introduced in the spirit of those orders. The Germans treated the Dominicans with contempt and ridicule who came into their lands preaching the papal sentences against Frederick II. Other bishops must have privately been pleased with this—the bishop of Worms was publicly reprimanded for allowing it.[185] There was no open break, however. The prelates appear not to have been bothered by the ban against Frederick II.

After the lengthy wait at Valenciennes, Cardinal Otto set out for the Upper Rhine; he ultimately hoped to reach Bavaria where he might enlist the aid of the duke, but his progress was halted at Strasbourg where Staufen forces hemmed him in.[186] According to Conrad de Fabaria, the legate instituted a wide-ranging reform of the monastery at Reichenau, and he was otherwise active in effecting changes.[187] On 19 December 1229 he was

---

[185] Winkelmann, *Acta Imp. inedita* I 495; Boos, *Wormser UB* I, Nrs. 151, 153a, 153b, 153c; Potthast, *Regesta* I, Nr. 8451; Böhmer-Ficker, *Regg. Imp.* V/2, Nr. 6784 (3 September 1229). A papal letter of 29 March 1233 speaks of the *"[fratres] Praedicatorum Warmaciens[es], qui, cum secundum compositionem cum [Henrico] episcopo Warmaciensi nuper initam recedere ipsos oporteat a domo, quam in civitate Warmaciensi construxerant, . . ."*; see Würdtwein, *Nova subs.* VI 32; Potthast, *Regesta* I, Nr. 9134.

[186] *Chron. Ebersheim.* 452; Eduard Winkelmann, "Die Legation des Kardinaldiakons Otto von S. Nicolaus in Deutschland, 1229-1231," *MIÖG* 11 (1890) 34.

[187] *Conr. de Fabaria* 182: *"Visitatores eciam per diversos missos ecclesias, cum multos perturbassent tam abbates quam monachos, immo eciam plebanos et clericos minoris ordinis, cohibuit, ne ad monasterium venientes, suos perturbarent fratres. Non hoc sine summi pontificis obtinuit permissione. Audivit enim, qualiter in nobili ecclesia Augiensi processerant, et quemadmodum fratres ipsius perturbaverant monasterii. Cum adhuc in dubio, utrumne nobis sicut aliis infligant ecclesiis, consulo itaque, ut simus cauciores in disciplina et moribus et honesta conversacione, quia, ut ait quidam sapiens."* See also *Chron. Ebersheim.* 452: *"Mittitur ab apostolico medio tempore legatus, cardinalis videlicet dictus Oddo, statum ecclesiarum Alemannie respecturus. Qui ob metum regis ad singulas dioceses declinare formidans, quippe quia controversia tunc movebatur inter papam et imperatorem, in Argentinam, in qua defendi poterat, est receptus. Deferuntur autem illuc ei quelibet huius terre negotia discutienda; sed inter multa sibi aperitur de huius ecclesie dilapidatione. Notorium enim erat quod populus et locus in quo residebant utrique proclamabant. Terminatis igitur eis secundum posse pro quibus venerat, visitatores instituit et iam reditum disponens, inter cetera statuta depositionem huius abbatis eis committit. Mandatum imperantis servatur, et cum aliquibus qui idem meruerunt ministris quasi sinister circa principium septimi anni deponitur. Fratrum quidam per diversa locati factum ignorant, et visitatores contra libertatem antiquam ecclesie sibi potestatem electionis usurpant."* For further comment, see F. W. Schirrmacher,

at Constanz where he demonstrated his concern for prostitution by issuing an indulgence to those who supported through their financial contribution the *sorores poenitentes S. Mariae Magdalenae in Alemannia.*[188]

Sensing the overwhelming opposition in his mission, however, he made no further attempts to reform the dioceses of Upper Germany. Early in 1230 he returned by way of Metz and Verdun to Lower Lorraine. *En route* to Metz he undoubtedly was overtaken by a letter dictated 26 October 1229 by Pope Gregory IX which directed him to ensure that a sentence of excommunication imposed by the archbishop of Trier against those clerics in the diocese of Metz who refused to assist their bishop in his struggles to get out from under the burdens of debt which had plagued his church for years.[189] A similar mandate was sent to the prelates and clergy in the diocese of Verdun, warning that if they failed to give financial support to Bishop Rudolf their metropolitan had received authority to compel them.[190] From Verdun he wrote an ordinance for the cathedral chapter at Metz on 24 January 1230, intending thereby to correct abuses which he had just noticed. The efforts by Bishop Conrad of Metz in 1220 to encourage the maintenance of the residence obligation by cathedral canons had apparently been unsuccessful, for the legate stated:

> *Sane dum Metis essemus, intelleximus, immo comperimus manifeste, quod licet ecclesia vestra, utpote nobilis et sollempnis, canonicorum numerum habeat congruum et decentum, qui beneficia percipiunt in eadem, paucos*

"Die Mission Ottos des Cardinaldiacons von St. Nicolaus in carcere Tulliano in den Jahren 1228-1231," *Forschungen zur Deutschen Geschichte* 8 (1868) 48-50; chronological corrections by Winkelmann, "Legation des Kardinaldiakons Otto" 34.

[188] Winkelmann, *Friedrich II.* II 228 note 4. On 4 June 1228 Pope Gregory IX had issued an injunction to all German prelates relative to protecting the Penitential Sisters against encroachments; see Potthast, *Regesta* I, Nr. 8203; also Nr. 8969. According to Hauck, *KGD* IV 1014, the Penitential nuns were established at Trier in 1238; André Simon, "L'Ordre des Pénitentes" (Unpubl. Dissertation, Fribourg [Switz.], 1918) 133, claims they were at Trier in 1227, making this one of their earliest establishments in Germany.

[189] Rodenberg, *MG Ep. s. XIII* I, Nr. 406; Auvray, *Registres de Gregoire IX* I, Nrs. 363, 366. On 8 November 1229 Gregory IX granted permission to Bishop John of Metz to claim for a term of three years the fruits of all benefices within his diocese which fell vacant within the next five years, in order that he might be able to pay his debts; cf. Rodenberg, op.cit. I, Nr. 408. As late as 30 May 1237 the church at Metz was struggling with the problem of debts, having borrowed money from a Roman merchant-banker named Juvenal Mannetti who at length sought papal help in recovering his money; cf. Auvray, *op.cit.* II, Nr. 3877.

[190] Clouet, *Hist. de Verdun* II 391 note 1; Rodenberg, *MG Ep. s. XIII* I, Nr. 407; Auvray, *Registres de Gregoire IX* I, Nrs. 364, 365. On 18 December 1232 Gregory IX gave instructions to an archdeacon of Toul and two other clerics that they relax the interdict which had been laid upon the diocese of Verdun and announce the lifting of the ban of excommunication imposed upon the bishop for his failure to pay his debts to Juvenal Mannetti and various other merchants of Rome, Sens and Florence; cf. Auvray, *op.cit.* I, Nr. 998.

tamen habet, qui ei serviant et respondeant ex condigno. Unde fit multociens, quod requit absque pudore referri, quod decanus vix sex vel septem de sexaginta habeat in matutinis officiis adiutores.[191]

Such an extreme case of absenteeism was presumably not unique to Metz; the declaration of the legate in fact reminds us of a similar statement by Archbishop Dietrich II of Trier in 1215 as he set about to restore the *vita communis* among the canons of his cathedral.

The solution ordained by Cardinal Otto was far more modest, however, and reflects the economic realities of the thirteenth century. Rather than appealing to some earlier ideal such as the Rule of Bishop Chrodegang of Metz, or pursuing the radical reform path taken by the archbishops of Salzburg and Magdeburg in the twelfth century in establishing chapters of Augustinian or Premonstratensian canons in their cathedral churches, the legate simply used the threat of the loss of income from prebends as the means of compelling obedience to the residence requirement.[192] Whoever did not maintain residence for at least half a year and perform the choir obligations incumbent upon his prebend would lose the income from the prebend for the entire year; the dean and the more senior members of the chapter should then decide how best to use that same income.

The legate also sought to curtail absenteeism which was due ostensibly to study outside of Metz, requiring solid evidence that the canon was actively and conscientiously pursuing the training which his absence from chapter obligations implied. Once again the dean was given discretionary power to withhold prebendal income in cases where fraudulent behavior was detected.[193] Restrictions were also placed on the improper disposition of

---

[191] Metz Bibliothèque Municipal MS A. 1. fol. 2ᵛ; Georg Heinrich Pertz, *Archiv* 8 (1849) 450; Winkelmann, "Legation des Kardinaldiakons Otto" 38-40; Böhmer-Ficker, *Regg. Imp.* V/2, Nr. 10098

[192] "*Cum igitur, sicut hii, qui altari serviunt, debent vivere de altari, sic sumpto a sensu contrario argumento, qui non deserviunt altari, vivere non debe[a]nt ex eodem, ut qui non laborat, sicut alibi dicitur, non manducet, providendum duximus statuentes, ut quicunque canonicis per dimidium annum continue vel per partes residentiam non fecerit et servierit in ecclesia memorata, ita quod matutinis aut missis sive in vesperis intersit, nisi peregrinationis aut alia necessaria et probabili causa poterit rationabiliter excusari, totius anni fructibus sit ipso iure privatus, ita quod liceat decano cum aliquibus de senioribus fructus eosdem auctoritate propria occupare in usus deservientium convertendos.*"

[193] "*Volumus insuper, ut nulli causa studii suffragetur, nisi prius per dimidium annum residentiam fecerit in ecclesia supradicta, ut superius est expressum, et extunc sine fraude in scolis per dimidium annum studens tanquam residens habeatur. Quod si post modum ab eo scolarum residentia fuerit interrupta, nisi probabili et rationabili causa fuerit excusatus, antequam fructus prebende percipiat et residentiam ulterius facere possit in scolis, ad faciendum in ecclesia dimidii anni estagium iterum teneatur. Quod si dubium oriri contigerit, que sit necessaria et probabilis causa, decani et capituli arbitrio decidatur vel illorum, quos*

cathedral prebends, recalling the statute of Cardinal-legate Conrad of Porto given at Mainz in 1225.[194] The almost identical nature of these statutes to those issued at Metz in 1220 suggests that the latter had proven ineffective; apparently it was hoped that the added authority of a papal-legate would have a more lasting impact upon the clergy of Metz.

By 10 February 1230 Cardinal-legate Otto was in Liège where he also sought to effect changes in the cathedral church. Noting the uneven distribution of prebendal incomes, he attempted to dissolve all existing prebends and then redistributing the resources equally among the *capitulares*. This overt assault on the privileges and incomes of the higher clergy of the diocese caused those who were adversely affected to place themselves under the protection of the king and to call the imperial advocate (*Reichsvogt*) William from Aachen. Fearing the outcome, the legate, with Bishop Jean, left Liège and fled to the fortress at Huy. There, on 13 February, he pronounced an interdict over the city. The bishop in turn ordered the clergy to leave the city and church services stopped.[195] According to the chroniclers, the whole affair was the result of a mis-perception by the legate: he mistakenly took the crowd which had gathered out of curiosity to witness his hurried departure for a mob sent to capture or even kill him by the clergy. Such a view has not stood up to modern scholarship, however. The populace of the region was especially hostile to papal representatives, regarding them as foreigners. Another legate, Bishop William of Modena, returning from Prussia, was held captive at Aachen at about this same time (late February 1230).[196] As a result of this act, Aachen also felt the sting of an interdict from Otto.

The imperialists blamed the bishop for the entire fiasco, citing his relationship with the papal-legate as especially offensive. They even went so far as to declare him deprived of all temporal rights in his diocese. Shortly thereafter, first Liège and then numerous other towns rebelled against him. Under these circumstances, the papal-legate left, moving

---

ad hoc decanus et capitulum deputarent. Volumus iterum et mandamus, ut hiidem fructus in deservientium usus cedant et distribuantur provide inter illos in tribus horis superius nominatis [deservientes] per decanum et aliquos alios, qui consilio capituli ad hoc fuerint deputati. Ad hec districtius inhibemus, ne aliquis eiusdem ecclesie canonicus prebendam suam obliget maxime ultra annum nec capitulum obliganti de cetero consentire presumat."

[194] Pope Gregory IX confirmed these statutes on 14 November 1231; cf. Böhmer-Ficker, *Regg. Imp.* V/2, Nr. 10098.

[195] *Chron. Albrici (a. 1231)* 928; *Chron. reg. Colon. cont. IV (a. 1228)* 261; *Aegidii Aureavall. (a. 1230)* 123; Hartzheim, *Concilia* III 538. See also the itinerary of the cardinal-legate reconstructed in Winkelmann, "Legation des Kardinaldiakons Otto" 34, and based on that, Böhmer-Ficker, *Regg. Imp.* V/2, Nr. 10098a. Further discussion in Finke, *Konzilienst.* 62.

[196] *Chron. reg. Colon.* 261; Böhmer-Ficker, *Regg. Imp.* V/2, Nr. 10136b.

slowly across Brabant through Mecheln, Thuin, Château Cambresis, and arriving at Tournai. All the while he organized visitations for northern Germany. Grouping several dioceses together, he appointed three visitors per district, including at least one Dominican among them: Merseburg, Magdeburg, Brandenburg, and Havelberg; Münster, Paderborn, and Osnabrück. He then took sail for Denmark and left them to their task, charging them with sending him reports.[197]

The departure of the papal-legate had left Bishop Jean of Liège in a most difficult situation, and yet he appears to have met the challenge head-on. On 2 June 1230 he convened a synod at Huy, to which all the prelates of his church were summoned.[198] Details are lacking, but the assembly undoubtedly dealt with adapting the cardinal's decrees to the needs and realities of church-life in Liège. Acts of violence against clerics and church property may also have been dealt with.

It is unknown to what extent the presence of the papal legate in Liège was felt in neighboring dioceses.[199] His efforts to effect changes within the German church must have been intended to extend beyond those areas for which we have documentation, however. It is thus intriguing to consider what other items might have been on the agenda when Bishop Wilbrand of Utrecht met with his diocesan clergy on 22 May 1230: the sole surviving record of this assembly is a confirmation of privileges for the monastery at Bethlehem.[200] A similar document dated only with the year 1230 records another synod at Hildesheim.[201] In addition to the juridical issue mentioned, it is probable that the matters discussed in a papal letter of 9 May 1230 to Bishop Conrad II—that of clerics and laymen who inflicted

---

[197] Winkelmann, *Phil. von Schw.* II 230-232; Böhmer-Ficker, *Regg. Imp.* V/2, Nrs. 10100, 10105-10107

[198] *Reineri Ann.* 680: "*Anno 1230 domnus Teodericus abbas Sancti Jacobi post 14 menses sue promotionis dominica in octavis pentecostes ad sinodum Hoi venit . . .*"; *Aegidii Aureavall.* 123: "*Hic [i.e. Episc. Johannes] . . . in octava pentecostes celebravit sollempnem primam missam in Walle sancti Lamberti anno Domini 1231, primam vero sinodum tenuit in Novo-Monasterio Hoyensi in epdomada Trinitatis. Ibi Theodericus Sancti Jacobi novus abbas diem clausit extremum*"; *Chron. Albrici (a. 1230)* 926: "*Apud Hoyum in pentecostes octavis Johannes Leodiensis episciscopus in ecclesia Novi Monasterii suam celebravit generalem synodum.*" Printed in Hartzheim, *Concilia* III 538. See also Binterim, *Concilien* IV 435; Hefele-Leclercq, *Conciles* V/2 1506.

[199] Johanek, "Pariser Statuten" 343, notes that he has found in the Bonn, Universitätsbibliothek MS S 755 fol. 63ʳ-63ᵛ, a previously unknown set of Cardinal-legate Otto's statutes which he is now preparing for publication.

[200] Sloet, *Oorkondenboek* 536, Nr. 534 ("*Actum . . . apud Traiectum in ecclesia maiori . . .*"); the document was witnessed by a large group of clergy, suggesting that they had been present at a synod.

[201] Hoogeweg, *UB Hilds* II, Nr. 292; Hartzheim, *Concilia* III 535-536 ("*in sinodo*").

injury upon other clerics, or who made transactions while under the ban of excommunication—was also dealt with.[202]

During the late summer of 1230, word came north that Frederick II had made peace with the pope on 23 July. Having happily ended a conflict over the bishopric of Riga, Cardinal-legate Otto was now able to return safely to Germany and to continue his reforms. Traveling to Bremen, he spent two months there, undoubtedly hearing reports and organizing further visitations. Out of the dioceses of Bremen and Verden he created another district; he also added Minden to the Münster group.[203] It is not to be doubted that he did the same with other North German dioceses.[204]

The Archbishopric of Bremen and the Stedinger

A diocesan synod is recorded for Bremen on 17 March 1230 which had as its primary purpose a political objective. Though couched in religious or theological terms, a call to arms issued by the archbishop against the independent peasant inhabitants of the Weser marsh-lands was intended to crush their resistance to his territorial lordship. Branding them as heretics and declaring them anathema, Archbishop Gerhard II summoned clergy and laity to a holy war against these *"Stedinger."*[205] Later that same year Cardinal-legate Otto and his Dominican assistant Gerhard gave enthusiastic support to the idea; thus, Gerhard also sought and obtained papal approval of his campaign. Not until April/May 1234 did the plans come to fruition, however, resulting in the complete destruction of this nascent peasant republic on the Lower Weser.[206]

---

[202] Hoogeweg, *UB Hilds* II, Nr. 278; cf. Idem. II, Nr. 230 (1227); Maring, *Diözesansynoden* 67.

[203] Winkelmann, *Friedrich II.* 232 note 4; Böhmer-Ficker, *Regg. Imp.* V/2, Nrs. 10111, 10112, 10116; Winkelmann, "Legation des Kardinaldiakons Otto" 36; *Westf. UB* IV 121-122.

[204] Cf. Böhmer, *Regg. Imp.* V/2, Nr. 10114, 10115, 10116.

[205] Ehmck, *Bremisches UB* I, Reg. Nr. 343; May, *REB* I 234, Nr. 852; Hermann Albert Schumacher, *Die Stedinger. Beitrag zur Geschichte der Weser-Marschen* (Bremen, 1865) 1-248, espec. 80-91, 222; Rolf Köhn, "Die Verketzerung der Stedinger durch die Bremer Fastensynode," *Bremisches Jb* 57 (1979) 15-85.

[206] Schumacher, *Stedinger* 117-122; C. Krollmann, "Der deutsche Orden und die Stedinger," *Alt-Preussische Forschungen*, Historische Kommission für ost- und westpreussische Landesforschung 14 (Königsberg, 1937) 1-13; Carl Wöbcken, "Die Schlacht bei Altenesch am 27. Mai 1234 und ihre Vorgeschichte," *Oldenburger Jahrbuch*, Verein für Landesgeschichte und Altertumskunde 37 (1933) 5-35. Archbishop Gerhard ordained that an annual celebration be held in the future to commemorate this victory. On the relationship of the Stedinger campaigns to other "secular" uses of the crusade, see Elizabeth T. Kennan, "Innocent III, Gregory IX, and Political Crusades: A Study in the Disintegration of Papal Power," *Reform and Authority in the Medieval and Reformation Church*, ed. Guy Fitch Lytle (Washington. D.C., 1981) 15-35, espec. 24-26.

On 4 November 1230 Otto issued regulations for the church at Bremen, particularly regarding the election, age and offices of the twenty-four *capitulares* in the cathedral chapter, and the administration of twelve obediences. As he did at Metz, the legate declared that the canons were obligated to maintain residence or lose the incomes from their benefices during unexcused absences: authorization could be given for pilgrimage, study away from Bremen, and chapter business.[207] The cardinal also established two confessors to whom the priests and laymen could go in cases of doubt.[208] This is the first known instance of a response in Germany to *c.* 10 of the Lateran IV decrees which had ordained that in all cathedral and collegiate churches appropriate men were to be chosen as coadjutors of the bishop for confessions—that is, episcopal penitentiaries. Hauck sees this innovation as due to the cardinal-legate, but finds little evidence that similar actions were taken elsewhere.[209] On 29 June 1231 Pope Gregory IX confirmed the statutes of his legate, including Otto's division of the archdiocese of Bremen into four archdeaconates.[210] Presumably the visitations of bishoprics in the province at the instigation of the cardinal-legate also led to some sort of disciplinary action.[211]

---

[207] Ehmck, *Bremisches UB* I, Nr. 156.

[208] Ehmck, *Bremisches UB* I 180, Nr. 155; Hodenberg, *Die Diözese Bremen* xxxix, sect. 24; Hauck, *KGD* IV 8: *"Similiter in qualibet synodo sollempni archiepiscopus vel decanus verbum dei proponat vel proponi faciat, ad minus ultima die capituli. Item statuantur in capitulo maiori duo confessores, ad quod sacerdos diocesis super dubio, si quod ipsis occurrerit in foro penitenciali, habeant recursum, et ad quod tam ipsi sacerdotes quam eorum subditi de ipsorum consilio recurrant. . . ."*

[209] Hauck, *KGD* V 165.

[210] Ehmck, *Bremisches UB* I 681, Nr. 357; Potthast, *Regesta* I, Nr. 8756. The division was not without controversy, however. On 26 August 1245, Pope Innocent IV commissioned the archbishop of Bremen to review the administrative divisions; complaints had come to the Curia from the dean of Bremen and the members of the cathedral chapter regarding the uneven nature of the *"obedientiae."* If some sort of adjustments to boundaries were deemed necessary, the prelate was empowered to make the changes; cf. May, *REB* I 267, Nr. 974; Potthast, *op.cit.* II, Nr. 11837a–26332.

[211] To the abbot of Bredelar and the Dominicans Conrad of Höxter and Ernst of Bremen, charged with the visitation of the dioceses of Münster, Osnabrück and Paderborn, the cardinal legate order ". . . *ut tam in civitatibus quam in dyocesibus . . . ad clericorum mundiciam et eorum, que ad ornatum altaris et que ad cultum divinum pertinent, reformationem specialiter intendatis, nichilominus inquirentes de statu et incontinentia, introitu vicioso et aliis manifestis excessibus, corrigentes et reformantes tam in capite quam in membris, prout vestra discretio faciendum, contradictores et rebelles per censuram ecclesiasticam compescendo."* See *Westf. UB* IV/1, Nrs. 176, 177 (12 May 1230). On 15 September 1230 from Bremen, the legate wrote the same three visitors, directing them to include the diocese of Minden on their itinerary as well; cf. Idem. IV/1, Nr. 181. One week later, Otto wrote the bishops of Münster, Osnabrück, Paderborn and Minden, informing them of his recent appointments and commanding the prelates to obey his visitors, despite the fact that the pope himself had previously given them (i.e., the bishops) the task of conducting visitations; cf. Idem. IV/1, Nr. 182.

Cardinal Otto's preference for the Dominicans became even more evident as he traveled from Bremen to Westphalia at the beginning of November 1230. He turned over to the Friar *Johannes Teutonicus* of Wildeshausen the business left undone during his two-months' stay, including the completion of the visitation of the diocese of Minden.[212]

The legate also appears to have created further opposition to himself and the papal program by using his authority to grant prebends to Italian clerics. It was probably at this time, while otherwise engaged in the archdiocese of Trier, that he claimed the right to confer a vacant prebend at the collegiate church of St. Florin upon a certain cleric named Deodatus, nephew of the papal notary *magister* Gotifridus. The opposition of the chapter to this provision is revealed in a papal letter dated 21 February 1233, in which Gregory IX directed Raynaldo de Puzalia, a papal subdeacon and a cathedral canon at Mainz, "*cum plenitudine iuris canonici*" to enforce that grant.[213] That the cardinal-deacon also used his authority within the province of Salzburg may be inferred from a letter which Gregory IX wrote on 18 December 1236 to Archbishop Eberhard, directing that the prelate see to it that he make satisfaction to Rufinus *nepos Ottonis tit. S. Nicolai in carcere Tulliano diaconi cardinalis* for the parish church at Pütten which Eberhard had withdrawn from the Italian cleric and given to one Conrad.[214] He apparently attempted to establish outsiders in the cathedral chapters at Paderborn,[215] Constanz, Halberstadt and Magdeburg as well.[216]

---

[212] Earlier literature, including Schumacher, *Stedinger* 88, and Ehmck, *Bremisches UB* I 185, saw in this John the fanatical heretic-hunter and penance-preacher, John of Vicenza. That it was instead the future fourth general of the Order is argued by Winkelmann, *Phil. von Schw.* II 233, and Böhmer-Ficker, *Regg. Imp.* V/2, Nr. 10117. See also Schirrmacher, "Mission Ottos des Cardinaldiacons" 55 note 1; Finke, *Konzilienst.* 63

[213] Würdtwein, *Nova subs.* VI 19; Potthast, *Regesta* I, Nr. 9100; Auvray, *Registres de Gregoire IX* I, Nr. 1116; Beier, *Päpstliche Provisionen* 67 note 4. Raynaldo de Puzalia had himself been the recipient of just such a papal provision in 1221 (see Ch. Four above, note 233). He remained a trusted papal agent within the German church: on 3 June 1236 Gregory IX again directed him to assist in securing a prebend for another Italian cleric, in this case *magister Marino subdiaconus suus clericus Iohannis tit. S. Praxedis presbyter cardinalis*; the prebend was to be "*aliqua praepositura vel alio beneficio competenti*"; cf. Würdtwein, *op.cit.* IX 11; Potthast, *op.cit.* I, Nr. 10177. On 16 September 1238 the pope once again referred to his agent, now the provost of St. Bartholomew's collegiate church at Frankfurt; cf. Potthast, *op.cit.* I, Nr. 10654.

[214] Potthast, *Regesta* I, Nr. 10276; Meiller, *RAS* 267, Nr. 438.

[215] *Westf. UB* IV 173, Nr. 207; Hanneken, "Paderborn DK" 161-162. In 1231 the pope ordered the archbishop of Cologne to instruct the bishop of Paderborn to excommunicate the members of the cathedral chapter because of their refusal to accept Gregorius Petrus Heinricus de Sancto Eustachio, a "*canonicus basilice principis apostolorum*" in Rome, who had tried in vain since 1229 to gain admission into their body.

[216] In Constanz Otto appointed a Lombard to the cathedral chapter against the wishes of the

Until Christmas Day, which he spent in Cologne, Cardinal Otto was busy in the provinces of Trier, Cologne, Magdeburg, and Bremen, correcting what he saw needing it and bringing to completion measures already begun. The interdict placed on Liège was finally lifted after several months without Divine Services, at the command of the pope who had to acquiesce to the emperor during the peace negotiations. The burghers of Aachen also did penance for their outrageous act against the bishop of Modena during Otto's stay at Cologne.[217]

The Impact of Cardinal-Deacon Otto on the German Church

The months that the papal-legate was in Germany during 1229 and 1230 had made a significant impact upon the church. The bishops found themselves being pushed aside in their own dioceses by legatine visitors. The prelates nevertheless obeyed Otto's commands, if unhappily, because they were based on the fullness of papal authority which he had received. In some instances this led to a complete overturning of ecclesiastical organs, as was the case with the legate's visitation of Münster, Minden, and Bremen, and the division of these bishoprics into archdeaconates (20 January 1231).[218] The reorganization occurred because the old archdeaconries were too closely bound to secular jurisdictions and were vulnerable to them. The clerics thus left without offices or functions by the bishops were forced to accept the changes, even though bitterness grew in those areas where the legate had intervened. The archbishop of Cologne, e.g., lost his right to ordain priests in the bishopric of Liège during an episcopal vacancy; Frederick of Halberstadt had to find a place for the Dominicans under pressure from the legate; Berengar of Speyer had to retract the grant of a prebend. Some even feared that the cardinal-legate would claim prebends in their churches for himself as he had in Naumburg.[219]

---

capitulares. The process dragged on for over four years (cf. Auvray, *Registres de Gregoire IX* I, Nr. 1877); at length the Italian was killed by the brother of him whom the chapter had wanted. In Magdeburg Otto granted a prebend to a poor cleric and excommunicated the members of the cathedral chapter who objected; in Halberstadt he gave support to a cleric who had been granted a provision by the pope. See Beier, *Päpstliche Provisionen* 67 note 4; Böhmer-Ficker, *Regg. Imp.* V/2, Nrs. 10130, 10131; Auvray, *op.cit.* I, Nr. 2211.

[217] *Chron. reg. Colon.* 261, 262; Winkelmann, *Friedrich II.* II 234-235.

[218] Böhmer-Ficker, *Regg. Imp.* V/2, Nr. 10112; on 29 June 1231 Gregory IX confirmed the action taken at Bremen, dividing the archdiocese into four archdeaconates (cf. Potthast, *Regesta* I, 752, Nr. 8756; Ehmck, *Bremisches UB* I, Nr. 356).

[219] Cf. Böhmer-Ficker, *Regg. Imp.* V/2, Nrs. 15004,10123-10124, 10122a, 10131; Winkelmann, *Friedrich II.* II 235; Remling, *UB Speyer* 189, Nr. 182: "*Notum esse volumus universitati vestre, quod quidquid fecimus circa Henricum clericum super ecclesia de*

In the previous year the legate had only touched the southwest dioceses belonging to the massive ecclesiastical province of Mainz, and then not as profoundly as he had wished. Perhaps the change of things which had occurred at Mainz in the meanwhile would assist his efforts. Archbishop Siegfried II of Mainz died 9 September 1230. His successor, the son of his brother Gottfried and an unnamed sister of Archbishop Dietrich II of Trier, included among his first acts in office the naming of a Dominican, Daniel from the Erfurt convent, as the visitor of the Thuringian priories. Seeing this as a most favorable sign of a predisposition for reform, Legate Otto summoned a provincial synod to be convened in Würzburg in early February 1231.

At Würzburg the general dissatisfaction at last came to a head. The synod was convened about mid-February 1231, but without the presence of many suffragans from the Mainz province. King Henry (VII) was there, as were many spiritual and secular princes from other provinces. Among them were the archbishop of Magdeburg and the bishop of Naumburg who probably carried a letter which Duke Albert of Saxony had sent to all the princes and prelates. They intended to read before the assembly a plea that the bishops preserve their ancient rights and liberties against the encroachments of Rome and her legates.[220] The effect of the letter upon the assembly was appreciable. The bishops, assured of secular support, reacted with a general rejection of the legate. This was the first time that such *gravamina* or complaints of the German church had been voiced in this fashion against Roman absolutism. The legate responded sharply, suspending the spokesmen for the dissenters—the bishop of Naumburg and the abbot of Corvey. Shortly thereafter, the synod broke up with the approval of the king. Otto left Würzburg, travelling as far as Regensburg

---

Medenheim ex mandato domini cardinalis perspectis diligenter privilegiis cenobii de Hemmenrode super eadem ecclesia, cum constaret nobis, sicut et antea constiterat, quod dicta ecclesia ex collacione predecessoris nostri bone memorie Cuonradi episcopi, imperialis aule cancellarii et consensu capituli nostri Spirensi pleno iure spectaret ad memoratum cenobium, ex mandato dicti cardinalis denuo accepto revocavimus." See also, Mazetti, *Bernger von Entringen* 51; Beier, *Päpstliche Provisionen* 67 note 4. Otto had in fact commandeered a prebend for himself in Naumburg; cf. Böhmer-Ficker, *op.cit.* V/2, Nr. 10128a.

[220] *Albrici Chron.* 928; Hartzheim, *Concilia* III 537. Hefele-Leclercq, *Conciles* V/2 1506-1507, sees Bishop Engelhard of Naumburg as the inspiration behind the protest letter; such seems clearly indicated in the papal letter to Bishop Conrad of Hildesheim in 1232 (Potthast, *Regesta* I, Nr. 9055). Binterim, *Concilien* IV 357, citing Schaten, *Ann. Paderbor.* II, *ad anno 1230*, notes that in January 1230 Cardinal-legate Otto sent his representatives out to visit the monasteries, chapters and parishes, with the mandate to abolish abuses and establish good regulations. For further discussion, cf. Hauck, *KGD* V 136 note 3, V 799, and IV 767 note 3.

with the abbot of St. Gall who had been given the task of accompanying him. The legate remained there for several weeks, livid over his treatment at the synod, and then continued on through Styria to Rome.[221]

Undoubtedly related to the presence of the cardinal-legate in the city of Würzburg in mid-February 1231, and to his use of Dominican friars in his efforts to effect reform within the German church, is a document issued on 16 February 1231 which records an agreement reached between the bishop and clergy of Würzburg on the one hand, and the newly established community of Preachers on the other, with the purpose of integrating the Dominicans into the pastoral work of the city and diocese. Following stipulations relating to their rights with respect to burials and preaching, their jurisdiction in the confession was also clarified:

> *Eos, qui immediate subsunt episcopo, puta eos, qui dicuntur synodales, recipient vice episcopi. Laycos autem, qui plebanis subsunt, et clericos, qui decanis subsunt, monachos et regulares canonicos, volentes eis confiteri, non recipient, nisi suis prelatis primitus sunt confessi.*[222]

The significance of this agreement for our purposes is that it represents a direct application of c. 21 of the Fourth Lateranum constitutions with its emphasized requirement of annual confession before one's *proprius sacerdos*.[223] Laymen and clerics, monks and canons regular were required as before to reveal their sins to their designated confessor; even the

---

[221] Winkelmann, *Friedrich II*. II 236-237. The pope confirmed the suspension of Bishop Engelhard on 6 December 1232 through a letter to Bishop Conrad of Hildesheim, and gave Engelhard one month to purge himself of the accusation; cf. Rodenberg, *MG Ep. s. XIII* I 399, Nr. 496; Potthast, *Regesta* I, Nr. 9055; Scheid, *Origines Guelf.* IV 33; Auvray, *Registres de Gregoire IX* I, Nr. 976. Conrad de Fabaria makes mention of the fact that the cardinal-legate held a synod at Mainz at this time; cf. *Casus S. Galli* 182: "*Cardinalis, cuius prius fuit habita mencio, concilium in Maguntina civitate habiturus, comprovinciales citaverat episcopos, et abbates, et diversi ordinis clericos, si non abbas consilio suo cum rege habito id irritasset. Precepit enim rex, ne quis in regno suo preter episcopos, quorum id erat officii, concilia celebraret: aliud faciens gracia sua careret. Disposuerat namque prefatus, Alemanniam, datis quibusdam edictic, spoliare. Videns vero, quia non, sicut disposuerat, haberet processum, ad securitatem sui accepto ducatu pacis, abbate sancti Galli duce et comite Ratisbonam venit cum pace; . . .*" Schirrmacher, "Mission Ottos des Cardinaldiacons" 57, argues for a separate synod which Otto summoned on the heels of the disaster in Würzburg; Winkelmann, "Legation Kardinaldiacons Otto" 32-33, on the other hand, makes the more compelling case that the St. Gall historian simply wrote Mainz when in fact he meant Würzburg as the synodal venue. On 2 May 1233 Gregory IX wrote to the convent at Corvey to inform them that he had relaxed the sentence of suspension which Otto had placed on their abbot, following the latter's personal visit to Rome and his humble petition for papal grace; cf. Auvray, *op.cit.* I, Nr. 1278.

[222] *Mon. Boica* XLV 65, Nr. 39.

[223] Gescher, "Synodales" 372-373.

bishop was the *proprius sacerdos* for a specific group of individuals within his diocese—for those who were directly accountable to him and are called *synodales*. Now, however, the Dominicans received a delegated confession jurisdiction in place of the Würzburg ordinary.

This charter also serves as the *terminus ante quem* for the publication of the statutes of the Council at Würzburg. We have no record of any diocesan synods for this bishopric before this time; furthermore, the exemption from attendance at provincial synods in 1218 may have been a negative factor in the reception of the full set of constitutions from Lateran IV. Nevertheless, the familiarity with the decree *De confessione facienda* which the document reveals gives us reason to conclude that some sort of formal publication had preceded the legatine synod of 1231.

Heresy in the Archdiocese of Trier—1231

One of those German prelates who remained away from the fiasco at Würzburg was Archbishop Dietrich II of Trier.[224] While the papal legate was being publicly criticized in mid-February 1231 for his abuse of authority, Dietrich issued several charters of confirmation to various religious houses of his archdiocese, actions witnessed by a variety of clergy and laity of his church.[225] Such acts have been recognized at Trier and elsewhere as having been done at synods; thus, it is probable that the traditional February synod was held at Trier in connection with the feast of *cathedra Petri* in 1231. Before the year had ended, however, another synod had been summoned, and with far more sensational consequences.

According to the *Gesta Treverorum*, a persecution of heretics throughout all of Germany began that year, and over the next three years many persons were burned. Among those areas affected by this outbreak of heterodox religiosity was the archdiocese of Trier, and the chronicler noted that in the

---

[224] That the legate had discussed ecclesiastical matters within the province of Trier with the archbishop may be inferred from the fact that on 20-21 January he issued charters from the metropolitan city: the first confirmed a statute of the cathedral chapter at Liège regarding the improvement of prebends there; the second contains a decision which he rendered in a dispute between an archdeacon of Trier and the monastery at Orval (cf. Böhmer-Ficker, *Regg. Imp.* V/2, Nrs. 10126, 10127; Goffinet, *Cartulaire* Nr. 215).

[225] Beyer, *MRUB* III, Nr. 386 (dated 20 February 1231 at Nothausen, this charter dealt with the sale of land); Nr. 387, dated simply February 1230/31, this dealt with the incorporation of a church at Helbingen into the monastery Freisdorf); Nr. 388, dated February 1230/1231, this dealt with a grant made to the monastery of St. Martin at Trier; Nr. 389, dated February 1230/1231, this dealt with the incorporation of the church of St. Gangolf into the infirmary of the monastery at Mettlach.

archiepiscopal city itself three schools or cells were discovered.[226]   The probable impulse for conducting the visitation which revealed these cells was a letter of Pope Gregory IX to the German prelates concerning their obligations with respect to heretics.   The copies sent to the archbishops of Salzburg (20 June 1231) and Trier (25 June 1231) are extant, revealing that they had received an injunction to make use of the papal decrees throughout their respective provinces, and that they were to publish the statutes ceremoniously each month.   They were also to see to it that their officials observed them, and to incorporate the statutes of the Senate of Rome into the capitularies of their towns and cities.[227]

The Trier chronicler (who was a Dominican friar) noted that the visitation of 1231 revealed some serious problems existing within the archdiocese.   It is most difficult to distinguish between that which might actually have been advocated by religious dissidents in the Middle Ages and that which was attributed to them by their persecutors.   We have noted above that both Waldensians and Cathari had spread into the provinces of Trier, Mainz, Cologne, and Salzburg before the Fourth Lateranum.   It has been suggested that the spread in Trier "was all the more certain, since nothing was done against them for so long.   They were observed for the first time in 1231.   And then it was obvious that the friends of the Waldensians had spread throughout the entire diocese."[228]   Most of what the heretics at Trier were purported to believe was in fact Waldensian: the use of vernacular Scriptures, the claim that any "ordained or unordained" person could consecrate, the attack against the pope and the clergy, the rejection of confirmation and unction, and the denial of the efficacy of intercession for the dead, fasting, and Church fast-days.   Perhaps the most

---

[226] *Gesta Trev.* 400-401: "*Anno Domini 1231. orta est persecutio hereticorum per totam Alemanniam, et exusti sunt plurimi per continuum triennium.   Nec Treverica dyocesis ab hac infectione excors fuit.   Nam in ipsa civitate Treveri tres fuisse scolas hereticorum publicatum est.*"   The account is printed in Hartzheim, *Concilia* III 539; Mansi, *Collectio* XXIII 241.

[227] Potthast, *Regesta* I, Nrs. 8753, 8754; Beyer, *MRUB* III, Nr. 432; Böhmer, *Acta Imp. inedita* II, 665, Nr. 959: "*solent heretici ad . . .*"   See also, Förg, *Ketzerverfolgung* 50; Heydenreich, *Metropolitangewalt* 109.

[228] *Gesta Trev.* 401-402: "*Et plures erant secte, et multi eorum instructi erant scripturis sanctis, quas habebant in Theutonicum translatas.   Et alii quidem baptisma iterabant; alii corpus Domini non credebant; alii corpus Domini a malis sacerdotibus non posse confici dicebant; alii indifferenter corpus Domini a viro et muliere, ordinato et non ordinato, in scutella et calice et ubique locorum posse confici dicebant; alii confirmationem et inunctionem superfluam iudicabant; alii summo pontifici, clero et relioni derogabant; alii defunctis suffragia ecclesie prodesse negabant; alii matres proprias, redimentes consanguinitatem, que ibi erat, per 18 denarios, in coniugium sumebant; alii pallidum hominem vel etiam cattum osculbantur, et adhuc peiora faciebant; alii dies omnes quipendentes, feriari aut ieiunare nolebant, unde diebus festis operabantur et parasceve carnes manducabant.   Et hec de articulis errorum dixisse sufficiat, non quod omnes dixerimus, sed quod precipuos tantum notaverimus.*"

alarming revelation, however, was the existence of Luciferian views. Nothing more is said concerning this alleged practice of Luciferianism at Trier, but other contemporary accounts reveal that similar charges had been brought in both the archdiocese of Mainz and the archdiocese of Cologne.[229] As at Trier, so also in Cologne, women—the descendants of that first woman who succumbed to the enticings of Satan—were closely associated with this so-called cult of Lucifer.

In an attempt to account for the rapid spread of such a cult, Aubrey of Trois Fontaines related its history as he had heard it.[230] Reports such as this one by a Cistercian monk must have gained sufficient credence to concern even the pope. On 13 July 1233 Gregory IX sent a letter to the

---

[229] Describing this activity in Cologne in the year 1233, Aubrey of Trois-Fontaines wrote: "*Et ultra Coloniam fuit quedam synagoga hereticorum, ubi responsa dabat ymago Luciferi, sed ubi catholicus clericus advenit et pixidem cum corpore Domini de sinu suo protulerit, pestifera ymago corruit. Item quod quedam specialis amica Luciferi, ad ignem deducta, sublata est a demonibus, et non comparuit.*" See further, Pixton, "Dietrich of Wied" (1972) 97; Hauck, *KGD* IV 890, maintains that Aubrey's story about the devil's image at Cologne appears to be an „*erbauliche Lüge.*" The other story about the disappearing special "*amica Luciferi*" appears again in *Radulf, Chron. Angl.*, in Fredericq, *Corp. doc.* I 61, Nr. 61.

[230] "*Est villa quedam, que dicta est Maestricht, inter Brabantiam et Coloniam; ibi adveniens quidam magister Toletanus, nigromanticus totus dyabolo deditus, dum sederet ad mensam inter clericos, quos voluit permisit comedere, quod voluit fecit dormire. Adheserunt ei octo vani clerici, postulantes ab eo ut iuvaret eos in explendis desideriis suis. Qui respondit talia sine circulo non posse adimpleri, et fecit maximum circulum cum characteribus suis, ita quod omnes octo posuit in ipso circulo. Tres autem sedes preparavit in una parte circuli et dixit clericis, quod ibi sessuri erant tres magi de ewangelio. Extra circulum vero preparavit et ornavit maxime sedile et floribus decoravit satis accurate. Et incipiens de media nocte operari, excoriavit cattum unum, et duas columbas scidit per medium; deinde tres demones illos advocavit, quod habebat pro regibus, et novissime magnum illum principem, quem Epanamon nominavit. Dixit quod ipsos ad parvulam cenam invitaverit, ut illos clericos iuvarent in petitionibus suis. Cattum excoratum tribus illis demonibus apposuit, quem titum in momento devoraverunt; duas columbas magno demoni apposuit, et statim devorate fuerunt. Habebat vasculum vitreum et coniuravit magnum demonem, ut se in tantum exinaniret, quod in illud intraret; quo facto cera signavit, alpha et omega superscripsit. Postea dictum est clericis, ut peterent quidquid vellent.*

Unus petivit, ut posset habere consensum cuiusdam nobilis mulieris, et concessum est ei; alter petivit familiaritatem ducis Brabantie, et obtinuit; et omnes alii quidquid petierunt optinuerunt preter unum, qui petebat consensum masculi cuiusdam nobilis adolescentis, quod dyabolus ad se pertinere negavit, nec sibi esse licitum in tam illicito desiderio ei prebere adiutorium, et ita ad aliud se convertit. Postea audientibus illis clericis, cepit ille magister multa contraria loqui de Christo cum demonibus suis et de omnibus christianis et ipsos clericos in maximam perversitatem induxit, circulum exire non permisit usque ad solis ortum; et in ipso egressu oportuit, ut quilibet diceret: 'Deus homo factus est, in hoc honore vivo'; alioquin rapuissent eum demones, et qui eos compellebat ad negandum misterium incarnationis, non poterat sanos educere de circulo sine confessione ipsius incarnationis.

Qui hec retulit dixit, quod a duobus vel tribus de illis clericis istud accepit. Per istos ergo accrevit et dilatata est infidelitas illa in culta Luciferi."

archbishop of Mainz (similar letters were received by the bishop of
Hildesheim and other suffragans of Mainz, by *magister* Conrad of Marburg,
by King Henry, and by Emperor Frederick II), in which were mentioned
additional allegations against the so-called cult of Luciferians in Germany.[231] The reference in this papal letter to the alleged claim by the

---

[231] Hartzheim, *Concilia* III 544; Mansi, *Collectio* XXIII 323-326; Potthast, *Regesta* I, Nr.
9230; Auvray, *Registres de Gregoire IX* I, Nr. 1391; Rodenberg, *MG Ep. s. XIII* I 432, Nr.
537 ad a. 1233: "*Vox in Rama. . . . Huius pestis initia talia perfereruntur: nam dum novitius
in ea quisquam recipitur et perditorum primitus scholas intras, apparet ei species quedam rane,
quam busonem consueverunt aliqui nominare. Hanc quidam a posterioribus et quidam in ore
damnabiliter osculantes, linguam bestie intra ora sua recipiunt et salivam. Hec apparet
interdum indebita quantitate, et quandoque in modum anseris vel anatis, plerumque furni etiam
quantitatem assumit. Demum novitio procedenti occurrit miri palloris homo, nigerrimos habens
oculos, adeo extenuatus et macer, quod consumptis carnibus sola cutis relicta videtur ossibus
superducta; hunc novitius osculatur et sentit frigidum sicut glaciem, et post osculum catholice
memoria fidei de ipsius corde totaliter evanescit. Ad convivium postmodum discumbentibus,
et surgentibus completo ipso convivio, per quandam statuam, que in scholis huiusmodi esse
solet, descendit retrorsum ad modum canis mediocris gattus niger retorta cauda, quem a
posterioribus primo novitius, post magister, deinde singuli per ordinem osculantur, qui tamen
digni sunt et perfecti; imperfecti vero, qui se dignos non reputant, pacem recipiunt a magistro,
et tunc singulis per loca sua positis, dictisque quibusdam carminibus, ac versus gattum
capitibus inclinatis: 'Parce nobis,' dicit magister, et proximo cuique hoc precipit, respondente
tertio ac dicente: 'Scimus magister'; quartus ait: 'Et nos obedire debemus'; et his ita peractis
extingunter candele, et proceditur ad fetidissimum opus luxurie, nulla discretione habita inter
extraneas et propinquas. Quod si forte virilis sexus supersunt aliqui ultra numerum mulierum,
traditi in passiones ignominie, in desideriis suis invicem exardentes, masculi in masculos
turpitudinem operantur, similiter et femine immutant naturalem usum in eum, qui est contra
naturam, hoc ipsum inter se damnabiliter facientes. Completo vero tam nefandissimo scelere
et candelis iterum reaccensis singulisque in suo ordine constitutis, de obscuro scholarum
angulo, quo non carent perditissimi hominum, quidam homo procedit a renibus sursum fulgens
et sole clarior, sicut dicunt, deorsum hispidus sicut gattus, cuius fulgor illuminat totum locum.
Tunc magister excerpens aliquid de veste novitii, fulgido illi dicit: 'Magister, hoc mihi datum
tibi do,' illo fulgido respondente: 'Bene mihi servisti pluries et melius servies, tue committo
custodie, quod dedisti,' et his dictis protinus evanescit. Corpus etiam Domini singulis annis
in pascha de manu recipiunt sacerdotis, et illud ad domus suas in ore portantes in latrinam
proiciunt in contumeliam Redemptoris. Ad hec infelicissimi omnium miserorum gubernantem
celestia pollutis labiis blasphemantes asserunt delirando, celorum dominum violenter contra
iustitiam et dolose Luciferum in inferos detrusisse. In hunc etiam credunt miseri, et ipsum
affirmant celestium conditurum, et adhuc ad suam gloriam precipitato Domino rediturum, per
quem cum eodem et non ante ipsum se sperant eternam beatitudinem habituros. Omnia Deo
placito non agenda fatentur, et potius agenda que odit.*" Cf. also Hefele, *Conciliengeschichte*
V (1863) 907ff., Binterim, *Concilien* IV 302; Raynaldi, *Annales eccl. ad a. 1233*, Nr. 45;
Böhmer-Will, *RAM* I 225, Nr. 93; Potthast, *Regesta* I, Nr. 9229-9231. Hauck, *KGD* IV 917
note 7, argues that the nonsense (*Verrücktheit*) mentioned in this letter probably came from
Conrad of Marburg himself; cf. letter of Mainz to the pope (*Chron. Albrici* 931; a papal letter
of 10 June 1233 to Conrad of Marburg acknowledges the receipt of a report about the heretics
which he, the archbishop and the bishop of Hildesheim had sent him, and urges Conrad to use
all measures possible to combat them.

heretics that Lucifer had been unjustly cast out of Heaven establishes a connection between them and the woman Luckardis at Trier. It is also evident that the charge claimed by the Trier chronicler to have been made at that city in 1231, that "some kissed the pallid man or even the cat, or did even worse things," was related to the practice which Pope Gregory IX described in much greater detail. It seems probable that the chronicler, writing shortly after 1242, had access to the papal letter of 13 July 1233, and that he attributed to specific individuals accused of heresy at Trier those teachings and practices which the Roman pontiff had made only general. The entire account seems to be aimed at making the heretics appear so perverse that anyone accused of religious deviance would be at once guilty of the most heinous of all offenses—homosexuality and sacrilege.

There are reasons for questioning whether the "cult" of the Luciferians as described in the orthodox literature of the period was a distinct religious aberration, however. The account given by Aubrey of Trois-Fontaines introduces the section on the Luciferians at Cologne by first recounting the death of Vigorosus of Baconia, the Cathar bishop of Toulouse. There seems to have been no clear distinction in the chronicler's mind between the Cathars and those whom he called "Luciferians." Furthermore, despite the reference to necromancy, the account which Pope Gregory IX gave of the initiation practices ascribed to the Luciferians mentioned two important elements of Cathar worship: the distinction made between the *perfecti* and the *imperfecti*, and the "kiss of peace." The kiss had nothing whatever to do with immorality, being rather the manner in which the Cathar *perfecti* greeted one another. At the end of their services, they again embraced and gave the kiss which was then given to the disciples or *credentes*.[232]

The high degree of dualism which was characteristic of Cathar teachings in the West after 1167, a doctrine in which Satan was accorded god-like status over/against the Christian deity, may in part explain the confusion in the minds of those who opposed them as to whom the Cathars actually worshipped. On the other hand, there appears to have been an almost deliberate twisting of the Cathar tenets by orthodox Catholic writers. From the eleventh century onward there was a tradition among protagonists of the True Faith which attributed to heretical groups the practice of Satan-worship and immorality. Scholars and chroniclers of the twelfth and thirteenth centuries were misled in much of what they wrote by the treatises of Augustine against the heretics of his own day. Many tried to make thirteenth-century heterodoxy fit fifth-century definitions. The accounts of Aubrey and the anonymous author of the *Vita Theoderici* at Trier may also belong to this school of medieval historians. The early thirteenth century

---

[232] Cf. Pixton, "Dietrich of Wied" (1972) 101-105; Borst, *Die Katharer* 199-200.

seems to have had an unusual preoccupation with stories of devils and occult powers which no doubt intensified under the pressure of religious persecution. It is therefore a very difficult task to determine whether the accounts of Satan-worship and immorality should be accepted.

In keeping with the papal mandate of June 1231, Archbishop Dietrich of Trier convened a synod to deal with those whose aberrant religious views had been uncovered during the visitation of his diocese.[233] Hauck regards this as one of the few thirteenth-century German synods to rise above the mechanical level,[234] although we have identified several others of this type as well. The *Gesta Treverorum* state that at the synod the metropolitan publicly announced that the heretics in his diocese had a bishop whom they called Dietrich, after his own name, and that the same practice was also observed elsewhere. He noted that they furthermore had a pope whom they addressed as "Gregory"; thus, if they should ever be asked about their faith, they might respond that they held the same views as pope Gregory and such-and-such a bishop, mentioning those of the established religion, but meaning their own.[235]

---

[233] *Gesta Trev.* 401-402; Hartzheim, *Concilia* III, 539; Mansi, *Collectio ampliss.* XXIII, 241. Binterim, *Concilien* IV 400, maintains that this was the same synod as that dated 1238; Hefele-Leclercq, *Conciles* V/2 1536, accepts 1231 date and rejects Binterim's equation. Arens, "Datierung" 95, notes that canons of this synod are no longer extant, and also the puzzling fact that the *Gesta* make reference to this one alone. Yet, he too finds it impossible to equate the 1231 and 1238 synods. The *Gesta* place the synod in the year 1231, while the year 1238 appears four pages later in the account. The critical study by Friedrich Bertheau, "Die Gesta Trevirorum vom Jahre 1152 bis zum Jahre 1259: Eine Quellenuntersuchung," (Unpublished Diss. Göttingen, 1874) 72-73, also rejects such an identification; he cites Hartzheim, *Concilia* III 539, which he claims is another document dated 1231 and agrees with the *Gesta* but is independent of it. K. Cüppers, "Zur Kritik der Gesta Trevirorum 1152-1259," *Münsterische Beiträge zur Geschichte*, Heft I (Paderborn, 1882) 29, believes that the author of the *Gesta Theoderici* had the use of the 1231 synod protocol when he wrote.

[234] *KGD* IV 9.

[235] *Gesta Trev.* 401-402: "*Eo tempore Treverensis archiepiscopus synodum tenuit, in qua ipse publice enunciavit, hereticos in sua dyocesi habere episcopum, quem cognominassent secundum suum nomen Theodoricum, et idem alibi fecisse de episcopis locorum; itemque habere eos communiter papam, quem secundum catholice ecclesie episcopum nuncuparent Gregorium, ut, si interrogarentur de fide, eam fidem se habere dicerent, quam haberet papa Gregorius et ille episcopus sic nominatus, nostrum nominantes et suum intendentes. In eadem synodo tres fuerunt heretici presentati, quorum duo sunt dimissi, unus exustus. In eadem synodo archiepiscopus ecommmunicavit omnes falsatores monetarum, tam iubentes, quam facientes. . . . . Nam exusta est ibi quedam Lucardis, que sanctissime vite putabatur, que incredibili lamentatione lugebat liciferum iniuste de celo extrusum, quem volebat replorare denuo in celum.*" A German translation of the *Gesta Treverorum* in given in Emil Zenz, ed., *Die Taten der Trierer: Gesta Treverorum* III (Trier, 1959) 53. Further discussion of this synod in Hauck, *KGD* IV 9 and 901; Idem V 140 note 2; Binterim, *Concilien* IV 295-301; Hefele-Leclercq, *Conciles* V/2 1536; Arens, "Datierung" 95.

According to the *Gesta* account, three heretics were presented at this synod, two of whom were released. The incorrigible one, apparently the Luciferian woman Luckardis, was burned. At the same synod, those found guilty of counterfeiting money—both those who ordered it and those who minted it—were condemned in the strongest terms. Pope Innocent III had striven actively to suppress heresy through imprisonment, confiscation, and banishment. The death penalty for convicted heretics did not form part of his legislation. In his letters to the episcopate, Gregory IX always demanded that the bishops follow the prescriptions of the Fourth Lateran Council, the papal constitutions, and the canonical penalties which he himself had instituted. At no time did he decree anything more stringent than confiscation, or exile, or both. While it may therefore appear contrary to papal policy that Archbishop Dietrich of Trier delivered up a woman to be burned in 1231, his actions must also be viewed against a general practice of early thirteenth-century Germany. When Emperor Frederick II declared the death penalty in 1232 for convicted heretics throughout the Empire, he merely legalized what was already a standing custom.[236]

News of the persecution of heretics at Trier reached Pope Gregory IX. On 21 October 1233, the Roman pontiff sent a letter to Archbishop Dietrich in which he praised the latter's efforts:

> We deplore and we are disturbed that Germany which until recently has been redolent like a garden of spiritual delights and has flourished with the verdure of Catholic faith and the piety of good works, now appears filled with thornbushes and is made hideous by the filth of offenses; and except the Lord had left behind in her the seed of benediction, sincere men, zealous for the faith, the labor of its correction would be uncertain, perhaps even hopeless. Now indeed, as we ascertain the truth, you and other prelates of churches, lifting up balm to its aches and, like the Samaritan in the Gospel, pouring wine and oil upon its wounds, are approaching with care, if perchance there be soundness of body.[237]

The optimistic tone of the letter was premature, however; in 1238 the archbishop found it necessary to legislate against heresy once more.[238] Nor was all well with respect to the clergy of Trier, either: on 9 February

---

[236] *MGH Leges*, ed. Georg Heinrich Pertz, II (Hannover, 1837; reprint Stuttgart, 1965) 288; Albert Clement Shannon, *The Popes and Heresy in the Thirteenth Century* (Villanova, Penna., 1949) 109.

[237] Potthast, *Regesta* I, Nr. 9315; Hartzheim, *Concilia* III, 540: *"Dolemus, et vehementi commotione turbamus, quod Teutonia, . . ."* Similar letters were sent to the archbishop of Mainz, the bishop of Hildesheim, and Friar Conrad of the Order of Preachers who was the provincial prior in Germany; cf. Potthast, *op.cit.* I, Nr. 9314; Würdtwein, *Nova subs.* VI 36.

[238] See below, Ch. Five, p. 417.

1233, Gregory had granted permission to the Dominican Friar Bernard to suspend all clerics in the provinces of Trier and Cologne who were accused of having sexual relations with nuns and secular canonesses.[239]

Lapses at the Abbey of Lorsch

Siegfried III of Mainz was equally determined as his uncle at Trier to restore discipline and order among his clergy. His efforts met with strong opposition in the Benedictine monastery at Lorsch, however. The poor administration of this abbey had already attracted the attention of Archbishop Siegfried II and Pope Gregory IX: at papal insistence, Siegfried II had found it necessary to intervene in several internal matters. Shortly before his death he also deposed the last abbot of Lorsch, Conrad, primarily for alienating property belonging to the house, but for his failure to maintain the proper discipline among his monks as well.[240]

No sooner had Siegfried III come to office than he sent a letter to the pope, declaring his doubts that the monastery would ever be able to reform itself. In response to this, the pontiff on 6 August 1231 transferred to the archbishop complete administration of the abbey.[241] At the same time the bishop of Hildesheim was given the assignment of a papal commissioner, with the task of making a thorough investigation of Lorsch and of reporting the true state of affairs to the Curia. The monks at Lorsch resisted any and all efforts by the archbishop to assume control of their house, against which Siegfried III threatened to secularize the monastery and to unite it with the cathedral chapter at Mainz. To the surprise of many, they accepted the proposal.[242]

The bishop of Hildesheim had meanwhile completed his investigation and had filed his report, arousing great concern in Rome. Thus, on 24 February 1233 the archbishop was directed to remove the Benedictines and to

---

[239] Goerz, *MRR* II, Nr. 2053; Potthast, *Regesta* I, Nr. 9086; Auvray, *Registres de Gregoire IX* I, Nr. 1085.

[240] Scriba, *Hess. Regg.* I 32, Nr. 330; Potthast, *Regesta* I, Nr. 8391 (4 May 1229); Böhmer-Will, *RAM* II 201, Nr. 580; Fink, *Siegfried III.* 65; Johann Peter Schunk, ed., *Beyträge zur Mainzer Geschichte* III (Mainz & Frankfurt, 1789) 369, Nr. 57; Johann Konrad Dahl, *Historisch-topographisch-statistische Beschreibung des Fürstentums Lorsch, oder Kirchengeschichte des Oberrheingaues, Geschichte und Statistik des Klosters und Fürstentums Lorsch, nebst einer historischen Topographie* (Darmstadt, 1812) 79; Hermann Bär, *Geschichte der Abtei Eberbach im Rheingau*, Im Auftrag des Vereins für Nassauische Alterthumskunde und Geschichtsforschung, II (Wiesbaden, 1858) 19; Valentin Al. Franz Falk, *Geschichte des ehemaligen Klosters Lorsch an der Bergstrasse* (Mainz, 1866) 94, 210.

[241] Potthast, *Regesta* I, Nr. 8779; Scriba, *Hess. Regg.* I, Suppl. 3, Nr. 2623; Böhmer-Will, *RAM* II 214, Nr. 24.

[242] Fink, *Siegfried III.* 65-66; Freherus, *Scriptores rer. Germ.* I 166.

establish Cistercians at Lorsch. If some so desired, they might remain as part of the new community; the others were ordered to find houses of Black Monks in the diocese.[243] The monks appeared to comply, but at the first opportunity they came back one night and drove out the new occupants. Archbishop Siegfried had to use force of arms to restore the Cistercians.[244] Other problems developed as well. In order to carry out the papal injunction with haste, Siegfried had appointed Abbot Raimund of Eberbach and three other Cistercian abbots to regulate affairs at Lorsch. They in turn had excommunicated the Benedictines. Feeling incompetent to deal with the matter to completion, however, they referred the archbishop to the general chapter of their Order. Siegfried petitioned the pope to intervene, which the latter did.[245]

The interests of the former inhabitants of Lorsch were furthered also by the opposition of the duke of Bavaria who claimed earlier rights of patronage and advocacy over the monastery. Siegfried was forced to excommunicate him; he in turn appealed to Rome. Thus, another commission was established to help resolve the differences.[246] The dispossessed Benedictines tried to persuade the pope to oppose the archbishop; when Siegfried failed to comply with the second commission's directives, they excommunicated him (18 January 1239).[247] The Black Monks also sought support from the duke of Bavaria to permanently regain their monastery. Displaying a total disregard for the authority of the archbishop, they harassed the Cistercians a second time, driving them out and threatening to kill any who returned.[248]

---

[243] Böhmer-Will, *RAM* II 224, Nr. 84; Fink, *Siegfried III.* 66, citing Freherus, *Scriptores rer. Germ.* I 158; date corrected by Potthast, *Regesta* I, Nr. 9104, citing Manrique, *Ann. Cist.* IV 443; Auvray, *Registres de Gregoire IX* I, Nr. 1095.

[244] Fink, *Siegfried III.* 67; Trithemius, *Ann. Hirsau.* 234; Dahl, *Beschreibung von Lorsch* 80 note 3, based on a MS document of Lorsch.

[245] Fink, *Siegfried III.* 67; Dahl, *Beschreibung von Lorsch* 80 note 3

[246] Böhmer-Will, *RAM* II 236, Nr. 162; Potthast, *Regesta* I, Nr. 9732; Auvray, *Registres de Gregoire IX* I, Nr. 2118; Fink, *Siegfried III.* 67-68; Dahl, *Beschreibung von Lorsch* 80; Rodenberg, *MG Ep. s. XIII* I, Nr. 600. The commission was given to Bishop Engelhard of Naumburg, the prior of the Augustinian canons-foundation at Zeitz, and *magistro J. Cemecae, scholastico Halberstadensi*. The latter was none other than John Zemecke (Johannes Teutonicus), the canonist whose *Compilatio quarta* had been a major vehicle in disseminating the decretals of Innocent III (including the constitutions of the Fourth Lateranum) throughout the Latin Church.

[247] Böhmer-Will, *RAM* II 252, Nr. 313; Fink, *Siegfried III.* 68; Dahl, *Beschreibung von Lorsch* 80. Siegfried appealed his own excommunication and was released by the pope 7 July 1239; cf. Gudenus, *CdMogunt.* I 551 ("*sine causa rationabili, nulla competenti monitione premissa.*")

[248] Fink, *Siegfried III.* 69; Dahl, *Beschreibung von Lorsch* 80 note 3.

Although Siegfried III expelled the truculent Benedictines, he could not effect a return of the Cistercians and the monastery was vacant for several years. The matter remained undecided during the vacancy which followed Gregory IX's death. Shortly after the accession of Innocent IV, however, Siegfried renewed his desires. On 5 May 1245 the pope granted him authority to fill the monastery with either regular or secular canons. The archbishop responded by inviting Premonstratensians from the church of All Saints in Strasbourg to come and occupy it, and he placed the house under a prior chosen by the brothers upon the presentation of the archbishop.[249]

Opposition to the Archbishop of Cologne

At some time during the year 1231, and presumably after the cardinal-legate had departed, a struggle broke out between Archbishop Henry of Cologne and his cathedral chapter. The cause was financial, having to do with arrangements made by the prelate with merchants—presumably money lenders,[250] and the chronicler reported that many ills ensued. Complaints concerning his qualifications to be archbishop reached Rome, for on 12 December 1231 Pope Gregory IX issued a reprimand to Henry regarding serious faults.[251] For this reason the pontiff had established a commission comprised of the bishop of Lausanne, the archdeacon of Cambrai, and the dean of St. John's at Liège to investigate the charges, so that whatever action had to be taken could be properly carried out. On 12 July 1232 the pope informed the inhabitants of the archdiocese of Cologne that an

---

[249] Potthast, *Regesta* I, Nr. 11649; Böhmer-Will, *RAM* II 283, Nr. 518; Fink, *Siegfried III*. 69; Berger, *Registres d'Innocent IV* 190, Nr. 1234; Freherus, *Script. rer. Germ.* I 168.

[250] *Chron. reg. Colon. (a. 1231)* 263: "*Archiepiscopus Coloniensis cum capitulo Sancti Petri dissentit; que dissensio multorum malorum seminium fuit.*" See the indulgence granted to the dean and chapter at Cologne by Pope Gregory IX on 5 February 1232, "*ut, cum eorum bona sint a bonis archiepiscopalibus penitus segregata, et quidam archiepiscopi Colonienses se diversis mercatorum societatibus obligarint recipiendo ab eis mutuo absque eorum consensu non modicam pecuniae quantitatem, nullus in eos propter hoc per litteras apostolicas praesumat suspensionis, excommunicationis aut interdicti sententias promulgare*"; Lacomblet, *NRUB* II 92, Nr. 180; Potthast, *Regesta* I, Nr. 8869.

[251] Auvray, *Registres de Gregoire IX* I, Nr. 748; Rodenberg, *MG Ep. s. XIII* I, Nr. 459: "*Speravimus ut sublimatus dignitatis honore oneris agnosceres gravitatem, sciensque te familie Domini preditum, subditos tuos verbo pasceres et exemplo. Sed quod non sine amaritudine multa referimus, tu proprium ministerium inhonorans te dignitate reddis indignum, dum carni spiritum et rationem sensualitati subicens, noxiis vanitatibus ventilaris et enecas filios quos susceperas educandos, ut taceamus turpitudines criminosas, que pudori relatui et auditui sunt horrori, licet eas fama immo infamia publica non desinat divulgare, faciens patientiam nostram a multis multipliciter exprobari, quasi culparum tuarum nos participes per diutinam tollerantiam faciamus, nisi horrendum scandalum de te ortum debita castigatione sedemus.*"

investigation of their shepherd was underway.[252]   That this inquest took considerable time and effort may be seen from the letter which Pope Gregory IX directed to Archbishop Dietrich II of Trier on 30 March 1233, instructing him to use his authority to prohibit his colleague at Cologne from alienating any property belonging to his church while the review of his stewardship was in progress.   This restriction of Archbishop Henry's ecclesiastical authority was to be made known publicly,[253] though the nature of the assembly at which this was done is not known.   Given the frequent synods at Trier, it is not improbable that one of his own served this purpose.   Although it was not always his fault, Henry of Müllenark was seldom at peace, either with his neighbors the princes, or with his own clergy.   It has been said of him that "he knew how to wield the sword better than the shepherd's staff."[254]   Further evidence of his neglect of spiritual matters may be seen in the letter noted above in connection with Trier, whereby the Roman pontiff granted authority to a Dominican preacher to suspend from office and benefice all clerics found guilty of fornicating with nuns and canonesses.[255]

Bishop Henry of Meissen also held a synod in 1231 (24 May), the record of which speaks only of administrative actions.[256]   Despite the fact that his predecessor, Bruno, had been forced to resign his office in October 1228,

---

[252] Lacomblet, *NRUB* II 93, Nr. 181; Potthast, *Regesta* I, Nr. 8971; Rodenberg, *MG Ep. s. XIII* I, Nr. 472.

[253] Auvray, *Registres de Gregoire IX* I, Nr. 1214; Rodenberg, *MG Ep. s. XIII* I, Nr. 520: ". . . *quatinas predictas inhibitionem et suspensionem publicari, et ecclesiam ipsam, si archiepiscopus ipse contra presumpserit, as solutionem alicuius pecunie propter hoc aliquatenus non teneri et contractum huiusmodi non valere.*" On 10 June 1233 the pope wrote to the prelates of the city and diocese of Cologne, commanding them to compensate Goswin of Volmarstein, the cathedral dean at Cologne, in the amount of 300 Marks sterling for his expenses incurred during the inquest into Archbishop Henry's negligent administration; should they fail to comply with this mandate, he had empowered the scholastics of St. Gereon at Cologne and Xanten, and another canon at St. Gereon, to compel their obedience; cf. Rodenberg, *op.cit.* I, Nr. 535. The following day Gregory dictated instructions to Archdeacon Hugh of Rheims, Archdeacon John Barat of Châlons, and the canon G. Goin of Rheims, urging them to use caution in relaxing the sentence of excommunication against any protestors to the previous appeal for financial support; see Rodenberg, *op.cit.* I, Nr. 536.

[254] The editorial comment belongs to Binterim, *Concilien* IV 432: „*[Er] wusste geschickter das Schwert als den Hirtenstab zu führen.*" Somewhat incongruent therefore is the papal letter of 18 December 1233 which confirmed reforms carried out at the cloister of Vilich-Rheindorf by the abbot of Heisterbach at the request of the archbishop of Cologne: owing to financial problems, the abbess's resources were incorporated into those of the cloister. Without the proper economic underpinnings, no religious community could hope to maintain a viable program of prayer and service, yet the mere granting of financial support did not ensure that a regimen of discipline would follow.

[255] See above, p. 388.

[256] Potthast, *Regesta* I, Nr. 9086; Rittenbach, *Bischöfe von Meissen* 142.

Henry does not appear in documents until 10 April 1230; presumably he was elected just shortly before that time, though the reasons for the delay are unknown.[257] Given the lengthy period of Bruno's ineffective leadership over the diocese, this same synod would have been the likely setting for any initial efforts to re-assert episcopal control. We have no record, of such, however.

A similar situation existed at Verden where for almost thirty years Iso of Wölpe had sat as bishop. Upon his death on 5 August 1231 the cathedral chapter elected its own provost, Luder of Borg, to be prelate. Among his first acts in office as *electus et confirmatus* was the confirmation of the rights and customs of the cathedral chapter, promising to acknowledge the privileges granted by his predecessors. Whereas Bishop Iso had conferred the office of archdeacon upon whomever he wished, Luder covenanted that the provostship of Bardowiek, the archdeaconate of Holdenstadt which was united with the provostship of St. Andreas in Verden, and the archdeaconates of Bevensen, Modestorf, Salzhausen, Hittfeld, Sottrum, and Schessel were to be given only to Verden cathedral canons.[258] The assembly at which this agreement was announced may have been a diocesan synod, although the details of the capitulation would have been worked out in advance. It clearly shows that in this diocese at least, serious ecclesiastical reform would be difficult to achieve.

Whether this new prelate understood fully the canonical implications of the constitutions of Lateran IV may be implied from a letter issued by Pope Gregory IX in the summer of 1235. The Roman pontiff directed the provosts of Heiligenroth and St. Anschar, and the dean of St. Anschar at Bremen, to relax the sentence of excommunication imposed in contradiction to the statutes of the General Council by Bishop Luder on a knight named Alardus, who had been accused of despoiling men of the bishopric of Verden.[259] We have no earlier evidence that the statutes of the Fourth Lateranum were published at Verden, in which case the bishop acted out of ignorance of the new legislation. The constitutions in question is not specified, but the issues addressed in *cc.* 32, 45 and 46 all seem applicable in this case.[260] In the event that he and his clergy had not been exposed to the full set of statutes at some earlier date, 1235 marks the *terminus ante quem* for their publication in his church. That such a delay could have oc-

---

[257] Fuchs, *Besetzung* 34.

[258] Von Hodenberg, *Verdener GQ* II, Nr. 56.

[259] Potthast, *Regesta* I, Nr. 10003; Ehmck, *Bremisches UB* I, Nr. 194.

[260] (*C. 32*) *Ut patroni competentem portionem dimittant clericis; (c. 45) Patronus qui clericum ecclesiae occideret vel mutilaverit, ius patronatus amittit; (c. 46) De taliis a clericis non exigendis.*

curred seems hardly likely, however, given the strong evidence from other German dioceses of much earlier introduction.

Were our record more complete, we might be able to perceive greater correspondence between reform activities being undertaken in one ecclesiastical province and those in another. This is not to imply that there was some overriding, coordinated plan followed by metropolitans: the nature of the German church of the thirteenth century was too diverse to suggest that there was even uniformity among the cloisters or foundations of a single diocese. Nevertheless, there are observable parallels between the province of Salzburg and those of Mainz and Trier which deserve notice. The known general chapters of 1218, 1221, 1224 and 1230 for Salzburg had their counterparts in 1222, 1224 and 1227 for Mainz, and in 1219/1220, 1230, and 1239 for Trier.[261] The 1230 assembly, held for the Benedictines of the province of Trier, addressed many of the same issues dealt with that same year for the Augustinian canons at Salzburg. In each case we see the strong hand of an archbishop committed to principles of reform.

On 5 April 1231, Archbishop Eberhard granted a forest to the monastery of St. Peter in Salzburg, an act witnessed by Bishop Rüdiger of Chiemsee, Provost Henry *Soliensis*, and at least twelve members of the cathedral chapter.[262] The size of the group which witnessed this act suggests that it was part of the business dealt with at a provincial synod. It is not improbable that further details relating to the erection of the bishopric of Lavant were also discussed, but any expectations which the metropolitan may have had about the ability of this new see to deal effectively with ecclesiastical matters may have been premature. Among the immediate challenges for Bishop Ulrich was the correction of a religious house within his own episcopal city: on 27 May 1232 the pope issued a mandate to the abbot of Sitich and the priors of Seitz and Geyrach that, at the request of the duke of Carinthia (*conquerente Carinthiae duce inductus*), they "*corrigant et reforment*" the monastery of St.Paul in Lavant "*tam in capite quam in membris.*"[263]

---

[261] Dopsch, *Geschichte Salzburgs* I 329 note 783; Hauthaler, *SUB* III, Nr. 809; J. Zeller, "Drei Provinzialkapitel aus der Kirchenprovinz Mainz," *Studien und Mitteilungen* 43 (1925) 73-98; Hilpisch, *Geschichte des Benediktinischen Mönchtums* 235-238. At one of the Mainz provincial chapters held at Hirsau the authority of Abbot Eberhard (1216-1227) was severely reduced on account of his numerous abuses; see *Germania Benedictina* V 285.

[262] Hauthaler, *SUB* III, Nrs. 780, 825; Hartzheim, *Concilia* III 541-542.

[263] Potthast, *Regesta* I, Nr. 8934; *AÖG* 32 (1864) 167, Nr. 902. On the development of the phrase "*tam in capite quam in membris*," see Karl Augustin Frech, *Reform an Haupt und Gliedern: Untersuchung zur Entwicklung und Verwendung der Formulierung im Hoch- und Spätmittelalter*, Europäische Hochschulschriften, Reihe III: Geschichte und ihre Hilfswissenschaften, vol. 510 (New York, 1992).

Papal Relations with the Province of Salzburg

Pope Gregory IX also wrote Eberhard of Salzburg on 22 November 1232 urging his energetic prosecution of heretics,[264] but his response was somewhat mild. The Inquisition was primarily the responsibility of the Dominicans who had become established in his archdiocese at Friesach in 1218 and at Pettau in 1231.[265] The archbishop instructed his judges and officials to support the Dominicans, but he insisted that those who had been accused by the Inquisition as well as those who actually admitted to heretical beliefs be punished according to canon law.[266] Even a renewed admonition from the pope did not alter Eberhard's position over against the inquisitors.[267] Apart from conflicts with certain nobles of his archdiocese,[268] the Salzburg church had in fact been relatively quiet after years of constant agitation by the archbishop. His many years of service to the church and loyalty to the papacy were rewarded in April 1232 when the pope granted him and his successors an indulgence allowing them to have the crucifix borne before them everywhere except in the city of Rome itself or anywhere where the pontiff or one of his legates was present.[269] The following year Gregory IX formally announced the canonization of Vigilius, former bishop of Salzburg († 784). Undoubtedly this bull was read at an assembly of the clergy and laity; Hartzheim regards the event as a synod.[270]

Between 21/30 August of that year Pope Gregory IX addressed letters to the cathedral chapter at Passau, to the archbishop, to the bishops of Chiemsee and Freising, and to the deans at Freising and Regensburg,

---

[264] Potthast, *Regesta* I, Nr. 9046; Meiller, *RAS* 259, Nr. 404. See also Potthast, *op.cit.* Nrs. 8994, 8995.

[265] Dopsch, *Geschichte Salzburgs* I 315 note 649.

[266] Dopsch, *Geschichte Salzburgs* I 315 note 650; Hauthaler, *SUB* III, Nr. 879.

[267] Dopsch, *Geschichte Salzburgs* I 315 note 651; Potthast, *Regesta* I, Nr. 8753.

[268] Cf. Potthast, *Regesta* I, Nr. 8902; Meiller, *RES* 255, Nr. 387.

[269] Potthast, *Regesta* I, Nr. 8913; Meiller, *RES* 256, Nr. 389: "... *cum tibi et successoribus tuis ferendi crucem in Salzeburgensi provincia sicut asseritur a sede apostolica sit indultum, salutiferae crucis vexillum ante te fecias ubique deferri nisi in urbe Romana et ubicumque fuerit summus pontifex aut legatus a suo latere destinatus.*"

[270] On 11 September 1230 Pope Gregory IX commissioned Bishop Conrad of Brixen and some abbots of the Cistercian order to inquire into the alleged miracles of the former archbishop of Salzburg, Virgilius; cf. Potthast, *Regesta* I 738, Nr. 8601; Auvray, *Registres de Gregoire IX* I, Nr. 489. Their investigation must have produced convincing evidence, for on 18 June 1233 the Roman pontiff announced the formal canonization, indicating that the saint's feast day (27 November) was to be celebrated throughout the entire church; Hartzheim, *Concilia* III 541; Potthast, *op.cit.* I 790, Nrs. 9237, 9238; Auvray, *op.cit.* I, Nr. 1414. Alone among the Austrian annals, the *Annales sancti Rudberti Salisburgenses* contain the terse note: "*1233. Sanctus Virgilius a papa Gregorio IX canonizatus est*"; cf. *MGH SS* IX 785.

announcing the resignation of Bishop Gebhard of Passau.[271]   Not until 1
July 1233 did the Roman pontiff transfer to Passau Bishop Rüdiger of
Chiemsee, long a trusted tool in the hands of the archbishop and the
papacy.[272]   Whether any sort of provincial synod was convened in 1232
in conjunction with the public proclamation of Bishop Gebhard's abdication
is unknown, but the close sequence of the bulls which declared the
canonization of St. Vigilius and the postulation of Bishop Rüdiger allow the
conjecture that in late summer/early autumn 1233 Archbishop Eberhard II
of Salzburg presided over a dazzling assembly of his provincial clergy (and
laymen?) at which he had the first major opportunity to be preceded into his
cathedral church by the crucifix in accordance with the papal privilege of
1232, at which he gave his seal of approval to the transfer of Rüdiger of
Radeck from Chiemsee to Passau, at which he announced the appointment
of Provost Albert of Salzburg as the new bishop of Chiemsee,[273] sanctify-
ing the entire assembly by the proclamation of the official canonization of
a former Salzburg prelate, St. Vigilius.

The only explicitly identified synod recorded anywhere in Germany for
1232 was the one held at Speyer by Bishop Berengar who died in November
that same year.[274]   Problems within the church at Augsburg surfaced as
well, but the role of the bishop in their resolution is unknown: on 11
November 1232 the pope confirmed a petition from the prior and convent
of St. Ursi (Irrsee) that no one under the age of twenty years be admitted
as a monk.[275]   There were discoveries made of heretics at Strasbourg and
Erfurt that same year, presumably in connection with the inquisitorial
activities of Conrad of Marburg, but it is also probable that similar to Trier,
episcopal visitations had been conducted; four heretics were burned at
Erfurt.[276]   On 19 October 1232 Pope Gregory IX granted to the bishop of

---

[271] Rodenberg, *MG Ep. s. XIII* I, Nr. 480; Auvray, *Registres de Gregoire IX* I, Nr. 859.

[272] Auvray, *Registres de Gregoire IX* I 806, Nrs. 1444-1445; Rodenberg, *MG Ep. s. XIII*
I, Nrs. 544, 545.

[273] *Ann. Salisb.* 786:   "*Albertus prepositus Salzpurgensis in episcopum Chiemensem ab
archiepiscopo eligitur; pro quo substituitur Chuno eiusdem ecclesie decanus.*"

[274] Remling, *Speyer UB* I 193, Nr. 187; *Wirtemburg. UB* III 303, Nr. 808; Hauck, *KGD*
IV 7 note 1; Duggan, *Bishop and Chapter* 35 note 96; Mazetti, *Bischof Berngar* 15.   The
extant record tells of a grant of property by the bishop to the cathedral chapter and to the
Cistercian monastery at Maulbronn "*ut persone ibidem Deo servientes ad honorem Dei et sue
sanctissime genetricis commodius valeant sustenari. . . . Acta sunt . . . presentibus abbatibus,
prepositis, decanis et universo clero nostre diocesis in nostra generali synodo constitutis et
nobilibus laicis.*"

[275] Auvray, *Registres de Gregoire IX* I, Nr. 956.

[276] *Ann. Erphord.* 82:   "*In Alemannia perfida heresis, que ibidem diu occulte pullulaverat,
est manifestata.   Quapropter circa Renum nonnulli et alibi innumerabiles heretici per
magistrum Cunradum de Marburc auctoritate apostolica examinati ac per sententiam secularem*

Strasbourg authority to enlist the help of some of the abbots of his diocese
in his task of degrading priests who had been found guilty of heretical actions.[277] But even the Benedictines of his diocese exhibited tendencies
towards un-discipline and spiritual decay: complaints undoubtedly led to an
episcopal visitation of the non-exempt monasteries, the result of which was
his determination to remove the Black Monks at the abbey of St. Leonardus
and to fill it with secular canons, *"cum monasterium . . . per malitiam
monarchorum nigrorum in eodem degentium ad miseriam devenisset . . ."*
On 2 April 1235 the pope confirmed this decision.[278]

The issues of heresy and lapsed religious within his province were
clearly on the mind of Archbishop Siegfried III as well when he convened
a provincial synod at Mainz on 13 March 1233.[279] The synod issued a set
of fifty-one decrees aimed at combatting heterodoxy, charging each bishop
with the responsibility of taking action against religious aberrations, and of
publishing the papal and imperial bulls against them at their diocesan
synods.[280] Whereas earlier scholars had placed them at a synod held later

---

*damnati cumbusti sunt igne. Fueruntque etiam presente eodem Cunrado Erphordie III. Non.
Maii [5 May 1232] quatuor cumbusti."*

[277] Rodenberg, *MG Ep. s. XIII* I, Nr. 485; Auvray, *Registres de Gregoire IX* I, Nr. 933.

[278] Schöpflin, *Alsat. dipl.* I, Nr. 482; Potthast, *Regesta* I, Nr. 9873; Auvray, *Registres de
Gregoire IX* I, Nr. 2504.

[279] *Ann. Erphord.* 85: *"Hoc etiam anno Sifridus Moguntinus habito consilio cum canonicis
Moguntinis pro sui predecessoris debetis, quibus episcopatus iam dudum Rome fuerat obligatus,
in tota sua diocesi redituum vicesimam partem a personis ecclesiasticis colligi mandavit, ac
super hoc dato privilegio se nunquam a clero suo diebus suis quicquam amplius petiturum.
Canonici etiam matricis ecclesie Moguntine fide iuratoria confirmaverunt se de cetero nullum
pontificem electuros, nisi in idem privilegium consensurum. Hic anno III. Idus Marcii Sifridus
Moguntine sedis archiepiscopus Moguntie concilium celebravit, pontificatus sui anno III."*
Derived from this is the account in *Chron. Reinhardsbrun.* 614. The synod is listed in Mansi,
Collectio XXII 323-324; Binterim, *Concilien* IV 371-372; Biskamp, *Mainzer DK* 68-71.
Böhmer-Will, *RAM* II 226, Nr. 95, places it at an unknown date before 18 June. A passage
in the Middle High German poem *Wartburgkrieg* also refers to the synod; cf. Karl Joseph
Simrock, ed., *Der Wartburgkrieg* (Stuttgart & Augsburg, 1858) 152, 292ff.

[280] The decrees were found in an undated synodal-protocol at the end of a Reichenau MS
closely written together in a thirteenth-century hand and preserved at Karlsruhe, Landesbibliothek (MS 109, fol. 52ᵛ-53ᵛ); published by Moné in *ZGO* 3 (1851) 131-142. Other known MSS
include München Staatsbibliothek, clm 213, fol. 195ʳ-196ʳ (*in margo*); clm 213, fol. 203ʳ-204ʳ
(dated 1234); Wien, Institut für österreichischen Geschichtsforschung, Fragment Nr. 37; for
these and other MSS relating to Mainz and Salzburg synods, cf. Johanek, "Synodalia" III 60-
130, espec. 62. Neither Schannat nor Würdtwein knew of these statutes, though Schannat does
print other decrees which make reference to these and are therefore somewhat related. The
copiest left the introduction and closing formulae off for want of space, thus eliminating the
date of these decrees. This can only be determined by comparison with other documents. Art.
3 refers to papal and imperial legislation according to which the confiscation of property of
heretics is introduced: this appears in the statute of Frederick II from 27 February 1232, Art.
1 and 2, from which is concluded that the Mainz synodal decree in this point is an execution

that same year—on 25 July, Kaltner has convincingly shown that they belong to the synod held on 13 March.[281] These statutes make reference to an older council, which now appears to have been that of 1209.[282] They reveal that finding qualified parish priests was difficult, having set the age of fourteen as the earliest date for conferring the *cura animarum* (*c.* 20).

The Dissolution of the Vita Communis at Mainz

As in other dioceses of the time, the archbishopric of Mainz was experiencing the negative effects of the growth in the power, influence and independence of the archdeacons.   Mainz was among those churches which still attempted to maintain the *vita communis* in the thirteenth century.   At various times during the previous century the practices which dated back to the Rule of Chrodegang had had to be reinforced by additional archiepiscopal decrees: in 1128, e.g., regulations were issued for the common refectory for all cathedral canons and vicars; in 1146 stipulations were given for the common dormitory.[283]   Militating against the survival of the *vita communis*, however, was the tendency which became widespread at Mainz and elsewhere in Germany during the twelfth century of allowing cathedral canons to acquire numerous prebends in other churches of the city and even

of the imperial decree. Inasmuch as the provincial synods of Fritzlar 1246 and Mainz 1261 cite many canons from this collection almost verbatim, it cannot be dated later than 1246. These also refer to older decrees which cannot all be identified. This proves, however, that there were earlier statutes for Mainz which have been lost. On 29 October 1232 Pope Gregory IX had issued the command to the archbishop of Mainz to send *religiosos viros* to all parts of his diocese to combat heresy; if those accused of religious aberrations were found guilty, the inquisitors were instructed to use the new statutes. See Potthast, *Regesta* I, Nr. 9031; Rodenberg, *MG Ep. s. XIII* I, Nr. 490.

[281] Moné sees the possibility that these statutes belong to the synod held 25 July 1233 at Mainz (Hartzheim, *Concilia* III 542, 544, 547; X 729); following him are Adolf Hausrat, *Kleine Schriften religionsgeschichtlichen Inhalts* (Leipzig, 1883) 294-296; Hefele-Knöpfler, *Conziliengeschichte* V 1086 note 3; Fink, *Siegfried III.* 57. Against this, Kaltner, *Konrad von Marburg* 148-149; Steinberger, "Mainzer Synoden" 616-617.

[282] Finke puts the older synod in the pontificate of Siegfried II (*Konzilienst.* 29, 36), supporting his thesis mainly on a reference in *c.* 50 of the 1233 statutes which draws on an earlier council: "*Item concilii Maguntini statutum innovanda sancimus, ut si . . . ,*" and also upon a letter of Innocent IV (11 February 1248) which refers to a statute of Siegfried III which he enacted at a council "*praedecessoris sui (i.e., Siegfried II) inherens vestigiis.*" (Rodenberg, *MG Ep. s. XIII* II, Nr. 495). Hauck argues for the pontificate of Arnold of Selenhofen, 1153-1160 (*KGD* IV 82-84; V, 143-4; *Abhandlung* 80ff.). Steinberger, "Mainzer Synoden" 616-620, rejects placing the older statutes before Lateran III, argues instead for the period 1200/1215 which gives our suggestion of 1209 further plausibility. Johanek, "Synodalia" I 33-35, remains uncommitted.

[283] Biskamp, *Mainzer DK* 9.

in outlying places such as Frankfurt, Bingen and Erfurt. The development of the rather independent position for archdeacons likewise weakened the community of the cathedral chapter.

In the twelfth century the archdeaconates in the Mainz church became attached to various provostships at collegiate churches; the fact that these provostships were controlled for the most part by cathedral canons meant that someone such as the cathedral *custos* was also the provost at St. John's collegiate church in Mainz, and at the same time an archdeacon. Joining him in the archiepiscopal administration were the cathedral provost, the cathedral dean and the cathedral cantor.[284] It had long been recognized that the duties of the provost in looking after the external affairs of the chapter necessitated his frequent absence from his obligations in the choir, but the assumption of duties outside the cathedral by the dean, the cantor and the scholastic—the very chapter officials charged with maintaining the "inner life" of the church, had disastrous effects upon discipline and the communal spirit.[285] As was true throughout the medieval Church, the example of those charged with correcting the errors of the clergy of the diocese preached a louder sermon than any homily delivered at diocesan or archiepiscopal synods.

Archbishop Siegfried III originally intended to hold them to the obligation of residence in the cathedral church, for on 30 October 1232 he obtained a commission from the pope to that effect.[286] This concern would certainly have come up at the synod held just four months after the papal letter had been sent, adding to the tension which existed between this prelate and his clergy. Four years later (July 1236) Siegfried reversed himself, allowing the archdeacons to maintain residence or not. Thereafter his concern was for the vicars set in their places.[287] These were needed to provide sufficient clerics in the choir, deficiencies in which had arisen as ever greater numbers of cathedral canons, and particularly the prelates,

---

[284] Biskamp, *Mainzer DK* 10, 19-20.

[285] Biskamp, *Mainzer DK* 10-11: „*Strenge Residenz und Innehaltung des gemeinsamen Lebens liess sich aber mit der Ausübung der Amtspflichten von Erzdiakonen schlecht vereinigen, und diese mochten auch wenig genug Neigung haben, das zu tun.*"

[286] Biskamp, *Mainzer DK* 10-11, 48; Böhmer-Will, *RAM* II 221, Nr. 69; Potthast, *Regesta* I, Nr. 9032: "*Tuis devotis precibis inclinati, compellendi archidiaconos ecclesie Maguntine ad debitam in eadem ecclesia residentiam faciendam et assignandi eis stalla in choro et loca in capitulo, secundum quod eorum exigunt dignitates, prout ad te pertinet, nec non et extirpandi pravas consuetudines ab eadem et instituendi honestas in ipsa auctoritate presentium liberam tibi concedimus facultatem.*" The letter of Gregory IX also in Rodenberg, *MG Ep. s. XIII* I, Nr. 491; Würdtwein, *Nova subs.* VI, Nr. 11.

[287] Böhmer-Will, *RAM* II 244, Nr. 224; Biskamp, *Mainzer DK* 48. By the 1250s absenteeism was chronic, and in 1254 the *vita communis* was abolished at Mainz; cf. Biskamp, *op.cit.* 11.

were taken away from the Divine Service by their activities as archdeacons.[288] By the thirteenth century the number of these vicars had become quite sizeable.

Siegfried III also was directly involved in the detection and disposition of heretics. On 29 October 1232 Gregory IX issued him a mandate, directing that he dispatch monks (*viros religiosos*) and men learned "*in lege Domini*" to all parts of his diocese, whose task it would be to inquire into aberrant beliefs. If they indeed found evidence of non-conformity, they were to proceed against such persons according to the statutes which had recently been sent from the apostolic see.[289] One of the possible consequences of this mandate was that the Dominican prior of Erfurt, Daniel, and a Rudolf, *plebanus de Vipeche* (Vippach), in the diocese of Mainz, conducted a visitation which resulted in the suspension and excommunication of Conrad, the parish priest at *Chimera*. On 11 March 1233 Pope Gregory IX directed Provosts Gerbodo of Mainz and Arnold of St. Severin in Erfurt, together with Conrad the scholastic at Mainz, to relax the sentences and to restore the benefices and their fruits to the dispossessed cleric.[290]

Archbishop Siegfried must also have taken action against the nuns of the cloister of Altenmünster near Lorsch during 1233, for on 30 March 1234 Pope Gregory IX issued a mandate to the cathedral provost and subdean at Cologne, and to the dean of St. Maria *ad gradus* in the same city, that they conduct a visitation of the house, correcting and reforming those things found to require such actions. At the same time, however, they were instructed to restore the possessions, rents, and other properties of the convent which Archbishop Siegfried had confiscated in an apparent move to force compliance with his directives.[291] They were also to see to it that Abbess Iuncta returned to her former position at the head of the house. Mention was made above of the resistance to reform which the archbishop experienced from the abbey of Lorsch. The episode with Altenmünster indicates how far the example of reprobate monks could affect neighboring religious houses.

---

[288] See Biskamp, *Mainzer DK* 9.

[289] Potthast, *Regesta* I, Nr. 9031; Würdtwein, *Nova subs.* VI 28; Böhmer-Will, *RAM* II 221, Nr. 68; Auvray, *Registres de Gregoire IX* I, Nr. 936. See also Julius Ficker, "Die gesetzliche Einführung der Todesstrafe für Ketzerei," *MIÖG* 1 (1880) 214; Kaltner, *Konrad von Marburg* 148.

[290] Potthast, *Regesta* I, Nr. 9120; Würdtwein, *Nova subs.* VI 21; Auvray, *Registres de Gregoire IX* I, Nr. 1183.

[291] Potthast, *Regesta* I, Nr. 9429; Würdtwein, *Nova subs.* VI 41; Auvray, *Registres de Gregoire IX* I, Nr. 1844.

From his predecessor Siegfried III had inherited massive debts which went
back to the time when Siegfried II had lived in exile in Rome during the
German throne controversy and the schism in his own church. In an effort
to relieve these burdens, Siegfried III had suggested sometime earlier that
each member of the Mainz cathedral chapter donate a half-tithe on his
benefice. The canons had objected, claiming that their incomes were
already too small and barely provided for their daily necessities; they further
pointed out that the wars had hurt their church buildings and reduced the
incomes from many of their properties. Nevertheless, the archbishop
insisted and the canons at length acquiesced, on the condition that he never
again request money from them; they furthermore stipulated that without
their approval, he was not to incur any new debts. They also swore a
common oath that in the future no archbishop would be elected except on
these conditions. The terms, and the archbishop's acceptance of them, were
publicly proclaimed at the synod. Ultimately, Siegfried had to compel some
of the cathedral canons to pay the half-tithe; he even sold the cathedral bells
in his effort to quit his see with the Italian creditors. His actions won him
no friends among the higher clergy of his church. In the end, he received
papal permission to hold a prebend in every collegiate church of the
archdiocese, a solution which the cathedral chapter approved in 1235.[292]

The National Synod at Mainz—1233

On 25 July 1233, another synod was held at Mainz, but of a totally different
nature. It dealt with charges of heresy against a prominent German count,
but it also demonstrated that at times the German prelates did take a stand
against papally-appointed legates. Since 1231 the archbishopric of Mainz
had been affected directly by the almost fanatical activities of *magister*
Conrad of Marburg. On the testimony of witnesses, Count Henry of Sayn
was summoned before Conrad's inquisitorial court to answer charges of
riding on a crab. The count refused to submit himself to such accusations,
however, asking that Archbishop Siegfried of Mainz convoke a synod with
his suffragans and clergy to consider the matter.[293] Inasmuch as the synod
coincided with an imperial diet, prelates from dioceses outside the province
of Mainz were also present, giving this assembly the appearance of a
German national council once more. In the presence of King Henry (VII)

---

[292] Binterim, *Concilien* IV 372.

[293] *Ann. Erphord.* 84: "*Anno Domini MCCXXXIII. VIII. Kal. Augusti rex et Moguntinus
et magister Cunradus de Marburc Moguntie conventum episcoporum et comitum atque
clericorum fecerunt pro quibusdam infamatis ab heresi. Inter quos comes de Seine accusatus
inducias expurgationis ulteriores obtinuit.*"

and the assembled spiritual and lay princes of Germany, Conrad of Marburg presented his case against the count of Sayn. The testimony of the witnesses was not convincing, yet the bishops were unable to render a final judgment. They suggested, therefore, that the synod send a report to the pope, while King Henry moved for an adjournment until the reply was received. Count Henry pressed for an immediate decision, but was restrained by Archbishop Dietrich II of Trier who is said to have declared: "My lord, the king, desires that the case be postponed." Then turning to the people gathered round about, the metropolitan announced that ". . . the count of Sayn departs from here un-convicted and as a good Catholic."[294]

This action by the archbishop of Trier left no doubt that Master Conrad had been less than convincing in his charges. It is all the more noteworthy, since Dietrich II himself had persecuted heretics at Trier and had received papal praise for his efforts. Conrad of Marburg withdrew from the synod, and the chronicler places in his mouth the words: "If he had been convicted, the situation would have been far different!" Indeed, it would have been—the conviction of a high noble such as Count Henry of Sayn might have been the signal for additional charges against others of his class by Conrad of Marburg and his low-born associates. What can be termed the "Conradian era" was over, however. Refusing the protection offered by the king, the master inquisitor left Mainz for Marburg and was brutally murdered within a few days after his defeat before the synod. In February 1234 the count of Sayn was vindicated of all charges against him of heresy.[295]

The July 1233 national synod was thus not the usual type of ecclesiastical assembly. Instead of dealing with general statutes for the ordering of the Church, it was convened for the purpose of treating a single issue. It demonstrated the moderation of some of the German prelates, revealing them as men who were not to be stampeded into mass hysteria over charges brought by a frenzied papal inquisitor. During and immediately after the synod, Archbishop Siegfried of Mainz tried to reason with Conrad of Marburg alone. The archbishops of Trier and Cologne joined him on yet another occasion as he interviewed Conrad, but the man refused to exercise any kind of restraint. Thus, in addition to the report of the synodal

---

[294] *Gesta Trev.* 402: *"Comite autem instantius petente, ut ad finem cause tenderetur, archiepiscopus Treverensis dixit ad comitem precise: 'Dominus meus rex vult, quod causa ista differatur;' et ad populum: 'Denuncio vobis, quod comes Seynensis hinc recedit pro homine catholico et inconvicto.' Et magister Conradus submurmurando ait: 'Si convictus esset, alia ratio esset.'"*

[295] *Gesta Trev.* 402: *"A quo conventu cum magister Conradus, spreto regis et episcopi Moguntini conductu, recederet reversurus in sua, in via interemptus est una cum socio suo Gerardo quodam. . . ."* See also *Ann. Erphord.* 85; Goerz, *MRR* II, Nr. 2105

proceedings at Mainz which the German primate sent to Rome, a second
letter was dispatched a few days later, telling the pope that Conrad's attitude
had become even more rigid and that further complaints against him were
being heard.[296] With the brutal (and apparently un-punished) assassination
of the inquisitor from Marburg, quiet and a sense of great relief returned to
much of Germany.

The only immediate responses to Archbishop Siegfried's command in
1233 to hold diocesan synods were the assemblies recorded at Constanz and
Eichstätt. The former was held under the newly-elected Bishop Henry I and
dealt with a disputed tithe.[297] A further indication that the new prelate
was pro-active with respect to correcting the faults of his clergy can be seen
in the papal indulgence which he received in January 1234: he was given
power to compel the prelates of those churches subject to his jurisdiction to
provide the stipulated procurations to him or his delegated representatives
when they were engaged in a visitation of the diocese, even those some
objected that they had never been required to do so.[298] We may infer
from this letter that the bishop was either in the process of mounting a
visitation, or else he had just completed one which had not been met with
the success and deference he had expected.

Bishop Henry III of Eichstätt, formerly the canon at Würzburg whose
father had assassinated Bishop Conrad of Querfurt in 1202, also distinguished himself in combatting moral lapses and concubinage among his
clergy: on 18 January 1235 Pope Gregory IX granted him the right to
reclaim for his church the houses and property which certain canons and
clergy of his diocese in the higher degrees of consecration had sold to their
housekeepers (*focariis*).[299] The papal letter was in response to an appeal

---

[296] Fink, *Siegfried III.* 58-60; Böhmer-Will, *RAM* II 229, Nr. 103; Idem 233, Nr. 131;
Förg, *Ketzerverfolgung* 82-83; *Chron. Albrici* 931; Ficker, "Einführung der Todestrafe" 219;
Henry Charles Lea, *The Inquisition of the Middle Ages, Its Origin and Operation* (New York,
1954) 340; *Annales Worm.*, *MGH SS* XVII 39f.; *Ann. Erphord.* 85; Pellens, *Dietrich von Wied*
52; Bertheau, "Die Gesta Trevirorum" 71; *Gallia Christiana* XVI 439.

[297] Joseph Vochezer, "Bischof Konrad I. von Konstanz," *ADB* 11 (Leipzig, 1880) 509-511,
notes without references that Henry I was concerned with maintaining order in his church: „.
. . kräftig handhabte er die Kirchenzucht und für ein sittenreinen Clerus war er eifrig bedacht."
Brehm, *Constanzer Synoden* 19, cites the synod mentioned in the forged charter for Weingarten
of 4 October 1236; cf. Ladewig, *Regg. Const.* I, Nr. 1487.

[298] Auvray, *Registres de Gregoire IX* I, Nr. 1722: "*Cum spiritualia seminantibus . . . (1
Cor. 9, 11).*"

[299] Heidingfelder, *Regg. Eichst.* 209, Nr. 688; Auvray, *Registres de Grégoire IX* I 1260,
Nr. 2415. Julius Sax, in his *Die Bischöfe und Reichsfürsten von Eichstätt 745-1806* I
(Landshut, 1884) 98ff., regarded Heinrich III as an outsider to the Eichstätt church and charged
him with moral depravity and concubinage, basing this on the above cited document which
proves just the opposite; cf. Heidingsfelder, *op.cit.* 204. That Henry held a prebend within
the cathedral chapter at Eichstätt is shown by the papal commission given to the bishop of

from the bishop; presumably he had buttressed his initial action on the decrees issued by the cardinal-legate Conrad of Porto in 1225 at the national synod held at Mainz, a copy of which would have been available at Eichstätt.

One of those obligated to attend Mainz provincial synods was Bishop Berthold of Chur who was assassinated on 25 August 1233 near Reuen. That he was a student of canon law may be seen from the fact that just prior to his death he made a grant of three codices to his church, listed simply as *"decreta," "decretales,"* and *"relationes super his."* The item *"decreta"* was probably a copy of Gratian, but the identity of the *"decretales"* has aroused some scholarly debate. Mayer argues that the work in question was that of Gregory IX. Affentranger rejects this as a faulty assumption, however, since the comprehensive collection of papal decretals which Raymond of Peñafort compiled in commission from Gregory IX did not appear until 1234, one year after Bishop Berthold's death.[300] The gift must therefore have been a decretal collection compiled since Gratian—perhaps one of the *Quinque compilationes antiquae*; the *"relationes super his"* were commentaries on Gratian and the decretals, but again otherwise unknown.[301] Unless his interests in canon law were purely academic, however, it is difficult not to conclude that this prelate also held diocesan synods with his clergy, despite the absence of documentary evidence.

According to Aubrey of Trois-Fontaines, Bishop Jean of Liège convened another synod on 28 June 1233 in the cathedral church of St. Lambert, at which time he made a gift of precious stones for its beautification.[302] One wonders whether the canons from St. Adelbert's church in Aachen were happy participants at this synod: the previous year Pope Gregory IX had

---

Würzburg and two other clerics on 3 December 1232, that they investigate the disputed election at Eichstätt between the Bamberg canon Hermann and the Eichstätt canon Henry; cf. Auvray, *op.cit.* I, Nr. 990.

[300] *Necrologium Curiense, Das ist: Die Jahrzeitbücher der Kirche zu Chur*, ed. Wolfgang von Juvalt (Chur, 1867) *ad 25 Aug.*; Mayer, *Geschichte des Bistums Chur* I 235; Affentranger, "Bischöfe von Chur" 160-161; see also Potthast, *Regesta* I, Nr. 9693, 9694 (dated 5 September 1234), in which Pope Gregory IX announces his sending of the *Decretales* to the faculties at Bologna and Paris.

[301] The medieval book lists for the bishopric of Chur offer no clues as to the identity of these three volumes; cf. Paul Lehmann, ed., *Mittelalterliche Bibliothekskataloge Deutschlands und der Schweiz*, Bd. 1: *Die Bistümer Konstanz und Chur* (München, 1918).

[302] *Chron. Albrici* 932-933; Hartzheim, *Concilia* III 542: *"Die Martis post dominicam Trinitatis, quedam mala per fulmen et tonitruum facta sunt, et sequenti die, hoc est feria quarta Kalendis Iunii apud Leodium Iohanne [Apianus] eiusdem civitatis episcopo generalem synodum in ecclesia sancti Lamberti celebranti, presentibus universis totius episcopatus ecclesiarum prelatis, ceciderunt lapides glaciei mire magnitudinis et maxime super predictam ecclesiam; fuerunt qui dicerunt grossitudinem istorum lapidum ad modum ovorum columbarum."*

confirmed a quarter tithe which had been imposed on them thirty years earlier by the papal legate Guy Poré.[303]   Bitter feelings undoubtedly persisted from the time of the legatine visit to Liège in 1230 as well. Whether the statute of 1236 which called for a *commune capitulum* three times yearly at Liège referred to monastic general chapters as prescribed in *c*. 12 of the Lateran IV constitutions, to a gathering of the members of the cathedral chapter, or was a continuation of the archaic usage meaning a synod, cannot be determined.   Synods were regular enough at Liège, however, that in 1240 the proper seating of the abbots of St. Truijen and Gembloux had to be regulated.[304]

Those attending the 1233 synod at Liège would also have been aware of Bishop Jean's efforts to reform various Benedictine houses in his diocese. The abbey of Neumünster at Huy had been established in 1101 by Peter the Hermit who died there in 1115.[305]   About the year 1231 Bishop Jean had ordered a visitation which had resulted in the prescription of corrective measures.   These had been incorrectly revoked, however, and on 10 March 1233 Pope Gregory IX issued a mandate to the dean of St. Maria *ad Gradus* in Cologne, and to the *magistri* W. of the church of the Holy Apostles in Cologne, and W., a canon at St. John in Liège, that they conduct a new visitation.[306]

More notorious was the house at Gembloux which had been visited by several teams of clerics over several years' time.[307]   At length Abbot Henry was removed for incompetence, but his successor John was equally unable to effect changes among the monks.[308]   He therefore went person-

---

[303] Potthast, *Regesta* I, Nr. 8897; Christian Quix, *Geschichte der Stadt Aachen (bis zum Jahre 1350) nach Quellen bearbeitet, mit einem Codex diplomaticus Aquensis* I/2 (Aachen, 1840) 108, Nr. 154.

[304] Hauck, *KGD* IV 8 note 1, places it in 1236, citing Muller, *Cartularium* 177, c. 21; perhaps this is the same as that given in Potthast, *Regesta* I, Nr. 9924, with date of 25 May 1235, citing Ennen, *Quellen* II, Nr. 160.

[305] Cottineau, *Repertoire* II 2059.

[306] Auvray, *Registres de Gregoire IX* I, Nr. 1164.

[307] Auvray, *Registres de Gregoire IX* I, Nr. 1766: ". . . *cum monasterium suum primo per . . . abbatem Floreffiensem, Premonstratensis ordinis, et collegam suum, secundo per fratrem B., ordinis Predicatorum, eiusdem collegam, demum vero per . . . abbatem de Villari, Cisterciensis ordinis, et H., archidiaconum Leodiensem, tam nostra quam dilecti filii nostri O., sancti Nicolai in Carcere Tulliano diaconi cardinalis, tunc Apostolice Sedis legati, et tua [i.e., episcopus] etiam auctoritate fuerit visitatum . . .*"

[308] "*H[enricus], quodam abbas ipsius, cuius malitia prefatum monasterium et aliorum habitantium in eodem erat ad etremam exina[ni]tionem fere perductum, fuisset, iustitia suadente, remotus: monachi ipsius monasterii . . . successorem, prava ponere in directa et aspera in vias planas, et idem monasterium, quod erat temporaliter et spiritualiter deformatum, reformare studentem, adeo affecerunt contumeliis et injuriis oppresserunt, quod coatus est regimen ipsorum relinquere, et ad monasterium de quo assumptus fuerat, remeare; cui dictus*

ally to Rome where he appealed for further help. On 31 January 1234 the pontiff commanded Bishop Jean "*in monasterio Gemblacensi corrigenda et reformanda corrigat et reformet.*" Those who resisted the bishop were to be subjected to ecclesiastical disciplinary measures in the hope that they would do proper penance and return to an obedient mode of conduct; if necessary, however, the incorrigibles were to be turned over to the secular authorities for punishment.

The abbey of St. Laurence was likewise embroiled in difficulties arising from the fact that its abbot "*ad ipsius monasterii regimen non absque vitio symoniace pravitatis assumptus, vitam ducens nimio dissolutam, bona eius dilapidabat enormiter ac in usus illicitos consumebat, . . .*"[309] For that reason complaints had reached the Curia which proceeded to appoint a visitation team which included *magister W* [ ], an archdeacon at Cambrai, and two associates. Their investigation triggered an appeal from the abbot. A second set of papal visitors, including the abbot of Floreffe in the diocese of Liège, resumed the process of correction at the monastery. At length, after many delays and canonical maneuvers, the pope appointed a third delegation on 22 November 1236 (consisting of the cathedral dean and scholastic at Cologne and the scholastic at Xanten) to resolve the matter without further ado.

In 1234 there are only two recorded synods, an apparent provincial one summoned at Mainz and a diocesan assembly at Hildesheim. Bishop Conrad of Hildesheim had been a strong supporter of the Inquisition in Germany led by *magister* Conrad of Marburg, a position which led to his being openly criticized by King Henry at an assembly of German prelates and princes held at Frankfurt-am-Main on 2 February 1234. The leader of the anti-Inquisition sentiment was Archbishop Siegfried III of Mainz who knew how to exploit that feeling in clerical circles. For a discussion of purely ecclesiastical matters, the prelates withdrew to a more suitable location—Mainz, where Siegfried called a synod for 2 April. The results of this synod were unhappy for the Inquisition, as defenders almost lost their lives and the case against the count of Sayn was abandoned.[310]

J. postmodum substitutus, rectitudinis zelo succensus,—circa ipsorum [monachorum] statum spiritualiter et temporaliter corrigendum se multipliciter exhibuit studiosum; sed terra cordis eorum sic ex toto in salsilaginem est conversa, sic malitie gelu constricta, quod nullo imbre doctrine, nullo rore gratie est ad ferendum fructus debitos emollita."

[309] Auvray, *Registres de Gregoire IX* II, Nr. 3379.

[310] *Gesta Trever.* 402: "*Post hec in purificatione sancte Marie factus est iterum conventus et curia sollempnis aput Frankinvort coram rege, 25 circiter episcopis, abbatibus et prioribus diversorum ordinum, prioribus etiam cleri et principibus innumeris congregatis; ubi adducta in medium causa comitis, comite presente, pro fide et innocentia comitis sacramenta presentibus episcopis, prelatis, abbatibus, Maioribus et Minoribus fratribus, clericis et monachis,*

Following the synod, Archbishop Siegfried sent a new report to the pope which contained the decisions reached there: the Inquisition preachers were not to be allowed to use pulpits in any of the German churches; all who had been accused by them were pardoned.[311] Recognizing the loss of support in this matter from Mainz, Gregory IX turned to his trusted agents in Germany, the archbishop of Salzburg, Bishop Conrad of Hildesheim, and the Cistercian abbot of Buch.[312] Given Bishop Conrad's role as a papal agent,[313] it was the cathedral provost at Hildesheim who presided over the diocesan synod held 26 October 1234 at Bockenem. Another document issued at an undated synod of this period may also be a product of this assembly.[314] The charter dated 1232 *in sollempni sinodo* at Hildesheim must be repositioned in 1236 because of the witnesses who are listed.[315] Bishop Conrad's value to the papacy can still be seen in 1238 when Pope Gregory IX gave him the mandate to investigate efforts by the Augustinian canons at Windhausen in the diocese of Halberstadt to reform their house: if he found evidence of failure, he was instructed to dissolve current community and to introduce Cistercian monks.[316]

The Bohemian Church in the 1230s

It is not known to what extent the Bohemian and Moravian bishops of the Mainz province attended synods summoned by their metropolitan. Nor do we have very much testimony of their own synodal efforts. We have suggested above that Bishop Andreas of Prague published the decrees of Lateran IV in 1216, but his forced exile soon thereafter prevented any serious attempt to implement the reform measures of Innocent III. A clear indication that the Lateran constitutions were known in those bishoprics is

---

principibus quoque laicis et baronibus universis, comes gloriossime expurgatus est." See also Fink, *Siegfried III.* 62-64; *Ann. Erphord.* 85-87; *MG SS* XVII 843; *Chron. Albrici.* 931, 932 note 9.

[311] *Chron. Albrici* 931-932.

[312] Hartzheim, *Concilia* III 554-556; Potthast, *Regesta* I, Nrs. 9977, 9978; Rodenberg, *MG Ep. s. XIII* I, Nr. 647; Fink, *Siegfried III.* 64. See also E.L.Th. Hencke, *Konrad von Marburg* (Marburg, 1861) 66, Nr. 69

[313] See the letter of Pope Gregory IX dated 11 October 1234, in which Bishop Conrad of Hildesheim and the Cistercian abbots of Georgental and Eberbach are given the mandate to investigate the miracles attributed to Elizabeth, the deceased landgravine of Thuringia, and to send their report to the Curia; Rodenberg, *MG Ep. s. XIII* I 486, Nr. 599; Potthast, *Regesta* I, Nr. 9721; Auvray, *Registres de Gregoire IX* I, Nr. 2114.

[314] Hauck, *KGD* V 166 note 3; Hoogeweg, *UB Hilds* II, Nrs. 398, 402.

[315] Hoogeweg, *UB Hilds* II, Nr. 347.

[316] Rodenberg, *MG Ep. s. XIII* I, Nr. 739; Auvray, *Registres de Gregoire IX* II, Nr. 4652 (15 December).

seen in the fact that the Benedictines and Premonstratensians refused to convene general chapters every three years as stipulated in *c.* 12. The papacy had periodically ordered visitations to improve ecclesiastical discipline, but realizing that reform must come from within, Gregory IX on 20 April 1234 commissioned the Benedictine abbots of Brevnov and Kladrau, and the Cistercian abbots of Pomuk and Plass in Bohemia, to summon a general chapter of the Black Monks within the course of the year and to repeat this practice annually.[317] The fact that Innocent IV repeated this mandate on 23 January 1246 suggests that it was not received with much enthusiasm. The resistance by the Bohemian canons regular to reform measures is also seen in the fact that the abbot of the Premonstratensians in Prague had to ask for papal assistance against the undiscipline of his monastery.[318]

The registers of Gregory IX are otherwise rather silent with respect to Prague and Olmütz, however. On 22 April 1227 the pontiff granted an indulgence to two canons at Prague who, having ignored the sentence of suspension from their benefices, celebrated the Divine Office.[319] Ten years later Gregory gave permission to Bishop Robert of Olmütz to celebrate the stigmata of St. Francis and others in his church.[320] Whether any sort of diocesan assembly was associated with the introduction of this new service we cannot say. It is consistent with Robert's training as a theologian, however, that he would choose to focus on some supernatural phenomenon as an innovation in the liturgical practices of his church.

The failure of the Benedictine monks in Bohemia to assemble themselves in triennial general chapters was not the least unique to that region of Germany. We have observed above that in Salzburg the regular convening of such meetings was directly tied to the determination of Archbishop Eberhard II. Conversely, the lack of evidence from the province of Cologne may in fact be testimony that the metropolitans there were not committed to the program to the same extent. On 4 May 1235 Pope Gregory IX wrote to the abbot of St. Jacob in Liège and the dean and scholastic of the cathedral chapter at Cologne regarding statutes which had recently been enacted for the reformation of the order of Black Monks throughout the Latin Church.[321] The fifty-four decrees were intended to

---

[317] Dudik, *Prag* 218-219; Erben, *Regesten* I 393, Nr. 836; Potthast, *Regesta* I, Nr. 9450.

[318] Boczek, *CdMor* III 61; cf. abbatial letter of 8 June 1234 in Erben, *Regesten* I, Nr. 839; Potthast, *Regesta* I, Nr. 9468.

[319] Potthast, *Regesta* I, Nr. 7882; Auvray, *Registres de Gregoire IX* I, Nr. 46.

[320] Potthast, *Regesta* II, Nr. 10308; Auvray, *Registres de Gregoire IX* II, Nr. 3598.

[321] Auvray, *Registres de Gregoire IX* II, Nr. 2552. A copy of this same letter was sent to the abbot of St. Mansuy in the diocese of Toul, to prior of Prato (St. Nicholas des Pres, diocese of Verdun), and to *magister* J. de Maderiis, a canon at Verdun. An earlier letter had

assist in the regeneration of the order,[322] though the restriction of notification to French-speaking clerics is somewhat puzzling.

That they were in fact intended for a wider audience may be inferred from the commission given on 25 May 1235 to the above-mentioned abbot of St. Jacob in Liège and his colleagues to ensure that general chapters of the Benedictine abbots and priors in the province of Cologne be celebrated each and every year in a venue well-suited for this purpose.[323] Had general chapters for this ecclesiastical province been held on a regular basis since 1215, problems such as those encountered by the bishop of Liège among the Benedictines of his diocese might have been dealt with before they had become acute.

The presumed new thrust given such assemblies in 1235 perhaps corresponded with a synod which the bishop of Osnabrück convened for his clergy and others in the same year,[324] while a synod at Utrecht in 1236 is the first one recorded since 1230.[325] We may assume that the conduct of the exempt Premonstratensian houses in the latter diocese had had a negative impact upon the Benedictine cloisters and secular clergy as well, and that church discipline would have been an item on the synod-agenda, but we have no corroborating evidence.[326] Equally problematic must have been the indulgence granted to the dean at Utrecht on 15 April 1236 that he be allowed to retain several benefices in contradiction to Church canons.[327]

Inasmuch as it was convened on the traditional day (22 February), we consider the assembly at which the archbishop of Trier confirmed the

---

been sent to the abbots of Derven and St. Dionysius at Rheims, and to *magister* G. de Lauduno, a canon at Rheims; cf. *op.cit.* II, Nr. 2548. The image of the vineyard, which Innocent III used in his summons to the Fourth Lateran Council, is still strongly represented: "*In medio ecclesie vinea Domini sabaoth, videlicet religio Nigro ordinis, quasi Paradisus, Dominus dextera divina plantata, sub primis ordinis patribus laudabiliter pululavit et palmites suos extendit a mari usque ad mare et a flumine usque ad terminos orbis terre; sed nunc, quod non absque amaritudine mentis audivimus et referimus cum dolore, in aliene vitis amaritudinem est conversa. . . .*"

[322] See Auvray, *Registres de Gregoire IX* II, Nr. 2549. The statutes were re-issued in 1237; cf. *op.cit.* II, Nr. 3045.

[323] Potthast, *Regesta* I, Nr. 9924; Ennen, *Quellen* II 162, Nr. 160; Hilpisch, *Geschichte des benediktinischen Mönchtums* 239.

[324] Hauck, *KGD* IV 8; Philippi, *Osnabrück UB* II, Nr. 328

[325] Hauck, *KGD* IV 8; Muller, *Cartularium* 177, c. 21.

[326] Cf. letter of Gregory IX to three Premonstratensian abbots from the dioceses of Utrecht and Cambrai dated 23 June 1232: "*. . . significamus, se ad reformationem eiusdem ordinis et observantiam regularem duxisse statuendum, ut, cum per incuriam aut negligentiam diffinitorum et visitatorum ipsius ordinis excessus excedentium remaneant incorrecti, quolibet anno in generali capitulo diffinitores et visitatores mutentur, novis qui religione praemineant veteribus subrogatis . . .*"

[327] Auvray, *Registres de Gregoire IX* II, Nr. 3104.

election of the new abbot of the Benedictine abbey of Laach in 1235 to have been a diocesan synod, even though Laach, and not Trier or Coblenz, was the venue.[328]   The possibility that diocesan synods often extended over two days allows the conclusion that the celebration at Laach immediately preceded or followed the more traditional meeting at Coblenz.   The authority of the prelate over/against the religious houses of his archdiocese could hardly have been better demonstrated than to have declared the new abbot's synodal obligations, to have consecrated him, and then to have presided over that large assemblage of monastic and secular dignitaries. We may also see the determination of the metropolitan behind a commission which Gregory IX conferred upon Dietrich II and his suffragans on 18 June 1235, directing them to remind all abbesses and nuns of the province who might have allowed a relaxation of monastic discipline that they had specific responsibilities in that regard (of which the pope himself had admonished them in the past); furthermore, that these same conventual leaders were to prevent individuals of questionable character from entering their houses, and that such not be recruited.[329]   Dietrich's concern for the care of souls may also be inferred from the plan announced the following year to create a separate bishopric of Prüm, the execution of which was never carried out.[330]

During January 1235 the papal chancery drafted four letters which dealt with matters pertaining to the archdiocese or province of Mainz, suggesting that in the immediately preceding months actions had been taken by certain prelates.   On 4 January, e.g., papal permission was granted to the bishop of Bamberg to withhold incomes from the benefices of those cathedral canons who failed to maintain the obligation of residence.[331]   The matter had been brought to the attention of the Curia by the bishop himself who

---

[328] Beyer, *MRUB* III, Nr. 498; Goerz, *RET* 39; Wegeler, *Kloster Laach* II 28. On 12 December 1236 the pope directed the archbishop of Trier to accept the resignation of the abbot at Laach because the latter had a *defectus natalium*, being the natural son of a cleric. If, however, the prelate determined that the monastery had been soundly administered in the past, and that the prospects for the future were equally positive, he was authorized to grant a dispensation from the defect and to appoint the former abbot *"propter illius merita"* to the office. See Auvray, *Registres de Gregoire IX* II, Nrs. 3402, 3403.

[329] Vatican Archives—Regesta Gregorii IX, 18 fol. 40', c. 116; Wampach, *UB Luxemburg* II 299, Nr. 278.

[330] Vatican Archives—Regesta Gregorii IX, a. 10, 18 fol. 159', c. 94; Manrique, *Ann. Cist.* IV 526; Potthast, *Regesta* I, Nr. 10170; Auvray, *Registres de Gregoire IX* II, Nr. 2643; Beyer, *MRUB* III 432, Nr. 560; Goerz, *MRR* II 581, Nr. 2224; Marx, *Erzstift Trier* I 233-234; Albert Heintz, *Die Anfänge des Landdekanates im Rahmen der kirchlichen Verfassungsgeschichte des Erzbistums Trier*, Trierer Theologische Studien 3 (Trier, 1951) 9.

[331] Auvray, *Registres de Gregoire IX* I, Nr. 2406.

thus gives us some small indication that between the known synods of 1228 and 1243 efforts were being made to effect reform within his church.

More obvious were the two mandates given to Archbishop Siegfried III on 19 January, authorizing him to grant dispensations to conventuals of his diocese who had gained entrance into their respective houses *"per vitium simoniae,"*[332] and to release from canonical sanctions those clerics within his diocese who had celebrated the Divine Office while suspended or excommunicated.[333]   Yet, even while the pope was strengthening the archbishop's hand in one vital area of administration, he was contributing to the undermining of discipline at Mainz in another: on 17 January 1235 permission was granted to Conrad, the scholastic at Mainz, to acquire additional prebends with an annual income of up to 100 Marks, even those to which the cure of souls was attached.[334]

Pluralist that he was, the scholastic at Mainz was undoubtedly affected by further reform measures which the archbishop of Mainz undertook relating to his cathedral chapter, and which may have been made public at a diocesan synod held ca. 1236/1237. Siegfried probably conducted a visitation of his own archdiocese as well, in part on his own authority and in part with a papal commission. He was assisted in this by the Cistercian abbot of Eberbach and the dean of St. Peter's. We have from this time various ordinances which Siegfried and his colleagues published: e.g., only those clerics present in the city and in the choir should receive the daily distribution of bread; in lifting the requirement of obedience, the canons were only to leave the cathedral enclosure accompanied by a mounted servant; whosoever went against this was to be punished by being prohibited

[332] Auvray, *op.cit.* I, Nr. 2410. Reference is made in the papal letter to the *"statuta generalis concilii."* The constitutions in question are *cc.* 63 (*De simonia*) and 64 (*De eadem circa monachos et sanctimoniales*) of the Fourth Lateranum. The latter is particularly applicable: *"Quoniam simoniaca labes adeo plerasque moniales infecit, ut vix aliquas sine pretio recipiant in sorores, paupertatis praetextu volentes huiusmodi vitium palliare, ne id de caetero fiat, penitus prohibemus, statuentes ut quaecumque de caetero talem pravitatem commiserit, tam recipiens quam recepta, sive sit subdita sive praelata, sine spe restitutionis de suo monasterio expellatur, in locum arctioris regulae, ad agendum perpetuam poenitentiam, retrudenda. . . ."*

[333] Auvray, *op.cit.* I, Nr. 2411.

[334] Auvray, *op.cit.* I, Nr. 2414. Conrad appears in a document of 23 July 1235 as the scholastic at Mainz (Böhmer-Will, *RAM* II 238, Nr. 187), but by 31 July 1236 he had succeeded to the office of dean (Idem. II 243, Nr. 223). He is last mentioned in that office in 1247 (Idem. II 293, Nr. 589). His sudden appearance in 1235 suggests that he may be identical with the Conrad who is documented as provost of St. Maria in Erfurt from 1 August 1221 (Dobenecker, *CdThur* II, Nrs. 1967, 2377).

from office, incomes, and administrating, until he reconciled himself with the chapter.[335]

He also gave specific instructions regarding clothing and demeanor. Important was the statute that no prelate was to hold more than one office, drawing on *cc*. 15, 16, and 29 of the Lateran IV decrees, yet those fortunate enough to have obtained a papal dispensation could obviously ignore this restriction. We have noted above that in 1232/1233 the archbishop had attempted to hold even the archdeacons to the obligation of residence, but that this measure proved ineffectual. By 1236/1237 he had conceded that they must be allowed great latitude in the carrying out of their administrative responsibilities. It had thus become necessary to appoint several vicars who performed the duties in the choir etc. In order that the cathedral chapter might have sufficient resources to support these archidiaconal substitutes, Siegfried also incorporated the church at Nordenstadt and the chapel of St. Lambert in the vineyard before the city into the cathedral chapter.[336] In this we may also see the implementation of *c*. 32 of the Council's decrees. Several years later (31 December 1241) he also granted income to the cathedral chapter to enable it to increase the number of prebends. Nevertheless, the biographer of Siegfried III of Eppstein notes that his relationship with the higher clergy of his church was painful.[337] Despite his pronouncements, there is no record of disciplinary punishments against his own canons.

On 19/20 February 1237 Siegfried's uncle, Archbishop Dietrich of Trier, announced from Coblenz the grant of lands to the monastery at Rommersdorf. Three days later he was present at Heidelberg on 22 February as the count Palatine of the Rhine enfeoffed the dynasts of Isenburg with the comital lands and title of Wied.[338] Either or both of these assemblies may have been part of a diocesan synod, inasmuch as they fell near or directly

---

[335] Böhmer-Will, *RAM* II 244, Nr. 225 ("*cum ordinate potestate, cum delegata nobis sede apostolica*"); Karl Georg Bockenheimer, *Der Dom zu Mainz* (Mainz, 1879) 67; Fink, *Siegfried III*. 75. On 28 September 1238 Pope Gregory IX granted a license to Arnold, a canon at St. Maria *ad Gradus* in Mainz to study canon and civil law outside the city for a period of three years. This privilege enabled Arnold to receive the ecclesiastical stipend during that time, with the exception of the *distributiones* which were reserved for those who maintained residence. Given the responsibility for administering this arrangement were the dean and *thesaurius* of St. Peter's and *W. de Echeburu*, a cathedral canon; see Rodenberg, *MG Ep. s. XIII* I, Nr. 732.

[336] Gudenus, *CdMogunt* II 769; Böhmer-Will, *RAM* II 244, Nr. 224. There is evidence of the *vita communis* at Mainz in a document of 6 December 1238; cf. Böhmer-Will, *op.cit*. II 252, Nr. 308, which records an indulgence granted to two cathedral canons at Mainz by the archbishop, releasing them from the obligations of presence and residence in return for a yearly payment of five Marks each to be used to acquire decorative articles for the cathedral.

[337] Fink, *Siegfried III*. 76-77.

[338] Lacomblet, *NRUB* II 111; Beyer, *MRUB* III, Nrs. 552, 584; Goerz, *RET* 40.

on that day which traditionally had been reserved for such occasions. The Heidelberg assembly must have been somewhat emotional, for the archbishop's once proud comital family had now come to the end of the male line and the *Grafschaft* Wied was passing into the hands of his sister's husband's family, the up-and-coming lords of Isenburg. It was the son of that marriage—Arnold of Isenburg—who succeeded Dietrich of Wied as archbishop of Trier in 1242.

Siegfried's suffragan, Bishop Hermann of Würzburg conducted a visitation during 1237/1238, as a result of which the Benedictine nuns' cloister at Billigheim (*Billikem*) had asked him to prescribe reforms. His solution was to introduce into the house Cistercian nuns, a practice used by many of his contemporaries in their efforts to break the pattern of decay found in so many traditional nunneries of the day.[339] He retained full rights to supervise and discipline the cloister in the future, however, rather than allowing it to claim exempt status.[340] A similar situation existed within the diocese of Speyer where efforts by the abbot of Odenheim had failed to correct the abuses of the Benedictine monks at that house. Either a request from the abbot or from the diocesan bishop resulted in the mandate given by Pope Gregory IX on 27 January 1238 to Bishop Conrad, authorizing him to reform the monastery "*in spiritualibus et in temporalibus.*"[341]

A sixteenth-century fragment preserved at the Landeshauptarchiv in Schwerin reveals that in 1238 Archbishop Gerhard of Bremen, together with the approval and support of Bishop-elect Frederick of Schwerin, issued regulations for two newly-created prebends in the Schwerin cathedral chapter.[342] The nature of this act suggests that it was done at a synod, although the location of that assembly, and whether it was diocesan or provincial, cannot be determined. Despite various papal directives in the early 1230s regarding the Stedinger, there is no record that synods had been held at Bremen since that of 1230 under the direction of Cardinal-legate Otto.[343] Associated with the synod of 1238 was the visitation of bishop-

---

[339] Ussermann, *Episcopatus Wirc.* 59-60, Nr. 64; Hauck, *KGD* IV 1000; Cottineau, *Repertoire* I 381; Cheney, *Episcopal Visitations* 40.

[340] ". . . *[plenarie retinentes] eiusdem loci iurisdictionem et dominium tam in temporalibus quam in spiritualibus . . . Salva in omnibus Cisterciensis Ordinis disciplina.*"

[341] Auvray, *Registres de Gregoire IX* II, Nr. 4067.

[342] *Mecklenburg UB* I 483-484, Nr. 487; May, *REB* I, Nr. 934. Cf. also the related documents in *Mecklenburg UB* I, Nrs. 486, 494.

[343] Cf. Potthast, *Regesta* I, Nrs. 9030, 9042, 9076, 9236; Rodenberg, *MG Ep. s. XIII* I, Nrs. 489, 539; Auvray, *Registres de Gregoire IX* I, Nr. 940. See also *Ann. Stad.* (*a. 1230*) 361: "*Bremensis archiepiscopus Stedingorum insolentium repressurus, die natalis Domini valido eos bello aggreditur, ibique frater eius Hermannus, dominus de Lippia, vir utique sapiens et illustris, solus occiditur. Unde subita confusione facta, totus ille bellicus apparatus*

rics by *visitatores a domino archiepiscopo*,[344] the first record of such since those conducted under the mandate from Cardinal-legate Otto in 1230/1231.

Albert of Stade—A Proponent of Reform

Contemporaneous to these events was Abbot Albert of Stade, a man whose use of the *magister* title between 1217 and 1224 suggests that he had acquired advanced training at some school.[345]   As a cathedral canon at Bremen and provost of the collegiate church at Ramesloh, he apparently acquired sufficient reputation that in August 1232 he was chosen by the brothers of the Benedictine convent of St. Mary at Stade to become their new abbot.[346]   Rather than receiving consecration from the archbishop of Bremen as his predecessors had done, however, Albert was given the abbatial blessing by the Cistercian monk, Baldwin of Aulne, who had just been appointed as bishop and papal legate in the mission diocese of Livonia, and was passing through northern Germany *en route* to his new post.   This exclusion of the metropolitan of Bremen and apparent preference for a Cistercian has given modern scholars to speculate whether Albert was already disillusioned with Archbishop Gerhard II.[347]

In his *Annales Stadenses*, written after 1240, Albert states unequivocally that in that same year he resigned his office at Stade and became a Minorite because of the complete lack of discipline in his house and of his inability to effect reform there.   This struggle probably began at the time of his becoming abbot in 1232, since which he had watched with great concern the loosening of the Benedictine Rule among his monks.   He undoubtedly thought of *c*. 58 in the Rule where it states that he who is commanded to follow, and does not, will be damned by that very God whom he has ridiculed.   Fearing such a consequence for his convent, Albert travelled to Rome in 1236 where he attempted to persuade Pope Gregory IX to place Stade under the Rule and Order of the Cistercians.   The pontiff responded by sending a letter to Archbishop Gerhard of Bremen, informing him of the

---

dissolvitur"; (a. 1233) 361: "Crux contra Stedingos ubique auctoritate apostolica praedicatur, et a multis accipitur. . . ."; (a. 1234) 361: "Heinricus dux Brabantiae et Florentius comes Hollandiae, Bremae existentes, contra Stedingos viriliter se accinxerunt, tamquam contra inimicos manifestos ecclesiae.   Nam sicut probatum est super eos, et per Mindensem, Lubicensem, Raceburgensem episcopos papae auribus intimatum, ipsi doctrina matris ecclesiae penitus vilipensa, . . ."

[344] Hauck, *KGD* IV 20, citing *Schlesw.-Holst. Reg.* I 255, Nr. 570; see also Hauck, *op.cit.* V 150.

[345] Lappenberg, *Hamb. UB* I 359, 418.

[346] *Ann. Stad. (1232)* 361; Karl Fiehn, "Albertus Stadensis," *Historische Vierteljahrschrift* 26 (1931) 536-572, espec. 537-538.

[347] Cf. Fiehn, "Albertus Stadensis" 541.

request, and warning him that if the monastery did not reform itself in accordance with the Rule of St. Benedict, it would in fact be placed under control of the White Monks: those Benedictines at Stade who were resistant to a major reform were to be transferred to some other house of their same Order, while against those who were completely out of control disciplinary measures should be taken.[348]

The archbishop appears to have taken the papal charge seriously, for on 21 July 1237 he announced that the following day Abbot Albert and the entire convent were to appear before him at his chapel in Stade. Rather than take a hard line at the assembly, however, the prelate was content with having the papal bull read aloud and then adding the admonition that the monks should reform their house to conform with the expectations of the Rule, or else he would have to see to the execution of the pope's alternative solution. Thus, Abbot Albert found himself in the unhappy position of having to combat the evils of his house without any real backing from either Rome or Bremen. One wonders to what extent the synod and visitations of 1238 addressed themselves to the issues raised by Albert.

Unhappily, the Benedictines of Stade, like many of their contemporaries elsewhere in Germany, rejected both the command to live according to the precepts of their founder and the Cistercian model which would have provided a more regulated life for them while (in theory) it also elevated their efforts to a higher plane of devotion and service.[349] The deeply entrenched attitudes resisted any efforts to alter the status quo. Albert waited three years to see some sign of improvement, at the same time keeping the archbishop apprised of the situation. Neither the prelate nor the cathedral chapter at Bremen appear to have taken the abbot's concerns seriously, however. At last, Albert abandoned his office and his house, rather than give up his vision of a more disciplined religious life.[350]

Apart from his own personal account, Albert's annals offer few details concerning the inner life of the ecclesiastical province of Bremen: at best they record the succession of suffragan bishops.[351] The most interesting

---

[348] May, REB I 251, Nr. 912; Potthast, Regesta I, Nr. 10328; cited in Ann. Stad. 366.

[349] Cf. Hauck, KGD IV 347f.

[350] Fiehn, "Albertus Stadensis" 542-543.

[351] E.g., Ann. Stad. (a. 1228) 360: "Heinricus Raceburgensis episcopus obiit, cui Lambertus, Bremensis canonicus et Hammaburgensis, successit. Hic unam missam die assumtionis beatae Mariae celebravit, et unum cimiterium dedicavit, et eodem anno obiit. Cui Godescalcus, eiusdem ecclesiae praepositus, successit"; (a. 1230) 361: "Bertoldus Lubicensis obiit, cui eiusdem ecclesiae decanus Iohannes successit"; (a. 1235) 362: "Godescalcus Raceburgensis episcopus obiit. Cui Petrus, eiusdem ecclesiae praepositus, successit"; (a. 1236) 363: "Petrus Raceburgensis episcopus moritur, cui Ludolfus, eiusdem ecclesiae camerarius, subrogatur"; (a. 1237) 363: "Brunwardus Zwerinensis episcopus obiit, cui Fridericus, antiqui Gunzelini filius, successit."

thing he had to report concerned a priest in Bremen named Marquard who surreptitiously entered the archbishop's residence and removed some items which he then burned; upon his capture, he was suspended from office.[352]

The Reform Decrees of Trier—1238

On 23 May 1238 Archbishop Dietrich II of Trier issued a charter of confirmation to the cloister at Machern regarding the grant of the rights of patronage at Kesten from the *ministeriales* Frederick *de Ponte* and his two nephews.[353] Among the obligations stipulated for the priest at Kesten was that he attend synods along with other pastors of the diocese,[354] an indication that the archbishop was still in the habit of holding regular annual assemblies with his diocesan clergy. That same prelate likewise maintained the provincial synodal tradition. On 21 September 1238 he presided over an assembly in the cathedral church at Trier which was attended by the suffragan bishops of Verdun, Metz, and Toul. The assembly published forty-five canons and placed strong censures and penalties on both laymen and clerics who failed to comply with the decrees of the prelates.[355] The first six articles were addressed primarily to laymen and dealt with such problems as the burning and robbing of cloisters and churches, persecuting priests, and disregarding ecclesiastical censures. The arsonists were to be declared excommunicate by all conventual churches, by the parish clergy, and by the monks and nuns (*c.* 1). Those caught robbing churches (*c.* 2) or receiving items stolen from them (*c.* 3) were to be given time to make proper restitution, after which they were to be declared excommunicate. In all these instances, only the pope could restore the offenders to full fellowship in the Church.

---

[352] *Ann. Stad. (a. 1238)* 363.

[353] Beyer, *MRUB* III 475, Nr. 621.

[354] "*Que videlicet persona ad presentationem dominarum instituenda ternebitur ad omnia quantum ad synodi et capitulorum frequentationem et iurium aliorum exhibitionem nobis et successoribus nostris necnon et loci archidiaconis debitorum, ad que tenentur pastores ceterarum parochialium nostre dyocesis ecclesiarum.*"

[355] Martène, *Thesaur. nov. Anecdot.* IV 183-184, published the first nine canons "*ex MS eccles. Mettensis.*" Later, Martène found a complete set in a MS of St. Victor which he published in *Collectio* VII 126. Hartzheim, *Concilia* III 558, appears to have had a different codex for his edition of the statutes: while he does not note the source, his chapter divisions are completely different from Martène's, and there are some variations in wording, especially at the beginning. Like Hartzheim, Mansi, *Collectio* Tom. II Suppl. Concil. 977, distinguishes between the council mentioned in the *Gesta Trev.* (1231) and that of 1238. Binterim, *Concilien* IV 401-403, disagrees, while Heydenreich, *Metropolitangewalt* 108-109, and Hauck, *KGD* V 140 note 2, see them as two distinct assemblies.

The continual struggle against clerical lapses was also evident. The clergy was forbidden to frequent taverns (*c.* 14, based on *c.* 16 of Lateran IV) or to play dice or games of chance (*c.* 20, also based on *c.* 16 of Lateran IV). Strictures were also given against those members of the secular clergy and orders who lapsed into carnal sin: clerics were to be refused ordination in the Church, participation in elections, and be made to appear before the archiepiscopal curia to answer charges brought by their ordinary (*cc.* 17, 18); monks or nuns were to be excluded from having a voice in chapter affairs and from any ordination within or outside their chapter (*cc.* 38, 39). The success of Archbishop Dietrich's reform of the diocesan clergy from 1215 onward through the re-institution of the *mensa communis* is also reflected in *c.* 29 which ordained that "Since, according to the Apostle, he who does not work shall not eat, we enjoin the prelates of the conventual churches that they compel their subordinates to a frequentation of the choir and to residency by means of withholding the benefices which they hold." It is clear from this statute that the common table had been unsuccessful as a tool for enforcing residence and presence requirements among the clergy.

Nor had the actions taken against heretical activity in 1231 been totally effective. All archdeacons, pastors, vicars, clerics, and laymen within the ecclesiastical jurisdiction of Trier were commanded to make known to the archbishop not only the names of the "*doctores huius sceleris,*" but also the "*auditores, receptores, fautores, et alii qui eos non accusant cum sciunt*" (*c.* 31). The problems involved in presiding over such a large flock as the archbishopric of Trier undoubtedly required a great deal of time and effort on the part of the shepherd. Unlike many German dioceses, Trier had few archdeacons, so that the area which each of them must superintend was also significant. And yet, those upon whom the archbishop relied were at times his opponents. In *c.* 36 it was declared that archdeacons were subject to episcopal jurisdiction, an indication that these dignitaries were already asserting their independence in an ever-increasing fashion. The immediate cause of their disobedience was the archbishop's *officialis*, an administrative extension of the prelate whose jurisdiction the archdeacons rejected.[356] *C.* 35 also sought to restore *publica poenitentia* as a means of curbing abuses such as the selling of remission from penance time at the end of confession. Indirectly, this statute may be an indication that *c.* 21 of Lateran IV (*Utriusque sexus*) was also being implemented within the province of Trier.[357]

---

[356] Hubert Bastgen, "Die Entstehungsgeschichte der trierer Archidiakonate," *Trierisches Archiv* 10 (1907) 23; Michel, *Gerichtsbarkeit und Verwaltung* 19; Pellens, *Dietrich von Wied* 44.

[357] Hauck, *KGD* IV 51 note 2; V 365-366.

The Trier statutes of 1238 are in many ways similar in content to the 1231 Trier and 1233 Mainz decrees. They form the basis upon which later synodal legislation at Trier built: in 1310, e.g., a provincial synod (c. 30) made reference to c. 45 of the 1238 synod, noting that *"propter multas abusiones annus gratiae fuerit alias revocatis."* Canons 43 and 44 of the 1238 synod deal with counterfeiters and excommunicates, repeating in part the prohibitions of 1231 and indicating that these were still matters of concern.[358] While serving those synods which came later, the 1238 synod also drew on earlier ones. As noted earlier, there are four references to legislation which was enacted prior to 1238.[359] Kentenich observes that the text of the 1238 statutes, as well as other records of juridical acts from the pontificate of Archbishop Dietrich II, reveal a remarkable familiarity with contemporary canon law, both in terms of their style and in their disposition.[360]

On 11 May 1239 Archbishop Dietrich of Trier declared *"quod licet in concilio nostro statuerimus Trevirensi"* the parishioners of Alflen who ordinarily attended services at the chapel at Grevenich were obligated to attend the mother church on the feasts of All Saints and Pentecost.[361] Although the privilege itself was one which could have been granted at a diocesan synod, the use of the term *concilium*, which does not appear as a synonym for *synodus generalis* or diocesan synod in any other Trier documents, supports the conclusion that this decision was made at a provincial synod—presumably that of 21 September the previous year. A more immediate possibility exists, however. On 20 March 1239 at Metz, Bishop-elect Jacques de Lorraine received episcopal consecration under the hands of Archbishop Dietrich, Bishop Roger of Toul and Bishop Rudolf of Verdun.[362] Just prior to this, Jacques had been one of sixty-six clerics who had received consecration as priests in the church of St. Matthias at Trier from Bishop Roger.[363] In short, for a period of several days during

---

[358] Binterim, *Concilien* IV 401-402.

[359] See above, pp. 240-241.

[360] Gottfried Kentenich, *Beschreibendes Verzeichnis der Handschriften der Stadtbibliothek zu Trier*, vol. 9: Die Juristischen Handschriften (Trier, 1919) viii.

[361] Goerz, *RET* 42; Idem., *MRR* III 27, Nr. 117; Beyer, *MRUB* III, Nr. 651.

[362] Heydenreich, *Metropolitangewalt* 57-58; Morret, *Stand und Herkunft* 34; Pixton, "Dietrich of Trier" (1972) 129. On Jacob of Lorraine as a not-unusual example of a German cleric who amassed prebends despite the prohibitions of Lateran IV, see Pfaff, "Domkapitel und Papsttum" 48; P.E. Guillaume, *Histoire diocésaine de Toul et Nancy* (1866) I 472f.; H. Thibaut de Monsabert & A. Haefeli, "Les Evêques de Metz," *Annales Soc. hist. archéol. Lorraine* 61 (1962) 3f.

[363] The *Notae stabulenses, MGH SS* XXIV 32, give the date as 26 Mar 1239 (the eve of Easter); either this date or that of the episcopal consecration appears to be in error. See Goerz, *MRR* III, Nr. 111a.

mid- to late-March 1239 a series of highly ceremonial ecclesiastical events brought together all the prelates of the province of Trier. It would thus not be inconsistent with circumstances observed in connection with other provinces to conclude that a provincial synod was held either at Trier or at Metz at this time.

Goerz includes (with date ca. 1240) in his register of documents relating to Trier an undated notice that the abbots of the Benedictine monasteries of St. Matthias and St. Evre in the dioceses of Trier and Toul respectively had published statutes which they and their Cistercian brethren, the abbots of Himmerode and Weiskirchen, had presented for adoption at the general chapter held at Trier.[364] If the pattern of triennial general chapters stipulated by Lateran IV was maintained through the end of the fourth decade of the thirteenth century, the probable year for this particular gathering was 1239, making this a complement to the provincial synod posited for that same year.

The Mainz Synod of 1239

Commencing on 2 July 1239, Archbishop Siegfried III of Mainz also held a synod, but of a far more dazzling nature than that of his uncle at Trier. Present were the bishops of Strasbourg, Würzburg, Eichstätt, Worms, Speyer, Paderborn, Verden, Havelberg, and Ratzeburg. With the exception of the latter two, all were suffragans of Mainz, allowing the conclusion that this was a provincial synod. Bishop Conrad of Hildesheim excused himself in a letter to the metropolitan, claiming that *"venire non possumus infirmitate detenti . . ."*[365] The occasion was probably the consecration of the cathedral which took place on the third day.[366] This project had

---

[364] Goerz, *MRR* III 45, Nr. 199; Bertholet, *Hist. de Luxembourg* V 17; Alphonse Guillaume Ghislain Wauters, *Table chronologique des chartres et diplômes imprimées concernant l'histoire de la Belgique, mise en ordre et publiée sous la direction de la Commission royale d'histoire* (Bruxelles, 1866f.) IV 343.

[365] *Ann. Erphord.* 97: *"Hoc anno VI. Nonas Iulii civitate Moguntina celebratum est concilium, presidente Conrado rege, imperatoris filio, ac eiusdem sedis archiepiscopo cum IX [fere] ceteris episcopis."* The request from Bishop Conrad of Hildesheim is printed in Hoogeweg, *UB Hilds* II, 259, Nr. 532. Hartzheim, *Concilia* III 568-569, prints the summons, the request for an excuse by Hildesheim, the statutes, and the consecration of the cathedral. See also Mansi, *Collectio* XXII, cc. 511-512; the *Liber pontificalis eccles. Eistetensis* printed in Gudenus, *CdMogunt* I 575; the *Liber sacristiae* in Joannis, *Regg. Mag.* I 599; Fink, *Siegfried III.* 46; Hauck, *KGD* IV 827; Riedel, *CdBrand* II 446, Nr. 12. That King Henry was not there has been proved by Julius Ficker, "Erörterungen zur Reichsgeschichte des 13. Jahrhunderts, II: Die Provinzialkonzilien zu Mainz 1239 und 1243," *MIÖG* 3 (1882) 347-349. Binterim, *Concilien* IV 375 says that the archbishop recognized this as the first such synod.

[366] The consecration was the *Moguntinensis ecclesia* according to the *Ann. Mogunt.*, *MGH*

taken almost fifty years since the great fire of 1190 had reduced the previous structure to a shell. Archbishop Siegfried himself had taken concern to aid in its rebuilding and had dispensed an indulgence to help finance it. He also gave the money from the sale of two houses to help replace the windows.[367]

The synod dealt with several issues, among them the decision not to publish the ban of excommunication which had been pronounced against Frederick II by the pope; a letter explaining this position was sent to the pontiff at the conclusion of the synod.[368] A conflict between the bishop of Eichstätt and his *ministeriales* and burghers was also resolved.[369] The occasion of the consecration of the Mainz cathedral served as an ideal opportunity for eight of the bishops to publish a letter offering an indulgence of forty days to those who gave financial assistance to the rebuilding of the cathedral at Halberstadt.[370] The summons to the synod had indicated that matters of church reform were also to be considered. To this end, the decrees of 1233 were reformulated and expanded, establishing thereby a core of synodal statutes which served later assemblies as well.[371]

Archbishop Siegfried III also became involved in the affairs of the bishopric of Olmütz. Late in 1239, Bishop Robert asked permission to

---

SS XVII 2, the *maior ecclesia Moguntina* according to the *Sakristeibuch* in Guden, *CdMogunt.* I 527. See further, Böhmer-Will, *RAM* II 256, Nr. 334; Friedrich Schneider, *Der Dom zu Mainz. Geschichte und Beschreibung des Baues und seiner Wiederherstellung* (Berlin, 1886) col. 26f.

[367] Ficker, "Eröterungen" 348.

[368] Hauck, *KGD* IV 827.

[369] *Ann. Erphord.* 97: "*In quo scilicet concilio episcopus Eistatensis querelando miserabiles exhibuit litteras, in quibus continebatur, quomodo sui ministeriales ac cives Eistetenses iam fere per annum pertinaciter in excommunicatione manentes diabolica atque heretica presumptione ac perversione ipsum episcopum cum clero sibi favente crudeliter expellendo abiecissent et laicas personas in episcopum ac prepositum et decanum elegissent ac eiusdem matricis ecclesie sacristiam infringendo spoliaverint, quomodo etiam ipsorum errorem magnates ac potentiores quidam de terra foventes perniciose in malicia confortaverint; ac qualiter suos fautores, si decesserint, cum musicis instrumentis ad sepulturam conducendo letanter sepeliant.*" See also Heidingsfelder, *Regg. Eichst.* 216-217, Nr. 706, who offers conjectures regarding both the causes and the outcome of this dispute. One possible grievance of the *ministeriales* was the recent reduction in the number of canonates in the cathedral church from fifty to thirty, an action which they regarded as particularly prejudicial to members of their class; cf. Heidingsfelder, *op.cit.* Nrs. 676, 677.

[370] Schmidt, *UB Halb* II 19, Nr. 684; Riedel, *CdBrand* I/2 446; Heidingsfelder, *Regg. Eichst.* 217, Nr. 707.

[371] Hauck, *KGD* V 144-147 note 2 and note 3; Idem., *Abhandlungen* 84-86. Hauck, op.cit. V 134, argues that the decrees of 1154 served as models for a long time, and that still in the thirteenth century they were referred to as the "old statutes of Mainz"—e.g., the Mainz synod of 1239 (= 1261 c. 11): "*antiquum statutum moguntini concili.*" *Cc.* 1-25 of 1261 are taken from 1239 set of statutes.

resign as the prelate of Moravia, giving as the cause his age. On 17 January 1240 the Gregory IX established a commission with power to receive the resignation in the name of the pope.[372] There was already strong evidence of disorder in the cathedral chapter; for this reason Archbishop Siegfried had ordered a visitation of the entire diocese in late November/early December 1239. As a result of this archiepiscopal inquiry, Dean John and the Olmütz cathedral chapter were excommunicated and suspended from office. In a letter to the pope, Siegfried blamed the entire situation on the bishop whom he had admonished several times. Robert's resignation was thus not entirely voluntary.[373] Administration of the see was assumed by Papal-legate Albert Behaim, the previously-mentioned cathedral canon at Passau and a Czech by birth.

Despite the fact that the Olmütz cathedral chapter could not legally hold a new election because they had been excommunicated by the archbishop soon after the general-visitation, they nevertheless met and elected their con-canon, *magister* William, archdeacon of Prerau, to be the new bishop. William was a member of the Czech nobility, well-educated and disciplined; moreover, he had probably been a notary of the Bohemian king Wenceslas I. The archbishop protested the irregularity of the election, and when the three-month deadline had passed without William's request for archiepis-copal confirmation, Siegfried of Mainz, with the king's prior knowledge, designated Conrad of Friedberg, a cathedral canon at Hildesheim, to be bishop. Conrad was consecrated with the approval of the Emperor Frederick II.

It was now the cathedral chapter's turn to protest, but their rejection of Bishop Conrad was short-lived as the new prelate quickly suppressed their revolt and took control of his episcopal city. The Olmütz canons thereupon turned to the Curia, which commanded the cathedral chapter at Breslau to investigate the matter.[374] Bishop-elect Conrad was also directed to appear personally in Rome, a summons which he refused to obey.[375] Given the uncertain loyalties of the king, Gregory IX allowed the entire process to be prolonged, and the extended vacancy in the papal office which followed the death of Gregory only compounded the problem. At the First Council of

---

[372] Friedrich, *CdBoh* III 302, Nr. 225; Boczek, *CdMor* II 364; Dudik, *Geschichte Mährens* 272-273; *Bistum Olmütz* 41-42.

[373] Cf. letter of Pope Innocent IV, dated 11 September 1243, in which he explains the problems at Olmütz to Bishop Nicholas of Prague, the abbot of Brno, and the dean of Prague: Erben, *Regesten* I 515, Nr. 1032; Boczek, *CdMor* III 29, Nr. 43; Potthast, *Regesta* II, Nr. 11129; Rodenberg, *MG Ep. s. XIII* II, Nr. 21; Dudik, *Geschichte Mährens* 272-273; Fink, *Siegfried III.* 77-78; *Bistum Olmütz* 41.

[374] Friedrich, *CdBoh* IV 58-59, Nr. 3.

[375] Dudik, *Geschichte Mährens* 276-277, 341-342.

Lyons in 1245 Conrad was declared deposed.[376] Opposition notwithstanding, Bishop Conrad convened a diocesan synod on 20 March 1243.[377]

Conrad of Friedberg had been accustomed to regular synods held under the direction of a watchful shepherd at Hildesheim. Despite his earlier request to be excused from the July 1239 synod at Mainz on account of poor health, Bishop Conrad of Hildesheim convened his own diocesan assembly on 20 September of that same year.[378]   In the neighboring diocese of Halberstadt the eleven-year hiatus continued, however. Bishop Ludolf had been elected following the death of Frederick II of Kirchberg in early May 1236, received consecration almost a year later, and spent the greater portion of his five-year pontificate in a power struggle with the margraves of Brandenburg.[379]   The cure of souls thus took a back seat to territorial politics. Not until 1260 do we find record of another diocesan synod.[380]

When one looks at the larger picture of synodal activity and related diocesan visitations, certain patterns appear. Just as not all monasteries and/or cloisters within a given diocese required simultaneous attention, so too not all dioceses were disturbed to the same degree by major or minor political events. There seems to be some correlation between the resumption of pastoral activity in one diocese and the appearance of similar evidence from a neighboring see as well. Thus, at the very time when the bishop of Hildesheim was exhibiting concern for his flock, Bishop Engelhard of Naumburg undertook a reformation or visitation of the monasteries in his diocese. The impetus came from the pope and the archbishop,[381] and the primary concerns seem to have focused on the proper discharge of clerical obligations, in this instance the choir service and the celebration of the Mass. Whether a synod was associated with this visitation is unknown, yet the findings of the bishop's investigation must surely have been announced to his diocesan clergy, together with the remedies prescribed.

---

[376] Cf. *Bistum Olmütz* 42-43; Frind, *Kirchengeschichte von Böhmen* 31.

[377] Friedrich, *CdBoh* IV 88-89, Nr. 18 ("*Actum in sinodo nostra in Puztemir*").

[378] Hoogeweg, *UB Hilds* II, Nr. 535 ("*synodo generali*"); Hauck, *KGD* V 169 note 1.

[379] Fuchs, *Besetzung* 95-96, 138-139.

[380] Schmidt, *UB Halb* II, Nr. 604.

[381] Hartzheim, *Concilia* III 569, citing *Paulus Langius in Chronico Citizensis ad a. 1239 apud Pistorium*: "*Eodem tempore, anno videlicet Domini 1239 Engelhardus Episc. noster ex mandato summi pontificis, et archi-episcopi nostri Alberti, fecit reformantionem sive institutionem novam suae dioecesis Monasteriorum et praecipue in cantu et celebratione divini cultus, et hoc propter abusiones, quae in ecclesiis inoleverant, multas confecitque desuper privilegium, quod ita incipit.*" The commission from the archbishop, dated 6 September 1239, is in Mülverstedt, *RAMagd* II 508, Nr. 1111. See also Cheney, *Episcopal Visitations* 29.

The Consequences of the Political Shift 1238-1239

The growing pre-occupation of some German prelates in 1238 and 1239 with political matters was symptomatic of the dramatic shift which had occurred. Despite several major disputes between the emperor Frederick II and the papacy since 1215, Germany had not been torn apart by papal-imperial conflicts to any degree comparable to the aftermath of the double-election of 1198 and the involvement of Innocent III in the political affairs of the Empire. Discipline and order all but disappeared in the German church, precipitated or compounded by the schismatic elections at Liège, Mainz, Cologne, Bremen, and elsewhere. Papal commands concerning political partisanship often pitted clergy against their prelates and made a shambles of normal church life. Monasteries became targets of lay depredations, churches failed to fulfill the essential tasks of the Divine Office, care of souls and exemplary Christian living. Only in the relative peace which came to prevail 1216-1218 with the disappearance of Welf opposition to a Staufen monarchy was there opportunity to effect significant changes within the structure and behavior of the German church. But the efforts which many German prelates had put forth to correct the deleterious effects of the civil war were dashed on the rocks of the renewed papal-imperial conflict during the late 1230s.[382]

To help combat Frederick II, Pope Gregory IX attempted to assert papal influence over every possible election to high ecclesiastical office. The *Chronicon Augustensis* noted that

> *Electiones episcoporum, personarum et aliarum dignitatum tunc a sede apostolica et legatus ejus taliter sunt suspensae, ut contra voluntatem eligentium is vel ille praeficeretur in qualibet dignitate, qui vel cuius amici tunc videbantur sedi apostolicae plus favere.*[383]

Those clerics loyal to the pope were in turn persecuted by the emperor. The evil times had returned. It is thus not surprising that the number of synods convened between 1240 and 1245 was appreciably smaller than for a similar period of time previously.

---

[382] Cf. *Chron. reg. Colon., cont. IV (a. 1238)* 272: "*Per idem tempus infra quadragesimam in Coloniensi, Trevirensi et Moguntinina provinciis et maxime in diocesi Leodiensi plurime guerre emergunt, propter quas incursus bellorum, depredationes et incendia multa fiunt. In fine eiusdem quadragesime obiit domnus Henricus Coloniensis archiepiscopus.*"

[383] Binterim, *Concilien* IV 280, citing Freherus, *Chron. Augustens.* I 520.

The Episcopal Schism at Liège—1238

In Ch. Two we examined in detail the impact which the schismatic imperial election of 1198 had upon the church at Liège. The consequences of partisan politics were felt in that diocese for years to come, necessitating visits by papal legates and a vigorous synodal activity by her bishops. Unhappily, Liège was particularly affected by the increased tension between the papacy and the Hohenstaufen rulers after 1238 as well. Bishop Jean II (d'Eppes) died in May of that year during the siege of the town of Poilevache.[384] His diocese had suffered greatly during his pontificate, owing to the hostility of the nobles toward him; twice he had been driven from his city by armed men.[385] The cathedral chapter and part of the clergy also sided with the opponents of the bishop, resulting in deplorable conditions within the Liège bishopric.

Following Jean's death the members of the cathedral chapter assembled on the feast of St. John the Baptist (24 June) for the new election. Whereas the interests of the Liège church demanded unity so that the new prelate might deal effectively with the belligerent nobles and correct the abuses of the clergy, the politicization of German life once again created a schismatic situation. The one party sought a bishop loyal to the pope, the other demanded a prelate willing to support Frederick II of Staufen. When pre-election negotiations failed to produce a consensus, the chapter appointed three *scrutinatores* as prescribed by the Fourth Lateranum.[386] These conducted a secret poll which revealed support for William of Savoy, procurator of the diocese of Valenciennes, and for Otto of Mark, provost at Aachen.[387]

---

[384] *Ann. Floreffiensis*, MGH SS XVI 627.

[385] See Joseph Ferdinand Damberger, *Synchronistische Geschichte der Kirche und der Welt im Mittelalter, kritisch aus den Quellen bearbeitet* X (Regensburg, 1857) 100.

[386] For the details of the schism at Liège in 1238, see J.R. Kirsch, "Das Lütticher Schisma vom Jahre 1238," *Römische Quartalschrift für christliche Alterthumskunde und für Kirchengeschichte* 3 (Rome, 1889) 177-203, espec. the bull of Gregory IX, dated 18 November 1238 (p. 187).

[387] *Chron. Albrici* 943, states that Jacques de Lorraine, the *primicerius* of Metz who was also provost at Liège, led the party which favored Otto; the opposition party was headed by Archdeacon Walther, brother of the count of Rethel. Otto was the son of Count Adolf of Mark and Margaret of Gelders who, in addition to being provost of St. Mary's collegiate church at Aachen, was provost of St. Servatius at Maastricht, provost of St. Mary's in Utrecht, and a cathedral canon at Cologne. Bishop Hugh II of Pierrepont, who occupied the chair at Liège 1200-1229, was the son of Hugh, lord of Pierrepont, and Countess Clementia of Rethel. Bishop Jean II was his nephew, being the son of William of Apia (Eppes) and Margaret, daughter of Hugh of Pierrepont and Clementia of Rethel (see Pelster, *Stand und Herkunft* 31-33; *Chron. Albrici* 852).

Matthew Paris wrote in his chronicle that the pope tried personally to secure Liège for William because he intended to give him the leading role in the struggle against Frederick II.[388] William, son of Count Thomas I of Savoy, was clearly one of the most powerful ecclesiastical princes of his day. His brother Thomas was, through his marriage to Johanna of Flanders, possessor of that county; his sister was Beatrice of Provence whose daughter Eleanor was married to King Henry III of England. William was known for his learning and intelligence, traits which gave him great influence. Henry III tried to secure the bishopric of Winchester for him, but to no avail. Having accompanied Eleanor to England, William left upon hearing that a party at Liège favored him for bishop of that see.[389]

Provost Otto of Aachen also sought to gain further support for his election. Although by Easter 1238 an appeal had gone to Rome from the cathedral chapter, seeking the help of the Curia in the resolution of the impasse, Otto approached the emperor Frederick II for the regalia. Without waiting for a papal decision, Frederick granted these to Otto at Brescia: Conrad of Staufen, the emperor's son, established Otto in the bishopric and presided at his enthronement in his cathedral church.[390] To William, Frederick II granted the city and county of Valenciennes where he already was procurator of the diocese.[391]

Under these circumstances Pope Gregory IX commissioned Archbishop Henry (of Dreux) of Rheims and Bishop Guido (de Lauduno) of Cambrai to conduct a thorough investigation of the election and to sent him a report. They were ordered to summon both the candidates and the electors peremptorily to appear before the Curia: Otto was to be required to appear personally, while William and the cathedral chapter might send procurators.[392] William probably went personally to Rome, nonetheless, immediately after Otto's investiture by the emperor.

The case had thus been transferred to Rome, but despite this Otto tried to obtain confirmation of his office from Archbishop-elect Conrad of Cologne. Conrad of Hochstaden had not yet received papal confirmation of his own election, nevertheless he was audacious enough to approve Otto's. This blatant act of disregard for canonical procedures prompted a

---

[388] *Matth. Paris. Chron.*, *MGH SS* XXVIII 151: *"Et tunc temporis vocatus est electus Willelmus electus Valentinus, procurante papa, quia ut dicebatur proposuit eum habere ducem exercitus sui contra imperatorem, ad episcopatum Leodiensem."*

[389] Kirsch, "Lütticher Schisma" 180 note 1.

[390] Böhmer-Ficker, *Regg. Imp.* V 477; *Aegidii Aureavall.* 27; Kirsch, "Lütticher Schisma" 180.

[391] Böhmer-Ficker, *Regg. Imp.* V 482, Nr. 2404.

[392] Kirsch, "Lütticher Schisma" 187, *Dokument* Nr. 1; Auvray, *Registres de Gregoire IX* II, Nr. 4587.

second letter from Gregory IX to the archbishop of Rheims (8 December 1238), stating that despite this confirmation the previous commission was still valid. Archbishop Henry of Rheims was directed to command the subjects of the church at Liège to wait until the investigation had been completed before they accepted anyone as their prelate.[393]

Unfortunately, Otto had already taken possession of several episcopal fortresses and had begun to act as if he were in fact a confirmed and consecrated bishop: he had demanded the oath of obedience from the clergy of Liège, had granted benefices to his supporters and had excommunicated those who opposed him. When members of William's party resisted a terrible civil war ensued.[394] The count of Flanders even invaded the bishopric to assist those trying to establish William's claims.[395] Once again the pope gave a mandate to the archbishop of Rheims (23 January 1239), empowering him to re-establish order in the bishopric, to annul all of Otto's un-canonical acts, and to take back all of the episcopal fortresses.[396]

Meanwhile, the first commission had sent its report on the election itself to the Curia. Pope Gregory appointed three cardinals to adjudicate the case between Otto and William, both of whom were still in Rome. Quickly seeing that his chances of success were nil, however, Otto left before the end of the suit; at this, the pontiff quashed Otto's election altogether and confirmed that of William. Notice of this action was sent to the cathedral chapter at Liège on 29 May 1239, with the command that the canons accept and obey William as their new bishop.[397] Since Otto was not prepared to accept this decision, the pope also gave to his commission power to excommunicate Otto and his supporters unless they abandoned their opposition.[398] Gregory also ordered the archbishop-elect of Cologne to go personally to Liège and to proclaim the decision to the clergy and people.[399]

---

[393] Kirsch, "Lütticher Schisma" 189, *Dokument* Nr. 2; Auvray, *Registres de Gregoire IX* II, Nrs. 4642, 4643.

[394] *Aegidii Aureavall.* 126-127: "*Interea vastabatur graviter episcopatus Leodiensis a vicinis praedonibus undique emergentibus dimicantibus inter se enormiter villis episcopalibus, quibusdam partes Ottonis, aliis ex adverso partes Wilhelmi tueri et confovere nitentibus: quia ut legitur non erat tunc rex in Israel, sed unusquisque quod bonum in oculis suis videbatur faciebat.*"

[395] *Chron. Matth. Paris.* 189.

[396] Kirsch, "Lütticher Schisma" 190, *Dokument* Nr. 3.

[397] Kirsch, "Lütticher Schisma" *Dokument* Nr. 4 (29 May 1239). William was also allowed to retain Valenciennes and other prebends in addition to the new bishopric; cf. Idem. Nr. 10 (8 June 1239).

[398] Kirsch, "Lütticher Schisma" 194, *Document* Nr. 6 (2 June 1239).

[399] Kirsch, "Lütticher Schisma" 196, *Dokument* Nr. 8 (3 June 1239).

William of Savoy appears to have left Rome shortly after late June/early July 1239, moving northward through his family's lands. On 3 August the pope dictated a letter to him regarding a situation with which he would have to deal immediately upon his entrance into his diocese—the reform of the monastery of St. Jacob's at Liège. The sad condition of this monastery shows the ill-effects of the schism within the Liège church, conditions which no one had been bold enough to correct. Many years earlier (1229/1231) Cardinal-legate Otto had quashed the irregular election of a monk named John as abbot of St. Jacob's.[400] In spite of this John had asserted his claim to the office and had misused his authority in every way. The papal bull gives the sad account of his behavior: he wasted resources, ignored the monastic regulations, and did not hold the monks to their vows. At length, two brothers from the house had gone to seek help from the pope. Thus it was that Gregory IX commanded William of Savoy to visit the monastery personally and to re-establish discipline and order.[401] But, William was able neither to assume his office as bishop of Liège nor deal with St.

---

[400] Problems at St. Jacob's were by no means novel: in 1209 the abbot had to be removed from office because of incompetence (cf. p. 158). The last entries in *Reineri Ann.* (a. 1229-1230) 680, give the background to the most recent situation: *"[1229] Fratre Waselino abbate transeunte ad ordinem Cisterciensem in Valle sancti Lamberti, domnus Theodericus de gremio ecclesie assumptus eligitur, et succedit abbas ad Sanctum Iacobum, et benedicitur a magistro Iacobo Aconensi episcopo.*

Anno 1230. domnus Theodericus abbas Sancti Iacobi post 14 menses sue promotionis dominica in octavis pentecostes ad sinodum Hoi venit, et sequenti 5. feria ibidem defunctus, in Valle benedicta monialium Cisterciensis ordinis sepultus est.

Predictus frater Waselinus de Florinis ad Sanctum Iacobum veniens, invenit ecclesiam obligatam 644 marcis et 700 modiis bladi. Quibus longo tempore multa fratrum penuria pacatis, quinque annis antequam recederet, flagellata est ecclesia tempestatibus, incendiid, et defectu panis, maxime exactionibus episcopi in quinquaginta marcis;proinde remanet debitum ipso recedente 26 marcarum et 45 modiorum bladi, meliorate tamen ecclesia devotione fidelium in calicibus, casulis, cappis sericis, luminaribus, fenestris vitreis, pavimento et cottidiani panis augmento."

[401] Kirsch, "Lütticher Schisma" 200, *Dokument* Nr. 16 (3 August 1239): *"Ex insinuatione . . . maioris et sanioris partis conventus monasterii Sancti Jacobi Leodiensis ordinis sancti Benedicti nos noveris accepisse, quod licet olim monasterium ipsum occasione electionis de J. qui pro abbate se gerit ipsius minus canonice celebrata fuisset diversis litigiis laceratum, et tandem auctoritate dilecti filii nostri O. Sancti Nicolai in carcere Tulliano diaconi cardinalis tunc in partibus illis apostolice sedis legato electio ipsa cassata tam electionis vitio quam electi idem tamen perjurus, symoniacus et pluribus aliis criminibus irretitus per ambitionis audaciam ipsius monasterii regimen adipiscens, dato virtutibus libello repudii cum vitiis sic contraxit, quod non tam monachus quam demoniacus dici possit, cum detinere presumat publice concubinam ex qua duas filias procreavit, et asserens secum super hoc authoritate apostolica dispensatum, abjecta prorsus modestia monachiali et incontinentie publice lassatis abenis, bona dicti monasterii dilapidare presumit eadem in usus illicitos convertendo, et alias non servando regularia instituta nec faciendo a subditis observari; . . ."*

Jacob's: he died, probably on 1 November 1239, at Viterbo.[402] William was clearly more of a *Staatsmann*—politician than a prince of the Church. Nevertheless, because of his connections to the princely families of the Rhine-Meuse region it had been anticipated that he would be able to benefit the church at Liège. Aegidius of Orval lamented his death, having hoped that he would be able to heal the wounds.[403]

After William's death there was a lengthy vacancy, indicating perhaps that the schism continued within the cathedral chapter. Eventually the chapter postulated the bishop of Langres, Robert of Thourotte (nothing more is heard of Otto)[404] who objected to this, preferring the relative peace of his own see to the intrigues and problems of Liège. Following papal urging to accept the postulation, however, Robert agreed, bringing to an end this painful chapter in the ecclesiastical history of Liège.[405] The outcome of efforts to reform St. Jacob's monastery is unknown.[406] That the new bishop was intent on maintaining a synodal tradition may be inferred from the document issued on 28 October 1242, wherein the Benedictine abbot of Afflighem in Brabant acknowledged his obligation to assist the bishop of Liège each year in his synod, by reason of the church at Genappe.[407]

---

[402] *Chron. Matth. Paris.* 179; *Ann. Floreff.* 627; *Aegidii Aureavall.* 127.

[403] *Aegidii Aureavall.* 126-127: "*Inter hec fama discurrente, domnum Guillermum a summo pontifice Gregorio confirmatum et consecratum in antistitem, nec existente qui episcopatui interim in tribulationibus subveniret, expectabatur fere per annum novus episcopus a clero et populo ardenti desiderio, sed heu! quam cito, volvente rota fortune, fraudati sunt a desiderio suo. Cum enim idem esset venerabilis antistes in reditu itineris tam periculosi, in dampnum tocius episcopatus Leodiensis in partibus Transalpinis diem clausit extremum anno Domini 1239 [mense Octobri], . . .*"

[404] Otto of Mark in fact renounced his clerical vows and returned to the secular world; he married Ermengarde of Holte (see Pelster, *Stand und Herkunft* 33). On 5 February 1245 Innocent IV directed Bishop Robert to grant a prebend which, despite a papal penalty, was still controlled by Otto of Mark in the cathedral chapter at Cologne, to another suitable person; cf. Kirsch, "Lütticher Schisma" 202, *Dokument* Nr. 19.

[405] See Kirsch, "Lütticher Schisma" 186-187; letter dated 2 August 1240 from Gregory IX to his legate in Germany, Idem. 202, Nr. 18; Potthast, *Regesta* I, Nr. 10923. Aubrey of Troisfontaines derives the family of Thourotte (Torota) from Count Robert of Dreux, son of King Louis VI: Robert's daughter Alaydis bore a son John (I of Thourotte, dép. Oise) to her third husband, the castellan John of Noyon. John I of Thourotte was the father of both Bishop Robert of Liège and Bishop Rudolf of Verdun; see Pelster, *Stand und Herkunft* 33; *Chron. Albrici (a. 1162)* 845f.; A. Lefranc, *Histoire de la Ville de Noyon*, Bibliothèque de l'Ecole des Hautes Etudes 75 (1888) 105ff. In addition to the papal/imperial overtones of the election, it was also a contest between the old established family of the counts of Rethel and a new challenger for the see of Liège.

[406] Reiner, the annalist at St. Jacob's, presumably died in 1230, thus depriving us of this valuable source for the inner life of the Liège church.

[407] Bormans, *Cartulaire de Liège* I, Nr. 348.

A document dated simply 1242 and printed in the *Addenda* of Volume III of the *Westfälisches Urkundenbuch* is taken from the *Repertorium* of the Münster cathedral chapter and contains the note: *"Item litera statutorum et ordinatorum per episcopum ad instar eorum que alias statuta et ordinata fuerunt in concilio provinciali Coloniensi."* The bishop in question in 1242 was Ludolf of Holte, but the older collections contain no reference to a provincial synod held near this time. The probability exists, however, that the assembly held 8 April 1240 at Cologne is that otherwise unknown provincial synod.[408] On that day, Archbishop Conrad of Cologne, together with Bishops Landulf of Worms, Engelbert of Osnabrück, and Ludolf of Münster, wrote a letter to Pope Gregory IX in which they declared their intention to remain loyal to the Church in the conflict between the papacy and Frederick II. They did, however, ask the Roman pontiff to consider Frederick's letter which had been sent with the Grand Master of the Teutonic Knights. The wording of the note in the *Repertorium* suggests that there were other matters of significance discussed and decreed at the Cologne provincial synod of 1240 which may have related to ecclesiastical discipline, and that these same statutes were repeated in 1242 at an assembly convened by bishop Ludolf of Münster with his own clergy.[409]

Unless the assembly of 1233 at which the bull of canonization for St. Vigilius was publicly read was in fact a provincial synod, the one which Archbishop Eberhard II of Salzburg convened on 5 April 1231 was without apparent successors until the synod held in 1240 at Straubing.[410] Among its business were efforts to deal with disturbers of Church order, and to bring an end to the decline in religious life. It also attempted to reach a peace agreement with Duke Otto of Bavaria, a decided anti-Staufen, but the *Landfriede* failed. Two years later another synod was held at Regensburg, but the issues dealt with were more civil than ecclesiastical.[411] The efforts by Eberhard II to establish regular synod attendance and his frequent use of papal support should caution us against underestimating the number of synods called and of those actually held between 1200 and 1246, as older scholars have done, however.[412]

---

[408] *Westf. UB* III, Nr. 103 Add. Nr. 366.

[409] Hermann Cardauns, *Konrad von Hostaden, Erzbischof von Köln (1238-1261* (Köln, 1880) 113-132, discusses „Die Kirche, das geistige Leben und die Kunst" in some detail, yet he is aware of neither the ticklish assignment given Conrad in 1239 with regard to the schismatic election at Liège, nor the provincial synod of 1240.

[410] *Ann. Salisb. (a. 1239)* 787; Mansi, *Collectio* XXII, col. 517-518; Binterim, *Concilien* IV 444; Meiller, *RAS* Nr. 371; Dopsch, *Geschichte Salzburgs* I 329, espec. note 686.

[411] Hübner, "Provinzialsynoden" 206.

[412] Johanek, "Synodalia" I 88, against the views of Hauck, *KGD* V 137 note 2.

For the most part, minor synods only are recorded from 1241 through 1245. Bishop Bernhard IV of Paderborn convened his clergy in such an assembly in 1241.[413]   That same year, on 28 February, Archbishop Dietrich II of Trier held a synod at Coblenz where he excommunicated all who had withheld gifts from the hospital of St. Nicholas which the Teutonic Order maintained near Coblenz.[414]   The following year, on 22 February (the traditional day), the last synod of his long pontificate was convened at Trier where he confirmed the privileges of the collegiate church of Carden-on-the Mosel.   Among them was exemption from the *cathedraticum* for those churches over which the foundation of Carden exercised patronage.[415] Sometime in 1242 and on 8 June 1243 Bishop Rudolf of Merseburg convened synods which dealt with the renunciation of fishing rights by the knight Rüdiger of Lüssen in favor of the monastery at Pforta, and the exemption of the church at Oetzsch from that at Dallschütz, with a compensation being paid to the mother church in the form of a hide of land at Dallschütz.[416]   Bishop Conrad of Hildesheim held synods on 21 February 1243 and on 9 April 1244,[417] and Henry of Catania, the newly-appointed bishop of Bamberg, held a synod shortly after his arrival from Rome in early fall 1243, for the purpose of getting to know his clergy and of reorganizing his bishopric.[418]   At a diocesan synod held 8 June 1243 at Naumburg, financial and legal matters were attended to.[419]   That Bishop Engelbert I of Osnabrück also summoned a synod in 1243/1244 may be inferred from a privilege granted in 1243 to the Cistercian monastery of Bersenbrück, exempting it from synodal obligations.[420]

---

[413] *Westf. UB* IV, Nr. 306.

[414] Beyer, *MRUB* III, Nr. 672; Goerz, *RET* 42; Johann Heinrich Hennes, ed., *Codex diplomaticus Ordinis Sanctae Mariae Theutonicorum. Urkundenbuch zur Geschichte des Deutschen Ordens* (Mainz, 1845) 113.

[415] Beyer, *MRUB* III, Nr. 698: "*Notum sit omnibus presentem paginam inspecturis, quod cum ratione visitationis vel synodi nostre in anno bisextili a capitulo Cardonensis super universis ecclesiis, quarum ius patronatus ad ipsum capitulum pertinere dinoscitur, . . .*"

[416] Kehr, *UB Merseburg* I, Nrs. 252, 254.

[417] Hoogeweg, *UB Hilds* II, Nrs. 676, 708; Binterim, *Concilien* IV 444; Hauck, *KGD* V 169 note 1.

[418] Hartzheim, *Concilia* III 569, citing Hoffmanns, *Annalium Bambergens.* Lib. IV; Krenzer, *Heinrich von Bilverstein* 23; Jäck, *Gesch. Bambergs* II, 34, place it in 1242, which Krenzer finds too early; Looshorn, *Bistum Bamberg*, fails to mention it; Guttenberg, *Bistum Bamberg* 175 notes that Heinrich of Catania remained in Italy until August 1243 during the efforts to get a new pope favorable to Frederick II; he was therefore not likely present at the Mainz provincial synod on 25 June as claimed by Heidingsfelder, *Regg. Eichst.* Nrs. 723-724.

[419] Dobenecker, *RdThur* III, Nr. 1090; see also Nrs. 1245, 1450, 1451.

[420] Hilling, *Diözesansynoden* 44; Philippi, *UB Osnabrück* II, Nr. 442.

During the last week of June (25-27) 1243 a provincial synod was held at
Mainz, several details of which have been preserved.[421] On the first day
a dispute arose over the proper seating of the prelates: attending were the
bishops of Hildesheim, Paderborn, Worms, Würzburg, Strasbourg,
Bamberg, Speyer, Halberstadt, and Eichstätt. Bishop Frederick II of
Eichstätt claimed that the chair next to the archbishop belonged traditionally
to his church, going back to the relationship between Saints Boniface and
Willibord, the founder of the Eichstätt bishopric; this privilege had been
challenged by the bishops of Hildesheim, Paderborn, and Worms. The
Eichstätt prelate defended his claims with the aid of the testimony of two
provosts and a dean—each according to his own statement almost 100 years
old, who declared that when the archbishop convenes a synod, the bishop
of Eichstätt and the metropolitan sat on one side of the cathedral, the
suffragans on the other; should the archbishop be sick, the Eichstätt bishop
presided, directed all business matters, proclaimed the decisions, and closed
the synod. On the basis of this testimony, bishop Frederick demanded a
formal proclamation of his church's prerogatives by the synod.

This declaration was made by the assembly the following day, 26
June.[422] After the prelates had taken their proper places, Bishop Frederick of Eichstätt then represented the archbishop in proclaiming the decisions
of the synod. Decrees were issued, dealing with robbers of churches and
the clergy. Those found guilty of such actions were not to be allowed to
enter any ecclesiastical corporations. Due to the preoccupation of the
metropolitan on 27 June, Frederick also consecrated the new chapter

---

[421] The only evidence of this synod is found in an entry in the *Pontificale Gundekarianum*
(Ordinariatsarchiv Eichstätt fol. 10ᵛ), printed in Schmid, *Dissertatio de conciliis Moguntinis*,
in Georg Christian Joannis, *Script. rer. Mogunt.* III 295; Hartzheim, *Concilia* III 569 (without
historical introduction); Idem IV 616 (with historical introduction); Mansi, *Collectio* XXIII
688; Gudenus, *CdMogunt* I 575. In Böhmer, *Regesten Conrads IV.* Nr. 11, this synod is
equated with that held in 1239. Ficker, "Erörterungen" 347-350, demonstrates to the contrary
the necessity of assuming two separate synods: that of 1239 met on 1-4 July (cf. Hartzheim,
Concilia III 568), while the 1243 assembly met on 25 June. Cf. further, Heidingsfelder, *Regg.*
Eichst. Nr. 723; Hefele-Knöpfler, *Conziliengeschichte* V 1098; Hauck, *KGD* IV 20 note 1;
Wetzer & Welte, *Kirchenlexikon* VIII 525; Michael Lefflad, ed., *Die Regesten der Bischöfe von*
Eichstätt II (Eichstätt, 1872) 11.

[422] Heidingsfelder, *Regg. Eichst.* Nr. 724; Hauck, *KGD* V 138 note 1; Ficker, "Erörterungen" 347-348; Fink, *Siegfried III.* 73. The only evidence we have of a long-standing right
of the bishops of Eichstätt to represent the archbishop during a vacancy is the consecration of
the bishop of Halberstadt, Conrad of Krosigk, on 1 January 1202 by Bishop Hartwig of
Eichstätt during the schism; cf. Heidingsfelder, *op.cit.* Nr. 521. That the rights to represent
Mainz go back to the relationship of St. Boniface to Willibord as was perceived in the
thirteenth century is questionable. Thus, there are serious doubts about the accuracy of the
report as transmitted to us. The bishops of Prague and Olmütz represented Mainz at the
coronation of the king of Bohemia in 1260.

buildings at the Mainz cathedral.[423] On 11 February 1248, Pope Innocent IV admonished Siegfried of Mainz to adhere without ceasing to the statute which he had published against arsonists and other persons who committed violent acts against church property and clerics at the provincial synod, even though some of these same individuals claimed exemption from his authority.[424] Since there were no larger assemblies involving the participation of suffragans between 1243 and 1248, the papal letter must have had reference to this synod. We may therefore conclude that its statutes were also known in the Curia.

The two clerical gatherings at Weimar and Fritzlar in the spring of 1244 were local synods for the Thuringian and Hessian clergy respectively. According to the *Chronica S. Petri Erfordensis moderna*, the first assembly was held *proxima dominica Letare* and dealt with the denunciation of Emperor Frederick II and the excommunication of the burghers of Erfurt who refused to break with the Staufen ruler; the Fritzlar synod held 30 May confirmed those declarations and also took the action of degrading the former Mainz cathedral *custos* and provost of the collegiate church of St. Peter at Mainz, Count Frederick of Eberstein, due to his continued support of the emperor. Touching upon matters of Church discipline and order, the archbishop also temporarily withdrew the prebends of some of the cathedral canons due to their neglect of obligations, took measures to correct the manner of administering the sacraments and improving the parish priest's office, and provided for greater security of the clerics, instructing that a night watch by two un-tonsured clerics be established; for their support he granted the lower chapel of the church of St. Gotthard.[425] A

---

[423] Heidingsfelder, *Regg. Eichst.* Nrs. 725, 726; Böhmer-Will, *RAM* II, 273, Nr. 446; Fink, *Siegfried III.* 74. Binterim, *Concilien* IV 379, notes the synod, but states that there is no record of the proceedings. Concerning the buildings consecrated at this time, cf. Schneider, *Der Dom zu Mainz* col. 28, espec. note 3

[424] Rodenberg, *MG Ep. s. XIII* II, Nr. 495: "*Ex parte tua, frater archiepiscope, fuit propositum coram nobis, quod licet Thuringorum et Hassanorum nationes tue diocesis, ab antiquo semper malitose pre aliis, inobedientes tibi fuerint et rebelles, post mortem tamen clare memorie H. Romanorum regis, cum non sit eos valeat cohercere, in tantum prevaluit malitia eorundum, quod nec Deum timentes nec hominem reverentes, tanta in libertatem ecclesiasticam tyrannide degrassantur, quod ausu diabolico ecclesias per incendia devastant, clericos spoliant [etc.]. . . . Quare tu predecessoris tui inherens vestigiis in provinciali tua synodo de suffrageorum tuorum consilio et assensu pro refrenanda dictorum malefactororum rabie statuiti, ut . . .*"; Fink, *Siegfried III.* 74.

[425] *Chron. S. Petri Erford.* 238: "*Maguntinus, ut Erphodenses adhuc durius arceret, in octava epyphanie omnem clerum cum religiosis civitatem exire compulit; qui postea in proxima sequenti dominica Letare in villa Wimaria cleri ac poluli conventum statuens, Fridericum imperatorem cum Erphordensibus denunciavit, ac post hoc III. Kal. Iunii in Vritslaria concilium faciens eadem confirmavit.*" Hartzheim, *Concilia* III 576-577, lists fourteen canons from this synod; Mansi, *Collectio* XXII, cols. 603-604; Binterim, *Concilien* IV 385; Fink,

copy of the entire set was sent to Innocent IV for confirmation, which he granted.[426] The 1310 statutes contain several citations from the 1244 decrees.[427]

Visitations Conducted at Papal Command

That same year (1244), at papal direction, Siegfried of Mainz also conducted visitations of the archdioceses of Mainz, Trier and Magdeburg, where he was to correct any abuses which he found.[428] The need for outside intervention in the affairs of the Magdeburg church seems connected to Archbishop Wilbrand of Käfernburg's constant wars with neighboring princes. His predecessor, Burchard of Woldenburg, had been elected near the end of October 1232 and died at Constantinople on 8 February 1235 during a pilgrimage to the Holy Land. At the time of his death, he had not yet received consecration as archbishop,[429] which meant that during those two and a half years he was incapable of convening a provincial synod. Wilbrand himself was consecrated at Viterbo by Gregory IX on 25 November 1235 and received the pallium of his office shortly thereafter.[430] Despite his ability to preside over provincial synods from this time onward, we have no record that he did so. There may thus have been a decided decline in church discipline within his archdiocese and the

---

Siegfried III. 74-5; Hauck, *KGD* V 138 note 1, and 144; Idem. IV 832-833. Against Hefele-Knöpfler, *Conziliengeschichte* V 1099, who date the synod in 1243 is Finke, *Konzilienst.* 18-24. See also Hauck, *Abhandlungen* 71-72. C. 47 was overturned by Urban IV on 9 November 1269; cf. *Regg. d'Urban* II, 9, Nr. 20. Hauck, *op.cit.* V 165, notes that the 1244 synod at Fritzlar established two penitentiaries in each diocese of the Mainz province; cf. Hartzheim, *op.cit.* III 604 (1261, c. 33). They are still visible in the fourteenth and fifteenth centuries. By October 1244 the clergy of Erfurt had returned to the city; cf. Fink, *op.cit.* 44.

[426] Cf. Leipzig Universitätsbibliothek MS 1062, fol. 35ᵛ-36ᵛ: "*Confirmatio statutorum moguntinensis diocesis*"; the item is without date or the name of the archbishop, and the conclusion is missing.

[427] Cf. Mainz, Stadtbibliothek 281, fol. 1ʳ-13ᵛ; Würzburg, Universitätsbibliothek M.p.th. q. 72, fol. 282ʳᵃ-292ʳᵃ; Leipzig Universitätsbibliothek MS lat. 1085 (14th c.), fol. 50ʳ-53ʳ. See also Johanek, "Synodalia" III 62.

[428] Gersdorf, *UB Meissen* I, xxii and Nr. 127: ". . . *quod cum status ecclesiarum in Magdeburgensi provincia multae deformationis tribulis opprimatur,* . . ."; on 26 September 1244, under the authority of the papal bull of 27 April 1244, he commissioned the bishop, cathedral provost and dean, and the cathedral canon Sifrid von Pegau to visit every church of the diocese of Meissen. The papal mandate itself is in Rodenberg, *MG Ep. s. XIII* II, Nr. 62.

[429] Cf. Fuchs, *Besetzung* 92.

[430] *Cat. aep. Magd., MGH SS* XXV 486. In a papal document dated 19 December 1235 the pope speaks of *Archiepiscopus Wilbrandus*, indicating that the latter had in fact received the pallium; cf. Mülverstedt, *RAMagd* II, Nr. 1047. See also Fuchs, *Besetzung* 93-94; M-Alpermann, *Stand und Herkunft* 12; Schäfers, *Amtsdaten Magdeburg* 44-45.

Magdeburg province by 1244, prompting the delegation of its correction to Siegfried of Mainz.

The visitation of Trier was clearly connected with the disorder which arose upon the death of Archbishop Dietrich II on 28 March 1242. For thirty years this committed metropolitan had striven to implement the principles of reform and ecclesiastical order articulated at the Fourth Lateranum, utilizing his own brother, his nephew, and other trusted members of his clergy in the process. He even planned for the perpetuation of his policies by securing the succession of that nephew, Arnold of Isenburg, to the archiepiscopal chair. Alas, those plans proved fragile when a dispute erupted among the members of the cathedral chapter during the new election: the majority of the cathedral canons elected their provost, Arnold, while a dissenting minority opted for Rudolf de Ponte [Jr.], provost of St. Paulin. King Conrad of Staufen, arriving at Trier shortly thereafter, granted the regalia to Rudolf, presumably because of an incident which had occurred earlier in March 1242, and also due to Arnold's relationship to Siegfried of Mainz.

At a time when the archbishops of Cologne and Mainz had already broken with Frederick II, Dietrich II of Trier remained loyal to the Staufen dynasty. Thus, when Conrad IV visited Trier during Lent 1242 he was received with honor by the ailing metropolitan. During this time a partisan of the Mainz archbishop, Siegfried of Honeck, killed one of the king's soldiers in the house of the Trier cathedral provost, Arnold of Isenburg, as the soldier attempted to seize Honeck and take him to the king. The commotion which followed saw the followers of Conrad drive the provost and his household out of his own residence and into the bishop's palace. The archbishop immediately attempted to still the disorder and to placate the king, aided by the lords of Bolanden and Falkenstein, nephews of the provost.[431]

It is an open question whether Arnold belonged to the anti-Staufen party at the beginning of March 1242, or joined it after Conrad's confirmation of Rudolf. Arnold's side claimed the *maior et sanior pars* of the chapter, including most archdeacons, and the provosts of Pfalzel, Münstermaifeld,

---

[431] Cf. *Gesta Trev.* 405-406; Goerz, *MRR* III 289, 290; Idem., *RET* 44; Stramberg, *Antiquarius* 705; Bastgen, "Beschwerdebrief" 75-76; Pixton, "Dietrich of Wied" (1972) 189-191; Paul Aldinger, "Die Erhebung Arnolds von Isenburg zum Erzbischof von Trier 1242," *Programm des königlich württemberg. ev.-theol. Seminars in Schönthal (1898)* 11-37; Franz-Josef Heyen, "Über die trierer Doppelwahlen von 1183 und 1242," *AMrKG* 21 (1969) 28-33. Arnold received papal permission 1242/1244 (document undated) to retain his archdeaconate during the schism at Trier (cf. Beyer, *MRUB* III, Nr. 812). He appears never to have given it up, however, a factor which contributed to the great friction which existed between himself and the other archdeacons.

and St. Florin. The dispute resulted in several canons' being seized in the cathedral in their clerical robes and led in a deplorable fashion through the streets, and then imprisoned. The cathedral church itself was turned into a fortress as the children of the church of Trier raged against their mother. Rudolf's party took control of the cathedral.[432]

Under these circumstances, a document issued by the cathedral chapter at Trier, together with the collegiate foundations of St. Paulin and St. Simeon, and the abbeys of St. Matthias, St. Mary and St. Martin, on 17 April 1242, has a particular significance. Recognizing the fact that the cessation of divine services which had recently been imposed by the prelates of the city in an effort to punish those who had committed violence against the clergy and against ecclesiastical establishments had also had a deleterious effect upon discipline in secular and regular communities alike, and fearing that the collapse of order within their diocese would bring down upon their heads the righteous indignation of an offended God, they had agreed upon a united action against the malefactors. The names of those accused of crimes against the churches of the diocese were to be submitted in writing by the clergy; these were then to be denounced publicly as excommunicated in all parish, foundation and conventual churches each Sunday, accompanied by the ringing of bells and the lighting of candles. Parish priests were ordered to admonish their flocks to shun those thus excommunicated, lest they too become guilty of aiding and abetting such offenders. The archdeacons were charged with being conscientious in exercising their jurisdiction over against the accused, and should they be lax therein, the archiepiscopal *officialis* was given license to assume their duties.

In three instances the declaration makes reference to the "*statuta concilii Trevirensis*" which were to be followed by the clergy in dealing with this crisis. The statutes are clearly *cc.* 1-6 of the provincial synod of 1238 which prescribed essentially the same procedures for dealing with those who committed crimes against the church of Trier and/or its clergy.[433] Here

---

[432] Rudolf de Ponte [Jr.] was the nephew of that Archdeacon Rudolf de Ponte who in 1200-1203 had been a major factor in the schismatic election at Liège; cf. Heyen, "Doppelwahl" 29-30; Binterim, *Concilien* IV 406.

[433] E.g., 1238 synod, *c.* 1: "*Quoniam crescente malitia perversorum hominum, adversus spirituales nequitias, santorum patrum canones ad reprimendas quorumdam insolentias non sufficiunt, novis morbis nova medicamenta praeparamus, necessitate eorum compulsi. Itaque praecipimus religiosorum locorum incendiarios et eorum receptores, singulis diebus dominicis excommunicatos nuntiari per omnes conventuales ecclesias, et per parochias, et monasteria monachorum et monialium.*" The 1242 adaptation states: "*Saniori freti consilio, talium machinationibus et crudelitatibus sine dispendio cultus divini, quantum possumus, obviare volentes, unanimi consensu contra eos secundum formam subscriptam decrevimus precedendum; videlicet, quod ecclesie singule et ecclesiastice persone suos malefactores, laicos tantum excommunicatos, legitime dent in scriptis, nec inscribant aliquem, nisi notorie reum, nec illos*

we find a clear example of an effort to adapt the decrees of an earlier synod to fit the exigencies of 1242; at least some of the statutes given in 1238 were themselves modifications of even earlier legislation by Archbishop Dietrich II, giving us some indication that in this diocese and province (as presumably elsewhere in Germany as well where archiepiscopal statutes existed) provincial synodal decrees were repeated and re-interpreted on occasions beyond their initial publication.

After months of much bitter hostility, the issue of the archiepiscopal election was at last resolved: Rudolf de Ponte [Jr.] agreed to renounce all claims to the archiepiscopal chair in return for the cathedral provostship; Arnold of Isenburg was confirmed and consecrated as archbishop. The pastoral needs of his church were great: the *mensa communis* which his uncle and predecessor, Archbishop Dietrich II, had instituted in 1215 had ceased; clerical discipline had declined dramatically. But instead of accepting that obligation to correct problems, Arnold became quickly known for a spirit hostile to reform measures. In 1246 the Trier cathedral chapter complained to him that he and his *officialis* were being too oppressive; it was furthermore asserted that he disturbed the jurisdiction of the archdeacons, thereby upsetting the order and discipline of his church. The complaint further noted that Arnold not only failed to convene synods of his own, but also hindered Archdeacon Henry of Bolanden from convening his synod (*Send*) at Andernach. The prelate was also charged with retaining prebendal incomes contrary to the laws of the church.[434]

If this declaration is correct in its various points, the assembly held on 19 February 1244 at Coblenz, which witnessed the incorporation of church property, is not to be construed as a synod.[435] If, on the other hand, it was such, then the complaint by the cathedral chapter two years later should be interpreted to mean that Arnold held no synods which were pastoral or juridical in nature. A search of the Trier cartularies fails to reveal any evidence of synodal activity between 1244 and 1261, at which time Archbishop Henry of Vinstingen resumed the tradition which Dietrich II of Wied had labored so tirelessly to perpetuate.

On 19 April 1244 Archbishop Gerhard II of Bremen declared that, in accordance with the decision of a *"capitulum generale,"* the canons at Bassum (Brixina) were to enjoy the same privileges regarding the making and execution of wills, and annates, as members of the cathedral chapter at

---

de quibus questio vel litigium pendet, inscribant et huiusmodi sic in scriptis dati, in singulis ecclesiis et monasteriis conventualibus cum proclamatione solemni singulis diebus dominicis nominatim, campanis pulsatis et accensis candelis excommunicati, publice iudicentur."

[434] Binterin, *Concilien* IV 408-9; Hontheim, *Hist. Trev. dipl.* I, 738; Heydenreich, *Metropolitangewalt* 108, citing Beyer, *MRUB* III, Nrs. 1389, 1407.

[435] Goerz, *RET* 44.

Bremen.   Witnessing this act were the provost, dean, *vicedominus,* scholastic, cantor and *thesaurarius* of the cathedral, the deans and chapter members of St. Willehad and St. Anschar, the abbots of St. Pauli in Bremen and of Rastad, and the priors of St. George in Stade and Osterholte.[436] It is clear from this assemblage of cathedral and collegiate clergy that this general chapter was not one such as Lateran IV prescribed for the Benedictines on a triennial basis, but in fact a diocesan synod.   The selection of Stade as the venue may have been intended to send the message to the brothers of the ill-famed house of St. Mary's monastery that it must submit itself to much-needed changes, yet the absence of the abbot of Stade at the synod leaves open the question.   Despite the defection of one of the leading ecclesiastical figures in the archdiocese in 1240 (Abbot Albert), there is no indication that any serious reform measures were undertaken. The synod of 1244 at Bremen thus appears to have retained the traditional function of an administrative assembly.

No synods are recorded for the German provinces or bishoprics in 1245, a fact not surprising due to the general Church council held at Lyons that same year.   In the thirty years since the Fourth Lateranum there had been a great deal of synodal activity.   Our study of those three decades has been approached in a chronological fashion in order to reveal relationships between diocesan and provincial synods of specific regions of Germany, and also to suggest the response to papal, legatine, and archiepiscopal stimuli. It would be incorrect to assume that the decrees of Lateran IV revived a totally moribund practice, however.   Comparing the last half century before the Council with the thirty years which followed allows us to assess the impact more correctly.

[436] May, *REB* I 263, Nr. 962.

CHAPTER SIX

SUMMA AEVI

Et venite, et arguite me, dicit Dominus: si fuerint peccata vestra ut coccinum, quasi nix dealbabuntur: et si fuerint rebra quasi vermiculus, velut lana alba erunt. Si volueritis, et audieritis me, bona terrae comedetis. Quod si nolueritis, et me ad iracundiam provocaveritis, gladius devorabit vos, quia os Domini locutum est.
(Prophetia Isaiae 1, 18-20)

. . . Primus dolor est, de deformitate praelarorum et subditorum, quia non erant, quales consueverant et debebant esse. . . . De eorum excessibus multa dixit.
(Innocent IV, a. 1245)

One of the fives "wounds" of the Church identified by Pope Innocent IV at the council which he convened at Lyons in June 1245 was the sins of the clergy, for which an urgent remedy was needed. Thirty years had passed since Innocent III had issued a similar declaration in his summons to the Fourth Lateran Council and in the opening address to that same assembly. We are thus prompted to ask, how did the German church of 1245 compare with its counterpart of 1215? What evidence can be produced that the reform decrees of the Fourth Lateranum had had any appreciable impact upon the discipline of German clerics, or had increased their commitment to the principles and ideals of their estate in general, or of their particular Order? Does the example of 1215 suggest that major changes in human behavior can be legislated?

Innocent III had hoped that the re-invigoration of synodal life within the Latin Church would facilitate the reforms needed to enable that institution to correct the abuses evident among the clergy and to meet the pastoral needs of the lay members, thereby combatting as well the growing popularity of heretical or anti-sacerdotal movements. Our extensive searches into the printed and unpublished sources for the six ecclesiastical provinces which made up the major portion of the medieval German church have revealed the following patterns for the period 1216-1245:

Table D: German Synodalia 1216-1245

PROVINCIAL SYNODS		DIOCESAN SYNODS	
BREMEN		Ratzeburg	24 May 1217
		Lübeck	April 1222?
		Bremen	17 March 1230
	1238		
		Bremen	19 April 1244
COLOGNE		Münster	1216/1217
		Liège	1217
		Utrecht	1217
	bef. 1 Aug. 1220		
		Cologne	1221
		Liège	1222
		Cologne	1223
		Osnabrück	1223
		Minden	11 April 1224
	June? 1224	Münster	April 1224?
	Sep. 1226	Münster	1226
		Liège	1229
		Utrecht	28 May 1230
		Liège	2 June 1230
		Liège	28 June 1233
		Osnabrück	1235
		Utrecht	1236
		Münster	1238
	8 April 1240	Liège	1240
		Osnabrück	1243/1244?
MAGDEBURG		Merseburg	1216
		Merseburg	1217
		Naumburg	9 Oct. 1217
		Merseburg	1218
	30 Aug. 1220	Brandenburg	1220?
		Naumburg	1222
		Merseburg	1222
		Meissen	Lent 1222
		Meissen	March 1223
	Sep. 1225	Merseburg	22 Dec. 1225
	Spring 1228		
		Meissen	24 May 1231
		Merseburg	1242
		Naumburg	8 June 1243
		Merseburg	8 June 1243

PROVINCIAL SYNODS		DIOCESAN SYNODS	
MAINZ		Constanz	1216
		Hildesheim	1216
		Prague	mid-1216
		Halberstadt	18 Oct. 1216
	(late) 1218	Halberstadt	1218
		Augsburg	early 1219?
		Strasbourg	by 1219?
		Speyer	by 23 Aug. 1219?
		Chur	by Apr. 1219?
		Paderborn	1219
		Hildesheim	1220
		Halberstadt	1220
	bef. 25 Aug. 1221	Constanz	26 March 1221
		Hildesheim	1221
		Hildesheim	1222
		Halberstadt	25-26 Mar. 1223
		Eichstätt	late Mar. 1223
		Worms	1223
		Mainz (Erfurt)	1223
		Worms	1224
		Hildesheim	29 Sep. 1224
		Hildesheim	22 Oct. 1224
		Halberstadt	14 March 1225
	30 Nov. 1225	Halberstadt	late Mar. 1225
		Halberstadt	1226
	1227	Hildesheim	2 June 1227
		Halberstadt	29 Nov. 1227
		Strasbourg	1227/1229
		Halberstadt	18 Feb. 1228
		Bamberg	1228
	mid-Feb. 1231	Verden	late 1231
		Speyer	1232
	13 March 1233	Constanz	1233
		Eichstätt	1233
	2 April 1234	Hildesheim	26 Oct. 1234
		Hildesheim	1236
		Mainz	1236/1237
		Halberstadt	(1239)
	2 July 1239	Hildesheim	20 Sep. 1239
		Paderborn	1241
	25-27 June 1243	Hildesheim	21 Feb. 1243
		Olmütz	20 Mar. 1243
		Bamberg	(Fall) 1243
		Hildesheim	9 April 1244
		Mainz (Weimar)	1244
		Mainz (Fritzlar)	1244

PROVINCIAL SYNODS		DIOCESAN SYNODS	
SALZBURG	24 Sep. 1216		
	(Fall) 1219	Freising	(before 1220?)
	Nov. 1220	Brixen	(before 1220?)
		Regensburg	(1220?)
		Gurk	(by 1220?)
		Passau	1220
	1222		
	1224	Passau	1224
	1225/1228	Brixen	ca. 1225/1228
	5 April 1231		
	1233		
	(early) 1240		
	1242		
TRIER	5/15 Sep. 1216		
	1219	Metz	(by 1219)
	Nov./Dec. 1220	Trier	1221
	Oct. 1222	Verdun	June 1222?
	1223		
	May 1224	Toul	Oct./Nov. 1224
		Trier	22 Feb. 1225
	1226		
		Trier	Feb. 1229
		Trier	Feb. 1230
		Trier	Feb. 1231
	1231	Trier	(late) 1231
		Trier	22 Feb. 1235
		Trier	Feb. 1237
	21 Sep. 1238	Trier	1238?
	20 Mar. 1239		
		Trier	Feb. 1241
		Trier	22 Feb. 1242
		Trier	Feb. 1244?

Despite strong evidence for some provinces and bishoprics, it seems clear that the carefully defined provincial and diocesan synods which Innocent III expected to be held annually were not convened.[1] In this respect the

---

[1] Hinschius, *KR* III 588, 591, thought that the holding of two synods per year was becoming more common in the thirteenth century; Hauck, *KGD* V 169, expresses skepticism regarding this; G. Schreiber, *Kurie und Kloster im 12. Jahrhundert* I (Stuttgart, 1910) 216 note 3, produces no evidence for the statement that „im Allgemein, wurden im 12. und 13. Jahrhundert zwei Diözesansynoden im Jahre abgehalten." See also Cheney, *English Synodalia* 18, who concludes that "The synod appears to have been a regularly recognized obligation, and its summoning in this period apparently was not so remarkable as to occasion comment; but we cannot be sure that the regulations were perfectly maintained in any province of the Western

German experience was not unlike that in England. Gibbs and Lang
concluded that only a few bishops really comprehended the ideal of Innocent
III's program.   The majority misunderstood the relative value of the
individual decrees: they often neglected the most important, or else
followed the letter but not the spirit.[2] The death of Innocent III prevented
his putting his reform machinery into operation, and even if he had been
allowed to remain in office longer, the renewal of the Church could not
have been accomplished in one pontificate. His successors, possessing the
same energy for reform as he, would have had to give the forces for reform
in the various countries even more drive. Above all they would have had
to ensure the holding of yearly provincial synods in letter and spirit: this
important tool could not be left unused.[3]

Many of the same characteristics of German synodalia 1170-1215 are
also discernable in the three decades which followed the Fourth Lateranum:
the continued regularity of diocesan synods at Halberstadt and Hildesheim
attest to an extremely strong tradition in those two bishoprics, but the
explicit references to these assemblies may also represent an idiosyncratic
trait of their respective chanceries. Poorly-illuminated synodal traditions
before the Council, on the other hand, often find little better documentation
thereafter.

Johannes Baur has noted that

> Synods allow us to feel clearly the pulse of the religious and public life of an
> age and of a people. They draw attention to contemporary problems. By
> means of the synodal statutes we gain a penetrating view into the juristic and
> cultural structure of this particular period of time.[4]

Such a conclusion is difficult to apply to the three decades covered by this
study, however. The Lateran IV decrees came back with bishops or their
representatives in 1216. Further impetus must have come from *Compilatio
quarta* which was published soon thereafter, and yet again from the *Liber
extra* which Gregory IX announced in 1234.[5]   Despite such official

---

Church."

[2] Gibbs/Lang, *Bishops and Reform* 147, 174ff., and following them, Tillmann, *Innozenz
III.* 164.

[3] Tillmann, *Innozenz III.* 164, citing Hauck, *KGD* V 135ff., for a discussion of how
infrequent synods were held in Germany 1216-1310.

[4] "Brixner Synoden" 305.

[5] Stelzner, "Gelehrtes Recht" 198, suggests that the acquisition of the earlier collections
(including copies of the constitutions of the Fourth Lateran Council) must have fallen before
1234. One must expect that once the *Liber extra* became available and had been declared the
"current and official" collection of papal decretals, extant copies of the constitutions and of
earlier *compilationes* were neglected, or were used in book-binding, etc. This reality makes

collections of Church decrees, and despite the rather large number of synods which we can document, only six actual sets of German synodal decrees are known for the period under study: Salzburg 1216, Salzburg 1224 (fragment), Bremen 1230, Mainz 1233, Trier 1238, and Mainz 1244. Numerous others (e.g., Bremen 1226, Trier 1216/before 1238) must have existed at one time in no more than single copies, accounting for their eventual loss and failure to have a long-term impact upon the churches in which they were enacted. With the exception of Mainz 1209 (and possible restatements after 1215), only the presumed provincial synod at Trier in 1216, the diocesan synod at Cologne in 1221, and the provincial synod at Mainz in 1233 exhibit any evidence of influence from the statutes published by Bishop Eudes of Paris in 1208.[6]

English studies, on the other hand, have identified fourteen sets of synodal statutes for the same period, with an additional five which may have been issued before 1245.[7] By comparison, then, the German output is meager indeed. The inescapable impression is that the Fourth Lateran Council failed to trigger the desired response among the German episcopacy, either because there was general indifference to the question of reform or because there was general unfamiliarity with the process of "statute making."

Despite the expressed reform-objectives of the general council which met at Lyons on 26 June 1245, the German church was little affected by it either, and there was no noticeable increase in synodal activity as a result. Unlike Lateran IV with its 404 bishops and over 800 abbots in attendance, the First Council of Lyons had only about 140 episcopal participants, and

all the more remarkable the fact that so many MSS containing the Lateran IV decrees are still extant.

[6] The Second Council of Lyons (1275) revived an interest in Eudes' statutes which thereafter influenced decrees issued by various German metropolitans; cf. Johanek, "Pariser Statuten" 338-341.

[7] 1219 Worcester I; 1217/1219 Salisbury I; ?1224 Winchester I; ?1222/1225 Synodal statutes for an English diocese; 1222/1228 Canterbury II; 1229 Worcester II; ?1225/1230 Constitutiones cuiusdam episcopi; 1228/1236 Durham I; 1224/1237 Coventry; 1225/1237 Exeter I; ?1239 Lincoln; 1240 Worcester III; 1240/1243 Norwich; 1238/1244 Salisbury II; ?1247 Winchester II; 1241/1249 Durham II; 1241/1255 York I; ?1228/1256 Salisbury III; 1239/1256 Ely. See Cheney, English Synodalia vii-viii, and corresponding sections in main text; Gibbs/Lang, Bishops and Reform 129-173, 183-184; Cheney, "Statute-Making in the English Church in the Thirteenth Century," Proceedings of the Second International Congress of Medieval Canon Law, Boston College, 12-16 August 1963 (Città del Vaticano, 1965) 399-414; reprint in Idem, Medieval Texts and Studies 138-157. Cheney, Synodalia 76-84, has shown that the statutes of Exeter (1225/1237) use Richard Poore's reworking of Bishop Eudes of Paris' 1208 decrees for Salisbury and Durham (1217/1219); ca. 1250 Bishop Fulk of London used both the Exeter statutes and again directly Eudes' originals. See further, Johanek, "Pariser Statuten" 339.

of these just two represented German sees—Robert of Liège and Nicholas of Prague[8].

As a pontiff convinced of the power of the written law in shaping society, Innocent III appears to have expected his own decrees to have had a profound impact upon his generation. More recent examples of "legislated behavior" may help us to appreciate the challenges of such an expectation, however. In the seventeenth century, Oliver Cromwell and his Puritan cohorts tried to impose their vision of a Christian society upon "Merry Olde England" and ended up having to declare martial law. Herbert Rowan has remarked that "most Englishmen soon hated this new tyranny of compulsory righteousness . . . [and] began to yearn for the return to the 'good old days'."[9] In the early twentieth century the United States Congress passed and submitted to the states the Eighteenth Amendment which prohibited the manufacture, sale or transportation of alcoholic beverages in the United States. Sixteen years later another Congress repealed that same law and the "Noble Experiment" was over. To have successfully implemented the law would have required over one million federal agents (whereas as no time did they exceed three thousand), and individual liberties would have had to be suppressed.[10]

Innocent III had neither the absolute power of an early-modern statesman, nor the bureaucratic machinery of twentieth-century America. His instruments of implementation were a diverse body of men who represented a wide variety of interests—temporal as well as spiritual. Some of them appear to have understood clearly the twin aspects of their office and to have utilized every tool at their disposal in effecting change among their clergy:[11] in this respect, Archbishops Eberhard II of Salzburg and Dietrich II of Trier towered above their contemporaries. With the exception of Eberhard, however, all the German prelates who had attended the Council in 1215 were dead by the time Innocent IV convened his at Lyons in 1245.

The dual nature of the medieval bishop's office frequently brought men to the episcopacy whose family ties were more significant than their spiritual qualities. Numerous bishops were chosen because their dynastic resources offered the best hope of defending the bishopric against aggressive acts by

---

[8] H-Bréholles, *Hist.dipl.Frid. II* VI 317; Hauck, *KGD* IV 848 note 5.

[9] *A History of Early Modern Europe 1500-1815* (Indianapolis, 1960) 262.

[10] Arthur S. Link, *American Epoch: A History of the United States since the 1890s* (New York, 1960) 344.

[11] Gibbs/Lang, *Bishops and Reform* 174-176, acknowledge as well that the weakness of Innocent III's position lay in the fact that he had to rely almost entirely on the archbishops and bishops for the execution of his program; the evidence for England suggests that although individual bishops understood and were inspired by Innocent's ideal, the vast majority did not share the pope's vision and failed to grasp the magnitude of the task entrusted to them.

other powerful families. E.g., the election of 1210 at Bremen brought to
the archiepiscopal chair Gerhard I of Oldenburg as a counterpoise to the
pretender, Bishop Waldemar of Schleswig. Similarly, his successor,
Gerhard II of Lippe, seldom exhibited a grasp of the spiritual dimensions
of his office: despite couching his "crusade" against the Stedinger in the
1230s in religious and theological terms, his destruction of this region of his
archdiocese had at bottom the avenging of his brother's death and the
extension of his own territorial authority.

Family politics and the struggles between the papacy and the Hohenstaufen at various periods during the decades 1216-1245 also contributed to the
character of the German episcopacy. Of the ninety elections which occurred
between those years, thirty-six were schismatic. Some of the worst of these
disputes were in Lorraine where, e.g., the murder of Bishop Rainald of
Toul in 1217 precipitated a period of contested elections, the result of which
was that the bishopric lay vacant—without a single, universally-recognized
and consecrated head—for approximately seventeen of the thirty years
covered in this study.[12]

Other dioceses were similarly without effective and proper episcopal
leadership and supervision for extended periods of time, e.g.,: Verdun—approximately nine years; Cologne—approximately seven and one-half years;
Utrecht—approximately twenty-four years; Brixen—approximately ten years;
Magdeburg—approximately nine and one-half years. Even though in many
cases the temporal or spiritual administration of these dioceses had been
conferred upon another party, the psychological and material impact of a
vacant see must have been pronounced. Where the vacancy occurred in an
archbishopric the chain of ecclesiastical leadership was particularly broken,
inasmuch as only a metropolitan in possession of the pallium could convene
provincial synods. Thus, the unwillingness of popes to grant immediate
conferral of this symbol frustrated one of the most crucial elements of
Innocent III's reform program: without the annual provincial synod and the
continuous reminder to diocesan bishops of their obligations relative to
implementing reform within their churches, the momentum generated in
November 1215 was quickly lost.

Most of the bishoprics were more stable than these above-mentioned,
but even in those where the shepherd was generally at his watch-post the
frequent change of the person of the bishop was an apparently negative
factor in the matter of reform and discipline. The average length of the

---

[12] The list of titles dealing with episcopal elections in Germany during the thirteenth century
includes Krabbo, *Besetzung* (1901); Aldinger, *Neubesetzung* (1901); Krabbo, *Ostdeutsche
Bistümer* (1906); von Wretschko, *Besetzung* (1907); Fuchs, *Besetzung* (1911); Haid, *Besetzung
Brixen* (1912); and Diegel, *Bischofswahlen* (1932).

pontificates for all those bishops who served 1215-1245 was 15.43 years. There were twenty-five, however, whose tenure of office was less than five years; thirty-six governed more than twenty. Given the slower pace of medieval life and the virtual absence of technological and institutional aids to effect desirable change, a short pontificate was clearly less apt to implement conciliar provisions and effect change than an extended one.

Eberhard II of Salzburg presided over his church for forty-six years, yet in spite of all apparent efforts he was unable to establish any enduring effect by his reform decrees of 1216: only one copy seems to have survived to the present, suggesting that they had but a small area of impact; they did not establish a tradition of legislation since they were not used by synods held during the second half of the thirteenth century.[13] The confusion which arose in the Salzburg church after the death of Eberhard in 1246 created a break in the synodal tradition.[14] Thus, for all intents and purposes the legislative activity of the Salzburg archbishops began in the last third of the thirteenth century, the impulse for which (as in other German provinces as well) came from the Curia. It commenced with the statutes of Cardinal-legate Guido of S. Lorenzo in Lucina given at the provincial synod of Vienna in 1267, and it continued at the provincial synods of 1274, 1281, 1298 and 1310.

Despite Archbishop Dietrich II of Trier's careful maneuvering to secure the succession of his nephew Arnold of Isenburg, the latter failed to carry on the vigorous program of his uncle and a similar break is discernable in that province. It remains somewhat puzzling that Albrecht of Magdeburg with his canonistic background made no apparent attempt to legislate for his province, yet, he appears representative of an age which saw in university training (and particularly training in canon law) an important tool for securing high Church offices. The example of Berthold of Andechs, the cathedral canon at Bamberg whom Innocent III rejected for an archprelacy in Hungary, was thus not lost on at least some German clerics. Excellent training in and of itself was no guarantee that a bishop or archbishop would grasp hold of the spiritual responsibilities of his office, however. We are reminded of the assessment made of Conrad of Scharfenberg, bishop of Metz and Speyer, that he was "more at home in the administration of the

---

[13] Johanek, "Synodalia" I 91; Idem, "Die Anfänge der Salzburger Provinzialstatuten im 13. Jahrhundert und die Herzöge von Österreich," *Bericht über den dreizehnten österreichischen Historikertag in Klagenfurt, veralstaltet vom Verband Österreichischer Geschichtsvereine in der Zeit vom 18. bis 21. Mai 1976*, Veröffentlichungen des Verbandes Österreichischer Geschichtsvereine 21 (1977) 217.

[14] Johanek, *Synodalia* I 89-93.

state than in performing the duties of his ecclesiastical office, and certainly
not devout."[15]

Salzburg, Mainz and Trier are the only provinces for which there is
sufficient evidence to allow us to argue that there was some sort of
systematic or comprehensive reform program; for Cologne, Bremen and
Magdeburg the data is too fragmentary and the extenuating circumstances
non-conducive. Given the violent and chaotic nature of internal conditions
up to 1250, it is not surprising that there was actually an increase in synodal
activity in the provinces of Cologne and Bremen thereafter.

A further element stressed by the Fourth Lateranum as a tool in
effecting needed reform within the religious orders was the holding of
general chapters where this had not been customary in the past. The model
for this was the Cistercian Order whose members became active participants
in efforts to revive a spirit of discipline and commitment among the
Benedictines and canons regular. Here again, however, there is only limited
evidence for implementation in Germany:

Table E: General Chapters, 1216-1245

SALZBURG PROVINCE:	1218, 1221, 1224, 1230
TRIER PROVINCE:	1219/1220. 1230. 1239
MAINZ PROVINCE:	1222, 1224, 1227, 1234/1235[16]
BREMEN PROVINCE:	
MAGDEBURG PROVINCE:	
COLOGNE PROVINCE:	1235[17]

Existing statutes from the provinces of Mainz, Salzburg and Trier reveal a
wide range of concerns with respect to Benedictine monks and nuns, as well
as Augustinian canons. Further research is needed to assess the impact of
such decrees upon individual houses, but the fact that the stipulations of the
1218 assembly at Salzburg were repeated verbatim in 1221 and 1224 may
be an indication that little if any change occurred during the three-year intervals. Specialized studies for the other provinces would give a more
complete picture as well.

---

[15] Eduard Winkelmann, "Konrad III., Bischof von Speyer," *ADB* 16: 620.
[16] Benedictine houses in Bohemia; thereafter annually?
[17] Thereafter annually?

The evidence cited for the province of Cologne seems consistent with conditions found in many other areas of the Latin Church in the mid-1230s, resulting in the decision by Pope Gregory IX to legislate decrees for all houses of Black Monks within the Roman obedience. Whether the command to hold annual general chapters in Cologne and in Bohemia had any more success that the triennial meetings prescribed by Innocent III has not been determined, however.

Each pope of the thirteenth century tried to reform the monasteries, yet their efforts failed to have much effect on the Benedictines. Despite the presence of abbots and priors at synods, monastic affairs were seldom revealed by an outside report and were unsuitable for discussion in diocesan synods. Thus, Innocent III's program included regular visits of non-exempt religious houses, not only by diocesans, but also by metropolitans or their representatives, as the best means of getting to the heart of internal matters.[18] The visible pattern for the period 1216-1245 is checkered:

Table F: Visitations 1216-1245

DATE	PROVINCE/DIOCESE/HOUSE	MANDATE
1217	Diocese of Toul	B[19]
1218	Province of Trier	P
1218	Province of Mainz	AB
1218	Abbey of Werden	P
(by 1219)	Province of Salzburg	AB
1220	Diocese of Regensburg	B
1220	Abbey of Gorze	P
1221	Province of Trier	P
1222	Province of Salzburg	AB
1222	Abbey of Heiligenthal	P
1222	Convent Nonnenmünster	B Worms
1223	Province of Trier	P
1223/1224	Diocese of Münster	B
1226	Province of Salzburg	AB
1228	Diocese of Regensburg	B
1228	Diocese of Passau	P

[18] See M. Lingg, *Geschichte des Instituts der Pfarrvisitation* (Kempten, 1888); Hauck, *KGD* V 181; Cheney, *Episcopal Visitations* 18-23. Gibbs/Lang, *Bishops and Reform* 151-153, note that in England, as contrasted with the Continent, very scandalous houses were extremely rare.

[19] B = Bishop; AB = Archbishop; P = Pope; PL = Papal Legate.

DATE	PROVINCE/DIOCESE/HOUSE	MANDATE
1228	Diocese of Naumburg	AB
1228/1229	Cloister of St. Julia	P
1230	Archdiocese of Bremen	PL
1230	Diocese of Minden	PL
1230	Diocese of Münster	PL
1230	Diocese of Osnabrück	PL
1230	Diocese of Paderborn	PL
1230	Diocese of Verden	PL
1230	Thuringia (Archdioc. of Mainz)	AB
1231	Archdiocese of Trier	AB
1231	Abbey of Lorsch	P
ca. 1231	Cloister Neumünster at Huy	B Liège
1232	Diocese of Strasbourg	B
1232	Erfurt Priories	AB Mainz
1233	Archdiocese of Mainz	AB
1233	Cloister Villich-Rheindorf	AB Cologne
1233	Diocese of Constanz	B
1233	Cloister Neumünster at Huy	P
1234	Altenmünster near Lorsch	P
1234	Abbey of Gembloux	P
1235	Diocese of Passau	P
1236/1237	Archdiocese of Mainz	AB
1237/1238	Cloister Billigheim	B Würzburg
1238	Monastery of Winthusen	P
1238	Province of Bremen	AB
1239	Diocese of Olmütz	AB Mainz
1239	Diocese of Naumburg	AB Magdeburg
1244	Archdiocese of Mainz	P
1244	Archdiocese of Trier	P
1244	Archdiocese of Magdeburg	P

Here again the evidence is rather meager. The chronicler at Trier had indicated that after a vigorous start in that province under Archbishop Dietrich II, by his own day (ca. 1250) visitations had generally been discontinued. The papal-legate John of Tusculum declared at the national synod held at Würzburg in 1287 that they had ended throughout Germany,[20] but this was an exaggeration.[21] His words reveal, however, that the

[20] C. 27 (*Ob defectum visitationis*), cited by Hauck, *KGD* V 181.
[21] Visitations are recorded for the diocese of Passau in 1259, Cologne 1260/1261, Cologne 1263, Mainz 1264, Mainz 1275, Mainz 1277; cf. Hauck, *KGD* V 181-182. Hauck cites nearly a dozen instances between 1271 and 1300 of metropolitan visitations undertaken by the

neglect was more common than the actual execution. Part of the problem may have been that the size of German bishoprics made personal visitations difficult, especially on an annual basis. Yet, not until 1263 do we find evidence of a German prelate asking permission to use representatives in this important task.[22]

The fact that papal mandates were given in so many instances between 1216 and 1245 should not be construed as a sign that the prelates themselves were generally unwilling implementers of the papal reform program, however. One of the puzzling aspects of this entire picture is the fact that, although Innocent III had declared that suffragan bishops were obligated to attend the annual provincial synods, and that diocesan prelates were equally expected to meet with their bishop in his annual synod, even as energetic an archbishop as Eberhard II of Salzburg felt it advantageous (or necessary) to buttress his summonses with a papal bull. It is not known whether other metropolitans followed a similar tack, but its use in the Salzburg church was at once a confession that the archiepiscopal authority had lost some of its clout by the early thirteenth century and an invitation to the Curia to strengthen its hold over the episcopacy without the mediation of the archbishops. Presumably a similar practice prevailed with respect to provincial or diocesan visitations: although the ultimate commission may have come from Rome, there are clear indications that this was often in response to an episcopal request. The result was the same, however: implicit in such actions was the admission that the prelate lacked the authority to compel his subjects to accept reform measures on his own, and that only the additional endorsement of the Roman pontiff could compel their obedience.[23]

Provincial and diocesan visitations were less apt to find mention in the sources unless some provocation required further assistance from papally-appointed visitors or *iudices delegati*. The picture which has been preserved is thus somewhat fragmented. Particularly notorious religious houses appear to have flourished in the dioceses of Liège, Toul and Worms, where there is evidence of repeated attempts to correct problems. In the end, the

archbishop of Mainz; cf. *KGD* IV 20, 799; V 150, 184. (cited by Cheney, *Episcopal Visitations* 45). Hageneder has likewise provided a handful of references to monastic visitations by the bishops of Passau and their representatives, 1258-1301; cf. *Geistliche Gerichtsbarkeit*.

[22] *Westf. UB* V/1 294, Nr. 628; Urban IV grants permission to the archbishop of Cologne. The following year a similar indulgence was granted to the archbishop of Mainz; cf. Böhmer-Will, *RAM* II 371, Nr. 188.

[23] Hauck, *KGD* IV 798-799, and V 132, 148, observed that neither the German monarchs nor the German prelates halted the advance of papal authority. The evidence cited suggests just the opposite: many invited it because of their own weak position over against their clergy.

solution was either to superimpose a more rigorous rule upon the existing
community or to dissolve the house completely and transfer in Cistercians
or canons-regular.

Contraditory Elements in Innocent III's Reform Legislation

Two aspects of Innocent III's reform statutes seem to have worked against
each other: 1) those statutes which stressed the right and responsibility of
diocesan bishops to correct their own clergy (*cc.   7-8, 14-21*); 2) those
statutes which clarified and strengthened the appeal processes (*cc.* 35-36).
C. 7 stipulated that ". . . no custom or appeal can impede the execution of
[prelates'] decisions, unless they go beyond the form which is to be
observed in such matters." We have seen that in 1224 the pope reprimanded the bishop of Münster for that very thing, and there were other instances
where bishops or archbishops had acted contrary to the Council's decrees.
The evidence cited in Chh. Four and Five clearly indicates that efforts to
provide swift and summary judgments in cases brought against undisciplined
clergy often were frustrated by appeals which extended action for many
years and created enormous debts for many churches. These debts were in
turn often paid off by allowing bishops and other prelates to retain prebends
which they had held before being elevated to their present position (or
which became vacant during a three-to-five year period of time), thereby
necessitating the appointment of under-paid and often unruly vicars to
perform the obligations incumbent upon the benefice.

Pluralism and the Cura Animarum

A detailed analysis of German cathedral and collegiate chapters at mid-
century would reveal that pluralism was just as pronounced as it had been
at the beginning of Innocent III's pontificate. Despite the condemnation of
the practice by the Council (*c.* 29), especially when it hampered one's
giving proper attention to the *cura animarum*, German clerics continued to
accumulate prebends, offices and ecclesiastical titles far beyond what was
needed to sustain them in their spiritual status.[24] Hannecken's study of

---

[24] For example, the provost of the cathedral chapter at Passau in 1241, Liuprand, was also
archdeacon of Carinthia and (since 1231) *plebanus* of Neustadt; cf. Krick, *Passauer DK* 4. His
more famous contemporary, Albert Behaim, was a canon at Passau, archdeacon of Lorch (since
1226), a cathedral canon at Olmütz, provost in Vienna Neustadt, *plebanus* of Ettling, Enns,
Weiten, Rastatt, Lauffen, Mannswerde, Waldkirchen in Austria, Landshut, Pfaffenhofen,
Sleisbach, Serven, Pondorf, and yet others, papal legate for Germany (since 1239), and in 1245
became cathedral dean; cf. Krick, *Passauer DK* 11. John of Brakel, a cathedral canon at
Hildesheim since 1218, held the chapter offices of *cellerarius* 1226-1252, *custos* 1246-1250,

Paderborn, e.g., indicates that during the thirteenth and fourteenth centuries the *nobiles* in the cathedral chapter joined forces with the *ministeriales* to exclude bourgeois or non-noble individuals from the body; the process was complete by 1341.[25] In the thirteenth century, as well as before and after, the Church was regarded as an institution which provided for the excess children of noble families, and the acquisition of offices and prebends enabled the clerical members of a dynastic family to maintain a status equal to that of her/his lay siblings.

The popes contributed to the decline in the *cura animarum* in Germany as well, since they had reserved the right to grant additional prebends to suitable individuals.[26] Moreover, the development of the papal bureaucracy in the thirteenth and fourteenth centuries was responsible for a large number of requests for benefices: because clerics who served in the Curia or in the households of cardinals required support which neither the papacy nor the cardinals could supply, ecclesiastical benefices from all over Christendom were pre-empted in order to supply the stipends.[27] Papal provisions had an especially severe impact in Germany: whereas one-sixth of all of those made under Honorius III fell upon German churches, under both Gregory IX and Innocent IV the ratio rose to one in every four.[28] But, even here the burden was borne unevenly: under Honorius the

---

provost at Ölsburg 1232-1246, and provost of St. Moritz 1252-1257. In 1257 he was elected bishop of Hildesheim; cf. Lamay, *Hildesheimer DK* 50-51. Henry of Schalkenberg, mentioned first as a canon at Hildesheim in 1231, appears as *capellanus episcopi* as well in 1235, provost in Alsberg in 1262, and as both a canon at Hildesheim and at Minden in 1263; cf. Hoogeweg, *UB Hilds* II, Nrs. 316, 327, 336, 337, 340; further, *Minden UB* I, Nrs. 253, 255, 279, 281, 304, 464, 769, 780. Liupold Rindesmaul, a canon at Bamberg since 1223, is documented as an archdeacon in 1237, as cathedral *custos* 1239-1253, and as provost at St. Jacob 1243-1253; cf. Guttenberg, *Bistum Bamberg* 304-305.

[25] "Paderborn DK" 166. H. Werner, "Die Geburtsstände in der deutschen Kirche des Mittelalters," *DGbll* 9 (1908) 263, found this to be true in Westphalian religious houses as well. Wilhelm Dräger, "Das Mindener Domkapitel und seine Domherren im Mittelalter," *Mindener Jahrbuch* 8 (Minden, 1936) 117, notes, however, that members of the lower nobility and burgher class predominated at Minden and Münster,

[26] E.g., Berthold of Pietengau, the *Vitztum* of Regensburg and later bishop of Passau, was granted a dispensation from the prohibition by Innocent IV; he is mentioned as *canonicus Augustiensis* and a nephew of Bishop Conrad of Speyer in a document dated 15 May 1245 (Berger, *Registres d'Inn. IV* 195, Nr. 1270; Janner, *Regensburg* 418). On the development of canonistic theory relative to *c.* 29 of Lateran IV (*De multa*), see Kenneth Pennington, "The Canonists and Pluralism in the Thirteenth Century," *Speculum* 51/1 (1976) 34-48, and Idem, *Pope and Bishops* 115-153.

[27] Pennington, *Pope and Bishops* 116. Gibbs/Lang, *Bishops and Reform* 170-173, argue that the failure of *c.* 29 is unique in the fact that it was due almost entirely to the practices of the popes themselves; if the actions of the bishops were not very successful in stemming the tide of pluralism, the popes were more to blame.

[28] Beier, *Päpstliche Provisionen* 28.

dioceses of northwestern Germany were affected most; under Gregory IX there is a very scattered pattern, with only the archdiocese of Cologne showing any appreciable disadvantage; but under Innocent IV, over one-third of all provisions made in Germany fell on three dioceses—Basel, Strasbourg and Constanz. Beyond that, the distribution is more pronounced in the western regions than in the eastern.[29] Presumably, the closeness of southwestern Germany to the Curia accounts for the great disparity.[30]

This enormous increase in the number of papal provisions, and the parallel survival of traditional pluralistic practices among the German clergy, resulted in the widespread use of vicars with all the abuses which that practice entailed (and against which the Fourth Lateranum had pronounced). Major efforts within the provinces of Mainz and Trier between 1216 and 1245 had failed to curtail absenteeism to any appreciable degree. The almost total disregard for the residence requirement in the cathedral chapter at Mainz in the final years before the dissolution of the *vita communis* can be seen in the possibility of the simultaneous absence of three prelates and several other *capitulares* (among them the archpriest) at a time when a document was issued by their fellow canons; upon their return they declared the charter null and void.[31] A similar situation could be found in the diocese of Regensburg where at Alte Kapelle there were eighteen canons, yet on feast days hardly five or six were present to perform choir and altar obligations; thus, a statute issued by the bishop on 1247 decreed that henceforth absences totalling no more than six weeks in a given year would be allowed only with the consent of the dean.[32]

Apart from Trier where Archbishop Dietrich II actually tried to re-institute at least part of the *vita communis* by requiring all members of his cathedral chapter to participate in a *mensa communis*, most remedies applied to the problem of absenteeism were conservative, similar and generally ineffective: withhold incomes from those ignoring the residence require-ment. The cathedral canons ate in a common refectory at Mainz, Bremen,

---

[29] Beier, *op.cit.* 25-26. On 30 September 1248 a document was issued at the command of the pope and the papal legate then in Germany, ordering the cathedral church at Constanz to provide thirty-eight prebends for designated individuals: fourteen had already been accommodated, but an additional twenty-four were waiting their turn; cf. Beier, *op.cit.* 32.

[30] Beier, *op.cit.* 26, 33.

[31] Gudenus, *CdMogunt* I 634 (dated 13 February 1253); cited in Biskamp, *Mainzer DK* 11.

[32] Janner, *Regensburg* 425. As early as 10 January 1236 Pope Gregory IX had confirmed a statute issued by the dean and chapter at Alte Kapelle ". . . *ut proventus beneficiorum canonicorum absentium in fabricam ecclesiae suae, nimia vetustate consumptae, et in solutionem eiusdem ecclesiae debitorum convertantur*"; see Auvray, *Registres de Gregoire IX* II, Nr. 2905.

Utrecht, Minden, Würzburg, Augsburg, Freising, and Halberstadt as the thirteenth century began, and at Freising, Hildesheim and Lübeck they also slept in a common dormitory. Such practices were severely challenged during the first half of the 1200s, however, and in many cases the *vita communis* disappeared altogether, yet another victim to the growing secular spirit among the German clergy. We have noted specifically the example of Mainz where all vestiges of the common life among the cathedral clergy had vanished by the time of the First Council of Lyons. Even the efforts of Cardinal-legate Otto in 1230 could not prevent a similar development at Minden.[33]

Other serious conditions prevailed even in those churches where absenteeism seemed less a problem, however. Mention was made in Ch. Two of the crisis which existed at Cologne until ca. 1217 because of a lack of consecrated priests who could officiate at the altar.[34] Presumably the stress which Lateran IV placed on the proper discharge of the *cura animarum* resulted in corrective measures at Cologne, but results were probably temporary at best. In 1250 the papal-legate Peter of Albano complained that the number of subdeacons and deacons in the cathedral chapter at Liège was so low "*quod non possit ad maius altare per canonicos deserviri.*"[35] He therefore ordained that six canons be given consecration as subdeacons and deacons in his presence. Such a calamity had not occurred overnight, but had resulted from the fact that new members of the chapter had refused to accept the "spiritual" obligations incumbent upon their prebends. The gradual attrition of canons possessing higher grades of consecration eventually resulted in the inability of the cathedral church to fulfill one of its most important functions.

This "secular" attitude also reached to the highest offices in the German church. Evidence from the bishopric of Toul shows that in at least one instance (and presumably others) individuals were instituted as abbots who had not even made their profession. The ambitious abbot of St. Gall squandered the resources of his house in his vain pursuit of an episcopal office. Perhaps most telling was Philip of Ortenburg, however, who was elected as archbishop of Salzburg in 1247 as the successor to Eberhard II, but refused to receive episcopal consecration despite all canonical regula-

---

[33] Cf. the legate's statute for the Minden cathedral chapter, *Westf. UB* VI 207: "*Item statuimus, quod precipue in refectorio et dormitorio honeste et disciplinate se habeant; qui aliter se habeat, a decano pro qualitate commissi graviter puniatur.*" Dräger, "Mindener DK" 20, argues that the dissolution occurred shortly after 1230 and was clearly evident by 1250; cf. *Westf. UB* VI 542, 677.

[34] See above, pp. 168-169.

[35] Cited in Görres, *Lütticher DK* 21.

tions.   On 5 September 1257 the cathedral chapter sent its provost and
another canon to Rome to protest before the Curia that Philip had sat, not
as a bridegroom but as an adulterer, for the past nine years. Philip was also
accused of having lost 10,000 Marks in games of chance. Having no
defense against the charges, he was excommunicated in 1256 and deposed
the following year.[36]

Papal Provisions

Although papal provisions were contested in many German churches during
the thirteenth century, there were instances where they were welcomed.
Beier found no evidence of political overtones before or during the
pontificate of Innocent III, but by the 1240s provisions were often employed
as a means of rewarding those who supported the papacy in its struggle
against the Hohenstaufen dynasty.   Strasbourg, one of the most heavily
affected dioceses, illustrates this policy in astonishing detail.   Henry of
Stahleck, bishop of Strasbourg (1244-1260), was the son and grandson of
men who had supported the Hohenstaufen, and who had been rewarded
through that service. Beginning his career as a canon at Mainz, a position
he owed to family ties with the church at Mainz, Henry extended his
ecclesiastical sphere of activity into Alsace by virtue of his mother's family
ties.[37] During the last great conflict between the Emperor Frederick II and
the Papacy, however, Bishop Henry stood on the side of Innocent IV. As
reward for his loyalty, he and his relations received numerous favors from
the Roman Curia, which are noted in the episcopal cartulary.

On 17 November 1246, Bishop Henry received permission to grant a
dispensation to a cleric named Frederick, the son of his maternal uncle—the
provost of Surburg, in order that a *defectus natalium* would not prevent this
Friedrich from acquiring prebends in addition to the parish church at
Bischofsheim. Among these other prebends were the *scolastria* at Surburg,

---

[36] Janner, *Regensburg* 457; Alfred von Wretschko, *Zur Frage der Besetzung des
erzbischöflichen Stuhles in Salzburg im Mittelalter* (Stuttgart, 1907) 6-7, 27-38, 78-79; Fischer,
Amtsdaten 60-62.   On 1 April 1251 Philip (at the time possessing the consecration as
subdiaconus) received the diaconal blessing at Prague from the hands of Bishop Nicolaus; cf.
Cosmae chron. 173.

[37] The scion of a Lower-Rhine family of nobles which took the fortress Dicke near
Grevenbroich (archdiocese of Cologne) as its seat, Henry of Stahleck became bishop of
Strasbourg in 1244, having previously been a canon both there and in Mainz, as well as an
archdeacon at Strasbourg; cf. Hessel, *Regg. Strassburg* II 92ff., significant corrections to which
are offered in my forthcoming article, "Die Herren von Stahleck aus den Geschlechtern von
Dicke und Brunshorn: Ein Beitrag zur Familien- und Territorialgeschichte des Niederrheins,
des Mittelrheins und des Elsasses."

a prebend in the church of St. Thomas in Strasbourg, and a third one unnamed.[38] The provost of Surburg in the year 1246 was one Frederick of Hagenau who, as early as 1233, appears as the *cellerarius* of the Strasbourg cathedral chapter.[39] His presence there as an office holder explains as well how Henry of Stahleck (the son of a female member of the von Hagenau family) gained entry into the Strasbourg cathedral chapter. After Henry became bishop, he rewarded his uncle by elevating him to the office of cathedral provost at Strasbourg, and by granting the above-mentioned prebends to Frederick's base-born son.

A letter dictated 9 March 1247 by Innocent IV conferred on Bishop Henry the power to seek prebends with an annual income of up to 100 Marks of silver within the ecclesiastical provinces of Mainz and Trier for Alexander and Richwin, sons of his sister.[40] On 27 February of the same year Innocent IV also issued a dispensation for one Frederick of Stahleck, an apparent brother of the Strasbourg bishop, allowing him to acquire additional offices and prebends.[41] On 7 January 1255 Bishop Henry received from Innocent IV permission to install his nephew Henry, the son of his brother Alexander and the parish priest at Ebersheim, in the cathedral chapter itself, provided of course that the chapter members gave their assent.[42] A further papal dispensation, granted 27 April 1258, gave Bishop Henry permission to exempt his nephew John, a cathedral canon at Strasbourg, from the papal decree which limited the number of prebends which a canon might possess at any given time.[43]

The last close relatives of Bishop Henry to benefit from his political alignment in the papal camp were the brothers Günther und Egelolf *de Landesperc*, who are mentioned in a document of 1254 as clerics and as

[38] Hessel, *Regg. Strassburg* II, Nr. 1168.

[39] Idem, II, Nr. 1006. In February 1251 he was in the process of surrendering the office of provost at Surburg; cf. Idem, II, Nr. 1353.

[40] Idem, II, Nr. 1190. On 15 July 1247 Bishop Henry III also received from the pope permission to acquire a dignity for his nephew, the cathedral canon at Worms Alexander, within his episcopal city or diocese; cf. Idem, II, Nr. 1227. It is undoubtedly the same person. That Alexander also received a position within the Trier church can be deduced from the fact that from 1251-1258 an Alexander appears as scholastic at St. Paulin in Trier; cf. Beyer, *MRUB* III 1117.

[41] Hessel, *Regg. Strassburg* II, Nrs. 1185, 1186.

[42] Hessel, *Regg. Strassburg* II, Nr. 1483. From the outset of Henry's pontificate his brother Alexander is mentioned in his immediate company, often as *frater domini episcopi*. See, Idem, II, Nr. 1400; Goerz, *MRR* III, Nrs. 306, 307, 1262; Herrmann, *Grafschaft Saarwenden* I, Nr. 118. For Alexander of Dicke as *frater domini episcopi*, cf. Hessel, op.cit. II, Nrs. 1208, 1286, 1313. In the year 1258 Henry appointed his brother to be the burgrave of Strasbourg, and declared that Alexander's son of the same name should follow him in that office; cf. Idem, II, Nr. 1531.

[43] Hessel, *Regg. Strassburg* II, Nr. 1536.

nephews of the prelate.[44]   Their father was undoubtedly the Günther I of Landsberg who appears 1230-1260 as a *ministerialis* of the Strasbourg church; their mother must then be the noblewoman Beligna, who is documented 1230-1251.

This favoring of episcopal relatives went far beyond the immediate family members, however. On 3 May 1247 Innocent IV granted permission to Bishop Henry to bestow the office of *mansivus* within the bishopric to whomever he wished, an office which at that particular time was held by the Archdeacon Hugo, a *consanguineus* of the bishop. This Hugo appears in a document from Trier in 1242 as *Hugo de Petra archidiaconus Argent.*; since 1223 he had been a cathedral canon at Trier as well. The dynasty to which Hugo belonged was that of Stein-Kallenfels, which was only distantly related to Henry's own through marriage.[45] Other *consanguinei* of Bishop Henry were also given benefices: on 17 April 1247 Innocent IV commissioned the prelate to obtain for his *consanguineus* Anselm, a cathedral canon at Speyer, a prebend in the cities or churches of Worms or Strasbourg. One month later Henry received from the pope permission to install this Anselm in the Strasbourg cathedral chapter itself. There is no evidence that this was ever done, since Anselm's name never appears among those cathedral canons who witnessed episcopal documents. On the other hand, a document dated 1249 provides evidence that Anselm had been elevated to the provostship of St. Martins in Worms.[46] Anselm appears for the first time in the year 1220 as a *prebendarius* at Speyer.[47] He was presumably a member of the noble dynasty of Stein-Kallenfels; as such he would have been a cousin to the Archdeacon Hugo of Strasbourg, with family ties to the bishop.

The recipient of a dispensation granted on 28 April 1249 by Innocent IV was a certain Everardus, a canon at Carden-on-the-Mosel, to whom further prebends were given.[48] Again, this cleric appears to be a member of the family of the lords of Oberstein who, through marriage, came to become a *consanguineus* of Bishop Henry. Other relationships are more difficult to

---

[44] Idem, II, Nr. 1444.

[45] Hessel, *Regg. Strassburg* II, Nr. 1209; Beyer, *MRUB* III, Nr. 756. For Hugo as a canon at Trier, see Idem, *MRUB* III 251, 273, 277, 360, 376, 385, 479, 829, 985, 996, 1017, 1179, 1210, 1241, 1262, 1272. At times he appears as *Hugo de Lapide.* On the family of Hugo, see Beyer, *MRUB* II lxxxiii; cf. also Walther Möller, *Stammtafeln westdeutscher Adelsgeschlechter im Mittelalter* III (Darmstadt, 1936) Table cxxiv.

[46] Hessel, *Regg. Strassburg* II, Nrs. 1203, 1213, 1298.

[47] Remling, *UB Speyer* I 1852, Nr. 140.

[48] Hessel, *Regg. Strassburg* II, Nr. 1302.

establish, however. On 27 November 1247 Bishop Henry III of Strasbourg was commissioned to allow his *consanguineus* Walther of Mietesheim to enjoy his prebends another five years, even should he retreat back into the ranks of the laity. Twenty years earlier, in the year 1228, Walther of Mietesheim appears as *advocatus Argent., liber*, and in 1233 he was apparently still a member of the laity.[49] In the years following, however, he became a cleric.

This amazingly complex set of family relationships reveals just how far the papacy was willing to go in order to reward loyal German prelates. At the same time it lays bare the problems of papal provisions. Clerics were being granted prebends which lay within various, separate ecclesiastical obediences. Thus, in a situation not unlike the lay world where the multiplication of fiefs led to a confusion of primary or liege obligations, resulting in the commutation of personal services to cash payments and a loosening of the personal bonds which had given stability and definition to eleventh and twelfth-century society, the thirteenth-century German church was becoming a congeries of ecclesiastical prebend-holders who received incomes from a wide range of offices and benefices, fulfilling few of the obligations incumbent upon those positions themselves, rather relying on surrogates who were underpaid and presumably perfunctory in their performance of duties.

Clerical Alternatives in the Thirteenth Century

If one were to use the examples of Conrad of Urach and Conrad of Krosigk from the early thirteenth century as illustrative models, then the alternative available for those members of the secular clergy disillusioned over the lack of discipline found among their contemporaries was to become a Cistercian monk. For Albert of Stade in 1240 it meant becoming a member of the Minorite Order. Presumably there were many other men and women in Germany who were able to find an outlet for their religiosity within the existing framework of the Church.[50] But the evidence presented in the preceding chapters also shows that resistance to reform measures such as those enacted at the Fourth Lateran Council came both from individual clerics within a given community, and from entire houses.

---

[49] Idem, II, Nrs. 1236, 932, 1006.

[50] Freed, *Friars and German Society* Table XV (233-237), lists but a handful of German clerics who became Franciscans before 1250: Bernhard of Poppenburg, a Hildesheim cathedral canon (1223); Albert of Stade (1240); Walter of Reutlingen, scholastic at Chur (1247).

We have considered the personalities of individual German prelates, discovering in the process a wide range of preparation for the episcopal office, and an equally wide range of attitudes towards its obligations. Clearly the personalities of individual popes was a factor in Church reform as well. One has to wonder how the relationship between the papacy and the German empire (including within it the German churches) might have been different had Conrad of Urach, cardinal-bishop of Porto and S. Rufina, accepted the proffered papal tiara in 1227.[51] Instead, the office of Roman pontiff was conferred upon his equally-illustrious colleague, Ugolino de Segni, the cardinal-bishop of Ostia and Velletri, who took the title of Gregory IX. The somewhat conciliatory pontificate of Honorius III was thus followed by a more aggressive one in which the Curia pressed its advantage over-against the prelates of Germany and other regions of western Christendom. Our search through papal registers has left the unmistakable impression that the Curia devoted far less time to reform-matters in the German church after 1226 than it did during the pontificates of Innocent III and Honorius III.

There can be little doubt that the political issues which tore apart German society between 1198 and 1218 greatly affected the ability of the institutional Church to perform its role to any degree of effectiveness. Even the papacy found itself forced to compromise on certain principles in order to achieve political objectives in Germany. The lofty rhetoric of papal missives and public pronouncements was sacrificed for the expedient of political advantage. Once the papal-Hohenstaufen conflict increased once again to a frenzied pitch in the early 1240s, any real opportunity for significant reform within the Church had passed. As had been true earlier in the century, the German clergy were forced to choose sides in the political sphere. The monarchs cared little for such subtle matters as spiritual regeneration or ecclesiastical discipline; they saw the German church as the source of tremendous power and the guardian of enormous resources which could be pressed into service in its behalf. The papacy, on the other hand, showed a similar willingness to abandon principles which its predecessors had sought to inculcate into the thinking and practice of the clergy.

Our study has of necessity restricted itself to but a few of the decrees of the Fourth Lateranum as they related to efforts among the German episcopacy to improve the discipline within their respective churches after 1215. Only occasionally have we considered the institution of more or better schools, and the establishment of episcopal penitentiaries or episcopal

---

[51] *Historia Villariensis*, ed. Edmond Martène & Ursin Durand, *Thesaurius novus* III 1275; Roth von Schreckenstein, "Urach" 365.

officiales.[52] The picture is thus far from complete, and these topics deserve an equally thorough investigation.

Ecclesiastical reform cannot be seen as a single act which one completes, and then moves on. Reform of any type is an on-going process which requires a willing heart (or at least a mind that is willing to overrule a stubborn heart). Our study has shown that there were several bishops during the three decades 1216-1245 whose heart was in tune with the program laid out by Pope Innocent III. But even the most energetic of these could not prevail against deeply entrenched abuses within the fabric of their respective churches. Often as not they found themselves treating just the symptoms, and not the root causes.

We have used as the theme of this study the metaphor of the "Watchman on the Tower," a phrase employed by both Pope Innocent III and members of the German episcopacy. In his first epistle to the Christian Saints at Corinth, St. Paul wrote:

> For if the trumpet give an uncertain sound, who shall prepare himself to the battle? So likewise ye, except ye utter by the tongue words easy to be understood, how shall it be known what is spoken? for ye shall speak into the air. There are, it may be, so many kinds of voices in the world, and none of them is without signification. Therefore if I know not the meaning of the voice, I shall be unto him that speaketh a barbarian, and he that speaketh shall be a barbarian unto me. Even so, forasmuch as ye are zealous of spiritual gifts, seek that ye may excel to the edifying of the church.[53]

Clearly, the German episcopacy responded to a variety of "voices" in the thirteenth century, and in so doing they gave an "uncertain sound" from their watchtower. The hoped-for renewal of the Church never came.

---

[52] According to Gescher, "Offizialatsstatut" 477, the archbishopric of Mainz, with its suffragans Speyer, Worms, Constanz and Strasbourg, led the way in the introduction of the *officialis*. The pattern seems more complex than that, however. Liège is documented with such an episcopal functionary in 1204 (Gescher, *op.cit.* 278); Mainz in 1209 (Carlen, "Offizialat" 221); Trier before 1212 (Corsten, "EB Johann I. von Trier" 133-134); Augsburg 1219 (Carlen, *op.cit.* 221); Halberstadt 1235 (Carlen, *op.cit.* 221); Speyer 1237 (Carlen, *op.cit.* 221); Worms 1243 (Carlen, *op.cit.* 221); Cologne 1252 [prior to 1224?] (Gescher, *op.cit.* 476); Constanz 1256 (Carlen, *op.cit.* 221); Chur 1273 (Carlen, *op.cit.* 221).

[53] 1 Cor. 14, 8-12.

EPILOGUE

THE FOURTH LATERANUM IN PERSPECTIVE

The foregoing study examines three levels of medieval Church government: 1) that directly administered by the papacy and/or the Roman Curia; 2) that of the ecclesiastical province; and 3) that controlled by diocesan bishops. The existence of the medieval German state or Empire is also discernable, though there was no corresponding element in ecclesiastical administration: there were in fact several imperial bishoprics which have been excluded from this study because they were part of provinces which lay predominantly outside the Empire.

The Fourth Lateran Council was a further extension of a tradition which originated in the primitive Church when disciples of Christ gathered at Jerusalem to establish policies with respect to the imposition of Old Testament prescriptions on pagan converts.[1] In the post-Apostolic era, bishops of the different Roman provinces developed the practice of gathering to discuss and reach decisions on matters of both theological and disciplinary nature, as e.g., the assembly of bishops from Asia Minor ca. A.D. 170 to treat the problem of Montanism. The conciliar or synodal practice was thus already fully developed in the Church before the conversion of Constantine I, who in 325 convoked a council of bishops from the entire Roman Empire at Nicaea, thus establishing the universal or "ecumenical" council.[2] Between the First Council of Nicaea and the Second Council of Nicaea (787) regular or extraordinary gatherings of bishops dealt with a host of issues, the most controversial of which tended to involve definitions of the Godhead. Seven of these councils were recognized by both the Orthodox Church of Byzantium and the Roman Catholic Church as authentically ecumenical, that is, representative of and binding upon all of Christendom.

Factors at once political and theological created a schism between East and West which ultimately ended the possibility of joint councils. Within each division of Christendom the conciliar tradition continued, however. In the Latin West a variety of councils was held from the ninth century on: the great royal-imperial assemblies of the Carolingian age, the general councils convened under papal auspices in the eleventh century and thereafter, provincial gatherings directed by a papal legate or the metropoli-

---

[1] Acts 15:1-30.

[2] Cf. J. Gaudemet, *La Formation du droit séculier et du droit de l'eglise aux IVe et Ve siècles* (Paris, 1957).

tan, and diocesan synods at which the clergy of a diocese assembled under the presidency of the local bishop.

Although the Greek Church later rejected the Fourth Council of Constantinople (869-870) as ecumenical, from the eleventh century the Latin Church ranked it with the seven earlier ecumenical councils as the eighth universal synod. Of the many other important councils convened directly by the papacy or by papal legates from the mid-eleventh century until 1179, the status of "ecumenical" is reserved by the modern Roman Church only for those held in the Lateran (I) in 1123 by Calixtus II, in 1139 (II) by Innocent II, and 1179 (III) by Alexander III. Eleventh-century canonists in the West also introduced the notion that all of the earlier ecumenical councils had been celebrated with papal authority. The *Dictatus papae* of Pope Gregory VII (1073-1085) even declared that no synod (i.e., council) may be called a general one without his order (*c.* 16). Stated in other terms, only the approbation of the Roman see could give a council the certainty of being consistent with the true traditions of the universal church.[3]

Whereas the early-Christian councils were pre-occupied with doctrinal matters, those of the Latin West from ca. 1050 to 1122 gave much greater attention to various aspects of "reform" as constantly re-defined in each new generation: such issues as simony, clerical continence, and lay investiture were paramount. As the dominance of lay princes—particularly by the German emperors—became less evident, councils and provincial synods alike took on a different character, giving greater attention to the internal affairs of the Church. The Third Lateran Council (1179), for example, attended by some three hundred bishops, including eighteen from Germany, stipulated that no persons should be consecrated as bishop before attaining the age of thirty, and it condemned the practice of pluralism where the cure of souls was involved.[4]

---

[3] On the *Dictatus papae*, cf. Karl Hoffmann, "Der 'Dictatus papae' Gregors VII. als Index einer Kanonessammlung," *Epistolae selecta* II.1 (1920) 201-208; S. Löwenfeld, "Der Dictatus papae Gregors VII. und eine Ueberarbeitung desselben im XII. Jahrhundert," *NA* 16 (1891).

[4] Cf. John Meyendorff, "Councils (Ecumenical, 325-787)," *Dictionary of the Middle Ages*, ed. Joseph R. Strayer, III (New York, 1983) 627-631; Robert Somerville, "Councils, Western (869-1179)," *op.cit.* III 632-639. For the development of the notion of general councils in the High Middle Ages and the relation of that concept to the ecumenical councils of the Roman church, see Horst Fuhrmann, "Das ökumenische Konzil und seine historischen Grundlagen," *Geschichte in Wissenschaft und Unterricht* 12 (1961), which in places corrects the work of Albert Hauck, "Die Rezeption und Umbildung der allgemeinen Synode im Mittelalter," *HVj* 10 (1907) 465-482. See also Remigius Bäumer, "Die Zahl der allgemeinen Konzilien in der Sicht von Theologen des 15. und 16. Jahrhunderts," *AHC* 1 (1969); Cheney, "The Numbering of the Lateran Councils in 1179 and 1215," *Medieval Texts and Studies* (1973) 203-208.

There was thus a substantial tradition of conciliar decrees regarding ecclesiastical reform previous to the accession of Innocent III in 1198. From the very outset of his pontificate he had hoped to convene a general council, but this remained an unrealized objective until he had re-established control over affairs in the Empire (or so he thought); only in April 1213 could he issue the bull *Vineam domini Sabaoth*, formally announcing the council for November 1215. The large number of those attending this assembly confirmed in fact the theories of papal primacy that had been developing for centuries in the Western Church, and that Innocent III utilized with consummate skill. In addition to the more than twelve hundred ecclesiastical figures present, representatives from many of the major states of Latin Christendom also witnessed the pomp and circumstance which transpired within the basilica of St. John Lateran during the course of an entire month. Noticeably absent, however, were envoys of the Greek Church, undoubtedly due to the Latin conquest of Constantinople in 1204; the Orthodox half of Christendom was thus represented in a figurative sense only.[5]

The constitutions of the Fourth Lateranum touched upon a wide spectrum of issues, making definitive statements with respect to orthodox beliefs and condemning heresy, strengthening the hand of metropolitans and bishops with respect to their clergy, extending greater control over conventuals, imposing restrictions upon lay encroachments into ecclesiastical matters, clarifying canonical processes (such as appeals), reducing by three the forbidden degrees of consanguinity, and instituting the practice of annual auricular confession for all individuals who had attained the age of accountability.[6] Johannes Haller has reminded us that the need for reform

---

[5] At the very beginning of the pontificate of Innocent III a general council was envisaged, in the correspondence between Rome and Byzantium, as a possible and desirable framework for reunion discussions; differences in intentions brought the dialogue to an abrupt halt, and it was only near the end of Innocent's pontificate that the council finally met, albeit under totally different circumstances. See Jedin, *Handbook of Church History* IV 166-167.

[6] Cf. Paul B. Pixton, "Councils, Western (1215-1274)," *Dictionary of the Middle Ages* III 639-642. On the importance of the Fourth Lateranum, cf. Hauck, "Rezeption und Umbildung der allgemeinen Synode" 465-482; Foreville, *Lateran I-IV* 296ff.; Antonio Garcia y Garcia, "El gobierno de la Iglesia universal en el concilio IV Lateranense de 1215," *AHC* 1 (1969) 50: "*El concilio IV de Latran es . . . el concilio ecumenico mas importante de toda le Edad Media.*" W. Imkamp, "Sermo ultimus, quem fecit Dominus Innocentius papa tercius in Lateranensi concilio generali," *Römische Quartalschrift* 70 (1975) 149-179. In addition to the larger works already cited, see Peter Browe, *Die häufige Kommunion im Mittelalter* (1938); Jean Dauvillier, *Le mariage dans le droit classique de l'église depuis le Décret de Gratien (1140) à la mort de Clement V (1314)* (1933); Solomon Grayzell, *The Church and the Jews in the XIIIth Century* (Philadelphia, 1933); T.P. McLaughlin, "The Teaching of the Canonists on Usury (XII, XIII and XIV Centuries)," *Medieval Studies* 1 (1939) 81-147, and 2 (1940).

within the Church was not peculiar to this or any other period of the Middle Ages, however; it extended across many centuries and was perhaps as old as the Church itself.[7] The model was that of reform-decadence and was essentially backward-looking: reform returned the institutions of the Church to a more perfect or correct former state.[8]

Alongside this conservative view of the *ecclesia* (or to use the Pauline model—the *corpus Christi*) was a forward-looking one which took on greater significance during the course of the twelfth century: in this view the past lost its quality of representing the absolute to which all contemporary institutions must look for legitimation, while at the same time innovations lost the stigma of being inherently bad. Representative of this new spirit were the reform orders which were a response to changing socio-economic conditions and to the greater expectations of the post-Gregorian period.[9]

During the twelfth century the papacy, the canonists and the theologians began to develop the concept of "*reformatio tam in capite quam in membris*" with reference to smaller ecclesiastical bodies such as cathedral chapters, monasteries, and foundations.[10] Between the time of Alexander III and Innocent III variations of this phrase became common in letters which emanated from the papal chancery, and given the latter pope's continual involvement in the operations of his Curia it was probably he himself who was responsible for its being introduced into the canon law books. Since his time practically all popes employed the phrase.[11]

For the orthodox thinkers of the twelfth century as well as for Pope Innocent III reform must conform to the hierarchical structure of the Church

---

[7] Cf. Johannes Haller, *Papsttum und Kirchenreform. Vier Kapitel zur Geschichte des ausgehenden Mittelalters*, I (2nd ed.; Berlin-Zürich-Dublin, 1966) 10; Frech, *Reform an Haupt und Gliedern* 92. Gerhard B. Ladner, "Erneuerung," in *Reallexikon für Antike und Christentum*, ed. Theodor Klauser, 6 (Leipzig, 1941†) col. 268, notes that „*Die Geschichte des mittelalterlichen Christentums ist eine lange Kette der Reformen.*"

[8] On the role of the primitive Church as a model for twelfth century reform, see Giles Constable, "Renewal and Reform in Religious Life," *Renaissance and Renewal in the Twelfth Century*, ed. Robert L. Benson and Giles Constable (Oxford, 1982) 51-56; Magnus Ditsche, "Die Ecclesia primitiva im Kirchenbild des hohen und späten Mittelalters," (Dissertation Bonn, 1958); Gordon Leff, "The Apostolic Ideal in Later Medieval Ecclesiology," *Journal of Theological Studies*, 2nd ser., 18 (1967) 58-82. See further, Giles Constable, "Seminar III. Reformatio," *Ecumenical Dialogue at Harvard. The Roman Catholic-Protestant Colloquium*, ed. S.H. Miller and G.H. Wright (Cambridge, 1964) 332; B. Bolton, *The Medieval Reformation* (New York, 1983) 13.

[9] Cf. Frech, *Reform an Haupt und Gliedern* 92-95; Constable, "Seminar III. Reformatio" 332-333; Idem., "Renewal and Reform" 38-39.

[10] Frech, *Reform an Haupt und Gliedern* 113ff., finds the first clear articulation of the meaning of this phrase (if not the actual words) in a letter written by Pope Alexander III to Archbishop Henry of Rheims ca. 1171.

[11] Frech, *Reform an Haupt und Gliedern* 365; Tillmann, *Innocenz III.* 256.

and of society: the head must direct the body; the members must follow where the head leads. Reform from below was unthinkable.[12] The mandates given by Innocent III and his immediate successors to their representatives essentially gave them a free hand to correct whatever abuses they encountered, though the Roman pontiffs generally thought in terms of the smaller units of ecclesiastical organization (e.g., "*in monasterio Gemblacensi corrigenda et reformanda corrigat et reformet*"): seldom if ever did they grant authority to reform entire dioceses from the prelate on down. Canons 6 and 7 of the Fourth Lateran Council reaffirmed the traditional role of the archbishops and bishops in the on-going process of reform: the *membra* were to be corrected by the *caput*.[13]

The Fourth Lateranum thus marked the high point in medieval reform legislation and is generally considered the most important Western council before Trent. It stands out as a unique event, representing the papal monarchy in all its majesty as Innocent III dealt with matters both temporal and spiritual. At the same time, however, this council may also have aroused greater expectations which suffered a serious set-back when this powerful Roman pontiff died so soon after its conclusion; a great deal of the momentum generated at Lateran IV was undoubtedly and irretrievably lost.[14]

To men trained in the tradition of canon law, the constitutions of the Fourth Lateranum, when coupled with the existing institutions of the Church, should have been capable of producing the *desideratum*—a regeneration of the Church. But the medieval world (and its modern successor) also had to deal with the sometimes unknown or unpredictable factor of human nature which often skewed the equasion. Thus, as we have seen, the legislation of Lateran IV had little appreciable impact on the German church in general, or upon the vast majority of German clerics as individuals. Imposed from above, the Lateran decrees failed in their intended purpose and remained for the most part mere bureaucratic statutes.[15]

1215 was not the last opportunity for the medieval Church to look into itself and to effect changes which would enable it to respond to the social,

---

[12] Frech, *Reform an Haupt und Gliedern* 34, 77, 102.

[13] Frech, *Reform an Haupt und Gliedern* 135, 151-159. S.C.J. Naslund, "Papal-Cistercian Relations: 1198-1241. With Particular Emphasis on France" (Dissertation, University of Illinois, 1976) 30, observes: "Reform of the Church for Pope Innocent meant total reform on every level of ecclesiastical life."

[14] Cf. Tillmann, *Innocenz III.* 164; Geoffrey Barraclough, *The Medieval Papacy* (1968) 135.

[15] Frech, *Reform an Haupt und Gliedern* 159; Gibbs/Lang, *Bishops and Reform* 153-158, 174ff.

economic and political forces which repeatedly intersected with it. Though it moved too slowly for some, it is to the credit of this immense institution that it was able to capture the enthusiasm of a Bernard or a Francis and to generate periodic reform from within its own ranks. Seen through the eyes of Innocent III in 1215, there were sufficient religious orders to suffice the Church—men and women both could choose from among the various interpretations of St. Benedict's Rule, opting for houses which were part of the larger Cistercian, Benedictine, Cluniac, Franciscan, or Dominican orders, or of the Premonstratensian, or other canons regular.[16] Unwittingly, he forced some expressions of late medieval spirituality outside the structures which flourished in his own day.

For almost three decades following the great council, the Roman pontiffs sparred with Frederick II over his promise to undertake a crusade and his intentions in Italy.   In 1241 the emperor exacerbated already-fragile relations by capturing more than one hundred prelates who were *en route* to a Roman council and by seizing papal territory and forcing Pope Innocent IV to seek refuge at Lyons. To deal with the renewed imperial threat, and to consider matters of ecclesiastical reform, a new crusade, aid to Constantinople, and measures against the Mongols—the "five wounds" of the Church, Innocent IV convoked a general council for Lyons in June 1245.[17]

Not surprisingly, attendance by bishops from areas ruled by Frederick II was sparse—from the Empire, only those of Prague and Liège. Thus, as Innocent IV rose on 28 June 1245 in the cathedral of Lyons to speak on the words of Jeremiah: "Behold, and see if there be any sorrow like unto my sorrow," he addressed a predominantly Spanish, French, and English assembly of one hundred fifty bishops. Joining them were abbots, generals of the new orders, and representatives of invited chapters, cities, and provinces   Although clerical abuses were among the issues covered in the twenty-two constitutions adopted by the council, political issues were predominant. The council was an attempt, only partly successful, to mobilize Christian opinion against the emperor.[18] It is characteristic of the

---

[16] This effort to retain papal control over medieval spirituality is discussed in broad terms by Jeffrey Burton Russell, *A History of Medieval Christianity: Prophecy and Order* (New York, 1968), espec. 1-9, 181-195.

[17] David Abulafia, *Frederick II: A Medieval Emperor* (Oxford, 1988) 342-366; Alfred Haverkamp, *Medieval Germany 1056-1273* (2nd ed.; Oxford, 1992) 260-261.

[18] See August Folz, *Kaiser Friedrich II. und Papst Innocenz IV. Ihr Kampf in den Jahren 1244 und 1245* (Strasbourg, 1905); James M. Powell, "Frederick II and the Church: A Revisionist View," *Catholic Historical Review* 48 (1962-1963) 487-497; Barraclough, *The Medieval Papacy* 135. On the preparation for the council, its course and its outcome, cf. Hans Wolter and H. Holstein, *Lyon I et Lyon II*, Histoire des Conciles Oecuméniques 7 (Paris, 1966).

First Council of Lyons that its decrees, to the extent that they touched upon internal Church affairs, were "entirely confined to technical questions of law and procedure," an indication of how far the legal spirit had increased at the curia. To what extent the decrees relating to judicial reform, limitations on the powers of judges-delegate, and responsible stewardship of Church property had any measurable impact upon the German church requires further detailed study.

The most significant aspect of the First Council of Lyons in the context of this present study, however, was the attack on the whole system of papal government, an attack which emananted from England but was supported within two years by a similar denunciation—the *Gravamina ecclesiae Gallicanae* of 1247—from France.[19] If, in other words, it had been a question in 1215 of the reform of the "members" by the "head," in 1245 it was realized that the "head" also was in need of reform. Papal taxation and papal provision to benefices—papal "extortion," as the critics now no longer hesitated to describe it—were the burden of both the English and the French complaints. But the charge went deeper when St. Louis himself intervened, asserting that the pope was doing new things, new and unheard of (*nova et inaudita*), and that this was the root cause of the evil in the Church.[20]

This charge of innovation clearly implied the subversion of the old ecclesiastical order, and fell into line with the charge of the Spiritual Franciscans that the Church, through papal action, was departing further and further from the example of the apostles and the apostolic precepts. It implied a condemnation of the whole centralized system of Church government as an excrescence, which—people would later say—must be removed to get back to the true ecclesiastical order. As yet people did not say this: they failed to draw the logical corollary, still hoped that the pope himself would draw a line and put things right. But the appeal of the English clergy in 1246 to a future council is significant, particularly as Frederick II, claiming that Innocent IV was not impartial and that the council of 1245 was not representative, had already made the same appeal.

---

[19] Cf. K. Schleyer, *Anfänge des Gallicanismus im 13. Jahrhundert* (Berlin, 1937).

[20] Barraclough, *The Medieval Papacy* 135. Frech, *Reform an Haupt und Gliedern* 186, notes that although the specific phrase "reform in head and members" was used in thirteenth century synodal statutes, it does not appear in the constitutions of the three general councils. He therefore questions the correctness of Francis Oakley's statement, *The Western Church in the Later Middle Ages* (Ithaca-London, 1979) 219: "The call for reform in head and members . . . had been bruited already in 1245 and 1274 at the first and second councils of Lyons." More correct, according to Frech, is Oakley's earlier statement (*op.cit.* 52) that "The cry for change, heard already at the first and second councils of Lyons, had swelled at the Council of Vienne into a far-reaching program of reform 'in head and members'."

It shows that people still thought the ecumenical council was above the pope, that there was a further recourse, a higher tribunal.[21]

Our study of Germany 1216-1245 confirms the view that for well over a century the clergy of the local churches had generally welcomed the extension of papal control into the provinces, and by their own petitions and appeals had done much to stimulate and accelerate the process. Archbishops, bishops, abbots, prioresses, and numerous others had all on occasion sought papal confirmation of their reforming efforts, or had turned to the curia when local opposition exceeded their power or patience. Such requests were still common at the beginning of the fourteenth century, but another attitude had also become apparent. From the waning decades of the thirteenth century there is evidence that clerical opposition to papal policy was beginning to increase—indications that certain groups of clergy were so disgruntled as to be willing, in moments of critical tension, to side with their rulers against the pope or, at least, to acquiesce in policies directed by their rulers against the Roman pontiff.

Like Innocent III, Pope Gregory X also entertained hope for a union with the Greek Church and ecclesiastical reform when he summoned a general council for 1274 at Lyons. At the same time he appears to have recognized that the policies of his immediate predecessors (particularly Innocent IV and Clement IV) had contributed to the growing disillusion with the papacy, a factor which now stood in the way of united Christian action against the Turks. The part played by the papacy in the destruction of the Hohenstaufen and the Empire had produced widespread pessimism: instead of zeal and belief in the papacy, there was general criticism. To engage this criticism head-on, Gregory requested that reports on conditions—*gravamina*—be submitted to the curia before the council as an aid to preparations.

Extant are those reports prepared by Humbert of Romans, the former general of the Dominicans; by an anonymous member of the Franciscan Order; and by Bishop Bruno of Olmütz.[22] These reports cast a revealing light on the state of Latin Christendom at the beginning of the last quarter of the thirteenth century. In particular, they reveal the disorder introduced into the Church by papal support of the Mendicants against the secular clergy, and the bitter feeling aroused thereby, as well as the weakening of the position of the parish priests towards the laity resulting from the preference given to the Friars.

---

[21] Barraclough, *The Medieval Papacy* 136. Against the appeal of Frederick II's envoy to the council, Thaddeus of Suëssa, to a future pope and a general council, Innocent argued that the emperor's actions had prevented many of those who had been invited from attending, and that the council was both general and legitimate.

[22] Frech, *Reform an Haupt und Gliedern* 186-187.

Although there is no hesitation about attacking the abuses of the Roman Curia, these writings nonetheless all demonstrate a curious hesitancy: while clearly holding the papacy responsible for many of the evils in the Church, they see at the same time no hope of regeneration except through the pope. In short, the papacy is being asked to reform itself.

In this sense the council of 1274 represented a middle point: the evils at the center of the Church were recognized, but the papacy was not attacked.[23] Most of the formulating of reform measures which emanated from it was done by the pope himself, aided by his trusted collaborators, the Dominican cardinal Peter of Tarentaise and the Franciscan cardinal Bonaventure. Among them were further prohibitions against the establishment of new religious orders, temporarily restricting those (such as the Carmelites and the Augustinian Hermits) that had been founded or confirmed since 1215; exempt, however, were the Dominicans and Franciscans whose service to the Church was readily apparent. Excessively long vacancies, especially those of benefices connected with the cure of souls, were to be stopped, and only worthy candidates were to be appointed to them. Pluralism was once again curtailed, and the obligation of residency was reinforced. In his closing address Gregory charged the bishops to pay greater attention to their pastoral obligations, reforming themselves first, then their clergy, and ultimately the entire Church.[24]

Among those who had written works preparatory to the council was Thomas Aquinas.[25] Though invited to participate in the council, he died *en route* and was buried in the Cistercian abbey of Fossanuova. Those nearly three hundred bishops who did attend, together with some sixty abbots, generals of orders, prelates and other prominent theologians of the Church received the papal decrees. The early death of the pontiff in January 1276 prevented his seeing the impact of his efforts, but his decrees

---

[23] Barraclough, *The Medieval Papacy* 136-138.

[24] Jedin, *Handbook of Church History* IV 205, notes that although the matter of Church reform was the most important of the three principal topics of the council, and the one for which the best preliminary work had been done, it was apparently the least actually discussed by the council fathers. In fact, the papal admonition to the prelates *"quod ipsi se corrigerent"*, appears as an afterthought, since the council had not specifically dealt with that issue; cf. Frech, *Reform an Haupt und Gliedern* 187. For the constitutions of this council, see Emil Göller, "Zur Geschichte des zweiten Lyoner Konzils und des Liber Sextus," *Römische Quartalschrift* 20 (1906) 14-24.

[25] *Contra errores Graecorum*, though written in 1260, clearly belongs to those writings upon which the papacy based its efforts in 1274; cf. edition by P. Glorieux (Tournai & Paris, 1957).

survived, becoming part of the *Codex iuris canonici* and affecting church law to the present day.[26]

The pontificate of Boniface VIII (1294-1303) and that pope's disastrous clash with King Philip IV of France marked an end to the extreme hierocratic views which had been prevalent since the days of Gregory VII and had reached their zenith under Innocent III. Boniface's successors were hard-pressed just to ward off the king's demands for the posthumous judgment and condemnation of that pope and for the assembly of a general council to achieve that end. Pope Clement V did in fact convene a council at Vienne in 1311-1312, the only general council held in the fourteenth century, and although he was largely successful in blunting the attack on the memory of Boniface VIII, it was at the price of surrendering to the demands of the king on the issue of dissolving the Order of Templars.

While in many respects the Council of Vienne resembled those of the earlier era and may be seen as the last in the great series of reform councils extending back at least to the Third Lateran Council (prefiguring as well the general councils of the modern era—Trent, Vatican I, and Vatican II), all of which were convoked by the papacy, given shape by papal concerns, and responsive, though in differing degrees, to papal control, at the same time it anticipated those councils of the fifteenth century which departed from the conciliar norm.[27]

In the well-established conciliar tradition, Clement V addressed the matter of the crusade against the Saracens, an issue made difficult by the decline in zeal for such an enterprise; a resulting concomitant of this decline had been a diminution of papal leadership over Latin Christendom. Also in the pattern of Innocent III and Gregory X, Pope Clement requested that lists of *gravamina* be submitted, along with recommendations for suitable corrective measures; in so doing, however, he opened the door for an attack on the papacy such as no previous council had experienced. Two bishops at least, William Lemaire of Angers and William Durant of Mende, assailed

---

[26] See Deno J. Geanakoplos, *Emperor Michael Palaeologus and the West (1258-1282). A Study in Byzantine-Latin Relations* (Cambridge, Mass. 1959); Stephan Kuttner, "Conciliar Law in the Making: The Lyonese Constitutions (1274) of Gregory X," *Miscellanea Pio Paschini* II (1949); H.D. Nichol, "The Greeks and the Union of the Churches. The Preliminaries to the Second Council of Lyons (1261-1274)," *Medieval Studies*, presented to A. Gwynn (Dublin, 1961) 454-480.

[27] Joseph H. Lynch, *The Medieval Church: A Brief History* (London and New York, 1992) 175. Barraclough, *The Medieval Papacy* 138, sees the Council of Vienne as closest in spirit to that of Lyons I, having been summoned essentially for political reasons.

the entire system of papal government, and there is evidence of other criticism from the body of the council.[28]

Although the reform decrees of the council reflected the efforts of the conciliar reform commission that Clement V had appointed to draw some general conclusions from the mass of material submitted and to recommend an appropriate legislative response, that response fell far short of the sweeping demands for reform *"tam in capite quam in membris"* that Lemaire and Durant had submitted. In his *Tractatus de modo concilio celebrandi*, and as part of his attempt to restore and defend the integrity of episcopal authority, Durant had argued quite plainly and openly, that if there were to be reform, it must start with the "head" of the Roman Curia, and that if there were no reform the blame would lie sqaurely with the pope and the cardinals and the synod. The first thing was to put an end to the sale of offices and dispensations, from which the Curia lived. The taxes the papacy levied from those to whom it granted benefices, *servitia* and annates, were no better than simony. But Durant went further, maintaining that the pope was bringing confusion into the whole ecclesiastical order by depriving the prelates of their rights—namely to hear suits arising in their dioceses, and to provide for their own clergy. Things had reached such a pass, he added, that the clerks of the papal chancery had precedence over archbishops. It was the pope's duty to respect the ancient law of the Church, and to change it only with the consent of the general council which should meet every ten years. The pope's primacy was not denied, both in the spiritual and in the temporal spheres. In short, what Durant demanded was the abolition of the papal *plenitudo potestatis*, of the unlimited powers which had grown up in the course of the previous century, and a return to the old

---

[28] In the bull *Regnans in excelsis* issued by Pope Clement V on 12 August 1308, the prelates summoned to the council two years hence were commanded to ". . . *diligenter inquirerent, deliberarent, scriberent, et in scriptis ad dictum Concilium defferrent omnia quae pro bono statu Ecclesiae . . . eis utilia viderentur."* See Frech, *Reform an Haupt und Gliedern* 197; F. Ehrle, *Bruchstück der Akten des Konzils von Vienne* ( ) 361-368; Emil Göller, "Die Gravamina auf dem Konzil von Vienne und ihre literarische Überlieferung," *Festgabe für Heinrich Finke* (Münster, 1904) 195-211; Müller, *Vienne* 387ff. Extant among others are memoranda from Giles of Rome, the Cistercian abbot Jacques de Thermis, and Raymond Lull; cf. M. Heber, *Gutachten und Reformvorschläge für das Vienner Generalkonzil 1311-1312* (Leipzig, 1896) 56-58. On the council itself, see J. Lecler, *Vienne*, Geschichte der ökumenischen Konzilien 8 (Mainz, 1965); E. Müller, *Das Konzil von Vienne 1311-1312. Seine Quellen und seine Geschichte*, Vorreformatorische Forschungen 12 (Münster, 1934); L. Veerecke, "La réforme de l'Eglise au concile de Vienne 1311-1312," *Studia moralia* 14 (1976) 283-335.

constitution, with a restoration of the independent authority of bishops and of synods.[29]

In urging a return of authority to the episcopacy, Durant appears to have been a traditional thinker, but in his advocation of regular general councils at ten-year intervals he was quite revolutionary. So fierce was his attack that he was arrested and kept in prison for seven years and more, in spite of protests from the French king; moreover, his teachings were suppressed. Clearly, the criticism at the Council of Vienne frightened the papacy. It is significant that in the three generations subsequent to the dissolution of the council on 6 May 1312 no new general council of the Church was summoned, and when the next general council—the sixteenth—met at Constanz in 1414 the situation was very different. For in fact none of the reform projects, neither those of 1274 nor those of 1311, came to anything. And after 1311, for the very lack of a constitutional means of airing grievances and seeking redress, the abuses of which William Lemaire and William Durant had complained, grew apace, furthered by the adverse conditions which faced the papacy after 1309 at Avignon.[30]

Although the general Church council was clearly the most spectacular of ecclesiastical assemblies in the Middle Ages (and the Fourth Lateranum towered above all others in terms of size and spectacle), diocesan and provincial synods represented Church government at a more immediate and effective level. Our survey of German synodalia in the four centuries which preceded the Fourth Lateran Council reveals that there was a strong tradition for both types of synods: the intent of Innocent III was to re-invigorate them as organs of reform.

The diocesan synod grew out of the *presbyterium* of the episcopal church.[31]   As long as this was the only parish church, performing the Divine Office and looking after the cure of souls for the entire diocese, the

[29] A. Posch, "Die Reformvorschläge des Wilhelm Durandus jun. auf dem Konzil von Vienne," *MIÖG* Erg-Bd. 11 (1929) 288-303; C. Fasolt, "A New View of William Durant the Younger's 'Tractatus de modo generalis concilii celebrandi'," *Traditio* 37 (1981) 291-324; Barraclough, *The Medieval Papacy* 138-139.

[30] Cf. Francis Oakley, "Councils, Western (1311-1449)," *Dictionary of the Middle Ages* III 642-656; Frech, *Reform an Haupt und Gliedern* 366-368; Barraclough, *The Medieval Papacy* 139-140. Though now somewhat dated, the bibliography provided by E.F. Jacob, "Reflections Upon the Study of the General Councils in the Fifteenth Century," in Ecclesiastical History Society, *Studies in Church History: Subsidia* I (Oxford, 1964), is still useful. On the claims of conciliarists with respect to papal subordination to general councils, cf. Francis Oakley, *Council Over Pope? Towards a Provisional Ecclesiology* (New York, 1969); Brian Tierney, *Foundations of Conciliar Theory* (Cambridge, 1955).

[31] Gescher, "Geschichte und Recht" 7; Phillips, *Diözesansynode* 35ff.; Hinschius, *KR* VII 132ff.; Werminghoff, *Verfassungsgeschichte* 219; Johann Baptist Sägmüller, *Lehrbuch des katholischen Kirchenrechts* I (Freiburg i. Br., 1914) 503.

bishop always had his clergy close about him. The dramatic change came with the extension of pastoral and sacramental activities into the country-side—various clerics left the *presbyterium* and assumed their new roles away from the episcopal city.[32] For the bishop as well as for these more remote places, contact and communication were vital. Out of this need there grew two instruments of ecclesiastical governance: the diocesan synod and the episcopal visitation.[33] The bishop travelled annually throughout his diocese in order to preach and dispense the sacrament of confirmation, and by means of his own observations and determinations become familiar with the religious and moral condition of the clergy and people.[34]

Yet, it must also have been desirable (even essential) for the bishop to assemble his clergy on occasion at the diocesan center, whether it be to determine more about its life, knowledge of doctrine and Church practices, or activities, or to discuss matters of concern relative to the cure of souls with his *presbyterium* which, despite the geographical separation, still constituted a strong unity in both the theoretical and the juridical sense, or to make known to the largest circle of his clergy new stipulations of his episcopal regime. These assemblies of the entire clergy of a diocese under

[32] This decentralization process began in the West in the fourth century and was still in full swing in the ninth century. See Hinschius, *KR* II 262ff.; Hauck, *DKG* I 222ff.; Idem. II 737ff.; Ulrich Stutz, *Geschichte des kirchlichen Benefizialwesens von seinen Anfängen bis auf die Zeit Alexanders III.* (Berlin, 1895; repr. Aalen, 1961) 4, 66ff.; Arnold Pöschl, *Bischofsgut unf Mensa Episcopalis, ein Beitrag zur Geschichte des kirchlichen Vermögensrechtes* I (Bonn, 1908) 11f.; Werminghoff, *Verfassungsgesch.* 23; Sägmüller, *Kirchenrecht* I 474; Cheney, *English Synodalia* 3-8. Speaking of the legal or constitutional role of diocesan synods, Hinschius, *op.cit.* III 328, remarks: „*Sie haben nicht . . . die Bedeutung einer Repräsentation von kirchlichen Körpern, sind vielmehr, wie dies auch ihr Ursprung ergiebt, aus dem Presbyterium des Bischofs herausgewachsen, und nehmen neben ihm nur die Stellung einer berathenden Versammlung ein.*"

[33] Phillips, *KR* VII 124ff.; Cheney, *Episcopal Visitations* 19-22. Lingg, *Pfarrvisitation* 4f., incorrectly saw St. Boniface as the originator of the episcopal visitation. Although the latter did not create this institution, he did re-vitalize an almost forgotten practice. See further, A.M. Koeniger, "Burchard I. von Worms und die deutsche Kirche seiner Zeit (1000-1025)," *Veröffentlichungen aus dem Kirchenhistorischen Seminar München*, ed. A. Knöpfler, II. Reihe, Nr. 6 (München, 1905) 111ff.; Stutz, *Kirchenrecht* 310; Sägmüller, *Kirchenrecht* II 308f.; Gescher, "Geschichte und Recht" 7.

[34] Hauck, *KGD* II 248, sees this as the origin of the episcopal *Sendgericht*; cf. also Koeniger, "Burchard I. von Worms" 120. S. Dill, *Roman Society in Gaul in the Merovingian Age* (1926) 393, observed that: "The independence which the monks enjoyed had produced many irregularities which, from the beginning of the fifth century, the Councils in Gaul set themselves to correct. . . . The discipline of all religious houses is to be under the inspection and control of the bishop. The abbots are under his spiritual power." Popes and canonists from Gregory I to Innocent III reaffirmed this principle (allowing at times for exemptions); cf. Cheney, *Episcopal Visitation* 19-23.

the presidency of the bishop or his representative are termed diocesan synods by both tradition and scholarly writings.[35]

It is therefore obvious that diocesan synods were not possible until the previously closed circle of clergy attached to the episcopal church was broken up by the creation of other churches within the episcopal city and upon the landscape which surrounded it. Although this process of decentralization began as early as the fourth century in the Latin Church, the earliest certain reference to a diocesan synod comes from the late sixth century, at Auxerre.[36] From this assembly also comes our oldest regulation concerning the frequency of episcopal synods, to which all diocesan priests were expected to come each year in mid-May.[37] Thereafter, however, references to diocesan synods disappear almost completely for a very long time: presumably they fell into desuetude during the unhappy decline of church life associated with the late Merovingian era.

The reform efforts of St. Boniface retrieved this forgotten institution from oblivion and re-introduced, among other things, the diocesan synod into the structure, law and practice of the medieval Church.[38] It was for him a significant and useful aid in creating a unified and vital organism out of the newly-reorganized bishoprics. At the very first German national synod which convened on 21 April 742 under his towering influence, the annual episcopal synod was re-established.[39] Charlemagne placed great emphasis on diocesan synods, and during his reign there was a substantial flowering of the practice.[40] Even in the post-Carolingian period there was

---

[35] Cf. Phillips, *Diözesansynode* 44ff.; Idem., *KR* VII 124, 132ff.; Gescher, "Geschichte und Recht" 86-88, publishes a Frankish *Ordo* for diocesan synods dating from the ninth century. The *presbyterium* which remained at the episcopal church, and formed but a small portion of the diocesan clergy, became the basis for the later cathedral chapter. See Phillips, *op.cit.* 35ff.; Hinschius, *KR* II 49ff.; Georg von Below, *Die Entstehung des ausschliesslichen Wahlrechts der Domkapitel mit besonderer Rücksicht auf Deutschland*, Historische Studien, Heft 11 (Leipzig, 1883) 17ff.; Gescher, *op.cit.* 17ff.

[36] *Concilia* I 180. Hauck, *KGD* I 126 note 1, 228 note 3; Idem. II 40 note 5; and Sägmüller, *Kirchenrecht* I 503, date the synod 573/603. Hinschius, *KR* III 583 note 5, argues for the year 585; this is accepted by Hilling, *Diözesansynoden* 1, and Maring, *Diözesansynoden* viii note 2.

[37] Hartzheim, *Concilia* I 180: "*C. 7: Ut medio Madio omnes presbyteri ad synodo in civitatem veniant et kalendis Novembris omnes abbates ad concilium conveniant.*" The abbots, it seems, held a separate assembly each year with the bishop, to which the secular clergy were not invited.

[38] Gescher, "Geschichte und Recht" 8. Boniface also made the ancient church practice of episcopal visitations an obligation; cf. Lingg, *Pfarrvisitation* 5f., 11; Koeniger, "Burchard I. von Worms" 112.

[39] Hartzheim, *Concilia* II 3; Hauck, *KGD* I 520ff.; Gescher, "Geschichte und Recht" 9.

[40] Phillips, *Diözesansynode* 45 f.; Idem. *KR* VII 138 note 6; and Hinschius, *KR* III 585 note 2, print the Carolingian capitularies relative to diocesan synods.

a considerable vitality in the institution, although our reconstruction of the German synodalia up to the year 1215 reveals a most uneven pattern.[41]

Given the circumstances of the three decades which followed the Fourth Lateran Council, one might hope for more consistent and continuous evidence of synods, and for greater indications that reform-legislation had emerged from the provincial assemblies. It is nonetheless not surprising that such was not the case.[42]

It is in fact a paradox of the later Middle Ages that although there was a dramatic increase in the number of sets of diocesan and provincial synodal statutes after 1250 (and particularly after 1310)—their proliferation in and of itself may be seen as testimony that reform was not easily achieved[43]—this very epoch also saw the emergence of widespread movements which seldom enjoyed the enthusiastic support of the institutional Church. Moreover, the German bishops and archbishops of the fourteenth century emerge from the records as being set on consolidating the territorial states whose foundations had been laid by their twelfth and thirteenth-century predecessors. This "state-building" was made immeasurably easier by the weakened nature of the German monarchy, a condition to which popes such as Innocent III, Gregory IX and Innocent IV had greatly contributed.[44] One may only speculate whether the survival of a stronger

---

[41] See above, Ch. One; also Hinschius, *KR* III 585; Hauck, *KGD* II 735f.; Idem III 38, 47, 581. The observation of Koeniger, "Burchard I. von Worms" 114, is nonetheless correct, that reports concerning diocesan synods „*bis tief ins 11. Jahrhundert hinein*" are infrequent.

[42] The comment found in Jedin, *Handbook of Church History* IV 172, that "While the Council's political decisions were not of lasting importance and soon appeared out of date because of events, its legislation persisted because it was taken into the general law of the Church. A vigorous synodal activity, instituted *everywhere* [italics added] right after the Council, contributed to this. More important still was the adoption of fifty-nine of the seventy decrees into the law book of Gregory IX. Lateran IX holds the first place after Trent in the conciliar sources of the modern *Codex Iuris Canonici*.", cannot be substantiated fully on the basis of the German evidence.

[43] Johanek, "Synodalia" I 2-3, cautions that synodal statutes from the medieval period do not always correspond to actual problems within the contemporary Church or society: many decrees were carried over from one synod to thge next, irrespective of their relevance.

[44] Cf. Al. Dominicus, *Baldewin von Lützelburg, Erzbischof und Kurfürst von Trier* (Coblenz, 1862); Jakob Marx, "Die Entstehung des Kurstaates Trier," *Trierisches Archiv* 3 (1898) 38-62; Fritz Michel, "Wie Entstand die Landeshoheit des Erzbischofs von Trier in dem Gebiet zwischen Lahn, Rhein, Sayn und Gelbach?," *Zeitschrift für Heimatkunde von Coblenz* Jg. 1 (1920); Fritz Rörig, "Die Entstehung der Landeshoheit der Trierischen Erzbischöfe zwischen Saar, Mosel und Ruwer und ihr Kampf mit den patrimonialen Gewalten," *WZGK*, Ergänzungsheft 13 (1906); Otto Rosbach, "Die Reichspolitik der Trierischen Erzbischöfe vom Ausgang der Regierung Friedrichs I. bis zum Ende des Interregnums," Teil I: 1183-1189, *Program des königlichen Gymnasiums zu Bonn* (1883) 1-23, Teil II (bis 1212), *Program Trier* (1888/1889); Friedrich Rudolph, "Die Entwicklung der Landeshoheit in Trier bis zur Mitte des 14. Jahrhunderts," *Trierisches Archiv*, Ergänzungsheft 5 (1905) 1-65; Hermann Hecker, "Zur

central government in Germany might not have prevented the rise of territorial states—among them the ecclesiastical principalities—and by so doing have forced the ecclesiastical princes to focus their time and energies more on the pressing spiritual matters of the early fourteenth century. But, just as a multitude of conditions contributed to the unhappy state of the German church which we have described in Ch. Two, so too no single factor can be blamed for similar conditions in the fourteenth and fifteenth centuries.

From the perspective of the late 1400s, the modern historian Jerome Blum offers this view:

> The Council of Constance in 1415 gave the medieval Church just one century to put its house in order. The history of this eleventh hour of the medieval Church is the history of the papacy's failure to correct abuses in the face of the mounting attack of concerned Christians, clerical and lay, on those abuses, and increasing anti-clerical sentiment, which was almost universal among European laymen by the eve of the Protestant Reformation.
>
> The ecclesiastical abuses were many and some were major. Three constituted corruption even by existing Church law. Simony, the sale of of the entire range of Church offices, including bishoprics, made the clergyman's vocation a commodity, his duties a matter of profit. Pluralism, the simultaneous holding of several major Church offices, bred indifference to responsibility, non-residence of clergy, and the execution of the cure of souls by deputy. . . .
>
> While drawing the fire of those who urged reform, corruption was more symptomatic of spiritual laxity than of depravity. The monastic clergy were at the end of a long road of decline from the spiritual vitality of the monasteries in the early and high Middle Ages. . . .
>
> The secular (non-monastic) were probably no worse with respect to ability, learning, devotion, and morality in 1500 than at any other time in the Middle Ages. That says very little in their favor, however. Those who were educated in divinity and canon law were drawn off into lucrative and powerful careers in Church and state. From them came the bishops and higher clergy. The bulk of the secular clergy were ill-educated and poor, and most of them worked their fields like common peasants, living lives neither longer nor less brutish than peasants. . . .

Geschichte der territorialen Politik des Erzbischofs Phillip I. von Köln," *Historische Studien* 10 (Leipzig, 1883); Manfred Stimming, "Die Entstehung des weltlichen Territoriums des Erzbistums Mainz," *Quellen und Forschungen zur Hessischen Geschichte* 3 (Darmstadt, 1915); K.H. Schmitt, "Erzbischof Adalbert I. von Mainz als Territorialfürst," *Arbeiten zur deutschen Rechts- und Verfassungsgeschichte*, Heft 2 (Berlin, 1920); Geoffrey Barraclough, *The Origins of Modern Germany* (Oxford, 1946; repr. New York, 1963) 240-352; Daniel Waley, *Later Medieval Europe: From St Louis to Luther* (London & New York, 1964) 73-94.

In Germany, where a strong central power did not emerge, there were fewer limitations on papal powers of appointment, ecclesiastical jurisdiction, and taxation. . . .[45]

The events of the early sixteenth century were not the inevitable consequence of the failure of 1415, let alone 1215. During the three centuries which separated the Fourth Lateran Council from Luther and his generation of critics there were numerous opportunities for the later medieval Church to correct those abuses which kept it from fulfilling that vision of regeneration which had been articulated by Innocent III at the council and re-iterated by other popes and reformers thereafter. The parameters of this present study are too narrow to allow the conclusion that at no time between 1215 and 1500 was there measurable improvement in the personal and collective performance of the medieval German church; additional studies are needed to determine whether the German response to the reform legislation of the three general councils subsequent to the Fourth Lateranum was any different from that which followed on the heels of Innocent III's great council.

[45] Jerome Blum, Rondo Cameron and Thomas G. Barnes, *The European World: A History* (2nd ed.; Boston, 1970) 118-120, 123. A similar picture is given by De Lamar Jensen, *Reformation Europe: Age of Reform and Revolution* (2nd ed.; Lexington, Mass., 1992) 44-47.

BIBLIOGRAPHY

Primary Sources—Manuscripts

Admont Stiftsbibliothek
  MS 22, fol. 245-246
Bamberg Staatsbibliothek
  MS Can. 19
  MS Can. 20 (P.II.7), fol. 63v-70v
  MS Patr. 132 (Q.VI.42) fol. 81-109
Bibliotheca Bodmeriana
  Cod. Bodmer 80 fol. 28-42
Brussels Royal Bibl.
  MS 4202 (2804)
Frankfurt
  MS Barth. 28, fol. 111ra-137rb
Fulda Landesbibliothek
  MS D.6
  MS D.14, fol. 128-144v
Giessen Universitätsbibliothek
  MS 1105, fol. 47ra-58vb (60)
Graz Universitäsbibliothek
  MS III 106
  MS III 138, fol. 233-246v
  MS 331, fol. 81-93v
  MS 374, fol. 284-319v
  MS 532, fol. 201 - 202
  MS 830, fol. 137-145v
Innsbruck Universitäts-Bibliothek
  MS 16, fol. 1r
Karlsruhe Landesbibliothek
  MS Reichenau 109
  MS 345, fol. 14-27'
Kassel Landesbibliothek
  MS *Jur 11, fol. 110ra
Koblenz Landeshauptarchiv
  MS Best. 162, Nr. 1401/3, fol. 129-136
Leipzig Universitätsbibliothek
  MS 968, fol. 232-261
  MS 1062, fol. 35^v-36^v
  MS 1065, fol. 1-65
Marburg Universitätsbibliothek
  MS C.2
Maribor (Marburg), Slovenia, Episcopal Library
  MS Q 18, fol. 30^r-32^r
Metz, Bibliothèque Municipal
  MS A.1, fol. 2^v

München Staatsbibliothek
 clm 213 fol. 203^b-208
 clm 1128 (S. Nicolai 87)
 clm 3879, fol. 150-267 (p. II) f. 1sqq.
 clm 5822 (Ebersb. 22), fol. 179ᵛ-180ʳ
 clm 7841, fol. 122-126
 clm 9596, fol. 128-
 clm 12 612, fol. 117ʳ-117ᵛ
 clm 27 421, fol. 211ʳᵛ
Prague, University Library
 MS XXIII.E.59 (antes Lobkowitz MS 439), fol. 1-23v
St. Florian Stiftsbibliothek
 Cod. XI 720, fol. 5ʳ-55ʳ
Trier Stadtbibliothek
 MS 1731
Wien, Nationalbibliothek
 MS 1467 [Univ. 279], fol. 142b-143a
 MS 2149 [Jur. can. 37], fol. 1a-10b
 MS 2183, fol. 87a-106a
Zurich Zentralbibliothek (Stiftsbibliothek—Grossmünster)
 C. 148 MS II, fol. 25r-43v, 46r-48v

Primary Sources—Published

Acta imp. inedita	=	*Acta imperii inedita saecula XIII et XIV. Urkunden und Briefe zur Geschichte des Kaiserreichs und des Königreichs Sicilien in den Jahren 1200-1400* I-II, ed. Eduard Winkelmann (Innsbruck, 1880, 1885).
Aegidii Aureavall.	=	*Aegidii Aureavallensis Gesta Episcoporum Leodiensium*, MGH SS XXV (Hannover, 1880).
Annalen Kolmar	=	*Annalen und Chronik von Kolmar*, vol. 75 of *Die Geschichtschreiber der deutschen Vorzeit*, transl. by H. Papst (Leipzig, 1897).
Ann. Admunt	=	*Annales Admuntensis—Continuatio Garstensis*, ed. W. Wattenbach, *MGH SS* IX (Hannover, 1851) 569-579.
Ann. Altah	=	*Annales Altahenses maiores*, ed. E. v. Oegele, *MGH SS rer. Germ.* (2nd. ed., 1891).
Ann. Brunwilar	=	*Annales Brunwilarenses*, *MGH SS* XVI (Hannover, 1859).
Ann. Elwang	=	*Annales Elwangenses*, *MGH SS* X (Hannover, 1852).
Ann. Erphord	=	*Annales Erphordenses*, in Böhmer, *Fontes* II (1845); later edition in *MGH SS* XVI (Hannover, 1859); *SS rer. Germ.* [42] (1899).
Ann. Essenbec	=	*Annales Essenbecenses*, *MGH SS* XXIX (Hannover, 1892).
Ann. Gotwic	=	*Annales Gotwicenses*, *MGH SS* IX (Hannover, 1851).
Ann. Herbipol	=	*Annales Herbipolienses*, *MGH SS* XXX (Hannover, 1896).
Ann. Marbac	=	*Annales Marbacenses*, ed. R. Wilmans, *MGH SS* XVII

(Hannover, 1861) 142-180.

Ann. Magunt.	=	*Annales Maguntinenses, MGH SS* XVII (Hannover, 1861).
Ann. maximi Colon.	=	*Annales maximi Colonienses, MGH SS* XVII (Hannover, 1861).
Ann. Mellic.	=	*Annales Mellicenses, MGH SS* IX (Hannover, 1851).
Ann. Nerresh.	=	*Annales Nerresheimenses, MGH SS* X (Hannover, 1852).
Ann. Osterhov.	=	*Annales Osterhovenses, MGH SS* XVII (Hannover, 1861).
Ann. Patherbr.	=	*Annales Patherbrunnenses,* aus Bruchstücken wieder hergestellt von P. Scheffer-Boichhorst (Innsbruck, 1870).
Ann. Pegav.	=	*Annales Pegavienses et Bosovienses, MGH SS* XVI (Hannover, 1859) 234-270.
Ann. Pragenses	=	*Annales Pragenses, MGH SS* III (Hannover, 1839).
Ann. Reinhardsbr.	=	*Annales Reinhardsbrunnenses,* ed. Franz X. Wegele, *Thüringische Geschichtsquellen* I (Jena, 1854).
Ann. Salisb.	=	*Annales S. Rudperti Salisburgenses,* ed. W. Wattenbach, *MGH SS* IX (Hannover, 1851) 758-810.
Ann. S. Blasii	=	*Annales S. Blasii et Engelbergenses, MGH SS* XVII (Hannover, 1861).
Ann. S. Disibodi	=	*Annales Sancti Disibodi,* ed. Georg Waitz, *MGH SS* XVII (Hannover, 1861).
Ann. S. Gereon. Colon.	=	*Annales S. Gereonis Coloniensis, MGH SS* XVI (Hannover, 1859).
Ann. S. Pauli Virdun.	=	*Annales S. Pauli Virdunensis, MGH SS* XVI (Hannover, 1859).
Ann. S. Steph. Frising.	=	*Annales S. Stephani Frisingenses, MGH SS* XIII (Hannover, 1881).
Ann. S. Vitoni Virdun.	=	*Annales S. Vitoni Virdunensis, MGH SS* X (Hannover, 1852).
Ann. Scheftlar.	=	*Annales Scheftlarienses maiores, MGH SS* XVII (Hannover, 1861).
Ann. Shir.	=	*Annales Shirenses, MGH SS* XVII (Hannover, 1861).
Ann. Spir.	=	*Annales Spirensis, MGH SS* XVII (Hannover, 1861).
Ann. Stad.	=	*Annales Stadenses, MGH SS* XVI (Hannover, 1859).
Ann. Veterocell.	=	*Annales Veterocellenses, MGH SS* XVI (Hannover, 1859).
Annalista Saxo	=	*Annalista Saxo,* ed. Georg Waitz, *MGH SS* VI (Hannover, 1844) 553-777.
Arnoldi Chron.	=	*Arnoldi Chronica Slavorum, MGH SS* XXI (Hannover, 1869).
Bernardi Cremif. Hist.	=	*Bernardi Cremifanensis Historiae, MGH SS* XXV (Hannover, 1880).
Böhmer, *Acta imperii sel.*	=	Johann Friedrich Böhmer, *Acta imperii selecta,* ed. J. Ficker (Innsbruck, 1870).
——, *Fontes rer. Germ.*	=	——, ed., *Fontes rerum Germanicarum—Geschichtsquellen Deutschlands,* 4 vols. (Stuttgart, 1845-1868).
——, *Regg. Imp. I*	=	——, *Regesta Imperii, I: Die Regesten des Kaiserreichs unter den Karolingern (751-918),* revised by Engelbert Mühlbacher (2nd ed.; Innsbruck, 1908).
——, *Regg. Imp. V*	=	——, *Regesta Imperii,* 5 vols., ed. Johann Friedrich Böhmer; Neubearbeitung von Julius Ficker und Eduard

		Winkelmann (Innsbruck, 1881-1991).
Brackmann, *Regesta*	=	Albert Brackmann, *Regesta pontificum Romanorum*. Germania pontificia I-II/1 (Berlin, 1911, 1913).
Bremisches UB	=	*Bremisches Urkundenbuch*, vols. I-II, ed. Dietrich Rudolf Ehmck & W. von Bippen, (Bremen, 1873, 1876).
Brower/Masen, *Antiq.*	=	Chr. Brower et Mason, *Antiquitatum et annalium Treverensium libri XXV*, 2 vols. (Liège, 1670).
Caes. Cat. archiep. Colon.	=	*Caesarii Heistebacensis catalogus episcoporum Coloniensis*, *MGH SS* XXIV (Hannover, 1879) 346-352; *Fontes rer. Germ.* II 281.
Caesarii Dialogus	=	*Caesarii Heisterbacensis Dialogus Miraculorum*, ed. Joseph Strange (Köln, 1851).
Caesarii Omasticon	=	*Caesarii Heisterbacensis Omasticon*, ed. Alfons Hilka as *Wundergeschichten des Caesarius von Heisterbach* I, III, Publikationen der Gesellschaft für Rheinische Geschichtskunde (Bonn, 1933, 1937).
Cartulaire d'Orval	=	*Cartulaire de l'Abbaye d'Orval*, ed. Hippolyte Goffinet, Collection de Chroniques Belges Inédites (Bruxelles, 1879).
Cartulaire de Metz	=	*Cartulaire de l'Eveché de Metz*, ed. Paul Georges François Joseph Marichal, I-II (Paris, 1904-1908).
Cartulaire de Liège	=	*Cartulaire de l'Eglise Saint Lambert de Liège*, ed. Stanislas Bormans and E. Schoolmeesters, Collection de Chroniques Belges Inédites, XXVI (Bruxelles, 1893).
Cartulaire de Saint Trond	=	*Cartulaire de Abbaye de Saint Trond*, ed. Ch. Piot (Bruxelles, 1870).
CdAF	=	*Codex diplomaticus Austriaco-Frisingensis. Sammlung von Urkunden und Urbaren zur Geschichte des ehemals freisingischen Besitzungen in Österreich*, ed. J. Zahn, Fontes rerum Austriacarum, Abt. 2, Bd. 31 (Wien, 1870).
Friedrich, *CdBoh*	=	*Codex diplomaticus et epistolaris regni Bohemiae*, ed. Gustav Friedrich, I: 805-1197 (Prag, 1904-1907); II: 1198-1230 (Prag, 1912), IV: 1241-1253 (Prag, 1962).
CdBrand	=	*Codex diplomaticus Brandenburgensis* I-II, ed. A.F. Riedel (Berlin, 1838, 1847).
CdLubec.	=	*Codex diplomaticus Lubecensis. Lübeckisches Urkundenbuch*, Section I, Part I: Urkunden der Stadt Lübeck, ed. Verein für Lübeckische Geschichte (1843; repr. Osnabrück, 1976).
CdMogunt.	=	*Codex diplomaticus sive anecdotorum res Moguntinas illustrantium*, 5 vols in 6, ed. Valentin Ferdinand de Gudenus (Göttingen, Frankfurt & Leipzig, 1743-1768).
CdMorav.	=	*Codex diplomaticus et epistolaris Moraviae*, ed. A. Boczek, 15 vols. (Olmütz, 1836-1903).
CdNassoic.	=	*Codex diplomaticus Nassoicus: Nassauisches Urkundenbuch* I, ed. Wilhelm Sauer (Wiesbaden, 1885-1887).
CdNeerlandicus	=	*Codex diplomaticus Neerlandicus*, 6 vols. (Utrecht, 1848ff.).
CdRatisb.	=	*Codex chronologico-diplomaticus Episcopatus Ratisbon-*

ensis I, ed. Thomas Ried (Ratisbonae, 1816).

CdRhM = *Codex diplomaticus Rheno-Mosellanus. Urkundensammlung zur Geschichte der Rhein- und Mosellande, Nahe- und Ahrgegend und des Hundsrückens, des Meinfeldes und der Eifel*, vol. I, ed. Wilhelm Günther (Coblenz, 1822).

CdSR = *Codex diplomaticus Saxoniae Regiae* (Leipzig, 1864) etc., I: Naumburg Urkunden ed. C.P. Lepsius (Leipzig, 1864); II: UB Meissen.

Chron. Albrici = *Chronica Albrici Trium Fontium, MGH SS* XXIII (Hannover, 1874).

Chron. Elwac. = *Chronicon Elwacense, MGH SS* X (Hannover, 1852).

Chron. Ebersh. = *Chronic. Ebersheimensis, MGH SS* XXIII (Hannover, 1874).

Chron. Erfurt. = *Chronicon Erfortensium, MGH Scriptores rerum Germanicarum* III (Hannover, 1899).

Chron. Magni presb. = *Chronici Magni presbyteris Continuatio,* ed. W. Wattenbach, MGH SS XVII (Hannover, 1861) 476-523.

Chron. minor Erph. = *Chronica minor Minoritae Erphordensis, MGH Scriptores rerum Germanicarum in usum scholarum* (Hannover, 1899).

Chron. Mont. sereni = *Chronicon Montis sereni,* ed. E. Ehrenfeuchter, *MGH SS* XXIII (Hannover, 1874) 138-226.

Chron. regia Colon. = *Chronica regia Coloniensis, (Annales maximi Colonienses) cum continuationibus in monasterio s. Pantaleonis scriptis alisque historiae Coloniensis monumentis,* ed. G. Waitz, *MGH SS rer. Germ.* (Hannover, 1880).

Chron. Reinhardsbrun. = *Chronica Reinhardsbrunnensis, MGH SS* XXX, Pars I (Hannover, 1896).

Chron. Salemit. = *Chronica Salemitana,* in Moné, *Quellensammlung* III 27.

Chron. S. Huberti Andag. = *Chronicon Sancti Huberti Andagimensis,* ed. L.C. Bethmann & W. Wattenbach, *MGH SS* VIII (Hannover, 1848) 565ff.

Chron. S. Petri Erford. = *Chronica S. Petri Erfordensis moderna,* ed. Oswald Holder-Egger, *MGH SS rer. Germ.* [42] (Hannover, 1899).

Chron. Ursperg. = *Die Chronik des Propstes Burchard von Ursperg, MGH SS rer. Germ.* (Hannover, 1916); see also *Burchardi et Cuonradi Urspergensis Chronicon, MGH SS* XXIII.

Chron. Villar. = *Chronica Villariensis Monasterii, MGH SS* XXV (Hannover, 1880).

Codex Udalrici = *Codex Udalrici Babenbergensis,* ed. Phillip Jaffé, *Bibliotheca rerum Germanicarum* V (Berlin, 1869) 17-469.

Conr. de Fabaria = *Conradi de Fabaria Casus Sancti Galli, MGH SS* II (Hannover, 1829).

Cont. Claustro-neuburg. = *Annales Mellicensium, Continuatio Claustro-neuburgensis* I, ed. W. Wattenbach, *MGH SS* IX (Hannover, 1851) 607-613; Secunda: 613-624; Tertia: 628-637.

Cont. Gerlaci abb. = *Continuatio Gerlaci abbatis Milovicensis, MGH SS* XVII.

CIC = *Corpus Iuris Canonici,* ed. Emil Friedberg (Leipzig, 1879-1882).

Cosmae chron. = *Cosmae chronica Boemorum Libri III--Continuatio Canonicorum Pragensium,* ed. Rudolf Koepke, *MGH SS* IX (Hannover, 1851).

Dalham, *Concil. Salisb.* = Florian Dalham, *Concilia Salisburgensia provincalia et diocesana* (Augsburg, 1788).

Dipl. Styriae = *Diplomataria sacra ducatus Styriae,* collegit Sigismund Pusch, edidit Erasmus Froelich (Wien-Prag-Triest, 1756).

Eccard, *Corpus hist* = J.G. Eccard, *Corpus historicum medii aevi,* 2 vols. (Leipzig, 1723).

Ekbert, *Sermones* = Ekbert of Schönau, *Sermones XIII contra Catharos,* in Migne, *PL* CVC.

Emonis Chron = *Emonis Chronicon, MGH SS* XXIII (Hannover, 1874).

Engel, *WzUrkReg* = Wilhelm Engel, ed. *Würzburgischer Urkundenregister vor dem Jahre 1400* (Würzburg, 1958).

Ennen, *Quellen* = Leonard Ennen & Gottfried Eckertz, eds., *Quellen zur Geschichte der Stadt Köln,* 6 vols. (Köln, 1860-1879).

Epist. Mogunt. = *Epistolae Moguntinae,* ed. Ph. Jaffé, *Monumenta Moguntina,* vol. V of *Bibliotheca* (Berlin, 1866).

Epitome const. Frising = *Epitome constitutionum ecclesiasticarum Dioesesis Frisingensis anno 789 typis impressa,* etc. (Monachii, 1826).

Erben, *Quellen-Mattsee* = Wilhelm Erben, ed., *Quellen zur Geschichte des Stiftes und der Herrschaft Mattsee,* Fontes rerum Austriacarum, Abt. 2, vol. 49, part 1 (Wien, 1860).

Fontes rer. Austr = *Fontes rerum Austriacarum. Oesterreichiche Geschichtsquellen,* herausg. von der historischen Kommission der Akademie der Wissenschaft in Wien; Abth. 2. Diplomataria et acta, 51 vols. (1855-1901).

Franz, *Chron. Pont. Leod* = Friedrich Franz, *Die Chronica Pontificum Leodensium. Eine verlorene Quellenschrift des XIII. Jahrhunderts* (Strassburg, 1882).

Fredericq, *Corp. doc. inq.* = P. Fredericq, *Corpus documentorum inquisitionis haeretiae pravit, Neerlandicae* I (Gent, 1889).

Freherus, *Germ. rer. script* = Marquard Freherus, *Germanicarum rerum scriptores aliquot insignes* I (Frankfurt, 1600; 3rd ed. Strassburg, 1717).

Friedberg, *CIC* = Emil Albert Friedberg, *Corpus Iuris Canonici,* edition lipsiae secunda (Leipzig, 1879-188).

——, *Can.-Samml.* = ——, *Die Canones-Sammlungen zwischen Gratian u n d Bernard von Pavia* (Leipzig, 1897; repr. Graz, 1958)

Fürstenberg. UB = *Fürstenbergisches Urkundenbuch,* I, ed. Sigmund Riezler (Tübingen, 1877); V, ed. Fürstenberg Fürstliches Archiv in Donaueschingen (1885).

Geschichtsschr. d. d. V. = *Geschichtsschreiber der deutschen Vorzeit,* Bd. II: 13. Jht., trans. of MGH edition by Karl Platner (Leipzig, 1881).

Gesta abb. Trudon. = *Gesta abbatum Trudonensium,* Continuatio III, *MGH SS* X (Hannover, 1852).

Gesta Alberonis Trev = *Gesta Alberonis archiepiscopi Treverensis auctore Balderico, MGH SS* VIII (Hannover, 1848) 234-260.

Gesta archiep. Magd = *Gesta archiepiscoporum Magdeburgensium,* ed. G. Schum,

MGH SS XXIV (Hannover, 1879) 367-489.

Gesta Godefridi archiep = *Gesta Godefridi archiepiscopi Treverensis, MGH SS* VIII (Hannover, 1848).

Gesta Halb = *Gesta episcoporum Halberstadensium*, ed. L. Weiland, *MGH SS* XXIII (Hannover, 1874) 78-123.

Gesta Leod. Abb = *Gesta episcoporum Leodensium Abbreviata, MGH SS* XXV (1880).

Gesta Traiect = *Gesta episcoporum Traiectensium, MGH SS* XXIII (Hannover, 1874).

Gesta Trev = *Gesta Treverorum, MGH SS* VIII (Hannover, 1848); *continuatio tertia et quarta, MGH SS* XXIV (Hannover, 1879).

Gesta Vird = *Gesta episcoporum Virdunensium, MGH SS* X (Hannover, 1852).

Glasschröder, *Pf. Urkk* = Franz Xaver Glasschröder, ed., *Urkunden zur pfälzischen Kirchengeschichte im Mittelalter* (München & Freising, 1903).

Gudenus, *Sylloge* = Valentin Ferdinand de Gudenus, ed., *Sylloge variorum diplomatariorum monumentorumque veterum ineditorum adhuc et res Germanicas* (Frankfurt, 1728).

——, *CdMogunt* = ——, ed., *Codex diplomaticus exhibens anecdota Moguntiaca*, 5 vols. (Göttingen, Frankfurt & Leipzig, 1743-1768).

Günther, *CdRhM* = W. Günther, *Codex diplomaticus Rheno-Mosellanus*, 6 vols. (Coblenz, 1822-1826).

Hamb. UB = *Hamburgisches Urkundenbuch* I, ed. Johann Martin Lappenberg (Hamburg, 1842).

Hansiz, *Germ. sacrae* = M. Hansiz, *Germaniae sacrae* I-II (Augsburg, 1727).

Harduin, *Acta concil* = J. Harduin, *Acta conciliorum* VI (Paris, 1714).

Hartzheim, *Concilia* = Johann Friedrich Schannat, ed. (cont. by Joseph Hartzheim), *Concilia Germaniae*, 11 vols. (Coloniae, 1759-1790).

Hehl, *Konzilien 916-1001* = Ernst-Dieter Hehl, ed., unter Mitarbeitung von Horst Fuhrmann, *Die Konzilien Deutschlands und Reichsitalien 916-1001*, Teil I: 916-960, MGH Concilia VI (Hannover, 1987).

Heinrici Chron. Lyv. = *Heinrici Chronicon Lyvoniae, MGH SS* XXIII (Hannover, 1874).

Hertel, *UB ULFMagd* = Gustav Hertel, ed., *Urkundenbuch des Klosters Unserer Liebfrauen zu Magdeburg*, Geschichtsquellen der Provinz Sachsen 10 (Halle, 1878).

Hess. UB (Baur) = *Hessisches Urkundenbuch aus dem Grossherzöglich-Hessischen Haus- und Staatsarchiv*, ed. Ludwig Baur, I (Darmstadt, 1846).

Hess. UB (Reimer) = *Hessisches Urkundenbuch*, Abth. II: *Urkundenbuch zur Geschichte der Herren von Hanau und der ehemaligen Provinz Hanau*, ed. H. Reimer, I (Leipzig, 1891).

Hess. UB (Wyss) = *Hessisches Urkundenbuch I: Urkundenbuch der Deutschordens—Ballei Hessen*, ed. Artur Wyss, Publicationen aus den Preussischen Staatsarchiven 3 (Leipzig, 1879).

484 BIBLIOGRAPHY

Himmelstein, *Synod. Herb* = Franz Xaver Himmelstein, ed., *Synodicon Herbipolense. Geschichte und Statuten der im Bistum Würzburg gehaltenen Concilien und Dioecesansynoden* (Würzburg, 1855).

Hist. Cremifan = *Historia Cremifanensis, MGH SS* XXV (Hannover, 1880).

Hist. dipl. Frid. II = *Historica diplomatica Friderici Secundi*, 6 vols., ed. Jean Louis Alphonse Huillard-Bréholles (Paris, 1852-1861).

Hist. Walciod = *Historia Walciodorensis Monasterii Continuatio, MGH SS* XIV (Hannover, 1883).

Hodenberg, *Brem. GQ* = Wilhelm von Hodenberg, ed., *Bremische Geschichtsquellen* I (Celle, 1858).

Hoogeweg, *Schriften Olivers* = Hermann Hoogeweg, ed., *Die Schriften des Kölner Scholasters, späteren Bischofs von Paderborn und Kardinalbischof von S. Sabina Oliverus* (Tübingen, 1894).

Horoy, *Honorius III opera* = César Auguste Horoy, ed., *Honorii III romani pontificis opera omnia* (Paris, 1872-1892).

Isengrani Ann. maiores = *Isengrani Annales maiores, MGH SS* XVII (1861).

Jaffé, *Bibliotheca* = Phillip Jaffé, ed., *Bibliotheca rerum Germanicarum* I (Berlin, 1864), III (1866), V (1879).

——, *Regestum Pontificum* = ——, ed., *Regestum Pontificum* [to 1198], 2 vols. (Leipzig, 1885, 1888).

Joannis, *Scr. rer. Mogunt* = Georg Christian Joannis, ed., *Scriptores rerum Moguntiacum* III (Francofurti ad Moenum, 1722-1727).

Kempf, *NRI* = Friedrich Kempf, ed., *Regestum Innocentii III papae super Negotio Romani Imperii* (Rome, 1947).

Lamperti mon. Hersf = *Lamperti monachi Hersfeldensis opera*, ed. O. Holder-Egger, *MGH SS rerum Germanicarum in usum scholarum* (3rd. ed. 1894).

Lechner, *Conc. Bamberg* = P. Lechner, ed., *Concilia, Synodi et comitia facta Bambergensia* (Bamberg, 1770).

Leibnitz, *Scr. rer. Br.* = Georg Wilhelm Leibnitz, ed., *Scriptores rerum Brunsvicensium*, 3 vols. (Hannover, 1707-1711).

Lippische Regg = *Lippische Regesten, aus gedruckten und ungedruckten Quellen*, ed. O.Preuss & A. Falkmann, I: 783-1300 (Lemgo & Detmold, 1860; repr. Osnabrück, 1975).

Magdeb. Schöppenchronik = *Magdeburger Schöppenchronik*, ed. K. Janicke, Chroniken der deutschen Städte VII (1869).

Mainzer UB = *Mainzer Urkundenbuch*, I: *Die Urkunden bis zum Tode Erzbischof Adalberts I. (1137)*, ed. Manfred Stimming (Darmstadt, 1972); II: *Die Urkunden seit dem Tode Erzbischof Adelberts I. (1137) bis zum Tode Erzbischof Konrads (1200)*, ed. Peter Acht (Darmstadt, 1971).

Manrique, *Ann. Cist* = Angel Manrique, *Annales Cistercienses. Kirchengeschichte von Erbauung Cisterz.* 5 vols in 2 (Regensburg, 1739-1741).

Mansi, *Collectio* = Johannes Dominicus Mansi, ed., *Sacrorum Conciliorum nova et amplissima Collectio*, 31 vols. (Florence, 1759-1789).

Martène, *Collectio* = Edmond Martène & Ursin Durand, eds., *Veterum scriptorum et monumentorum amplissima Collectio* VII (Paris, 1733).

——, *Thes. novus* = ——, eds., *Thesaurius novus Anecdotorum* I (Paris, 1717); IV (1733).

Mecklenburg UB = *Mecklenburgisches Urkundenbuch*, ed. by Verein für Mecklenburgische Geschichte und Altertumskunde, I: 786-1250 (Schwerin, 1863); II: 1251-1280 (Schwerin, 1864); III, 1865.

Mencken, *Scr. rer. Germ* = J.B. Mencken, *Scriptores rerum Germanicarum, praecipue Saxonicarum*, 3 vols. (Leipzig, 1728-1730).

Monumenta Boica = *Monumenta Boica*, published by the Academia Scientiarum Boica
vol. 28/1: *Monumenta Patavia* (München, 1829).
vols. 37-46, 60: *Monumenta Episc. Wirz.* (München, 1864-1905, 1916; repr. 1964).
vol. 50: *Urkunden des Hochstifts Eichstätt* (München, 1932).

MGH Epist. s. XIII = *MGH Epistolae saeculi XIII e Registris Pontificum Romanorum*, ed. Carl Rodenberg, I (Hannover, 1883); II (1887).

MGH Lib. de lite = *MGH Libelli de lite imperatorum et pontificum saeculi XI et XII conscripti*, I-II (1891, 1892).

MGH LL = *Monumenta Germaniae Historica, Leges.*

MGH SS = *Monumenta Germaniae Historica, Scriptores.*

MGH SS rer. Germ = *Monumenta Germaniae Historica, Scriptores rerum Germanicarum in usum scholarum.*

Migne, *PL* = Jacques Paul Migne, ed., *Patrologiae Cursus Completus, Series Latina*. 218 vols. (Paris, 1855ff.).

Ex Mirac. S. Marci = *Ex Miraculi Sancti Marci, MGH SS* IV (Hannover, 1841).

MC = *Monumenta historica ducatus Carinthiae. Geschichtliche Denkmäler des Herzogtums Kärnten*, ed. August Ritter Jaksch von Wartenhorst, vol. I: *Die Gurker GQ 864-1232* (Klagenfurt, 1896); II: *Die Gurker GQ 1233-1269* (Klagenfurt, 1898); III: *Die Kärnten GQ 811-1202* (Klagenfurt, 1904); IV: *Die Kärnten GQ 1202-1269* (Klagenfurt, 1906).

Möser, *Sämmtliche Werke* = Justus Möser, *Sämmtliche Werke*, Theil VIII: *Osnabrückische Geschichte*, Part IV: *Urkunden* (Berlin, 1843).

MRR = *Mittelrheinische Regesten oder chronologische Zusammensetzung des Quellenmaterials für die Geschichte der Territorien der beiden Regierungsbezirke Coblenz und Trier*, ed. Adam Goerz, vols. I-III (Coblenz, 1876-1886).

MRUB = *Urkundenbuch zur Geschichte der jetzt die Preussischen Regierungs bezirke Coblenz und Trier bildenden mittelrheinischen Territorien*, ed. Heinrich Beyer, Leopold Eltester and Adam Goerz, 3 vols. (Coblenz, 1860-1874).

Muller, *Cartularium* = S. Fz. Muller, Het oudste Cartularium van het sticht Utrecht (Utrecht, 1892).

NRUB   =   *Urkundenbuch für die Geschichte des Niederrheins oder des Erzstiftes Cöln, Fürstenthümer Jülich und Berg, Geldern, Meurs, Cleve und Mark und der Reichsstifte Eltern, Essen und Werden*, 4 vols., ed. Theodor Joseph Lacomblet (Düsseldorf, 1840-1858).

Oorkondenboek Utrecht   =   *Oorkondenboek van het Sticht Utrecht tot 1301* I, ed. S. Fz. Muller & A.C. Bouman (Utrecht, 1920). Deel I: 695-1197

Oorkondenboek Gelre   =   *Oorkondenboek der Graafschappen Gelre en Zutfen*, ed. Ludolf Anne Jan Wilt Sloet van de Beele, ('s Gravenhage, 1872-1876).

Otton. Fris. cont. Sanbl.   =   *Ottonis Frisingensis Chronica, continuatio Sanblasiensis, MGH SS* XX (Hannover, 1868).

Poncelet, *Actes*   =   Edouard Poncelet, ed., *Actes des Princes-Evêques de Liège Hughes de Pierrepont 1200-1229*, Recueil des Actes des Princes Belges (Bruxelles, 1946).

Potthast, *Regesta*   =   August Potthast, ed., *Regesta Pontificum Romanorum* I (Berlin, 1874).

Raynaldi, *Ann. eccles*   =   Odorico Raynaldi, *Annales ecclesiastici ab anno 1198*, ed. Mansi, I (Lucae, 1747).

Rechtsbook van Utrecht   =   *Rechtsbook van den Dom van Utrecht*, ed. Muller (Haag, 1895).

RAM   =   *Regesta archiepiscoporum Maguntinensium. Regesten zur Geschichte der Mainzer Erzbischöfe von Bonifatius bis Heinrich II.*, aus dem Nachlass von Johann Friedrich Böhmer, bearbeitet und herausgegeben von Cornelius Will, vol. I (Innsbruck 1877), II: 1161-1288 (Innsbruck, 1886; reprint 1966).

RAMagd   =   *Regesta archiepiscopatus Magdeburgensis*, ed. Georg Adalbert Mülverstedt, 3 vols. and Index (Magdeburg, 1876-1899).

RAS   =   *Regesta archiepiscoporum Salisburgensium inde ab anno MCVI usque ad annum MCCXLVI. Regesten zur Geschichte der Salzburger Erzbischöfe Conrad I., Eberhard I., Conrad II., Adalbert, Conrad III. und Eberhard II.*, ed. Andreas von Meiller (Wien, 1866).

RdBoh   =   *Regesta diplomatica necnon epistolaria Bohemiae et Moraviae* I, ed. C.J. Erben (Prag, 1855).

RdThur   =   *Regesta diplomatica necnon epistolaria historiae Thuringiae*, 4 vols., ed. Otto Dobenecker (Jena, 1896-1934).

REB   =   *Regesten der Erzbischöfe von Bremen* I, ed. Otto Heinrich May, Veröffentlichungen der historischen Kommission für Niedersachsen, Bd. XI (Hannover, 1937).

REK   =   *Die Regesten der Erzbischöfe von Köln im Mittelalter*, Veröffentlichungen der historischen Kommission für Niedersachsen 11, 4 vols., ed. Richard Knipping, Wilhelm Kisky & Friedrich Wilhelm Oediger (Bonn, 1901-1915).

RET   =   *Regesten der Erzbischöfe von Trier von Hetti bis Johann II.*, ed. Adam Goerz (Trier, 1859-1861; reprint Aalen, 1969).

Regg. Bamb = *Die Regesten der Bischöfe und des Domkapitels von Bamberg*, ed. Erich Freiherr von Guttenberg, Veröffentlichungen der Gesellschaft für Fränkische Geschichte, VI. Reihe (Würzburg, 1932).

Regg. Const = *Regesta episcoporum Constantiensium—Regesten zur Geschichte der Bischöfe von Constanz 517-1496*, ed. Paul Ladewig & Theodor Müller (Innsbruck, 1887-1895).

Regg. der Juden = *Regesten zur Geschichte der Juden im Fränkischen und Deutschen Reiche bis zum Jahre 1273*, ed. Albert Dresdner, Ludwig Lewinski & Julius Aronius (Berlin, 1873).

Regg. Eichst = Franz Heidingsfelder, ed., *Die Regesten der Bischöfe von Eichstätt* (Innsbruck, 1915-1917); re-issued in Veröffentlichungen der Gesellschaft für fränkische Geschichte, VI. Reihe, Bd. 1 (Erlangen, 1938).

Regg. hist. Westf = *Regesta historica Westfaliae accedit Codex diplomaticus. Die Quellen der Geschichte Westfalens, begleitet von einem Urkundenbuch*, vol. I: bis zum Jahre 1125; vol. II: 1126-1200, ed. Heinrich August Erhard (Münster, 1847, 1853; new printing Osnabrück, 1972); continued as *Westfalisches Urkundenbuch*.

Regg. Hon. III = *Regesta Honorii papae III (1216-1227)* I, ed. Petrus Pressutti (Rome, 1888).

Regg. MBr = *Regesten der Markgrafen von Brandenburg aus dem Askanischen Hause*, ed. H. Krabbo & G. Winter, Veröffentlichungen des Vereins für die Geschichte der Mark Brandenburg (1910-1955).

Regg. Strassburg = *Die Regesten der Bischöfe von Strassburg bis zum Jahre 1202*, ed. Paul Wentzcke, vol. I, Part 2 of *Die Regesten der Bischöfe von Strassburg*, ed. Hermann Bloch (Innsbruck, 1908); vol. II: 1202-1305, ed. Alfred Hessel & Manfred Krebs (Innsbruck, 1928).

Registres de Gregoire IX = Lucien Henri Louis Auvray, ed., *Les Registres de Gregoire IX* (Paris, 1896ff.).

Reineri Ann. = *Reineri Annales*, *MGH SS* XVI (Hannover, 1859).

Repertorium Fontium = *Repertorium Fontium historiae medii aevi, primum ab Augusto Potthast digestum, nunc cura collegii historicorum e pluribus nationibus emendatum et auctum*, II (Rome, 1962), IV (Rome, 1976), V (Rome, 1984).

Richeri Gesta = *Richeri Gesta Sennones*, *MGH SS* XXV (Hannover, 1880).

SUB = *Salzburg Urkundenbuch*, 3 vols., ed. Willibald Hautaler & Franz Martin (Salzburg, 1910-1918), Bd. I: *Traditionskodizes* (1910; repr. Aalen, 1987).

Scriba, *Hess. Regg* = H.E. Scriba, *Regesten zur Landes- und Ortsgeschichte des Grossherzogthums Hessen*, 4 vols. (Darmstadt, 1847-1850).

Statuta ord. Cist = *Statuta Capitularum Generalium Ordinis Cisterciensis ab anno 1116 ad anno 1786*, ed. Joseph Marie Canivez,

488   BIBLIOGRAPHY

I: 1116-1220 (Louvain, 1933).

Steiner, *Synodi August* = Joseph Anton Steiner, *Synodi Dioecesis Augustanae* I (Mindelheimii, 1766).

Sudendorf, *Regestrum* = Hans Friedrich Georg Julius Sudendorf, ed., *Regestrum, oder merkwürdige Urkunden für die deutsche Geschichte* I (Jena, 1849-1854).

Summa contra haereticos = The *Summa contra haereticos* ascribed to Praepositinus of Cremona, ed. Joseph N. Garvin & James A. Corbett, Notre Dame University Publications in Medieval Studies XV (Notre Dame, Indiana, 1958).

Tanner, *Decrees* = Norman P. Tanner, ed., *Decrees of the Ecumenical Councils*, I: Nicea to Lateran V (Washington, D.C., 1990).

Theiner, *Vetera* = August Theiner, ed., *Vetera Monumenta Slavorum medidionium* I (Rome, 1858).

Thietmari Chron. = *Thietmari Merseburgensis episcopi Chronicon*, ed. R. Holtzmann, Scriptores rerum Germanicarum, N.S. 9 (1935).

Trithemius, *Ann. Hirsaug* = Johannes Trithemius, *Annalium Hirsaugiensium* (St. Gall, 1690).

Thurgau UB = *Thurgauisches Urkundenbuch*, ed. J. Meyer (Frankenfeld, 1882).

UB Augsburg = *Die Urkunden des Hochstifts Augsburg 969-1420*, ed. Walther E. Vock (Augsburg, 1959).

UB Babenb. = *Urkundenbuch zur Geschichte der Babenberger in Österreich*, vorbereitet von Oskar Frh. von Mitis, bearb. von Heinrich Fichtenau und Erich Zöllner, I (1950), II (1955).

UB Eberbach = *Urkundenbuch der Abtei Eberbach im Rheingau*, ed. Karl Rossel, I (Wiesbaden, 1862).

UB Erfurt = *Urkundenbuch der Erfurter Stifter und Klöster, Teil I (706-1330)*, ed. Alfred Overmann, Geschichtsquellen der Provinz Sachsen,Bd. 5 (Magdeburg, 1926).

UB Halb = *Urkundenbuch des Hochstifts Halberstadt und seiner Bischöfe*, ed. G. Schmidt, Publicationen aus den preussischen Staatsarchiven 17 and 21, 2 vols. (Leipzig, 1883, 1884)

UB Hilds = *Urkundenbuch des Hochstifts Hildesheim und seiner Bischöfe*, Theil 1, bis 1221, ed. Karl Janicke (Leipzig, 1896); Theil 2, ed. Hermann Hoogeweg (Hannover & Leipzig, 1901).

UBLOE = *Urkundenbuch des Landes ob der Enns*, II (Wien, 1856); III (Wien, 1862); IV (Wien, 1867).

UB Luxemburg = *Urkunden- und Quellenbuch zur Geschichte der altluxemburgischen Territorien bis zur burgundischer Zeit*, ed. Camillus Wampach, II (Luxemburg, 1938).

UB Lübeck = *Urkundenbuch des Bistums Lübeck I, Codex diplomaticus Lubecensis—Lübeckisches Urkundenbuch* II. Abt., ed. Wilhelm Leverkus (Oldenburg, 1856).

UB Magd = *Urkundenbuch des Erstifts Magdeburg*, Teil I: 937-1192, ed. Friedrich Israël, with Walter Möllenberg, Ge-

schichtsquellen der Provinz Sachsen und des Frei-
staates Anhalt, N.R. Bd. 18 (Magdeburg, 1937).

UB Merseburg   =   *Urkundenbuch des Hochstifts Merseburg* I (962-1357),
ed. Paul Kehr, Geschichtsquellen der Provinz Sachsen
und angrenzenden Gebiete, vol. 36 (Halle, 1899).

UB Meissen   =   *Urkundenbuch des Hochstifts Meissen* I, ed. E.G. Gersdorf, Codex diplomaticus Saxoniae Regiae II/1
(Leipzig, 1864).

UB Naumburg   =   *Urkundenbuch des Hochstifts Naumburg I: 967-1207*, ed.
Felix Rosenfeld, Geschichtsquellen der Provinz
Sachsen. N.R. 1 (Magdeburg, 1925).

UB Osnabrück   =   *Urkundenbuch des Bistums Osnabrück* I, ed F. Philippi
(Osnabrück, 1892).

UB Stadt Magdeburg   =   *Urkundenbuch der Stadt Magdeburg*, vol. I to 1403, ed.
Gustav Hertel, Geschichtsquellen der Provinz Sachsen
und angrenzender Gebiete, vol. 26 (Halle, 1892).

UB Steiermark   =   *Urkundenbuch des Herzogtums Steiermark*, ed. J. Zahn
(Graz, 1875).

UB Strassburg   =   *Urkundenbuch der Stadt Strassburg* I-II, Wilhelm Wiegand, ed.(Strassburg, 1879, 1886).

Urkk. Speyer   =   *Urkunden zur Geschichte der Stadt Speyer*, ed. Alfred
Hilgard (Strassburg, 1885).

Urk.reg. Würzburg   =   *Urkundenregister zur Geschichte der kirchlichen Verwaltung des Bistums Würzburg im hohen und späten
Mittelalter (1136-1488)*, (Regesta Herbipolensia II) ed.
W. Engel, Quellen und Forschungen zur Geschichte
des Bistums und Hochstifts Würzburg IX Würzburg,
1954).

Verdener GQ   =   *Verdener Geschichtsquellen*, ed. Wilhelm von Hodenberg
I-II (Celle, 1856-1857).

Vita Altmani   =   *Vita Altmani episcopi Pataviensis*, ed. G.H. Pertz, *MGH
SS* XII (Hannover, 1856).

Vita Adelberti   =   *Vita Adelberti II. Moguntini*, ed. Ph. Jaffé, *Bibliotheca
rer. Germ.* 3 (1866) 565-603.

Vita Bernwardi   =   *Vita Bernwardi, MGH SS* IV 767 (Hannover, 1841).

Vita Godehardi   =   *Vita Godehardi episcopi Hildenesheimensis auctore
Wolfherio, MGH SS* XI (Hannover, 1854) 167-218.

Vita Meinwerci   =   *Vita Meinwerci episcopi Patherbrunnensis*, ed. F. Tenck-
hoff, *MGH SS rer. Germ.* (1921); earlier ed. in *MGH
SS* XI (1854).

Vock, *Urkk. Würzburg*   =   Walter E. Vock, ed., *Die Urkunden des Hochstifts
Augsburg 969-1420* (Augsburg, 1959).

Weech, *Cod. Salemit.*   =   F. von Weech, *Codex diplomaticus Salemitanus. UB des
Klosters Salem*, 3 vols. (Coblenz, 1883ff).

Westfälisches UB   =   *Westfälisches Urkundenbuch*, a continuation of Erhard's
Regesta Historiae Westfaliae, ed. by Vereine für
Geschichte und Altertumskunde Westfalens, vols. III-
VI (Münster, 1859-1898).

Wirtemburg. UB   =   *Wirtemburgisches Urkundenbuch*, ed. by the Königliches
Staatsarchiv in Stuttgart, I-II (Stuttgart, 1849, 1858).

Wormser UB   =   *Wormser Urkundenbuch. Monumenta Wormatiensa*, ed.

		Heinrich Boos I (Berlin, 1893).
Würdtwein, *Nova subs.*	=	Stephanus Alexander Würdtwein, *Nova subsidia diplomatica ad selecta iuris ecclesiastici Germaniae et historiarum capita elucidanda* (Heidelberg, 1785).

Secondary Works

ADB	=	*Allgemeine Deutsche Biographie* (2nd ed.; Berlin, 1967-1971; reprint of 1st ed.; 1875-1912).
Aldinger, *Neubesetzung*	=	Paul Aldinger, *Die Neubesetzung der deutschen Bistümer unter Papst Innocenz IV., 1243-1254* (Leipzig, 1901)
Bachmann, *Gesch. Böhmens*	=	Adolf Bachmann, *Geschichte Böhmens*, I: bis 1400, Geschichte der Europäischen Staaten (Gotha, 1899).
Bastgen, *Trierer DK*	=	Hubert Bastgen, *Die Geschichte des trierer Domkapitels im Mittelalter*, Goerres-Gesellschaft zur Pflege der Wissenschaft im katholischen Deutschland, Sektion für Rechts- und Sozialwissenschaft, Heft 7 (Paderborn, 1910).
Baumbach, *Arnold v. Selenhofen*	=	F. Baumbach, *Arnold von Selenhofen, Erzbischof von Mainz* (Dissertation Göttingen, 1871).
Benson, *Bishop Elect*	=	Robert L. Benson, *The Bishop Elect: A Study in Medieval Ecclesiastical Office* (Princeton, 1968).
Bernhöft, *Ratzeburg*	=	Hans Bernhöft, *Das Prämonstratenser Domstift Ratzeburg im Mittelalter. Verfassung, ständisches, Bildung* (Ratzeburg, 1932).
Bertram, *Bistum Hildesheim*	=	A. Bertram, *Geschichte des Bistums Hildesheim*, I-II (Hildesheim, 1899, 1916).
Bertholet, *Hist. de Lux.*	=	J. Bertholet, *Histoire ecclésiastique et civile du duché de Luxembourg*, 8 vols. (Luxembourg, 1741-1743).
Bienemann, *Conrad v. Scharfenberg*	=	Friedrich Bienemann, *Conrad von Scharfenberg, Bischof von Speyer und Metz und kaiserlicher Hofkanzler 1200-1224* (Strassburg, 1887).
Bierbaum, *Diözesansynode*	=	M. Bierbaum, *Die Diözesansynode des Bistums Münster* (Freiburg, 1928).
Binterim, *Concilien*	=	Anton Joseph Binterim, *Pragmatische Geschichte der deutschen National-, Provincial-, und vorzüglichsten Diöcesanconcilien, vom vierten Jahrhundert bis auf das Konzilium zu Trient*, vols. IV-V (Mainz, 1840-1843).
Biskamp, *Mainzer DK*	=	Elard Friedrich Biskamp, *Das Mainzer Domkapitel bis zum Ausgang des 13. Jahrhunderts* (Marburg, 1909).
Bitterauf, *Trad. Freising*	=	Theodor Bitterauf, *Die Traditionen des Hochstifts Freising*, Bd. 1: 744-926; Bd. 2: 926-1083, Quellen und Erörterungen zur Bayerisch- und Deutsche Geschichte, N.F. 4 (München, 1909).
Bogumil, *Bistum Halb.*	=	Karlotto Bogumil, *Das Bistum Halberstadt im 12. Jahrhundert. Studien zur Reichs- und Reformpolitik des Bischofs Reinhard*, Mitteldeutsche Forschungen 69 (Köln/Wien, 1972).
Börsting, *Bistum Münster*	=	Heinrich Börsting, *Geschichte des Bistums Münster* (Bielefeld, 1951).

Borst, *Katharer* = Arno Borst, *Die Katharer*, Schriften der Monumenta Germaniae Historica, XII (Stuttgart, 1953).

Boshof, *Erzstift Trier* = Egon Boshof, *Das Erzstift Trier und seine Stellung zu Königtum und Papsttum im Mittelalter* (Köln, 1972).

Brackmann, *Halberstadt DK* = Albert Brackmann, *Urkundliche Geschichte des Halberstädter Domkapitels im Mittelalter* (Dissertation Göttingen, 1898).

Braun, *Bischöfe von Augsb.* = Placidius Braun, *Geschichte der Bischöfe von Augsburg*, I (Augsburg, 1813).

Brem, *Gregor IX.* = Ernst Brem, *Gregor IX. bis zum Beginn seines Pontificates* (Heidelberg, 1911).

Browe, *Pflichtkommunion* = Peter Browe, *Die Pflichtkommunion im Mittelalter* (Münster, 1940).

Calmet, *Hist. eccles.* = Auguste Calmet, *Histoire ecclésiastique et civile de Lorraine* I (Nancy, 1728).

Cardauns, *Konrad v. Hostaden* = Hermann Cardauns, *Konrad von Hostaden, Erzbischof von Köln (1238-1261)* (Köln, 1880).

Cheney, *English Synodalia* = Christopher R. Cheney, *English Synodalia of the Thirteenth Century* (Oxford, 1941).

——, *Texts and Studies* = ——, *Medieval Texts and Studies* (Oxford, 1973).

——, *Episcopal Visitations* = ——, *Episcopal Visitations of Monasteries in the thirteenth Century* (Manchester, 1931).

Chevalier, *Répertoire-Bio* = Ulysse, Chevalier, *Répertoire des Sources Historiques du Moyen Age: Bio-Bibliographique* II: J-Z (Paris, 1907).

Claude, *Erzbistum Magdeburg* = Dietrich Claude, *Geschichte des Erzbistums Magdeburg bis in das 12. Jahrhundert*, Part I: Die Geschichte der Erzbischöfe bis auf Ruotger, Mitteldeutsche Forschungen vol. 67/1 (Cologne & Vienna, 1972).

Clouet, *Histoire eccles.* = Louis Clouet, *Histoire ecclesiastique de la province de Trèves et des pays limitrophes, comprenant les dioceses de Trèves, Metz, Toul, Verdun, Reims et Chalons* (Verdun, 1844-1861).

——, *Histoire de Verdun* = ——, *Histoire de Verdun et du pays verdunois* (Verdun, 1867-1870).

Cottineau, *Repertoire* = L.H. Cottineau, *Repertoire Topo-Bibliographique des Abbayes et Prieures*, 2 vols. (Macon, 1939).

Coulet, *Visites pastorales* = Noel Coulet, *Les Visites pastorales. Typologie des sources du moyen age occidental*, Directeur: L. Genicot, Fasc. 23 A-IV.1* (Turnhout, Belgium, 1977).

Curschmann, *Diözese Brand.* = Fritz Curschmann, *Die Diözese Brandenburg*, Germania Sacra (Leipzig, 1906).

Dictionnaire Cist. = *Dictionnaire des Auteurs Cisterciens*: M-O (1978).

DHGE = *Dictionnaire d'histoire et de géographie ecclésiastique* VI (1932): "Bamberg—VIII. Synodes" by Hans Burchard, col. 471.

Diegel, *Bischofswahlen* = Albert Diegel, *Der päpstliche Einfluss auf die Bischofswahlen in Deutschland während des 13. Jahrhunderts* (Berlin, 1932).

Dopsch, *Gesch. Salzburgs* = Heinz Dopsch, *Geschichte Salzburgs: Stadt und Land*, vol. I (Salzburg, 1984).

Duggan, *Bishop and Chapter* = Lawrence G. Duggan, *Bishop and Chapter. The*

Governance of the Bishopric of Speyer to 1552. Studies Presented to the International Commission for the History of Representative and Parliamentary Institutions (New Brunswick, N.J., 1978).

Falck, *Mainz im Ma.* = Ludwig Falck, *Mainz im früh- und hohen Mittelalter*, II: Geschichte der Stadt Mainz (Düsseldorf, 1972).

Feine, *Kirchl. RG* = Hans Erich Feine, *Kirchliche Rechtsgeschichte*, I: Die katholische Kirche (Weimar, 1951; 4th ed., Köln & Graz, 1964)).

Ficker, *Engelbert* = Julius Ficker, *Engelbert der Heilige, Erzbischof von Köln und Reichsverweser* (Köln, 1853).

Fink, *Siegfried III.* = Erich Fink, *Siegfried III. von Eppenstein, Erzbischof von Mainz 1230-1249* (Rostock, 1892).

Finke, *Konzilienst.* = Heinrich Finke, *Konzilienstudien zur Geschichte des 13. Jahrhunderts, Ergänzungen und Berichtigungen zu Hefele-Knöpfler „Conciliengeschichte"* Bde. V-VI (Münster, 1891).

Fischer, *Amtsdaten* = Wilhelm Fischer, *Die Personal- und Amtsdaten der Erzbischöfe von Salzburg (789-1519)* (Dissertation Greifswald; Anklam, 1916).

Förg, *Ketzerverfolgung* = Ludwig Förg, *Die Ketzerverfolgung in Deutschland unter Gregor IX.*, Historische Studien, ed. Ebering, 218 (Berlin, 1932) 1-98.

Foreville, *Lateran I-IV* = Raymonde Foreville, *Lateran I-IV*, vol. 6 of Geschichte der ökumenischen Konzilien (Mainz, 1970).

Frensdorff, *Dienstmänner* = [   ] Frensdorff, *Das Recht der Dienstmänner des Erzbischofs von Köln*, Sonderabdruck aus den Mitteilungen des Stadtarchivs von Köln (Köln, 1883).

Friedberg, *Canones-Samml.* = Emil Friedberg, *Die Canones-Sammlungen zwischen Gratian und Bernhard von Pavia* (Leipzig, 1887).

Frind, *Bischöfe von Prag* = Anton Frind, *Geschichte der Bischöfe und Erzbischöfe von Prag* (Prag, 1873).

Fuchs, *Besetzung* = Wilhelm Fuchs, *Die Besetzung der deutschen Bistümer unter Papst Gregor IX. (1227-1241) und bis zum Regierungsantritt Papst Innocenz IV. (1243)* (Berlin, 1911).

Gallia Christ. = *Gallia Christiana in provincias ecclesiasticas distributa*, ed. Dion. Sammarthanus (Paris 1716-1785).

Gams, *Series Episc.* = Bonifacius Gams, *Series Episcoporum Ecclesiae Catholicae* (Ratisbon, 1873).

Ganzer, *Papsttum und Bistum* = Klaus Ganzer, *Papsttum und Bistumsbesetzungen in der Zeit von Gregor IX. bis Bonifaz VIII., Ein Beitrag zur Geschichte der päpstlichen Reservationen*, Forschungen zur Kirchlichen Rechtsgeschichte und zum Kirchenrecht IX (Köln-Graz, 1968).

Germania Benedictina = *Germania Benedictina*, Bd. II: Bayern, ed. Jos. Hemmerle (Augsburg 1970); V: Baden-Württemburg, ed. Franz Quarthal (Augsburg, 1975); VI: Niedersachsen, Norddeutschland, ed. Ulrich Faust (Augsburg, 1979).

Germania Pontifica = *Germania Pontifica*. 1. Provincia Salisburgensis et Episcopatus Tridentinus,

ed. Albert Brackmann (Berlin, 1911).
2. Provincia Maguntinensis. Teil 1: Dioeceses Eichstetensis, Augustensis, Constantiensis I; Teil 2 : Dioeceses Constantiensis II et Curiensis et episcopatus Sedunensis, Genevensis, Lausannensis, Basiliensis, ed. Albert Brackmann (Berlin, 1923 and 1927).

Gibbs/Lang, *Bishops/Reform* = Marian Gibbs & Jane Lang, *Bishops and Reform 1215-1272* (Oxford, 1934).

Glaeske, *Erzbischöfe H-Br* = Günter Glaeske, *Die Erzbischöfe von Hamburg-Bremen* (937-1258), Quellen und Darstellungen zur Geschichte Niedersachsens, Bd. 60 (Hildesheim, 1962).

Görres, *Lütticher DK* = Joseph Görres, *Das Lütticher Domkapitel bis zum 14. Jahrhundert* (Berlin, 1907).

Grundmann, *Relig. Bewegung.* = Herbert Grundmann, *Religiöse Bewegungen im Mittelalter* (2nd ed.; Berlin, 1935).

Groten, *Priorenkolleg* = Manfred Groten, *Priorenkolleg und Domkapitel von Köln im Hohen Mittelalter. Zur Geschichte des kölnischen Erzstifts und Herzogtums*, vol. 109 of Rheinisches Archiv (1980).

Guttenberg, *Bistum Bamberg* = Erich Freiherr von Guttenberg & Alfred Wendehorst, *Das Bistum Bamberg. Die Reihenfolge der Bischöfe* (1937; reprint in Germania Sacra II/1, Berlin, 1966).

Hageneder, *Gerichtsbarkeit* = Othmar Hageneder, *Die geistliche Gerichtsbarkeit in Ober- und Niederösterreich. Von den Anfängen bis zum Beginn des 15. Jahrhunderts*, Forschungen zur Geschichte Österreichs 10 (Linz, 1967).

Haid, *Besetzung Brixen* = P. Kassian Haid, *Die Besetzung des Bistum Brixen in der Zeit 1250-1376* (Wien & Leipzig, 1912).

Hantsch, *Gesch. Österr.* = Hugo Hantsch, *Die Geschichte Österreichs* I (3rd ed.; Graz & Wien, 1951).

Harzem, *Prioren* = Hansheinz Harzem, *Die 'Prioren' im mittelalterlichen Köln* (Dissertation Universität Köln, 1949).

Hauck, *KGD* = Albert Hauck, *Kirchengeschichte Deutschlands* (3rd/4th ed., Leipzig, 1906; 8th unaltered ed., Berlin, 1954).

Havet, *L'heresie et le Bras* = Julien Pierre Eugene Havet, *L'heresie et le Bras Seculier au moyen âge jusqu'au trézième siècle* (Paris, 1881).

Hefele, *Concilien* = Karl Joseph Hefele, *Conciliengeschichte*, 9 vols. (Freiburg im Breisgau, 1850-1890). vol. 4: 1879.

——/Knöpfler, *Concilien-gesch.* = ——, *Conciliengeschichte*, 2nd ed., revised and augmented by Alois Knöpfler (Freiburg, 1886).

——/Leclercq, *Conciles* = ——, *Conciliengeschichte*, trans., augmented and corrected by H. Leclercq (Paris, 1913).

Heussen, *Batavia Sacra* = Hugo Franciscus van Heussen, *Batavia Sacra sive Regestae apostolicorum Virorum qui fidem Bataviae primi intulerunt* (Bruxelles, 1714).

Heydenreich, *Metropolitan* = Johanne Heydenreich, *Die Metropolitangewalt der Erzbischöfe von Trier bis auf Baldewin*. Marburg Theologische Studien (Marburg, 1938).

Heyen, *St. Paulin* = Franz-Josef Heyen, *Das Stift Sankt Paulin von Trier*, Germania Sacra, Neue Reihe VI (Berlin, 1972).

Hilling, *Diözesansynoden* = Nikolaus Hilling, *Die westfälischen Diözesansynoden bis*

		zur Mitte des 13. Jahrhunderts: Ein Beitrag zur geistlichen Verfassungsgeschichte der Bistümer Münster, Paderborn, Osnabrück und Minden (Lingen, 1898).
Hinschius, *KR*	=	Paul Hinschius, *Das Kirchenrecht der Katholiken und Protestanten in Deutschland* III (Berlin, 1869-1897; repr. Graz, 1959).
Hirn, *Kirchen-Verhältnisse*	=	Josef Hirn, *Kirchen- und reichsrechtliche Verhältnisse des Salzburgischen Suffragenbistums Gurk* (Krems, 1872).
Hodenberg, *Diöcese Bremen*	=	Wilhelm von Hodenberg, *Die Diöcese Bremen und deren Gaue in Sachsen und Friesland*, 3 vols. (Celle, 1858-1859).
Hofmeister, *Bischof und DK*	=	Philipp Hofmeister, *Bischof und Domkapitel nach altem und neuem Recht* (Abtei Nerresheim/Württemberg, 1931).
Hontheim, *Hist. Trev. dipl.*	=	Johann Nikolas von Hontheim [Honthemius], *Historia Treverensis diplomata et pragmatica*, 3 vols. (Aug. Vind. & Herbipoli, 1750-1757).
——, *Prodromus Trev.*	=	——, *Prodromus historiae Trevericus diplomaticus* I (Augsburg, 1757).
Hurter, *Innocenz III.*	=	Friedrich Hurter, *Geschichte Innocenz des Dritten* I (Hamburg, 1841).
Jäck, *Bistum Bamberg*	=	H[einrich] J[oachim] Jäck, *Die Geschichte Bambergs von der Entstehung des Bistums im Jahre 1006 bis auf unsere Zeiten* (Bamberg, 1809-1810).
Janner, *Regensburg*	=	Ferdinand Janner, *Geschichte der Bischöfe von Regensburg*, 2 vols. (Regensburg, 1883-1884).
Jedin, *Handbook*	=	Hubert Jedin, *Handbook of Church History*, IV: From the High Middle Ages to the Eve of the Reformation, trans. Anselm Biggs (New York, 1970).
Juritsch, *Babenberger*	=	Georg Juritsch, *Geschichte der Babenberger und ihrer Länder* (Innsbruck, 1894).
Kahlkoff, *Wolfger v. Passau*	=	P. Kahlkoff, *Wolfger von Passau 1191-1204* (Weimar, 1882).
Kaufmann, *Caesarius*	=	Alexander Kaufmann, *Caesarius von Heisterbach: Ein Beitrag zur Culturgeschichte des zwölften und dreizehnten Jahrhunderts* (2nd. ed; Köln, 1862).
——, *Caesarius-Werken*	=	——, *Wunderbare und Denkwürdige Geschichten aus den Werken des Caesarius von Heisterbach*, Teil I (Köln, 1888).
Kauffungen, *Meissen DK*	=	K. Kauffungen (gen. Brunn), *Das Domkapitel von Meissen im Mittelalter*, Mitteilungen des Vereins für die Geschichte der Stadt Meissen VI/2 (Dissertation Leipzig, 1902).
Kehrberger, *Synodalstatuten*	=	Eduard Otto Kehrberger, *Provincial- und Synodalstatuten des Spätmittelalters. Eine quellenkritische Untersuchung der Mainzer Provinzialgesetze des 14. und 15. Jahrhunderts und der Synodalstatuten der Diözesen Bamberg, Eichstätt und Konstanz* (Stuttgart, 1938).
Kentenich, *Verzeichnis*	=	Gottfried Kentenich, *Beschreibendes Verzeichnis der Handschriften der Stadtbibliothek zu Trier, vol. IX: Die Juristischen Handschriften* (Trier, 1919).

Kerschbaumer, *Sankt Pölten* = Anton Kerschbaumer, *Geschichte des Bistums Sankt Pölten*, I: Vorgeschichte (Wien am Graben, 1875).

Kieckhefer, *Repression* = Richard Kieckhefer, *Repression of Heresy in Medieval Germany* (Philadelphia, 1979).

Kist, *Erzbistum Bamberg* = Johannes Kist, *Fürst- und Erzbistum Bamberg. Leitfaden durch ihre Geschichte von 1003-1943* (Bamberg, 1953).

Kneschke, *Adels-Lexikon* = Ernst Heinrich Kneschke, *Neues allgemaines Deutsches Adels-Lexikon* I-IX (1859-1870; repr. 1973).

Kohlmann, *EB Ludolf* = Friedrich Kohlmann, *Erzbischof Ludolf von Magdeburg. Sein Leben und politische Tätigkeit 1192-1205* (Halle, 1885).

Krabbo, *Besetzung* = Hermann Krabbo, *Die Besetzung der deutschen Bistümer unter Friedrich II. (1212-1250)*, Part I to 1227 (Berlin, 1906).

——, *Ostdeutsche Bistümer* = ——, *Die Ostdeutschen Bistümer, besonders ihre Besetzung unter Kaiser Friedrich II.* (Berlin, 1906).

Kuhle, *Neubesetzung* = Otto Kuhle, *Die Neubesetzung der deutschen Bistümer unter Papst Innozenz III.* (Berlin, 1934).

Kuttner, *Repertorium* = Stephan Kuttner, *Repertorium der Kanonistik (1140-1234)* (Città del Vaticano, 1937).

Kyriander, *Annales Trev.* = Wilhelm Kyriander, *Annales, sive Commentarii de origine et statu antiquissimae civitatis Augustae Treverorum* (Biponti, 1603).

Lacombe, *Prévostin* = Georges Lacombe, *La vie et les oeuvres de Prévostin*, Bibliothèque thomiste, 11 (Le Saulchoir (Belgium), 1927).

Lamay, *Hildesheimer DK* = G. Lamay, *Die Standisverhältnisse des HildesheimerDomkapitels in Mittelalter* (Dissertation Bonn, 1909).

Lappenberg, *Ratzeb./Schw.* = J.M. Lappenberg, *Zur Geschichte der Bistümer Ratzeburg und Schwerin*, Jahrbücher 10 (1845).

Lepsius, *Hochstift Naumburg* = Carl Peter Lepsius, *Geschichte der Bischöfe des Hochstifts Naumburg vor der Reformation* I (Naumburg, 1846).

Lewin, *Siegfried II.* = Heinrich Lewin, *Der Mainzer Erzbischof Siegfried II. von Eppstein* (Bern, 1895).

LTK = *Lexikon für Theologie und Kirche* (2nd ed.; Freiburg im Br., 1930-1938).

Lingg, *Pfarrvisitation* = Max Lingg, *Geschichte des Instituts der Pfarrvisitation* (Kempten, 1888).

Lipf, *Verordnungen* = Joseph Lipf, *Oberhirtliche Verordnungen und allgemeine Erlasse für das Bistum Regensburg vom Jahre 1250-1852* (Regensburg, 1853).

Löhnert, *Amtsdaten Trier* = Kurt Löhnert, *Personal- und Amtsdaten der Trierer Erzbischöfe des 10. - 15. Jahrhunderte* (Greifswald, 1908).

Looshorn, *Bistum Bamberg* = Johann Looshorn, *Geschichte des Bistums Bamberg von 1102-1303* I-II (München, 1886, 1888; reprint 1967).

Lüntzel, *Diözese Hildesheim* = H.A. Lüntzel, *Geschichte der Diözese und Stadt Hildesheim*, 2 vols. (Hildesheim, 1858).

Machatschek, *Hochst. Meissen* = E. Machatschek, *Geschichte der Bischöfe des Hochstifts Meissen* (Meissen, 1884).

Manitius, *Latein. Literatur* = Max Manitius, *Geschichte der lateinischen Literatur des Mittelalters* III (München, 1931).

Maring, *Diözesansynoden*	=	Johannes Maring, *Die Diözesansynoden und Domherren-Generalkapitel des Hochstifts Hildesheim bis zum Anfang des XVII Jahrhunderts: Ein Beitrag zur geistlichen Verfassungsgeschichte des Bistums Hildesheim* (Hannover, 1905).
Marx, *Erzstift Trier*	=	Jacob Marx, *Geschichte des Erzstifts Trier* II/2 (Trier, 1862).
Masch, *Bistum Ratzeburg*	=	G.M.C. Masch, *Geschichte des Bistums Ratzeburg* (Lübeck, 1835).
Mayer, *Bistum Chur*	=	Johann Georg Mayer, *Geschichte des Bistums Chur* I (Stans, 1907).
Mazzetti, *Bischof Berngar*	=	Ludwig Mazzetti, *Die Verfassungsrechtliche Stellung des Bistums und der Stadt Speyer zur Zeit des Bischofs Berngar von Entringen, 1224-1232* (Speyer, 1927).
Meier, *Halberstadt DK*	=	Rudolf Meier, *Die Domkapitel zu Goslar und Halberstadt in ihrer persönlichen Zusammensetzung im Mittelalter*, Studien zur Germania Sacra I (Göttingen, 1967).
Meyer v. Knonau, *Jahrbücher*	=	Gerold Meyer von Knonau, *Jahrbücher der deutschen Geschichte—Jahrbücher des deutschen Reichs unter Heinrich IV. und Heinrich V. II: 1070-1077* (Leipzig, 1894).
Michel, *Gerichtsbarkeit*	=	F. Michel, *Zur Geschichte der geistlichen Gerichtsbarkeit und Verwaltung der Trierer Erzbischöfe im Mittelalter*, Veröffentlichungen des Bistumsarchiv Trier III (Trier, 1953).
Morret, *Stand und Herkunft*	=	Benno Morret, *Stand und Herkunft der Bischöfe von Metz, Toul und Verdun im Mttelalter* (Düsseldorf, 1911).
von Muchar, *Steiermark*	=	Albert von Muchar, *Geschichte des Herzogtums Steiermark* V (Grätz, 1850).
M-Alpermann, *Stand und Herkunft*	=	Gerhard Müller-Alpermann, *Stand und Herkunft der Bischöfe der Magdeburger und Hamburger Kirchenprovinz im Mittelalter"* (Dissertation; Greifswald, 1930).
Münster, *Konrad v. Querfurt*	=	Thomas Münster, *Konrad von Querfurt, kaiserlicher Hofkanzler, Bischof von Hildesheim und Würzburg* (Leipzig, 1890).
Obersteiner, *Gurk*	=	Jakob Obersteiner, *Die Bischöfe von Gurk 1072-1822*, Aus Forschung und Kunst, vol. V (Klagenfurt, 1969).
Oediger, *Bistum Köln*	=	Friedrich Wilhelm Oediger, *Das Bistum Köln von den Anfängen bis zum Ende des 12. Jahrhunderts*, Geschichte des Erzbistums Köln, vol. 1 (2nd ed.; Köln, 1972).
——, *Bildung*	=	——, *Über die Bildung der Geistlichen im späten Mittelalter*, Studien und Texte zur Geistesgeschichte des Mittelalters, 2 (1953).
Oswald, *Passau DK*	=	Josef Oswald, *Das alte Passauer Domkapitel. Seine Entwicklung bis zum dreizehnten Jahrhundert und seine Wahlkapitulationswesen*, Münchner Studien zur Historischen Theologie 10 (München, 1933).
Palazzini, *Dizionario*	=	Pietro Palazzini, *Dizionario dei concili* (Roma, 1963).
Pellens, *Dietrich v. Wied*	=	Karl Pellens, *Der Trierer Erzbischof Dietrich II. von Wied*

		(1212-1242) (Dissertation Fribourg, Switzerland, 1958).
Pelster, *Stand und Herkunft*	=	W. Pelster, *Stand und Herkunft der Bischöfe der Kölner Kirchenprovinz im Mittelalter* (Köln, 1909).
Phillips, *Diözesansynode*	=	George Phillips, *Die Diözesansynode* (Freiburg, 1849).
Pontal, *Liste des MSS*	=	Odette Pontal, *Liste des manuscrits contenent des statuts synodaux de l'ancienne France classé par dioceses*, Bulletin d'information de l'Institut de Recherche et d'Histoire des Textes, Nr. 11 (Paris, 1962).
——, *Statuts synodaux*	=	——, *Les Statuts synodaux*, Typologie des Sources du Moyen Age, Fasc. 11 (Turnhout, 1975).
——, *Statuts du XIIIe S.*	=	——, *Les Statuts Synodaux Francais du XIIIe Siècle précédes d'l'historique du synode diocésain depuis ses origines I: Les Statuts à 1229* (Paris, 19); Tome II: Les Statuts de 1230 à 1260 (Paris, 1983). Collection de Documents inédits sur l'Histoire de France, Section de Philologie et d'Histoire jusqu'a 1610, vol. 15.
Prutz, *Friedrich I.*	=	H. Prutz, *Kaiser Friedrich I.*, 3 vols. (Danzig, 1871-1874).
Remling, *Bistum Speyer*	=	Franz Xaver Remling, *Geschichte der Stadt und des Bistums Speyer* I (Mainz, 1852).
Rittenbach, *Meissen*	=	Willi Rittenbach & Siegfried Seifert, *Geschichte der Bischöfe von Meissen 968-1581*, Studien zur katholischen Bistums- und Klostergeschichte, VIII (Leipzig, 1965).
Röhrich, *Adolf I. von Köln*	=	Viktor Röhrich, *Adolf I., Erzbischof von Köln* (Dissertation Königsberg, 1886).
Röhricht, *Deutschen im HL*	=	Reinhold Röhricht, *Die Deutschen im Heiligen Lande* (Innsbruck, 1894).
Rosenstock, *Rechtsliteratur*	=	Eugen Rosenstock, *Ostfalens Rechtsliteratur unter Friedrich II.* Texte und Untersuchungen (Weimar, 1912).
Roth, *Visionen und Briefe*	=	F.W.E. Roth, *Die Visionen und Briefe der heiligen Elisabeth, sowie die Schriften der Äbte Ekbert und Emecho von Schönau* (2nd ed., Brünn, 1886).
Santifaller, *Brixener DK*	=	Leo Santifaller, *Das Brixener Domkapitel in seiner persönlichen Zusammensetzung im Mittelalter*, Schlern Schriften 7 (Innsbruck, 1924).
Sawicki, *Bibliographia*	=	Jacobus Theodor Sawicki, *Bibliographia synodorum particularium*, Monumenta Iuris Canonici, Series C: Subsidia 2 (Città del Vaticano, 1967).
Sax, *Eichstätt*	=	J. Sax, *Versuch einer Geschichte des Hochstifts und der Stadt Eichstätt* (Nürnberg, 1857).
——, *Bischöfe*	=	——, *Die Bischöfe und Reichsfürsten von Eichstätt 745 bis 1806* (Landshut, 1884-1885; rev. by J. Bleicher, Eichstätt, 1927).
Schäfers, *Amtsdaten Magdeb.*	=	J. Schäfers, *Personal- und Amtsdaten der Magdeburger Erzbischöfe* (Dissertation Greifswald, 1908).
Schannat, *Hist. Wormat.*	=	Friedrich Schannat, *Historia Episcopatus Wormatiensis* (Frankfurt, 1734).
Schaten, *Ann. Paderbor.*	=	R.P. Nicolas Schaten, *Annalium Paderborensium*, Pars I-II

(Monasterium, 1774-1776).

Scheid, *Origines Guelficae* = *Origines Guelficae, opus praeeunte*, G.W. Leibnitz, J.G. Eccard, J.D. Gruber emissum studio Chr. L. Scheidii, 5 vols. (Hannover, 1750-1780).

Schneider, *Domkapitel* = Philipp Schneider, *Die bischöflichen Domkapitel, ihre Entwicklung und rechtliche Stellung im Organismus der Kirche* (Mainz, 1885; 2nd ed., Mainz, 1892).

Schönbach, *Erzählungslit.* = A.E. Schönbach, *Studien zur Erzählungsliteratur des Mittelalters*, Part IV: Über Caesarius von Heisterbach I, Sitzungsberichte der Österreichischen Akademie der Wissenschaft in Wien, Phil.-Hist. Classe, Band CXLIV (1902), 9. Abhandlung, 4-45.

Schöntag, *Augsburg DK* = Ilse Schöntag, *Über die persönliche Zusammensetzung des Augsburger Domkapitels im Mittelalter* (Diss. Breslau; Zeulenroda, Bernhard Sporn Verlag, 1938)

Schöttgen/Kreysig, *Dipl.* = Chr. Schöttgen & G.Chr. Kreysig, eds., *Diplomataria et scriptores historiae Germanicae medii aevi*, 3 vols. (Altenburg, 1753-1760).

Schroeder, *Discipl. Decrees* = Henry J. Schroeder, *Disciplinary Decrees of the Great Councils: Text, Tralsations and Commentary* (London, 1937).

Schrödl, *Bistum Passau* = Karl Schrödl, *Passavia Sacra. Geschichte des Bisthums Passau bis zur Säkularisation* (Passau, 1879).

Schulte, *QL* = Johann Friedrich Schulte, *Die Geschichte der Quellen und Literatur des Canonischen Rechts von Gratian bis auf die Gegenwart* I-II (Stuttgart, 1875, 1877).

Schwemer, *Innocent III.* = Richard Schwemer, *Innocent III und die deutsche Kirche während des Thronstreits von 1198-1208* (Strassburg, 1882).

Scr. rer. Germ. = *Monumenta Germaniae Historica, Scriptores rerum Germanicarum in usum scholarum.*

Simon, *Stand und Herkunft* = Johannes Simon, *Stand und Herkunft der Bischöfe der Mainzer Kirchenprovinz im Mittelalter* (Weimar, 1908).

Simonsfeld, *Jahrbücher I* = H. Simonsfeld, *Jahrbücher des deutschen Reichs unter Friedrich II.* I: 1152-1158 (Berlin, 1908).

Sindern, *Kloster Corvey* = Heinrich Sindern, *Beitrag zur inneren und äusseren Geschichte des Klosters Corvey von 1160-1255* (Dissertation Münster, 1939).

Sinnacher, *Säben und Brixen* = Franz Anton Sinnacher, *Beyträge zur Geschichte der bischöflichen Kirche Säben und Brixen in Tyrol*, 3 vols. (Brixen, 1821, 1822, 1823). vol. 4, 1824-1826.

Sparber, *Bistum Sabiona* = Anselm Sparber, *Das Bistum Sabiona* (Brixen, 1942).

——, *Fürstbischöfe* = ——, *Die Brixner Fürstbischöfe im Mittelalter. Ihr Leben und Wirken* (Bozen, 1968).

Specht, *Unterrichtswesens* = Franz Anton Specht, *Geschichte des Unterrichtswesens in Deutschland* (Stuttgart, 1885).

Staber, *Regensburg* = Joseph Staber, *Geschichte des Bistums Regensburg* (Regensburg, 1966).

Steichele, *Bistum Augsburg* = A. Steichele, *Das Bistum Augsburg historisch und statistisch beschrieben* (Augsburg, 1864ff.).

Tabouillot, *Hist. de Metz* = Jean François & Nicolas Tabouillot, *Histoire de Metz, par* des Religieux Bénédictins de la Congrégation de S. Vanne, Preuves de l'histoire de Metz (Metz & Nancy, 1769).

Tangl, *Teilnehmer* = Georgina Tangl, *Die Teilnehmer an den allgemeinen Konzilien des Mittelalters* (2nd ed.; Köln, 1969).

Thiéry, *Toul* = A.D. Thiéry, *Histoire de la Ville de Toul et de des évêques* (Paris, 1843).

Thiekötter, *Münster DK* = H. Thiekötter, *Die ständische Zusammensetzung des Münsterschen Domkapitels im Mittelalter* (Dissertation Münster, 1933).

Tillmann, *Innocenz III.* = Helene Tillmann, *Papst Innocenz III.*, Bonner Historische Forschungen, Bd. 3 (Bonn, 1954).

Trusen, *Gelehrten Rechts* = Winfried Trusen, *Anfänge des gelehrten Rechts in Deutschland. Ein Beitrag zur Geschichte der Rezeption, Recht und Geschichte* 1 (Wiesbaden, 1962).

Ussermann, *Germaniae Sacrae* = Aemilian Ussermann, *Germaniae sacrae prodromus seu collectio monumentorum res Allemannicus illustrantium.* (St. Blasien, 1790-1791).

——, *Episcopatus Bamb.* = ——, *Episcopatus Bambergensis sub S. Sede apostolica chronologice et diplomatice illustratus opera et studia* (St. Blasien, 1802).

——, *Episcopatus Wirc.* = ——, *Episcopatus Wirceburgensis sub metropoli Maguntina chronologice et diplomatice illustratus* (St. Blasien, 1794).

Vochezer, *Waldburg* = Joseph Vochezer, *Geschichte fes fürstlichen Hauses Waldburg in Schwaben*, 3 vols. (Kempten, 1888-1907).

Wattenbach, *Deutschlands GQ* = Wilhelm Wattenbach, *Deutschlands Geschichtsquellen im Mittelalter bis zur Mitte des 13. Jahrhunderts*, 2 vols. (5th ed.; Berlin, 1885-1886). 6th (Berlin, 1893ff.).

——/Schmale, *DGQ* = ——, *Deutschlands Geschichtsquellen*, revised by Franz-Josef Schmale (Köln, 1963).

Weinfurter, *Bistumsreform* = Stefan Weinfurter, *Salzburger Bistumsreform und Bischofspolitik im 12. Jahrhundert. Der Erzbischof Konrad I. von Salzburg (1106-1147) und die Regularkanoniker* (Köln/Wien, 1975).

Wenck, *Hess. Landesgesch.* = Helfrich Bernhard Wenck, *Hessische Landesgeschichte, mit einem Urkundenbuch* II (Darmstadt & Giessen, 1783f.).

Wendehorst, *Bistum Würzburg* = Alfred Wendehorst, *Das Bistum Würzburg. Die Bischofsreihe bis 1254*, Germania Sacra N.F. I: Die Bistümer der Kirchenprovinz Mainz (Berlin, 1962).

Wenner, *Rechtsbeziehungen* = J. Wenner, *Die Rechtsbeziehungen der Mainzer Metropoliten zu ihren sächsischen Suffraganbistümern bis zum Tode Aribos (1031)*, Görres-Gesellschaft zur Pflege der Wissenschaft im katholischen Deutschland, Sektion für Rechts- und Sozialwissenschaft, 46 (Paderborn, 1926).

Wentz, *Bistum Brandenburg* = G. Abt & Gottfried Wentz, *Das Bistum Brandenburg*, Germania Sacra I/1 (Berlin, 1929).

——, *Bistum Havelberg* = ——, *Das Bistum Havelberg*, Germania Sacra I/2 (Berlin & Leipzig, 1933).

——, *Erzbistum Magdeburg* = ——, & Berent Schwinekoper, *Das Erzbistum Magdeburg*,

Abt. 1: Magdeburg, Germania Sacra: Die Bistümer der Kirchenprovinz Magdeburg (Berlin & New York, 1972).

Werminghoff, *Verfassungsg.* = Albert Werminghoff, *Verfassungsgeschichte der deutschen Kirche im Mittelalter* I-II (Leipzig, 1907, 1913).

Widmann, *Gesch. Salzburgs* = Hans Widmann, *Geschichte Salzburgs*, I: bis 1270, Deutsche Landesgeschichten 9 (Gotha, 1907).

Winkelmann, *Friedrich II.* = Eduard Winkelmann, *Geschichte Kaiser Friedrichs II. und seiner Reiche* (Berlin, 1863-1865).

——, *Philipp v. Schw.* = ——, *Philipp von Schwaben und Otto IV. von Braunschweig*, 2 vols. (Leipzig, 1873; 3rd ed., Darmstadt, 1962).

Wretschko, *Besetzung* = Alfred von Wretschko, *Zur Frage der Besetzung des erzbischöflichen Stuhles in Salzburg im Mittelalter* (Stuttgart, 1907); also in Mitteilungen der Gesellschaft für Salzburger Landeskunde 47 (1907) 189-303.

Zatschek, *Urkundenlehre* = Heinz Zatschek, *Studien zur mittelalterlichen Urkundenlehre: Konzept, Register und Briefsammlung* (Brünn, 1929).

Zimmermann, *Legationen* = Heinrich Zimmermann, *Die päpstliche Legationen in der esten Hälfte des 13. Jahrhunderts* (Paderborn, 1913).

Zoepfl, *Bistum Augsburg* = Friedrich Zoepfl, *Das Bistum Augsburg und seine Bischöfe im Mittelalter* I (Augsburg, 1955).

Literature—Unpublished

Affentranger, "Bischöfe von Chur" = Urban Affentranger, "Das Leben und Wirken der Bischöfe von Chur in der Zeit von 1122 bis 1250" (Dissertation Salzburg [typewr.], 1975).

Czumpelik, "Gurk" = Rudolf Czumpelik, "Die persönlichen Verhältnisse der Bischöfe von Gurk im Mittelalter" (Dissertation [typewr.] Wien, 1947).

Gescher, "Geschichte und Recht" = Franz Gescher, "Geschichte und Recht der kölnischen Diözesansynoden" (Jur. Dissertation [typewr.] Köln, 1923).

Johanek, "Synodalia" = Peter Johanek, "Synodalia. Untersuchungen zur Statutengesetzgebung in den Kirchenprovinzen Mainz und Salzburg während des Spätmittelalters," 3 vols. (Habilitationsschrift [typewr.] Würzburg, 1977).

Klein, "Salzburg DK" = Herbert Klein, "Die Standesverhältnisse des Salzburger Domkapitels im Mittelalter (bis 1400)" (Dissertation [typewr.] Wien, 1923).

Klink, "Konstanz DK" = Karl Erich Klink, "Das Konstanzer Domkapitel bis zum Ausgang des Mittelalters" (Dissertation [typewr.] Tübingen, 1949).

Mayrhofer, "Sedisvakanzen" = Emma Walpurga Mayrhofer, "Die Sedisvakanzen im Erzstift Salzburg" (Dissertation [typewr.] Salzburg, 1969).

Pixton, "Dietrich of Wied" (1972) = Paul B. Pixton, "Dietrich of Wied, Archbishop of

Trier 1212-1242: A Study in Princely Politics and Church Reform" (Dissertation [typewr.] University of Iowa, 1972).

Schaller, "Das geistige Leben" = Hans Martin Schaller, "Das geistige Leben am Hofe Ottos IV. von Braunschweig," address delivered 3 July 1974 to the Ausseninstitut der Universität Braunschweig.

Tröster, "Säben-Brixen" = Hans Tröster, "Studien zur Geschichte des Episkopats von Säben-Brixen im Mittelalter" (Dissertation [typewr.] Wien, 1948).

Wisplinghoff, "EB Friedrich I." = E. Wisplinghoff, "Friedrich I., Erzbischof von Köln (1100-1131)," (Dissertation [typewr.] Bonn, 1951).

Frequently Cited Journals

Archiv = *Archiv der Gesellschaft für ältere deutsche Geschichtskunde*, 12 vols. (Frankfurt & Hannover, 1820-1874); superseded by *Neues Archiv*.

AGHA = *Archiv für die Geschichte des Hochstifts Augsburg*

AGAW = *Archiv für die Geschichte und Altertumskunde Westfalens*, herausg. von P. Wigand, 7 vols. (Hamm & Lemgo, 1826-1838).

AGNrh = *Archiv für die Geschichte des Niederrheins*, herausg. von Th. Jos. Lacomblet; fortges. von W. Harless, 7 vols. (Düsseldorf, 1831-1869).

AHC = *Annuarium Historiae Conciliorum: Internationale Zeitschrift für Konziliengeschichte* (München, 1969ff.)

AKKR = *Archiv für Katholisches Kirchenrecht* (Mainz, 1855ff.).

ANrh = *Annalen des historischen Vereins für den Niederrhein* (Köln, 1855ff.)

AÖG = *Archiv für Kunde österreichische Geschichtsquellen* (für Österreichische Geschichte), herausg. von der Kommission der. k. Akademie der Wissenschaft, 87 vols. (Wien, 1848-1899).

AmKG = *Archiv für mittelrheinische Kirchengeschichte* (Mainz, 1949ff.).

AVNAG = *Annalen des Vereins für Nassauische Altertumskunde und Geschichtsforschung* (Wiesbaden, 1827ff.).

AVN = *Vaterländisches Archiv des historischen Vereins für Niedersachsen* (Hannover, 1836-1851).

DA = *Deutsches Archiv für Erforschung des Mittelalters namens der Monumenta Germaniae Historica* (Köln & Wien); supercedes the *Neues Archiv*.

DGbll = *Deutsche Geschichtsblätter. Monatschrift für Erforschung deutscher Vergangenheit auf landesgeschichtlicher Grundlage* (Gotha, 1849ff.).

FDG = *Forschungen zur deutschen Geschichte*, 26 vols. (Göttingen, 1862-1886).

HGbll = *Hansische Geschichtsblätter* (Leipzig, 1871ff.)

HJb = *Historisches Jahrbuch der Görres-Gesellschaft* (Münster, 1880-1882; Müchen, 1883ff.).

HSt = *Historische Studien*, herausg, von E. Ebering (Berlin, 1896ff.).

Hyppolytus = *Hyppolytus. Archiv für Diözesan-Geschichte des Bistums sprengels St. Pölten* (1894ff.).

HZ = *Historische Zeitschrift*, herausg. von H. v. Sybel u.a. (München, 1859ff.).

JbLN = *Jahrbuch für Landeskunde von Niederösterreich* (Wien, 1976ff.).

MGbll = *Geschichtsblätter für Land und Stadt Magdeburg. Mitteilungen des Vereins für Geschichte und Altertumskunde des Herzogtums und Hochstifts Magdeburg*

                        (Magdeburg, 1866ff.).

MIÖG   = *Mitteilungen des Instituts für österreichische Geschichtsforschung* (Innsbruck/-
                        Wien, 1880ff.).

MRhWGA   = *Monatschrift für Rheinische-Westfalische Geschichtsforschung und Altertums-
                        kunde*, ed. Richard Pick, vols. 1-7 (Bonn/Trier, 1875-1881). Title varies:
                        also *Monatschrift für die Geschichte Westdeutschlands.* Superseded by
                        Westdeutsche Zeitschrift der Geschichte und Kunst.

NA   = *Neues Archiv der Gesellschaft für ältere deutsche Geschichtskunde*, 26 vols.
                        (Hannover, 1876-1901). Superseded by *Deutsches Archiv für Geschichte
                        des Mittelalters.*

Studien und   = *Studien und Mitteilungen zur Geschichte des Benediktiner Ordens und seiner
   Mitteil.   Zweige* (Salzburg/München, 1880ff.); vols. 4-31 bear title, *Studien und
                        Mitteilungen aus dem Benediktiner- und Zistenzienser-Orden* (1883ff.)

Traditio   = *Traditio* (New York, 1943ff.).

WZGK   = *Westdeutsche Zeitschrift für Geschichte und Kunst* (Trier, 1882-1913).

ZGAW (T)   = *Zeitschrift für Geschichte und Altertumskunde Westphalens und Rheinlands*,
                        herausg. von L. Tross, 3 vols. (Hamm, 1824-1826).

ZGAW   = *Zeitschrift für vaterländische Geschichte und Altertumskunde*, herausg. von
                        dem Verein für Geschichte Westfalens (Münster, 1838ff.).

ZGO   = *Zeitschrift für die Geschichte des Oberrheins*, ed. Franz Joseph Moné
                        (Karlsruhe, 1850ff.).

ZHV   = *Zeitschrift des Harzvereins für Geschichte und Altertumskunde* (Wernigerode,
                        1868ff.).

ZSRG   = *Zeitschrift der Savigny-Stiftung für Rechtsgeschichte*, Kanonistische Abteilung
   KanAbt   (Weimar, 1911ff.).

ZVN   = *Zeitschrift des historischen Vereins für Niedersachsen* (Hannover, 1854ff.).

INDEX OF NAMES

INDEX OF SUBJECTS

Studies in the History
of Christian Thought

EDITED BY HEIKO A. OBERMAN

50. HOENEN, M. J. F. M. *Marsilius of Inghen*. Divine Knowledge in Late Medieval Thought. 1993
51. O'MALLEY, J. W., IZBICKI, T. M. and CHRISTIANSON, G. (eds.) *Humanity and Divinity in Renaissance and Reformation*. Essays in Honor of Charles Trinkaus. 1993
52. REEVE, A. (ed.) and SCREECH, M. A. (introd.) *Erasmus' Annotations on the New Testament*. Galatians to the Apocalypse. 1993
53. STUMP, Ph. H. *The Reforms of the Council of Constance (1414-1418)*. 1994
54. GIAKALIS, A. *Images of the Divine*. The Theology of Icons at the Seventh Ecumenical Council. With a Foreword by Henry Chadwick. 1994
55. NELLEN, H. J. M. and RABBIE, E. *Hugo Grotius – Theologian*. Essays in Honour of G. H. M. Posthumus Meyjes. 1994
56. TRIGG, J. D. *Baptism in the Theology of Martin Luther*. 1994
57. JANSE, W. *Albert Hardenberg als Theologe*. Profil eines Bucer-Schülers. 1994
58. ASSELT, W.J. **van**. *The Covenant Theology of Johannes Cocceius (1603-1669)*. An Examination of its Structure. *In preparation*
59. SCHOOR, R.J.M. **van de**. *The Irenical Theology of Théophile Brachet de La Milletière (1588-1665)*. 1995
60. STREHLE, S. *The Catholic Roots of the Protestant Gospel*. Encounter between the Middle Ages and the Reformation. 1995
61. BROWN, M.L. *Donne and the Politics of Conscience in Early Modern England*. 1995
62. SCREECH, M.A. (ed.). *Richard Mocket, Warden of All Souls College, Oxford, Doctrina et Politia Ecclesiae Anglicanae*. An Anglican Summa. Facsimile with Variants of the Text of 1617. Edited with an Introduction. 1995
63. SNOEK, G.J.C. *Medieval Piety from Relics to the Eucharist*. 1995
64. PIXTON, P.B. *The German Episcopacy and the Implementation of the Decrees of the Fourth Lateran Council, 1216-1245*. Watchmen on the Tower. 1995

Prospectus available on request

E. J. BRILL — P.O.B. 9000 — 2300 PA LEIDEN — THE NETHERLANDS